BEYOND
CHRISTENDOM

BEYOND CHRISTENDOM

Globalization, African Migration, and
the Transformation of the West

JEHU J. HANCILES

ORBIS BOOKS
Maryknoll, New York 10545

Founded in 1970, Orbis Books endeavors to publish works that enlighten the mind, nourish the spirit, and challenge the conscience. The publishing arm of the Maryknoll Fathers and Brothers, Orbis seeks to explore the global dimensions of the Christian faith and mission, to invite dialogue with diverse cultures and religious traditions, and to serve the cause of reconciliation and peace. The books published reflect the opinions of their authors and are not meant to represent the official position of the Maryknoll Society. To obtain more information about Maryknoll and Orbis Books, please visit our website at www.maryknollsociety.org.

Library of Congress Cataloging in Publication Data

Hanciles, Jehu, 1964-
    Beyond christendom : globalization, African migration, and the transformation of the West / Jehu J. Hanciles.
        p. cm.
    Includes bibliographical references.
    ISBN 978-1-57075-790-7
    1. Globalization—Religious aspects—Christianity. 2. Emigration and immigration—Religious aspects—Christianity. 3. Christianity--Forecasting. I. Title.
    BR115.G59H36 2008
    270.8'3—dc22
                                                            2008013931

To

Andrew F. Walls,

who taught me to see the world through African eyes

Contents

Part II
Migration and the New World Order

Part III
Mobile Faiths

List of Figures

Acknowledgments

When I embarked on this project six years ago I had no idea what a formidable and challenging undertaking it would turn out to be. But I was never on my own. Indeed, while I take full responsibility for all deficiencies manifest in this final product, it came to fruition only because so many provided vital assistance or input in countless ways. Among all those who traveled with me on this journey, the following deserve particular mention.

From the start, Sherwood Lingenfelter (provost at Fuller Theological Seminary) and Douglas McConnell (dean of the School of Intercultural Studies, Fuller Theological Seminary) gave full backing to the venture and secured the initial grants required to get it off the ground. Their support and generous counsel on managing the project were indispensable. The bulk of the research conducted in cities throughout the United States was made possible only by a major grant from the Louisville Institute. I thank Jim Lewis, director of the Louisville Institute, for his understanding and accommodation. I am also grateful to Wendy Walker and Christine Cervantes, who administered the grants on Fuller's behalf and whose budgetary expertise ensured smooth operational progress.

During my research trip to Africa in 2003, I received generous help and hospitality from Samuel Ngewa as well as Douglas and Ayiku Carew at the Nairobi Evangelical Graduate School of Theology (Kenya). I also owe the success of my Ghana trip to the organizing skills of Kingsley Larbi. My heartfelt thanks go to all the pastors, university professors, and graduate students in these two countries who, through interviews and personal interaction, provided vital information and insights into the migrant factor within contemporary African Christianity. Few were more gracious and accommodating than Pastor Oscar Muriu (Senior Pastor, Nairobi Chapel, Kenya), Pastor Prince Obasi-ike (Regional Co-Coordinator, Redeemed Christian Church of God, Kenya), Apostle Michael Ntumy (Chairman, Church of Pentecost, Ghana), and Pastor Mensa Otabil (International Central Gospel Church, Ghana). In his inimitable way, Tokumboh Adeyemo, with whom I spent valuable time, affirmed my work and enlarged my understanding of the terrain.

Full realization of the project's wide-ranging objectives within the United States required the involvement of seven research assistants, almost all in doctoral programs or with newly acquired PhDs: Emmanuel Bellon, James Kissi-Ayittey, Moses Biney, Joseph Ezeigbo, Daniel Imo, Damaris M'Mworia, and Mary Wangila. I am indebted to each of them for their keenness, enterprise, and commitment to the cause. I am also deeply grateful for the special assistance provided by Doris Frimpong, who translated the congregational survey form into French, and Joenita Paulrajan, who helped with the compilation and analysis of the statistical data.

My heartfelt appreciation goes to all the pastors and congregants in the African congregations around the country who gave generously of their time for interviews, sustained interaction, and meaningful feedback. Among the many African pastors I personally interviewed and engaged in repeated conversations, five in particular did much to facilitate the research and accommodate my uncommon demands: Bishop Darlingston Johnson (Bethel World Outreach Church, Maryland); Pastor Oladipo Kalejaiye (International Christian Center, Los Angeles, California), Pastor Joe Kamanda (Schekina Christian Center, Chicago), Pastor Tayo Badejoko (Courage Christian Center, Philadelphia), and Pastor Bayo Adewole (Jesus House, Chicago).

My colleagues in the School of Intercultural Studies at Fuller provided encouragement and helpful feedback on presented material. But I owe a special debt of gratitude to Wilbert R. Shenk and Bryant Myers, both of whom read the original manuscript with meticulous thoroughness and gave invaluable scholarly feedback. I also benefited greatly from the expertise of leading Old Testament scholar John Goldingay, whose insights and bibliographical knowledge augmented my reflections on the importance of migratory movements in Scripture. Within the community of African scholars, no one did more to stimulate, encourage, and inspire my efforts than Ogbu U. Kalu (McCormick Theological Seminary). His shrewd understanding of African realities was a great resource. Very special thanks also go to Lamin Sanneh (Yale University), Jon Bonk (Overseas Ministries Study Center, United States), Jacob K. Olupona (Harvard University), and Gerrie ter Haar (Institute of Social Studies, The Netherlands) all of whom readily consented to provide commendations for this book; and my deepest appreciation to Joel Carpenter (Nagel Institute, Calvin College, Grand Rapids, Michigan) for writing the foreword.

Publishing a book on Christian mission that cuts across major disciplines and explores novel phenomena in a way that questions received wisdom calls for an editor with keen perception of the emerging global Christian landscape. Even before he saw a single chapter, Bill Burrows responded with excitement and enthusiasm to my ideas and ruminations. For reasons that remain unclear to me he was confident that the story was worth telling and that I would get it done. I could not have asked for a more experienced, supportive, and congenial editor.

Throughout this long journey I was always assured of the prayerful encouragement and caring support of my wider Sierra Leonean family, many of whom also provided affectionate hospitality during my many research trips around the country: Emeric and Sylvia Palmer, Hudson and Gina Jackson, David and Molley Macauley, Patrick and Elaine Hume-Dawson, Modupe and Renee Taylor-Pearce, Randolph and Hudrie Leigh, Charles and Marvel Sawyer, Maurice and Olabisi Hanciles. *Oonar all tenki!* Outside this circle, I recall with gratitude the solicitous encouragement of Eugene and Daniela Matei. Above all, I thank Biffoh (my wife), whose loving support and unstinting devotion are the greatest blessing a husband can ask for. To Sade and Shola, my deepest thanks for your many concessions.

A Note on Sources and Documentation

Documenting sources became a great challenge in this book for several reasons, which coalesce around the attempt to utilize the most up-to-date statistical and social-scientific research and other materials, many of which are published online or in other untraditional formats. In the footnotes, I give full publication information the first time I refer to a source. Subsequent references will be in the format of author/short title/page number. In the case of traditional journals, books, and newspapers, this presents little difficulty; I follow the standard academic format.

In the case of online reports from research institute publications and similar data, the issue is not so simple. My goal, however, is to give sufficient information to guide the reader to the Web sites from which I gathered the data. Because Uniform Record Locators ("URLs") change, index numbers for specific documents are altered, documents are posted, taken down, revised, reposted, and so forth, knowing how best to indicate where a reader can go for additional information or to check my interpretations is difficult. URLs with 150 characters and the date I consulted the Web site are pedantic and are likely to produce fruitless searches. My goal is to give a full name of the organization providing the data and its basic URL. If an online document, for instance, is published by a U.S. government agency or the United Nations or is added as an online premium to a magazine like *The Economist,* I give the full name of the agency providing the data or indicate that I am using material from, for example, a research unit of *The Economist.* Thus, a note might inform the reader that I have gotten the statistics used in the text from the U.S. Census Bureau, Washington D.C., the 2008 Statistical Abstract of the United States published by the U.S. Census Bureau (www.census. gov/compendia/statab/), no. 1269, "U.S. Government Foreign Grants And Credits By Country: 1990 to 2006." Would that the titles, locations, and providers of all data were so easy to document.

The bibliography at the end of the book is a "Selected" bibliography. I have not tried to list every book, newspaper or magazine article, or Web document I have consulted or cited in the book. It is, instead, a record of the most important materials I have read and used in the preparation of this book, whether I cite them in the text or not. In particular, I have given references to sources such as daily newspapers or weekly magazines in footnotes, but have not usually listed them in the bibliography.

Foreword

Joel B. Carpenter

A Caribbean missionary couple lived just down the block from me right here in Grand Rapids, Michigan. No, they were not here on furlough or retired from an overseas post. They were missionaries to Grand Rapids. Dr. Antonio and Wanda Rosario came here from the Caribbean—he from the Dominican Republic and she from Puerto Rico—and they led an effort that resulted in six new Adventist congregations, one of them meeting on Saturdays in the same church building where I worship. Now the Rosarios have moved to Indianapolis to share the gospel with more people and start more churches. Their story, as missionaries to America, seems quite unusual but, in truth, it is not. Such things are happening all over the United States, in virtually every town and city.

Most Americans have heard by now of their nation's rapidly changing population, what Newsweek magazine called "the browning of America." In another twenty years or so, our demographers tell us, the population of the United States as a whole will look much like that of Texas or California today, with no race or ethnic group having a majority. The United States is becoming the world's foremost receiver of people on the move. They have left their homes to escape violence and to seek a better future for their children. This time, however, the immigrants are not only from Europe but from every part of the world. Here in western Michigan, in addition to a recently arrived Bosnian community and a rapidly growing Latino population, we have communities of immigrants from Liberia, the Sudan, and Ethiopia; and from South Korea and Vietnam as well. Few of us, however, have a sense of the global forces that are driving these migrations. And hardly any of us have looked into the religious dimensions of these historic movements.

This book by Jehu Hanciles, who is himself an immigrant from Sierra Leone, could not be timelier. He argues that the rapid exchange of ideas, investments, people, and products that we know as globalization is having a very surprising effect. While we Americans often think of it as bringing Coca Cola to the world and exporting factory jobs to lower-wage nations, Hanciles argues that globalization is propelling a great increase in personal mobility, and that people on the move are bringing their own ideas and outlook with them.

The great majority of the new immigrants to the United States are Christians, Hanciles informs us, but their faith is not merely another American cultural import. It partakes of their unique views of life and of God's work in the world.

The United States would be moving much more rapidly toward a post-Christian status, he argues, were it not for these fresh infusions of believers. With a focus on the hundreds of African immigrant congregations arising in our cities and suburbs, Hanciles gives us an intimate look at the new missions movement happening in our land. It will change the character of American Christianity, he insists, and perhaps, of Christianity worldwide.

Introduction

This book is based on research and reflections that date back to 2001. In some ways, however, it is the fruit of a journey that began when I left my native Sierra Leone in 1990. Since then I have lived as a migrant in three different countries. I remain part of that formless mass sometimes referred to as the African diaspora. Not that any of the material contained here is autobiographical. Yet in some ways much of it is, insofar as my personal story is reflected in the lives of countless migrants who have learned the truth of that poignant commentary on second-century Christians: that "for them any foreign country is a motherland, and any motherland is a foreign country."[1]

The material contained in this study explores the interconnection of globalization, migration, and religious expansion. It advances the argument that while Western initiatives and projects appear to dominate the contemporary world order, the processes of globalization incorporate powerful trends and religious phenomena that originate in the non-Western world and will potentially impact the West in significant ways. In particular, it examines the way in which recent transformations within global Christianity combined with global migration flows (specifically South–North movement) point to the West as a major frontier of religious interactions and missionary engagement. A detailed assessment of African migrations and the formation of African immigrant congregations in the United States provides the main case study.

The work is of necessity interdisciplinary in approach and coverage. Core material and analytical tools are derived from three major disciplines or discourses: globalization, migration, and mission studies. The processes of globalization provide the basic framework, while the character, composition, and dynamic of international migrations inform the study's core assumptions about the potential of African movements. But it is the inextricable connection between migration and mission in the Christian experience that provides the rationale and seedplot. This linkage is rooted in the biblical tradition and factors prominently in the history of Christian expansion. The fact that this connection is largely overlooked in mission studies has something to do with the unwarranted distinction between "church" and "mission" that has marked Western theological reflection for at least two hundred years.

In the interest of full disclosure, my primary discipline is history, and a historical perspective shapes the treatment of all subject matter. But the integrative

---

1 "Letter to Diognetus," in *Early Christian Writings: The Apostolic Fathers* (New York: Penguin Books, 1987), 145.

1

approach adopted in this study is thoroughgoing. By this I mean that material incorporated from each major discipline forms an indispensable piece of the whole. Academic disciplines do not exist in water-tight compartments, and cross-fertilization is common; but each discipline revolves around core concepts and theories. In this case, I have not simply pressed into service certain pieces of this or that discipline in order to provide a semblance of cross-disciplinary engagement. Globalization, migration, and mission form constitutive building blocks of the book, which helps to explain why it is divided into three sections, each of which roughly corresponds to one major discourse. In this book, also, I use the concepts "Western" and "non-Western" as broad categories that provide convenient reference points for discussing global processes. This is not to suggest that either is a homogenous monolith. As I explain later (see chapter 1) each is used not so much to identify a particular entity as to qualify a certain reality.

In any case, this book is written from a non-Western (and for the most part African) perspective. I have tried to be as balanced as possible in my arguments and reassessments, fully cognizant of the fact that my own views are far from unassailable. One major shortcoming of such a wide-ranging treatment is that, however discriminating the effort, it is liable to make sweeping judgments and obscure the more nuanced insights of the theses I take issue with. I hope I have made up for this somewhat by being forthright in my own rationale and bias. By the same token, there are many non-Western readers who may be offended by the idea that I can claim to speak for them. I do not; but, then again, the charge is not baseless.

Part 1 probes key points of debate within the discourse of globalization and queries the widespread notion that processes of globalization perpetuate structures of Western (principally American) hegemony. Undoubtedly, contemporary globalization embodies the most powerful transformative processes of our time, but it has deep historical roots and denotes a complex reality that is still evolving. While vital aspects certainly reflect American economic dominance, America is no more immune to the disruptions caused by evolving global structures than other industrial nations. And far from being a one-directional, single, unified phenomenon, the processes of globalization are multidirectional, inherently paradoxical, and incorporate movement and countermovement. This dynamic allows for what is sometimes referred to as "globalization from below": non-Western cultural movements, both secular and religious, with a global reach that impact the West.

To make the case more directly, I critically evaluate global-culture (or cultural-homogenization) arguments that uphold Western culture as a universal ideal. The "global-culture" thesis maintains that, as a result of the inexorable spread of Western modernization and/or American consumer culture, we are witnessing the emergence of a global culture or universal civilization. This perspective is peculiarly Western, and it typifies the notion that globalization is a one-directional, managed process with a fixed ideal. I interrogate a number of specific theories reflective of this viewpoint, including the well-known "secularization theory," Peter Berger's "four faces of global culture," Francis Fukuyama's "end of history," and Benjamin Barber's "Jihad versus McWorld." Samuel Huntington's much-debated "clash of civilizations" argument also receives strong attention because it forcefully challenges the single global-culture paradigm.

Each of these arguments pays serious attention to the religious aspects of globalization. Indeed, with varying degrees of emphasis, all highlight the growing religious gap between the West and non-West that significantly troubles the single global-culture perspective. It is also intriguing to note that the universal-culture argument is ultimately rooted in religious concepts and convictions. The idea was in large measure spawned by Christendom—the experience and understanding of Christianity as a territorial and tribal faith. This Christendom construct was produced not by the conversion of the emperor Constantine I, as commonly believed, but by the mass conversions of Germanic peoples (ancestors of Western Europeans). How this is so is explained in great detail.

Within a Christendom framework, European peoples conceived of their culture or civilization as Christian; which also meant that Christianity was coterminous with European territories. In its crudest expression this conception linked the spread of Christianity with the territorial expansion of European control and culture. This deeply ethnocentric outlook spawned racist ideologies such as "white man's burden," "manifest destiny," and "divine providence," all of which rationalized the conviction that the superior values, ideals, and material benefits of European civilization should be spread around the world. Efforts at the global expansion of Christendom—the spread of European culture as a normative expression of the Christian faith—represents the most comprehensive attempt in the history of the world to impose the civilization of one race or people on all others.

I will contend, however, that Christendom was bankrupted as a universal ideal by expanding colonial interests and the missionary encounter with the immutable diversity of non-Western societies. Even more important, this encounter contributed to the emergence of non-Western movements and initiatives, some of which are now acting reflexively back on Western societies. No single development in the last fifty years demonstrates this unintended consequence more definitively than the reshaping of global Christianity that has seen Africa, Latin America, and Asia emerge as the new heartlands of the faith. The nature of this extraordinary shift, its implications for the study of Christianity, and the significance of the African element within it are given thorough consideration. Among other things, the claim that the non-Western experience and expressions of the faith represent the "next Christendom" is roundly rejected as an example of a widespread tendency to imprison understanding of the new global Christian realities within Western intellectual categories.

Part 2 (comprising chapters 6-10) considers the crucial role of international migrations in the reshaping of the contemporary world order. The aim is to provide a thoroughgoing assessment of migration as a vehicle of cultural and religious transformation, starting with the extraordinary movements and displacement of peoples instigated by European overseas explorations and empire. Christian expansion and migratory movement have historically been intimately intertwined; and, throughout the history of the faith, migrant movement has been a causative factor in both Christian advance and Christian decline. The great century of Western missionary expansion (1814-1915), for instance, involved the overseas migration of an estimated forty to sixty million Europeans—the majority of whom were economic migrants! In effect, the extensive penetration and spread of various forms of Christianity in the southern continents—Latin America, Africa, parts of Asia, and the Pacific—itself provides one of the most compelling historical examples of the profound historical link between migration and mission.

But it is important to our story that these momentous events and their unanticipated repercussions are viewed through a biblical lens or, at least, assessed with a biblical understanding (provided in chapter 6). Within migration or immigration studies, acknowledgment of the strong connection between migration and the intensification of religiosity or religious commitment is fairly recent. But the connection is a timeless one. Historian Timothy Smith memorably declared that "migration [is] often a theologizing experience."[2] This much is evident from the biblical (and missiological) appraisal of migration provided here. The Bible depicts every known form of migration, and themes of displacement and uprootedness form a powerful subtext in the biblical narrative of divine intervention in human history. I will argue that not only is migrant movement crucial to the unfolding of the divine plan of salvation, but it also furnishes the basis for a biblical critique of global cultural hegemony.

So integral is mobility to human development and human interactions that it is recognized as one of the oldest forms or causes of globalization. The encounter between different groups of people (whether through conquest, trade, or displacement) inevitably expands the horizons of knowledge on both sides and fosters interconnectedness—causing the world to "shrink." Most significantly, when people move, they carry their ideas, beliefs, and religious practices with them. Peter Stearns aptly describes such movements as cultures in motion.[3] The impact and implications of such movements can be profound. Regardless of whether the cultural encounters that occur in migration are marked by coercion or by fruitful accommodation, the cultural groups involved are seldom left unchanged. The movement of peoples thus has the capacity not only to foster cultural diversity but also to significantly alter demographic, economic, and social structures. This capacity makes migration a potent source of social transformation and an active ingredient in the great dramas of history.

But the scale and velocity of human migration in the contemporary period are without historical precedence, giving rise to the conviction that we live in "the age of migration." Importantly, the unprecedented magnitude and scope of contemporary international migrations have produced new conceptual models and perspectives which throw significant light on the nature and dynamic of global flows. Even the traditional definition of "migrant" has come under sharp scrutiny with implications for our understanding of migrant roles. My primary concern, however, is with South–North migrations and the significance of the African element within it.

Since the 1970s, the number of African migrants has risen dramatically as

---

2. Timothy L. Smith, "Religion and Ethnicity in America," *American Historical Review* 83, no. 5 (December 1978): 1174f.

3. Peter N. Stearns, *Cultures in Motion: Mapping Key Contacts and Their Imprints in World History* (New Haven: Yale University Press, 2001).

escalating conflicts, brutal regimes, and economic collapse (related to globalization) have induced colossal displacements of peoples. The possibility that the phenomenal growth of Christianity in Africa is impacted by such tremendous transfers of population is acknowledged but not pursued here. What is explored is Africa's contribution to the massive escalation of South–North movement from the 1960s. As an aspect of cultural globalization, nonwhite migration represents a significant example of global processes which originate outside the Western world and impact Western societies. The religiosity of the new immigrants potentially transforms the religious movement into missionary engagement. At the very least it implicates secular (largely post-Christian) Western societies as sites of new religious interactions. In this regard, the vigorous debate over the assimilation of massive nonwhite immigration into Western societies, including the emergence of new models of assimilation, is thoroughly evaluated. Old patterns persist, but the dynamics of contemporary globalization self-evidently foster new modes of immigrant assimilation within Western societies that will hardly leave the latter unchanged.

Part 3, the final section of the study, explores the religious implications and impact of massive South–North migration on Western societies. Precisely because the North–South divide is as religious as it is economic, massive South–North migration is creating new religious communities and new religious trends within Western societies that present significant challenges to cherished ideals and portend an enduring impact on its wider cultural ethos. Since massive Muslim immigration into Western societies represents the most conspicuous example of these trends, I felt compelled to devote a whole chapter to it in order to elucidate key points of argument. The issues are exceedingly complex and analysis is vexed. But few aspects of contemporary globalization provide a more thorough repudiation of the universal-civilization ideal and the predictions of the secularization theory than the relentless furor and widespread angst that have attended the vibrant growth of these Muslim communities within Western societies.

For quite distinct reasons, the experiences of Muslims in Europe and America differ in significant ways. In Europe the vast majority of immigrants are Muslims (a consequence of empire), and extensive secularization, signifying the massive erosion of Christian beliefs and practice, means that the rapid growth of Islam is more readily perceived as a direct threat to values associated with liberal democracy. Popular misconception of Islam as a uniform, foreign entity combined with the equally mythical notion that European society constitutes a monolithic cultural mass continue to plague the assimilation/integration question. This issue is fully examined. Calls for the "Europeanization" of Islam typically ignore the possibility that this would of necessity imply the "Islamization of Europe." For a European Islam molded by the active incorporation of democratic ideals, individual rights, and gender equality will also have wider appeal and greater missionary potential.

In the United States, the Muslim population forms a very small proportion of recent immigrants (the majority of whom are Christian) and join a population of unparalleled religious diversity. Muslim immigrants in America also tend to be highly educated professionals living in middle class suburbs, in striking contrast to their counterparts in Europe who largely form an underclass. Here the pathways to reconstructing an Islamic identity are much less troubled, even in the face of resolute anti-Islam sentiments within the wider public and America's belligerent interventions in the Middle East. But here, perhaps even more so than in Europe, it is the very conditions of security and freedom provided by democratic society that allows Muslim communities and the Islamic faith to thrive—often in ways that are not possible within the Islamic world. In the final analysis, Islam has become a permanent feature of Western society. As in the fabled story, the emperor has new clothes; whether the new garments are truly invisible is open to debate, but, one way or another, the emperor's status and identity can never be quite the same again.

The Christian dimensions of this story have not attracted the same level of media or academic coverage, but they are equally compelling. Moreover, the high levels of Muslim and Christian immigration into Western societies may turn out to be quite interconnected in their impact. Not least because *the most significant counterforce to Islam in Europe is likely to come less from secularism or from Europe's homegrown, fairly moribund, Christianity than from the steady influx of Christian immigrants (from Africa, Latin America, and Asia).*

Christianity is the most migratory of religions, and there is a strong argument to be made that the tide of South–North migrations has a greater implication for Christianity than any other world religion. For one thing, South–North migrations are significantly shaped by colonial linkages, and not only did those same colonial powers (Japan excepted) claim to be Christian, but colonial expansion was intimately related to the Western missionary project. In any case, the fact that the southward shift in global Christianity's center of gravity coincides with this epochal reversal in the direction and flow of global migrations is of historic consequence. It is fairly obvious that every missionary is a migrant in some sense; but I will also argue that *every Christian migrant is a potential missionary.*

Since South–North migration predictably draws on historical links between ex-colonies and ex-colonial states, the African Christian presence in Europe is more long-standing and self-evident. It is a well-known fact that the largest church in Britain and the largest church in all of Europe are both African (specifically Nigerian) founded and led. African Christian communities in Europe were also the first to receive detailed scholarly attention, notably Gerrie ter Haar's *Halfway to Paradise: African Christians in Europe* (Fairwater: Cardiff Academic Press, 1998).

In the United States, where voluntary African immigration in sizable numbers is a more recent phenomenon and constitutes a minor fraction of post-1965 immigration, African immigrants have been completely ignored by most studies on immigration, including the few that take religion into account. The trend was recently broken with the publication of *African Immigrant Religions in America* (2007), edited by Jacob Olupona and Regina Gemignani, which explores the social and cultural impact of flourishing African religious communities (Christian and Muslim) in the North American context.[4] My own assessment provides

---

4. See Jacob K. Olupona and Regina Gemignani, *African Immigrant Religions in America* (New York: New York University Press, 2007).

detailed examination of African (Christian) immigrants in the United States: their profile, assimilation patterns, religious congregations, troubled relations with African Americans, and missionary engagement with American society.

The study of African Christian immigrants and their proliferating congregations within America's quite diverse religious landscape is compelling for at least three reasons. First, and most obviously, the United States is a de facto immigrant country; its very existence is a powerful testimony to the link between migration and religious expansion in the history of Christianity. As I demonstrate in chapter 12, successive waves of massive immigration not only account for momentous changes in America's history, but they have also been the main source of transformation of America's religious landscape. Partly because the dominant hermeneutic in the history of Christian missions conceives of "missions" in terms of expansion from a fixed geographical center, the ways in which initiatives or movements from outside have impacted American religious life and may even have contributed to the strong missionary impulse within American Christianity have received scant attention. At the very least, massive Christian immigration throughout the nineteenth century is perhaps the most important single reason why the decline of Christianity in America at the end of the twentieth century is less substantial than Europe's—America, as Andrew Walls comments, simply "started its Christian decline from a much higher base than Europe did."[5]

Second, Africa is a major heartland of the Christian faith and also a prominent emitter of international migrants. It is therefore of no little consequence that the United States is now the primary destination for Africans who migrate to Western industrial nations. In fact, the African foreign-born population (mainly from West Africa)—touted as "the last source of new Americans"—constitutes one of the fastest growing immigrant groups in the United States. This means that African Christians form a significant component in the vast body of Christian immigrants whose arrival coincides with a decline in American Christianity.

Third, America has been the chief Western missionary-sending nation (in sheer numbers) since the Second World War. Thus, its transformation into a missionary-*receiving* nation by virtue of immigration makes for intriguing analysis. I take the view that massive nonwhite post-1965 immigration will potentially have a greater and more lasting impact on America's religious life and heritage than any previous wave (with the possible exception of the first wave from Western Europe). Already, the new immigrants have transformed America into the most religiously diverse nation on the planet. Less well known is the fact that the majority of the new immigrants (at least 60 percent according to one survey) are Christians (from Africa, Asia, and Latin America) who are expressing their Christianity in languages, customs, forms of spirituality, and community formation that are almost as foreign to Americans as other religions. The new immigrant Christian communities are effectively "de-Europeanizing" American Christianity.

Readers who care to negotiate the first and second parts of this book will

---

5. Andrew F. Walls, "Mission and Migration: The Diaspora Factor in Christian History," *Journal of African Christian Thought* 5, no. 2 (December 2002): 10.

have a better appreciation of why it was necessary to scrutinize and evaluate issues pertaining to globalization and migration before addressing the missionary potential of South–North migratory flows. To date, Western missiological thinking has paid negligible attention to international migrations, even though human migrations have played a critical role in the expansion of the Christian faith from its very inception. If the discipline (of mission history, at least) has got away with it so far, it is only because the Western missionary project has been identified so extensively with visible structures of economic and political dominance. But no other dimension of contemporary experience captures more fully the magnitude, momentum, and motivations of this emerging non-Western missionary movement than migration.

Non-Western missionary initiatives are not new. In fact the tendency for missionary historiography to account for the spread of Christianity almost exclusively in terms of Western initiatives, and to overlook the decisive contributions of indigenous agency, is one of its most significant failings. By 1986, Nigeria alone could claim three thousand official missionaries (five hundred of whom were sent by the Evangelistic Missionary Society in West Africa).[6] But such efforts reflect the Western model of missions and barely represent the tip of the iceberg of the African missionary movement. Incidentally, the mission agency approach is rapidly losing ground even within Western missions. Reference in this book to the emergence of a non-Western missionary movement reflects a global perspective and points to a phenomenal upsurge of migrant movements, which have fostered relatively new sustained encounters between post-Western Christianities and the post-Christian West. Without a full grasp of the salient features of contemporary global migrations—including the impact of transnationalism, the legacies of Western colonialism, and the unique experiences of the migrants themselves—appraisal of the new non-Western missionary movement will be significantly impaired.

All of which brings us to the main and final point of this book. In the same way that unprecedented European migrations from Christianity's old heartland provided the impetus for the European missionary movement, phenomenal migrations from Christianity's new heartlands (in Africa, Latin America, and Asia) have galvanized a massive non-Western missionary movement. This latter movement implicates the West as a new frontier of global Christian expansion and represents a major turning point in the history of the Christian faith. Perhaps no other continent epitomizes this dynamic more fully than Africa. Africa is at the same time a major heartland of Christianity and a prominent theater and source of international migrations. Africans are also notoriously religious, form community instinctively, and (according to research) maintain strong homeland ties long after they emigrate. In the United States, at least, African immigrants include a conspicuously high proportion of highly educated men and women in their prime of life (see chapter 13). All these qualities contribute to missionary effectiveness. In the event, African immigrant congregations in Western societ-

---

6. Samuel Wilson and John Siewart, eds., *Mission Handbook: North American Protestant Ministries Overseas* (Monrovia, CA: MARC, 1986), 20.

ies represent an important example of how South–North migration provides the structure and impetus for a full-fledged, if largely unstructured, non-Western missionary movement.

The final two chapters of this book combine description and critical assessment of over seventy African immigrant churches in six major U.S. cities (Los Angeles, Metropolitan New York, Philadelphia, New Jersey, Washington D.C., and Chicago). The data and findings presented here are drawn from extensive ethnographic research conducted as part of the Mobile Faith project from 2003 to 2006. This project was designed and spearheaded by me, and the first leg involved a research trip to Africa in Spring 2003 aimed at exploring the interaction between migrant movement and Christian expansion within Africa as well as between Africa and the West. I interviewed and interacted with sixteen African Christian leaders and pastors (in Kenya and Ghana) whose ministries or movements reflected sustained international mission enterprise in the previous decade. Their testimonies provided abundant confirmation that the massive migrant movement taking place within and from the African continent was a prime catalyst in a new era of global missionary initiatives from Africa.

This initial finding provided the direction and framework for subsequent research in the United States. To search for and re-search the rapidly proliferating African immigrant congregations throughout the United States required the sacrificial commitment of eleven paid research assistants. The cities included in the research were chosen by a combination of deliberate choice (insofar as they represent major centers of African immigration) and circumstance (the research possibility being limited to the availability of research assistants). Some major centers of African immigration in the United States, like Atlanta and Houston, were only excluded for lack of resources. Regrettably so. The research involved three main components: interviews of founding pastors and leaders of the churches, participant observation of Sunday worship, and congregational surveys in up to thirty African immigrant congregations.

The findings are significant. The rate of growth of many African immigrant churches, all of which reflect an intense spiritual orientation, is quite astonishing. Most important, virtually all incorporate a strong missionary purpose beyond the strong preoccupation with cultural self-maintenance that is the hallmark of the immigrant congregation. My research confirms that pastors and members share bold visions of multicultural outreach and a conviction that America is a mission field. This missionary vision, as we shall see, is often expressed in concrete strategies and new models. At the same time, missionary engagement with the wider American society faces formidable obstacles, not the least of which is *race*. In America, as in all Western societies, Africa is the face of poverty, disease, calamity, and degradation. In the American situation, moreover, the long history of racial oppression and race division adds a further dimension. How this and other challenges complicate the missionary encounter is closely examined.

In the final analysis, this African missionary movement has wider significance beyond the encounter with any one Western context. Typically urban-based and dependent on social networks, African immigrant congregations are also veritable centers of transmigration or transnationalism. This, coupled with the fact that being in America often affords the most enterprising pastors ample resources for full-fledged international ministries, means that these flourishing African Christian communities potentially bridge North and South Christianities. At the very least, this study indicates that no evaluation of the future of global Christianity will be complete without taking into account the significance and potential of this emerging non-Western missionary movement, in which Africans play a vital role.

Part I

TRANSFORMING
THE MARGINS

1

Globalization

Descriptions, Debate, and Destinies

> I am a part of all that I have met;
> Yet all experience is an arch wherethro'
> Gleams that untravell'd world, whose margin fades
> For ever and for ever when I move.
> —Alfred Lord Tennyson, "Ulysses"

Modern history is littered with imprudent predictions about technology and its possibilities. In 1899, for instance, the commissioner of the United States Office of Patents recommended that his office be abolished on the grounds that "everything that can be invented has been invented." We do well to note that the late nineteenth century was characterized by a spectacular wave of technological innovation and scientific invention, including the invention of the telephone (1876), the first bicycle (1878), the discovery of the malarial parasite (1880), the invention of the wireless telegraph (1891), and the invention of the first car (1891). Even so, to twenty-first century ears the commissioner's declaration appears startling in its foolhardiness, to say the least.

On the other end of the spectrum, it is easy to find utopian projections of a future infinitely renewed by technological innovation and human ingenuity. These include grandiose predictions of an idyllic future in which the most mundane tasks would be transformed by technological progress. Indeed, over time technological breakthroughs have inspired even more fanciful hype and expectations that transcend earlier beliefs. Visions of the smart automated home, for instance, have long beguiled the scientific imagination. It will come as a surprise to some readers that as early as the 1890s the alluring fantasy in which typical household chores require the mere press of a button already existed. Only the details have been ratcheted up in keeping with technological advancement. Thus, in the more contemporary version of this prospect, Internet-capable appliances order groceries before they run out.

The point here is not that long-term technological predictions should be eschewed or ignored, but rather that we peer into the future through lenses conditioned by particular experiences and attendant dreams—even when the former transcends the latter. Ours is a world in which the margins and ideals of human existence constantly shift, so that each mark of progress is attended by a sense of ideals lost, and the miracles of human achievement must constantly bow before the new vistas of knowledge and ambition. Hence the deep poignancy of the mariner's reflection that "all experience is an arch wherethro' gleams that untravell'd world, whose margin fades forever and forever as I move." This perception is preeminently relevant to the study of globalization, a phenomenon that embodies and amplifies some of the most spectacular advances in technology in recent experience yet leaves us wrestling most intensely with age-old problems.

The term "globalization" has been in fashion for over three decades, and its immensely complex dimensions remain the focus of endless analysis and numerous monographs. Needless to add, the very concept is celebrated as much as it is contested, in part because it can mean all things to all people. In part also because of the widespread tendency to adopt the term as blanket coverage for any significant contemporary social change, so that it has become associated with a bewildering array of human actions and experiences. Such indiscriminate use, as Martin Albrow correctly surmises, reflects the limits rather than the extent of current understanding (1997). For its apologists, globalization impacts virtually every aspect of human life, from the critical to the mundane, and is poised to sweep all before it. Artful illustrations like that of the man in Jerusalem who places his cellular phone up to the Western Wall so a relative in France can say a prayer at the holy site are considered compelling. Detractors, however, associate the phenomenon with delirious fantasies evoked by unbridled hype surrounding the Internet revolution (think "e-solution"). Globalization, they scoff, is not (or never was) global. For some critics what passed for globalization is already passed. Thus, John Ralston Saul insists that the remarkable, unexpected, recovery of nationalism in various forms—including America's determination to act unilaterally (thus nationally) in the war with Iraq—signals a "post-globalization" era. In this view the menacing inequalities that continue to bedevil world economy, the dot.com bust, and the devastating September 11 event, are among key reasons why the G word stands for "globaloney."

Probably the safest conclusion that can be drawn from the plethora of studies on globalization is that reality is more complicated than theory. There is no golden, one-size-fits-all, theoretical model; and no approach appears to be uncontested. Yet, despite the faddishness surrounding usage of the term, the concept furnishes us with a powerful analytical tool for understanding what is undeniably one of the most powerful, transformative forces shaping our everyday lives. To attempt a fulsome examination of globalization in one chapter would be imprudent. What follows is an attempt to provide a very general description of the phenomenon with a focus on its historical, political, and economic dimensions. I also aim to spotlight key aspects of the continuing debate and identify some elements of the non-Western experience.

Explaining Globalization

The proliferation of definitions of globalization in the literature bears ample testimony to its complexity and unwieldiness. Summary definitions are plentiful, but James H. Mittleman (2000) notes that the best generally highlight two inter-related realities: first, the growing consciousness of the world as a single place, related to the escalating experience of interconnections or interdependence accompanied by growing borderlessness; second, the compression of time and space, evidenced among other things by the shrinking of distances through air travel and the Internet, the instant access to distant events granted by electronic transmission of information or images, and the de-localization of goods and products through international trade. Helpful definitions of globalization include the following:

- The intensification of worldwide social relations which link distant locali-ties in such a way that local happenings are shaped by events occurring many miles away and vice versa.
- The compression of the world and the intensification of consciousness of the world as a whole.
- A widespread perception that the world is rapidly being molded into a shared social space by economic and technological forces and that developments in one region of the world can have profound consequences for the life chances of individuals or communities on the other side of the globe.
- The rapidly developing and ever-densifying network of interconnections and interdependences that characterize modern social life.
- Increasing global interconnectedness, so that events and developments in one part of the world are affected by, have to take account of, and also influ-ence, in turn, other parts of the world. It also refers to an increasing sense of a single global whole.
- As experienced from below, the dominant form of globalization means a historical transformation: in the economy, of livelihoods and modes of existence; in politics, a loss in the degree of control exercised locally—for some, however little to begin with—such that the locus of power gradually shifts in varying proportions above and below the territorial state; and in culture, a devaluation of a collectivity's achievements and perceptions of them. This structure, in turn, may engender either accommodation or resis-tance (Mittelman 2000).

(Mittleman's definition is noteworthy because it attempts to capture an under-standing of globalization from "below," that is, one representative of the views and experiences of the majority of the world's peoples most of whom are on the margins of the new global order in economic and political terms.

The Historical Question

Is contemporary globalization a unique phenomenon or simply the latest mani-festation of a trend with long historical roots? How this question is answered has important bearing on assumptions and projections related to the phenomenon. All too often, in popular literature and some scholarly assessments, the historical antecedents of contemporary globalization are completely obscured by an over-whelming emphasis on its uniqueness and novelty. In this approach contempo-rary globalization, signifying a period of global integration and interconnection, is the historical successor of the "Cold-War" era, which was defined by division and partition. In other words, it is just over twenty years old.

Until recently, one of the most prominent examples of this view was the best-selling book by award-winning *New York Times* journalist Thomas L. Friedman, *The Lexus and the Olive Tree: Understanding Globalization* (1999). In a volume that reads like an extended editorial, Friedman permits himself the barest reference to a "previous era of globalization"—from the late 1800s to the late 1920s—during which Great Britain was the dominant global power. In his thinking, the preceding era of globalization was succeeded by a "long time-out" of roughly seventy-five years, which ended with the Cold War. This curious assessment discounts epochal twentieth-century developments with far-reaching implications for the contemporary world order, including the for-mation of the United Nations, the creation of the World Bank and Interna-tional Monetary Fund, and decolonization. While Friedman allows that there are many similarities between the previous era of globalization and the present one, he intones that the present era of globalization is "not only different in degree" but "in some important ways . . . also different in *kind* [italics added]" (1999: xv). He avers that anyone who wants to understand the post-Cold War world must "start by understanding that a new international system has suc-ceeded it—globalization."

This approach points to the spectacular developments and unique manifesta-tions of the current order, but it is impoverished by a weak historical perspec-tive and ultimately signals an understanding of contemporary globalization that identifies it with Americanization. In his more recent exploration of globaliza-tion, *The World Is Flat: A Brief History of the Twenty-First Century* (2005), Friedman, to his credit, radically revises his historical understanding and postu-lates three eras of globalization: the first era (1492 to circa 1800) dominated by countries; the second (1800 to 2000) driven by multinational companies; and the third (2000 to the present) driven by a "diverse—non-Western, nonwhite—group of individuals." Friedman's updated analysis coheres in some respects with the arguments pursued here about the deep historical roots of globalization, its inher-ently paradoxical nature, and (to a lesser extent) its multidirectional quality. One major difference is that Friedman attributes salience to non-Western elements only in the current era of globalization. Further, as in his earlier (1999) work, his journalistic approach means that his account is fixated on the more spectacular and conspicuous manifestations of the phenomenon—principally its economic dimensions—and is heavily America-centered. Most important, Friedman's his-torical typology is highly artificial. It bizarrely conceives of contemporary glo-balization as roughly eight years old!

To be sure, opinion as to the specific historical origins of globalization varies considerably, but most analysts agree that what is called globalization today has long historical roots. Some venture that the globe began to shrink when funda-mental forms of human interaction associated with large-scale society—including conquest, trade, and migration—enmeshed the fate of distant communities or groups.[1] In effect, processes of globalization date to the very beginning of civilization itself some five thousand years ago. Others contend that the emergence of major empires such as ancient Rome and China, which controlled and economically integrated huge swaths of the globe, represented early forms of globalization. From yet another perspective, globalization originated with the emergence of capitalism in Western Europe in the sixteenth century, a development that facilitated major technological breakthroughs and aided European colonial expansion. Such assessments, David Held et al. (1999) note, are complicated further by the argument that since globalization is a highly differentiated or multidimensional phenomenon, different aspects necessarily have different starting points.

Perhaps a more useful approach to this historical question lies in tracing the emergence of *global consciousness*: the growing awareness that the world we inhabit is a single (social) place. From time immemorial, various human societies have operated with some conception of the inhabited world—a "worldview." But even as recently as five hundred years ago actual knowledge of the world's physical or geographical extent was greatly circumscribed and shrouded in mythology. The great pre–sixteenth-century civilizations, including the Chinese, Hindu, Roman, and even Islamic civilizations, engendered large-scale transregional interactions but remained "discrete entities" with limited interdependence.[2] Similarly, the great monotheistic religions (Judaism, Christianity, and Islam) imagined the universe as a single bounded entity created by and subject to the sovereignty of a Supreme Being, yet theological presuppositions remained hostage to the boundaries of human knowledge and experience—even while (for Christianity and Islam) this universalistic vision constantly motivated expansion efforts that pushed those boundaries.

As a concept, globalization connotes processes of change that transcend territorial limits (including that of empires) or cultural differentiations, with the clear implication that the limits of impact and action are the globe itself. "Globe" in this sense, as Martin Albrow notes, is less a literary reference than a metaphor for the finitude of the particular space that human beings inhabit. In effect, globalization is less a *chronological* reference—indicative of innovation, progress, or sequential developments—than a *spatial* reference. That said, insofar as it represents "overall historical transformation," it involves relativity to some past state of affairs—to nineteenth-century colonialism, for instance, which did not achieve full world relevance.[3] This image or (technologically dependent) visualization of the world as a single, undifferentiated entity—a globe—is a fairly recent development, but it arrived in a series of steps taken by Western peoples.

Until the age of Western European exploration, the various regions and peo-

---

1. Joseph S. Nye and John D. Donahue, eds., *Governance in a Globalizing World* (Washington, DC: Brookings Institution Press, 2000).
2. See Anthony D. Smith, *Nationalism and Modernism: A Critical Survey of Recent Theories of Nations and Nationalism* (New York: Routledge, 1998); Held et al., *Global Transformations*, 33.
3. Albrow, *Global Age*, 90f.

ples of the world existed in almost complete isolation, and the current world order would have been unimaginable to them.[4] Europeans had no idea of the existence of the Americas; Japan was largely unknown to the rest of the world outside a handful of Dutch merchants; and Africa had only the most superficial contacts with the Far East or Europe. In fact, European sailors were convinced that beyond Cape Bojador (a projection on the Saharan coast, at the height of the Canary Islands) was a "Green Sea of Darkness" from which no one ever returned. Like many epochal transitions in human history, the events that transformed this speckled world order have a strong air of inadvertence.

The Chinese (under the Ming dynasty) were the first to initiate systematic overseas exploration in the early fifteenth century. Between 1405 and 1433, Chinese ships under the famed Admiral Zheng He, a Muslim eunuch, sailed as far as India and moored off the eastern coast of Africa not far from Mombassa (in 1418). Internal problems, exorbitant expedition costs, and the legendary Chinese isolationism rendered such efforts abortive.[5] By 1436, the construction of seagoing ships was banned by imperial edict as China turned its back on the world. It is intriguing but futile to speculate what the world would have been like today without that imperial edict. In 2005, perhaps to signal a newfound determination to restore the glories and technological exploits of an ancient past, China celebrated the six hundredth anniversary of Zheng He's extraordinary expedition with fanfare. But the fact remains that with China's preemptive disengagement, worldwide exploration from the late fifteenth century became a Western European prerogative.

Attended by technological breakthroughs and momentous advances in scientific knowledge, this age of European exploration stimulated a series of events over the next four centuries which progressively fostered global awareness. In *Understanding Globalization* (1997), Robert Schaeffer identifies three landmark events that provide meaningful reference points for our discussion. As I aim to demonstrate, however, each momentous step in the emerging consciousness of the world as a single place was ironically accompanied by determined efforts to divide it or carve it up into spheres of competing political dominance. These twin (somewhat paradoxical) forces—integration and divisive domination—I would argue, remain central elements of contemporary globalization.

The Treaty of Tordisellas

The first European nation to engage in overseas exploration was the relatively tiny and thoroughly Roman Catholic country of Portugal. From the start Portuguese efforts were linked to the militarist expansion of Christendom, and presiding popes—whose authority, as God's representatives on earth, extended throughout the known world—granted the Portuguese monarch the right to claim the newly *discovered* lands as Portuguese possession. Spain, a staunch economic rival and

---

4. E. J. Hobsbawn, "The World Unified," in *The Globalization Reader*, ed. Frank Lechna and John Boli (Malden, MA: Blackwell, 1999).

5. See Held et al., *Global Transformations*, 90; also Andrew Ross, *A Vision Betrayed: The Jesuits in Japan and China, 1542-1742* (Maryknoll, NY: Orbis Books, 1994).

emerging power in its own right, quickly emulated Portuguese efforts and was rewarded with similar papal endorsements.

The intense rivalry between the two Iberian powers made a collision of their colonial ambitions inevitable. This came in 1492 when Christopher Columbus, an Italian-born navigator sponsored by the Spanish crown, "discovered" land not already claimed by the Portuguese and named it the "West Indies" because he thought he had reached the West coast of India. Spanish claim to the new territory was immediately challenged by Portugal under the terms of previous papal decrees. Spain appealed to Pope Alexander VI (a Spaniard by birth), who not only endorsed its claim but also, by the bull *Inter Caetera*, sanctioned Spanish authority over all territory more than one hundred leagues (roughly three hundred miles) west and south of the Portuguese Cape Verde Islands. This decision, symbolized by a line drawn through the Atlantic, effectively divided the non-European world between the rival Iberian powers.

Lacking our more sophisticated understanding of the world, Alexander VI did not draw a corresponding line through the Pacific. In the event, the Portuguese protested this pro-Spanish decision, and by the Treaty of Tordesillas (1494) the dividing line was moved 270 leagues (710 miles) farther west. Seemingly offhand, this concession enabled Portugal to claim the whole of Brazil when it was *discovered* six years later by the Portuguese explorer Pedro Alvares Cabral (1467-1520).

Pope Alexander VI's stance was momentous. It signified a vastly enlarged understanding of the world as an aggregate of different regions and peoples, a single interconnected entity—albeit with poorly understood boundaries—with hitherto unexplored potential for expansionist projects that would bring distant peoples within the same orbit of influence (ecclesiastical and otherwise). Equally significant, from a historical point of view, this new era of globalization was marked by competing political projects aimed at dividing the newly discovered lands into spheres of colonial control. Genocidal, rapacious, and unprecedented, European colonialist expansion climaxed four centuries later. Not for the last time, as we shall see, a decisive advance in the consciousness of the world as one place was accompanied by determined efforts to divide it.

Global Timekeeping

The process of European colonial expansion now under way would be hugely bolstered by the industrial revolution, which brought massive improvements in the technologies of transportation and communication and caused the world to shrink even further. This process eventually led to the second notable event in the growth of global consciousness: the emergence of a global system of timekeeping.

As Schaeffer explains, when European sailors began sailing across the oceans in the late fifteenth century they had only the most rudimentary navigational aids. Latitude was relatively easy to determine, but inability to fix their "longitude" meant that once out of sight of land sailors could not fix their position with any accuracy. Thus, they risked shipwreck or running out of vital provisions before they could make their way back. By 1670, scientists knew the circumference of the earth and could measure longitude by time. But not only were the earliest watches and clocks unreliable; they also ran at different speeds set by the individual craftsmen. Yet, because European colonial expansion was linked to "vital economic interests," there were huge incentives to produce a watch that could determine longitude at sea and keep accurate time for several weeks. European governments offered huge rewards for such an invention.

In the 1760s both British and French watchmakers developed the required technology, setting zero longitude on their maps at Greenwich (a town on the Thames River in London) and Paris, respectively. British dominance of the seas meant that the British conception of time became more widely used and "the world eventually adopted a British system of time and space, symbolized by the adoption of the Greenwich meridian as zero degrees longitude" (Schaeffer 1997: 7). By 1883, 72 percent of the world's sailors (mariners) used maps drawn to the Greenwich meridian. But this British system of timekeeping was not immediately accepted as a global standard. Railway companies in Europe and the United States each kept their own time, which played havoc with travelers schedules and was hazardous for trains using the same track. Increased transcontinental travel accentuated the need to end the confusion and chaos of railway usage. The pressures to adopt a single system of time and space were all too compelling.

In October 1884, at a conference held in Washington D.C. and attended by twenty-five countries, the British system of timekeeping was eventually adopted (over French objections) and an international dateline was set over the Pacific. Thus began a global system of time zones. Even today this global system is not accepted everywhere: China rejects the "British time" and uses a time set in Beijing. But the widespread use of maps and globes drawn to the Greenwich meridian immeasurably bolstered global consciousness and the processes of globalization. The adoption of the Greenwich meridian virtually brought the whole world into one system of timekeeping that would henceforth govern international travel, global communications, and long distance interaction. By the early twentieth century, the effects of this phase of globalization were patently evident. The World Missionary Conference, which met in Edinburgh, in 1910 declared elatedly:

> Nations which were as far apart as if they had been on different planets, so far as exerting a practical influence upon each other is concerned, have been drawn together, and the whole world for the first time has become one. By means of the various applications of steam and electricity, the world has become one neighbourhood. The nations and peoples have been drawn into closer touch with each other through trade and commerce, through the growing volume of travel, through the migration of students from land to land, through the influence of international societies of various kinds, through the activity of the press, through the development of international law, as well as through foreign missions. . . . As a result of all this intermingling, the nations and races are acting and reacting upon each other with increasing directness, constancy, and power.[6]

---

6. *World Missionary Conference, 1910: Report of Commission 1—Carrying the Gospel to All the Non-Christian World* (Edinburgh: Oliphant, Anderson & Ferrier, 1910), 344.

But if Pope Alexander's 1474 actions simultaneously reflected a new global consciousness and energized efforts by emerging powers to divide and dominate the world, so did the 1884 event. The same year that a global system of time zones was established saw the opening of the 1884-85 Berlin Conference, a meeting of European powers held to resolve years of fiercely competitive territorial expansion. Agreements reached at this Berlin meeting allowed the various European powers to divide various parts of the globe among themselves in what John Isbister has described as an "orgy of imperialist gluttony." Already under way by the late 1870s, this process of colonial expansion—involving six European nations (England, France, Belgium, Germany, Italy, and Portugal) as well as America and Japan—was predatory and explosive. By the onset of the First World War, notes Isbister, these eight nations had "annexed 17% of the world's territory at an average rate of 240,000 square miles every year."[7] The most dramatic of all the new acquisitions was the arbitrary division of Africa into European spheres of influence—a process that *The Times* dubbed "the Scramble for Africa."

Moon Landing

The emerging networks of colonial domination, economic exchange, and transcontinental interaction continued apace, creating a shrinking world in which the fates of distant communities became more irrevocably intertwined and interconnected. European missionary efforts, it is worth noting, were significantly implicated in these transformations. The missionary project widened European knowledge of the newly (and, in some cases, yet to be) acquired lands considerably. It also benefited equally from the processes of technological advancement. In 1793, for instance, it took the British Baptist missionary William Carey (1761-1834) five months to get to India from England; by 1923, the same journey took three weeks.

The growing consciousness of the world as a single place received a further boost with what Schaeffer identifies as the third significant event: the 1969 moon landing, celebrated by astronaut Neil Armstrong as "one giant leap for mankind." Schaeffer observes, "The astronauts' photographs of the Earth, spinning in space, gave currency to the idea of the world as a global place. After we saw these pictures, it became difficult not to imagine the world as Columbus, Pope Alexander, or Neil Armstrong did."[8] Armstrong's giant leap was a truly global event. With the possible exception of mainland China, people all over the world, from New Zealand to Zambia, followed this historic event closely (on radio if not television). It is difficult now to recapture the palpable angst that surrounded the episode and its aftermath, not to mention the morbid fascination that kept diverse peoples of the planet fixated on this exalted scientific achievement in outer space. At the time, the event evoked powerful, if oversimplistic, sentiments of human

---

7. See John Isbister, *Promises Not Kept: The Betrayal of Social Change in the Third World,* 5th ed. (Bloomfield, CT: Kumarian Press, 2001), 73.

8. Robert K. Schaeffer, *Understanding Globalization: The Social Consequences of Political, Economic and Environmental Change* (New York: Rowman & Littlefield, 1997), 11.

solidarity and focused renewed attention on the need to make the earth a better place.

President Richard Nixon was among the first to express the view that this arrival on the moon "would inspire man to work harder for a solution of the troubles of his own planet."[9] Glenn Seaborg (chairman of the Atomic Energy Commission) was no less enthusiastic:

> I find the moon landing an amazing scientific and engineering feat. . . . It personally reinforces my feeling about the great power and potential of science and technology and my belief that through cooperation and concerted efforts man is capable of solving almost any problem, of meeting almost any challenge. I hope the moon landing will have such an uplifting effect on people all over the world and help unite us toward meeting some of our goals here on earth."[10]

Even President Abdel Nasser of Egypt, who only days earlier had voiced strong condemnation of American Middle East policy, praised the moon landing achievement, noting grimly: "We are against American policy, we are not against technology and scientific knowledge."[11]

But this hugely significant global event also coincided with the bipolar division of the world and the competing quest for world domination known as the "Cold War," a term popularized by the presidential adviser and financier Bernard Baruch. The "War" dated to 1947, when the brief alliance between the United States and the Soviet Union during the Second World War disintegrated into intense hostility and antagonism. This state of affairs lasted until the collapse of the Soviet Union in 1991 (and still continues on a small scale in some parts of the world such as Cuba and the Korean peninsula). The Cold War divided the major powers of the world into two antagonistic blocs and complicated international relations for over three decades. It was waged through a variety of means, including economic manipulation, massive ideological propaganda, and military operations. It was also attended by intense and escalating technological competition.

For all the near-universal sense of celebration that accompanied it, the moon-landing event occurred at the height of the Cold War and was a major milestone in the "space race"—the ideological rivalry between the United States and the Soviet Union for technological supremacy and global dominance. Dating to the Soviet launch of Sputnik 1, the first artificial satellite to be put into orbit (in October 1957), this race took the form of competing efforts by the two powers to explore outer space, send humans into space, and land people on the moon using rocket science. The military possibilities and the profound psychological benefit of success made the space race perhaps the most exalted aspect of the Cold

---

9. Walter Rugaber, "Nixon Makes 'Most Historic Telephone Call Ever,'" *New York Times*, July 21, 1969.

10. "Reactions to Man's Landing on the Moon Show Broad Variations in Opinions," *New York Times*, July 21, 1969.

11. "Nasser Hails the Landing on Moon as a Great Feat," Special to the *New York Times*, July 21, 1969.

War rivalry. Thus, the first moon landing by a human in 1969 signaled human achievement as much as it crowned entrenched global division. Giving expression to this little-acknowledged fact, historian Lewis Mumford wrote, in the *New York Times* on July 21, 1969, "Like most conspicuous scientific and technical achievements of our age . . . the moon landing program . . . is a symbolic act of war, and the slogan the astronauts will carry, proclaiming that it is for the benefit of mankind, is on the same level as the Air Force monstrous hypocrisy—'Our Profession is Peace.'"

The three events identified by Schaeffer are more illustrative than exhaustive. And since they spotlight the actions of Western peoples and powers, there is a real danger that they will be construed as validation of the widely held notion that contemporary globalization is a one-directional, Western-managed process. Certainly, the outstanding contribution of Western initiatives to the processes of globalization cannot be denied; and it would be well-nigh impossible to account for some present-day manifestations without this element. Yet to reduce the phenomenon of globalization to Western efforts would represent a significant distortion.

To start with, the spread of global consciousness, which is the focus of the above discussion, is not fully contemporaneous with the emergence or experience of globalization. The two are intertwined to a considerable extent, but the latter tends to lag behind the former. The fact that Schaeffer makes the fifteenth century the starting point has its own problems. There are good reasons for doing so, but it is dubious to treat developments in any period of history, no matter how momentous, as if they constitute a complete break from the past. (This problem is evident in attempts to associate the emergence of contemporary globalization with the end of the Cold War era). As already mentioned, both the rise of empires and the spread of universalizing religions like Islam and Christianity represent significant forces of globalization antecedent to Western expansionist projects. Indeed, the spread of Islam in previous centuries, itself a globalizing factor, had a lot to do with European efforts at overseas exploration. In addition, often overlooked is the fact that Western societies were directly impacted by encounters and interactions with the non-Western world, engendered by the Western initiatives. (For more on this, see chapter 5).

The view taken here is that globalization is not a managed process. This is not to say that it is unmanageable, but rather to reject the notion that any region (or nation) of the world is immune to, or stands outside of, the processes associated with the phenomenon. The issue of global population growth easily illustrates this point.

Living Room and Room for Living

Since the late eighteenth century, when Thomas R. Malthus (1766-1834), an English economist and clergyman, propagated the view that populations tend to increase faster than the means of subsistence, concerns about the growth of the world's population (vis-à-vis the capacity of the globe) have produced considerable debate and not a few saturnine predictions. The dizzying details of this complex subject need not detain us. What warrants our brief attention is the way in which this issue underlines our sense of inhabiting a single social place with finite resources. Among the best-known facts, there are just over six billion people in the world today, but the world continues to grow at a record pace—by the size of New York City (roughly eight million) every month. Worldwide population growth in the last fifty years is greater than in the previous four million years. Human population increase in the 1990s alone exceeded the total global population in 1600.

Analysis of how many people the world can support is very complex, but twelve billion seems to be the most widely accepted figure. Not that the debate is over. Yet, even if the world population levels off at ten to eleven billion as United Nations' analysts project, the impact that increased pollution and human abuse of the environment will have on the capacity of the world is anybody's guess, not to mention the inevitable effects of our growing numbers and appetites. The heart of the dilemma, as Bill McKibben points out, is not one of "space" but of *resources*: everyone on earth, he explains, could fit into half of Rhode Island, if people were willing to stand. Yet it is manifestly clearer than ever before that significant mismanagement or overexploitation of the world's limited resources in any part of the globe can have major repercussions for the rest.

In short, the population question illustrates the fact that interdependence is intrinsic to the processes of globalization, and also that the margins are not merely at the mercy of the center. True, the richest 20 percent worldwide (disproportionately located in the North) consume sixteen times as much and use seventeen times the energy as the poorest 20 percent. Even more sobering is the thought that the earth's natural limits means that *it will be virtually impossible for the world's poor to follow the economic trajectory of the world's currently rich.*[12] Yet it is of no small importance that almost all of the world's current demographic growth comes from outside the West, as population growth has declined sharply in the developed industrial nations (in almost all cases to well below the replacement level of 2.1 births per adult female). This demographic imbalance— aging populations and low birth rates in advanced industrial countries combined with explosive population growth in the developing world[13]—portends crises and dilemmas that are hugely significant. Global destinies are far more intertwined than is often thought.

Ultimately, regardless of how far back in the past one dates the phenomenon of globalization, current manifestations are decidedly striking in terms of magnitude, complexity, and velocity, and many important aspects are unprecedented. But the historical perspective remains crucial, for contemporary globalization as embodies continuities and discontinuities with the past. Attentiveness to this historical dimension also serves as a useful safeguard against the sort of unqualified assessment made by the U.S. commissioner mentioned at the beginning of this chapter.

---

12. Isbister, *Promises Not Kept*, 231.

13. See the excellent study involving an interdisciplinary group of twenty-nine scholars based in the United States, Canada, and Western Europe—Wayne A. Cornelius, et al., eds., *Controlling Immigration: A Global Perspective*, 2nd ed. (Stanford: Stanford University Press, 2004).

Ready or Not: Aspects of the Non-Western Experience

In this book, I have opted to use the terms "Western" and "non-Western" to describe specific realities. I am quite aware that use of these concepts can be hopelessly unhelpful because they connote singularity and monolithic sameness, when nothing could be further from the truth. Use of the term "West" is arguably more defensible, aside from the obvious fact that it begs the question, "west of what?" Most descriptions point to "the people of Western Europe and their descendants in North America"[14] or to the heritage of Western Christendom (essentially the Western Roman Empire). In Samuel P. Huntington's usage, "the West" includes Europe, North America, and other countries in which Europeans settled, such as Australia and New Zealand.[15] The term "non-Western" potentially suffers both from the fact that non-Western societies lack any such cohesion and from the odium of describing those entities in terms of what they are *not* (i.e., Western). Huntington circumvents these pitfalls by adopting the distinctly unglamorous phrase, "the rest."

My reasons for adopting the label "non-Western" are quite varied. First, there is the obvious consideration that it is convenient and that such broad categories do serve a theoretical purpose; otherwise coherence and lucidity are sacrificed to multiple frames of reference and endless caveats. In much of this book a central concern is to delineate experiences and characteristics that, generally speaking, distinguish the West from much if not all of the non-Western world, although necessarily with important exceptions. That said, the conditions and worldviews that characterize and shape much of life in non-Western societies are arguably beyond the reference and understanding of most Westerners. Even more important, Western claims to universality and notions of cultural homogeneity distinguish its worldview from just about everybody else on the planet.

Second, it is sadly true that we are often more adept at defining our identities in terms of what we are not than based on a secure sense of what we are. What, after all, is a European identity? (As the debate surrounding the accession of Turkey, a 99-percent Muslim country, to the European Union indicates, this is a fraught question). Third, the alternative concepts are, in my view, equally if not even more problematic. The once popular "third world" is now gradually falling into disuse and has accrued deeply stereotypical connotations of underdevelopment, chronic poverty (combined with conspicuous consumption by ruling elites), economic dependence, illiteracy, political instability, and overpopulation. Quite frankly, I find the widely used "global South" oxymoronic. Also, like its variants—"two-thirds world" and "the South"—its application tends to be wholly economic and demographic.

These considerations hardly get away from the fact that the non-Western concept covers a vast panoply of distinct and diverse peoples, histories, and cultural

---

14. See Theodore H. Von Laue, *The World Revolution of Westernization: The Twentieth Century in Global Perspective* (New York: Oxford University Press, 1987).

15. Samuel P. Huntington, *The Clash of Civilizations and the Remaking of World Order* (New York: Simon & Schuster, 1996), 46.

realities. But this is precisely why I find it appealing. Taken at face value, the "non-Western world" is largely synonymous with the developing world (including the Asian Tigers who, for all their economic development, include largely rural populations). But, unlike other options, "non-Western" extends beyond mere economic, geographical, and demographic reference to *cultural* and *existential* significance. One can point to certain features that are indigenously present almost everywhere—such as an emphasis on communality and the attendant veneration of ancestors—but the non-Western world is palpably pluralistic and immeasurably diverse. The worldviews and philosophies of its multitudinous societies and cultures are not lacking a universal vision, but it is the contextual and the particular that frame their worldviews and define existence. In this regard, the term "non-Western" serves not so much to identify an entity as to qualify a reality—a reality that exists in enduring antithesis to the Western world in at least one critical respect: *claims to universality or normativity are conspicuously absent.*

The Limits of Experience, and Experiencing the Limits

Undoubtedly, Western domination in various forms and disguises represents a major strand of globalization, and relationships of control, exploitation, and dependency remain entrenched within the new global order. If globalization is often used as a "blame word" by many, especially among the world's poor and powerless,[16] it is because important dimensions negatively impact "livelihoods and modes of existence." Clearly, what is termed globalization is not experienced the same way throughout the world. The increased velocity of human interaction and growing global interdependence means that an increasing number of events simultaneously impact distant parts of the world or leave few aspects of daily life untouched. However, regardless of our mode of existence and geographical location, we are more conscious of some aspects of globalization than of others. While the average American, say, might be keenly sensitive to the potential impact of off-shore "outsourcing" and the threat of terrorism, the average sub-Saharan African is more acutely attuned to the spread of the AIDS virus and the impact of non-governmental organizations (NGOs).

Furthermore, we do not all experience these "global" events the same way. International migration is arguably one of the most pervasive strands of contemporary globalization—one out of every thirty-four persons in the world is an international migrant[17]—and few people in the world are immune to the effects of migration. Yet, while immigrant experiences within wealthy Western societies get the most media attention, the vast proportion of global migration takes place *within* the non-Western world in the form of South–South migration. The impact of such massive people movements and displacements on the impover-

---

16. See Roland Robertson, "Globalization and the Future of Traditional Religion," in *God and Globalization: Religion and the Powers of the Ethics of the Common Life*, ed. M. L. Stackhouse and P. J. Paris (Harrisburg, PA: Trinity Press International, 2000), 61, 63.

17. By 2005 there were an estimated 191 million international migrants—*Trends in Total Migrant Stock: The 2005 Revision* (United Nations, 2006).

ished economies and dilapidated infrastructures of societies in the developing world beggars the imagination.

Equally significant, "there are many phenomena, especially on a local level that are either outside globalization or mingle only indirectly with global processes."[18] This limitation is powerfully illustrated by the disparateness of access to the Internet, a circumstance that essentially divides the world into the "wired" and the "unwired." Undoubtedly, Internet users worldwide remain a privileged elite—in 2006 global usage was still under 16 percent. But Internet usage is lowest in Africa, where only 2.6 percent of the population are users— compared to 10 percent for Asia, 10 percent for the Middle East, 14 percent for Latin America and the Caribbean, 36 percent for Europe, and 67 percent for the United States.[19] The disparity is even more obvious when it is considered that, though it accounts for 14 percent of the world's population, the African continent is home to only 2.3 percent of Internet users worldwide.

To be sure, this situation is far from static. Between 2000 and 2005, Internet usage in Africa rose faster than anywhere else in the world (423.9 percent), except the Middle East (454.2 percent). But such statistics need heavy qualifications. The proliferation of Internet cafes in Africa's cities is unmistakable. But who uses them? For now, mainly foreigners and tourists who can afford the prohibitive charges. In Latin America, too, it is noteworthy that most Internet users "are white, male, urban and upper class."[20] In effect, for much of the developing world, the digital divide is being reconfigured, not bridged.

Accounts of the impact of globalization on the "developing world" tend to lopsidedly emphasize either positive or negative aspects. In reality the phenomenon portends mixed blessings. Among other things, transformations associated with globalization have facilitated greater access to information and communication networks that can empower disadvantaged groups and provide tools of positive change. Globalization is also held to be "a powerful force for poverty reduction."[21] Transnational corporations (TNCs), which account for one-third of the world's capital, can boost the economy of poor countries by providing thousands of jobs and skills training, importing advanced technology, and contributing to a better business climate.[22]

But few would deny either that globalization, most patently economic globalization, has a "dark side" or that what can be a powerful force for good is daily

---

18. Mittelman, *Globalization Syndrome*, 226.

19. See Internet Usage Statistics for Africa, in the Internet World Stats (http://www.internet worldstats.com/stats1.htm). According to Ron Nixon, by 2007, still less than 4 percent of Africa's population was connected to the Internet, and the majority of these were in North African countries and South Africa (see Ron Nixon, "Africa, Offline: Waiting for the Web," *New York Times*, June 22, 2007).

20. Jose Vargas, "Bridging the Digital Divide in Latin America," *Global Future* (First Quarter, 2001).

21. *World Bank Development Report: Building Institutions for Markets* (New York: Oxford University Press, 2002), 6. It cites China, India, Uganda, and Vietnam as models/examples.

22. See Pamela K. Brubaker, *Globalization at What Price? Economic Change and Daily Life* (Cleveland: Pilgrim, 2001), 20; Miriam Adeney, *God's Foreign Policy: Practical Ways to Help the World's Poor* (Vancouver: Regent College Publishing, 1998).

deformed by corporate greed, unrestrained self-interest, exploitation, and crime. The globalization of crime is an obvious example. Illicit financial flows (or "dirty money") siphon "hundreds of billions of dollars out of nonwestern countries into Western countries" based on a global system "developed in the West and advanced by the West."[23] Raymond Baker describes this as "the most damaging economic condition hurting the poor."[24] The impact on non-Western societies is horrendous: including severe and worsening poverty, devastating civil wars, diminished trade, failed states, rampant government corruption, and limited investment. Yet, as Baker explains, the costs to Western societies are equally staggering—including the failure of the foreign policy objectives, uncontrollable illegal drug use, gang warfare, terrorism, high-level corruption, and massive tax evasion.[25]

All over the world, numerous communities "are threatened locally by the changes [associated with globalization] and feel victimized by them."[26] TNCs are often exploitative of workers, ignore environmental damage and pollution, and put profit before the dignity of life. For instance, it has been known for many years that the drug eflornithine cures sleeping sickness (trypanosomiasis), a deadly disease spread by the tsetse fly which drives victims mad before killing them. Trypanosomiasis devastates parts of central Africa and about three hundred thousand people are infected every year. However, medical production of eflornithine was stopped when early hopes that it would help to fight cancer were dashed; it mattered little that the drug saves lives in Africa. Reproduction of the drug only resumed when it was discovered that it eliminates facial hair in women[27]—a major source of profit! The profit motive is undeniably indispensable for research investment, but such displays of capitalism bereft of conscience are deeply alienating and account for the most bitter criticisms of economic globalization.[28]

Ultimately, however, globalization involves *marginalization and exclusion*. This can be understood in different ways. Ankie Hoogvelt argues perceptively that contemporary globalization has "recast traditional patterns of inclusion and exclusion between countries by forging new hierarchies which cut across and

---

23. Raymond W. Baker, *Capitalism's Achilles Heel: Dirty Money and How to Renew the Free-Market System* (Hoboken, NJ: John Wiley & Sons, 2005), 194, 202. See also Moisaés Naâim, *Illicit: How Smugglers, Traffickers and Copycats Are Hijacking the Global Economy* (New York: Doubleday, 2005). Illicit financial flows cover an extensive, perhaps boundless, range of nefarious activities including smuggling, credit fraud, prostitution, large-scale bribery, mispricing, dummy corporations, money laundering, and tax evasion.

24. Baker, *Capitalism's Achilles Heel,* 248.

25. Ibid.,162-206.

26. Max L. Stackhouse and Peter J. Paris, eds., *God and Globalization,* vol. 1, *Religion and the Powers of the Common Life* (Harrisburg, PA: Trinity Press International, 2000).

27. Donald G. McNeil, "Cosmetic Saves a Cure for Sleeping Sickness," *New York Times,* February 9, 2001.

28. See Klaus Schwab, "Capitalism Must Develop More of a Conscience," *Newsweek,* February 24, 2003. It is noteworthy that only 10 percent of global spending on medical research and development is directed at the diseases of the poorest 90 percent of the world's people (*Human Development Report 2003* [New York: Oxford University Press, 2003], 12).

penetrate all societies and regions of the world."[29] As such, global economic divisions are less geographical (or regional) than hierarchical. The "developing world" or "third world" is not a geographical entity but a social reality. The richest nations have "third world" spheres within their domains and the most poverty-stricken countries boast wealthy elites who can participate in the economies of the world system (even if their countries cannot).[30] Mittelman concurs that under globalization "entire zones of the global political economy, except for their dominant strata, and pockets in the developed world are left out."[31] In this respect at least, globalization is paradoxically regressive—in the sense that it has engendered (on an infinitely larger scale) the old feudal order, in which the upper classes of nobles and lords in various regions have more in common with each other than with the peasants in their geographical space.

Undoubtedly also, the forces of economic globalization have contributed to egregious inequalities within nations. How this is so is complicated and has a lot to do with the fact that economic globalization is driven by hypercapitalism. It is therefore significant that the United States is not only the most developed (capitalistic) economy but also the most unequal society in the industrialized world: by 2001, 13.7 percent of its population (more than thirty-six million) lived in poverty; and 40 percent of its wealth was owned by the top 1 percent.[32] This writer finds it hard to comprehend the virtues of an economic model in which the net worth of a single individual (Microsoft founder Bill Gates) equaled the total net worth of the bottom 50 percent of American families in the year 2000.

Perhaps even more significant is the fact that the processes of globalization have engendered staggering inequalities *between* geographical regions of the world. The shameless abuses and gross disadvantages to which poor nations (in addition to their own internal crises, of course) have been subjected as a price for incorporation into a global economy dominated by the rich industrial countries and the international institutions they control has no parallels in history. The debt crisis of the 1980s is crucial to the story.[33] For "third world" countries, efforts to service monstrous, often immorally acquired debts resulted in a net reverse flow of funds from the South to the North and impoverished the indebted nations further. Radical market-oriented reforms (notoriously "structural adjustment programs") imposed by the North, ostensibly to stimulate economic growth, further devastated already vulnerable economies and evoked bitter accusations of recolonization. The most significant outcome of all these developments has been the

---

29. Ankie Hoogvelt, *Globalization and the Postcolonial World: The New Political Economy of Development* (Baltimore: Johns Hopkins University Press, 1997), xii.

30. Ibid., 84.

31. Mittelman, *Globalization Syndrome*, 241.

32. Noreena Hertz, *The Silent Takeover: Global Capitalism and the Death of Democracy* (New York: Free Press, 2001), 8f., 43f. Hertz adds that less than twenty-five years previously 40 percent of the wealth was owned by the top 13 percent.

33. For a helpful account, see, among many others, Isbister, *Promises Not Kept*, 179-84; Hoogvelt, *Globalization and the Postcolonial World*; and Walden Bello, "Structural Adjustment Programs: 'Success' for Whom?," in *The Case against the Global Economy and for a Turn toward the Local*, ed. J. Mander and E. Goldsmith (San Francisco: Sierra Club Books, 1996).

enforced integration of southern countries into a North-dominated economy—a process in which the International Monetary Fund (IMF) and World Bank played crucial roles.

It is a fact that economic globalization creates winners and losers, or more precisely a world in which few win and many lose. "Participation in global economic policymaking," notes the *Human Development Report 2000*, "is embedded in a world of grossly unequal economic power." Statistical representations of this reality are a commonplace and, due in part to their propaganda value, a weapon of choice for critics of all stripes. They are best seen as snapshots of an enormously complex landscape. Among the most commonly cited are the following:

- The rich countries (comprising 15 percent of the world population) account for about 60 percent of the world GDP.[34]
- These same rich countries use 70 percent of the world's energy, 75 percent of its metals, 85 percent of its wood, and consume 60 percent of its food.[35]
- Together, the top one-fifth of the world's population accounts for 86 percent of all private consumption expenditures; the richest 20 percent worldwide consume sixteen times as much, and use seventeen times the energy, as the poorest 20 percent.[36]
- The hundred poorest countries, with one-fifth of the world's population, receive only 1 percent of financial flows;[37] so these countries lack the foreign capital to take advantage of increased market access.[38]
- In today's market-driven economy, 20 percent of the world's people receive 83 percent of the world's income.[39]
- The richest 1 percent of the world's people receive as much income as the poorest 57 percent.[40]
- Wal-Mart, the world's largest retailer, has revenues as large as the economies of 160 countries combined.[41]

The marginalizing effect of globalization is perhaps most insidious in the case of Africa. No other region is more negatively affected by GATT (General Agreement on Tariffs and Trade) policies. It is no secret that the same rich nations who sing the praises of liberalism and free market and insist that developing countries adhere to its tenets have implemented protectionist policies and erected high trade barriers to the products of the developing countries, particularly agricul-

---

34. Bruce Scott, "The Great Divide in the Global Village," *Foreign Affairs* (Jan./Feb. 2001), 163.

35. Hoogvelt, *Globalization and the Postcolonial World*, 87.

36. Brubaker, *Globalization at What Price?* 32.

37. Ibid., 22.

38. Scott, "Great Divide," 164.

39. Ronald J. Sider, *Rich Christians in an Age of Hunger: Moving from Affluence to Generosity* (Nashville: Word, 1997).

40. *Human Development Report 2000* (New York: Oxford University Press, 2000), 19.

41. Brubaker, *Globalization at What Price?* 58.

ture, essentially depriving struggling economies of their few comparative trade advantages.[42] In 2002, the thirty industrial countries of the Organization for Economic Cooperation and Development (OECD) spent $311 billion on domestic agricultural subsidies, which is more than the combined domestic products of all the countries of sub-Saharan Africa; and the World Bank calculated that the European Union's annual subsidy to dairy farmers comes to $913 per cow, which far exceeds sub-Saharan Africa's per capita GDP of $490! while South Africa alone loses $100 million in annual exports to America and Europe subsidies on sugar production.[43]

By 1990 Africa had about 13 percent of the world population but contributed less that 1.7 percent to world production.[44] Africa also represents the most conspicuous exemplar of Ankie Hoogvelt's provocative thesis that the world economy was far more integrated and interconnected at the height of European colonialism that it is under contemporary globalization. Hoogvelt contends that the economic expansion of the colonial era, which brought significant populations of the periphery (regions of Africa, Latin America, and Asia) "into an *expanding* and intensifying network of economic exchanges with the core [Western Europe, North America, and Japan]" has given way to an intensification of economic interaction *within* the core which has rendered the periphery "structurally irrelevant."[45] He insists that even if the four "Asian Tigers"—Singapore, Hong Kong, Taiwan, and Korea (with a combined population of 72 million)—were added to the "core" countries, the decline in economic activity between core and periphery is still significant. Undoubtedly, many of Africa's myriad problems and implacable pathologies are of local origin and have internal causes,[46] including endemic civil wars, ethnic strife, inept authoritarian regimes, and the AIDS epidemic (by 2006 there were almost twenty-five million people living with HIV in sub-Saharan Africa—63 percent of the global total).[47] (For a fuller discussion of Africa's crises, see chapter 9). Yet, simply to blame the continent's internal woes for its marginalization within the global order is to suggest that the forces of globalization require ideal conditions to work, a claim easily refuted by examples in Europe and elsewhere. Globalization appears to have brought little gain for the continent and arguably portends greater threat than promise in the short term.

---

42. See Jack Beatty, "Do as We Say, Not as We Do," *Atlantic Monthly* (February, 2002).

43. See Andrés Martinez, "Who Said Anything about Rice? Free Trade Is about Cars and Playstations," *New York Times*, August 10, 2003; editorial, "Harvesting Poverty: Napoleon's Bittersweet Legacy," *New York Times*, August 11, 2003.

44. Kidane Mengisteab, *Globalization and Autocentricity in Africa's Development in the 21st Century* (Trenton, NJ: Africa World Press, 1996).

45. Hoogvelt, *Globalization and the Postcolonial World*, 18f., 68-89.

46. See Paul Kennedy, *Preparing for the Twenty-First Century* (New York: Vintage Books, 1993).

47. *Aids Epidemic Update: Special Report on Hiv/Aids* (Geneva: UNAID/WHO, 2006), 6. In Swaziland, the country with the highest HIV incidence in the world, one-in-three adults (33 percent) is infected. By 2001, HIV-AIDs had killed 17 million Africans (more than 3.7 million of whom are children); see *Time Magazine*, February 12, 2001, 55. However, 2.1 million Africans died of the disease in 2006 alone.

Indeed, there is an argument to be made that Africa's prospects of wholesome integration/participation in the new global order seem particularly bleak.[48]

Whose Globalization?

In recent decades the United States has flexed its huge superpower muscles with scant regard for the world's approval, stimulating vigorous debate about its imperial status. "Respected analysts on both the left and the right," comments Joseph S. Nye (dean of Harvard's Kennedy School of Government), "are beginning to refer to 'American empire' approvingly as the dominant narrative of the twenty-first century."[49] He adds that not since Rome has one nation loomed so large above the others. In similar vein, Dimitri K. Simes (president of the Nixon Center in Washington) observes that "whether or not the United States now views itself as an empire, for many foreigners it increasingly looks, walks, and talks like one, and they respond to Washington accordingly."[50]

But many political analysts query the notion of America as an imperial power. Nye himself points out that while the United States may be more powerful than Britain was at its imperial peak it has less control over what occurs inside other countries than Britain did at the height of its empire. Throughout its colonies, for instance, the British officials had control of schools, taxes, laws, and even elections. Furthermore, America's habitual reluctance to invest in or commit to nation building and peacekeeping are incompatible with a wholesome global role beyond narrow self-interest. Significantly, the United States spends sixteen times as much on its military as it does on international development (which remains at 1 percent of the federal budget). Nor, in fact, does the United States dominate trade, antitrust, or financial regulation issues. In all these areas it has, perforce, to cooperate with the European Union, Japan, and others.[51] And the growing impact of China's emerging economy on the world economy further undermines long-standing notions of American preeminence.[52] Others also point out that U.S. contribution to world output has declined from about 40 percent in 1950 to 28 percent in 1999.[53]

In a word, the world is not standing still. For one thing, growing anti-Americanism around the world means that, while American influence and bargaining power are immense in geopolitical terms, individual nation states have complete freedom to protect their independence and act in their own interests—even in the face of American bully tactics. Importantly, American suprem-

---

48. Mittelman, *Globalization Syndrome*, 241.

49. Joseph S. Nye, "U.S. Power and Strategy after Iraq," *Foreign Affairs* 82, no. 4 (July/August 2003): 60-73.

50. D. K. Simes, "America's Imperial Dilemma," *Foreign Affairs* 82, no. 6 (November/December 2003): 91-102.

51. Nye, "U.S. Power and Strategy after Iraq," 65-71.

52. For a helpful evaluation, see "China and the World Economy," *The Economist*, July 30, 2005.

53. Isbister, *Promises Not Kept*, 192.

acy, like all forms of hegemony, invites resistance in the form of alternative counter-hegemonic power blocs. Growing regionalism, it is argued, will chip away at U.S. preeminence and make it more sensible to conceive of a "multi-polar" world in which the United States is *primus inter pares*. Charles A. Kup-chan (professor at Georgetown University and a senior fellow at the Council on Foreign Relations) insists that "as the EU fortifies its governmental institutions and takes in new members . . . , it will become a formidable counterweight to the United States on the world stage," for "centers of power by their nature compete for position, influence, and prestige."[54] Andrew Moravcsik (Harvard University professor of government) also contends that while Europe may pos-sess weaker military forces than does the United States, it is stronger in almost every other dimension of global influence.[55] If America is the military super-power, Europe is the "civilian" superpower.

Interestingly, this spirited debate among political analysts and foreign rela-tions experts over the question of American imperialism appears to have had little impact on the fairly pervasive notion that globalization is a one-directional process, aided by technological innovations produced in the West, and largely synonymous with American capitalist expansion and cultural imperialism. Part of the problem lies in the fact that globalization is often conceived in exclusively economic terms: as a singular process aimed at the creation of a single market system dominated or manipulated by a handful of rich nations. From this point of view, U.S. economic hegemony and principal status in the Breton Woods institu-tions (the IMF and World Bank) render all other arguments moot. Economic glo-balization is, perforce, essentially a Western or principally American project.

This "economy is all" approach is notably evident in arguments and pro-nouncements on the extreme ends of the globalization debate, that is, among the phenomenon's most ardent believers and die-hard skeptics. For the former, globalization is a capitalist reality that signals the inevitable spread of neo-liberal enterprise and the move toward an integrated global market, in which the nation state will be supplanted as the primary economic unit.[56] In this sense, global-ization is "an all-powerful god; a holy trinity of burgeoning markets, unsleep-ing technology, and borderless managers."[57] This narrow perspective typically underlies grand theories of globalization which depict it as a homogenizing force synonymous with Americanization.[58] (The contentious issue of an emerging global culture/civilization, reflective of the inexorable spread of Western mod-ernization and American consumer culture, is taken up in the next chapter.)

Such hyperbolized claims provide easy targets for detractors who point to the intensification of North–South inequalities, the resilience of the nation-state,

---

54. Charles A. Kupchan, "The End of the West," *Atlantic Monthly* (November, 2002).

55. Andrew Moravcsik, "Striking a New Transatlantic Bargain," *Foreign Affairs* 82, no. 4 (July/ August, 2003): 84. He contends that a "bipolar world," in which Europe is seen as providing an alternative, complementary leadership base, is closer to reality.

56. For a more elaborate description of this "hyperglobalist" position, see Held et al., *Global Transformations*, 3-5. This approach is also evident in Friedman's *World Is Flat* (2005).

57. Saul, "Collapse of Globalism," 33.

58. See Robertson, "Globalization and the Future of Traditional Religion," 55f.

growing regionalism, resurgent nationalism, and the inherent contradiction in a vision that promises the worldwide spread of democracy, on the one hand, while projecting a decline in the power of the nation-state (an entity indispensable for democracy), on the other. But for critics also, much of what passes for globalization amounts to a vaunted economic experiment aimed at sustaining the primacy of the West in world affairs. This is one reason why many in the "third world" conceive of economic globalization as a process tantamount to recolonization, or worse.[59] In effect, detractors and true believers share the same basic premise.

This is arguably one reason for the ironic contradictions that plague the anti-globalization movement. Apart from the fact that it utilizes the tools of globalization to sustain its campaign against it, anti-globalizers have done more than most groups to spread and strengthen awareness of globalization at the popular level. Hugely responsible for disseminating notions of globalization as a Western-managed phenomenon, the anti-globalization movement is itself a *Western* movement. Its numbers and activities are overwhelmingly dominated by Westerners, and its most militant expressions and activism are to be found in the United States. As Roland Robertson observes, "the American form of antiglobalism may well become globalized," which in turn might lead to "the perspective that *anti*globalism is a form of Americanization."[60] Thus, we are left with that familiar dynamic in which the West is presented as both the problem and the solution.

The widespread depiction of globalization as more or less a thirty-year-old monolithic Western economic experiment is problematic for other reasons. Globalization, as we have noted, is a multidimensional phenomenon. This is to affirm that it reflects "a multiplicity of driving forces" or, in Mittelman's phrase, a "syndrome of processes." In other words, it is simultaneously cultural, economic, political, and so on.[61] Identifying these dimensions can be arbitrary, for while they represent highly differentiated processes, almost all overlap in the arena of human activity and interaction. Even ecological globalization is not without political, social, and economic implications. At the same time, it would be a mistake to assume that developments or changes in one domain will necessarily be duplicated in others. The facile assumption that developments within the world economy explain what might happen in other areas is one of the reasons why the globalization debate remains so fraught.

Undoubtedly, some vital aspects of contemporary globalization reflect American economic dominance. It might even be true to say that economic globalization is *America-centric*. By 1900 the United States was the richest country in the world, and in the tumultuous years following the devastations of the Second World War, it alone accounted for 50 percent of world GDP. Today the U.S. economy is reportedly as large as the next three (Japan, Germany, and Britain). With

---

59. Hoogvelt (*Globalization and the Postcolonial World*) makes a convincing case that the world economy was far more integrated and interconnected at the height of European colonialism than it is at present, that where once non-Western societies were *structurally exploited*, they are now *structurally irrelevant*.

60. See Robertson, "Globalization and the Future of Traditional Religion," 62.

61. Mittelman, *Globalization Syndrome*, 12; also Nye and Donahue, eds., *Governance in a Globalizing World*, 4-6; and Held et al., *Global Transformations*, 23-26.

only 5 percent of the world's population, it accounts for 43 percent of the world's economic production, 40 percent of its high technology, and 50 percent of its research and development. Added to economic dominance is undisputed military supremacy. The fact that America spends as much on defense ($399 billion) as the next twenty top-spending nations combined (including Russia, China, Japan, the U.K., France, and Germany)[62] may be as much a tribute to global preeminence as it is to national phobias.

In fact, America is no more immune to the disruptions caused by evolving global structures than other industrial nations.[63] It is noteworthy, from a historical perspective, that the United States is itself a product of seventeenth- and eighteenth-century globalization. Present-day America is notoriously averse to encroachment of its sovereignty by transnational institutions like the United Nations or an International Criminal Court. But the global nature of an increasing number of issues—including human rights, terrorism, and crime, environmental degradation or global warming—need solutions that are beyond the capacity of individual nation states, no matter how powerful they are. By its very nature, global terrorism makes a mockery of national sovereignty not only because it is lacking nationalist ideology and interests but also because it appears to thrive on the very conditions that derive from economic hegemony. In any case, addressing the global disorder it portends requires powerful Western states to form strategic alliances and collaborate with impoverished non-Western nations. In an age of AIDS, the West Nile virus, global warming, off-shore "outsourcing," and massive nonwhite immigration, not even the most powerful nation on earth can claim secure sovereign autonomy. Interestingly, the same forces of globalization that were applauded for the reinvigoration of Western economies in the 1990s are now blamed for the relentless export of jobs from America, Britain, and Germany to India, China, and Mexico.[64]

Transforming the Center

The point at issue is that the processes of globalization are inherently paradoxical. They incorporate

- movement (colonial expansion, the spread of economic modernization) and counter-movement (third world nationalism, North-to-South migration, religious revitalization)
- hegemony (American "hard" power, the dominance of transnational corporations) and resistance (rampant anti-Americanism, "soft protest," or "consumer activism")

---

62. Karen Yourish, "The Cost of Empire," *Newsweek*, July 21, 2003, 27.
63. Mittelman, *Globalization Syndrome*, 18.
64. See "A World of Work: A Survey of Outsourcing," *The Economist* (November 13, 2004): 3-6.

- forces of integration (the European Union) and fragmentation (growing ethnic nationalism, even "ethnic cleansing")

The unending debate over the impact of globalization on the nation-state reflects this paradoxical element. Statehood, as some like Connie McNeely argue, remains "fundamental to the structure and organization of the international system";[65] yet transnational or subnational agencies and regional cooperation increasingly impact or limit political sovereignty, and non-state actors like transnational corporations, globalized criminal enterprises, and international NGOs play a significant role in world politics.[66]

But perhaps the most significant paradox within globalization lies in the interpenetrative conjunction between global and local. It cannot be stressed too strongly that globalization is unfeasible without localization. The term *glocalize* (from a Japanese term meaning "global localization") has been employed by Roland Robertson and others to signify this reflexive, multidirectional, relationship.[67] To put it differently, the face of the global is in the local. Genuinely globalizing movements like Pentecostalism, which impact the local order in societies throughout the world, are marked by this interpenetrative conjunction. As Byron Klaus argues, Pentecostalism enjoys a global appeal precisely because it "has been the quintessential indigenous religion, adapting easily to a variety of [local] cultures."[68] Transnational products, from McDonald's to evangelical worship, are adapted to local taste and requirement in order to ensure global appeal. Thus, McDonald's provides McBurrito in Mexico, McLlahua sauce in Bolivia (a local chili sauce that accompanies every meal) and the Maharaja Mac in India (a vegetarian version of the Big Mac—beef and pork being problematic in that context).[69]

The recent success of electronic giant LG electronics provides a powerful illustration. Sales of the company's cell phones received a major boost after CEO Kim Ssang, inspired by a trip to the Middle East, made a phone for Muslims which "rings five times a day on the prayer hours and has a compass that points to Mecca."[70] A visit to India also inspired Ssang to develop the ideal refrigerator for a nation of vegetarians: it has an extra large crisper and small freezer. The product was a hit. CEO Ssang's new philosophy of learning from the "field" or local contexts—he began spending 70 percent of his time traveling around the

---

65. Connie McNeely, "The Determination of Statehood," in *The Globalization Reader*, ed. J. Lechner Frank and John Boli (Malden, MA: Blackwell, 2000), 199.

66. Held et al., *Global Transformations*, 9; Nye, "U.S. Power and Strategy after Iraq," 62. See also Geoffrey Garrett, "Partisan Politics in the Global Economy," in *The Globalization Reader*, ed. Frank J. Lechner and John Boli (Malden, MA: Blackwell, 2000), 227-35.

67. Roland Robertson, *Globalization: Social Theory and Global Culture* (London: SAGE, 1992).

68. See Byron D. Klaus, "Pentecostalism as a Global Culture: An Introductory Overview," in *The Globalization of Pentecostalism: A Religion Made to Travel*, ed. Murray W. Dempster, Byron D. Klaus, and Douglas Petersen (Irvine, CA: Regnum Books International, 1999), 127.

69. Richard Tiplady, ed., *One World or Many? The Impact of Globalisation on Mission* (Pasadena: William Carey Library, 2003).

70. "Global Enterprise," *Newsweek*, December 20, 2004, E6.

globe—is seen as the main reason for LG's spectacular growth. According to *Newsweek*, it became both the world's fastest growing mobile-phone maker and its most profitable appliance maker with projected sales of $13 billion in 2004.

In truth, the global-local nexus is not always benign or mutually beneficial; for the forces of globalization, as James Mittelman explains, embody both transformation and resistance. The local is a site of adaptation and negotiation but also of resistance and protest, including those culturally conditioned, sustained, and often undeclared forms of resistance (individual and collective) that Mittelmen terms "soft protest."[71] The diffusion of the democratic ideal around the globe, for instance, has been attended by contextual appropriation and implementation. In many places its mechanisms have contributed to the promotion of indigenous culture and have fostered the rise of civil society groups that coalesce around emotive causes and initiate powerful organized resistance to forms of hegemony. As such, while dominant global processes can undermine and disrupt local livelihoods, the deepening of global-local interdependence also means that local developments or initiatives can have global consequences or can represent instruments of change. Globalization often transforms the role of the margins.

In the final analysis, the widespread notion that globalization is a managed process with a fixed ideal ignores its inherent ambiguities, contradictoriness, and open-endedness. There is strong scholarly consensus that much about the potential and possibilities of globalization remains unknown. One major study concluded that "there is no a priori reason to assume that globalization must simply evolve in a single direction or that it can only be understood in relation to a single ideal condition."[72] Amid the hype and contention it is easy to overlook the fact that, long historical roots notwithstanding, globalization embodies a complex reality that is still evolving. Global transformations do not simply favor hegemonic actors or entities; they also empower the periphery and marginalize the center in profound ways.

A central contention of this book is that, despite entrenched notions of Western provenance and dominance within the globalization discourse, non-Western initiatives and movements are among the most powerful forces shaping the contemporary world order. This argument is specifically applied to recent reconfigurations within global Christianity, with the growing presence of African migrants in America's hugely diverse religious landscape forming the main focus. Such a claim explicitly challenges the entrenched vision of a new global order inexorably molded according to a Western image.

---

71. Mittelman, *Globalization Syndrome*, 176. Such resistance, he adds, is often mounted by those "whose modes of existence are threatened by globalization."

72. Held et al., *Global Transformations*, 11; Robertson, "Globalization and the Future of Traditional Religion," 54. For similar arguments, see Albrow, *Global Age*, 90-93. Albrow even cautions against conceiving of the phenomenon as a "process" since there is no inherent logic to the concept "which suggests that a particular outcome necessarily will prevail."

2

Globalization of Culture

"We Are the World"

> Ours are not Western values; they are the universal values of the
> human spirit. . . .
>
> —British Prime Minister Tony Blair
> "Address to the U.S. Congress" (July 17, 2003)

In the late 1960s, the secularization thesis was at its height of influence in Western academic circles. Propounded by a relatively small group of powerful Western academics extrapolating from assessment of trends in Western Europe and North America, this thesis (based on arguments dating back to early twentieth-century sociological thinking) maintained that modernization and the spread of scientific rationality will cause an inevitable and irreversible decline in religious belief and practice throughout the world. Foundational to this theory was the entrenched, if unstated, conviction that Western ideals and experiences are paradigmatic and sufficient for global projections and calculations. Even if, in this case, concrete evidence indicative of comparable erosion in formal religious observances and allegiance within the non-Western world was lacking (see p. 113 below). We might call this tendency to ascribe global significance to a particular Western event, the "World Series" approach![1]

Not for the first time, but more patently than usual, academic pronouncements proved to be out of touch with reality. Contrary to the prognosis inherent in the secularization thesis, the world we live in today is as inundated by religious novelty, flux, and dynamism as it has ever been; and the rate of religious upsurge appears to be intensifying. All the major religions—Christianity, Islam, Judaism, Hinduism, Buddhism—are resurgent, and all have produced vibrant renewal movements.

Far from undermining religious beliefs, writes Samuel Huntington, the global spread of economic and social modernization has actually triggered "a global revival of religion" on every continent. Perversely, from a secular rationalist point

---

1. The "World Series," one of America's most revered sporting events, is a best-of-seven contest for the national championship in baseball. The fact that this is a national tournament (mainly confined to American teams) renders the description "World" (first used in 1903) a glaring misnomer and evocative of overblown cultural hubris.

of view, Islamism (or radical Islam) has been strongest in the more advanced and seemingly more secular Muslim societies such as Algeria, Iran, Egypt, Lebanon, and Tunisia or in countries experiencing rapid economic growth, including Jordan, Tunisia, and Morocco.[2] This pattern actually fosters the view that Islamism increases with modernization. Christianity also is experiencing explosive growth in non-Western societies, often in contexts of abject poverty but also drawing considerable stimulus from increased middle-class participation. Certainly in South Korea, remarkable Christian growth from the 1970s coincided with economic prosperity and modernization. And in other rapidly Westernizing Asian countries like Japan, Taiwan, Hong Kong, and Malaysia, folk religion and traditional faiths are reportedly thriving.[3] Clearly, the gods have not retired in the face of scientific modernity!

Not surprisingly, by the end of the twentieth century, a growing number of notable Western intellectuals had firmly rejected the secularization thesis and declared its falsification even in the case of the Western world.[4] Among the most prominent defectors was American sociologist Peter Berger, who now avers that "strongly felt religion has always been around [and] what needs explanation is its absence rather than its presence"; he adds that "modern secularity is a much more puzzling phenomenon than all these religious explosions," which is to say that "the University of Chicago is a more interesting topic for the sociology of religion than the Islamic schools of Qom."[5] Not unlike recent converts to a new religion, others were even more severe in their denunciation of their abandoned faith. *Atlantic Monthly* columnist David Brooks, a self-described "recovering secularist," castigated his media colleagues—many of them journalists and policy analysts "who are paid to keep up with these things"—for ignoring that the "great Niagara of religious fervor is cascading down around them while they stand obtuse and dry in the little cave of their parochialism."[6] He recommended six steps for other recovering secularists:

1. Accept the fact that you are not the norm.
2. Confront your fear (of uncontrolled religious conflict).
3. Get angry (at secular fundamentalists) for their parochialism and ignorant convictions.
4. Resist the impulse to find a materialistic explanation for everything.

2. Huntington, *Clash of Civilizations*, 101. See also Daniel Pipes, "God and Mammon: Does Poverty Cause Militant Islam?" *The National Interest* (Winter 2001/2002): 14-21.

3. Rodney Stark and Roger Finke, *Acts of Faith: Explaining the Human Side of Religion* (Berkeley: University of California Press, 2000).

4. See Peter L. Berger, ed., *The Desecularization of the World: Resurgent Religion and World Politics* (Grand Rapids: Eerdmans, 1999); Rodney Stark, "Secularization: The Myth of Religious Decline," *Fides et Historia* 30, no. 2 (1998): 1-19; Grace Davie, *Europe, the Exceptional Case: Parameters of Faith in the Modern World* (London: Darton Longman & Todd, 2002).

5. Peter L. Berger, ed., "The Desecularization of the World: A Global Overview," in idem, ed., *Desecularization*, 1-18, here 11-12.

6. David Brooks, "Kicking the Secularist Habit," *Atlantic Monthly* 291, no. 2 (March 2003): 26.

5. Acknowledge that you have been too easy on religion.
6. Understand that America was never very secular anyway.

We must note, however, that the falsification of the secularization thesis has done little to deflate the air of academic respectability that shrouds secular rationalism. Indeed, advocates of secularization have maintained a lively debate with rational choice theorists over the significance of religious plurality—a new dimension of religious life in the West.[7] The former insist that the reality and experience of religious pluralism "necessarily undermines the plausibility of all forms of religious belief," while the latter (who utilize the principles of supply-side, or market, economics) counter that religious pluralism or competition stimulates rather than depresses religious participation by enabling the religious needs of increasing diverse populations to be met. More recently the claims of this religious market model have come under withering critique based on studies that indicate that while the correlation between religious pluralism and religious participation fits the American situation, it is sharply contradicted by experience in other postindustrial societies. As Pippa Norris and Ronald Inglehart (2004) note, conspicuous examples include countries such as Ireland, Poland, and Italy, where there is high religious participation despite the fact that the Catholic Church enjoys a virtual religious monopoly.

The point, however, is that secular rationalism remains a force to be reckoned with. Paradoxically, this is precisely because Western secularism is a de facto "religion" with universalistic claims, utopian hopes, promises of salvation, strongly held creeds (including individual rights, gay rights, liberal democracy, and liberal progressivism), committed proselytization (especially via the public media), active "congregants" in academic institutions, and its own fundamentalist core.[8] And while the movement remains a predominantly European phenomenon, it is also enjoying some growth in the United States, where self-confessed adherents now reportedly represent more than 7.5 percent of the population.[9] For these reasons alone recent efforts to revise or update the secularization thesis are of great significance. By far the most compelling attempt is *Sacred and Secular* (2004), the richly detailed and thought-provoking study jointly authored by political scientists Pippa Norris and Ronald Inglehart.

Poverty and Prayer

Norris and Inglehart accept that the traditional secularization theory has notable defects, but they contend that it would be a mistake to reject it altogether. What is needed, they explain, is a theoretical revision that, rather than predict a

---

7. Davie, *Europe,* 15f., 42-45.

8. See Kenneth Minogue, "Religion, Reason and Conflict in the 21st Century," *The National Interest* (Summer 2003): 127-32.

9. David Klinghoffer, "That Other Church," *Christian Century* 49, no. 1 (January 2005): 62; see also Pippa Norris and Ronald Inglehart, *Sacred and Secular: Religion and Politics Worldwide* (New York: Cambridge University Press, 2004), 93.

deterministic decline of religious forms, accounts for the variation in religious practices around the world or addresses the issue of why some societies are far more religious than others. In this regard they propose "a theory of secularization based on existential security." Rich and poor nations, they argue, differ critically not only in human development levels but also in "living conditions of human security and vulnerability to risks." By human security they mean not merely military strength or territorial safety but the vast array of dangers and risks that threaten survival or undermine well-being—including poverty, illiteracy, corruption, disease epidemics, environmental disasters, insufficient public services, political instability, pollution, humanitarian crises, and so on. "Human security," Norris and Inglehart argue, is critical for religious participation and strong adherence to religious values and beliefs. In their view, human development is even more crucial for security than economic development. This assessment represents a refinement of the classical secularization theory, which linked the inevitable loss of spiritual faith to modernization and economic prosperity. More specifically, it is the absence of human security that drives religiosity: to wit, *the experience of growing up in less secure societies will heighten the importance of religious values* while, conversely, *experience of more secure conditions will lessen it.*[10]

To rephrase, in poor agrarian societies, where daily life is precarious and characterized by innumerable risks and vulnerabilities, the need for religious participation and focus on spirituality is high, whereas affluent and secure postindustrial nations register the lowest levels of religiosity. As societies transition from agrarian to industrial economies and then develop into postindustrial societies, "the conditions of growing security that usually accompany this process tends to reduce the importance of religious values."[11] Incidentally, the sharpest decline in religiosity occurs when a society shifts from an agrarian to an industrial economy; the transition to postindustrial is accompanied by a less dramatic erosion in religious participation.

The authors eschew the deterministic outlook of the classical secularization theory and insist that this is not a linear process. All forms of religion do not necessarily disappear as societies develop or modernize. Clearly, some rich nations are more religious than others, in part because the equitable distribution of resources is just as critical a factor as a nation's (or society's) economic development. More to the point, socioeconomic inequality in many wealthy nations leaves sizable portions of the population at risk—noticeably the unemployed, the disabled, the homeless, single parents, and ethnic minorities—and such groups evince a higher propensity for religiosity. Moreover, even in highly secular societies, religious traditions and the worldviews historically associated with them continue to shape the wider culture and values long after institutional allegiance

---

10. Pippa Norris and Ronald Inglehart, *Sacred and Secular: Religion and Politics Worldwide* (New York: Cambridge University Press, 2004), 18 (italics in original).

11. Ibid. The classification of agrarian, industrial, and postindustrial to describe levels of societal modernization draws on descriptions in the 1998 Human Development Index (p. 48).

has waned. This historical heritage also helps to explain variations in religiosity among societies with similar levels of development.

Ultimately, however, the theory of "existential security" is in agreement with the basic rationale and prediction of the secularization theory: modernization and economic prosperity erode religious beliefs and practices. Norris and Inglehart attest that while secularization is not a deterministic process, it is "largely predictable."[12] What, then, are the global implications or consequences of this process from the "existential security" perspective?

Here Norris and Inglehart deviate sharply from the traditional secularization thesis. Social vulnerability and lack of human development, they argue, drive not only religiosity but also *population growth*. Partly due to their strong religious orientation, also partly as a "survival strategy"—since more children die—poorer "traditional" societies emphasize family values and encourage large numbers of children; so fertility rates remain exceptionally high (two or three times the replacement level). Conversely, secularization and human development have a negative impact on demographic growth. In rich industrial societies, people live longer and have fewer children, to the point were fertility rates drop below the replacement level. Consequently, people who are religious account for a growing proportion of the world's population. This makes for a profound paradox: modernization and human development promote secularization and erosion of religiosity but "the world as a whole is becoming more religious."[13]

To demonstrate the efficacy of these arguments Norris and Inglehart make skillful use of data from the World Values Survey, a project that conducted a series of representative national surveys of the values and beliefs of the publics in seventy-nine countries comprising five billion people (more than eighty percent of the world's population) from 1981 to 2001. It is important to note that not all of the countries feature in all of the surveys and, as the authors admit, countries where opinion surveys have the longest tradition—Western Europe, North America, and Scandinavia—received the most comprehensive coverage. There is room here only to present some of the most pertinent (and least complex) findings or conclusions:

- Sixty-four percent of those who live in agrarian societies considered religion "very important," compared to 34 percent in industrial societies and 20 percent in postindustrial nations.
- Almost half (44 percent) of the public in agrarian societies attend a religious service at least once weekly, compared to 25 percent and 20 percent in industrial and postindustrial societies, respectively.
- The most religious societies in the world are overwhelmingly non-Western—Ireland and the United States being the only exceptions—and the least religious, most secular states include wealthy postindustrial European societies (like Denmark, France, Finland, Norway, and Sweden), many post-Communist nations, and Japan.

---

12. Ibid., 109.
13. Ibid., 23.

- "All groups in agrarian societies are more religious than *any* single group in postindustrial societies."
- In the period 1970-1998, there was a substantial decrease in regular attendance at weekly religious services in European societies surveyed, with Catholic nations registering the greatest shrinkage—though, significantly, religious participation in Protestant European nations was already "extremely low" at the start of the study.
- In industrial societies, religion remained stronger among the more vulnerable populations, which typically include women, older people, poorer households, and the less educated. In postindustrial societies "*the poor are almost twice as religious as the rich.*"
- Importantly, while people in wealthy postindustrial societies attach decreasing significance to religious values and do not support traditional religious institutions or authorities, they value private or individualized spirituality and even show "increasing interest in the meaning and purpose of life."
- In agrarian societies the young are fully as religious as the old (all groups being equally subjected to low levels of existential security), whereas in affluent postindustrial societies the young (presumably enjoying higher levels of development than previous generations) are much less religious than the older generations. (Religious values held in later life, Norris and Inglehart contend rather controversially, are largely shaped by the prevailing conditions that shaped childhood and early adolescence. This claim challenges the fairly widespread axiom that people naturally become more religious as they get older).
- There is an ever-widening gap in religiosity between poor and affluent societies: not because the former are becoming more religious—religiosity in agrarian societies remained relatively constant (statistically at least)—but because wealthy nations have become increasingly secular over the years.
- Contrary to the key Enlightenment claim (championed by Max Weber) that scientific rationality will destroy spiritual belief and the idea of the mysterious, "societies with greater faith in science also often have *stronger* religious beliefs."
- Human security is consistently linked to secularization: "as lives become more secure and immune to daily risks, the importance of religion gradually fades away."

These assessments reflect painstaking research, and the study is replete with important insights. The authors' perspective on the widening gap between the West and the non-West in terms of religiosity and cultural values is important; and the exploration of the religious landscape in Europe and America is quite authoritative. The study's central premise that human security is critical for religiosity is compelling, and the case is powerfully made. Few would question that collective or individual needs and aspirations as well as external forms of crisis significantly influence religious movement and commitment. Lewis Rambo (1993) has offered an insightful treatment of this issue. Some of the arguments, notably on the links between economic development and religion, will remain open to debate. Further, the focus on a grand (universally applicable) theory, while helpful in itself, inevitably appears facile and unsatisfactory from certain regional perspectives.

But the study's central theory is not without critical problems. At the risk of oversimplifying its complex arguments, it essentially makes the claim that the prevalence of (or propensity for) religious practice and beliefs within a society is a function of material deficiencies: insufficient schools, inadequate medical care, want of electricity and running water, daily hardships, and unreliable political representatives. In this sense it reprises the age-old notion that religion is a human invention, a product of our deepest fears and insecurities. Alleviate the latter, and religion or the need for it gradually disappears.

This materialist viewpoint is well entrenched in Western thinking and dates back to the Roman poet Lucretius (99-55 B.C.E.), who declared, "fear made the gods." Thus, the study's importance notwithstanding, it presents not a new theory but a rather old idea dressed in the highly respectable garb of the modern scientific method (statistics and all). There is a crucial rejection of the key Enlightenment claim that the spread of scientific knowledge will dissipate spiritual belief; but in the final analysis we are left with a depiction of religion or religiosity as an ailment that only the unalloyed benefits of Western modernity and economic prosperity can cure; or, at the very least, of religion as a public contagion born of poor human development that the material blessings of industrial advancement reduces to manageable individual infections.

The religiosity of agrarian preindustrial societies and the growing secularization of most developed nations are beyond question; and the study's most insightful contributions come from probing the divergences and implications. But other questions remain. Can a phenomenon as complex as religiosity be explained simply by the want of human security (and by implication the absence of full-blown modernity)? Is not the perception of risk and vulnerability itself conditioned by religious perspectives and experience? To what extent does the implicit use of Western models and measures of progress impair a true assessment of well-being across the various cultural divides? What makes the disorders associated with industrial and postindustrial society (including the breakdown of family life, the weakening of moral restraints, and hyper-consumerism) less inimical to the human condition than the perceived threats of the preindustrial world? In the new global context, what are the limitations of a localized understanding of human security? Can data from a twenty-year period—any twenty-year period—possibly provide conclusive analysis of modes of existence around the globe?

The Human Development Index utilized by Norris and Inglehart provides valuable information on standards of living around the world. But, surely, how specific details of need translate into what the authors term "existential security" involves subjective judgment, in part because perceptions of well-being and risk are not value free. It is for this reason that some have strongly criticized the conventional measures of economic development such as the Gross Domestic Product (GDP) as flawed instruments that distort the truth about economic well-being.[14]

---

14. See T. Halstead and C. Cobb, "The Need for New Measurements of Progress," in *The Case*

According to a recent study of more than sixty-five countries published in the British *New Scientist* magazine, Nigeria has the highest percentage of happy people, followed by Mexico, Venezuela, El Salvador, and Puerto Rico.[15] It also concluded that factors that make people happy vary from one country to the next—personal success and self-expression are seen as the most important in the United States, while fulfilling the expectations of family and society is valued more highly in Japan. On this same issue, a *New York Times* op-ed piece criticized the American belief that "happiness is essentially a personal emotion, not an attribute of a community or a country"; it pointedly added that "thinking of happiness as a quotient of cultural and environmental factors might help us to understand the growing disconnect between America's prosperity and America's sense of well-being."[16]

The African experience helps to illustrate a different point. The Human Development Index data on the continent read like a veritable litany of woes. Africa consistently boasts the worst statistics on the planet. According to the HDI 2005 report, thirty of the thirty-two countries ranked lowest in the world are in Africa; absolute poverty (the share of people living on less that $1 a day: 46 percent), infant mortality rate, and the percentage of people without access to improved water sources are higher on the sub-continent than anywhere else; life expectancy is the lowest in the world; and the continent is home to more than 80 percent of people living with HIV/AIDS in the world (thirty-six million at the end of 2000)—not to mention that the disease has killed seventeen million Africans since the epidemic began in the 1970s. The pathologies and colossal problems afflicting the continent no doubt factor into the massive accessions to both Christianity and Islam on the continent in recent decades. However, in the case of Christianity, phenomenal growth—from 9.2 percent in 1900 to 45 percent by 2000[17]—has a lot to do with Christianity's association with modernization. Even now, the unprecedented impact of neo-Pentecostal movements is considered a function of their ability to connect converts to "the modern world of commodities, media and financial flows."[18]

My point is that, far from weakening the importance of religious values, the encounter with modernity—albeit limited—has had little impact on African religiosity. Perhaps this is because African religious values, beliefs and participation are all of one piece with its cultural matrix and existential reality, not a discrete compartmentalized dimension of daily life—as a brief drive through most African cities will confirm. As John Mbiti (1990: 1) comments, "religion penetrates into all the departments of life so fully that it is not easy or possible always to isolate it. A study of these religions' religious system is, therefore, ultimately a

---

against the Global Economy and for a Turn Towards the Local, ed. J. Mander and E. Goldsmith (San Francisco: Sierra Club Books, 1996), 197-206.

15. "Nigeria Tops Happiness Survey," *BBC News,* October 2, 2003.

16. "Net National Happiness," *New York Times,* October 6, 2005.

17. Michael Jaffarian, "The Statistical State of the Missionary Enterprise," *Missiology* 30, no. 1 (January 2000): 15-32.

18. Ruth Marshall-Fratani, "Mediating the Global and Local in Nigerian Pentecostalism," *Journal of Religion in Africa* 38, no. 3 (1998), 299.

study of the peoples themselves in all the complexities of both traditional and modern life."[19]

Western thinking may struggle with the idea that Africans display high levels of religiosity not because they inhabit a palpably insecure sociopolitical environment but because they are quite simply religious; or that religion is a driving force behind much of African life, including its anarchic sociopolitical environment, and not simply a salve for daily hardships or want of modernity's comforts. Stephen Ellis suggests, for instance, that it is impossible to fully understand the anarchy that has plagued many parts of Africa in recent years without reference to the religious dimension or spiritual order.[20] In the event, the basic problem lies not with the reality but with a blinkered, untutored, outsider perspective.

To their credit, Norris and Inglehart at least recognize that the "predominant religious tradition of a given society tends to leave a lasting imprint on religious beliefs and other social norms."[21] Thus, even in societies where secularization has made profound inroads the religio-cultural heritage remains deeply influential. This at least opens the door to the argument that in some cases religious values shape attitudes to existential realities and not the other way around. They also eschew what I have termed the "World Series" approach and condemn the tendency to generalize from distinctive American experiences. This conviction that the rest of the world is not poised to mechanically follow the trajectory of Western historical experiences gives their analysis a certain freshness. What they perhaps ignore is the possibility that the encounter with Western-style modernity factors into this religiocultural cleavage. As Samuel Huntington maintains, the spread of socioeconomic modernization has not bankrupted religious life; rather it has revitalized it (see next chapter). Still—and this is most important—Norris and Inglehart surmise correctly that religious differences are "*increasingly* salient" in the growing cultural divergence between rich and poor countries.[22] We shall return to this point later.

Under the impact of globalization, the extensity and capacity of processes of cultural exchange and interaction have never been greater. Recent decades have witnessed a dramatic rise in the spread and pervasiveness of the values associated with Western secular society. Much less attention has been paid to the impulses and initiatives in the reverse direction; impulses that, principally through massive migration movements, significantly extend the reach and penetration of religious activities associated with non-Western societies. The latter movement forms the focus of this book. If the entrenched religiosity and unbridled spiritual outlook of poorer (mainly non-Western) societies constitutes a key component in arguably the most fundamental cultural divide of the new global order, then the admixture of migration and religious expansion represents one of the most important aspects of contemporary globalization.

---

19. For a detailed, graphic, representative example of how African religiosity pervades urban space, see Maureen Iheanacho and Allison Howell, *By His Grace: Signs on a Ghanaian Journey* (Akropong, Ghana: Amara-Zaane, 2005).

20. Stephen Ellis, *The Mask of Anarchy: The Destruction of Liberia and the Religious Dimension of an African Civil War* (New York: New York University Press, 1999).

21. Norris and Inglehart, *Sacred and Secular*, 220.

22. Ibid., 217.

But such movements—conceived as "alternative globalizations" or globalization from below—have received short shrift in the globalization discourse. The dominant perspective, reflected in enormous amount of print, holds that Western cultural models and values set the standard for the rest of the world and drive the processes of cultural globalization. For all its pervasiveness, this notion is unsustainable, and what follows is an interrogation of its central theories and core claims in an attempt to explain why this single global culture thesis is misleading.

Cultures Matter

With a few notable exceptions, the crude notion of "West is best" is no longer explicit in public discourse; but, in the United States and elsewhere, more sophisticated versions of this claim are well established in academic discourses. An increasingly common view attributes human progress—defined in terms of economic development, material well-being, and political democracy—to superior cultural values. Termed the "cultural paradigm," this approach is posited as furnishing a more plausible model for explaining (or addressing) poverty and development around the world than previous explanatory constructs such as colonialism, dependency, or racism. It formed the focus of a Harvard-sponsored symposium entitled "Cultural Values and Human Progress" (held in April 1999), which drew on the notion that cultural values and attitudes are increasingly viewed as "facilitators of, or obstacles to, progress."[23]

With the exception of an anthropologist who described himself as a heretic at a revival meeting, there were few dissenting voices among the distinguished group of scholars who convened for the meeting (including the obligatory sample of non-Western scholars). The subsequently published volume, titled *Culture Matters: How Values Shape Human Progress* (2000), reflected a variety of perspectives but upheld the link between Western cultural values or Westernization (the adoption of Western values, ideals, norms, etc.) and economic prosperity. Included among the topics of discussion were levels of corruption, work ethics, and family values. On almost every issue one contributor or the other found that Western approaches or examples—particularly those of Protestant societies in Europe and North America—were ideal. In a regrettable display of reverse ethnocentrism, the African contributor vociferously condemned African religiosity (or susceptibility to the "influence of invisible forces") as one of the chief reasons for African backwardness.[24]

Interestingly, the Norris/Inglehart study included an assessment that compared work ethic, ethical values, and moral values across religious cultures. They found that "in poorer developing nations, where work is essential for life . . . ,

---

23. Lawrence E. Harrison, "Introduction," in *Culture Matters: How Values Shape Human Progress*, ed. Lawrence E. Harrison and Samuel P. Huntington (New York: Basic Books, 2000), xxi.

24. Daniel Etouga-Manguelle, "Does Africa Need a Cultural Adjustment Program?," in *Culture Matters: How Values Shape Human Progress*, ed. Lawrence E. Harrison and Samuel P. Huntington (New York: Basic Books, 2000), 65-77.

people place by far the highest emphasis on the value of work" and that Muslim cultures "display by far the strongest work ethic." This assessment sharply contradicts the fundamental claims of the Harvard symposium. In fact, the Norris/Inglehart study concluded that *those living in Protestant societies today display the weakest work ethic.*[25] Protestant societies also turn out to be less ethical than Muslim societies on matters of obeying the law, honesty in public life, and corruption, while Eastern religious structures displayed the highest ethical standards. On moral values—specifically abortion, suicide, and euthanasia—Catholic and Muslim societies are "significantly more traditional" or, rather, more life affirming.

I mention these arguments mainly to illustrate the salience and centrality of the culture debate for our discussion. I could not agree more with the Harvard project's raison d'être: *culture matters.* However, given the thrust of its publication, "culture matters" turns out to be academic-speak for *Western culture matters.* Claims by a particular society to cultural supremacy by virtue of economic ascendancy are not new. As Richard Shweder reminded the forum participants, "throughout history, whoever is wealthiest and the most technologically advanced thinks that their way of life is the best, the most natural, the God-given, the surest means to salvation, or at least the fast lane to well-being in this world."[26] Given that the cultural dimension of globalization is arguably the most pervasive and unprecedented, the stakes have never been higher. And no aspect of the debate is more problematic than the now commonplace assertion that globalization is a homogenizing force ushering in a single global culture or universal civilization.[27]

White Man's Burden

The global culture or cultural homogenization thesis turns on at least three convictions: first, that economic dominance and technological supremacy are driving the inexorable spread of Western modernization (particularly American consumer culture) in a way that erodes local cultures and indigenous identities around the world; second, that non-Western peoples aspire to be more like northern Europeans; third, that distinct cultural attributes account for the progress and prosperity of some nations and not others. The current reasoning, comments Huntington, is that the West, "as the first civilization to modernize . . . , leads in the acquisition of the culture of modernity" and "as other societies acquire similar patters of education, work, wealth, and class structure . . . , this modern Western culture will become the universal culture of the world."[28] So entrenched are

---

25. Norris and Inglehart, *Sacred and Secular*, 160-73; quotations from 160-61, 163.

26. Richard A. Shweder, "Moral Maps, 'First World' Conceits, and the New Evangelists," in *Culture Matters: How Values Shape Human Progress*, ed. Lawrence E. Harrison and Samuel P. Huntington (New York: Basic Books, 2000), 167.

27. For a useful summary of the main assumptions and arguments of the "global culture" argument, see Held et al., *Global Transformations*, 342-63.

28. Huntington, *Clash of Civilizations*, 68.

these assumptions among the higher echelons of Western society, so seductive is the hold they exert on Western self-assessment, that British prime minister Tony Blair, addressing the U.S. Congress in 2003, could state without guile or spin, "ours are not Western values; they are the universal values of the human spirit."

Proponents unfailingly note that the world's economy is dominated by roughly two hundred transnational corporations (TNCs), many of which have larger sales revenues than the entire economies of most countries.[29] TNCs, which grew in number from seven thousand in 1970 to forty-four thousand in 1998, control two-thirds of the world's trade in goods and services and account for one-third of the world's capital. The annual values of sales of each of the six largest TNCs are now exceeded by the GDPs of only twenty-one nation-states. It is noted, *ad nauseam*, that 51 percent of the largest economies in the world today are corporations, not countries—the U.S.-based Wal-Mart, the world's biggest retailer, was ranked as high as no. 12 by the turn of the twenty-first century. Then there are the even more mammoth multinational corporations (MNCs).[30] As Noreena Hertz (2001) notes, the one hundred largest MNCs are thought to control about 20 percent of global foreign assets. Moreover, a small group of around twenty to thirty large multinational corporations, the majority of which are U.S.-based, dominate global markets for entertainment, news, television, and so on, acquiring a very significant cultural and economic presence on virtually every continent.

From the early 1980s, a frenzy of mergers and acquisitions within the media industry has left a decreasing number of powerful corporations with greater monopolistic control and unbridled global ambitions.[31] This process has not only produced "planetary giants" in the world of publishing and literature (notably Rupert Murdoch's News Corporation) but has also, because it significantly reduces choice and consumer autonomy, further intensified the drive toward cultural homogenization. As a matter of fact, this oligarchic acquisitiveness is driven by "the quest for a single product that can be owned by a single proprietor and sold to every living soul on the planet" (Barber 1995: 138). The dominance of these huge corporations, it is believed, will foster the spread of liberal democracy and stimulate the worldwide diffusion of a consumerist ideology that will increasingly undermine traditional cultures and ways of life. Intrinsic to this assessment is the crucial but often overstated argument that, in an increasingly borderless world, the global reach and economic dominance of such huge corporate entities has significantly eroded (even displaced) the function of nation-states.[32]

Precisely because they conceive of globalization almost exclusively in

---

29. TNCs are firms with *controlling* operations in more than one country, and since they are subject to the laws and customs of the multiple countries in which they operate, having a base in one particular country is less critical to their identity.

30. Multinational corporations maintain domestic identity and a central office in a particular country but operate in more than one country often through subsidiaries or joint ventures with individual companies.

31. For a thoroughgoing treatment, see Benjamin R. Barber, *Jihad vs. McWorld: Terrorism's Challenge to Democracy* (New York: Ballantine, 1995).

32. See Kenichi Ohmae, *The End of the Nation State: The Rise of Regional Economies* (London: HarperCollins, 1995).

economic terms, proponents of cultural homogenization see the process as immutably American. Globalization, declares Thomas Friedman (1999: 311f.), "has a distinctly American face" and it is "globalizing American culture and cultural icons." "We Americans," he continues, "are the Apostles of the Fast World, the enemies of tradition, the prophets of the free market and the high priests of high tech." And what makes this combination of Americanization and globalization so immensely powerful is the unparalleled ability to project its culture, values, economics, technologies, and lifestyles everywhere. "I . . . found India," he offers in *The World Is Flat* (2005: 5), "and I thought many of the people I met there were Americans. Some had actually taken American names, and others were doing great imitations of American accents at call centers and American business techniques at software labs." With equal conviction, though without Friedman's bovine self-glorification, Barber (1995: 60-61) intones that "global pop culture *is* American"; that "selling American products means selling America: its popular culture, its putative prosperity, its ubiquitous imagery and software, and thus its very soul"; that, for consumer goods corporations like Coca-Cola, KFC, Nike, McDonald's, Marlboro, and so on, "in a quite literal sense, we *are* the world" (1995: 68).

Another key plank of the argument is America's indisputable dominance of world trade in films and unassailable preeminence as the biggest exporter of television programs. It has more than triple the combined exports of the next three biggest exporters, all the while maintaining an extremely low level of foreign imported programming.[33] Indeed, argues Barber, "the Americanization of global television is proceeding even faster than the globalization of American films."[34] Barber astutely acknowledges that "market omnipresence is not the same as determinative influence," yet he is unable to resist the pronouncement that American films are "likely to inspire a vision of life and to affect habits and attitudes."[35] The trans-nationalization of the music industry is also depicted as simultaneously the story of the diffusion and export of American-style popular music, artists, and genres and a range of associated aspects of culture and subcultures from which it grew.[36] Even the Internet—widely hailed as the ultimate instrument of globalization—is largely controlled by two American giants: AOL Timer Warner and Microsoft.

And so on and so forth. Even critics allow that through powerful entertainment and information technologies American cultural products are sweeping the globe as "literally the entire planet is being wired into music, movies, news, television programs, and other cultural products that originate primarily in the film and recording studios of the Unites States."[37] Under this onslaught, the argument goes, traditional cultures throughout the world are being inexorably eroded while their rich heritage (in traditional music, for instance) is being undermined, or else

---

33. Held et al., *Global Transformations*, 359.

34. Barber, *Jihad vs. Mcworld*, 101.

35. Ibid., 97.

36. Held et al., *Global Transformations*, 352; see also, Barber, *Jihad vs. McWorld*, 104-11.

37. See R. Barnet and J. Cavanagh, "Homogenization of Global Culture," in *The Case against the Global Economy and for a Turn toward the Local*, ed. Jerry Mander and Edward Goldsmith (San Francisco: Sierra Club Books, 1996), x, 550.

mined for an international market driven by capitalist visions and consumerist impulses. It is noteworthy that while international record companies are "much agitated about protecting their own intellectual property from pirates" they "feel no compunction about uprooting the music of indigenous peoples from its native soil and treating it as a free commodity."[38] This "hyperimperial American culture," others insist, is not only "laying waste to indigenous cultures" but also "represents an onslaught on indigenous identities."[39]

This process of Americanization, as some like Friedman intuit, is as much about pull as it is about push. People all over the world want in on American globalization for a number of reasons, not least because it symbolizes modernity and fulfills fantasies inspired by American film and television media in the first place. Thus, while they are aware that there are alternative ways to live their lives, "they know about the American lifestyle, and many of them want a big slice of it."[40] Friedman offers little beyond anecdotal evidence to support these totalizing claims, but he is adamant that the global juggernauts of McDonald's or Taco Bell proliferate around the world because "they offer people something they want."[41] Ultimately, therefore, with the possible exception of Islamic theocracies, few parts of the world have escaped the flooding of certain global brands or icons of mass cultural production (Nike, Coca-Cola, IBM, Michael Jordan, Levi jeans, etc.).

It only remains to mention that the spread of the English language—more precisely American—is also considered intrinsic to this process of cultural homogenization.[42] The global culture, argues Barber (1995: 84), speaks American English. This form of English "has become the world's primary transnational language in culture and the arts as well as in science, technology, commerce, transportation, and backing." Thus, even the debate over America's global leadership and, for that matter, fulminations against American imperialism in the media are conducted in English. "English, the American-accented version," adds Friedman (1999: 312) simply, "has become the world's language."

The broad outline painted above is a limited summary of the carefully packaged arguments and reams of data marshaled by various proponents of the single global culture thesis.[43] It will therefore be helpful to assess specific theories of cultural homogenization which invest it with conceptual force or a clear theoretical framework. Three in particular deserve attention: the first, Peter Berger's "four faces of global culture," reflects sociological analysis, while the other two, Francis Fukuyama's "end of history" and Benjamin Barber's "Jihad versus McWorld," utilize political theory.

---

38. Ibid., 75f.

39. Ziauddin Sardar and Merryl W. Davies, *Why Do People Hate America?* (New York: Disinformation Company, 2002), 124f.

40. Friedman, *Lexus and the Olive Tree*, 235.

41. Ibid., 236.

42. Held et al., *Global Transformations*, 346.

43. Among other prominent works not discussed here, see George Ritzer, *The Mcdonaldization of Society: An Investigation into the Changing Character of Contemporary Social Life* (Thousand Oaks, CA: Pine Forge, 1996).

Faces of the New Global Culture

American sociologist Peter Berger's "four faces of global culture" represents one of the best-known systematic efforts to depict cultural globalization as largely a process of Americanization.[44] In a more recent presentation of his ideas, Berger insists that his analysis provides a "picture" rather than a theory of cultural globalization. He also makes the notable concession that contemporary cultural globalization is multicentered. In the final analysis, however, he remains firmly convinced that the emerging global culture is "heavily American in origin and content," that while "it is not the only game in town" it is likely to remain "the biggest game going . . . for the foreseeable future."[45]

The first of Berger's four faces is *Davos Culture* (so-named after the annual World Economic Summit that meets in the Swiss luxury resort, Davos). This culture is representative of up-and-coming participants in the global economy, "a global network of ambitious young people in business and the professions . . . who speak fluent English, dress and act alike, at work and at play, and up to a point think alike—and hope that one day they might reach the elite summits" (2002: 3-4). The homogeneity imposed by participation in the global economy, however, does not necessarily extend to their personal lives, and many "manage an art of creative compartmentalization, seeking to combine participation in the global business culture with personal lives dominated by very different cultural themes" (2002: 4). Berger insists on American provenance of Davos identity but allows that, with powerful centers in Tokyo, Hong Kong, and Singapore (Shanghai and Bombay as potential additions), the centers of "Davos" culture "are no longer exclusively Western."

The second face of global culture identified by Berger is *Faculty Club International*, manifest in the internationalization of the values, ideologies and concerns of the Western intelligentsia. This "faculty club" "seeks and actively creates markets throughout the world to promote the ideas and behaviors invented by Western (mostly American) intellectuals, such as the ideologies of human rights, feminism, environmentalism, and multiculturalism, as well as the politics and lifestyles that embody these ideologies" (2002: 4). It spreads its beliefs and values through the educational system, the legal system, various therapeutic institutions, think tanks, and at least some of the media of mass communications. Incidentally, it internationalizes not only the ideas and agenda of the Western intelligentsia but also "the conflicts in which this intelligentsia has been engaged in home territories."[46]

This assessment bears a faint echo of arguments dating back to the mid-1970s, when dependency theories were used to explain the continuing institutional and

---

44. Peter L. Berger, "Four Faces of Global Culture," in *Globalization and the Challenges of a New Century: A Reader,* ed. Patrick O'Meara, Howard D. Mehlinger, and Matthew Krain (Indianapolis: Indiana University Press, 2000).

45. Peter L. Berger, "The Cultural Dynamics of Globalization," in *Many Globalizations: Cultural Diversity in the Contemporary World,* ed. Peter L. Berger and Samuel P. Huntington (New York: Oxford University Press, 2002), 2-4.

46. Berger, "Four Faces," 422.

theoretical dependence of third world academics on their counterparts in the first world.[47] Berger himself acknowledges the neo-Marxist flavor of his argument by stating that the culture of the Faculty Club International incorporates relationships of dependence, in which "an indigenous 'comprador class' (on the margins)" carries out "the agendas devised in the cultural centers of the 'metropolis.'"[48]

The third face of global culture in Berger's analysis is *McWorld Culture* (or popular culture), essentially the globalization of American cultural symbols and consumer products, from music and movies to fast food "by business enterprises of all sorts." Utilizing quasi-religious terminology to good effect, Berger distinguishes between two types of consumption: "sacramental" and "nonsacramental" (2002: 7). The latter is free from cultural implications and aspirations—"sometimes a hamburger is just a hamburger"—whereas the former represents an effort to "participate vicariously in American-style modernity," a visible sign (so to speak) of inward aspirations. Over time a switch from "sacramental" to "non-sacramental" often takes place, but there is no way of deciding a priori which type of consumption will prevail. Furthermore, depending on local perception, indigenous reactions to the impact of this popular American culture range from uncritical social acceptance to militant (religious or nationalist inspired) rejection.[49]

Berger describes *Evangelical Protestantism*, his fourth face of global culture, as "the most important popular movement serving . . . as a vehicle of cultural globalization."[50] A movement of outstanding scope, this feature, especially in its Pentecostal version "has been exploding in parts of the world to which this religious expression has always been alien, indeed, almost unknown" (2000: 425)—notably in Latin America, sub-Saharan Africa, and Chinese societies. This, observes Berger, is in clear contrast to resurgent Islam, which "has been limited to countries that have always been Muslim and to Muslim Diaspora communities" (2000: 425). Evangelical Protestantism's contribution to an emerging global culture is indicated by a membership (or conversion) process that "transforms people's attitudes to family, sexual behavior, child rearing, and, most importantly, to work and general economic attitudes."[51] The movement "not only facilitates social mobility in developing market economies . . . but also facilitates actual or anticipated participation in the new global economy" (2002: 8).

Berger is convinced that evangelical Protestantism is "the carrier of a pluralistic and modernizing culture whose original location is in the North Atlantic societies."[52] While the movement itself has been successfully indigenized everywhere it has penetrated, its leaders are conscious of being part of a global movement and maintain increasing cross-national contacts between themselves and with the centers of evangelicalism in the United States. Moreover, the "spirit" it

---

47. See Priscilla Weeks, "Post-Colonial Challenges to Grand Theory," *Human Organization* 49, no. 3 (1990): 236-44.

48. Berger, "Four Faces," 4.

49. Berger, " Cultural Dynamics," 9.

50. Ibid., 8.

51. Ibid.

52. Berger, "Four Faces," 425.

expresses has "unmistakably Anglo-Saxon traits, especially its powerful combination of individualistic self-expression, egalitarianism (notably between men
and women), and the capacity for creating voluntary associations" (2000: 8).
In effect, evangelical Protestantism is a globalizing cultural phenomenon that
incorporates both Americanization and indigenization, reflecting both the tensions and convergences of cultural globalization.

Berger's analysis is thoroughgoing and penetrating. He incorporates familiar
arguments, notably that the new global culture "has a built-in affinity with the
modernization process" and that the two are identical in many parts of the world
today.[53] But his identification of religion as a powerful force in contemporary globalization diverges from other proponents and challenges the traditional rejection
of the cogency of religious dynamism within Western social scientific analyses.

Importantly also, he rejects the notion of Western or American cultural imperialism; though he allows that the "faculty club culture" demonstrates this trait.
The United States, he opines, exerts considerable power and influence but "its
culture is not being imposed on others by coercive means." In his view, Americanization is comparable to the Hellenization of a significant part of the world "at
a time when Greece had virtually no imperial power."[54] This argument is unhelpful. Prominent Greek thinkers like the famously xenophobic Aristotle depicted
non-Greeks ("barbarians") as subhuman or slaves by nature who are destined to
be ruled by Greeks. In any case, one does not have to subscribe to the notion of
an American empire to appreciate the fact that intentional structured efforts by
American corporations and institutions to project or impose American cultural
assumptions and values are inherent in the processes Berger describes.

International non-governmental organizations (INGOs), for instance, are
often an important and not always benign instrument of Western cultural projection. Described as organized civic groups with operations in more than one country, INGOs mainly originate in industrialized countries and provide more aid
than the entire UN system. Their numbers grew from six thousand to twenty-six
thousand in the 1990s.[55] In many parts of the developing world (notably Africa)
they dominate critical spheres of public service and often wield more power and
influence than emasculated impoverished governments.[56] One particularly critical assessment of their impact stipulated that some "are used to propagate western values" in much the same way that "Christian missionaries did in the nineteenth century."[57] Also, relying solely on outside resources, they often promote
Western-defined solutions that cause social disruption on the ground.

Berger's arguments also reveal some unresolved tensions between his conviction, on the one hand, that the emerging global culture is predominantly American and his tacit acceptance, on the other, that the process lacks inevitability,

---

53. Berger, "Cultural Dynamics," 9.

54. Ibid., 3.

55. See L. David Brown et al., "Globalization, NGOs, and Multisectoral Relations," in *Gover-nance in a Globalizing World*, ed. Joseph S. Nye and John D. Donahue (Washington, DC: Brookings Institution Press, 2000), 271-96.

56. See Mengisteab, *Globalization and Autocentricity*.

57. "Sins of the Secular Missionaries," *The Economist* (January 29, 2000): 27.

particularly on account of the salience of indigenization. The more recent and refined version of his article is adequate for making the case. He proposes that what the four faces have in common is "individuation" (distinct from the ideology of individualism), by which he means that "all sectors of the emerging global culture enhance the independence of the individual over against tradition and collectivity."[58] In the case of "McWorld culture," he accepts that "much of the consumption of this popular culture is arguably superficial, in the sense that it does not have a deep effect on people's beliefs, values, or behavior." And, while maintaining that this emerging global culture is "heavily American in origin and content," he insists that "the idea of a mindless global homogenization greatly underestimates the capacity of human beings to be creative and innovative in the face of cultural challenges."[59] In essence, the "picture" Berger provides lacks a compelling imagery.

The End of History?

When pressed to its logical conclusion, the global culture argument not only sanctions Western or American cultural hegemony but also implicitly degrades alternative worldviews or cultural systems. Pundits like Thomas Friedman are emphatic that "when it comes to the question of which system today is the most effective at generating rising standards of living, the historical debate is over—the answer is free-market capitalism."[60] This reasoning is redolent of Cold War bipolar rivalry—a winner-take-all competition for world domination between two *Western* ideologies—and reflects an entrenched link between contemporary globalization and the end of the Cold War. Globalization, as such, functions as a model of American-defined triumphalism: to wit, "with the end of the Cold War, globalization is globalizing Anglo-American-style capitalism," as well as "American culture and cultural icons."[61] In this view, cultural globalization is emphatically a unidirectional movement with a fixed singular ideal.[62] Francis Fukuyama's "end of history" thesis provides the most sophisticated and provocative exemplar of this approach.[63]

His arguments triggered a robust debate in subsequent issues of *The National Interest* (issues 17 and 18) and the journal later published a special edition containing the original essay and a number of responses to it as well as Fukuyama's own response entitled "Second Thoughts." Fukuyama's thesis eventually appeared in book form.[64] Fukuyama argues that the end of the Cold War (and the collapse of

---

58. Berger, "Cultural Dynamics," 9.

59. Ibid., 7, 11.

60. Friedman, *Lexus and the Olive Tree*, 86.

61. Ibid., 308.

62. Indeed, Friedman describes free market ideology and the rules that govern it as "the Golden Straitjacket" (ibid., 86).

63. See Francis Fukuyama, "The End of History?," *The National Interest* (Summer 1989).

64. See Francis Fukuyama, *The End of History and the Last Man* (New York: Free Press, 1992).

Soviet Communism) signified the triumph of Western liberal democracy as "the ideal that will govern the material world in the long run." In his view, the threat posed by Communist China to liberalism had already begun to lose its potency. While China could not as yet be described as a liberal democracy (at least at the time he wrote in 1989), the pull of the liberal idea is gaining strength with the total discrediting of Marxist-Leninism as an economic system and the Chinese economy's growing openness to the outside world. Precisely because "the basic *principles* of the liberal democratic state could not be improved upon," the inevitable "universalization of Western liberal democracy as the final form of government" represented "the end point of mankind's ideological evolution" (1989). In a word, "the end of history." "History" is understood here in the Hegelian-Marxist sense of the "progressive evolution of human political and economic institutions" culminating in an absolute moment.[65]

With this culmination, large-scale conflict between developed states—that is, states no longer in history—becomes a diminishing likelihood. Quite simply, "agreeing on ends, men would have no large causes for which to fight. They would satisfy their needs through economic activity, but they would no longer have to risk their lives in battle."[66] History ends with the emergence of the so-called universal homogenous state, itself a Marxist concept, which Fukuyama defines as "liberal democracy in the political sphere combined with easy access to VCRs and stereos in the economic" (1989). In the original Marxist understanding, of course, the universal autonomous state represents a utopian entity in which "all prior contradictions are resolved and all human needs are satisfied."

Notably for our discussion, the victory of this Western idea (or ideal) is not confined to politics. There is an unquestionable, if complicated, relationship between economic development and the emergence of liberal democracy, not least because countries that have achieved advanced economic development tend to "look increasingly similar to one another."[67] Thus, "the ineluctable spread of consumerist Western culture" will underpin the universal homogenous state. As a case in point, the essential elements of economic and political liberalism have been "successfully grafted onto uniquely Japanese traditions and institutions" and the "desire for access to the consumer culture, created in large measure by Japan, has played a crucial role in fostering the spread of economic liberalism throughout Asia, and hence in promoting political liberalism as well." Modern economic

---

65. See Francis Fukuyama, "Second Thoughts: The Last Man in a Bottle," *The National Interest* (Summer 1999).

66. Fukuyama, *End of History*, 311; also 328f. The same idea is reflected in Thomas Friedman's "Golden Arches Theory of Conflict Prevention," which stipulates that "when a country reaches the level of economic development where it has a middle class big enough to support a McDonald's network, it becomes a McDonald's country. And people in McDonald's countries don't like to fight wars anymore, they prefer to wait in line for burgers;" see Friedman, *Lexus and the Olive Tree*, 196.

67. Fukuyama, *End of History*, 125, 133.

development, insists Fukuyama, "is forcing the homogenization of mankind, and is destroying a wide variety of traditional cultures in the process."[68]

Importantly, Fukuyama discounts religion and nationalism (or forms of racial and ethnic consciousness) as viable alternatives to modern liberalism. He admits that religious resurgence around the world within major faiths "attests to a broad unhappiness with the impersonality and spiritual vacuity of liberal consumerist societies." But while religions like Christianity and Islam (which emphasize universal human equality) may be compatible with democracy, they are difficult to reconcile with key liberal values like recognition of universal rights and freedom of conscience.[69]

Moreover, religion has proven quite inadequate as a public instrument or a political instrument of public good, and past experiments in religiously based societies—specifically in the European context—failed miserably to provide peace and stability. Christianity (a "slave ideology" that conceives of true human freedom only in the afterlife) did contribute to the rise of democracies; but, claims Fukuyama, the privatization of the faith fostered by Protestantism led to secularization of its goals even before liberalism materialized. In the event, modern liberalism "vanquished religion in Europe."[70] The only existing theocracies (systems in which religion is fused to political ideology) in the contemporary world are Orthodox Judaism and Islam. But neither is capable of creating a free society. Islam, the more potent of the two, "has indeed defeated liberal democracy in many parts of the Islamic world"; but, despite universalistic claims and recent resurgence, Islam is in-exportable to non-Islamic parts of the world.[71] "The days of Islam's cultural conquests," Fukuyama declares, "are over." In effect, history reaches its terminus, and humanity attains its fullest sense of self-realization and contentment only in the absence of religion—at least as a driving force in human affairs.

The argument against nationalism (itself a Western construct) is less clear-cut. Fukuyama raises doubt as to whether in fact nationalism represents an irreconcilable contradiction in the heart of liberalism. He argues that ethnic and nationalist tensions are strong indicators that the liberalism project is incomplete. Such tensions tend to reflect the experience of "peoples who are forced to live in unrepresentative political systems that they have not chosen." More to the point, few nationalist movements in the world today embody a coherent political ideology beyond parochial self/group-interest or survival, much less offer a comprehensive agenda for socioeconomic organization. Indeed, in the long run, nationalism could itself be "modernized" and thus, like religion before it, fade away as a political force.[72]

---

68. Ibid., 235; also 108.

69. Ibid., 217.

70. Ibid., 271.

71. Ibid., 45f., 243.

72. Ibid., 271. Not that national groups or interests will disappear, but while yet retaining "their separate languages and senses of identity . . . , that identity would be expressed primarily in the realm of culture rather than politics."

So it is that the Western model of modern liberal democracy represents history's end point, signified by the emergence of a single form of sociopolitical organization that is free from contradictions (problems unsolvable within the system itself) and "*completely satisfying* to all human beings in their most essential characteristics" (Fukuyama 1992: 136). The superiority and finality of this order are underlined by the fact that it fulfills the fundamental human desire for "recognition" (of personal dignity and individual identity typically found in religion and nationalism) and "freedom" (including autonomous choice and unrestrained pursuit of material abundance). On the basis of this evaluation Fukuyama is convinced that there are "no serious ideological competitors left to liberal democracy." The superiority and power of this model lie in the "very strong *predisposition* for all human societies to participate in it." Where the model has persistently failed to materialize, notably in Latin America and Africa, the obstacles are either cultural or inadequate political will.[73]

This brief summary hardly does justice to the masterful brilliance of Fukuyama's arguments and the force of his complex ideas. But those ideas are inescapably and palpably Eurocentric: signified, *inter alia*, by universalistic claims, strong historicism, the celebration of individualism, an evolutionary understanding of progress, and the exaltation of secularism. What the carefully constructed analysis adds up to is a more sophisticated version of the single global culture argument, mounted in this case on the twin corollaries of modern economic development and liberal democracy: "the creation of a universal consumer culture based on liberal economic principles."[74]

When they were first published in *The National Interest* (in 1989), Fukuyama's ideas provoked vigorous debate and a storm of criticism among Western intellectuals.[75] More than one respondent described the rigid connection that Fukuyama stipulated between the decline of Communism and the global triumph of liberalism as dubious and highly questionable; others insisted that what, in fact, has ended or is ending is modernity or the "Enlightenment project" and with it the very idea of the "end of history." In his book, which appeared some three years later, Fukuyama's arguments are more nuanced, without quite the same radical edge. He even allows for the possibility (albeit remote in his thinking) that liberal democracy might yet prove inadequate and thus signal not the "end" but yet another ephemeral historical moment.

Two striking and somewhat paradoxical elements in Fukuyama's proposal are worth noting in passing. The first is its strongly religious (more accurately, Christian) character—explicit in its focus on eschatological fulfillment and millenarian expectation.[76] Fukuyama provides little indication about what exists beyond his-

---

73. Ibid., 103-8, 136, 211, 215-22.

74. Ibid., 108.

75. See the Fall 1989 edition of *The National Interest*. The thesis also stimulated the publication of another volume in which a groups of scholars interacted with Fukuyama's ideas from a variety of perspectives; see Timothy Burns, ed., *After History? Francis Fukuyama and His Critics* (Lanham, MD: Rowman & Littlefield, 1994).

76. Though, as G. M. Tamás rightly points out, the hope for an end to history enshrined within modernity is very different from the Christian expectation of a final judgement followed by eternal

tory's terminus but he emphasizes the crucial historical linkages between Christianity and the emergence of liberal democratic societies in Western Europe.[77] In fact, one would be forgiven for thinking that the "end of history" idea ironically revives an ancient tradition vividly depicted in the biblical story of the building of the tower of Babel (a tradition examined in chapter 6). The second element is the proposal's structural and epistemological dependence on Marxist concepts and imagery, including the vision of a materialistic secular utopia, an aspect that led Huntington to make the telling comment that Fukuyama's thesis "itself reflects not the disappearance of Marxism but its pervasiveness."[78]

Ultimately, one has to admire the intellectual and culture hubris reflected in the assertion that the economic-political order prevalent among a particular people is not only vastly superior to all others throughout history—for those "who live in longstanding liberal democracies . . . have trouble imaging a world that is better than [their] own"[79]—but is also destined for universal dominion. It is necessary to point out that this assessment combines a secular vision of the future with the cultural paradigm argument, which links a people's propensity for progress and economic development to specific cultural attributes. Without reopening the complex debate, Fukuyama's proposal raises a number of questions:

- How can the consummation of human happiness and contentment be ascertained without reference to something outside of, or transcendent to, the human condition—that is, beyond material existence, the autonomous self, and pursuit of greater and greater freedom (what he terms "the liberal *idea*").[80]
- Are not the interrelated attributes of happiness, success, and satisfaction indubitably culturally defined and conditioned?
- Free to choose, will intelligent human beings abandon diversity for a monolithic homogenous experience of life that implicitly discredits other alternatives and therefore devalues choice?
- Is it not equally likely that the spread of liberal democracy (and its sanction of personal freedoms) will allow religious identities to flourish and thus strengthen particularity rather than homogeneity?
- How does one reconcile the values of equality and relativity at the heart of modern liberal democracy with the claims of cultural superiority and self-assertiveness?
- Does not the fact that most countries associated with the ideals of liberal democracy have experienced profound demographic decline in recent decades impair the vision of a universal future defined by that ideal?
- How plausible is such a future anyway, given the view that planet earth could

---

heavenly peace and the radical claims of the gospel—G. M. Tamás, "A Clarity Interfered With," in *After History? Francis Fukuyama and His Critics*, ed. Timothy Burns (Lanham, MD: Rowman & Littlefield, 1994), 81-109.

77. Fukuyama, *End of History*, 196f.

78. Samuel Huntington, "No Exit: The Errors of Endism," *The National Interest* (Fall 1989). Fukuyama himself admits (*End of History*, 131) that he presents "a kind of Marxist interpretation of history," albeit one that "leads to a completely non-Marxist conclusion."

79. Fukuyama, *End of History*, 46.

80. Ibid., 45.

not possibly sustain on a global level the lifestyles associated with countries in which liberal democracy currently flourishes?

In view of the tacit devaluation of indigenous non-Western cultures in Fukuyama's proposal, another tension in his argument deserves comment. In his famous 1989 article, Fukuyama reasons that "consciousness and culture" (not simply material self-interest) are crucial factors in shaping a people's economic development. At the same time he is convinced that the spread of Western capitalism and the desires stimulated by its consumer culture will allow liberalism to displace indigenous cultures in the non-European world. These two points do not quite add up. If material self-interest by itself lacks sufficient force to shape a people's destiny, then surely it is not inevitable that an appetite for Western goods and technology will be accompanied by the abandonment of indigenous culture in favor of wholesale appropriation of Western ideals. As one critic observed:

> The people of the developing world want vcrs, but they will not be bought off with them, and they do not want them for the purpose of erasing their convictions and their cultures. For they have moral and social traditions of their own, living traditions, and they are more and more coming to the conclusion that modernization must not mean the immolation of these traditions. . . . I think we shall all be surprised by how far these societies travel along the new technological and economic paths without becoming what we would call liberal.[81]

Interestingly enough, and perhaps in response to such criticism, Fukuyama makes two important concessions in his book that point to critical weaknesses in his prognosis. (1) Many Asian societies have accepted Western principles of liberal democracy without abandoning Asian cultural traditions—quite simply, the long-predicted breakdown of Asian traditional values has thus far failed to materialize. In fact, he notes that if economic growth in America and Europe falters relative to that in Asia, and if "Western societies continue to experience the progressive breakdown of basic social institutions like the family," Asians are likely to attribute their economic success more to their own than to Western culture. (2) The "ever-increasing homogenization of mankind being brought about by modern economics and technology" is attended everywhere by "resistance to that homogenization, and a reassertion, largely on a sub-political level, of cultural identities that ultimately reinforce existing barriers between people and nations."[82] It is to this second point that we now turn our attention (the merits of the first point are taken up in the next chapter).

---

81. Leon Wieseltier, "Spoilers at the Party," *The National Interest* (Fall, 1989).
82. Fukuyama, *End of History*, 242, 243-44.

The Mullahs and the Mall

The cultural homogenization thesis implicitly discounts the salience of cultural resistance and, in its cruder forms, upholds a winner-take-all outlook that makes little allowance for the durability of competing ideological worldviews or counter-movements. Yet it is manifestly evident that the same processes of modernization and attendant market consumerism judged to constitute a driving force behind the emerging global culture have also triggered entrenched resistance in the form of profound cultural, often religious, movements centered on acute concerns about indigenous identity.

To their credit, many proponents of cultural homogenization note the rising swell of antagonistic reactions and opposition directly stimulated by forms of cultural globalization. But few engage the crucial implications of their arguments. Fukuyama merely concedes that the process of homogenization is attended by resistance and "a reassertion . . . of cultural identities" (1992: 244). Friedman (1999) similarly acknowledges that the backlash against (cultural) globalization is a universal phenomenon rooted in a variety of impulses, including but not limited to fundamentalist hatred.[83] He even advocates what he calls "healthy glocalization," whereby a culture, when it encounters other strong cultures, absorbs influences that naturally fit into and can enrich it while *resisting* those things that are truly alien.[84]

But the most rigorous analysis of the oppositional forces unleashed by the forces of cultural globalization is provided by political scientist Benjamin Barber in his bestseller *Jihad vs. McWorld* (1st ed., 1995). Like the others, Barber validates the notion and reality of a global culture and endorses the view that its template, style, and products are American. In fact he depicts the struggle of Jihad against McWorld as a war not *between* civilizations but a war *within* civilization, the "dialectical expression of tensions built into a single global civilization."[85]

The forces of McWorld are "integrative modernization and aggressive economic and cultural globalization"; the forces of Jihad are "disintegrative tribalism and cultural fundamentalism."[86] At first sight, the two are diametrically opposed—one driven by "universalizing markets" the other by "parochial hatreds"; one signifying secular materialism, the other fanatical religious traditions; one embodied by the "mall," the other by "mullahs." But, argues Barber, they are dialectically conjoined in the sense that both represent responses to modernity and reflect or reinforce modernity's virtues and vices.[87] McWorld is essentially the "culmination of a modernization process"; thus, Jihad is not only its adversary but also its child. Both "are locked together in a kind of Freudian moment of ongoing cultural struggle, neither willing to coexist with the other,

---

83. Friedman, *Lexus and the Olive Tree*, 280-82; also, 320-29.
84. Ibid., 236.
85. Barber, *Jihad vs. McWorld*, xvi.
86. Ibid., xii.
87. Ibid., 157.

neither complete without the other." Most important, both are antagonistic to the nation-state and subversive of democratic institutions. Ultimately, therefore, they are mutually reinforcing instruments of anarchic global disorder.

Barber's assessment of "McWorld" is studiously negative. In his view, the unfettered forces of McWorld are tyrannical (they present a form of "soft imperialism") and conducive to spontaneous greed. McWorld is also far more successful at globalizing the vices of the West (including its cultural icons, ideology of consumption, and tolerance for social injustice and inequality) than its virtues (democracy and human rights). Its global capitalism undermines democratic institutions, destroys indigenous cultures in the name of secular materialism and modernization, dismantles the foundations necessary for a meaningful moral existence, and sacrifices equality and justice on the altar of profit. Throughout the world, noticeably in poverty-stricken neighborhoods, McWorld's very logic and mechanics create ideal conditions for Jihad—an environment of despairing rage and resentment.

In Barber's usage, Jihad is freed from exclusive application to Islamic fanaticism or holy war. It is a universalizing construct evocative of "cultural fundamentalism" or "dogmatic and violent particularism." Its twin pillars are religion and nationalism. It is generally rooted in ideologies of self-determination and local identity and manifest in aggressive hostility to the modernizing and colonizing culture of McWorld. The movements of Jihad have a plurality of forms: they are evident in subnational and separatist movements within European democracies (like Spain and France); they flourish within many Asian nations where modernization has succeeded without the benefit of democracy (like Japan and Singapore); and they thrive within "transitional democracies" in Eastern and Central Europe, including those created by the breakup of the Soviet empire. But by far the most potent expressions of Jihad—"essential Jihad"—are "fundamentalist" movements found within most world religions.

In short, Jihad is to be found not only within Islam but in the multiplicity of efforts throughout the world to preserve indigenous traditions and cultural identity in the face of the imperialistic modernizing and homogenizing pressures of McWorld. Its agents and adherents exist in America (in the very heart of McWorld) as well as in Israel, Iran, and India. An "American Jihad" exists in the fundamentalism of the Christian Right and in white militias; it is also represented in "the millions of American Christian families who home-school their children because they are so intimidated by the violent commercial culture awaiting their kids as soon as they leave home."[88] Like disciples of Jihad everywhere, theirs is a hatred born of fear, their zealotry motivated by opposition to modern values and the spiritual poverty of markets. Even when they utilize the implements of McWorld (notably its high-tech communications), it is to make war on the present "to secure a future more like the past."

Barber's arguments are not without contradictions. For instance, his analysis helps us to see why orthodox Islamic groups in the United States can make common cause with Christian fundamentalist groups on a number of moral ques-

---

88. Benjamin Barber, "Beyond Jihad vs. McWorld," *The Nation* (2002).

tions (such as homosexuality and abortion) but not why the latter are the bitterest opponents of the former in terms of cultural values and religious understanding. Often, as the case of Hindus and Muslims in India suggests, Jihad's bitterest enemy is not McWorld but alternative forms of Jihad. The juxtaposition of Jihad and McWorld works against Barber's efforts to divest the former of its deeply Islamic connotations simply because the latter is, in his understanding, intrinsically American. Jihad is perforce anti-Western/American and anti-globalization, which makes it curious that anti-globalization protesters are "children of McWorld" whose "objections are not Jihadic but merely democratic."[89] When completely delinked from its Islamic roots, Jihad becomes a loose and slippery concept, so that, ultimately, the struggle between McWorld and Jihad represents the ambivalence (about the merits and costs of Western defined progress) within each culture and within each individual.[90]

Barber rightly acknowledges the tyrannical and destructive nature of McWorld and the despairing rage and rebellion it inevitably invokes. But in aligning McWorld with the processes of modernization and essentially with Western civilization, and associating anti-modernity almost exclusively with religious "fundamentalist" expression, his arguments fail us badly. The facts of the case do not appear to support this dichotomy. It is no secret that the current wave of militant Islam began with the 1970s oil boom. In addition, very few of the really poor Islamic countries have become centers of militant Islam, while a disproportionate number of terrorists and suicide bombers "have higher education, often in engineering and the sciences."[91] Recent studies also reveal that "75 percent of anti-Western terrorists come from middle-class or upper-middle-class homes" while "65 percent have gone to college and three-quarters have professional or semiprofessional jobs."[92] Barber's suggestion that both Jihad and McWorld reflect tensions within the same globalized world is much closer to reality.

Barber argues passionately that neither Jihad nor McWorld is conducive to a democratic secure future. In the struggle over human destiny, both portend a "new global disorder"; and "only the globalization of civic and democratic institutions" is likely to offer a way out of this global war. This "civic globalization" would secure the economic blessings of modernity for those who desire it and at the same time allow cultural diversity and religious distinctiveness to flourish— for spiritual malaise is an impediment to creating a civil society. Victory for the planet against the twin destructive forces of Jihad and McWorld requires the creation of a diverse democratic world "in which the practice of religion is as secure as the practice of consumption."[93]

But Barber is in no doubt about the alternative future confronting humankind; and in this he solidly identifies with other proponents of globalized culture. He predicts that while the extremist actions of Jihad continue to grab the headlines, in the long run the forces of McWorld and the spread of Western civilization

---

89. Ibid., xvi.
90. Ibid.
91. Pipes, "God and Mammon," 14-21.
92. David Brooks, "Trading Cricket for Jihad," *New York Times*, August 4, 2005.
93. Barber, *Jihad vs. McWorld*, xiii, xxxii, 275.

may prove unstoppable. Global culture will overcome parochialism and integrate partial identities.[94] He adds that Jihad's efforts to "escape out of history"
are ultimately futile, for "time has not been a friend to either religion or morals
in recent centuries" and "history has been a history of individuation, acquisitiveness, secularization, aggressiveness, atomization and immoralism."[95] This judgment reveals a striking affinity with Fukuyama's thesis. We are left, once again,
with that most Western of visions: a future that is de-pluralized and secular. And
since that future represents the past of a particular people, it makes one wonder
whether, in fact, it is not Jihad that wins out in the end.

---

94. Ibid., 20, 82f.
95. Ibid., 214, 215.

3

Cultures of Globalization

Funny Thing about Elephants

> The first blind man put out his hand and touched the elephant's side.
> "How smooth!" he said. "An elephant is like a wall."
> —The Blind Men and the Elephant
> (Indian Folktale)

There are many versions (and creative revisions) of the well-known Indian fable about the blind men and the elephant.[1] One of the many "original" versions goes like this:

A long time ago in the valley of the Brahmaputra River in India there lived six men who were much inclined to boast of their wit and lore. Though they were no longer young and had all been blind since birth, they would compete with each other to see who could tell the tallest story. One day, however, they fell to arguing. The object of their dispute was the elephant. Now, since each was blind, none had ever seen that mighty beast of whom so many tales are told. So, to satisfy their minds and settle the dispute, they decided to go and seek out an elephant.

Having hired a young guide, Dookiram by name, they set out early one morning in single file along the forest track, each placing his hands on the back of the man in front. It was not long before they came to a forest clearing where a huge bull elephant, quite tame, was standing contemplating his menu for the day. The six blind men became quite excited; at last they would satisfy their minds. Thus it was that the men took turns to investigate the elephant's shape and form.

As all six men were blind, neither of them could see the whole elephant and approached the elephant from different directions. After encountering the elephant, each man proclaimed in turn: "O my brothers," the first man at once cried out [as he rubbed the animal's side], "it is as sure as I am wise that this elephant is like a great mud wall baked hard in the sun."

"Now, my brothers," the second man exclaimed with a cry of dawning

---

1. American poet John Godfrey Saxe (1816-1887) produced one of the most well known adaptations.

recognition [as he felt the animal's tusk], "I can tell you what shape this elephant is—he is exactly like a spear."

The others smiled in disbelief.

"Why, dear brothers, do you not see," said the third man [as he touched its tail]— "this elephant is very much like a rope," he shouted.

"Ha, I thought as much," the fourth man declared excitedly [as he put his hand on the animal's limber trunk], "this elephant much resembles a serpent."

The others snorted their contempt.

"Good gracious, brothers," the fifth man called out [as he felt the elephant's ear], "even a blind man can see what shape the elephant resembles most. Why he's mightily like a fan."

At last, it was the turn of the sixth old fellow and he [as he wrapped his hands around the animal's leg] proclaimed, "This sturdy pillar, brothers mine, feels exactly like the trunk of a great areca palm tree."

Of course, no one believed him.

Their curiosity satisfied, they all linked hands and followed the guide, Dookiram, back to the village. Once there, seated beneath a waving palm, the six blind men began disputing loud and long. Each now had his own opinion, firmly based on his own experience, of what an elephant is really like. For after all, each had felt the elephant for himself and knew that he was right! And so indeed he was. For depending on how the elephant is seen, each blind man was partly right, though all were in the wrong.

Much about the globalization discourse is evocative of this saga. Few other areas of study are as inundated with so many half-truths masquerading as grand theories and persistent overgeneralizations founded on one particular event or experience. The grandiose claims and predictions that attended early writings and discussions on the phenomenon linger, and the widespread tendency among Western intellectuals to ascribe Western particularities to the entire phenomenon shows no signs of abatement—for one thing it produces too many best-sellers. In many respects, the "globalization is Americanization" view is deeply ideological. It fundamentally confuses Western aspirations with the needs of the non-Western world and, by misconstruing certain parts for the whole, bankrupts our understanding of the infinitely complex and paradoxical processes of globalization.

It needs to be stated that the concept of a global culture or "universal civilization" is a peculiarly Western one—one of many assumptions that distinguish the Western worldview from that of every other major culture.[2] In this regard, the global culture thesis essentially reprises the centuries-old Eurocentric notion of "civilization." For, in that strange monopoly of meaning so common within Western discourse, "civilization" (used in an unqualified sense) typically meant

---

2. Meic Pearse, *Why the Rest Hates the West: Understanding the Roots of Global Rage* (London: SPCK, 2004); see also Huntington, *Clash of Civilizations*, 66.

Western civilization: an advanced and sophisticated cultural entity by which non-European cultures, deemed "barbarian" or backward, were judged.

Thus, the nineteenth-century ideology of "white man's burden," in tandem with notions of "manifest destiny" or "divine providence," provided rationalization for the belief that the superior values, ideals, and material benefits of this civilization (crucially identified with Christianity) should be spread around the world (see pp. 164-65 below)—hence the entrenched but inaccurate historical assessment prevalent among Western intellectuals that this Western expansion amounted to what Huntington (1996: 53) terms "the unidirectional impact of one civilization on all others." That this view is shared even by a robust critic of a Western-derived global culture like Samuel Huntington is indicative of its entrenched nature.

Inarguably, the combined impact of the European colonial and Christian expansion projects generated massive transformations and radical social change in many parts of the world. But, as we shall see, the encounter with the non-Western world also had profound, reflexive consequences for Western societies. Among other things, it uncovered the hollowness of many universalistic claims/ideals associated with Enlightenment thinking (notably equality and liberty);[3] it also revolutionized Western scholarship and led to the establishment of new disciplines like anthropology, linguistics, and comparative religions. On the religious plane, the missionary encounter with Africa and Asia bankrupted the Christendom ideal of one nation/one faith and revitalized older religions like Hinduism (see chapter 4). It also exposed the contextual nature of theological reflection and laid the foundation for major transformations within global Christianity. Ultimately, the colonial project was a qualified failure, and the civilizing program of Western Christianity met with qualified success. Without denying the reality of neocolonialism, both were attended by unintended consequences.

All of this raises many questions conspicuously muted within current global culture rationalizations: whether the global reach of Western ideas and products will be without implications for Western societies themselves; whether the allure of modernization and Western notions of progress has left the vast majority of the non-Western world so blinded to the unpalatable legacies and incongruities of Western economic models and attendant lifestyles that they are willing to sell their cultural soul for a mess of foreign pottage; whether, as Fukuyama (1989) concedes, the rich non-Western cultures so offhandedly devalued will not yet provide answers for the "impersonality and spiritual vacuity of liberal consumerist societies"; whether the encounter with modernity in those same non-Western cultures might not, as the Japanese experience already suggests, yield unprecedented trajectories and models of progress.

The discrediting of the secularization thesis discussed at the beginning of the previous chapter provides salutary warning about the precariousness of judging the rest by the rubric of the West. Contemporary globalization, as we have already noted, creates winners and losers and reinforces enduring forms of marginalization and exclusion. Against this background, the image of elevated West-

---

3. See Dorinda Outram, *The Enlightenment* (New York: Cambridge University Press, 1995).

ern societies assiduously projecting their own ideals and values (by virtue of economic dominance) all the while existing in relative isolation immune to potent cultural currents from without—including the inevitable backlash engendered by all manner of grievances and discontent nurtured in part by the unbridgeable gap between reality and the ubiquitous images of hyper-consumerism associated with McWorld—is a blatant myth.

As already acknowledged, the transcending processes of globalization increasingly impinge on our daily lives and livelihoods—albeit in different ways and to varying degrees—and continue to strengthen our consciousness of the world as a single social space. This global consciousness is attended by strong convergence, notably the greatly increased facility for distant societies to share in (or be deeply impacted by) the same experiences. This can be planned as in the case of, say, a FIFA World Cup Finals event, or incidental, as in horrible tragedies like the Asian Tsunami (of December 2004), which took the lives of at least two hundred thousand people from thirteen countries and elicited a global response. The Asian region bore the brunt of the disaster (at least 128,000 people died in worse-hit Indonesia) but, since the worse hit areas included popular tourist resorts, societies and households in distant lands remain linked by the memory of the tragedy.

Totalizing explanations like the single global culture thesis point to vital aspects of contemporary globalization: that certain Western brands and products have worldwide presence; that through American dominance of mass media there is global awareness of particular values and lifestyles (including hyper-consumerism); that much of the world has been integrated into a global economic system (decreasingly?) dominated by the West; and that Western economic ascendancy remains a driving force behind the spread of modernity. But these conditions, some of which are open to question, represent only aspects of the "syndrome of processes" which contribute to globalization.

Reason in Search of Reality

From a certain perspective, the term "global culture" is somewhat oxymoronic, if one accepts that culture fundamentally represents a set of distinctive attitudes, beliefs, preferences, customs, and inherited institutions that distinguish one collective from others. It is not enough to say that "global" is in contradistinction to "local," since there can be no *global* without local expression and particularity of experience. Moreover, related arguments ignore the profound complexity of cultural interaction and encounter and, as Held et al. (1999: 373) note, fail to take into account "the ways in which cultural products are locally consumed, locally read and transformed in the process." Sociologist John Tomlinson (1999: 84) points out that to equate the worldwide presence of certain cultural goods with the emergence of a global culture implies a rather "impoverished concept of culture"; for culture "simply does not transfer in [a] unilinear way," immune to forces of interpretation, indigenization, or translation. The point of these observations is that in all cultural interactions people interpret and appropriate new concepts and experiences in terms of preexisting views and values.

Insofar as it entails the movement of "objects, signs and people across regions and intercontinental space," the globalization of cultures has a long history.[4] This historical dimension is most obvious when we consider the role human migration has played in cultural diffusion and interaction. When people move, they carry their ideas, beliefs, and religious practices with them; and the processes of exchange and interactions often see cultural practices take root in lands quite distant from the original site. This partly explains why the unprecedented "global reach and volume of cultural traffic through contemporary telecommunication, broadcasting and transport infrastructures" coincides with an equally unprecedented rise in the volume and velocity of global migrations.

Yet it is the very pervasiveness of cultural forms of contemporary globalization that makes the question of cultural homogenization so acute and complex. Are we indeed witnessing the imposition or spread of specific (presumably Western) cultural products and values throughout the world in a way that is inevitably transforming non-Western peoples' self-understanding and nullifying local beliefs or traditions? Put differently, is it valid to claim that the new American-dominated global infrastructures of cultural diffusion—including TNCs, television, movies, and NGOs—exercise such a powerful influence that the products and ideas they represent (or peddle) significantly transcend and erode national identities so that it is plausible to conceive of the emergence of a *global culture*?

One may grant that economic dominance and technological supremacy allow certain Western (chiefly American) cultural products, lifestyles, and inherent values to be projected around the globe in a way that has the propensity to subvert local production, and also that such cultural goods and lifestyles not only stimulate consumerist appetites but also inspire in far-flung societies around the globe modernist visions of prosperity and progress that compel quite similar aspirations. Yet it still requires a huge conceptual leap from such premises to the conclusion that the end result of such processes is inevitable Western-style cultural homogenization at the expense of local traditions and indigenous identity.

Taking the High Road

Significantly, many of the experiences implied in the so-called global convergence of culture bespeak a "high profile" understanding of globalization, which is to say that they are confined to the more affluent sectors of the developing and developed world—arguably less than 5 percent of the global population—whose education, tastes, aspirations, and purchasing power mean that they have more in common with each other than with others in their own countries. Berger's four models—Davos culture, faculty club international, McWorld culture, and Protestant evangelicalism—described in chapter 2 help to make the case.

Quite clearly, "Davos culture" is restricted to an affluent segment, a *relatively* small number of people linked by air travel, use of the Internet, and other technologically advanced means of communication. Huntington observes that "almost all these people hold university degrees in the physical sciences, social sciences,

---

4. Held et al., *Global Transformations*, 329.

business, or law, work with words and/or numbers, are reasonably fluent in English, are employed by governments, corporations, and academic institutions with extensive international involvement, and travel frequently outside their own country."[5] He also estimates that this Davos culture is shared by perhaps as few as one-tenth of 1 percent of the world's population.

Needless to say, the faculty club represents an equally if not more rarified model of elite interaction and participation in both social representation and global distribution. Eminent sociologist Immanuel Wallerstein once noted that from the period 1850 to 1914 and probably even to 1945, at least 95 percent of all scholars and all scholarship originated in five countries: France, Great Britain, the Germanies, the Italies, and the United States.[6] To be sure, the forces of globalization have radically transformed academia: most obviously by fostering a wider and faster spread of ideas but also through innovative instruments of instruction, and the internationalizing of many elite Western universities. In recent years there has been a sharp decline in the number of foreign students arriving in American universities, accompanied by a corresponding rise in countries like Britain, France, and Germany. Yet foreign students not only "contribute some $13 billion a year to America's GDP" but also supply "the brainpower for its research machine and energy for its entrepreneurial economy." Added to these are significant increases in the number of and access to higher education across the developing world (with countries like China determined to match or surpass the most advanced Western universities).[7]

But the "structures of *academic* dependency" endorsed by Peter Berger himself provide more than a hint that, amid notable transformations, much remains the same. Thus, at least for now, America accounts for seventeen of the twenty top universities in the world; its universities also currently employ 70 percent of the world's Nobel Prize winners and produce 30 percent of the world's output of articles on science and engineering. More to the point, while there are more than eighty million students in higher education worldwide only about 3.5 million people are employed to teach or look after them. The world's intelligentsia, much less its Western representatives, are a privileged few indeed.

Berger's other two "faces of global culture" (evangelical Protestantism and McWorld culture) have a much wider utilization and certainly impact the rank and file of the local order in societies throughout the world. Yet closer examination of the particular values and consciousness on which Berger predicates his case for cultural convergence confirms a high-profile understanding. His analysis focuses mainly on *leaders* of evangelical Protestantism, among whom similar aspirations and voluntary international interaction arguably foster a degree of sameness in doctrinal emphasis, pastoral image, and even preaching mannerisms. Yet global

---

5. Huntington, *Clash of Civilizations*, 37.

6. Cited by Walter Mignolo, "Globalization, Civilization Processes, and the Relocation of Languages and Cultures," in *The Cultures of Globalization*, ed. F. Jameson and M. Miyoshi (Durham, NC: Duke University Press, 1998), 32-53.

7. "A Survey of Higher Education," *The Economist* (September 10, 2005): 15.

evangelicalism is a polycentric movement with no pope or Mecca, and it would be foolish to ignore its entrenched sectarianism and proliferating fiefdoms.

Global evangelicalism, in fact, provides a more salient model of the interpenetrative conjunction of the global and the local than Berger allows. Take worship, a fundamental component of the movement. Undoubtedly, the same kinds of songs could be heard in congregations from New York to Nigeria—though the discerning observer may note variations in musical interpretation and kinds of worship. But not only do musical inspiration and influence flow in multiple directions—through migrant movement and professional collaborations—this is also one area where local production and indigenous expression persistently thrive in the face of, and even because of, global flows.

As for "McWorld culture," Ziauddin Sardar and Merryl W. Davies (2002: 124f.) note pointedly that it is really "those with the most prolific purchasing power—the children of the privileged, affluent elite" who are genuine partakers of America cultural symbols and consumer products. Even Berger admits that while popular culture penetrates broad masses of people all over the world, "control of these enterprises [of American cultural production] is exercised by elites."[8] To be sure, many individuals and groups around the world embrace Westernization at the expense of indigenous identity. But many more utilize or partake in Western/American products while rejecting the values they represent or turn them to different ends. Berger also concedes that "in principle an individual could wear jeans and running shoes, eat hamburgers, even watch a Disney cartoon, and remain fully embedded in this or that traditional culture."[9] In Huntington's more evocative phrase, "somewhere in the Middle East a half-dozen young men could well be dressed in jeans, drinking Coke, listening to rap, and, between their bows to Mecca, putting together a bomb to blow up an American airliner."[10]

The fact is that for vast populations in the world—particularly but not limited to the developing world—fast-food chains, televisions, *genuine* Levi jeans, Nike shoes, even telephones, are outside the frame of daily existence, in which the struggle to "make ends meet" is the foremost preoccupation. The genuine partakers of America cultural symbols and consumer products reflect not so much cultural homogenization as the menacing divisions engendered by economic globalization.

English, Please!

As already noted, a major plank of the cultural homogenization argument is that English is the indisputable language of the future—an ascendancy attributed less to the important legacy of the British empire than to the world dominance of America as a cultural and economic colossus. There is much to commend this

8. Berger, "Cultural Dynamics," 6.
9. Ibid., 7.
10. Huntington, *Clash of Civilizations*, 58.

view. Language is clearly "one of the prime tools of cultural expression" and the supreme symbol of national/ethnic identity.[11] As such, the global spread and appeal of the English language would seem to have clear implications for cultural globalization. "Never in human history," comments renowned linguist Joshua Fishman, "has one language been spoken (let alone semi-spoken) so widely and by so many."[12] Yet the claim or prediction that the growing prominence of English in global interactions will contribute to the erosion of indigenous cultures and local identities everywhere seems exaggerated.

In the first instance, such a claim overlooks the principle of translation and indigenization (discussed in chapter 4). In various regions and localities around the world, spoken English is subject to powerful local cultural and linguistic influences that impact its structure, syntax, vocabulary, and word sounds. Americans and the English are not the only peoples divided by the same language. Outside elite circles (where advanced educational attainments produce a certain affinity), English speakers from different parts of the world, say Japan and Jamaica, would struggle to understand each other fully. The English-speaking world is a world of "different Englishes."[13]

Inarguably, English, as Huntington observes, is the world's way of communicating interculturally in the same way that the Christian calendar is the world's way of tracking time and Arabic numerals, the world's way of counting. As he goes on to argue, the emergence of a lingua franca "is a way of coping with linguistic and cultural differences not a source of eliminating them. It is a tool for communication not a source of identity and community."[14] Thus, the use of English for intercultural communication "helps to maintain and, indeed, reinforces peoples' separate cultural identities." People use English to communicate with peoples of other cultures "precisely because [they] want to preserve their own culture" (Huntington 1996: 62).

In reality, therefore, the relationship between expansive use of English and globalization can be more complicated than at first appears. In regions where language differences underpin national distinctions and impede interaction, the spread of English can foster regional cooperation over and against global flows. Fishman confirms that "the kinds of interactions identified with globalization, from trade to communications, have also encouraged regionalization and with it the spread of regional languages," a process that extends to the rise of "pockets of localization and local-language revival resistant to global change."[15] In eastern Africa, for instance, two strangers encountering each other for the first time will most likely start their conversation in Swahili, not English.

Global migration flows are also hugely significant. The spread of English (and French to a lesser extent) arguably facilitates the international migrant move-

11. Sardar and Davies, *Why Do People Hate America?* 120.

12. Joshua A. Fishman, "The New Linguistic Order," in *Globalization and the Challenges of a New Century: A Reader*, ed. Patrick O'Meara, Howard D. Mehlinger, and Matthew Krain (Indianapolis: Indiana University Press, 2000), 435.

13. Huntington, *Clash of Civilizations*, 60.

14. Ibid., 61.

15. Fishman, "New Linguistic Order," 436.

ment and augments the capacity of non-Western cultural movements to impact the Western world. At the same time, migration movement can contribute to the erosion of particular languages, especially were the migrants constitute an isolated and relatively small group within the host culture. But in countries like the United States, where there are massive immigrant populations of Spanish, Korean, and Chinese speakers, language erosion is far less inevitable. Not only are many of these communities densely concentrated and segregated, but they are also served by their own television and radio stations and have access to home-land productions via satellite and Internet technology. Add to this the fact that immigrant populations have a much higher birth rate than native populations and it is hardly overstating the case to suggest that other major language groups are holding their own even in the largest heartland of the English language. Between 1980 and 1990, Spanish speakers grew by 50 percent (30 percent of New York is Hispanic), Chinese speakers by 98 percent, Korean speakers by 127 percent and Vietnamese speakers by 150 percent.[16]

It has to be said that, for the most part, second- and third-generation immi-grants in English-speaking countries consciously embrace English as their first language. But this does not in and of itself translate into cultural assimilation. It fosters bilinguality and reflects multilayered identities.[17] Take the younger gen-eration of Hispanic Americans. One observer notes that they "want to be spoken to in English even as they remain true to their Latino identity."[18] Based on this perception, the recently launched SíTV (in the United States), a twenty-four-hour cable channel that targets young Latinos (ages eighteen to thirty-four) adopted the motto "Speak English. Live Latin." Its Web site boldly proclaims that "SíTV goes beyond tradition by catering to today's English-speaking Latinos who con-sume English media but still want shows that speak to their Latino roots." It claims to deliver entertaining programming "on subjects that are important to young Latino and multicultural audiences whose culture is an integral part of their identity." The channel has enjoyed tremendous success, quickly reaching ten million households.[19]

On the global level, it is a sobering fact that over one billion people speak Chinese as their mother tongue, compared to about 372 million who speak Eng-lish. Indeed, global demographic trends in the last few decades suggest that the number of English speakers is declining relative to the proportion of people speaking Mandarin and Hindi. Renowned language specialist and senior edi-tor at *The Atlantic Monthly*, Barbara Wallraff, contends that English is likely to cede its place as the world's second-most-spoken language to Hindi and Urdu (two south Asian languages) by 2050.[20] By that time also, Spanish and Arabic may be as common as English. Even the posited link between English and the widespread use of the Internet appears to be unsafe. Wallraff highlights indica-

---

16. Barbara Wallraff, "What Global Language?" *Atlantic Monthly* (November, 2000): 52-66.
17. See Stephen Castles and Mark J. Miller, *The Age of Migration: International Population Movements in the Modern World,* 2nd ed. (New York: Guilford Press, 1998).
18. Jennifer Ordoñez, "Speak English. Live Latin," *Newsweek,* May 30, 2005, 30.
19. Ibid.
20. Wallraff, "What Global Language?" 55.

tions that "non-English speakers are the fastest growing group of new Internet users" and that "Internet traffic in languages other than English will outstrip English-language traffic in the next few years."[21] In the final analysis, to ascribe universality (even as prognosis) to a language spoken by less than 10 percent of the world's population surely betrays a certain conceit or just blind confidence that the "elephant is a tree."

Attending the Clash of Civilizations

In his best-selling *The Clash of Civilizations: Remaking of World Order* (1996), a book based on an article that first appeared in *Foreign Affairs* in the summer of 1993, eminent political scientist Samuel Huntington provides a robust and systematic contestation of the global culture thesis. His alternative "civilizational paradigm" presents a radically different analytical framework for understanding contemporary global realities, and it continues to provoke debate. Basically, Huntington's analysis postulates a fragmented global cultural landscape defined by competing "civilizations" and incorporates the remarkable assertion that, after centuries of overwhelming dominance and global influence, the West is actually fading as a power and will continue to decline relative to other civilizations.

Huntington rejects the correlation between Western civilization and modern culture as false and maintains that, far from creating an increasingly secular global society in which religion is a spent (public) force, the spread of modernization has helped to stimulate a global religious resurgence that fosters cultural parochialism.[22] Almost all non-Western cultures, he rightly observes, have existed longer and all have a long record of borrowing from other civilizations—through discriminate processes of assimilation and adaptation—to enhance their survival. Thus, the response of non-Western societies to Westernization and modernization covers the spectrum of rejection, amalgamation, absorption, and substitution.

More to the point, many non-Western societies have modernized without abandoning their own cultures. In fact, argues Huntington, modernization in many ways "promotes de-Westernization and the resurgence of indigenous culture" (1996: 76). This happens in two ways: at the societal level, modernization accelerates economic and political advancement generating renewed confidence in the society's culture; at the individual level, the weakening of traditional systems creates feelings of alienation and crisis of identity which in turn stimulate a turn toward religion (as a primary source of identity *re*-creation). In sum, under the pressures of modernization, the world "is becoming more modern and less Western" (1996: 78). And it is precisely the forces of integration hyperbolized by global culture arguments that are generating "counter forces of cultural assertion and civilizational consciousness" (1996: 36).

---

21. Ibid., 61. According to Global Reach (a marketing communications consultancy), English-language users accounted for 35.8 percent of the world online population in 2004 (non-English users, 64.2 percent); see Global Internet Statistics (by language) (http://global-reach.biz/globstats/index.php3).

22. For his full argument, see Huntington, *Clash of Civilizations*, 68-78, 96-97.

Huntington's core argument, however, is that the post–Cold War world is a multipolar, multicivilizational world. A world in which the most important distinctions among peoples are not ideological, political, or economic but *cultural*; and the most important, the most dangerous conflicts are not between social classes or other economically defined groups but "between peoples belonging to different cultural entities." Tribal wars or ethnic conflicts within civilizations will remain rife, but increasingly the most potent anarchic conflicts will be between states or groups from different civilizations. The rivalry of the superpowers is replaced by the clash of civilizations.

Like Barber, Huntington highlights religion as one of the most significant forces shaping the contemporary world order. But where Barber's utilization of religion is largely confined to movements hostile to modernizing culture, Huntington's employment of the term is far more comprehensive. Religion, he explains, is a major constituent of civilizations—in human history the world's great religions have been associated with major civilizations—thus the revitalization of religion throughout much of the world is reinforcing civilizational differences. But the global religious revival is not limited to fundamentalist movements. As dramatic as these may be, they are "only the surface waves of the much broader and more fundamental religious tide that is giving a different cast to human life at the end of the twentieth century" (Huntington 1996: 96).

The use of civilization*s* (plural) is critical and signifies conceptual divergence from the singular form adopted in universal civilization arguments. Civilization in both usages refers to a distinct cultural entity—"culture writ large" or "the highest cultural grouping of people" (Huntington 1996: 41). But there the parallel ends. Use of civilizations (plural) denotes strong rejection of the notion of an ideal model or a single standard. The new multicivilizational world order is defined by multidirectional interactions of seven or eight major civilizations: namely, the Sinic, Japanese, Hindu, Islamic, Orthodox, Western, Latin American, and possibly African. Of the major civilizational fault lines, the central civilizational clash and "the central axis of . . . world politics" is between the power and culture of West (the hitherto dominant civilization) and the power and culture of non-Western civilizations (Huntington 1996: 29).

The difference between these two is acute. The concept of a universal civilization, as we have already noted, is a peculiarly Western one. Even more important, the particular values that are prominent in the West (most conspicuously individualism) are least esteemed by the rest. Thus, what the West upholds as universal non-Westerners denounce as imperialistic, and the West's (especially America's) determination to promote its values and institutions around the world increasingly generates reactions ranging from skepticism to implacable hostility. Other areas of tension include efforts by the West to maintain its military superiority by enforcing nonproliferation policies and to stem the rising tide of immigration.

Perhaps Huntington's most arresting argument is that, while the West remains overwhelmingly dominant and will retain its primacy well into the twenty-first century, power is already shifting to non-Western civilizations; that inexorable, if gradual, changes in the balances of power among civilizations will see Asian societies (particularly China) increasingly ascendant. These same transformations will witness increased cultural assertiveness among non-Western societies accompanied by growing rejection of Western culture and the decreasing ability of the West to project or impose its values and concepts.[23]

For many centuries, explains Huntington, non-Western peoples sought to appropriate the values and institutions of the West in a bid to emulate its success. By the end of the twentieth century, however, such attitudes had begun to change with the rise of indigenization movements stimulated by a variety of factors. These factors include opposition to Western domination; worldwide religious revival; the widespread belief among East Asians that their newfound economic prosperity is attributable not to the importation of Western culture but rather to their adherence to their own culture; and (rather paradoxically) the adoption of the principles of democracy by non-Western societies, which often encourages popular mobilization against Western-oriented elites and has seen left-wing parties voted into power (in Latin America).

But, if the central division within the clash of civilizations is between the West and the rest, the most antagonistic relations, in Huntington's assessment, will be between the West and the "challenger civilizations" of Islam and China.[24] These two cultural traditions are much older; they are also "very different from and in their eyes superior to that of the West" (1996: 185).

A decade after Huntington's prognosis, China's global aspirations and hegemonic rise within Asian are far more evident; though it remains to be seen whether a Sinic-Islamic alignment centered on opposition to the West (which he projects[25]) will flourish. It is no secret that China is the fastest growing of the emerging economies in the world (which include India and Russia). A 2005 survey concluded that China "is beginning to drive, in a new and pervasive way," much that goes on in the world economy—including global inflation, interest rates, bond yields, house prices, wages, profits and commodity prices. China's integration into the world economy, it notes, is having "a bigger global impact than other emerging economies, or than Japan did during its period of rapid growth from the mid-1950s onwards" and its effects "could last for another couple of decades."[26] It has also not gone unnoticed that the long-standing rivalry between Japan and China for supremacy in East Asia and control of "the oil-rich seas and strategic shipping lanes that lie between them" has ratcheted up ominously in recent years, leading many experts to warn of inevitable collision in the foreseeable future.[27]

Huntington's account predated the spate of dastardly terrorist attacks on America and Europe, so perhaps of even greater significance is his insistence that the clash of civilizations between the West and Islam will be the most intense and momentous. The phrase "Islamic threat" is a far more loaded and sinister concept now than it was in the mid-1990s when Huntington's ideas were first published.

---

23. Ibid., 81-101, 183-206.

24. Ibid., 184f.

25. Ibid., 238-40.

26. "China and the World Economy: From T-Shirts to T-Bonds," *The Economist*, July 30, 2005, 61, 63.

27. Norimitsu Onishi and Howard W. French, "Japan's Rivalry with China Is Stirring a Crowded Sea," *New York Times*, September 11, 2005.

It is also surrounded by unhelpful hype and misinformation fed by glaring prejudices and misconceptions evident in media coverage on both sides. The popular and most persistent view portrays the prevailing confrontation as one between a modern secular West and traditionally minded or militant Islamist extremists. Huntington's assessment depicts a broader and more ominous picture.

The clash of these two civilizations, he declared, is not only rooted in centuries of deeply conflictual relations but is also ingrained in the very nature of the two civilizations and the religions associated with them. Moreover, in recent decades a number of factors—among these the collapse of Communism, migration, Islamic resurgence, and efforts by the West to universalize its values—have contributed to a sharp decline in tolerance within both Muslim and Christian societies for each other. And, following the 1979 Iranian Revolution, an inter-civilizational quasi war developed between Islam and the West, a war that, in its military aspects, has followed the now predictable pattern of Islamic terrorism versus Western air power. Significantly, the level of violence in this intercivilizational war has already exceeded that between the United States and the Soviet Union during the Cold War.

As is to be expected, Huntington's analysis provoked fierce debate and a bevy of articles. Several aspects of his thinking met with strong criticism.[28] Some of the most notable objections include the following:

- The power of the nation-state (as a primary actor in international affairs) is eviscerated or reduced to insignificance.
- The world's civilizations are treated as though they exist in clearly demarcated boundaries and water-tight compartments.
- It panders to a myth of unity that treats hugely fragmented or fissiparous entities like Islam, Christianity, and the West as monolithic homogenous units and, by extension, downplays the intense rivalries and power struggles that have long persisted within such entities.
- His focus in inter-civilizational interactions and conflicts obscures both the intensely local (as opposed to foreign) preoccupations of radical elements within those civilizations and the huge role that contextual factors play in shaping their agenda.
- His assessment grossly exaggerates civilizational differences and ignores historic examples of collaboration (including American complicity with Islamist regimes in recent history).
- It greatly underestimates the enduring power of secularism and the attractiveness of consumer culture.
- It misrepresents the genesis of contemporary conflicts (which have less to do with historic tribal hatreds than with the acquisition of power and control of resources) and ignores the ability of diverse peoples to coexist.

---

28. See, among others, Vinoth Ramachandra, *Faiths in Conflict? Christian Integrity in a Multicultural World* (Downers Grove, IL: InterVarsity Press, 1999); Fouad Ajami, "The Summoning," *Foreign Affairs* 72, no. 4 (1993): 2-9; John R. Bowen, "The Myth of Global Ethnic Conflict," in *Globalization and the Challenges of a New Century: A Reader*, ed. Patrick O'Meara, Howard D. Mehlinger, and Matthew Krain (Bloomington: Indiana University Press, 2000).

Middle East specialist Fouad Ajami (whom Huntington singles out as an example of "intellectual migrants to the West" who are enthusiastic proponents of the global culture idea) was scathing in his denunciation of Huntington's attitude toward nation-states and his readiness to assign ascendance to indigenous and religious phenomena. For Ajami, the nation-state, Western modernity, and secularism are enduring realities whose tenacity belies the pull of tradition or civilizational fidelities. "The things and ways that the West took to 'the rest,'" he declared, "have become the ways of the world. The secular idea, the state system and the balance of power, pop culture jumping tariff walls and barriers, the state as an instrument of welfare, all these have been internalized in the remotest places."[29] Such assertions further strengthen the point already made that despite massive evidence to the contrary, secularism and its high priests remain a major force within Western life and intellectual discourse.

This is not the place to rehash the animated, sometimes acrimonious, and still ongoing debate about the emergent world [dis]order. Some of the criticisms leveled against Huntington seem to miss the force and nuance of his arguments— including the claim that he ignores examples of intercivilizational collaboration. But most have merit. Treating hugely diversified entities like Christianity, Islam, or the West as if they were homogenous calcified realities does represent a defect in his analysis. While recent acts of terrorism have fostered renewed collaboration and convergence at the higher political levels between America and Europe, it is hard to ignore the divergent interests and intransigent transatlantic rivalry between the two. And Huntington's argument that the long-standing opposition between Europe and America has, in the twentieth century, given way to a "sense of broader identity" and the emergence of a broader entity (the West) of which America is leader, is unconvincing.[30] Then again, Huntington's civilizational theory points to broader issues of cultural affinity and historical heritage that are equally hard to ignore, not least from a non-Western perspective.

For instance, Huntington's civilizational paradigm dictates a rigid connection between Western civilization and Christianity (or Christendom) which leads him to draw quite erroneous conclusions about the fate and fortunes of global Christianity. He concedes that both Christianity and Islam have "significantly expanded their numbers in Africa, and that a major shift toward Christianity occurred in South Korea" (1996: 65). But, he surmises, "in the long run Mohammed wins out." Due largely to spectacular rates of population growth and a disproportionately youthful population, Islam will emerge as the most powerful non-Western movement—accounting for 30 percent of the world population (compared to 25 percent for Christianity)—by 2025.

This conclusion represents a highly dubious reading of contemporary global realities and stems from the faulty assumption that Christianity is a central component or expression of Western civilization. In fact momentous shifts within global Christianity in recent decades have witnessed massive ongoing recessions

---

29. Ajami, "Summoning," 6.

30. For more recent appraisals, see Andrew Moravcsik, "Striking a New Transatlantic Bargain," *Foreign Affairs* 82, no. 4 (July/August 2003): 74-89; and Kupchan, "End of the West."

from the faith within Western societies and spectacular growth in the non-Western world. So much so that Christianity is now decidedly a non-Western religion, with Africa and Latin America as newly emergent centers. By the most conservative estimates, less than 40 percent of the world's Christians reside in the West. (For more on this subject, see chapter 5.)

West and Non-West: Minding the Gap

For all its foibles, real and perceived, Huntington's assessment is a tour de force of contemporary sociopolitical analysis. He demonstrates a profound grasp of the intricacies of global politics and cultural realities that this writer finds fresh and persuasive for the most part. Detractors accuse him of being a "pandemonium prophet," of endorsing a global vision of implacably antagonistic cultural entities that is potentially self-fulfilling because the more the communities of the world believe in and act on it the more likely it is to come to pass.[31] In my own judgment, however, Huntington's appraisal of the contemporary world order is superior to, and certainly more refined than, the winner-take-all prognosis of the single-civilization construct. Furthermore, I suspect that what troubles some critics is its gritty warts-and-all realism. The startling, messy, possibly irrational, and potentially unmanageable collisions of Huntington's civilizational paradigm sit uneasily with any mind-set conditioned by Enlightenment values of progressivism and anthropocentric omnipotence. Yet, in many respects, the alternative vision of a single civilization—in which all indigenous spirit, all sense of identity and local heritage, as well as the creative impulses that stem from the genius of particular experiences and views of the world, are at the very least sublimated by a monolithic prefabricated way of life—is a far more fearsome prospect. It leaves us with only one of the parts of the elephant. The tail perhaps?

But it is Huntington's studious exploration of the cultural fault lines between the West and the rest (perhaps overstated in places but persuasive nonetheless) which I find most compelling because it coheres with my own analysis of the religious factor in South–North migrations.

The persistent and pervasive Western idea of the universality of its particular cultural values not only perpetuates ignorance and rejection of the "other" but also sanctions a *refusal to understand*. Western values or concepts of democracy, individualism, free markets, human rights, liberalism, privatized religion, and limited government hold some attraction and will be emulated by particular non-Western societies in varying degrees of accommodation and with varying success. But they are neither universal nor universally desirable—any more so than ancestor veneration, communalism, or extended family systems. True, some concepts such as freedom or sovereignty, even human rights, have universal application, but they are never free from cultural baggage and the need for contextual appropriation. In that connection, Ramachandra's suggestion that the concepts such as human rights and democracy, which originated from Europe,

---

31. Ramachandra, *Faiths in Conflict?* 37.

have as much universal validity as natural science strikes me as disingenuous and unhelpful. Further, their resonance is severely undermined when the self-styled champions of liberal democracy display egregious inconsistency in applying its principles and substance both within and without their national borders. In short, Western distinctives are not destined for global ascendancy. As Huntington (1996) reminds us, "the West won the world not by the superiority of its ideas or values or religion . . . but by its superiority in applying organized violence."

Barbarians at the Gates

The word "barbarian" has long been emblematic of civilizational difference and ingrained ethnocentrism. The Greeks used *barbario* to mock the foreign sounding Semites, Arabians, and North Africans. And, at the time of their first encounter and long afterwards, the Chinese and Japanese regarded Europeans as barbarians. In time, widespread use saw the term employed to dismiss "alien cultures and even rival civilizations . . . because they were unrecognizably strange." Perhaps, as Meic Pearse (2004) intimates, the current understanding of barbarian to mean someone violent, primitive, uncouth or uncivilized owes much to the Romans, who employed *barbari* to describe the bearded hordes (ancestors of contemporary Europeans) living beyond the frontiers of the empire and hence beyond "civilized" (from *civis*, the city) life. The irony of course is that the Romans themselves "were capable of cruelties all the more extreme and terrifying for being so ruthlessly efficient and organized," and they "would doubtless have defended themselves against charges of barbarism because their violence was so well orchestrated and disciplined, unlike the wild fury of the tribal war-hosts."[32] In any case, there is even greater irony in the fact that centuries later descendants of these *barbari* would unselfconsciously deprecate non-European cultures as barbaric, and even conceive of their particular culture (still marked by ancient residue) as universal.

Proponents of the cultural paradigm and prophets of a single global culture (American-/Western-style) can point to the vast wealth, technological superiority, and pleasures of life that characterize Western societies. They can also reasonably argue that it is the allure of these and other attainments that attract the hordes of immigrants beating at the door and motivate countless nameless migrants to brave the most hazardous and life threatening conditions in a bid to make it to the "promised land" (or, at least, the consumers' paradise).[33] This same conscious confidence in the "unique comforts" and hyper-prosperity of life in the

---

32. Pearse, *Why the Rest Hates the West*.

33. A series of attempts by hundreds of Africans from all over sub-Saharan Africa (who had already risked their lives crossing the Sahara desert) to storm through the Moroccan border at the enclave of Ceuta into Spanish territory led to more than forty people being injured and five deaths. The BBC notes that "many migrants are caught and many drown while attempting to make the sea crossing to enter Spain illegally"; for instance, see "Troops Sent to Spain Enclaves," *BBC News*, 2005, http://news.bbc.co.uk/go/pr/fr/-/1/hi/world/africa/4295248.stm (accessed September 29, 2005); and "New Storming of Spanish Enclave," *BBC News*, 2005, http://news.bbc.co.uk/1/hi/world/africa/4289818.stm (accessed September 29, 2005).

West is one reason why many Westerners react with a mixture of bewilderment and supercilious indifference to anti-Western sentiments. (An aspect which is even more true of American reactions to anti-Americanism).

Insofar as the hordes outside the gates, so to speak, are viewed with scorn or somewhat fearful disdain (see chapter 8), the analogy to ancient Rome may not be entirely inappropriate. Western views and perceptions of the masses of people who reside beyond the West tend to be deeply uncomplimentary. Notions of "uncivilized" or "barbaric" easily form with the aid of television-mediated images and thirty-minute documentaries that generally fixate on the unfamiliar and outlandish. It is necessary to qualify this observation. In my experience, the niceties and hollow platitudes of political correctness prohibit actual public description of non-Western customs or cultural practices as barbaric. But a mental viewpoint is formed nonetheless, a corollary of the understanding that a civilizational ideal exists. In modern society also, images typically pass for truth, so this mental viewpoint is invested with vivid impressions: of female "circumcision" (or, as "rights" campaigners would have it, female genital mutilation); of child soldiers; of hand and foot amputations (even of babies) by rebel forces; of arranged marriages; of multitudes of pot-bellied, skeletal, fly-infested children, victimized by famine; of vile dictators masquerading as democratically elected presidents; of innumerable brutalities and daily life assailed by unremitting nightmarish hardships. Such associations are not unjustified, but they mask considerable ignorance, even amongst the educated, about the non-Western world.

Unfortunately, the Western media on which most depend for knowledge of the "other" is often too ideologically driven to rise above stereotypically negative and, especially in the case of Islam, degrading images. As Ramachandra notes, Islamic countries and constituencies, of course, return the favor by propagating equally nasty stereotypes of the West, thus completing the circle of a mutually reinforcing trend.[34] But propaganda wars and ideologically inspired typecasting aside, attitudes in the non-Western world are arguably much better informed. Western (again, particularly American) domination of television media and movies means that Western lifestyles, preferences, and values—at least Hollywood's versions of them—are beamed into homes and communities around the world. The perceptions of hyper-prosperity thus fostered and the understanding of the American/Western attributes, all refracted through the cultural lenses of the particular viewers, often generate imperfect visions of daily life in the West. But it is far more likely to be a closer approximation of the truth.

Most Westerners would like to think that the accumulated impressions of the West formed among non-Western peoples would necessarily coalesce into a uniformly flattering, if somewhat overblown, appreciation of Western culture. There are many non-Westerns for whom this is quite true: conspicuous among them, Davos elites and aspirants, intellectual migrants to the West, and middle-class youths around the world who ardently seek and ape American-inspired pop culture. But if many aspects of Western culture meet with powerful resistance by groups even within the West itself (often on religious grounds), it should hardly

---

34. Ramachandra, *Faiths in Conflict?* 34-35, 43f.

be surprising that negative reactions to the Western values abound throughout the non-Western world. Admiration and craving for the unique comforts and fleshpots of the Western society are often mingled with abiding resentments of Western power (economic, political, and military) and apprehension (or repulsion) at many aspects of its moral culture and canon of values. Indeed, Pearse finds that non-Westerners are just as likely to employ the term "barbarian" to describe Westerners, "for despising tradition, the ancestors and the dead. For despising religion, or at least for treating it lightly. For the shallowness and triviality of their culture. For their sexual shamelessness. For their loose adherence to family and, sometimes, also to tribe. For their absence of a sense of honor."[35]

All this is not to suggest that the current world is hopelessly divided into two antagonistic cultural blocs. Rather it is foolhardy to ignore the cultural gulf that exists between the West and the non-West—in outlook, values, and preferences. After centuries of encounter, interaction, exchange, and Western dominion, non-Western sensibilities and priorities differ strikingly from Western preferences in critical respects.

Undoubtedly, the fissures and cleavages that continue to attend the cultures of globalization jostle for attention alongside processes of convergence and, like the *yin-yang* of Chinese philosophy, neither aspect is assured of existence without the other. Overwhelming media focus on the menace of global terrorism and the specific actions of radical Islamic groups, a preoccupation endlessly fueled by the ongoing war on Iraq, deflates much attention from the broader issues of intrinsic cultural differences between the West and the rest which Huntington explored. Popular characterization of the war on terrorism within some sectors of Western society as an effort by Western powers and their allies to defend particular "universal values" (meaning the values of Western secular modernity) or more crudely, in language redolent of the Cold War, as a conflict between "good and evil," embody more subtle forms of the myth of a single civilizational standard.

Interestingly, the single global culture thesis (that now finds its greatest champions among secularists and its most forceful expression in the secularization thesis) is ultimately rooted in religious concepts and convictions. The concept of the secular (descriptive of temporal and material existence) versus the "eternal" (otherworldly, or religious) is a creation of Christendom—partly, at least. As a Western phenomenon, secularization refers to the decreasing influence of religion (religious institutions, beliefs, and practices) in public life. This process presumes a condition in which all of society, and therefore public life, was Christian or subject to religious authority—in a word, Christendom. As we shall see, efforts at the global expansion of Christendom were significantly undermined by the political and economic priorities of colonial rule. By limiting, even prohibiting, Christian expansion when it threatened colonial interests, the powers of Christendom effectively severed religious profession from civic identity/allegiance and tacitly sanctioned religious plurality. In this sense, colonialism bankrupted Christendom and opened the way for secularization.[36]

---

35. Pearse, *Why the Rest Hates the West*, 34; for a detailed exposé of these issues, see 38-51.
36. See Walls, "Mission and Migration," 8.

But we digress. Christendom also fostered the Western idea of a universal civilization. Since Christian profession was binding on the whole of society and coterminous with tribal territory, the spread of the Christian faith was understood in terms of territorial expansion. And since European peoples conceived of their culture or civilization as Christian—tribal allegiance being inseparable from Christian identity—the universal spread of European civilization and the biblical mandate to spread the gospel throughout the world were understood as one and the same thing. Colonial domination and missionary enterprise became deeply intertwined. Efforts at the global expansion of Christendom—the spread of European Christianity as a normative expression of the Christian faith—represents the most comprehensive attempt in the history of the world to impose the civilization of one race or people on all others. Never was one civilization so dominant and so determined to create a new world order fashioned after its particular image. The ultimate demise of Christendom did not exhaust the idea of a single global culture, but its lessons need not be ignored.

4

The Birth and Bankruptcy of Christendom

A Missiological Reflection

Almighty God raises up certain good men to be rulers over nations in order that he may by their means bestow the gifts of his righteousness upon all whom they are set. . . . So, my most illustrious son, watch carefully over the grace you have received from God and hasten to extend the Christian faith among the people who are subject to you. Increase your righteous zeal for their conversion; suppress the worship of idols; overthrow their buildings and shrines; strengthen the morals of your subjects by outstanding purity of life, by exhorting them, terrifying, enticing, and correcting them, and by showing them an example of good works. . . .

—Letter dated 601 c.e. from Pope Gregory I
to King Æthelbert of Kent (England)[1]

For over a millennium, from roughly the eighth to the early twentieth century, the dominant model of Christianity was "Christendom": Christianity understood as territorial faith, the church construed as "the whole of human society subject to the will of God."[2] The emergence of Christendom as the prevailing expression and experience of the Christian faith among European peoples was a lengthy and complex process accompanied by modifications and exceptions. But its central features are easily described. Within Christendom (in its most fully developed form), the church was the entire society and the entire society was the church. Christian identity was not based on personal faith but was derived from the fact of belonging to a particular "Christian" nation or tribe. Becoming a member of the church was as involuntary as being born, and the life of the faith was equated with the ordinary process of socialization. To be a member of society was to be a Christian, to be a Christian was to be a member of society. Christendom repre-

---

1. Bede, *The Ecclesiastical History of the English People* (New York: Oxford University Press, 1994), 59 (Book 1.32).

2. R. W. Southern, *Western Society and the Church in the Middle Ages* (Harmondsworth: Penguin, 1990), 22.

sented Christianity as tribal religion. The introduction and spread of a feudal social structure with an emphasis on reciprocal obligations and binding oaths further strengthened the process: religious allegiance, already inseparable from tribal identity, became fused with political loyalty.

Exonerating Constantine! Conversion of the West

Contemporary usage of the term "Christendom" is wide and varied; the concept is applied not only as an explanatory model for Western European Christianity but also more broadly as a catchall description of situations anywhere in the world where Christian forms and structures are firmly entrenched within a society. Misapprehension of the concept is matched by the fog of confusion that persists about its origins. The most prevalent view links the emergence of Christendom to the Roman emperor Constantine's endlessly debated conversion to Christianity in 313 C.E. (the emperor postponed baptism until he was on his deathbed), an event that dramatically changed the fortunes of the church. This Constantinian explanation is heavily dependent on the writings of Eusebius (c. 275-339), bishop of Caesarea, renowned scholar and adviser to Constantine, whose unfinished *Life of Constantine* heaped panegyrical praises on the emperor's public achievements and left out damning details about his personal life.

It is well known that Constantine did not make Christianity an official religion of the Roman Empire. That honor belongs to his predecessor Emperor Galerius, who issued an edict of toleration in 311. But, after his fabled conversion, Constantine lavished imperial favors on the Christian church and conferred on it a highly favored status. Until his death in 337, he publicly associated himself with Christianity, interfered forcefully in the church's affairs, and directed the enormous resources of the empire to Christian ends.

Imperial favor and munificence radically transformed the relationship between the church (hitherto a dispersed and persecuted community of believers) and the Roman state from one of hostility and conflict to one characterized by concord and harmonious coexistence. As depicted in Eusebius's boldly sanguine description, empire and church began to converge in identity and common purpose: "a new and fresh era of existence had begun to appear" in which the fortunes of "the one catholic Church" and the empire (nay, the destiny of nations) were guided by a pious emperor who governed as God's chosen instrument. For Eusebius, Constantine I was "the servant of God," "the conqueror of nations," and the archetypal Christian ruler. His reign signaled a new dispensation in the history of humankind and brought the Roman Empire within divine providence; "God himself had given him the empire of the world."[3]

Eusebius's hagiographic account is short on historical accuracy and long on literary inventiveness, but it does provide some insight into the view of the

---

3. See Eusebius, *The Life of the Blessed Emperor Constantine* (Internet Medieval Sourcebook), http:www.fordham.edu/halsall/basis/vita=constantine.html.

emperor harbored by a deeply grateful fourth-century church. Constantine's lofty military and political achievements are beyond dispute, and there is no conclusive basis for doubting his conversion to Christianity, though the fact that he murdered his father-in-law, wife, and son troubles the image of saintliness. But the Constantinian explanation for the emergence of Christendom is problematic for other reasons.

The changed fortunes of the church under Constantine's rule made it desirable, even necessary, for all Romans ("Roman citizens," that is) to become Christian.[4] But that left massive hordes of peoples unconverted or indifferent. Not only were there non-Christians among high ranking officials in Constantine's own government, but polytheism, which some argue Constantine never officially renounced, also continued to flourish in the empire during his reign and long afterwards. While Constantine succeeded in uniting the empire—no mean political feat—his efforts at creating what Eusebius termed "one catholic church" were far less successful. Bitter divisions and competing understandings of the *ecclesia* (church) troubled catholicity, and significant sections of sincere believers such as the North African Donatists outrightly rejected imperial authority or interference. Given this state of affairs, it seems unfair to hold Constantine responsible for Christendom, even if his stalwart initiatives on behalf of his newfound faith provided inspiration for successive generations of Christian rulers.

A much stronger case has been made, primarily by Scottish scholar Andrew Walls, for dating the origins of Christendom to the conversion of the Germanic tribes of northern and western Europe whom the Romans derisively called barbarians.[5] Conversion of the Germanic peoples to the Christian faith was a complex, uneven, variegated development involving migration, resettlement, invasions, planned missionary action, and military conquest. While some such as the Vandals and Ostrogoths readily adopted the Christian faith (perhaps owing to greater exposure to Roman ways), the conversion of groups like the Franks and Anglo-Saxons was a prolonged process involving violent conflicts and use of naked brute force. Some groups adopted Roman civilization even while they plundered the empire; others were co-opted into the over-stretched Roman army to bolster defenses and even participate in the Roman administration, which meant that they imbibed deeply of Roman culture and political life. All in all, the spread of Christianity was fitful and gradual. Conversion of the Scandinavian tribes of northern Europe (today Denmark, Norway, and Sweden) came only in the tenth to thirteenth centuries.

With few exceptions, however, the Christianization of Germanic peoples followed a general pattern in which the conversion of the ruler or chieftain was followed immediately or shortly after by mass conversion of the entire tribe or all the ruler's subjects. The English were a case in point.

---

4. Richard Fletcher, *The Barbarian Conversion: From Paganism to Christianity* (New York: Henry Holt, 1997), 37.

5. Andrew F. Walls, "Ecumenical Missiology in Anabaptist Perspective," *Mission Focus: Annual Review* 13 (2005): 191-98; idem, *The Missionary Movement in Christian History: Studies in the Transmission of Faith* (Maryknoll, NY: Orbis Books, 1996), 19-20.

In the sixth century a group of monks was sent by Pope Gregory I (c. 540-604) to convert the pagan Anglo-Saxons to Christianity.[6] The group, headed by Augustine (not to be confused with the famous African bishop and theologian), reached Kent in 597 and settled in the capital, Canterbury. King Æthelbert's wife was already a Christian; but forsaking the traditions of his ancestors—customs and beliefs that "the whole English race have held so long"—was no small matter for a king. Yet, if conversion to Christianity was long in coming, acceptance of the faith could not have been more total. The Venerable Bede, the great Anglo-Saxon historian and our principal source for the conversion of the English people to Christianity in the seventh century, records:

> At last the king, as well as others, believed and was baptized, being attracted by the pure life of the saints and by their most precious promises, whose truth they confirmed by performing many miracles. Every day more and more began to flock to hear the Word, to forsake their heathen worship, and, through faith, to join the unity of Christ's holy Church. It is related that the king, although he rejoiced at their conversion and their faith, compelled no one to accept Christianity; though none the less he showed greater affection for believers since they were his fellow citizens in the kingdom of heaven.[7]

How much weight should be given to the observation that King Æthelbert made no effort to compel the conversion of his subjects is difficult to say. Royal conversion was followed by a mass movement to Christianity. Within a matter of months more than ten thousand English individuals were baptized;[8] and under royal authority the faith was disseminated throughout the kingdom and beyond. Augustine became the first Archbishop of Canterbury.

This pattern of royal conversion followed by mass movement to Christianity recurred with remarkable regularity among other Germanic peoples. Individual conversions, either through ecclesiastical initiatives or the patient labor of medieval missionaries, did not disappear but the top-down approach in which the ruling classes (who wielded the instruments of coercive power) were the primary targets of Christian mission became the dominant missionary strategy. This approach was successful in part because, as Richard Fletcher observes, collaboration between missionary and ruler was mutually beneficial. He explains:

> The missionary received protection, endowments . . . for Christian communities, the status that came from association with a king, the infectious example of a royal conversion, access to royal powers of coercion, a share in royal rights to various services performed by subjects. . . . Kings acquired new grandeur and renown, were introduced to new techniques of rule in

---

6. See Bede, *Ecclesiastical History*, 1.22-33; Fletcher, *Barbarian Conversion*, 112-19.

7. Bede, *Ecclesiastical History*, 1.26.

8. Fletcher, *Barbarian Conversion*, 117.

literacy and legislation, benefited from notions or rituals which enhanced authority and the mystique of royalty.[9]

Fletcher adds, instructively, that there were at least three reasons why some rulers resisted conversion to Christianity: (1) the fear that they might not be able to persuade their followers to follow suit, (2) apprehensions about angering the ancestors or breaking with ancestral traditions, and (3) a reluctance to abandon the prevalent and time-honored worship of plural deities in favor of the exclusive human worship demanded by monotheism. Thus, even in the rejection of the Christian faith the ruler's decision and the bond of tribal allegiance were crucial; and it is worth adding that polytheism persisted among Germanic peoples long after conversion to Christianity.

In the early stages of the Christianization of Europe, mass conversions were the norm because royal decree played a pivotal role in missionary expansion. Later on, notably after the conversion of the Franks, mass movements remained commonplace because territorial expansion by Christian rulers, inevitably involving mission by the sword, meant the sudden and forcible inclusion of large numbers of people within Christian domain. The most conspicuous example of such efforts in which the spread of the Christian faith was unashamedly linked to brutal subjugation and imperial expansion was that of Charlemagne (c. 747-814), the Frankish king crowned emperor on Christmas Day 800 C.E.

But there was an even more fundamental element at play in these mass conversions. Among European peoples, the Christian faith was adopted not on the basis of individual assent to a new belief system but as the religion of the entire clan, tribal group, or kingdom. Tribal allegiance and communal identity rested on the immutable bond of *custom* or *customary law*, and religion formed an integral part of the body of customs that bound the society together. The bond of custom precluded disparate forms of religious allegiance within the group. Thus, conversion to the new faith took place not as the private decision of individuals but as a public act involving the entire society. As Walls comments,

> the conversion of tribal peoples knew a far stronger law than any other Emperor could enforce, that of custom. Custom is binding upon every child born in to a primal community; and non-conformity to that custom is unthinkable. A communal decision to adopt the Christian faith might take some time in coming; there might be uncertainty, division, debate for a while but once thoroughly made, the decision would bind everyone in that society. A community must have a single custom.[10]

The adoption and experience of the Christian faith as custom or customary law meant that there could only be one church within the whole community. In other words, conversion did not involve joining a visible, separate, church community; the converts remained in their previous social structure (extended

---

9. Ibid., 237.
10. Walls, *Missionary Movement*, 20.

family, clan, or tribe).[11] The identification of the church with the whole of organized society thus became a distinguishing feature of European Christianity.[12] The conversion of "barbarians" gave rise to *Christendom*, the experience of Christianity as territorial faith and tribal religion.

To be sure, mass conversions meant that understanding of the new faith remained superficial and that, even under the most enthusiastic Christian ruler, the creation of a Christian society was a fitful and arduous process. The forms and expressions of Christianity encountered by Germanic people bore the stamp of the culture and concepts of the Hellenistic-Roman world into which it had been translated from its early Jewish origins. Greek and Latin were the languages of religious discourse and church liturgy. But the spread of the faith among Germanic tribes, the vast majority of whom lived beyond the influence of Roman civilization, coincided with the disintegration of the western empire. The conversion of Germanic peoples therefore required extensive cross-cultural translation efforts and the abandonment of cherished Christian forms and practice. The message of Christianity had to be communicated in the vernacular and reformulated using thought forms and traditions that were wholly drawn from the primal world.[13]

The prominent role that rulers played in establishing the faith also created an intimate connection between cross and crown, and political enforcement became an accepted means of regulating Christian doctrine and devotion. But the process of adaptation and reformulation of Christian beliefs and practice in accordance with Germanic needs and ideas took centuries; and the process of consolidating the Christian faith or inculcating new standards of Christian behavior among Germanic peoples was a long and laborious one. The precepts and practice of the new faith jostled for space with a vast body of primal beliefs and customs—including polytheism, magic, divine healing, amulets, ancestorship, death, and the afterlife—which retained their hold long after public conversion and even found new vitality within the new Christian dispensation.[14] Still, the tensions between cherished traditional customs and the claims of Christianity produced a variety of responses in different places and at different times. Reality often lagged behind ideal. In addition, throughout the medieval period, vigorous reform movements repeatedly emerged to deepen or renew Christendom. These initiatives culminated in the Protestant reformations of the sixteenth century.[15]

The Christendom ideal of one society, one faith, also engendered strong intolerance of religious dissent and, by implication, explicit disavowal of religious plurality. Mission in the service of Christendom ultimately aimed at the creation of Christian society, where it was deemed non-existent—that is, outside Europe. The

---

11. Isnard Wilhelm Frank, *A History of the Medieval Church* (London: SCM, 1995), 15.

12. Southern, *Western Society,* 16.

13. See Walls, *Missionary Movement*, 68-75.

14. For a helpful survey, see Fletcher, *Barbarian Conversion*, 228-84; also Ramsay MacMullen, *Christianity and Paganism in the Fourth to Eighth Centuries* (New Haven: Yale University Press, 1997), 103-49.

15. Renowned Reformation historian Roland Bainton argues that the Reformation was "above all else a revival of religion" and that it represented "the last great flowering of the piety of the Middle Ages" (*The Reformation of the Sixteenth Century* [Boston: Beacon, 1985], 3).

long-term presence of Jewish and Muslim communities within Europe itself indicates that this understanding was subject to practical considerations and exceptions. For instance, the Jewish population was close-knit, prosperous, and played a significant role in the medieval economy, most notably as moneylenders. Muslims who remained under Christian rule were generally those who lacked the means to migrate and were therefore confined to the lower classes, where their presence had little impact on the wider society. But, while there is little evidence of systematic efforts by the church to convert Europe's Muslim population, strict guidelines governed religious interaction. Religious minorities, including Jews, had limited rights. Intermarriage was forbidden, and apostates from Christianity to Islam risked the death penalty. Most significant, the flowering of Christendom coincided with the upsurge of religiosity in the eleventh and twelfth centuries that gave rise to the Crusades.[16] Jews were subjected to bloody persecution and mass expulsions; and Muslims fared no better. The reconquest, in 1492, of the last Muslim stronghold in Europe (the small enclave of Granada in Spain) was followed by forced baptisms. Europe now embodied the Christian faith.

Taking Christendom on the Road: The Western Missionary Movement (1500-1950)

Christendom emerged as a coherent system across western and central Europe—from the Atlantic to the eastern borders of Romania and Slovakia.[17] With the final collapse of the Eastern Roman (Byzantine) Empire before the Muslim Turks in the thirteenth century, Western Christendom became the predominant representation of Christianity.[18] When Granada, the last Muslim enclave on mainland Europe, fell to Spanish armies, western Europe achieved the culmination of Christendom. Europe was now territorially Christian, and Christianity was decidedly European. Since church and nation were coterminous in scope, European peoples also experienced Christianity as a territorial ideal—"the area subject to Christian custom and the law of Christ."[19] The Christian religion became so thoroughly melded with European ways and customs, that European culture was seen as Christian culture. As Walls puts it, "the domestication of Christianity in the West was so complete, the process of acculturation there so successful, that the faith seemed inseparable from the categories of European life and thought."[20]

This reality also fostered an enduring conviction that there is one essence or normative expression of the faith. Europe could now, and for another four centuries at least, claim to be the heartland of the Christian faith. As late as the early

---

16. Fletcher, *Barbarian Conversion*, 320f.

17. Walls, "Ecumenical Missiology," 193.

18. Walls, *Missionary Movement*, 20.

19. Walls, "Ecumenical Missiology," 193.

20. Andrew F. Walls, *The Cross-Cultural Process in Christian History: Studies in the Transmission and Appropriation of Faith* (Maryknoll, NY: Orbis Books, 2002), 49.

twentieth century, the prolific and staunchly Catholic Hilaire Belloc (1870-1953) could declare without qualification: *Europe is the faith and the faith is Europe.*[21]

These considerations shaped the Western missionary movement in profound ways. Christianity remained in essence a tribal religion and, not unlike tribal encounters, efforts at spreading of the faith among other peoples were strongly marked by aggression, self-assertiveness, and triumphalism. At stake in the expansion of Christianity was not only the salvation of non-Christian peoples (narrowly conceived) but also the dignity and supremacy of the sending tribe or "Christian nation." As we have seen in Pope Alexander VI's division of the non-European world (see pp. 18-19 above), the conception of Christianity as territorial faith also engendered a bifocal vision of the world in which the kingdom of Christ on earth was a visible, self-defined, territorial reality in contradistinction to "heathendom," or the territories of unbelievers. Since Europe was representative of the church, "mission" involved efforts to spread the gospel in non-European lands.

It is difficult to overemphasize the impact of this territorial dichotomy on Western missionary strategy and thinking and on the self-understanding of Western Christians. Christian mission became deeply intertwined with—indeed, often served as justification for—territorial expansion and political domination. Advancing the colonial objectives of crown and country, even through brutal military action, and extending European civilization (invariably tied to economic exploitation) overlapped with the cause of Christ. Missions unwittingly became the face of nationalism in part because individual Western nations were convinced that their imperial acquisitions were providentially ordained for the expansion of the gospel of salvation. The implications were paradoxical. While the conversion of non-European peoples to the Christian faith was taken quite seriously, missionary action became fettered to political aggression and economic exploitation; and while European missionaries often made extraordinary sacrifices in their efforts to preach the gospel in distant lands, the missionary project was blighted by nationalist competition and ingrained attitudes of cultural and racial superiority toward non-European peoples.

Significantly, appropriation of the term "mission" to describe the *sending* of ecclesiastical agents to distant territories coincided with European missionary expansion. Prior to the sixteenth century, the Latin term *missio* ("to send") existed in the church lexicon as descriptive of activity within the Holy Trinity—to wit, the sending of the Son by the Father or of the Holy Spirit by the Son. This arcane theological concept was first adopted by Ignatius Loyola (1491-1556), the extraordinarily gifted founder of the Society of Jesus, to describe Jesuit efforts outside Europe. Founded in 1540, the Society incorporated a vow of "special obedience to the Pope regarding the missions" and became the church's dominant missionary force, as active in winning back Protestant lands in Europe as it was in extending the Catholic faith in Africa, Asia, and America. Those efforts were linked to European colonialism and sanctioned by powerful Catholic monarchs. The term "missions" as a description of European overseas enterprise (both Catholic and

---

21. Hilaire Belloc, *Europe and the Faith* (New York: Paulist, 1920), ix.

Protestant) would henceforth be invested with heavy connotations of colonial dominance or imperial aggression.

Fifteenth- to Eighteenth-Century Roman Catholic Initiatives

The mentality of conquest and buoyant self-confidence derived from the full realization of Western Christendom informed the earliest efforts at European exploration and commercial expansion; and the intimate relationship between cross and crown shaped efforts at spreading Christianity. Heartened by the recent conquest of Granada, grateful popes were only too willing to bless the colonial adventures of the monarchs of Spain and Portugal in the name of Christian expansion. Papal sanction took the form of *padroado* (Spanish, *patronata*), official declarations that granted the rulers of Spain and Portugal complete ecclesiastical and economic control over the newly "discovered" lands. The *padroado*, a system that lasted long after the empires of the two European powers had waned and crumbled—for some five hundred years, in fact—epitomized the mission and vision of Christendom. Non-European lands and peoples were to be conquered and brought under the sway of European civilization and Christian domination. The 1481 bull *Aeterni regis clementia* issued by Pope Sixtus IV perfectly illustrates the wide-ranging authority and vast privileges granted to the Portuguese crown:[22]

> Navigation of the oceans of recent discovery is restricted to Portuguese ships.
> The Portuguese are the true lords (*veri domini*) of the lands discovered or yet to be discovered.
> The Portuguese may freely trade with unbelievers, even Muslims, provided they do not supply them with arms or anything of the kind.
> The Portuguese crown may found and erect churches, monasteries and other places of religious usage; the clergy who minister in such places will have full power to minister the sacraments and to pronounce absolution. Spiritual power and authority from Cape Bojador and Nam as far as the Indies belongs to Portugal in perpetuity.

From the European perspective, the newly discovered lands not only represented heathendom but also signified another "world," a "new world" at the boundaries of (European) "civilization."[23] *New* meant "new" to Europeans; "new" also implied unmarked by the imprint and imprimatur of European ideals, way of life, religious practices, and institutions. Faced with peoples in the Americas who were incomprehensibly and irremediably different, Europeans immediately questioned whether they were human beings with souls. The expansion of Christendom required both territorial conquest and the superimposition of European

---

22. Quoted in Stephen Neill, *A History of Christianity in India: The Beginnings to A.D. 1707* (New York: Cambridge University Press, 1984), 111f.

23. Abdul R. JanMohammed, "The Economy of Manichean Allegory: The Function of Racial Difference in Colonialist Literature," in *"Race," Writing, and Difference*, ed. Henry Louis Gates, Jr. (Chicago: University of Chicago Press, 1986), 83.

culture—deemed Christian and destined for universal dominance. With some notable but short-lived exceptions, including early Jesuit missions in China and Japan (see p. 161 below), this outlook marked the encounter. Almost everywhere, attitudes of instinctive (self-preserving) contempt and cultural superiority rapidly evolved into widespread racism.

Still, the conversion of non-European peoples to the Christian faith was taken quite seriously. From the outset, members of the orders or secular clergy were included in state-sponsored expeditions. These priests typically represented a mere fraction of the whole, but to focus on their numbers is to miss the point. Within a Christendom framework, as McKennie Goodpasture explains, the church was fully present in each shipload of merchants and mercenaries. It was not "a separate, voluntary body of believers but included everyone on shipboard . . . ; it was "part and parcel of the state."[24] Thus, when Spanish explorer Hernán Cortés landed in Mexico (from Cuba) with six hundred soldiers on Good Friday, 1519, the entire group knelt on the beach in prayer before embarking on the conquest of the Aztec empire. Each man a soldier in the service of the Spanish Crown; each man a soldier of Christ!

For Europe's Roman Catholic Church, the timing of the discovery of this vast "new world" confirmed divine purpose and providence. Here, indeed, was a God-given opportunity not only to recoup tremendous losses to Protestantism but also to extend the kingdom of God on earth. As Adrian Hastings explains, Iberian colonial ventures were shaped by the conviction that, "If God had held back any knowledge of this vast world from Christians until now and then bestowed it entire[ly] upon the Catholic kings, this demonstrated almost incontrovertibly the entirely special role that Spain was called upon to play in sacred and human history."[25]

In the long run, both Roman Catholic and Protestant missionary initiatives were shaped by this vital impulse: "a very special sort of sacred imperialism, a conviction of the hand of providence, of manifest destiny."[26] By the mid-seventeenth century, extensive Roman Catholic efforts had seen the establishment of indigenous Christian communities in Africa, Asia, and the Americas. But, after two and a half centuries of expansion, the Roman Catholic missionary movement became a spent force. Above all, the mass expulsion of thousands of Jesuit priests from Spanish and Portuguese colonies in the late 1750s and 1760s—a politically motivated move that signaled the internal contradictions of Christendom—dealt a crippling blow to Roman Catholic missions.

Eighteenth-Century Protestant Initiatives

Strikingly, the emergence of a major missionary movement among European Protestants coincided with the decline of Roman Catholic initiatives. In stark

---

24. H. McKennie Goodpasture, *Cross and Sword: An Eyewitness History of Christianity in Latin America* (Maryknoll, NY: Orbis Books, 1989), 1.

25. Adrian Hastings, "Latin America," in *A World History of Christianity*, ed. Adrian Hastings (Grand Rapids: Eerdmans, 1999), 334.

26. Ibid.

contrast to the massive Roman Catholic (Iberian-led) missionary effort, Protestant nations and churches had not mounted any sustained effort to spread the gospel in distant lands by the end of the seventeenth century.[27] How and why this was so had something to do with the nature of Christendom.

The sixteenth-century Protestant reformations shattered the structural uniformity of medieval Catholicism (embodied by the institution of the papacy) and paved the way for the emergence of national Christian identities. But the Protestant reformations left the underlying construct of Christendom intact. Indeed, Roland Bainton goes so far as to argue that the Protestant movement may be regarded as "the *renewal of Christendom*" insofar as it made "religion and even confessionalism a paramount issue in politics for another century and a half."[28] Since the church remained identified with the whole of organized society, the Christendom ideal of one nation—one faith remained unchanged. The bloody and devastating Thirty Years War (1618-1648), fulminated by ecclesiastical fragmentation, reflected the attempt by different rulers to impose confessional unity within their territories. Besides, the Peace of Westphalia, which ended the Thirty Years War decreed that each region had to follow the religion of its ruler. Among Protestants, however, this outlook was somewhat in tension with a more subjective, personalized view of salvation.

Europe would henceforth, to all intents and purposes, be a continent characterized by two dominant forms of faith, each adopted as the official religion within the territorial limits of particular nation-states. Protestantism was now "confined chiefly to the Teutonic peoples," or peoples of Germanic origin (including the English, Scots, Dutch, Germans, and Scandinavians), and it was mainly through the efforts of these people that the Protestant forms of Christianity would be "propagated by *migration* and conversion."[29] The point at issue is that Christendom remained the dominant model of Christianity among western European peoples, whether Catholic or Protestant, and the Western missionary movement reflected that fact. Yet, paradoxically (as I explain below), the European missionary movement helped to expose the limitations of Christendom as an exportable model or universal ideal.

Celebrated Christian historian Kenneth Latourette advanced six explanatory reasons for the two centuries time lag between Roman Catholic and Protestant foreign missionary endeavor.[30] First, complex internal struggles, doctrinal controversies, as well as the enormous challenge of reforming the church absorbed the energies of the Protestant movement in the early decades. Second, several of the early leaders of Protestantism (including Martin Luther) disavowed any obligation to carry the Christian message to non-Christians. Third, separation from the Roman Catholic Church precipitated a number of wars in which Protes-

---

27. For a helpful discussion of mission consciousness, or the lack thereof, among the Protestant reformers and groups, see David J. Bosch, *Transforming Mission: Paradigm Shifts in Theology of Mission* (Maryknoll, NY: Orbis Books, 1991), 241-43.

28. Bainton, *Reformation of the Sixteenth Century*, 4 (emphasis added).

29. Kenneth Scott Latourette, *Three Centuries of Advance, A.D. 1500-A.D. 1800*, vol. 3, *A History of the Expansion of Christianity,* 3rd ed. (Grand Rapids, MI: Zondervan, 1970), 32-33.

30. Ibid., 25-29.

tants were fighting for their very existence. Fourth, the comparative indifference of Protestant rulers to spreading the Christian message among non-Christians. Fifth, having rejected monasticism, Protestants lacked the orders which had been the chief agents for propagating the faith for more than a thousand years. Finally, until the seventh and eighteenth centuries, Protestants had relatively little contact with non-Christian peoples.

Two of these explanations (the fourth and sixth) support the argument that Protestant missions, like the earlier Catholic efforts, were framed by the ideals of Christendom and coincided with empire. From a Christendom standpoint, valid missionary engagement required contiguity with, or access to, territory deemed non-Christian. Unlike the Iberian powers flanked by Islamic lands, the newly formed Protestant states lacked direct contact with non-Christian peoples prior to overseas exploration and colonial expansion. Latourette insists that the more extensive contact of Roman Catholics with non-Christian peoples is the most important of all the reasons for the preponderance of Roman Catholicism in the expansion of Christianity in the three centuries after 1500 C.E. Roman Catholic missionary enterprise derived stimulus from the "Crusades" but it was also galvanized in no small measure by the overseas ventures of the Iberian monarchs, which led to the conquest of vast territories and populations. Protestant powers did not acquire similar territorial possessions for another two hundred years. This leads to the next point.

Among the main Protestant groups, mission enterprise was equally inconceivable without the collaboration of the political authorities. To be sure, there were significant exceptions to this. The earliest demonstrations of missionary consciousness came from marginalized groups like the Anabaptists, who disavowed the Christendom framework and rejected civil involvement in the life of the church.[31] In addition, the Puritan separatists who migrated to the New World (from the 1620s) identified the spread of the gospel as one of their primary objectives. But Puritan commitment to the Christendom ideal, embodied in the vision of a "Holy Commonwealth," engendered an extremely negative attitude toward the indigenous population and favored aggressive colonization. This state of affairs stifled the missionary impulse. In the event, the impact of Puritan settlement on the native population was not unlike that of earlier Iberian experiments in the New World.[32] Remarkable evangelistic efforts such as that of the Mayhew family on Martha's Vineyard (from 1642) and John Eliot's "Praying Towns" in New England were eventually scuttled by hostility and bloody war between the settlers and the native Indians. As American historian Mark Noll observes, "with some

---

31. Anabaptist groups upheld a "believers-only" church (not one comprised of the whole society), insisted on the complete separation of church and state, and viewed Europe as a mission field. They were vigorously persecuted by both Roman Catholics and other Protestant groups for their pains. Severe persecution stimulated constant dispersion and eventually mass migration to the New World in the eighteenth century (initially to Pennsylvania); see Frank H. Epp, "The Migration of the Mennonites," in *Mennonite World Handbook: A Survey of Mennonite and Brethren in Christ Churches*, ed. Paul N. Kraybill (Lombard, IL: Mennonite World Conference, 1978), 10-19.

32. Roger Daniels, *Coming to America: A History of Immigration and Ethnicity in American Life* (New York: HarperPerennial, 1991), 6.

exceptions, British contacts with the Native Americans did much more to harm than to help the spread of the faith."[33]

State-sponsored Protestant missionary initiatives date to 1705 when King Frederick IV of Denmark (apparently in emulation of Roman Catholic rulers) sent two German Protestant missionaries—Bartolomaeus Ziegenbalg (1682-1719) and Henry Plütschau (1677-1747)—to preach the gospel among his Indian subjects on the tiny Danish settlement of Tranquebar in southeast India.[34] Thus, like Roman Catholic initiatives, official Protestant missions emerged as a function of political domination and territorial expansion. The intimate association between missionary enterprise and territorial appropriation, in both Roman Catholic and Protestant endeavors, reflected or preserved the ideal of Christendom. There were tensions, of course. For instance, the emphasis on individual conversion was somewhat at variance with the patent desire to carve out Christian settlements out of the irrevocably pluralistic material of non-Western societies. But the Western missionary enterprise was marked by the dye of Christendom in its fundamental assumptions, operational strategy, and long-term objectives. Few aspects demonstrated this more clearly than its decidedly nationalistic character.

Missionary Nationalism[35]

With no exception, European nations (Roman Catholic and Protestant) believed that their territorial acquisitions were divinely ordained for the expansion of the gospel of salvation. Thus, the same spirit of nationalist competition that spurred European economic expansion also energized the missionary project to a huge extent. Missionary enterprise was also imbued with the conviction of manifest destiny: the sense that one's particular nation or tribe was uniquely called to fulfill divine purpose. Furthermore, foreign missionaries generally looked to their respective home governments for political protection in the same way that they depended on their respective home countries for sustenance. This intrinsic nationalism sat uneasily with the universal claims of the gospel, but it helps to account for the dynamism and purposefulness that characterized the missionary movement. (This element strongly coheres with my argument in chapter 1 that the processes of globalization have always incorporated or fostered fragmentation of competitive divisiveness). As Brian Stanley attests,

> the paradoxical and distinctly unpalatable reality about the history of Christian mission seems to be that its commitment to universality . . . has been strongest when combined with a lively sense of the calling of particular peoples—whether Britain, or Germany, or Portugal, or France, or

---

33. Mark A. Noll, *American Evangelical Christianity: An Introduction* (Malden, MA: Blackwell, 2001), 74.

34. Stephen Neill, *A History of Christian Missions* (New York: Penguin, 1990), 194.

35. I owe this phrase to Adrian Hastings; see Hastings, "The Clash of Nationalism and Universalism within Twentieth-Century Missionary Christianity," in *Missions, Nationalism, and the End of Empire*, ed. Brian Stanley (Grand Rapids: Eerdmans, 2003), 14-33.

South Africa, or the United States—to take a leading role in discharging that responsibility.[36]

Missionary nationalism took at least two obvious forms. First, it was evident in an anxious desire to establish territorial monopoly for one's country, religious order, or mission society. Second, and more egregiously, it was manifest in what Hastings describes as "an aggressive shared contempt for anything non-European," including hostility to local nationalisms or the promotion of indigenous clergy to positions of authority (2003: 19). The impact of missionary nationalism on the structure and outlook of the Western missionary movement was virtually the same among Catholics and Protestants.

Under the *padroado* (or *patronata*), the nation-states of Portugal and Spain were each granted a sphere of territorial influence and missionary control that allowed them to impose nationalist structures and prevent the involvement of missionaries from rival nations. National loyalties impacted missions significantly. The main missionary orders were themselves dominated by particular national groups: Franciscans and Dominicans were mainly Spanish, while the Jesuits were mainly Portuguese. They also depended on royal patronage. Fierce rivalry and competition ensued in contexts such as China, where the different orders operated within the same country but in discrete territorial enclaves determined by distant European authorities. Nationalist competitiveness was further enhanced by divergent missionary methods or approaches.

Eventually the major orders became fully internationalized. Even then, national provinces were created so that oversight of missionary operations in the territories belonging to a particular European nation fell to the corresponding national directorate. Missionaries from one European nation were typically unwelcome in the territory of another European nation, whether or not they belonged to the same order. Thus, only Belgian White Fathers were sent to the Belgian Congo; and only French White Fathers worked in French West Africa. And, since "Christian" Europe was generally divided into Roman Catholic and Protestant nations, Roman Catholic governments were typically reluctant to allow Protestant missionary initiatives within their territories (and vice versa). The establishment, in 1622, of the *Congregatio de Propaganda Fide*—in an effort to consolidate oversight of missions and all mission-related activities of the Roman Catholic Church—did little to change this dynamic.

From the early stages, the Protestant missionary movement (specifically its evangelical wing) embodied efforts at internationalization cooperation. For instance, the first missionaries sent out in 1802 by the London-based Church Missionary Society (to Sierra Leone) were Germans, as were the missionaries sent to the colony of Tranquebar by the Danish king. But, despite such instances of international collaboration, Protestant missions operated for the most part as national ventures informed by nationalist loyalties. "Almost every nineteenth-century Protestant missionary body," insists Hastings, "had a strong national

---

36. Brian Stanley, "Christianity and the End of Empire," in *Mission, Nationalism, and the End of Empire,* ed. Brian Stanley (Grand Rapids: Eerdmans, 2003), 5.

character and base."[37] In a manner that bore striking resemblance to the aims of the *padroado*, Protestant nations engaged in strenuous competition to break up the Iberian empires only to establish equally exclusive and monopolistic dominance over the non-European world, using national trading companies.

In China, where Christian missions benefited from the "unequal [economic] treaties," Protestant missionaries, no less than their Catholic counterparts, looked to their respective governments to provide protection and demand reparations for property damaged by anti-imperialist insurgents. Missionary societies were national creations, and celebrated missionaries like David Livingstone were national figures who embodied nationalist ideals.[38] Moreover, colonial expansion, which was in essence an exercise in national aggrandizement, directly influenced missionary numbers. The larger the territorial acquisition, the stronger the sense of divine providence and the greater the sense of missionary commitment. Among nineteenth-century evangelicals in Britain, these assumptions gave rise to the idea of "imperial trusteeship": the conviction that Britain's status as a world power with newly acquired territory was "a trust given for missionary purposes."[39] Livingstone was convinced that "it is the mission of England to colonize and to plant Christianity with her sons on the broad earth which the Lord has given to the children of men."[40] He urged that "colonization from a country such as ours ought to be one of hope, and not despair. . . . The performance of an imperative duty to our blood, our country, our religion and to human kind."[41]

The fact that Britain, a nation of forty million, produced the most foreign missionaries overseas (about ten thousand by 1900) had a lot to do with the strong missionary impulse generated by its vast colonial acquisitions. This equation testifies to the strength of missionary nationalism (commitment to a tribal religion) in efforts to expand Christendom.

Ultimately, even noteworthy instances of international collaboration among Protestants tended to founder in the shoals of nationalism. At the first meeting of the "Evangelical Alliance" (in August 1846), attended by eight hundred Christians representing fifty-two denominations from Europe and the United States, a promising vision of internationalism was scuttled by national differences related to the question of African slavery.[42] Britain had by this time already abolished slavery, and its representatives adamantly opposed the inclusion of any slaveholder as a member of the Alliance. But the majority of the American delegates were opposed to slavery—an institution that remained very much a part of American social and economic life—with strong backing from the church for the

37. Hastings, "The Clash of Nationalism," 21.

38. See Andrew F. Walls, "The Legacy of David Livingstone," in *Mission Legacies: Biographical Studies of Leaders of the Modern Missionary Movement*, ed. Gerald H. Anderson (Maryknoll, NY: Orbis Books, 1994), 145.

39. Brian Stanley, *The Bible and the Flag: Protestant Missions and British Imperialism in the Nineteenth and Twentieth Centuries* (Leicester: Apollos, 1990), 68.

40. Quotation taken from Oliver Ransford, *David Livingstone: The Dark Interior* (London: J. Murray, 1978), 159.

41. Ibid., 159; cf. Tim Jeal, *Livingstone* (New York: Putnam, 1973), 383.

42. See David M. Howard, *The Dream That Would Not Die: The Birth and Growth of the World Evangelical Fellowship 1846-1986* (Exeter: Paternoster, 1986).

most part. According to official proceedings, "it was eventually decided to abandon the idea of an ecumenical [i.e., international] alliance and adopt the British suggestion of loosely linked *national* organizations which were not responsible for each other's action" (Howard 1986: 13; italics added).

The World Missionary Conference of Edinburgh in 1910, spearheaded by two prominent evangelical leaders from different nations, Joe Oldham (Britain) and John Mott (United States), showcased Protestant missionary internationalism. It is not well known that this new spirit of international cooperation and ecumenicity among Protestant bodies was ignited in part by protests from Asian Christians against divisive denominationalism. But even this model of international cooperation ran into considerable difficulties. The 1910 meeting gave birth to the International Missionary Council (formed in 1921), which quickly evolved into a network of *national* Christian councils in Asia, Africa, and Latin America. International missionary collaboration ultimately collapsed during the First World War, as German missionaries (who represented a small but significant proportion of Protestant missions worldwide) were expelled from the colonial territories of other European powers, an experience that helped to create an even more virulent form of German nationalism based on racial superiority and Christian identity.

With the waning of British power and the rise of American preeminence, Christian missions became even more blatantly linked to empire (political dominance and economic supremacy) and bonded to national identity. As in the case of Britain, the number of American overseas missionaries rose dramatically with the spread of American influence and political power after the First World War. The American Protestant missionary force increased from about twelve thousand career foreign missionaries in 1935 to some thirty-five thousand by 1980 (a threefold increase in forty-five years);[43] and American Christians also affirmed a correlation between foreign missions and America's call to global dominance (see p. 165 below). Perhaps even more than earlier European missions, American initiatives were informed by "belief in the American way of life as supreme expression of Christianity."[44] Proponents believed that, as the representative of "the purest Christianity," America was uniquely equipped to "impress its institutions upon mankind."[45] With Christian missions now typified by unprecedented use of communications technologies and capitalist business methods, the view later emerged that American versions of Christianity constitute a product that can be exported along with other American consumer brands.

Thus, under American hegemony, Christendom was updated, branded, and refitted for global sampling! In particular, mission was increasingly "marketed" with triumphalist slogans (*"evangelize the world in the present generation"*), Europeanized portrayals of the gospel ("The Jesus film") and military imagery

---

43. See Joel A. Carpenter, *Revive Us Again: The Reawakening of American Fundamentalism* (New York: Oxford University Press, 1997), 184f.

44. Hastings, "Clash of Nationalism," 32.

45. Josiah Strong, *Our Country: Its Possible Future and Its Present Crisis* (New York: Baker & Taylor Co., 1885; rev. ed. 1891), 222.

(notably the popularization of the term "crusade" to describe evangelistic outreach). The territorial duality of Christendom remained unchanged.

How the Western Missionary Movement Bankrupted
the Christendom Construct

A summary evaluation of the nature and impact of the Western missionary movement, its complicated links with empire, and the intrinsic link with swelling European, and European-instigated migrations is provided in chapter 7. The assessment provided above is intended to demonstrate the indelible impact and imprint of the Christendom idea on Western foreign missions. Christendom did not give birth to the missionary movement. The missionary impulse, which mandates the preaching of the gospel among all peoples throughout the whole world (with the specific aim of religious conversion), is intrinsic to the Christian faith. Indeed, as I argue above, the Christendom construct emerged out of the spread of Christianity among western European peoples. The vast army of men and women—by 1900 the latter outnumbered the former—who went to distant lands as part of the official missionary force from Western nations were driven by a wide variety of reasons, motives, and causes. Their stories furnish us with compelling accounts of self-sacrifice, heroism, exemplary humanitarianism, and human ingenuity as well as egregious examples of overweening conceit, unscrupulous exploitation, and ethnocentric or nationalist hubris.

The central argument here is that Christendom, the idea of a Christian nation or the experience of Christianity as a territorial faith, welded to the conviction that there is one essence or normative expression of the faith, fundamentally shaped the assumptions, attitudes, strategies, and objectives of the Western missionary movement—and to a large extent still does. Serious criticism of the state of Christianity within Europe arose from time to time. Eighteenth-century evangelicals, for instance, were convinced that many sections of Western society needed to be won back to the faith or reevangelized. The emergence of Methodism embodied the fruit of this conviction. But, in the long run, it was the foreign missions movement that captured the imagination, fueled by (and in turn fueling) nationalist fervor and designs.

William Carey (1761-1834), whose manifesto helped to launch the most dynamic phase of the missionary movement, shared the general evangelical view that "a very great degree of ignorance and immorality abounds" among "those who bear the Christian name" (in England).[46] But his call to missionary action focused sharply on the "heathen" in distant territories and coupled the spread of the gospel with the extension of European civilization. In his words:

---

46. William Carey, *An Enquiry into the Obligation of Christians to Use Means for the Conversion of the Heathen* (London, 1792), 65. Papists, he added, "are in general ignorant of divine things, and very vicious. Nor do the bulk of the church of England much exceed them, either in knowledge or holiness; and many errors, and much looseness of conduct, are to be found amongst dissenters of all denominations."

Can we as . . . Christians, hear that a great part of our fellow creatures, whose souls are as immortal as ours, and who are as capable as ourselves . . . are enveloped in ignorance and barbarism? Can we hear that they are without the gospel, without government, without laws, and without arts, and sciences; and not exert ourselves to introduce amongst them the sentiments of men, and of Christians? Would not the spread of the gospel be the most effectual mean[s] of their civilization? Would not that make them useful members of society?

The enormous, complex, and extraordinary machinery that was the Western missionary movement was activated by the discovery of distant lands where there was no Christian civilization, specifically its western European form. "Foreign missions" emerged as a response to the biblical mandate to preach the gospel throughout the whole world. But this universal vision was invested with the prevalent and ingrained assumption that "the realities of Christendom represent the original"[47]—to put it crudely, real Christians looked and behaved like Europeans. Thus, the ultimate aim of mission was to replicate or reproduce the church as it existed in Europe—in a word, to "re-create a Christian nation or culture." In David Bosch's apt phrase, "mission was the road from the institutional church to the church that still had to be instituted."[48]

But one of the most complex ironies of the Western missionary movement was that though it was invested with (even animated by) Christendom ideals, its most spectacular failures were often due in large measure to those same ideals; and where it succeeded, it did so in spite of them. In the most extreme cases, the experience and understanding of the faith engendered by Western Christendom actually paralyzed missionary engagement. The outlook of the Dutch Calvinists who settled in South Africa from the mid-seventeenth century is a case in point.[49] These Dutch settlers (who became known as Boers or Afrikaners) identified Christianity with the European race and culture, "a birthright of Europeans." They were strongly averse to sharing their faith with African peoples, whom they regarded as barbaric and (as members of the black race or "children of Ham") condemned by God to perpetual servitude. Disingenuously, such ingrained convictions of religious purity, ethnic superiority, and racial dominance made it easier to sustain violent aggression against the indigenous tribes and spawned the system of *apartheid* ("separateness"). But the model of Christendom reflected in Boer Christianity all but precluded missionary engagement. And, since conversion to Christianity meant abandonment of African culture, the social barrier to conversion was immense.

---

47. Wilbert R. Shenk, *Changing Frontiers of Mission,* American Society of Missiology Series 28 (Maryknoll, NY: Orbis Books, 1999), 51f.

48. Bosch, *Transforming Mission*, 332.

49. For a valuable summary treatment, see Jonathan N. Gerstner, "A Christian Monopoly: The Reformed Church and Colonial Society under Dutch Rule," in *Christianity in South Africa: A Political, Social, and Cultural History,* ed. Richard Elphick and Rodney Davenport (Berkeley: University of California Press, 1997), 16-30.

There were reportedly only four converts among the Khoikhoi in the seventeenth century, all of whom eventually renounced their new faith.[50]

Massive European expansion and missionary effort from the sixteenth century onwards meant that by the mid-seventeenth century the Christian faith was no longer an exclusively European phenomenon. But Christianity remained strongly associated with European civilization and colonial expansion. Whether declared or not, the ultimate aim of these massive European expansion projects, in which the missionary movement play a vital role, was the global spread of European institutions and culture. For the missionary movement, however, the effort to recreate Christendom or extensions of it in non-European contexts proved largely futile and patently incompatible with the global spread of the gospel. Even more important, the hugely complex encounter with the non-Western world subverted Christendom and robbed it of its force. If the bankruptcy of the Christendom model remained obscured long after its limitations were in evidence, it was mainly because the Western missionary movement was both the chief instrument of purveyance and the main architect of its downfall. Again, this is plain from both Roman Catholic and Protestant efforts.

Early Roman Catholic Efforts

The collapse of Jesuit-led efforts in Asia in the seventeenth century provided early indications. The missionaries adopted a strategy that focused on conversion of rulers or ruling elites as the best way to safeguard both foreign missionary presence and the establishment of the church. But they also incorporated the principle of cultural adaptation, which meant adopting cultural traditions and religious concepts from the indigenous environment to ensure effective cross-cultural transmission of the message of the gospel. This latter approach, however, violated key Christendom ideals, ideals that sanctioned European ecclesiastical domination and territorial influence. To European minds conditioned by the reality and experience of Christendom, critical accommodation to Chinese or Japanese culture merely produced paganized Christianity. The general understanding that cultural normativity was detrimental to the spread of the gospel lay well in the future. The European church was too strongly wedded to structures of power and cultural particularity for its ecclesiastical authorities, even those committed to the expansion of the faith, to detect this profound principle.

In India, the Portuguese encounter with the Thomas (or Malabar) Christians in Southern India also demonstrated the deficiency of Christendom as a tool of expansion. The Thomas Christians represented a much older Christian tradition, dating back to the first apostles. They looked to the Chaldean patriarchate in Baghdad for ecclesiastical oversight and practiced Nestorian theology. In fact, they had never heard of the pope! Portuguese attempts to enforce the *padroado,* which gave them sole political and ecclesiastical authority (see p. 92 above) were stoutly resisted. The clash of the two Christianities lasted for centuries, fed by

---

50. Ibid., 25.

profound misunderstandings, Portuguese political ambitions, and implacable antagonisms.[51]

In Africa too, Portuguese efforts to Romanize the Ethiopian Church met with strong hostility. But it was in the African Kingdom of Kongo, a promising Christian experiment involving mass conversions and a turning of political structures to Christian ends, that the designs of Christendom unraveled most dramatically. Portuguese commercial interests, which focused on the African slave trade, formed part of the story. But, despite enthusiastic support from the *Bakongo* (Kongolese) ruling class, the life of the infant church was endangered from the start by the exclusive ecclesiastical domination legitimized by the *padroado*. Lacking the power of self-government and dependent on a distant power for ecclesiastical oversight, the church maintained a fragile existence. Foreign missionary disdain for the indigenous culture and religious traditions and a refusal to ordain African clergy proved nearly fatal. For a brief period, the emergence of the Antonian movement—a precursor of early-twentieth-century African prophet-healing movements that bypassed foreign missionary control and reinterpreted European forms within an African religious worldview—injected new life into a church already caught up in the social upheaval of the period.[52] The church tragically collapsed, deferring the establishment of Christianity as an African religion by several centuries. Some note that Simon Kimbangu's "The Church of Jesus Christ on Earth," which emerged two centuries later in Belgian colonized Congo, bore striking similarities to the Antonian movement in a way that suggests an enduring influence or, at the very least, a shared heritage.

Only in Latin America was Christendom transplanted with significant success. Here, the church emerged as a powerful social institution, foreign in form and control (indigenous peoples were excluded from the priesthood) and wholly identified with the forces of political oppression and economic exploitation. Even so, it proved impossible to completely stifle indigenous expressions and appropriations of the faith. As the Virgin of Guadalupe movement in Mexico clearly indicates, the official church remained under rigid Spanish control, but Catholic devotion and spirituality survived on Mexican terms.

The Protestant Missionary Movement

With regard to the requirements and vision of Christendom, Protestant missionary enterprise was little different from Roman Catholic initiatives because the ties with colonial expansion were just as intimate and national loyalties just as strong (even in the absence of a *padroado* agreement). From the start, the reproduction of Christendom as an aim of mission was subverted by the dynamics of colonial expansion.[53] Again, the Americas (and Australia, to a lesser extent) were significant exceptions. In North America, massive European immigration, decimation of

---

51. See Robert E. Frykenberg, "India," in *A World History of Christianity*, ed. Adrian Hastings (Grand Rapids: Eerdmans, 1999), 148-91; also Neill, *History of Christianity in India*.

52. See John K. Thornton, *The Kongolese Saint Anthony: Dona Beatriz Kimpa Vita and the Antonian Movement, 1684-1706* (New York: Cambridge University Press, 1998).

53. For more on this thesis, see Walls, *Cross-Cultural Process*, 194-214.

the indigenous population through warfare and imported diseases, and extensive colonization allowed the reproduction of Christendom, epitomized by ecclesiastical enclaves and the Puritan vision of a "holy commonwealth." As we shall see later, legislative efforts by successive American governments to preserve a dominant white Anglo-Saxon Protestant culture (in the face of Roman Catholic immigration) lasted well into the twentieth century.

But Britain, the leading Protestant missionary nation throughout the nineteenth century, could not duplicate in her overseas possessions the near complete replication of European life and institutions that characterized the Iberian experiments in Latin America or the colonization of North America and Australia. Not least because military subjugation of the vast territories and diverse peoples and kingdoms in Africa or Asia was out of the question. In fact, the nature of British colonial governance meant that not only Christian subjects but also huge populations of Muslims and Hindus were granted the protection of the British flag as colonial subjects. Owing to the enormous expanse of the British empire, the Queen of England had become the world's leading Islamic ruler by the end of the nineteenth century.[54] And in British colonial Africa, where Islamic infrastructures were vital to colonial governance, the exigencies of colonial rule often made it expedient to prohibit Christian missions in Muslim areas, to the chagrin of missionary societies.[55] (African Islam, in fact, enjoyed greater fortunes and flourished under British rule more than any other time previously). But if the nature and expediency of colonial rule compromised Christendom, missionary action proved to be quite damaging. This was evident in three main areas: vernacular translation, indigenous Christian initiatives, and the encounter with religious pluralism.

Vernacular Translation

It is striking that Western missionaries not only opposed efforts by non-Westerns to adapt their faith to indigenous culture but also labored assiduously to spread Western forms of Christianity, seemingly oblivious to the fact that fundamental aspects of Western Christianity were produced by prolonged vernacular translation involving extensive interpenetration between the gospel and the primal world of medieval Europe. But the extensive campaign to erect carbon copies of the Western church on the ruins of non-Western indigenous culture and religious systems failed to reckon with the translation principle.[56] According to this principle, effective cross-cultural transmission of the faith requires repeated acts of incarnation whereby the *Word* becomes flesh (literally speaks the vernacular

54. Ibid., 219; Andrew F. Walls, "Africa as the Theatre of Christian Engagement with Islam in the Nineteenth Century," *Journal of Religion in Africa* 29, no. 2 (1999): 167.

55. "It is a disgrace to British rule in tropical Africa," it was observed at the World Missionary Conference (in Edinburgh, 1910), "that it should anywhere favor Islam and discourage the extension of Christian missions" (*World Missionary Conference 1,* 209; see also 210, 214, 221).

56. For a thorough examination of the principle of translation, see Lamin Sanneh, *Translating the Message: The Missionary Impact on Culture* (Maryknoll, NY: Orbis Books, 1989); also Walls, *Missionary Movement,* 26-42.

and takes on indigenous cultural form) in each successive locality. This allows the Christian faith to be experienced and expressed within the language, thought forms, and contextual realities of diverse distinctive cultures and, thus, also to transform culture from inside. (For more on this, see pp. 141-42, 152-53, 154-55 below.)

The translation principle explicitly rejects the idea, enshrined in Christendom, that Christianity has a definitive cultural expression, that non-Christian peoples must embrace another culture as a a condition for salvation. To editorialize John 14:6:

1. Christ cannot be the *way* if he does not know where we are coming from or meet us where we are.
2. Christ cannot be the *truth* if he is not providing answers to the particular questions we are asking.
3. Christ cannot be the *life* if he does not embody our humanity (framed by our specific contextual experiences and cultural heritage).

Within this understanding, the Christian message is proclaimed "without the presumption of cultural rejection."[57] The gospel encounter necessarily produces a diversity of expressions or answers, each qualified by comparison with the original (biblical) act of translation. Moreover, the pre-Christian religious universe takes on fresh significance, since the new can be comprehended only by means of and in terms of preexisting ideas and values,[58] and the missiological perspective shifts from an emphasis on "the Church being *expanded*" to "the church being *born anew* in each new context and culture."[59]

It is clear that the operation of the "translation principle" has been a fact and a factor in the cross-cultural expansion of the Christian faith from early beginnings.[60] The history of Christian missions testifies to the inexhaustible potential of the gospel to respond to the peculiar needs, questions, and spiritual quest of the world's peoples, including non-European peoples. There were many European missionaries (both Roman Catholic and Protestant) who intuitively grasped the indispensability of translation and recognized that the European garb of missionary Christianity was a temporary vehicle. But the association with political power and the spirit of cultural domination which characterized the Western missionary movement blinded most to the principle and its possibilities, for the process of translation necessarily marginalizes the foreign missionary.

In the event, the message proved to be the undoing of the messengers. A decidedly negative view of non-Western cultures, notwithstanding, Western Protestant missionaries, who stressed the authority of Scripture and employed literacy as a

---

57. Sanneh, *Translating*, 31.
58. Walls, *Missionary Movement*, 28.
59. Bosch, *Transforming Mission*, 454.
60. Walls, *Missionary Movement*, 3-78; also Kwame Bediako, *Theology and Identity: The Impact of Culture upon Christian Thought in the Second Century and in Modern Africa,* Regnum Studies in Mission (Irvine, CA: Regnum Books International, 1999).

tool of mission, undertook massive efforts at vernacular translation of the Bible.[61] By the end of the nineteenth century, the Bible had been translated in whole or in part into roughly three hundred languages. Such efforts at translation proved quite subversive to foreign missionary dominance and control mechanisms in a number of critical ways. As Bishop Samuel Adjai Crowther (c. 1806-1891), who spearheaded an extraordinary missionary campaign in southeast Nigeria, recognized, "the 'Sword of the Spirit' placed in the hands of the congregations in their own tongue . . . will be carried into their homes, be a companion in the secret chamber of the faithful, and a comfort to the sick on his bed whenever the most zealous and energetic Missionary fails to be present."[62]

Translation highlighted foreign missionary dependence on indigenous agency and furnished indigenous Christians with an independent source of authority apart from the European missionary. In the African context, as Allan Anderson points out, indigenous believers soon discovered that the Bible "seemed to lend much more support to traditional African customs than to the imported cultural customs of the European missionaries."[63] The process also drew, perforce, on pre-Christian ideas and concepts (including indigenous names for God) and by so doing validated the plausibility of the non-European religious universe and worldviews. Nowhere else, remarks Lamin Sanneh, "were missionaries more anticipated than in the field of scriptural translation," for "all over that vast field we find evidence of deep and long preparation, in the tools of language as in the habits of worship and conduct, and in the venerable customs of the forebears."[64]

In the long run, vernacular translation "nourished ethnic consciousness,"[65] discredited the notion that European expressions of the Christian faith and gospel are normative,[66] and contributed immeasurably to the rise of indigenous Christian movements that rejected both European control and the paraphernalia of European Christianity. To be sure, theological freedom from Western intellectual hegemony proved to be a far more daunting proposition than political or ecclesiastical independence. In Africa in the 1960s there was still widespread realization that, despite the emergence of vibrant African church movements, the growth of African Christianity was stunted by a "foreign, prefabricated theology, which has . . . not grown out of the life of a living Church in Africa."[67] But vernacular translation undermined Christendom not only because it gener-

61. Neill, *History of Christian Missions*, 216.

62. Dandeson C. Crowther, *The Establishment of the Niger Delta Pastorate during the Episcopacy of the Rt. Rev. Bishop S. A. Crowther* (Liverpool: Thomson, 1907), 31.

63. Allan H. Anderson, "A 'Failure in Love'? Western Missions and the Emergence of African Initiated Churches in the Twentieth Century," *Missiology* 29, no. 3 (July 2001): 281.

64. Sanneh, *Translating*, 157.

65. Brian Stanley, "Twentieth Century Christianity: A Perspective from the History of Missions," in *Christianity Reborn: The Global Expansion of Evangelicalism in the Twentieth Century*, ed. Donald M. Lewis (Grand Rapids: Eerdmans, 2004), 64.

66. Lamin Sanneh, "Christian Missions and the Western Guilt Complex," *Christian Century* (April 8, 1987): 332.

67. Report of the First Assembly of the AACC in Kampala (1963), quoted in John Parratt, ed., *A Reader in African Christian Theology* (London: SPCK, 1987), 89.

ated or affirmed diversity of Christian forms and expressions but also because it exposed the awful spiritual and theological liabilities of Christian life clothed in "borrowed robes." In Desmond Tutu's arresting rhetoric, the African found that "the white man's largely cerebral religion was hardly touching the depths of his African soul; he was being given answers, and often splendid answers, to questions he had not asked."[68]

The postcolonial era witnessed renewed efforts among Western-trained non-Western theologians to explore the relationship between the Bible, indigenous culture, and primal religions and to examine critical aspects of the non-Western experience (including suffering, poverty, and oppression) in the light of Scripture. Out of the non-Western Christian engagement have emerged innovative theological reflections that have tremendously enriched global Christianity—no less than Western offerings—precisely because they are fomented by radically different historical experiences, cultural understandings, and spiritual insights. The concept of *contextuality* (or *contextualization*), for instance, introduced by the Taiwanese theologian Shoki Coe in the early 1970s, became a staple of the theological lexicon. Wilbert Shenk contends that, since "theology in the West had long lost its missionary direction . . . the movement to develop contextual theology could emerge only outside the historic Christian 'heartland' under non-Western leadership."[69] It took time for the realization to take root, but the discovery that genuine Christian theology grows out of a people's contextual experience of Jesus Christ negated the transplantation of Christendom.

Indigenous Christian Movements

Perhaps no aspect of the Western missionary movement has had more far-reaching unintended consequences than the role of vernacular translation in the spread of nationalism—a concept grounded in the idea of the autonomous nation within a designated territory, to which individuals belong and owe primary loyalty.[70] Adrian Hastings argues convincingly that the idea of nationhood has biblical origins, and he links the spread of nationalism to the impact of the Bible.[71] It is one of the great ironies of history that European colonial expansion—a process that typically involved usurping the right of other nations to self-government—was greatly impelled by European nationalism and national interest. In the event, the Protestant missionary movement "contributed substantially to the emergence of nationalism" in China, India, and Africa, "through the introduction of Western

---

68. Desmond Tutu, "Black Theology and African Theology," in *A Reader in African Christian Theology*, ed. John Parratt (London: SPCK, 1987), 48.

69. Wilbert R. Shenk, "Contextual Theology: The Last Frontier," in *The Changing Face of Christianity: Africa, the West, and the World*, ed. Lamin O. Sanneh and Joel A. Carpenter (New York: Oxford University Press, 2005), 193.

70. See Anthony D. Smith, *Nationalism and Modernism*. Nation refers to a group people with a shared language, history, and cultural heritage.

71. Adrian Hastings, *The Construction of Nationhood: Ethnicity, Religion, and Nationalism* (New York: Cambridge University Press, 1997).

education, social reforms, and political ideas."[72] In particular, missionary education, provided with an aim to Christian conversion, stimulated national sentiment, race pride, and adamant religious protest. In Africa and Asia, a significant
proportion of the first generation of nationalist leaders were products of missionary education.

With the exception of South Korea, where Western missionaries were willing
collaborators of indigenous nationalism (in the face of Japanese colonial domination), the rise of national sentiment and religious protest often took European missionaries by surprise and elicited deep hostility. In a groundbreaking document
entitled "On Nationality" (1868), Henry Venn, Church Mission Society secretary
(1841-1872) and arguably the greatest missionary statesman of the nineteenth
century, enjoined missionaries to "study the national character of the people
among whom you labor, and show the utmost respect for national peculiarities."
He also suggested "that as the native church assumes a national character it will
ultimately supersede the denominational distinctions which are now introduced
by Foreign Missionary Societies."[73] But Venn's foresight was exceptional within
the missionary movement and went against the grain of European missionary
consciousness. By the end of the nineteenth century, "mission fields" around the
world were experiencing, to varying degrees, a bitter "clash of nationalisms" that
saw the widespread emergence of indigenous Christian initiatives.

In China, where the link between Christian missions, nefarious and exploitative commerce, and humiliating (unequal) treaties inflicted deep wounds, Chinese nationalism emerged as an anti-imperial, anti-Western movement profoundly
antagonistic to Christian missions—which were widely regarded an embodiment
of Western imperialism. After more than a century of European mission toil and
sacrifice, Chinese intellectuals who had received Western education turned to
Communism as the ideal instrument for the creation of a new China.

In Africa, nationalist reaction and expression typically originated among
local clergy, who had the most exposure to missionary education and were most
conscious of European dominance and ethnocentrism. Incipient African nationalism, dating to the 1870s, drew considerable inspiration from European ideas,
including Henry Venn's vision of autonomous African churches.[74] It was also
shaped by ideological currents that flowed across the Atlantic with the migration
of black American Christians, among whom the experience of racial segregation
and racism in church life had already sparked vigorous movements of religious
protest and separatism by the late eighteenth century. Those currents gave rise
to Ethiopianism. Expressed in a variety of forms, the Ethiopian movement combined religious protest, racial identity, rejection of European domination, and a
vision for the evangelization of Africa by Africans.[75] African religious nation-

---

72. Stanley, "Christianity and the End of Empire," 7. See also idem, *The Bible and the Flag,*
133-35.

73. For more on the circumstances surrounding this document and its negligible impact on
missionary predisposition or action, see Jehu Hanciles, *Euthanasia of a Mission: African Church
Autonomy in a Colonial Context* (Westport, CT: Praeger, 2002), 123-45.

74. See ibid., 147-95.

75. Hanciles, *Euthanasia of a Mission*; see also Ogbu Kalu, "Ethiopianism in African Chris-

alism powered the phenomenal rise of independent church movements, which transformed the African religious landscape and sowed the seeds of political independence movements.

Discovering the Challenge Religious Plurality

Sustained contact and enforced interaction with the rich religious plurality of non-Western societies also underscored the fragility of Christendom. As a matter of fact, the impact of the European missionary movement stimulated reform within major religions such as Hinduism and (along with colonialism) helped to foment Hindu and Buddhist nationalism. Since Christendom, by definition, precluded religious plurality of the sort that flourishes outside Europe, early missionaries had no preparation for the particular concerns and predicaments that Christian engagement in such contexts evoked. The encounter with these ancient religious systems of Asia (Hinduism, Confucianism, and Buddhism) generated deep theological questions about Western understandings of the Christian faith, conversion, and the Scriptures. Agonizing missiological debates about the right approach to other faiths highlighted the futility of the triumphalist expectations that typify a Christendom mind-set and pointed to the critical role that non-Western Christianity, molded by intimate interaction with alternative religious systems, must play in the global witness of the church. As Andrew Walls recognizes, "pluralism may be a new issue for the West; it has been the normal experience for most of the world's Christians."[76]

Even in Latin America, where the structures and traditions of Christendom where transplanted wholesale, the Christendom mold began to show deep cracks after political independence (in the 1820s) and the dismantling of the close alliance between church and state. In truth, some postcolonial governments tried to preserve the old colonial powers, and the white-dominated clergy (appointed by the ex-colonial rulers) fought to retain former privileges. The strong identification between church and the colonial state meant that strong antireligious feelings also surfaced in the chaotic period that followed independence, leading to religious persecution of the church by new governments in countries such as Colombia, Chile, and Uruguay. But throughout the region, even in areas where the new governments were not hostile to religion, new legislature divested the church of many privileges and new polices saw the appointment of indigenous bishops.

Gradually also, energetic Protestant communities and movements began to spread, especially in countries of high immigration (such as Brazil and Argentina), ending the Roman Catholic Church's virtual monopoly. From 1930 to 1960, Protestants grew from 1 percent to 10 percent of the Latin American church, the most phenomenal increase occurring among Pentecostals. The vigorous critique

---

tianity," in *African Christianity: An African Story*, ed. U. Kalu Ogbu (Trenton, NJ: Africa World Press, 2007), 227-43.

76. Walls, *Missionary Movement*, 147.

of the old Christendom structures of cultural dominance and economic exploitation reflected in liberation theology heralded a new epoch; and, as was the case in Africa and Asia, the experience of ecclesiastical freedom fostered a rediscovery of the indigenous culture. The transition from colonial to Latin American control and the emergence of religious pluralism signaled the nullification of the *padroado* and the demise of Christendom.

Today, the non-Western Christian landscape is replete with churches, denominations, and movements that are veritable replicas of Western forms or parlous imitations of Western prototypes. And there are those who see the existence of such Christian communities, which have preserved imported ecclesiastical structures, ceremonial patterns, and liturgical practices (typically dating to the colonial period), as conclusive evidence that the Western missionary movement, aided by colonialism, successfully transplanted European Christianity. This view, which is a variation of the single global culture perspective discussed in the previous chapters, does not stand up well to scrutiny. The structures bequeathed by European missionary expansion certainly endure, but closer inspection indicates indigenous cultural accretions. Perhaps to a lesser degree than indigenous initiatives (which typically provide the cutting edge of Christian growth), even transplanted Catholicism or Protestant denominationalism also betray the stamp of non-Western spirituality and values in worship, forms of leadership, and even theological orientation. Witness the formidable cleavage within the worldwide Anglican Communion over issues of homosexuality, or even the startling contrast in dynamism and spiritual outlook between immigrant ("ethnic") churches and national churches within the same denomination in Europe and North America.

The ultimate achievement of the Western missionary movement was its pivotal role in the dramatic shift in global Christianity's center of gravity, which has witnessed the emergence of the non-Western world as the new heartland of the faith (see next chapter). It is not the first time in the history of Christianity that massive cross-cultural transmission of the faith has produced an epochal transformation.[77] As in earlier shifts, the ideas and constructs that dominated in the previous age are radically modified or else eliminated in the new age as the contexts and priorities of the new center(s) invest the faith with new attributes and expressions. The massive de-Christianization in the old heartlands ultimately points to the provisional nature and ultimate failure of the Christendom model—at least from a missiological point of view—and its successful transplantation would surely have threatened the survival of the faith elsewhere. One central reason for this failure is a diminished sense of mission to its own society and culture; and this loss of missionary function is rooted in the entrenched association between Christianity and Western culture or national identity. Quite simply, over time, Christian practice is de-linked from Christian faith.[78]

---

77. See ibid., 16-25.

78. For a meaningful treatment of this issue, see (among others) David E. Bjork, "The Future of Christianity in Western Europe," *Missiology* 34, no. 3 (July 2006): 309-24; J. D. Gort, "Theological Issues for Missiological Education: An Ecumenical-Protestant Perspective," in *Missiological Education for the Twenty-First Century: Essays in Honor of Paul E. Pierson*, ed. John Dudley Woodberry, Charles Edward van Engen, and Edgar J. Elliston (Maryknoll, NY: Orbis Books, 1996),

In the final analysis, "the drive to extend Christendom worldwide and maintain Western hegemony carried the seeds of its own destruction. And the discontinuities unleashed their own disintegrating impact."[79] If the Christendom notion of one normative expression of the faith belongs to a passing era, perhaps no concept is more definitive of the new epoch than *diversity of forms and expressions*. This is so specifically because the globalization of the Christian faith, the crowning achievement of the Western missionary movement, has transformed it not only into a non-Western religion but also into a religion defined by local expressions and marked by cultural plurality. As it turns out, this development restores a biblical ideal that was obscured and subverted by the Christendom project.

67-75; Wilbert R. Shenk, "The Training of Missiologists for Western Culture," in *Missiological Education for the Twenty-First Century,* 120-29.

79. Wilbert R. Shenk, "The 'Great Century' Reconsidered," *Missiology* 12, no. 2 (April 1984): 142.

5

Twentieth-Century Transformations

Global Christianity and Western Intellectual Captivity

> The best converts on the soil of uncivilized heathenism, according to the evidence received, represent a beautiful type of piety. . . . And just as many a parent has re-learned religious lessons by coming into touch with the piety of childhood, so it may well happen that the Christianity of Europe is destined to be recalled, if not to forgotten truths, at least to neglected graces, by the infant Churches that are just beginning to live their lives on the basis of mercy, the commandments, and the promises of God.
> —World Missionary Conference, 1910: Report of Commission 4
> *The Missionary Message in Relation to Non-Christian Religions*

The understanding that global Christianity experienced a massive and profound demographic shift in the second half of the twentieth century that has seen Africa and Latin America emerge as the new heartlands of the faith is now a widely accepted (and celebrated) dictum. So much so, in fact, that further appraisal is likely to have a deadening, rather than stimulating, effect. But appraise it we must. A rehashing of the basic facts is, alas, unavoidable; but a thorough reevaluation of this momentous development is crucial for at least three reasons: First, it is necessary to counter misleading assessments that analyze the "shift" in terms of a secular framework or within Western intellectual constructs. Second, the reshaping of the global Christian landscape provides critical support for the argument that non-Western initiatives and movements are among the most powerful forces shaping the contemporary world order. Third, an evaluation of Africa's emergence as a major heartland of the Christian faith helps to explicate its central role in the growing non-Western missionary movement linked to global migrations.

The widespread coverage and scholarly attention that the changing face of global Christianity has received in the last decade obscure the fact that pronouncements of this epochal transformation date to the 1960s, to a time, in fact, when the secularization thesis was ascendant in Western academic institutions and was beginning to influence popular opinion. On April 8, 1966, the cover of *Time Magazine* captured the core issue for its millions of readers with the question, *"Is God Dead?"* In the late 1960s, a handful of scholars who had spent several years studying African Christianity began pointing to trends that were strikingly at odds with the claims of secularization theories. In particular, these scholars noted the phenomenal growth and unprecedented dynamism of Christianity in Africa. Never before, averred David Barrett (1968: 192) have "strong and complex traditional societies, mass conversions of whole peoples from among those societies . . . and widespread circulation of vernacular scriptures combined together on the extent and scale found in contemporary Africa."

Alluding to the same phenomenon, Harold Turner asserted in the early 1970s that "Western studies of Christianity remain distorted insofar as they take little account of Christian forms in non-Western cultures and of local and contemporary forms of all cultures."[1] He also called attention to the striking similarity between non-Western Christian forms—"especially in the multitudinous African phenomena"—and that of the early church. The contrast with evaluations of European Christianity could not have been more startling. To one scholar writing in the late 1950s, Christianity "seem[ed] to many a thing of the past, part of the vanishing order of the old Europe, and the new powers shaping the world are non-Christian or even anti-Christian."[2]

At the time, however, the voices highlighting developments in the non-Western world were largely ignored outside a small circle of specialists, in part because trends within Western society indicating erosion in religious allegiance appeared far more axiomatic and of global significance. Within a matter of a few decades, however, the claims of the secularization thesis were looking much less compelling and increasingly contested. This was not because trends in Western societies had altered; on the contrary, indications of a massive erosion of the Christian faith in its traditional heartlands (Western Europe at least) had become even more irrefutable. But the tremendous explosion of religious vitality in non-Western societies was ever more evident, though it would be some time before the phenomenon drew significant attention from Western scholarship.

The exalted vision enshrined in Western Christendom and championed by the Western missionary movement for over four centuries had been finally achieved: Christianity had become a truly global faith, with "Christians and organized Christian churches in every inhabited country on earth."[3] Quite extraordinarily, the attainment of this long-cherished aim was accompanied by Christianity's transformation into a non-Western religion. Yet, as Samuel Huntington's "clash of civilizations" thesis illustrates, the centuries-old correlation between Chris-

---

1. Harold W. Turner, "The Contribution of Studies on Religion in Africa to Western Religious Studies," in *New Testament Christianity for Africa and the World*, ed. M. E. Glasswell and E. W. Fasholé-Luke (London: SPCK, 1974), 170.

2. Christopher Dawson, *The Historic Reality of Christian Culture: A Way to the Renewal of Human Life* (New York: Harper, 1960), 16.

3. David B. Barrett, George Thomas Kurian, and Todd M. Johnson, *World Christian Encyclopedia: A Comparative Survey of Churches and Religions in the Modern World*, 2nd ed. (New York: Oxford University Press, 2001), 3.

tianity and Western civilization remains entrenched. The reality, however, is impossible to deny: massive decline of the traditional faith within Western society and spectacular growth in the southern continents means that the face of global Christianity is now distinctly nonwhite.

State of the Faith: The Western Experience

The statistical data are now all too familiar, and what is presented here is intended to portray a general picture. According to the *World Christian Encyclopedia* (2001), the church in Europe and North America is losing members at a rate of six thousand members a day (just over 2.2 million a year).[4] The level of apostasy is much higher with regard to church attendance: roughly 2.7 million church attendees in Europe and North America cease to be practicing Christians every year (an average loss of seventy-six hundred every day). These extraordinary developments are substantiated by numerous reports.

Take the case of Britain. By 1986 overall church attendance was declining by approximately 2 percent every year, and only 11 percent of people attended church regularly.[5] In 2001, the head of the Catholic Church in England and Wales declared that Christianity has been "all but eliminated" as a source of moral guidance in people's lives.[6] A year later, the governing body of the Church of Scotland (the Kirk) declared that its church was losing seventeen thousand members a year and "could cease to exist within 50 years unless urgent action is taken to curb falling membership."[7] The Church of England is faring no better. Some twenty-six million English describe themselves as Anglicans (which would make the Church of England the largest body in the worldwide Anglican Communion), but official church figures puts the number of regular churchgoers at 2.75 million or 5.6 percent of the population[8]—attendance fell below one million in 1997 for the first time in recorded history.[9] Archsecularist Steve Bruce goes as far as to predict that "three decades from now, Christianity in Britain will have largely disappeared."[10]

In truth, questions remain about the nature and extent of the decline of Christianity within European societies. The issues are complex. English sociologist Grace Davie, who researches patterns of religion in Europe, makes the crucial point that it is misleading to account for religious belief solely in terms of church attendance

---

4. Ibid., 5.

5. Wilson and Siewert, eds., *Mission Handbook*, 26.

6. "Christianity 'Almost Vanquished in U.K.,'" *BBC News,* September 6, 2001.

7. "Kirk Is Given Just 50 Years Unless Fall in Membership Is Halted," *The Scotsman,* April 18, 2002.

8. "Factfile: Anglican Church around the World," *BBC News,* June 16, 2006 (http://news.bbc.co.uk/2/hi/3226753.stm).

9. Steve Bruce, "The Demise of Christianity in Britain," in *Predicting Religion: Christian, Secular, and Alternative Futures,* ed. Grace Davie, Linda Woodhead, and Paul Heelas (Burlington, VT: Ashgate, 2003), 54.

10. Ibid., 61.

or institutional allegiance.[11] As she puts it, "an unwillingness to attend a religious ✓ institution on a regular basis . . . does not mean necessarily a parallel abdication in religious belief." Moreover, weekly church attendance in Europe varies considerable from country to country: ranging from a high of 56.9 percent in Ireland to a low of 2.7 percent in Denmark.[12] And while only 20.5 percent of Europeans on average attend church once a week some 77.4 percent believe in God.

Much less compelling is the "mythical age of faith" argument, which asserts that "claims about a major decline in religious participation in Europe are based in part on very exaggerated perceptions of past religiousness."[13] This argument, in my view, misconceives the nature of Christian identity in societies where the reality of Christendom and principles of allegiance rendered regular church attendance a problematic index of faith commitment. It is also worth noting that low church attendance did not prevent participation in bloody religious wars that devastated much of Europe in the wake of the Protestant reformations. Also germane is Davie's observation about the modern European propensity for "vicarious religion"—induced, one might add, by latent notions of a Christian nation.[14]

Emerging trends in religious behavior in Western European societies remain enormously complex, and no conclusive assessment is intended here. Yet the fact that the Roman Catholic Church, Europe's largest Christian constituency, has declined by more than 30 percent in the last twenty-five years, points to a pattern of erosion that is impossible to deny.[15] As American journalist T. R. Reid put it, "Western Europe, home of the world's biggest religious denomination, the Roman Catholic Church, and the birthplace of most major Protestant faiths, has largely turned its back on [the Christian] religion."[16] To put it more forcefully, current trends indicate a significant depreciation not only of the church's privileged position in European societies but also of the ability of Christian institutions to influence individual lifestyles and societal norms—a stunning tribute to secularization. The aforementioned Church of Scotland report was quite candid on this point: "Although the Kirk is still respected for its social work and ministers are in demand to perform marriages, baptisms and funerals, as an institutional force it has been 'eased to the margins' [and] the Church no longer has the 'right to be heard' that it once did."

American Exception — Just Less of the Same?

Analysis of the U.S. experience remains even more contentious and fraught with competing assessments. America's prominence in the world, the global ramifications of its political actions, and the ubiquitousness of its symbols and images mean that perceptions easily get confused with reality. And this is true whether those perceptions are favorable or not. On the matter of American religiosity there appears

---

11. Davie, *Europe,* 41.
12. Ibid., 6.
13. See Stark, "Secularization"; see also Bruce, "Demise of Christianity in Britain," 53-63.
14. Davie, *Europe,* 19f.
15. Evan Osnos, "Islam Shaping a New Europe," *Chicago Tribune,* December 19, 2004.
16. T. R. Reid, "Hollow Halls in Europe's Churches," *Washington Post,* May 6, 2001.

to be a general axiom: in highly secularized societies (mainly Europe) America is viewed as very religious, whereas in deeply religious societies it is largely denounced as very secular. On either side, the perception intensifies if America is viewed unfavorably. Thus, "Europeans who think that 'America is too religious' are more inclined to be anti-American," while a higher proportion of Pakistanis who think that America is insufficiently religious view America unfavorably.[17] For the record, nearly two-thirds of Americans (64 percent) say religion is important to them and the vast majority (90 percent) pray at least once a week.[18]

For a long time, the fact that America reflects higher rates of church attendance and more overt public religiosity than Europe produced a general consensus of American "exceptionalism" among scholars. Even now, Christianity's loss of position in Europe appears far more conspicuous than it does in the United States. Interestingly, and of great relevance to the main arguments in this book, massive Christian immigration throughout the nineteenth century is perhaps the most important single reason why the decline of Christianity in America at the end of the twentieth century is less substantial or apparent than that in Europe. America, as Andrew Walls comments, simply "started its Christian decline from a much higher base than Europe did."[19]

Even so, appearances may be deceiving. The typical assessment of church attendance (once a week) in the United States is 43 percent[20]—which is much higher than in Europe (20.5 percent). In addition, 95 percent of Americans say they believe in God (compared to 77.4 percent in Europe). But more rigorous surveys have concluded that "Americans over-report their actual church attendance by a marked degree"; that actual attendance is closer to 24 percent and "falling slowly."[21] Robert D. Putman (2000) estimates that church attendance in America has fallen by roughly 25 to 50 percent in the last four decades. Church membership, a less demanding form of involvement, has declined less sharply, though mainline denominations register an alarming falloff rate. The United Methodist Church is believed to have lost almost one thousand members a week since 1965, and one general assessment goes so far as to suggest that "60 percent of all existing Christian congregations in America will disappear before the year 2050."[22]

Quite obviously, these generalized observations hardly do any justice to the complexities of American religious life and participation. Davie's caution about equating religiosity with institutional allegiance is germane. Some who leave traditional denominations simply join newer charismatic churches, and a growing trend toward "privatized religion," argues Putnam (2000), means that increasing

17. "In the World of Good and Evil," *The Ecomomist*, September 16, 2006, 37-38.

18. *Faith-Based Funding Backed, but Church-State Doubts Abound: Religion in American Life* (The Pew Research Center, 2001).

19. Walls, "Mission and Migration," 10.

20. Eddie Gibbs and Ian Coffey, *Church Next: Quantum Changes in Christian Ministry* (Downers Grove, IL: InterVarsity, 2001), 13; see also, *Faith-Based Funding Backed*.

21. See Tom Sine, *Mustard Seed Versus McWorld: Reinventing Life and Faith for the Future* (Grand Rapids: Baker Books, 1999), 134; Robert D. Putnam, *Bowling Alone: The Collapse and Revival of American Community* (New York: Simon & Schuster, 2000), 65-79.

22. Gibbs and Coffey, *Church Next*, 20.

numbers of people make a habit of church shopping (or "surfing") and devalue commitment to a particular community of believers.

In 2006, Baylor University's Institute of Studies of Religion published a survey it described as the "the most extensive and sensitive study of [American] religion ever conducted."[23] According to its findings, "barely one in ten Americans (10.8 percent) is not affiliated with a congregation, denomination, or other religious group." Yet its estimates put average church attendance (once a week) at roughly 36 percent.[24] People who are evangelical Protestant by religious affiliation account for a third (33.6 percent) of Americans; but "only 15 percent of the population use the term 'Evangelical' to describe their religious identity." Nearly half of Americans (47.2 percent) identify themselves as "Bible-believing"; but considerably fewer (28.5 percent) subscribe to the label "born-again" or consider themselves "theologically conservative" (17.6 percent).

Black Protestants demonstrate the highest and most consistent levels of belief and practice. Not a single black participant in the study denied that "God exists"; 74.1 percent pray once a day; 54.4 percent read Scriptures weekly or more often, and 43.1 percent attend religious services weekly or more often. African Americans are also more likely than whites to describe themselves as "Bible-believing" (63 percent, compared to 46 percent of whites) and "born-again" (43.9 percent; compared to 27.2 percent of whites). Some no doubt will attribute enduring black religiosity to the economic and social problems that continue to plague African American communities. Yet it is also possible to argue that the spiritual vitality of black Christianity in the United States owes something to the fact that in the American context the black church signified the limits of Christendom: delinked from structures of dominance and marked by a minority status.

The Baylor study charges that the rate of religious decline (or growth of secularization) is somewhat slower than previous assessments maintained.[25] But its findings confirm the general view that people under age thirty-five are hugely underrepresented in American Christianity: "persons aged 18-30 are three times more likely to have no religious affiliation (18.6 percent) than are persons aged 65 or older (5.4 percent)." Indeed, among American evangelicals, strong concerns have been voiced about the capacity of Christian teenagers to retain a Bible-believing faith in the face of "a pervasive culture of cynicism about religion."[26] Even without the massive abandonment of the faith by American youth feared by some, the current pattern of low church attendance among the eighteen to thirty age group portends even greater religious decline in coming decades, since a whole new generation is being raised with little or no Christian memory.

The Baylor study also confirms two widespread claims: first, that post-

---

23. *American Pietism in the 21st Century: New Insights to the Depth and Complexity of Religion in the U.S.* (Waco: Baylor Institute for Studies of Religion, 2006). Baylor University, which describes itself as "the largest Baptist university in the world," has an evangelical identity.

24. The 2001 Pew-sponsored report, *Faith-Based Funding Backed,* gives a slightly higher estimate of 43 percent.

25. *American Pietism,* 7-8.

26. Laurie Goodstein, "Evangelicals Fear the Loss of Their Teenagers," *New York Times,* October 6, 2006.

denominationalism—the growth of non-denominational congregations coupled with the fact that increasingly fewer people describe their Christian affiliation in terms of denominational allegiance—is on the rise; second, that the charismatic movement (the main engine of Christian growth in recent decades) has "pla-teaued" in all Western countries. A surprisingly small proportion of Americans identify with the label "charismatic" (7.3 percent) or "Pentecostal" (5.8 percent).[27] Other research indicates that the explosive growth of charismatic (or "new para-digm") churches reflects "transfer growth" or a "circulation of the saints,"[28] mean-ing that a good proportion of their members are Christians from other churches.

In sum, while the rate of Christianity's decline in America must remain a matter of debate and speculation and appears slower than in Europe, the fact of the decline itself is fairly evident.[29] In the United States, Christian vitality is undermined by a combination of secularism, a pervasive consumer culture, a pragmatic materialism that devalues the supernatural and worships technology, and a widespread tendency to conflate American ideals with Christian identity and the mission of the church. As American professor of evangelism and church growth George G. Hunter III explains, much of what passes as Christianity in the United States is "Christo-paganism," a form of civil religion blending patriotism, morality, materialism, contemporary wisdom, and idolatry of culture.[30] It is pre-cisely because Western societies once claimed the label "Christian" that the new reality is widely described as "post-Christian."

As David Lyon suggests, a good case could be made for limiting reliance on statistical figures to assess the power of faith.[31] Clearly, no amount of survey data will convince determined skeptics. Among these are critics of the seculariza-tion theory wary about premature confirmation of the theory's claims. But this concern neglects the fact that the theory's core prediction encompasses all forms of religious life and expression, not just Christianity. Thus, it would take a lot more than sheer numerical decline in church membership or affiliation—aspects that are difficult to measure with absolute certainty—to satisfy the theory's core assumptions. Moreover, even though the general trend of Christian recession seems clear, enormous variations persist among denominations, regions, coun-tries, and even ethnic groups.

It would also be misleading to equate the erosion of Christian beliefs and allegiance in Western societies with a decline in religiosity. Astonishingly, one assessment claims that over five hundred new religions are reportedly created

---

27. *American Pietism*, 16.

28. Donald E. Miller, *Reinventing American Protestantism: Christianity in the New Millen-nium* (Berkeley: University of California Press, 1999), 161. Miller claims that some 23 percent of this transfer growth is from Roman Catholic churches. He also explains that the typical member of a new paradigm church is "middle-income and white, with some college education and at least one child."

29. Andrew Walls observes that because the United States "ended the nineteenth century a more Christian country by most measures than it had been at the century's beginning," it "started its Christian decline from a much higher base than Europe did" ("Mission and Migration," 10).

30. George G. Hunter, *How to Reach Secular People* (Nashville: Abingdon, 1992), 24.

31. David Lyon, *The Steeple's Shadow: On the Myths and Realities of Secularization* (Grand Rapids: Eerdmans, 1987), 116.

each year in California alone.[32] Moreover, in America, as in Europe, the decline in Christian allegiance and church membership is at odds with what one *Newsweek* article described as "a flowering of spirituality."[33] "Spirituality" is a notoriously slippery concept that is often used in contrast to organized forms of religion; but it frequently connotes latent religiosity. And there is much to be said for the argument that it is the church that (captive to the worldview of modernity) has become secularized in a society that remains very spiritual.[34]

A further problem arises when one considers that general assessments of such notoriously complex phenomena as religious belief and identification tend to ignore powerful subcurrents. Under the impact of nonwhite immigration, other world religions are growing faster than Christianity in many parts of the West, and religious vitality among immigrant groups is conspicuous. This includes Christian immigrants (see chapter 12). Yet, until recently, studies of American religion have ignored the impact of massive immigrant influx on the American religious landscape and the extent to which it may be providing a counterweight to the downturn in Christian observance and church attendance. As a case in point, massive Hispanic immigration is a major reason why the Roman Catholic Church in the United States has avoided the fate of Catholicism in Europe.

Europe, too, is confronted with the growing presence of immigrants, who bring with them both religious plurality and religious dynamism, "at precisely the moment when the historic religions in Europe are losing control of both the belief systems and lifestyles of many modern Europeans."[35] But, unlike in the United States, where the majority of new immigrants are Christian, the majority of post-1960s immigrants in Europe are Muslim. Islam represents Europe's fastest growing religion and its second largest faith. The number of Muslims on the Continent has tripled in the last thirty years—estimates in 2005 ranged from 20.5 million (or 5.4 percent) to 51 million (roughly 7 percent)—and an even higher rate of growth is forecast for the near future. Islam's growing presence in Europe not only presents a major test of Europe's liberal values (which emphasize freedom of religion); it also represents a significant countertrend to secularism. See chapter 10 for a detailed discussion.

But among Europe's new immigrants are also huge numbers of Christians whose presence has contributed to an explosive growth in the number of churches. Largely confined to major metropolitan centers, these immigrant congregations display extraordinary spiritual vigor and dynamism, in startling contrast to most churches in the older denominations. Already in 2001, the number of African Christians throughout Europe was estimated to be in excess of three million.[36] A recent assessment of church growth and attendance in England reports that

---

32. Sine, *Mustard Seed Versus McWorld*, 125.

33. Jerry Adler, "Spirituality 2005," *Newsweek*, August 29/September 5, 2005, 49.

34. For his full argument, see John Drane, *The McDonaldization of the Church: Consumer Culture and the Church's Future* (Macon, GA: Smyth & Helwys, 2001), 59-61.

35. Davie, *Europe*, 38f.

36. Report of the Council of African Christian Communities in Europe (CACCE) at the 1999 meeting in Belgium, quoted in Roswith Gerloff, "Religion, Culture and Resistance: The Significance of African Christian Communities in Europe," *Exchange* 30, no. 3 (2001): 277.

in 2005 nonwhite groups accounted for 58 percent of churchgoers in London (outside London the percentage drops to 31).[37] A century ago, Charles Spurgeon's five-thousand-seat Metropolitan Tabernacle at Elephant and Castle (south London) was the largest Baptist church with thousands of white English worshipers; today the largest Baptist church in Britain is composed of African immigrants.[38] The Nigerian-led Kingsway International Christian Center has the largest congregation (over ten thousand in the entire United Kingdom, while the Redeemed Christian Church of God (a Nigeria-based movement), which established its first church in Britain in 1989, had grown to 141 churches with a total of eighteen thousand members by 2005.[39]

As I will argue (see chapter 11), *the most significant counterforce to Islam in Europe is likely to come less from secularism or from Europe's homegrown, fairly moribund Christianity than from the steady influx of Christian immigrants (from Africa, Latin America, and Asia)*. In Europe, the most vital forms of Christianity many Muslims will encounter will be products of non-Western immigrant influx. And where the Muslim encounter with Western secularism will remain antagonistic and fraught, this new Muslim–Christian encounter is likely to be far more cordial for two reasons. First, a sizable proportion of immigrant Christians hail from contexts of religious plurality characterized by peaceful coexistence with Muslims as neighbors, relatives, schoolmates, and fellow professionals. Second, Christian immigrants may well find that they have more in common with Muslim immigrants than they do with highly secularized Western Christians—notably with regard to public morality, family values, attitudes to the transcendent, the authority of Scripture, and a worldview that repudiates the secular distinction between the spiritual or supernatural and material existence.

Perhaps the most powerful testimony to the dynamism and drive of contemporary African Christianity is the fact that the largest single Christian community in all of Europe (the former heartland of the faith) is the Embassy for the Blessed Kingdom of God to All Nations (in Kiev, Ukraine), founded by Sunday Adelaja, a Nigerian pastor. Established in November 1993 as a Bible study group of seven people meeting in Adelaja's apartment, the new group registered as a church three months later with only forty-nine members.[40] Yet, by 2002, after adopting an outreach strategy that targeted the marginalized groups in Ukrainian society, the church had grown to twenty thousand. Over one million Ukrainians have reportedly been converted to Christianity as a result of its ministry.[41] The spread and impact of such African Christian initiatives in Europe point to the flip side

---

37. "London Is Different!," *Quadrant*, January 2007.

38. Lindsay Bergstrom, "Worldwide Baptists Survive, Reflect Century of Cultural Change," Associated Baptist Press, January 6, 2005.

39. See Mark Sturge, *Look What the Lord Has Done! An Exploration of Black Christian Faith in Britain* (Bletchley: Scripture Union, 2005), 93.

40. Sunday Adelaja, "Go to a Land That I Will Show You," in *Out of Africa*, ed. C. Peter Wagner and Joseph Thompson (Ventura, CA: Regal Books, 2004), 37-55.

41. See the Web site of the Embassy of the Blessed Kingdom of God for all Nations, www .godembassy.org.

of the recent historic shift in global Christianity's center of gravity: phenomenal accessions in the non-Western world.

The Queen of the South

In 1500, only 19 percent of the world's population was Christian. After a millennium of dramatic advances and spectacular recessions (mainly due to the spread of Islam), Europe had emerged as the major heartland of Christianity. Europe was thoroughly Christian and Christianity was thoroughly European. Over the next four centuries, an age of extraordinary international migrations and unprecedented colonial expansion, Europe extended its territorial dominance and exported its religion to far-flung corners of the world with unforeseen consequences (see chapter 7). For all its shortcomings, the European missionary project had a phenomenal global impact. By 1900, one-third of the world's population was Christian. Many more had been influenced by its ideals and message. But Christianity remained predominantly a religion of white people (who accounted for 80 to 90 percent of Christians),[42] and its status as a European or Western religion remained ingrained.

Yet, in the span of a century, the corresponding percentages of Christians in the West (Europe and North America) and non-West have been dramatically reversed. In 1900, less than 20 percent of Christians in the world were nonwhite and *less than one-fifth* (18 percent) resided outside Europe or North America. By 2000, over 60 percent of all Christians resided outside the West, a figure projected to rise to 70 percent by 2025. In 2006, there were almost as many Christians in Latin America as there were in the entire world in 1900. And it is estimated that in the next quarter of a century (by 2025) Africa and Latin America will together account for half the Christians in the world.[43] By 2050, reckons Philip Jenkins (2002), only about one-fifth of the world's Christians will be white.

Christianity's global spread and numerical gains in the last four decades have been largely driven by the Pentecostal-charismatic movement. In the thirty years between 1970 and 2000, the number of "Pentecostal-charismatics-neo-charismatics"—admittedly, a very fluid category at best—reportedly burgeoned over 600 percent. By 2006, this group accounted for at least one in every four Christians (or 27.4 percent) in the world.[44] But it is noteworthy that the growth of Christianity in the non-Western world has not been limited to Pentecostal-charismatic groups but encompasses older mainline denominations—the very segment that, in Western societies, has experienced the most dramatic decline in membership. In Africa, Latin America, and Asia, the overwhelming majority of Christians are to be found in the Anglican, Methodist, Baptist, and Catholic churches. By the turn of the twenty-first century, one in three of all Mennonites

---

42. Barrett, Kurian, and Johnson, *World Christian Encyclopedia*, 3.

43. Peter W. Brierley, *U.K.C.H. Religious Trends No. 3* (London: Christian Research, 2001), 4.

44. David B. Barrett and Todd M. Johnson, "Status of Global Mission, A.D. 2006, in the Context of 20th and 21st Centuries," *International Bulletin of Missionary Research* 30, no. 1 (January 2006): 29.

(38 percent) was African; and the majority of Roman Catholics (40 percent) were in Latin America. By 2025, Africa, Asia, and Latin America may account for almost three-quarters of all Catholics.

Figure 1
Growth of Global Christianity (1900-2025)

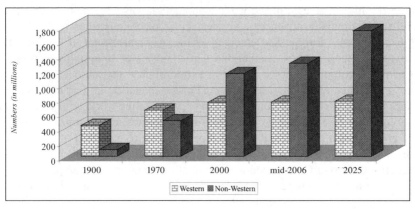

If these developments have transformed Christianity into a non-Western faith, they also call into question the entrenched European identity (or branding) of traditional denominations. Noting that over half of all Mennonites are to be found outside Europe and North America, Wilbert Shenk suggests that "a massive redefinition in Mennonite identity is called for."[45] This candid admission highlights the profound nature of the recent "shift." The case of worldwide Anglican Communion is the most striking. The word "Anglican" literally means "English"; but the overwhelming majority of active members of the 78 million-strong worldwide Anglican Communion are non-English and live outside England. One in every two is African (a total of 44 million), while active Anglicans in England number fewer than 3 million.[46] Nigeria has more practicing Anglicans than any other country (including Britain) and seven times the 2.3 million Episcopalians in the entire United States.[47] While the number of Anglicans in Nigeria has grown by over 250 percent in the last three decades, the number of Anglicans in North America (roughly 4 million) has remained stagnant or declined.[48]

In fact, nowhere has Christianity's explosive growth over the last century been as dramatic as in Africa, making Africa the "poster-child," so to speak, of

---

45. Wilbert R. Shenk, *By Faith They Went Out: Mennonite Missions, 1850-1999,* Occasional Papers/Institute of Mennonite Studies (Elkhart, IN: Institute of Mennonite Studies, 2000), 95.

46. David Van Biema, "Blunt Bishop," *Time,* February 19, 2007, 52; "Factfile: Anglican Church around the World," *BBC News,* June 16, 2006.

47. Kenneth L. Woodward, "The Changing Face of the Church: How the Explosion of Christianity in Developing Nations Is Transforming the World's Largest Religion," *Newsweek,* April 16, 2001, 48.

48. See Philip Jenkins, "Defender of the Faith," *Atlantic Monthly* 292, no. 4 (November 2003): 48.

this epochal shift. The African experience epitomizes the shift not only in terms of its sheer demographic scale but also in its unexpectedness and missionary significance. It is hard to believe that just a century ago, after centuries of notable European missionary efforts that had seen thriving Christian communities in West and East Africa, serious doubt remained in European missionary minds about the prospects of Christianity in Africa. Why this was so is perhaps best explained using the findings and reports of the first World Missionary Conference held in Edinburgh in 1910.

The Edinburgh 1910 Conference, Africa, and the "Shift"

Convened at the height of Western imperial expansion, this historic meeting bristled with optimistic self-confidence and a sense of urgency. "It is possible today as never before," its proceedings averred, "to have a campaign adequate to carry the Gospel to all the non-Christian world *so far as the Christian Church is concerned.*"[49] As we shall see below, this optimism was only slightly tempered by a muted recognition that the spiritual state of the "Home Church" was not fully in keeping with its missionary obligation. In keeping with a Christendom outlook, the Edinburgh 1910 meeting conceived of the world in terms of two distinct (territorial) blocs: "Christian" and "non-Christian." Brian Stanley explains that there was tense debate in the run-up to the meeting over the specifics of which lands and peoples constituted "Christendom"; but it was never in dispute that the two worlds, "Christendom" and "heathendom," must be differentiated on a territorial or geographical basis.[50] The meeting was convened not to assess mission to the world but "to consider missionary problems in relation to the non-Christian world." In other words, its sole focus was how to meet the challenge of carrying the gospel from Christian lands (Christendom) to non-Christian lands (heathendom). The designation "world" in the conference title referred not to the mission field but to the missionaries. It is hardly surprising, then, that non-Western representation at this meeting was limited to a handful of Indian, Chinese, and Japanese Christians. Not a single African was present.

European missionary agencies had never, as a rule, devoted their best resources or sent their finest and brightest to Africa.[51] It was Asia, particularly China, with its teeming masses and civilizational splendors, that had long captured the European imagination. A preoccupation with statistical calculation in missionary thinking meant that India and China were identified as "the two great mission fields of the world." Edinburgh 1910 participants were reminded that "two and a half times as many people await the Gospel in China as make up the entire

---

49. *World Missionary Conference 1910, 1,* 10 (emphasis in original).

50. See Brian Stanley, "Defining the Boundaries of Christendom: The Two Worlds of the World Missionary Conference, 1910," *International Bulletin of Missionary Research* 30, no. 4 (October 2006): 171-76.

51. See Walls, *Cross-Cultural Process,* 117.

population of Africa."[52] Yet a continent three times the size of Europe could not be ignored, no matter its internal complexities or perceived demerits.

The report on Africa estimated that it had some 150 million souls (including as many as 60 million Muslims) "awaiting the arrival of [Christian] messengers."[53] It allowed that some four million African Christians survived from apostolic times in Egypt and Ethiopia; but these Christian communities, it added matter-of-factly, "have long ceased to be missionary."[54] (The missionary significance of more recently formed indigenous Christian communities in West and East Africa was studiously ignored.) From the perspective of Edinburgh 1910, therefore, "the bulk of the population of Africa is immersed in darkness." Yet "no part of Africa [was] shut against the true missionary"; in pagan Africa "not only is the way open, but those to whom the way leads are awaiting the arrival of messengers."[55]

As we shall see, this view was seriously tempered by other grave misgivings. But it is worth explaining that while this estimation of the ripeness of Africa for the gospel reflected an unbounded confidence that no part of the world was absolutely closed to European missionary endeavor, it was also influenced by two added considerations. First, that the continent's immense, once seemingly impenetrable expanse no longer posed a formidable barrier to European advance. Its great waterways were now being navigated by flotillas of European steamers; networks of railways had been or were being built to facilitate access to its vast interior; and, under colonial administration, road construction was proceeding at a rapid pace. Huge swaths of the continent remained "accessible only by long and weary marching through bush or forest or tropical savannah or arid scrubland" (World Missionary Conference 1960: 211); but the "Dark Continent" was no longer the impenetrable mystery of lore. This turn of events perhaps explains the conference's curious statement that the greatest progress of Christianity in sub-Saharan Africa had been achieved within the past decade.

The second basis for optimism about the spread of Christianity in Africa had to do with the strong conviction that the cultures of "animistic societies" were incapable of mounting long-term resistance to sustained Christian missionary effort. By the early twentieth century the term "animism" (coined by British anthropologist Sir Edward B. Tylor in 1871) described belief systems and ritual practices that appeared to revolve around the worship of souls and spirits, including ancestral and nature spirits. Like the far more generic "heathenism," animism betrayed the ingrained ethnocentric bias of Western thinking, but it was also applied with greater authority because of its pseudo-scientific pedigree. In common usage, the term was pejoratively applied to the culture of peoples whom Europeans deemed to be in the lowest stages of human development, and thus the farthest removed from Western civilization. The beliefs and practices associated with animism were considered not only pagan but also crude, primitive, and

---

52. *World Missionary Conference 1910, 1*, 84, 204.
53. Ibid., 9, 206f.
54. Ibid., 207.
55. *World Missionary Conference 1910*, 1:9.

irrational. In European missionary parlance, animism was the chief form and expression of "heathenism," and it became a catchall label for the ways of life prevalent in non-Western societies.

(It is worth noting in passing that the designation "primal religions" is generally considered a better alternative to more derogatory labels such as "animistic," "primitive," or "pagan." Perhaps even broader in scope, the term "primal religions" applies to "the most basic or fundamental religious forms in the overall history of mankind" [cited in Cox 1996: 57]. Its application also involves the important recognition that the phenomenon in question is worldwide and not confined to any one region in the world. This robs the concept of the ethnocentric bias to which the other alternatives readily lend themselves. As John V. Taylor puts it, "so many features of African religion occur elsewhere in the globe and in the history of human belief that we may reasonably claim that we are dealing with the universal, basic elements of man's understanding of God and of the world."[56])

Animism received considerable attention at the 1910 conference, with "the Bantu tribes in Africa" forming the main focus.[57] European missionaries were the chief source of information and insights about animistic societies and practices—there is simply no indication that the opinion of non-Western Christians was directly sought on this matter. The views were wide-ranging and there was a difference of opinion on critical issues like the religious significance of animism. But there was unanimity of opinion on at least one point: namely, that "animistic heathenism is essentially weak through intellectual and moral bankruptcy, and . . . it inevitably goes down before the sustained attack of Christian missionary effort."[58] Herein lay the second explanation for the highly positive evaluation at Edinburgh 1910 of Africa's readiness for the gospel. Put simply, Africa promised an abundant harvest for missionary labor precisely because "here, as in no other continent, there was a mass of dark, illiterate, dissevered, and degraded Paganism to be enlightened and uplifted into the Church of Christ."[59]

For all that, European missionary opinion was quite divided on the crucial question of whether animism had religious significance. A minority insisted that animism has "no religious content" and is devoid of any "preparation for Christianity"—a fact deduced from the absence of "adequate words to express *trust, faith, holiness, purity, repentance,* and many other abstract ideas."[60] The majority of the missionaries also denied "the presence of any religious help or consolation in animistic beliefs and rites."[61] Yet most accepted that animistic reli-

---

56. John V. Taylor, *The Primal Vision: Christian Presence amid African Religion* (London: SCM, 1994), 26. For more on primal religions, see Walls, *Missionary Movement,* 119-39; Phillipa Baylis, *An Introduction to Primal Religions* (Edinburgh: Traditional Cosmology Society, 1988); James L. Cox, "The Classification 'Primal Religions' as a Non-Empirical Christian Theological Construct," *Studies in World Christianity* 2, no. 1 (1996): 55-76.

57. *World Missionary Conference 1910, 4,* 6-37. For an extensive review, see J. Stanley Friesen, *Missionary Responses to Tribal Religions at Edinburgh, 1910* (New York: Peter Lang, 1996).

58. *World Missionary Conference 1910, 4,* 36.

59. *World Missionary Conference 1910, 1,* 242.

60. *World Missionary Conference 1910, 4,* 24 (emphasis in original). For subsequent interpretation of this conclusion by African scholars, see Friesen, *Missionary Responses,* 4-8.

61. Friesen, *Missionary Responses,* 10.

gions present certain points of contact for the preaching of the gospel,[62] including widespread belief in the existence of a Supreme Being, widespread belief
in an afterlife (even immortality of the soul), the idea and practice of sacrifice,
the use of prayer, and the existence of a rudimentary moral sense and a dim
consciousness of sin. How "points of contact" is different from "preparation for
Christianity" (which a good proportion of European missionaries found inappli-
cable) is unclear. This produced a general consensus that "the native conception
of things" ought to be studied and proper account taken of such "points of contact" when preaching the gospel in non-Western societies.

In this regard, Edinburgh 1910 demonstrated a noteworthy advancement in
European missionary thinking, compared to as little as half a century earlier.[63]
And the pronounced ethnocentrism of its assessment aside, the overall evaluation
of animism hints presciently at the epochal transformation to come. However
dimly it was perceived at the time, the arguments about receptivity of "animistic societies" to the gospel anticipated the massive accessions to the faith in the
southern continents, which lay just beyond the horizon. The new Christian communities in Africa, Latin America, Asia, and the Pacific, which now constitute
the new heartlands of global Christianity, have been drawn overwhelmingly
from adherents of primal religions. In this statement from the Edinburgh 1910
meeting, there is even a subtle hint at the remarkable Christian transformation
that would take place on the African continent: "There is some ground for thinking that the specific doctrines of the evangelical creed appeal more directly to the
African mind than to the heathen mind in any other quarters of the world."[64]

The reports of the Edinburgh 1910 conference even contain the startling
suggestion that the new Christian communities emerging throughout the non-
Western world may one day become centers of spiritual vigor from which the
Western church may learn a thing or two (see full statement at the head of the
chapter).[65] This observation was made more in the spirit of an addendum than
as a matter for serious consideration. But there was also candid recognition that
Western Christendom was already experiencing discernible spiritual decline. It
was reported that

> the growing spirit of commercialism and materialism which characterizes
> the age had cast its influence over the Church. . . . It is a time of doubt and
> hesitation among many Christian ministers and teachers. . . . The life of
> the Church suffers from lack of clear conviction and of resolute loyalty to
> Christ throughout the whole sphere of duty. While the missionary obliga-

---

62. Ibid., 24-28.

63. One late-nineteenth-century European observer not only described Africa as a "land of
fetishes" where "all consciousness of 'the Eternal Power and Godhead'" was completely eclipsed
and added that whereas other nations in times past had shared this condition "the peculiarity of
Africa is that it has somehow gone further in departing from God"; see "The Negro," *Church Missionary Intelligencier* (August 1873).

64. *World Missionary Conference 1910, 4,* 31.

65. Ibid., 36f.

tion of the Church may be formally acknowledged, it is viewed with widespread apathy and indifference.[66]

Alas, these tantalizing observations yield their significance only in retrospect. The Edinburgh 1910 event occurred at the high-water mark of European missionary expansion. Its outlook mirrored the age of empire, and its ideals reflected the overheated self-confidence of a movement at full tide. The structure, focus, and core proposals of the conference were too clearly premised on the resolute assurance that Europe and North America constituted the centers of the faith and the fulcrum of its expansion. Its contributors and participants were fully conscious of the new global order. They noted that "the whole world has become one neighborhood" where "the nations and races are acting and reacting upon each other with increasing directness, constancy, and power."[67] But the new forces of globalization made little difference to a Christendom mind-set that envisaged a world divided into two distinct territorial realities and championed a missionary agenda involving universal expansion—"the evangelization of non-Christian lands"—from a fixed dominant center (the Western world).[68] This was implicit in the recognition that "we must not press upon other races undesirable and unessential features of our Western Church life" as well as in the affirmation that "missionary enterprise is the projection abroad of the Church at Home." In its grand vision, nothing less than the fate of "Christianity as a world religion" was at stake; but the outcome of this "decisive hour for Christian missions" depended, as far as human means go, solely on the actions and resources of the Western Church.

But the grand surge of the Western missionary enterprise on which Edinburgh 1910 placed all its bets never happened. Within a decade, the so-called Christian nations of the Western world turned on each other with ferocious destructiveness in one of the bloodiest wars in the history of humankind. European Christianity never recovered from the self-inflicted wounds of two World Wars, and the European missionary movement lost its vigor. By the 1920s, American missionary initiatives had risen to fill much of the gap, remarkably extending the fortitude and follies of Christendom (see chapters 4 and 7). But the global Christian landscape was already undergoing a radical reshaping of its demographic and cultural contours, a process that has ushered in a whole new chapter in the history of world Christianity. If the African experience within this global transformation has been among the most astonishing, this is in part because the overall forecast for African Christianity in the opening decades of the twentieth century was emphatically gloomy.

---

66. *World Missionary Conference 1910, 1*, 348.
67. Ibid., 344, 345.
68. Ibid., 344, 348.

The Significance of African Christianity: More Than Numbers!

The upbeat pronouncements at the 1910 World Missionary Conference about the ripeness of Africa for the gospel (discussed above) were virtually negated by palpable apprehension about the prospects for meaningful Christian expansion on the continent. There was one solitary reason for this disquiet: Islam. With an estimated sixty million Muslims on the African continent, Islam accounted for at least 40 percent of the non-Christian population. The conference noted that Christianity and Islam were the two forces contending for the soul of Africa; and it gave Islam the upper hand by some margin. Extensive missionary feedback indicated not only that Islam was "in many respects the more aggressive" of the two but also that "the absorption of native races into Islam is proceeding rapidly and continuously in practically all parts of the continent."[69] The official conclusion was unambiguous: the African continent faced a defining moment in its religious history, and "if things continue as they are now tending, Africa may become a Mohammedan continent."[70]

Almost a century later, the situation on the ground confounds this prognosis. Islam in Africa had, indeed, registered vigorous growth, but Christianity just (or nearly) as much. The African "mission field" reviewed at Edinburgh 1910 boasted the smallest number of Christians of any continent (with the exception of Oceania). Yet, by the end of the century Africa had transformed into an area "experiencing the fastest church growth of any region" in the world.[71] From roughly 9.9 million (9.4 percent of the population) in 1900, the number of African Christians had mushroomed to about 360 million (over 40 percent of the population) by 2000.[72] Such a rate of growth has no parallels in the history of Christianity. While the church in Europe and North America is reportedly losing an estimated six thousand church members a day, African Christians are increasing at a rate of twenty-three thousand new Christians a day (or 8.5 million a year).[73] When defections from the faith are accounted for, the net increase—that is, the number of new converts—still averages 1.5 million a year. And if current projections are accurate, this number will double by 2025, by which time there will be more Christians in Africa than on any other continent in the world.[74]

Such statistical evaluations obscure complex realities on the ground that involve massive dislocations, multiple allegiances, and endless sectarian divisions. But the significance of African Christianity extends far beyond numerical

---

69. Ibid., 20, 364. Incidentally, reports also confirmed that the migratory movement of Muslim traders was a major factor in the spread of Islam. "Mohammedan traders," it was declared, "are finding their way into the remotest parts of the continent, and it is well known that every Mohammedan trader is more or less a Mohammedan missionary" (p. 21).

70. Ibid., 20.

71. See John A. Siewert and E. G. Valdez, eds., *Mission Handbook* (Monrovia, CA: MARC, 1997), 34.

72. Barrett, Kurian, and Johnson, *World Christian Encyclopedia*, 5; see also Jaffarian, "The Statistical State of the Missionary Enterprise."

73. Barrett, Kurian, and Johnson, *World Christian Encyclopedia*, 5.

74. Barrett and Johnson, "Status of Global Mission," 28.

growth and rate of expansion. Indeed, to focus on these elements obscures other salient aspects of the African Christian experience, for example:

- Christian expansion has taken place against a background of massive upheaval, widespread violence, disease epidemics, and recurrent social change.
- Modern African Christianity is primarily a product of African agency and initiatives.
- The most vigorous growth took place *after* the heyday of Western missionary enterprise and *after* colonialism.
- The emergence of African Christianity as a popular religious movement owes much to continuity with African primal religions; notably in the widespread use of vernacular names for the Christian God, the preoccupation with spiritual power, and the centrality of healing.
- African Christian movements have adopted implements of modernity without abandoning indigenous values or worldviews.
- While the processes of globalization have marginalized the African experience in some ways, they have also facilitated the global spread of African forms of Christianity (a central argument of this book).

At the very least, Africa has taken center stage in the study of Christianity in a way that would have been unimaginable a century ago. Andrew Walls argues that when "we take the recent accession to Christianity in Africa along with the recent recession from it in the West, African Christianity must be seen as a major component of contemporary *representative* Christianity, the standard Christianity of the present age, a demonstration model of its character. That is, we may need to look at Africa today in order to understand Christianity itself." He adds that "Africa may be the theater in which some of the determinative new directions in Christian thought and activity are being taken."[75]

A full examination of the merits and implications of this observation is beyond the scope of this work. But there can be no doubt that the story of modern African Christianity is integral to any meaningful appraisal of global Christianity and its future prospects.

Take the issue of primal religions. While the Edinburgh 1910 conference gave insightful attention to what was termed "animistic religions," a full appreciation of the significance of primal religions was impeded by European perspectives and Enlightenment rationality. It observed, for instance, that "the beliefs and observances of Animism are dictated by physical necessity alone" and that "it is a physical salvation that is sought after," an assessment that reflected the dichotomy between the physical/material and spiritual imposed by enlightenment thinking but quite foreign to the primal worldview.[76] The ethnocentric preconception attached to the use of "animism" possibly blinded the overwhelming European participants to the fact that the world out of which their own ancestors

---

75. Walls, *Cross-Cultural Process*, 119.
76. For more on this, see ibid., 123.

were originally converted was a world of primal religions—a world defined by polytheistic worship, evil spirits and demons, and ancestor veneration.[77] Nor was there any recognition that the remarkable receptivity of primal religions to the Christian gospel has been a continuing theme in Christian history. The conference expressly declared that "in all his labors . . . the missionary must never attempt to combine Animism with Christianity" for "a syncretism is impossible." In fact, *the overwhelming majority of Christian converts in the history of the faith have been adherents of primal religion!*

The point is that the story of African Christianity fully demonstrates the critical importance of primal religions to Christian expansion.[78] Africans, notes Lamin Sanneh, have "best responded to Christianity where the indigenous religions were strongest, not weakest, suggesting a degree of compatibility with the gospel."[79] Indeed, he adds, Christian expansion on the continent has been "virtually limited to those societies whose people had preserved the indigenous name for God." Perhaps more obviously so in the African experience than anywhere else (in the last two centuries), the encounter between the message of the gospel and the primal tradition, rather than the purposeful replacement of the one by the other, has proven to be indispensable for the emergence of dynamic Christian movements.

An enduring primal religious consciousness helps to explain why African Christians take the supernatural claims of the gospel seriously. Pervasive religiosity and an intense spiritual worldview dictate an emphasis on the power of the gospel to provide physical healing as well as to save, to deliver (from evil forces or daily dilemmas), to set free from sin, to transform conditions in this life, and to guarantee happiness in the next. Extensive cultural affinity between the African and the biblical world also fosters literal interpretations of the Bible and reinforces expectations about spiritual manifestations and divine intervention in daily life (through dreams, prophecy, miraculous action, etc.). At the very least, the intellectual decision to follow Christ (across Christian traditions) is often accompanied by strong belief in the immediacy of the divine and the experience of the supernatural.

On the whole, African Christianity has displayed a remarkable capacity to adapt and to readjust to shifting sociopolitical predicaments, constantly reshaping its religious maps to achieve congruence between physical realities and spiritual need within situations of powerlessness. The compartmentalized and rationalistic faith of Western Christianity—largely confined to a few hours every week and scrupulously confined to material realities—turned out to be too anemic for

---

77. This story is touched on briefly on p. 89 above; see also Walls, *Missionary Movement*, 68-75.

78. See Walls, *Cross-Cultural Process*, 116-35; idem, *Missionary Movement*, 79-101; Kwame Bediako, *Christianity in Africa: The Renewal of a Non-Western Religion* (Maryknoll, NY: Orbis Books, 1995); Kwame Bediako, "Understanding African Theology in the 20th Century," in *Issues in African Christian Theology*, ed. Samuel Ngewa, Mark Shaw, and Tite Tienou (Nairobi: East African Educational Publishers, 1998), 56-72.

79. Lamin Sanneh, *Whose Religion Is Christianity? The Gospel beyond the West* (Grand Rapids: Eerdmans, 2003), 18, 31f.

African needs. Whether celebrating its religious heritage (epitomized by prophet-healing movements) in an effort to wrest the gospel from the possessive clutches of a dominating European culture or demonizing traditional religion (evident in the Pentecostal-charismatic movement) in a bid to appropriate modernizing spiritual principles, Africa's Christians have always taken the engagement with traditional culture or the primal world very seriously indeed. Therein lie its real strength and significance, the qualities that will likely preserve it against the "acids of modernity" and define its place in the history of Christianity. "It may well be," declares Kwame Bediako, "that in Africa the opportunity which was lost in Europe for a serious and creative theological encounter between the Christian and primal traditions can be regained."[80]

Western Intellectual Captivity

The southward shift in global Christianity's center of gravity is extraordinary by any reckoning. It represents perhaps the most remarkable religious transformation of the twentieth century, though it will be some time before understanding of its global ramifications catches up with the veracity of its global dimensions. But, regardless of whether one allows for American exceptionalism or treats statistical representations of religious phenomena as dubious, its fundamental implications for the study and evaluation of global Christianity in the twentieth century are all too pressing. "By becoming a non-Western religion," asserts Bediako, "*Christianity has also become a true world faith.*"[81] Yet the mere fact that the poor, powerless, and persecuted now represent the face of global Christianity requires a radically new understanding of its nature, potential, and pervasiveness. For that matter, evaluating the significance of these developments for global Christianity depends on how one understands the "shift" itself.

In part because of what has been loosely described as "structures of academic dependency,"[82] the most widely published interpretative analyses of the "shift" have been produced by Western scholars. Many provide insightful evaluation of its unprecedented nature, profound historical significance and far-reaching implications for the traditional theology curriculum.[83] But some of the most influential treatments either privilege a secularist perspective or utilize an inter-

---

80. Bediako, "Understanding African Theology," 68.

81. Bediako, *Christianity in Africa*, 265 (emphasis added).

82. These structures include the control by the Western academy of scholarly journals and organizations through which the bulk of information is disseminated and "the political and ideological [domination] of social theory and its consequent political use."

83. Among the most helpful, see Harold A. Netland and Craig Ott, *Globalizing Theology: Belief and Practice in an Era of World Christianity* (Nottingham: Apollos, 2007); Dana L. Robert, "Shifting Southward: Global Christianity since 1945," *International Bulletin of Missionary Research* 24, no. 2 (April 2000): 50-58; Wilbert R. Shenk, *Enlarging the Story: Perspectives on Writing World Christian History* (Maryknoll, NY: Orbis Books, 2002); idem, "Toward a Global Church History," *International Bulletin of Missionary Research* 20, no. 2 (April 1996): 50-57; Andrew F. Walls, "African Christianity in the History of Religions," *Studies in World Christianity* 2 (1996): 183-203; idem, *Missionary Movement*, 16-25, 68-75, 143-59.

pretative framework based on Western paradigms, or (typical for discourse on global phenomena) employ the "World Series" approach, in which the Western or American experience is projected on a global scale so that developments in the non-Western world are reduced to pale replicas of Western versions or treated as residues of Western expansion.

At least three approaches incorporating one or more of these viewpoints were discussed in the first three chapters: from a secularist perspective, Pippa Norris and Ronald Inglehart (2004) attribute high levels of religiosity (most prevalent in non-Western societies) to the experience of social vulnerability and lack of human development (see chapter 2); turning the secularization thesis on its head, Samuel Huntington (1996) attributes the massive religious resurgence in the non-Western world to the spread of Western economic modernization (see chapter 3); and Peter Berger (2002) argues that "evangelical Protestantism," which he identifies as a facet of cultural globalization, originates from and has its center in America (see chapter 2).

These viewpoints are not limited to political scientists and sociologists. Some Western religious scholars also utilize a secularist framework in their analysis of global religious developments. In *Exporting the American Gospel: Global Christian Fundamentalism*, for instance, Steve Brouwer, Paul Gifford, and Susan Rose explain the explosive growth of Pentecostal-charismatic movements in Africa, Latin America, the Caribbean, and Asia as manifestations of the global spread of American Christian fundamentalism, a movement "intertwined with the homogenizing influences of consumerism, mass communication, and production."[84] All these examples, however, impinge only indirectly on the issue of the recent demographic shift within global Christianity. By far the best-known assessment of this "shift" that employs a Western conceptual model is Philip Jenkins's *The Next Christendom: The Coming of Global Christianity*.

Jenkins's hugely popular book provides penetrating analysis of the changing contours of global Christianity and contains perceptive insights into what Jenkins terms "Southern Christianity." Yet its assessment is seriously marred by an approach that makes the Western Christian experience a definitive template or roadmap for understanding the radically different phenomena and transformations now unfolding in the non-Western world. Curiously enough, Jenkins condemns Western-centered appraisals of non-Western phenomena. He attests that "Northerners rarely give the South anything like the attention it deserves, [and] when they do notice it, they tend to project onto it their own familiar realities and desires." This turns out to be self-fulfilling commentary! He also predicts that "as southern churches grow and mature, they will increasingly define their own interests in ways that have little to do with the preferences and parties of Americans and Europeans." Yet, by adopting "Christendom" as a descriptive framework for his study of the emerging Southern Christianities, Jenkins completely ignores his better instinct.

In his account (2002: 215f., 11, 12), he insists that "the New Christendom is

---

84. Steve Brouwer, Paul Gifford, and Susan D. Rose, *Exporting the American Gospel: Global Christian Fundamentalism* (New York: Routledge, 1996).

no mirror image of the Old" but rather represents a "truly new and developing entity," also that the new shape of global Christianity forces us to see the whole religion in a radically new perspective, "as if . . . seeing it for the first time." But, inevitably, his analysis of the "new" draws almost exclusively on the "old." Indeed, he sees Christian–Muslim conflict in the present order as one of the closest analogies between the old Christendom and the new. He refers to "forces of Crusade, from the Christian Third World" and the possibility of "a wave of religious conflicts reminiscent of the Middle Ages, a new age of Christian crusades and Muslim jihads." He speculates that "the new Christian world of the south could find unity in common religious beliefs"—a modern Christendom based on "a powerful Christian identity in culture and politics." He is also convinced that "distinctively Christian politics [are] flourishing in the Third World"; and he ventures that the explosive growth of Christianity in the South will see the emergence of "a new wave of Christian states, in which political life is inextricably bound up with religious belief"—all of which signifies that the new (Southern) Christianity will be dealing with the same issues that confronted the old (Western) Christianity.

Jenkins's secularist perspective is also quite manifest. His prognosis duplicates the quintessential secularist premonition of an otherwise bright future sabotaged by medieval-like clashes of belief, missionary armies, and rampant religious conflict. He anticipates the possibility that the massive religious upsurge in the South will implode with bloody conflicts (engendered by population growth and attitudes to religious conversion) between the Christians and Muslims. This understanding grotesquely tags "Southern Christianity" as a destructive force within the new world order; it is all the more striking, given the nature of current global conflicts (including the "war on terror"), that he makes no reference to Western nations in this prognosis. At the same time, Jenkins makes room for the central secularization claim that such unbridled religiosity will inevitably succumb to the forces of modernization. For "what we are now witnessing in the global South is very much what occurred in the North when it was passing through a comparable stage of social development" (2002: 76). In other words, "as Southern economies develop, their demographic patterns will presumably come to resemble those of the older industrial nations" and trends now evident in the West will "eventually be replicated in the global South." As such, "African and Asian societies might undergo the same kind of secularization that Europe experienced in the eighteenth century, when concepts like witchcraft and prophecy gradually fell out of favor."

Since a detailed examination of the secularization theory is provided in chapter 2, further comment here would be superfluous. Arguments presented in the previous chapter about the limitations of Christendom as a durable or exportable model already attest to its inapplicability to the non-Western Christian experience. Lamin Sanneh makes the case most forcefully in connection with the African experience:

African Christianity has not been a bitterly fought religion: there have been no ecclesiastical courts condemning unbelievers, heretics, and witches to

death; no bloody battles of doctrine and polity; no territorial aggrandizement by churches; no jihads against infidels; no fatwas against women; no
amputations, lynchings, ostracism, penalties, or public condemnations of
doctrinal difference or dissent. The lines of Christian profession have not
been etched in the blood of enemies. To that extent, at least African Christianity has diverged strikingly from sixteenth- and seventeenth-century
Christendom.[85]

The utter inaptness of the Christendom concept aside, its usage also implicitly imprisons the study of non-Western Christianity within a Western theological framework and thus impoverishes understanding of its nature and
significance.

It cannot be emphasized too strongly that the Christendom concept holds little
value for understanding burgeoning non-Western Christianities. By any reckoning, the suggestion that "Southern Christianity" might evolve into a monolithic
entity defined by a common identity in culture and politics is quite bizarre. The
expressions and experiences of faith subsumed under "Southern Christianity"
are characterized by multitudinous and multifarious movements, divergent initiatives, and shifting identities, not to mention a propensity for endless sectarian
divisions. Even the cutting edge of growth is remarkably multicentered. Timothy
Shah attests that "for reasons deeply rooted in its belief and identity, evangelicalism does not constitute a single monolithic movement in the Third World but a
multitude of movements that divide and sub-divide in an endless ecclesiastical
mitosis."[86] The experience of Christendom perhaps predisposes Westerners to
think of religious phenomena in terms of a permanent center and structures of
unilateral control. In this new Christian epoch this outlook is patently unhelpful.
Non-Western (or "Southern") Christianity has no pope, no Rome, and, for that
matter, no Mecca.

In the final analysis, the dramatic shift that has transformed global Christianity into a non-Western religion calls for radically new conceptual tools and even
a new vocabulary. Many terms that derive their freight of meaning from the
Western experience and perspective—including "Christendom," "fundamentalist," "conservative," "liberal," and "postmodern"—have limited applicability and often undermine full comprehension when indiscriminately applied to
non-Western realities. Indeed, non-Western Christian experiences, perspectives,
and initiatives directly challenge long-standing conceptual dichotomies favored
within Western theological discourse: such as secular/religious, modern/tradi-
tional, conservative/liberal, church/mission. Full appreciation of the profound
implications of the recent "shift" for the study of global Christianity requires a
recognition that the new heartlands of the faith in the non-West are radically different in character and function from the preceding heartlands in the West. It also
requires an appreciation of the degree to which the supposedly one-directional

---

85. Sanneh, *Whose Religion Is Christianity?* 39.

86. Timothy S. Shah, "Evangelical Politics in the Third World: What's Next for the 'Next Christendom'?" *Brandywine Review of Faith & International Affairs* 1, no. 2 (2003): 28.

expansion of Western colonialism and missions paradoxically unleashed powerful forces of change within non-Western societies that now act back on the West.

The old heartlands exemplified political domination, territorial control, national religion, cultural superiority, and a fixed universal vision. In sharp contrast, the emerging heartlands of the faith embody vulnerability and risk, religious plurality, immense diversity of Christian experience and expression, and structures of dependency. The forms of Christianity that now flourish in the non-Western world are not only post-Christendom, they are *anti-Christendom*. The Christian experience is de-territorialized, and Christianity often exists as a minority faith. While it may give some marginalized groups a public voice or even align itself with a political movement, the church is divested of intrinsic political power or status. In many areas Christians are far more likely to be the persecuted and dispossessed rather than the persecutors or the powerful. Missionary initiatives are bereft of instruments of domination, and military action by political rulers in defense of the Christian faith is unheard of.

Moving beyond Christendom will have profound and still largely unexplored ramifications for the future shape and impact of global Christianity. What, for instance, will be the nature of Christian encounter and engagement in the wider global context, given the economic and political forces shaping non-Western contexts? If the future of the faith is tied in with the fortunes of Christianity in the new heartlands, how should we understand its missionary potential? And how will the new experiences and understandings of faith impact the study of Christianity or frame missiological reflection?

For the most part, massive and purposive Western involvement in the non-Western world was pursued with little thought to the ramifications for, or potential impact on, Western societies themselves. Western missions were conducted with hardly any consideration for the possibility that the spread of the Christian faith in the non-Western world would produce fresh theological enterprise that would challenge Western theological orthodoxies or new Christian expressions and initiatives that would radically undermine Western universal claims. There was the vaguest hint at the Edinburgh 1910 meeting that the Christianity of Europe may in time "be recalled, if not to forgotten truths, at least to neglected graces" by the newly emerging non-Western churches (World Missionary Conference 1910, 4:112), but few Western missionaries could have anticipated (or welcomed) the possibility that the churches over which they sought or exercised paternalistic control would in time exceed the old heartlands in growth and dynamism, much less produce reverse missionary movements that recast the West as a mission field.

Today, the claim that "the Christianity typical of the twenty-first century will be shaped by events and processes that take place in the southern continents, and above all by those that take place in Africa"[87] is unlikely to attract strong disagreement. But to fully understand how and why developments within African

---

87. Walls, *Missionary Movement*, 85; see also idem, *Cross-Cultural Process*, 119.

Christianity may have significance well beyond Africa requires critical assessment of the inextricable connection between missionary expansion and international migration. This migration–mission nexus is not new. But under the impetus of contemporary globalization it is now being demonstrated in extraordinary ways. The unprecedented migrations of peoples that accompanied European empire-building and missionary movement holds important clues to the nature and timing of the "shift" in global Christianity's center of gravity and the new initiatives associated with it. In fact, the emergence of a massive non-Western missionary movement is directly rooted in worldwide changes triggered by European expansion and movement in the sixteenth to nineteenth centuries.

As I will show, the link between migration and missionary expansion has been a prominent feature of Christianity from the beginning. Even more important, it has strong roots in the biblical tradition. How this is so deserves careful examination; for it is crucial that the assessment of historical developments is informed by a biblical perspective.

Part II

MIGRATION AND THE NEW WORLD ORDER

6

"A Wandering Aramean Was My Ancestor"

Exile, Migration, and Mission in Biblical Perspective

> Exile is a time for maintaining identity . . . a time for hope, not triumphalism . . . a time for new obedience. . . . Exile was and is a catalyst for translating the faith.
>
> —Ralph W. Klien, *Israel in Exile* (1979)

Human migration is a fact of history; indeed, migration has been described as "an irrepressible human urge."[1] For thousands of years, the unpredictability and precariousness of normal life made migration and relocation the norm in human existence. Myriad factors, from little-understood ecological changes (including occurrences of famine and natural disasters) to overly aggressive neighbors and the perennial round of military violence, necessitated recurrent movement. Mobility was essential to survival. Long after the development of large-scale agricultural cultivation of land (c. 5500 B.C.E.) allowed the formation of high-density populations, permanent settlement with the requisite social hierarchies and formal political structure remained an exception in human experience. For as long as human beings have inhabited the planet, relocation, displacement, and population transfers have marked the human condition.

It therefore comes as no surprise that the "spirit of migration" permeates the biblical record and defines biblical religion. The image of the sojourner, indeed of life as a sojourn (splendidly depicted in Psalm 121) is a dominant theme,[2] to such an extent, in fact, that the greatest peril to religious vitality and experience of the divine comes not from the trauma of violent displacement or the precariousness of exile and exodus but from the false sense of security derived from "having 'arrived' at the full and final expression of . . . doctrine, worship, and

---

1. W. R. Böhning, "International Migration and the Western World: Past, Present, Future," *International Migration* 16, no. 1 (1978): 18.

2. See James Limburg, "Psalm 121: A Psalm for Sojourners," *Word & World* 5, no. 2 (1985): 180-87.

exhortation."[3] Even those who question the historicity of the biblical story are forced to acknowledge that exile and exodus shape "the subtext of the narratives and rhetoric of the Hebrew Bible" to the point of "narratological obsession."[4] Not only do we encounter every major form of migration in the biblical account, but also the biblical story and message would be meaningless without migration and mobility.

Crucially, the interface between human mobility and divine purposes in the biblical story is unmistakable and compelling. The inextricable link between migrant movement and the *missio dei* (the mission of God) arguably confirms the historicity of many events. It is also strongly paradigmatic of the biblical God's intimate involvement in human affairs. In other words, to claim that the God of the Bible is a God of mission is to accept that he makes himself known to human beings through ordinary, culturally conditioned experiences. And, as already noted, few experiences are more basic to the human condition than migration. Significantly, migration and exile form bookends (of sorts) to the biblical record: the earliest chapters record the expulsion of Adam and Eve from the Garden of Eden (Gen 3:23), and the last book contains the magnificent vision of the apostle John, who is exiled on the island of Patmos (Rev 1:9).

The Old Testament: Light to the Nations

Andrew Walls rightly suggests that the book of Genesis might well have been named the book of "migrations."[5] The expulsion of Adam and Eve from the Garden—the first recorded migration—sets in motion further consequential migration events linked to human need and divine action. Cain is condemned to be "a fugitive and a wanderer on the earth" (Gen 4:12);[6] and a major ecological disaster imposes refugee status on Noah, along with his family and any number of living creatures. This ordeal ends with the divine proclamation "be fruitful and multiply, and fill the earth" (Gen 9:1), a "global" mandate that forms the background of the "tower of Babel" episode (Genesis 11). The latter event, so evocative of divine intervention in history, highlights the actions of a specific group of migrants who settle in Babylon (11:2). It also furnishes a compelling interpretative framework for global migration: "from there the Lord scattered them abroad over the face of all the earth" (11:9). Here too we encounter, through a subtle rhetorical usage, not a fearful and insecure deity who regards humans as a threat but a God so elevated and exalted that he must *descend* to catch sight of efforts that, from a human standpoint, represent a pinnacle of accomplishment.

---

3. See Donald Senior and Carroll Stuhlmueller, *The Biblical Foundations for Mission* (Maryknoll, NY: Orbis Books, 1983), 20.

4. Robert P. Carroll, "Exile! What Exile? Deportation and the Discourses of Diaspora," in *Leading Captivity Captive: "The Exile" as History and Ideology*, ed. L. Grabbe (Sheffield: Sheffield Academic Press, 1998), 63, 64.

5. Walls, "Mission and Migration," 3.

6. All quotations from the Bible, except where stated, are from the New Revised Standard Version.

"Let Us Make a Name for Ourselves"

The migration motif is prominent in the Babel incident, and from one perspective it appears to extend the theme of exile and banishment as divine punishment for human sinfulness. However, it is possible to see this story not as a further act of divine retribution but rather as denoting a divine act of liberation. *Babel* (from Assyrian, meaning "gate of the gods"), argue some non-Western scholars, is a symbolic reference to imperial arrogance and efforts at universal domination.[7] Thus, the story portrays efforts by the powerful to build economic or political towers of Babel that "perpetuate the unjust economic order of the world and control the destiny of humanity."[8] José Míguez-Bonino suggests that God's action not only thwarts the "project of false unity of domination" but also liberates "the nations that possess their own places, languages, and families."[9] In other words, "the act of defeating the 'imperial project' is at the same time an act of deliverance: the peoples can return to their own nation, place, and language!"

We should bear in mind that the dispersion and multiplication of the races is already described in the previous passage (Genesis 10). This sequencing is significant. The "tower of Babel" signifies *anti-migration*. A central aim in the building project is to forestall further movement: "otherwise we shall be scattered abroad upon the face of the whole earth" (Gen 11:4). The Babel project stands in opposition to the diasporic scattering of the nations and peoples in a way that allows them to experience the God of Heaven through a multiplicity of contexts and a diversity of cultural experiences. As the Apostle Paul declared centuries later, "from one ancestor he made all nations to inhabit the whole earth, and he allotted the times of their existence and the boundaries of the places where they would live [i.e., cultural environment], so that they would search for God" (Acts 17:26-27). Cultural diversity is a strongly biblical idea; the notion of a single global culture is not.

This is not the place to tackle the complex idea of "culture," except to recognize that it reflects the specific biological, environmental, and historical realities that distinguish human societies. It is within the particularity of culture that human ideas, human genius, and human creativity find their fullest expression. It is also within the particularity of cultural existence that the God of Heaven is revealed and encountered.

All human cultures are, of course, deformed by human sinfulness and are in need of redemption; but no culture or cultural system has a greater capacity than any other for facilitating response to, or experience of, the divine. From a Christian perspective, it is not necessary to abandon one's culture (or switch cultural traditions) in order to experience salvation through Jesus Christ. God has no favorite culture! As the prophet Amos reminded the people of Israel, they were

---

7. José Míguez-Bonino, "Genesis 11:1-9: A Latin-American Perspective," in *Return to Babel: Global Perspectives on the Bible*, ed. John R. Levison and Priscilla Pope-Levison (Louisville: Westminster John Knox, 1999), 15.

8. Choan-Seng Song, "Genesis 11:1-9: An Asian Perspective," in *Return to Babel: Global Perspectives on the Bible*, ed. John R. Levison and Priscilla Pope-Levison (Louisville: Westminster John Knox, 1999), 31f.

9. Míguez-Bonino, "Genesis 11:1-9," 15.

no dearer to God than the Africans (Amos 9:7). So integral is cultural specific-
ity to God's plan of universal salvation that it endures until the end of the ages
when "a great multitude . . . , from every nation, from all tribes and peoples and
languages, [stand] before the throne and before the Lamb" (Rev 7:9).

Babel, in essence, is a metaphor for cultural absolutism. It stands for monolithic human social projects that perpetuate a singular experience and attempt to
impose the name and language (or culture) of one group on all others. It exemplifies the secular ideal: idolatry of human achievement ("let us build"), the quest
for immortality ("a name"), and hegemonic advancement of one cultural group
("one language") at the expense of messy, cacophonic, cultural diversity—see
chapter 3.

The declaration, "let us build . . . a tower with its top to the heavens, and let us
make a name for ourselves" (Gen 11:4), also represents *the antithesis* of mission and
redemption. The biblical concept of "mission"—which basically denotes actions
and events (not always self-evident) related to God's plan of salvation—implies
movement, sending, boundary crossing, and *translation*. It originates in divine initiative: the acts of self-disclosure, self-revelation, and ultimately the self-emptying
of the incarnation whereby God is made manifest and encountered within specific
cultural contexts. Insofar as it involves human agency, mission inevitably requires
cross-cultural movement, or the crossing of boundaries, in which the primary
experience is of vulnerability and risk, a readiness to live on another's terms—features typified by migration and resettlement. Structures of domination and violent
subjugation may facilitate mission up to a point; but they ultimately epitomize the
spirit of Babel. They are emblematic of the finality, reliance on human structures,
triumphalism, and false sense of security that imperil the continuing experience of
God's power and salvation available to all humanity.

"Go to the Land That I Will Show You"

Throughout the Old Testament, God's salvific intentions and designs repeatedly
unfold within the trauma and travail of displacement, uprootedness, and migration.
Much of this has to do with the recurrence of violent conflicts and brutal warfare,
which, then as now, triggered uprootedness, refugee movement, and widespread
displacement of peoples. At the same time, recipients of the divine commission and
favor were for the most part individuals and communities in whose lives migration or displacement, and the experience of being aliens in a foreign land, fea-
tured prominently. Undeniably, migration and displacement exposed these biblical
migrants to alien influences and myriad possibilities of spiritual contamination,
even apostasy (cf. Gen 35:2-4; Deut 12:29-32). Yet, in richly textured detail, the
lives of many Old Testament figures make it plain that the disempowerment and
vulnerability intrinsic to the migrant experience often stimulate religious quest and
provide the subtext for spiritual transformation, in part because they afford heightened receptivity to new revelations of the divine. In other words, while migration
generally bespeaks dislocation and travail, it often also portends fresh hope and
aspirations, new possibilities and opportunities.

The Old Testament patriarchs (and matriarchs) were frequently migrants (Gen 12:1-4, 10-16; 26:3; 28:10-15; 26:1). Abraham, the prototypical migrant, models the profound integration of mobility, spiritual pilgrimage, and the unfolding of divine purposes. It is difficult to imagine how the biblical drama would have unfolded if Abraham had refused to move when God told him to do so—on two separate occasions (Acts 7:2; Gen 12:1). In response to the first divine call (though the Genesis passage seems to indicate that the decision to move to Canaan was made by his father, Terah, not Abraham), Abraham left the city of Ur in his native country of Chaldea (Mesopotamia), and after traveling some three hundred miles north, his family settled in Haran, a celebrated city in western Asia.[10] The second call proved far more consequential. In response to the divine summons, Abraham left the rather settled existence of a city dweller (first in Ur, later in Haran) to embark on a migratory tent-dwelling existence, taking with him a large household of several hundred souls. This archetypal migrant is proclaimed a model of faith because he "went, even though he did not know where he was going . . . , [and] made his home in the promised land like a stranger in a foreign country" (Heb 11:8 NIV).

It is the life of migration and movement that defines Abraham's religious life and legacy. Walls notes that "it is as a nomadic pastoralist that he experiences those divine encounters that become the basis of Israel's religion"; that "maybe he could never have heard the voice of the God of Heaven so clearly in Ur or in Haran [where] the noisy presence of the gods of the land would have obtruded too much."[11] In the course of that religious pilgrimage, a lifetime of wanderings, the earlier promises are repeated and enlarged. Abraham stumbled more than once (spiritually speaking), but in his life migration and movement emerge as metaphors of faith and obedient trust. It is in this regard that he is "the father [ancestor] of all of us" who also believe (Rom 4:16). It is also as a migrant that Abraham, called "the friend of God" (Jas 2:23), made such a wide and deep impression on the ancient world that references to his life "are interwoven in the religious traditions of almost all Eastern nations."[12]

Abraham's experience was not isolated. The migrant theme remains strong in the lives of the other patriarchs. The "forced" migration of Joseph not only translates into a personal spiritual odyssey but also sets the stage for the emergence of the Hebrews as a captive people whose exodus and subsequent wanderings became an archetypal biblical metaphor of God's people as a mobile community of faith guided by God's promises. Nor did settlement in the promised land nullify the intimate association between chosenness and the experience of being aliens and refugees, pilgrims and sojourners. As the story of Ruth indicates, migration and displacement remained very much a part of normal existence. Moreover, the nation of Israel was repeatedly enjoined to deal justly with the aliens and the dispossessed among them, not only in remembrance of their experience as slaves in

---

10. M. G. Easton, *Baker's Illustrated Bible Dictionary* (Grand Rapids: Baker Book House, 1981), 319.

11. Walls, "Mission and Migration," 3.

12. Easton, *Baker's Illustrated Bible Dictionary*, 13.

Egypt (Deut 24:17) but also as a witness to their calling as a people of God (Deut 27:19; Jer 22:3; Ezek 22:7).

Even so, worse acts of spiritual delinquency and apostasy in the life of the nation of Israel appear once they are settled in the promised land. Little wonder that both Israel's prophets and its people repeatedly looked back on the period of migration and unsettledness in their nation's life as a time of religious fervor and commitment (Hos 2:14-15)—though such recollections were rather selective. In any case, migration and dispossession became etched in the collective memory of the Israelites as emblematic of God's covenant faithfulness and redemptive promise. This much is indicated by the liturgical pronouncement enjoined on each Israelite in the ritual of sacrifice: *"a wandering Aramean was my ancestor"* (Deut 26:4-5).[13] In the event, the consolidation of Israelite settlement under a monarchy—an unstable unity vulnerable as much to external aggression as internal dissension—proved relatively short-lived and ended in mass deportation, captivity, and exile.

By the Rivers of Babylon

No other episode in the Old Testament Scriptures has been the focus of more scholarly attention and debate than the Babylonian exile of the Jewish people (from 605 to 539 B.C.E.). This tragic event involved death, destruction, and widespread disorder. But worse, far worse, than the carnage and devastation involved in the series of mass deportations instigated by Babylonian conquest under King Nebuchadnezzar was the searing spiritual, theological, and psychological impact of captivity.[14] What of the promise of an eternal dynasty to David? What of the promise of land as Israel's inheritance? The Sinai covenant had been broken, but was it fair to visit the sins of the fathers on the children? Were exile and captivity Yahweh's punishment for Israel's unfaithfulness or a consequence related to the abandonment of the local deities (under King Josiah's reforms)? By any reckoning, the destruction of Jerusalem and the Babylonian exile constituted an unmitigated catastrophe of earth-shattering proportions. The very core of Israel's historic faith was dealt a colossal blow. Mass apostasy loomed.

The exact numbers involved in the deportations are impossible to determine, partly because of conflicting biblical figures (2 Kgs 24:14, 16; Jer 52:28). Scholarly estimates range from twenty thousand to as high as eighty thousand.[15] The destruction of the nation also produced a massive tide of refugees, some of whom found their way to Egypt and other lands. The Babylonian exiles found themselves in the heart of a superpower, in cities festooned with great displays of affluence, where also pagan gods were worshiped in magnificent temples. They were selected for deportation because they were the cream of the crop—representatives of Israel's political, religious, and intellectual leadership. Nonetheless, they were alien cap-

---

13. See John Bright, *A History of Israel* (Louisville: Westminster John Knox, 2000), 90-92.

14. See Ralph W. Klein, *Israel in Exile: A Theological Interpretation,* Overtures to Biblical Theology (Philadelphia: Fortress, 1979), 1-8; Bright, *History of Israel,* 331-39, 347-50.

15. Daniel L. Smith, *The Religion of the Landless: The Social Context of the Babylonian Exile* (Bloomington, IN: Meyer-Stone Books, 1989), 31f.

tives from a provincial and relatively backward nation whose existence and religious life had been wrecked by Nebuchadnezzar's battering rams. As captives they
experienced "pain and turmoil and the hard service" (Isa 14:6), but in time they
were allowed to lead moderately normal lives and form a community (Jer 29:5-7;
Ezek 8:1; 33:30). The pressures to completely assimilate, to abandon the old religion
in favor of the more cosmopolitan Babylonian cults, and to exploit new economic
opportunities, must have been immense. The story of Daniel affords us a glimpse
of the nature of the challenge: the intensive assimilation program involving change
of name, wholesale reeducation, and a new diet (Dan 1:3-8).

The record is sketchy; but, as would be expected, huge numbers of Jews
accommodated themselves to life in Babylon at the expense of their religious or
cultural heritage. Yet the experience of displacement and exile also produced a
new community of faith committed to cultural preservation and determined to
retain religious identity; a resolve that expressed itself in both in the pain of nos-
talgic longing and theological hatred toward the oppressor (Psalm 137). In exile,
religious faith (or covenant relationship with Yahweh) had to be more deliberately
explored and explicitly expressed because the visible structures and symbols of
that faith where no longer available. The experience of migration also produced
new theological questions and demanded new religious explanations. This exilic
faith community emphasized Sabbath observance and circumcision (which the
Babylonians did not practice) as marks of distinctiveness.[16] Among them, the
voices of the prophets Jeremiah and Ezekiel provided a rationale for the tragedy
of exile and sowed seeds of hope for a new future. The natural craving for public
worship and the basic need for religious assembly to listen to the ministry of the
prophets and receive religious instruction, also increased the significance of the
synagogue—an institution of unknown origins.[17]

As foreigners in a distant land, the Jewish exiles also became more keenly
aware of world events, and they were forced to re-examine their faith in Yahweh
in the light of wider historical developments and the fortunes of other nations.
Out of the ashes of the old national cult emerged a broadened theological vision
in which Yahweh was recast as the God of history and the God of all nations.
In effect, the experience of exile made it necessary to translate the faith from
the parochial nationalistic claims of a tribal religion into a universal framework.
This task of adaptation and translation was superbly undertaken by the prophet
generally known as Second Isaiah (see Isaiah 40-43). The universal relevance
of Israel's chosenness or covenant relationship with Yahweh was dramatically
proclaimed through forthright reminders that the God of Israel is the Creator and
Lord of the whole world:

> Why do you say, O Jacob,
>   and speak, O Israel,
> "My way is hidden from the Lord,

---

16. Bright, *History of Israel*, 349; Smith, *Religion of the Landless*, 36.

17. Bright, *History of Israel*, 436-37. In time, the dispersion of Jews to "every nation under
heaven" (Acts 2:5) led to the proliferation of synagogues, which outlived the temple and became the
most enduring institution for regular worship in Judaism.

and my right is disregarded by my God"?
Have you not known? Have you not heard?
The Lord is the everlasting God,
    the Creator of the ends of the earth.
                                        (Isa 40:27-28)

Look to Abraham your father
    and to Sarah who bore you:
for he was but one when I called him,
    but I blessed him and made him many. . . .
I will bring near my deliverance swiftly,
    my salvation has gone out
    and my arms will rule the peoples;
the coastlands wait for me,
    and for my arm they hope.
                                        (Isa 51:2, 5)

As the books of Daniel and Esther demonstrate, enforced mobility and exile necessitated missionary encounters (cf. Dan 2:26-30; Esth 2:5-11; 8:11-17). In the book of Jonah in particular, the universal implications of Israel's faith are portrayed quite vividly. In the crucible of exile, non-Israelites or Gentiles were affirmed as having a place among God's people. God's universal plan of salvation was now boldly proclaimed (Isa 56:4, 6-7). As part of the reformulation of its belief system, the exilic community came to understand that Yahweh "will gather others to them besides those already gathered" (Isa 56:8). In essence, exile and displacement prompted missionary consciousness: "You are my witnesses, says the Lord" (Isa 43:10). The narrowly nationalistic interpretations of religion did not disappear, nor did the experience of exile produce consistent missionary endeavor in a modern sense.[18] But the connection between Israel's election and universal mission was established; presence among foreign nations served a missionary purpose. Israel's fortunes were tied to the history of the nations.[19]

Strikingly also, it is in this context of exile and displacement, a situation in which God's people are compelled to openly reckon with the universal (or international) dimensions of their covenant relationship with Yahweh, that Yahweh's plan for the salvation of the world unfolds. And it does so through the most profound, provocative, and poignant imagery of the Old Testament: the image of the "Suffering Servant" (Isa 49:1-6; 52:13-53:12), an instrument of Yahweh who will be "a light to the nations" (42:6), bear the sins of humanity (53:6, 12), and pour himself out to death (53:12). The endless debate about this enigmatic figure need not detain us here. Insofar as it points to the life and death of Jesus Christ, it clearly identifies God's universal salvation not with dominance, aggression, or conquest of the nations but with vulnerability, powerlessness, and even openness to rejection (53:2). To the foreign exiles surrounded by symbols of global power

---

18. Ibid., 359, 443, 445f.

19. Johannes Verkuyl, *Contemporary Missiology: An Introduction* (Grand Rapids: Eerdmans, 1978), 91.

and faced with taunts about the defeat of their God, this message no doubt had an even more immediate resonance. God's mission and redemptive purpose advance even in the situation of defeat, humiliation, and weakness that is intrinsic to the experience of migration and exile.

Back in Palestine a sizable population remained. Again, the numbers are unknown; though it is suggested that this Jerusalem remnant was numerically greater than the deportees. Their lot was miserable and desperate. The temple lay in blackened ruins, famine threatened their survival, and the sense of desolation inflicted on their hearts and souls by the catastrophic destruction of their nation was indelible (Lamentations 5). There were no doubt faithful worshipers among them, but the spiritual crisis caused by the eradication of the long-standing symbols and institutions of faith was all-pervasive. All rituals and sacrifices associated with the worship of Yahweh ceased;[20] only corrupted versions of the old faith remained. This Jerusalem remnant, too, mourned over the fate that had befallen their nation and longed for its restoration. But it settled into a precarious existence, barely sustained by fading memories of yesteryears. Settledness, such as it was, bred religious decay. William M. Ramsay puts it quite elegantly: "The Jew in his own land was rigidly conservative; but the Jew abroad has always been the most facile and ingenious of people."[21]

The rest of the story is well known. The faith of Israel survived and reemerged in a renewed and more vigorous form not among the settled Palestinian population but in the exilic community; the deportees who had endured the trauma of displacement refashioned their religious identity. The future of Israel lay not with the settled homeland population, the Jerusalem remnant, but with the migrants and exiles. The Jerusalem inhabitants were convinced that the exiles had "gone far from the Lord," that "to us this land is given for a possession" (Ezek 11:15). But they were grievously mistaken. The foreign exiles emerged as "the true remnant," favored by Yahweh (Jer 24:4-7).[22] Though few in number, writes John Bright, these exiles "were the ones who would shape Israel's future, both giving to her faith its new direction and providing the impulse for the ultimate restoration of the Jewish community in Palestine."[23]

Postexilic return and restoration saw the reestablishment of a Jewish cultic society in the homeland. Judaism emerged as a coherent faith community: its worship centered on the rebuilt temple; its way of life was marked by heavy emphasis on observance of the law. With the gradual formation of a canon of Scripture comprising the Book of the Law and the other books of the Old Testament, the office of the prophet went into permanent eclipse. Entirely surrounded by Gentile nations, and fearful of losing its distinctive character, Judaism tended to be exclusivist, inward looking, and hostile to foreigners. But the new impulse produced by the reinterpretation of the faith during exile did not die; the new sense of world mission existed in tension with the old particularistic ethos. There

---

20. See Smith, *Religion of the Landless*, 32-35.
21. William M. Ramsay, *St. Paul: The Traveler and Roman Citizen* (1898; rev. ed.; Grand Rapids: Kregel, 2001), 37.
22. Senior and Stuhlmueller, *Biblical Foundations for Mission*, 27f.
23. Bright, *History of Israel*, 345.

were those, notes Bright (2000: 445), "who felt an obligation to win Gentiles to the faith and who chafed at the narrowness of their brethren and their failure to take their mission to the world seriously." Once again, the migrant factor proved crucial; for "missionary activity was encouraged and furthered by the large number of Jews already living abroad in the diaspora."[24] Particularly noteworthy were the Pharisees, a new religious lay group committed to winning converts to Judaism. Out of these migrant communities of the diaspora would emerge Paul of Tarsus, the great apostle to the Gentiles.

The New Testament: Into All the World

One can be forgiven for thinking that during his ministry Jesus not only lived his life as a strict Jew but also focused his attention primarily on the Jewish community. The case might even be made that he went so far as to reject ministry among Gentiles. Before healing the Canaanite woman, Jesus informs her that he was "sent only to the lost sheep of Israel" (Matt 15:24); he instructs his disciples on one occasion to "go nowhere among the Gentiles" (Matt 10:5); and he appears to criticize the conversion efforts of the Pharisees (Matt 23:15). From this perspective, it is only after his resurrection that explicit statements related to a global mission appear. But closer examination reveals that Jesus' ministry exemplified critical elements that challenged and undermined the exclusivist and self-serving understanding of God's people and God's purpose that characterized Judaism.[25] The summary of Jesus' life and ministry provided by the Gospel writers contains a sometimes subtle but ever-present dynamic of boundary-crossing engagement with those on the margins of society, reinterpretations (or translation) of Scriptures that emphasized God's will for all humanity, a radical enlargement of the concepts of God's people and God's reign, and an interface between movement and mission epitomized by Jesus' alienation from his own family, village, and community (Mark 6:4-5; John 7:5).

"I Haven't Seen Faith Like This in All Israel!"[26]

No sooner was he born than the infant Jesus was caught up in refugee movement, as his parents fled to Egypt from Bethlehem to escape state-sanctioned infanticide. When the family returned to Palestine, they settled "in a town called Nazareth" in lower Galilee. So Jesus began his ministry not in Jerusalem, the celebrated religious center of the Jewish faith, but among the diaspora communities. Nazareth was an obscure agricultural village, "so insignificant to the religious life of Judaism that the Hebrew bible never mentions it";[27] and modern

---

24. Senior and Stuhlmueller, *Biblical Foundations for Mission*, 30.

25. For a thorough examination of the link between Jesus' ministry and the universal missionary consciousness of the early church, see Senior and Stuhlmueller, *The Biblical Foundations for Mission,* 141-60.

26. Matthew 8:10, New Living Translation.

27. Miguel A. De La Torre, *Reading the Bible from the Margins* (Maryknoll, NY: Orbis Books, 2002), 110.

scholarship continues to debate its actual existence. In any case, Jesus lived most of his life in Galilee, a region that had formed the northern part of the kingdom of Israel. From the eighth to the second century B.C.E., Galilee was successively controlled by the Assyrians, the Babylonians, the Persians, and the Seleucids; so for centuries the region was dominated by foreign (non-Jewish) influences and exposed to constant migrant movement. The prophet Isaiah described it as "Galilee of the nations" (Isa 9:1). In Jesus' day, in fact, Galilee was populated by migrants and the dispossessed and "an abundance of orphans, widows, poor, and unemployed."[28] The enduring impact of foreign influences on the region was such that Galileans could be recognized by their distinctive accent (Matt 26:73).

In sum, Jesus called his disciples and conducted most of his ministry in a context characterized by the incessant movement of merchants, traders, and migrants. Many of Jesus' parables and teachings reflect this atmosphere of constant mobility—the never-ending intrusion of journeys, the hustle and bustle of incessant social interaction and daily transactions: there was the man "going down from Jerusalem to Jericho" who was left half dead by robbers and was helped by a traveling Samaritan (Luke 10:25-37); the "merchant in search of fine pearls" (Matt 13:45); the man who, "going on a journey, summoned his slaves and entrusted his property to them" (Matt 25:14); the younger son who "gathered all he had and traveled to a distant country" (Luke 15:13). Jesus' ministry is also portrayed as repeatedly breaking through the self-imposed boundaries of Judaism. He is shown "provocatively associating with those members of Jewish society considered outside the law and, therefore, excluded from participation in the religious and social community of Israel."[29] These included tax collectors (Mark 2:15-17); the despised Samaritan (Luke 17:11-19); and women (John 4).

In Galilee there were many more Gentiles than Jews, so it is reasonable to assume that the "large crowds" often said to be traveling with or following Jesus included Gentiles (Matt 4:25; Mark 3:7; Luke 14:25; John 12:20-21). In the event, contact with Gentiles was inevitable; even if the recorded encounters are relatively few, and the Gentiles "always approach Jesus; never the reverse."[30] Those encounters, however, typically elicited a positive response and often produced unexpected outcomes or declarations. The Gospels record Gentile–Jewish comparisons (in favor of the former) that surely left Jesus' Jewish audience flabbergasted: a Roman centurion, a foreigner, is praised for possessing faith that surpassed that of any Israelite (Matt 8:10); Gentile towns (Sodom, Tyre, and Sidon) are favorably compared to Jewish cities that Jesus roundly condemns for rejecting his ministry (Matt 11:20-24); the Queen of Sheba (possibly from modern-day Ethiopia) and the Assyrian city of Nineveh are also upheld as exemplars of responsiveness to the God of Abraham (Luke 11:31, 32).

These examples hint at Jesus' strong awareness of Galilee's teeming Gentile population. The same is true of his radical reappraisal of Israel's privileged

---

28. Norberto Saracco, "The Liberating Options of Jesus," in *Sharing Jesus in the Two Thirds World*, ed. Vinay Samuel and Chris Sugden (Grand Rapids: Eerdmans, 1984), 34.

29. Senior and Stuhlmueller, *Biblical Foundations for Mission*, 147.

30. Ibid., 142.

or "elect" status whereby he repeatedly affirmed that God's plan of salvation embraces all peoples. In one instance, when he is sought out by Greek delegates, Jesus declares, "and I, when I am lifted up from the earth, will draw all people to myself" (John 12:32). On another occasion, he pronounced, even more pointedly, that while Jews will be thrown out of the kingdom of God, "people will come from east and west, from north and south, and will eat in the kingdom of God" (Luke 13:29). Here, too, we must note that in a context marked by religious plurality and diversity of cultures, Jesus' message and ministry do not validate any particular cultural system. It is the person of Jesus that becomes the basis for salvation for all, on the same terms, regardless of cultural background, religious heritage, or racial distinction (John 14:6).

All this is to suggest that Jesus' life and ministry embodied the interconnection of mission, boundary-crossing movement, and the alienation of exile and migration. The incarnation itself should be considered a veritable act of migration or relocation. The emptying of status to take on the form of a servant (Phil 2:7) has clear parallels in the experience of migration and displacement, which typically involves the diminishing of self. The same equally applies to the abandonment of one domain of existence to start life in an entirely different context where the experience of being "one with" (John 1:14) but also "not of" (Matt 8:27; Luke 8:37) is attended by alienation and hostility. How the God of the universe, by taking on human form (Phil 2:7), went into voluntary exile, confounds human comprehension. But we are afforded a glimpse of the extreme alienation involved in this agonizing cry: "'My God, my God, why have you forsaken me?'" (Mark 15:34).

The intimate link between mission and migration is also echoed in the fact that the long-awaited Messiah emerged in "a region where the unclean Gentiles outnumbered the Jews."[31] In that sense, Jesus' ministry models the migration–mission correlation. Moreover, the Gospels leave no doubt that Jesus' life experiences included the travail of a refugee, the pain of uprootedness, the hostility that greets the unwelcome stranger, and the isolation of homelessness. In Jesus' own words, "foxes have holes, and birds of the air have nests; but the Son of Man has nowhere to lay his head" (Luke 9:58). This personal odyssey ultimately led to the cross and an empty tomb. The migrant model portrayed in Jesus' ministry powerfully illustrates the emphasis on weakness and nondominance of the *missio dei*. Nothing could be further removed from the triumphalist and aggressive model of mission so prominent in the last millennium.

No Longer Strangers and Aliens in the Household of God[32]

The prominence of migration and exile in shaping religious development and missionary purpose in the Old Testament narrative foreshadowed the reality of the church as God's pilgrim people among the nations. This is to say that in the New Testament the intersection of migration and mission is further extended and capsulated in the establishment of the church, the new Israel, which, not

---

31. De La Torre, *Reading the Bible*, 31.
32. Ephesians 2:19.

unlike the old, comprised "aliens and strangers" (1 Pet 2:11 NIV). Soon after its inception, the Christian faith developed a missionary vitality and vision that was unparalleled in its dynamism and reach. Within a decade agitated detractors complained that its adherents "have caused trouble all over the world" (Acts 17:6 NIV). This hyperbolic testimonial masks the considerable reluctance of the early Jewish believers to move beyond Jerusalem or outside the Jewish orbit. But it also indicates the extraordinary mobility and social impact of the new Christian community. In this new dispensation, in fact, the link between migration and mission is utterly conspicuous and proves to be decisive for the survival of the Christian faith.

In the period immediately following Christ's bodily resurrection and ascension into heaven, the new (Jewish) believers formed themselves into a new community and confined themselves to Jerusalem. The Pentecost event, at which "devout Jews from every nation under heaven" heard God's deeds of power proclaimed in their native languages (Acts 2:4-11), pointed to a new dispensation, but Jesus' explicit command to "go into all the world and proclaim the good news to the whole creation" (Mark 16:15) was largely disregarded. This state of affairs changed abruptly when Stephen's bold and public testimony that Jesus of Nazareth was the Messiah led to his death and vigorous persecution of the primitive church (Acts 7 and 8). Persecution produced dispersion and migration. This dispersion no doubt radiated in all directions, but the biblical record focuses on the migrant movement to the north and west: to Phoenicia, Cyprus, and Antioch (Acts 11:19).[33] It is also clear that the efforts of itinerant missionaries led to the establishment of new Christian congregations in various towns throughout the regions of Judea, Galilee, and Samaria (Acts 8; 9:31; 10:1-48). But the unplanned migration movement stimulated by persecution produced momentous developments that radically altered the life of the church and decided the future of the faith; even if this was not immediately evident.

As noted above, the new faith was centered in Palestine and adherents were mostly Jews. In expression and experience, it was profoundly shaped by Jewish ideas, Jewish traditions, and Jewish institutions. The new congregations of believers met in synagogues established in Palestine and Jewish diaspora communities. There were notable Gentile converts like Cornelius, the Roman centurion and "God-fearing" proselyte (Acts 10:22, 34-48), but the movement remained a solidly Jewish phenomenon. In fact, there were powerful elements within the new faith who maintained that non-Jewish converts must be subject to the entire Jewish law and regulations in order to be accepted into the new faith (Acts 11:2-3). They became known as "the circumcision faction" (Gal 2:12). Once again, confinement to a fixed cultural center and immobilization within a particular cultural tradition imperiled rather than facilitated universal designs. Migration changed all that.

Among the believers dispersed in the wake of Stephen's martyrdom were unnamed Jews from Cyprus and Cyrene (present-day Libya). Having grown up in Greek lands, these migrant refugees "had a wider outlook on the world than

---

33. See Ramsay, *St. Paul*, 298.

Palestinian Jews,"[34] and when they got to Antioch they took an unusual step. Unlike other migrant Jewish believers, who "spoke the word to no one except Jews," the Cypriot and Cyrenaic Jews made a point of preaching the gospel to Hellenists or Greeks who joined the new congregation in Antioch (Acts 11:19-21). The act of migration unleashed missionary purpose and galvanized cross-cultural expansion.

This cross-cultural breakthrough also necessitated translation and adaptation of the faith. Up to this point, the message of the gospel had been proclaimed in exclusively Jewish concepts—Jesus was presented as the Messiah, the Savior of Israel[35]—that made no sense to Hellenistic pagans. In a radical move, the Cypriot and Cyrenaic believers appropriated a title from the Hellenist religious world. They proclaimed "the Lord Jesus" (Acts 11:20), "Lord" being a well-known title for Hellenistic cult divinities. As Walls (1996) explains, "it is doubtful whether unacculturated pagans in the Antiochene world could have understood the significance of Jesus in any other way [since] none of us can take in a new idea except in terms of the ideas we already have." The Hellenistic element in this new assembly was conspicuous enough to attract public attention and local gossip, especially since, as we must suppose, the new Greek believers now began to explain their newfound faith to their pagan neighbors. Since they frequently mentioned "Christ," popular society called the new believers "Christians" (Acts 11:26). Migration had precipitated cross-cultural mission and a vital act of translation that opened a vast new world of religious expansion. The future of the Christian faith lay not in the enclosed Jewish world centered in Jerusalem but in the world of the diaspora, the world of the Hellenists.

Meanwhile, the inclusion into the Christian movement of Gentiles who had no previous association with Judaism generated considerable controversy and long-term divisions within the church. The central body in Jerusalem, which maintained oversight of the primitive church—in much the same way that the Jewish rulers in Jerusalem exercised religious jurisdiction over diaspora Jews (cf. Acts 9:1-2; 22:5)—ruled after much debate that Gentile converts need not conform to the strict laws of Judaism in order to be accepted as followers of Christ (Acts 15:22-29). The regulatory codes urged on Gentile Christians—abstinence from sacrificial meat offered to idols, from blood, from what is strangled and from fornication—reflected instructions that had long governed foreigners who lived in Israel, and these regulations were imposed in the interest of meaningful fellowship. Circumcision, the definitive hallmark of Jewish birth and identity, was ruled a nonrequirement.

In Christ, therefore, cultural barriers to full experience of God are dissolved. Gentiles, once considered "aliens from the commonwealth of Israel, and strangers to the covenants of promise" (Eph 2:12), now have complete access to the full revelation of God. To claim membership in "the household of God, built upon the foundation of the apostles and prophets" (Eph 2:19-20), Gentiles do not have to become Jews or fulfill Jewish cultural requirements. Christ did not come into

---

34. Ibid., 50.
35. Walls, *Missionary Movement*, 34.

the world to abolish any cultural tradition, whether Jewish or Gentile. What was abolished by his sacrificial death was the "the law with its commandments and ordinances" (Eph 2:15) which had created a "dividing wall" of hostility between elect and nonelect. To understand the message of the gospel and experience salvation in Christ, non-Jews can make full use of the roadmaps within their own religious experience and culture, for Christ embraces all of humanity. In himself, however, Christ created "one new humanity" in which cultural divisions are reconciled (Eph 2:15).

The Jerusalem resolution recorded in Acts 15, therefore, signaled the fulfillment of a centuries-old divine promise: "my house shall be called a house of prayer for all peoples (Isa 56:7). Yet the church, the new household of faith, retains an intrinsic migrant identity; for the new humanity created in Christ remains *aliens and strangers in the world* (1 Pet 2:11 NIV).

Salvation to the Ends of the Earth[36]

The Antioch episode marked the beginning of the Gentile mission, but the man whose missionary passion and commitment made him *the* apostle to the Gentiles, who also became the greatest champion of a universal Christian mission, was Saul of Tarsus (later Paul the apostle). The basic outline of Paul's spiritual journey is well known: his strict Jewish upbringing and rigorous religious training (Acts 23:6; Phil 3:5); his rabid persecution of Jewish Christians; his role in Stephen's brutal death, which indicates that "he was already a person of influence in Jerusalem, marked out as a leader by his intense and devouring enthusiasm, especially where something exceptional or dangerous had to be done";[37] his dramatic conversion experience on the Damascus Road during a 130-mile journey in pursuit of Jewish adherents of the new faith; his summoning by Barnabas to Antioch to help supervise the growing Gentile congregations there; his struggle for Gentile rights, expansive religious vision, and tireless efforts to preach the gospel of Christ throughout the Greco-Roman world, based on the unshakable conviction that "everyone who calls on the name of the Lord shall be saved" (Rom 10:13).

It is frequently acknowledged that Paul was uniquely prepared to be "a minister of Christ Jesus to the Gentiles" (Rom 15:16). A "Hebrew born of Hebrews" (Phil 3:5), but also a Roman citizen born in the city of Tarsus, "a center of extensive commercial traffic with many countries along the shores of the Mediterranean, as well as with the countries of central Asia Minor,"[38] Paul was a transnational. He had dual nationality, the pervasiveness of Hellenistic culture notwithstanding, and he inhabited two worlds or cultures (Jewish and Hellenist). He received the best Hellenistic education—Tarsus was a highly regarded learning center associated with a famous university—as well as the most intensive religious training available within Judaism. His upbringing in a city where daily life reflected the

---

36. Acts 13:47.
37. Ramsay, *St. Paul*, 42.
38. Easton, *Baker's Illustrated Bible Dictionary*, 537.

confluence of diverse cultures and transnational movement no doubt contributed to his cosmopolitan understanding of the world.

As a diaspora Jew, also, he was freed from the suffocating parochialism of the Jewish culture in Jerusalem, while yet an expert on the law, a pinnacle of religious education. His intimate familiarity with the pagan Hellenistic world (including its intellectual tradition) combined with firsthand knowledge of the Jewish tradition. This explains his unique ability to translate God's promise to Abraham, now fulfilled in Christ (Acts 13:32), into a conceptual framework that could be grasped by Gentiles. As Ramsay surmises,

> he had been trained to a far wider outlook on the world than the people of Jerusalem could attain to. He knew the pagan world from inside, its needs, its desires, its religious longings, its weaknesses, and its crimes. He could appreciate the universality of the Savior's life and message to the world in a more complete way than any of the Palestinian Christians.[39]

Since he grew up in a strongly Pharisaic household, we must suppose that Paul's conversion to Christianity and lifelong commitment to the Gentile campaign caused bitter estrangement from his relatives—an experience perhaps hinted at in the declaration, "I regard everything as loss because of the surpassing value of knowing Christ Jesus my Lord" (Phil 3:8) or in his admonition to the church at Colossae, "fathers, do not provoke your children, or they may lose heart" (Col 3:21). Ramsay (2001) comments that the fact that Paul's nephew learned about a plot to kill him (Acts 23:16) meant that the nephew must have been among those hostile to Paul, since this was the only way he would have had free and confidential access to the group that hatched the plan. The point I wish to make is that the experience of alienation from his family and rejection by his own people (Acts 13:45, 50-51; 14:19; 17:5; 20:3; 21:27-28) adds poignancy to Paul's extraordinary career as a missionary migrant.

Paul never lost sight of Jerusalem, nor his mission disconnected from the ministry of the other apostles. But largely because of his extraordinary missionary efforts, the message of the gospel was rescued from proprietary association with any one culture. His mission theology emphasized that the gospel represents "the power of God for salvation to everyone who has faith" (both Jew and Gentile). It also indicates that the traditions and religious instincts embedded within the fabric of every culture (Rom 2:14-16; Acts 17:23-27) provide the material for translation of the gospel message, whereby the *Word* becomes flesh in each successive context. As a result, remarks Walls (1996: 25), "people separated by language, history, and culture recognize each other in Christ" without the imposition of one expression of faith on the other.

It is worth reiterating that from a biblical point of view, there is no such thing as *a Christian culture*: no single culture is ever fully aligned with the values of the kingdom of God; neither are those values hereditary. Furthermore, Christ embodied full humanity, not particular expressions of it. It is the act of incarna-

---

39. Ramsay, *St. Paul*, 45.

tion that provides the prototype for the (cross-cultural) expansion of the faith, not the specific cultural situation or experience that framed the original biblical act. All cultures penetrated by the gospel reveal aspects of God's reign and not others. It is in the sum total of those diverse experiences and expressions of the *Word made flesh* that we catch the fullest glimpse of God's full design and purpose. In effect, the translatability of the Christian faith and gospel locks diversity and unity in perennial tension: each living Christian community is a model of the whole and the whole is a reflection of the individual parts.

Migration and Mission: Any Foreign Country a Motherland

Christianity, then, is the most universal of faiths precisely because it is "the ultimate local religion."[40] That also makes it the definitive migratory religion. The migrant movement that spearheaded the Gentile mission took Christianity into a new cultural universe, quite distinct from the Jewish world in which the faith was born. Within a matter of decades, Gentile believers far outnumbered Jewish Christians and Christianity was transformed into a Gentile faith—Jesus the Messiah and Savior of Israel also became Jesus the Lord. As Walls (1996) explains, this expansion across cultural frontiers, largely facilitated by migration, allowed Christianity to survive as a separate faith; for the Jerusalem center disappeared with the destruction of the Jewish state in the holocausts of 70 and 135 C.E. This was the first of many "shifts" in Christianity's center of gravity, engendered by migration and cross-cultural expansion. Walls identifies six historical phases in which transformation by cultural diffusion gave the Christian faith continued existence, each stage investing it with new cultural attributes (reflective of translation) and each phase effectively widening its impact:[41]

1. The Jewish age, marked by *Jewish* practices and ideas
2. The Hellenistic-Roman age, marked by the idea of *orthodoxy*
3. The barbarian age, marked by the idea of a *Christian nation*
4. The western European age, marked by the primacy of the *individual*
5. The age of expanding Europe and Christian recession, marked by *cross-cultural transplantation* but also accompanied by massive recession from the faith among European peoples
6. The Southern age, featuring *extensive penetration of new cultures* in Africa, Latin America, the Pacific, and parts of Asia.

Each one of these epochal transformations is marked by extensive migration. In the centuries that immediately followed the Gentile breakthrough, the faith spread mainly through kinship and commercial networks, migrant movements (some stimulated by persecution), and other forms of mobility. As Walls explains, "migrant communities who retained ties to their home locality, while traveling

---

40. Robert, "Shifting Southward," 56.
41. Walls, *Missionary Movement*, 16-25.

from one part of the [Roman] empire to another, for trade, or work, or some other reason," were critical to the spread of Christianity within the Roman Empire.[42] A well-known description of second-century Christians captured this dimension quite distinctly: "Though they are residents at home in their own countries, their behavior there is more like that of transients; they take their full part as citizens, but they also submit to anything and everything as if they were aliens. For them, any foreign country is a motherland, and any motherland is a foreign country."[43]

The thousand years from 500 to 1500, which saw the entrenchment of Christianity as the faith of western Europe, involved turbulent Germanic migrations and "vast movements of peoples," notably in the Eurasian landmass.[44] During this period also, a vast network of trade routes by land and sea provided a vital outlet for Christian migrant movement, of traders as well as missionaries, which saw the emergence of Christian communities across the Asian landmass and in South Arabia. The end of this thousand-year period witnessed the beginning of the momentous expansion of Europeans from the heartlands of Christianity to other parts of the world, a development that laid the foundation for the most recent "shift" within global Christianity.

The rest of this book explores the hugely consequential connection between migration and mission in the history of Christian missionary expansion, starting with the age of European migrations in the sixteenth century. That story links the most remarkable of all migrations in human history with the greatest Christian missionary expansion to date. Yet this world-changing event produced far-ranging unintended consequences, including a new age of global migrations that coincides with the massive growth of Christianity in the Southern continents. These latter developments equally portend momentous changes within the new world order. The issues are complex, and detailed examination of contemporary migratory trends is integral to the story. If the biblical (and historical) record is anything to go by, contemporary migrant movement and cross-cultural expansion will be no less vital to the future of the faith than such phenomena have been in the past. Never has Christianity been more global or marked by greater cultural diversity; and not even the modern putative towers of Babel can change this reality—though not for want of trying.

---

42. Walls, "Mission and Migration," 4.

43. "Letter to Diognetus," in *Early Christian Writings: The Apostolic Fathers* (New York: Penguin Books, 1987), 144-45.

44. Kenneth Scott Latourette, *The Thousand Years of Uncertainty* (Grand Rapids: Zondervan, 1970), 3; Walls, "Mission and Migration," 5.

7

The Making of a New World Order

Empire, Migration, and Christian Mission

The conquest of the earth, which mostly means the taking it away
from those who have a different complexion or slightly flatter noses
than ourselves, is not a pretty thing when you look into it too much.
What redeems it is the idea only . . . ; and an unselfish belief in the
idea. . . .

— Joseph Conrad, *Heart of Darkness* (first published 1902)

For a period of over 450 years international migration was shaped by European
initiatives, ambitions, and priorities. The spread of European domination was
often destructive in effect if not in intent and was unmistakably bloody. Indeed,
it was made possible by extraordinary levels of organized violence—a timely
reminder that "for much of humanity in human history, the experience of globalization has been a bloody one."[1] But the outflow of people, ideas, institutions, and
skills involved was phenomenal in scale and impact. Europeans represented only
one-fifth of the world's population in 1800 (Asia accounted for 64.9 percent) and
just under a quarter in 1900 (see fig. 2).[2] Yet, by 1915, 21 percent of Europeans
resided outside Europe, and Europeans effectively occupied or settled in over a
third of the inhabited world. This migration movement was driven by a complex
array of factors: including technological innovations in oceanic travel (especially
the use of steam from 1850); the need to relieve population pressures at home
and augment white settler communities abroad; capitalist competition and the
development of market economics (by 1914 "there were over 30,000 commercial
ships plying the oceans of the world");[3] nationalist rivalries; rising expectations
about securing a better life; and Christian missionary activity.

Yet the "age of sail" began with Chinese ventures. Until the imperial edict
of 1433 ended Chinese sea-bound explorations, China was unsurpassed in ship

---

1. Held et al., *Global Transformations*, 89.
2. "World Population Growth, 1750-2150," Population Reference Bureau. See also W. M. Spellman, *The Global Community: Migration and the Making of the Modern World* (Stroud, England:
Sutton, 2002), 21, 73, 75; Böhning, "International Migration," 13.
3. Spellman, *Global Community*, 104.

construction, navigational technology, and long-distance ocean travel. Western Europeans, long dazzled by Chinese civilization but, unlike the Chinese, determined to expand their commercial reach—in part to circumvent the formidable barriers posed by Islam to Europe's south and east—duplicated and improved on the available nautical knowledge and technology. By the 1490s the tiny Iberian kingdom of Portugal, favored by the Atlantic seaboard, emerged as the principal navigating power. Other European powers followed and so began a new era of European exploration and colonial expansion, attended by massive migrations. Maritime technology and ocean travel allowed commercial activity, movements of peoples, and interaction of cultures on a scale and diversity without precedence in human history.

Figure 2
World Population Distribution by Region (1800-2050)

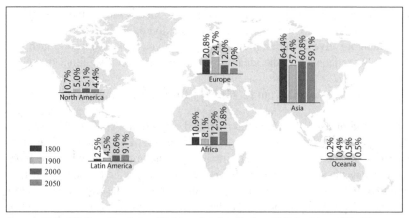

Source: United Nations Population Division, *Briefing Packet, 1998 Revision of World Population Prospects.*

This period of international migration (from 1500 to the present) is typically divided into four phases: mercantile (1500-1800), industrial (1800-1925), limited migration (1925-1960), and postindustrial (after 1960).[4] While useful in some respects, this typology is obviously Eurocentric. It also reflects a wholly economic understanding of international migration. Admittedly, European initiatives and economic interests were critical, but the movement and violent displacement of non-European peoples often dominated events and held the key to outcomes. During the so-called mercantile period (roughly 1500-1800), for instance, the most significant migrant movement that took place was the massive transcontinental transfer of Africans. In sheer numbers this movement of Afri-

---

4. See Douglas Massey, "Why Does Immigration Occur? A Theoretical Synthesis," in *The Handbook of International Migration: The American Experience* (New York: Russell Sage Foundation, 1999), 34-52.

cans exceeded that of European out-migration by about five to one.[5] Furthermore, a full grasp of the complex forces that shaped the emerging world order requires attentiveness to political dimensions, the machineries of imperial expansion, and the consequences of colonial domiance.

Admittedly, historical periodization reflects particular interpretations of history and therefore tends to be arbitrary and subjective. What is offered here is no different. To better capture both the economic and political factors and highlight non-European elements, I have revised the standard periodization as follows:

- 1500 to 1850: European expansion and the Atlantic slave trade
- 1800 to 1960: high imperialism and industrial growth
- From the 1960s: global migrations

European Colonial Expansion and African Slavery (1500 to 1850)

From the outset, European overseas explorations were linked to conquest and settlement. During this phase Europeans appropriated and occupied huge portions of the Americas, Africa, Asia, and Oceania. Migration was driven by Europe's mercantile needs and centered on the establishment of plantations for the large-scale cultivation of sugar, cotton, coffee, and tobacco, which made vast profits for Europe's merchants and cemented the political hegemony of Britain and France. Only a relatively small number of Europeans (perhaps several hundred thousand) migrated during this period as settlers, artisans, entrepreneurs, and administrators. But plantation economy was labor intensive, and the insatiable demand for cheap labor became the motivating force for the organized and wholesale transfer of millions of people.

The world changed dramatically. The gradual and systematic colonization of North America, Latin America, and Australia represented the most comprehensive territorial appropriation. European settlement terminally transformed the demographic and cultural composition of Latin America—even though over 90 percent of all European immigrants settled in just three countries: Argentina, Brazil, and Uruguay. Conquest was followed by the superimposition of European institutions and ways of life and the creation of an economic infrastructure that remained dependent on Europe long after colonialism ended. In regions that boasted robust political systems or established monarchies (such as China and South Asia) or where climate and disease posed huge challenges (notably western Africa), European settlement was limited. But even these areas were brought under European hegemony, exploited for European economic needs, and thoroughly exposed to European ideologies, institutions, and culture.

In the Americas, European incursions and policies had a genocidal impact (both physical and cultural) on the indigenous inhabitants. Sizable numbers succumbed to forced labor, while whole populations were decimated by imported diseases such as smallpox and measles. This brutal devastation limited the pool

---

5. Böhning, "International Migration," 13.

of Indian slaves, and within a century it was necessary to import indentured European labor, mainly drawn from among convicts and the desperately poor. This source too proved woefully inadequate: escape was relatively easy and replacing those who had served their indentured term was increasingly difficult. Still, the export of European slaves continued, in small numbers, until the end of the seventeenth century, mainly of women, who were used in brothels rather than sold.[6] European merchants belatedly turned their attention to Africa, where the Portuguese had broken Muslim monopoly of the trans-Saharan slave trade and established a lucrative trade in African slaves. In "the largest intercontinental migration up to that point in history" some ten to twelve million Africans (typically men and women in their prime) were brutally enslaved and transferred to the Americas in a period lasting more than three centuries.[7]

In addition to the immediate calculus of misery, this massive population transfer had a profound and enduring historical impact. It manifestly subverted Africa's economic potential, thoroughly disfigured European–African (race) relations, and permanently transformed the cultural, social and demographic complexion of the Americas. Slavery remained economically significant well into the nineteenth century, long after the abolition of the trade by Britain (the leading slave-trading nation) in 1807 and the Emancipation Act of 1833, which outlawed slave ownership in British dominions.

As noted in chapter 4, religious impulses and Christian missionary initiatives were intimately intertwined with these processes of European colonial expansion. Thus, the need to outflank the formidable Islamic presence in North Africa by the sea and form alliances with Christian monarchs rumored to exist beyond Muslim lands was all of one piece with the desire to break Islamic monopoly of, and appropriate, lucrative avenues of trade in gold and slaves across the Sahara. But if Christian mission was entangled with the unfolding saga of conquest, colonization, and pillage, it was not simply because philandering adventurers dominated expansion efforts. Few sixteenth-century monarchs were as concerned about purity of faith and the Christianization of newly conquered peoples as Queen Isabella of Spain (1451-1504). Yet her vision epitomized the fateful blend of mission and the needs of empire. In her own words,

> because we desire that the said Indians be converted to our Holy Catholic Faith and taught in its doctrines; and because this can better be done by having the Indians living in community with the Christians of the island, and by having them go among them and associate with them, by which means they will help each other to cultivate and settle and increase the fruits of the island and take the gold which may be there and bring profit to my kingdom and subjects. (Goodpasture 1989: 7-8)

Still, the association between Christian expansion and empire was deeply complex, and missionary objectives ultimately and irreconcilably clashed with the needs or designs of empire. In Japan and China, enterprising Jesuit mis-

---

6. Basil Davidson, *The African Slave Trade,* rev. ed. (London: Little, Brown, 1980), 64.

7. Philip D. Curtin et al., *African History* (London: Longmans, 1991), 215-17.

sionaries arrived well in advance of imperial structures and adopted strategies that involved subordinating European identity and ecclesiastical traditions to the culture and customs of the indigenous society. Missionary effort involved mastery of difficult languages, translation of the liturgy and sacred Scriptures into non-European concepts and religious symbols, painstaking adaptation to local conventions (including dress codes), and submission to local authorities. The process was never completely free from the dye of Europe, but neither did it lead to unalloyed Europeanization. Rather, it produced new forms of Christianity acceptable in an Asian context but incomprehensible in form and expression to distant Europe. Opposition from local religious authorities notwithstanding, these early experiments in translation of the faith met with remarkable success. For several decades, the gospel advanced and converts were won.

But this state of affairs proved short-lived. In the seventeenth century, the Jesuit-led efforts in Asia collapsed catastrophically. The reasons for this include growing unpopularity of the Jesuit order in Europe and bitter rivalries between the Jesuits and other Catholic orders. But the Jesuit approach of cultural accommodation, exemplified by the missionary-scholar Matteo Ricci (1552-1610), proved deeply unpopular in Rome. Papal envoys were eager to portray the papacy as a distant power with political influence. They were equally adamant about the subordination of the Asian churches and Christians to Rome. Rejecting the vernacular option, papal sanctions uniformly sought to impose European forms and structures. So complete was this association between ecclesiastical authority and political dominance that a Spanish captain fearful of losing his cargo to Japanese authorities warned his interlocutors that European missionaries were advance agents of a powerful foreign power.

Alerted to the threat posed by the church (as a foreign institution subject to decisions made in a distant land), Japanese and Chinese emperors responded with implacable hostility and vigorous efforts to extirpate Christianity. In the words of Emperor Tokugawa Ieyasu (1543-1616) of Japan, in a 1614 decree, "Christians have come to Japan . . . longing to disseminate an evil law and to overthrow right doctrine so that they may change the government of the country and obtain *possession of the land*."[8] As explained earlier, the scepter of empire and the shadow of Christendom proved decidedly inimical to Christian expansion. In Japan, Christianity never fully recovered from vigorous persecution by successive emperors. In China, missionary operations were dealt such a severe blow—a 1724 imperial edict prohibited Christianity—that they would not be revived again for a century.

In Brazil, Jesuit missions created large communities of Christianized Indians settled in mission villages (or *reductions*) removed from colonial control and exploitation. This purposeful subversion of empire and transplanted Christendom lasted for two centuries until the expulsion of the order from Spanish and Portuguese territories in the mid-eighteenth century.

---

8. Cited in Otis Cary, *A History of Christianity in Japan: Roman Catholic, Greek Orthodoxy, and Protestant Missions* (Rutland, VT: C. E. Tuttle, 1976), 176-77 (italics added).

Industrial Growth and High Imperialism (1800 to 1960)

The second phase of international migration was also defined by European movement, political expansion, and economic needs. The escalation of European migration and resettlement went hand in hand with an explosion of imperial expansion and colonial acquisitions through which Europeans extended or intensified their economic and political domination of non-European peoples and renewed their efforts to impose key aspects of European culture around the world. By 1900, Britain alone ruled more than a quarter of the world's people and could claim that the sun never set on its empire. European rivalries and competition for far-flung colonies drastically altered the global political landscape. In short order, new political states (or dependencies) were arbitrarily and whimsically created in African, Asia, and the Middle East with scant regard for demographic or cultural realities on the ground. In Africa especially, a good many were cartographical anomalies reflecting "international" borders that divided peoples of the same "nation."

In sheer numbers, however, European migration dominated this period. Massive European migrations were necessary to service the ravenous needs of empire, and out-migration increased with Europe's industrial development and scientific advancement. From 1800 to 1925, between fifty and sixty million Europeans moved to overseas destinations. Of these, 60 percent (or thirty-three million people) settled in the United States alone, and 85 percent settled in just five countries: Argentina, Australia, Canada, New Zealand, and the United States. This, the most remarkable migration in human history up to that point, was instigated by a combination of industrialization (rapid urbanization and technological breakthroughs in oceanic transport) and massive population growth in Europe. Between 1750 and 1850 alone Europe doubled its population from 270 to over 460 million.[9] In fact, the process of industrialization created massive displacements of rural populations as the implementation of new manufactures and a factory system cost many farmers and artisans their livelihoods. Swelling rural-to-urban migrations caused overpopulation in the cities and stimulated European out-migration to America.

To this European movement was added the forcible or coerced intercontinental transfers of non-European peoples from and to areas under the direct or indirect control of European powers. The abolition of the African slave trade by the 1830s intensified rather than lessened the search for huge labor resources elsewhere. During this period, slavery was gradually replaced by the use of indentured workers. Recruited (often forcibly) and contracted for work overseas for several years at a time, these workers became the chief source of labor for plantations, mines, and railway construction in Europe's expanding industrial project. In the British and Dutch colonies, the indentured labor system compensated for the loss of slave labor and generated a goodly supply of cheap and docile labor.[10] Most lived in conditions of semi-slavery and worked under severe constraints.

---

9. Spellman, *Global Community*, 73f.; also Daniels, *Coming to America*, 16.
10. Böhning, "International Migration," 15.

British and Dutch authorities recruited Chinese laborers for various construction projects. Britain also recruited workers from India to work in the Caribbean, East Africa, Fiji, and Malaya. According to one estimate, the indentured system involved twelve to thirty-seven million workers between 1834 and 1941.[11] Thus, for an almost unbroken period of four hundred years, European economic growth and industrial expansion were serviced to a great extent by the blood, sweat, and lives of non-European peoples throughout its extensive colonies.

Indian migration, for instance, was virtually nonexistent before the advent of colonialism. That changed rapidly and consequentially. Between 1830 and 1916, records W. H. Spellman, 1.5 million Indians were incorporated into Britain's expanding empire as semi-free indentured workers. This process saw the emergence of Indian populations in areas as far-flung as East and South Africa, the West Indies, and the South Pacific. By the end of the twentieth century roughly nine to ten million Indians were living outside their country.[12]

Chinese out-migration was also stimulated by European imperial expansion and followed China's humiliating defeat at the hands of the British in the two Opium Wars (1839-1842 and 1856-1860). By the end of the nineteenth century, well over two million Chinese were contracted and shipped to the Americas, South-East Asia, and South Africa. The vast majority came from two provinces, Guangdong and Fujian. By the Second World War almost nine million Chinese lived outside China. In the United States and elsewhere, Chinese "coolies" (a most derogatory term) worked under brutal conditions and faced extreme discrimination. Today, the largest Chinese community outside mainland China is located in America. The demand for indentured labor and Japan's own colonial ambitions also saw the migration of about one million Japanese to the Pacific (Hawaii), South America (mainly Peru and Brazil), and the United States.

Empire and Protestant Missions

The collusion between Christian missions and Western empire building was complex and tension-ridden, but undeniable. The two largely coincided in both geographical extension and historical existence. The association, to be sure, emerged gradually and fitfully, and was attended by vigorous debate in the early stages. But the pull of common interests in major causes like abolition and spread of education, as well as the strong awareness of reciprocal advantage (exemplified in the juxtaposition of Christianity, civilization, and commerce), ultimately overrode conflicting purpose and deep misgivings. The Western missionary project not only derived considerable impetus from the expansion of Western prestige and power, but it also spearheaded the spread of Western knowledge, culture, and values—all of which facilitated colonial subjugation. Besides, colonial structures and initiatives came to be regarded as vital for effective missionary enterprise on account of what colonial presence guaranteed: the establishment of law and order, safeguards for religious freedom, and unlimited access to new regions.

---

11. Cited in Castles and Miller, *Age of Migration*, 54.
12. Spellman, *Global Community*, 116.

Furthermore, as was the case with Roman Catholic initiatives, serious-minded Protestants were convinced that the timing and gains of imperial ventures reflected "divine providence," even "manifest destiny." The doctrine of "divine providence" was prominent among nineteenth-century British evangelicals (the group that supplied the vast majority of European missionaries up to World War I). This doctrine rested on the conviction that Britain's emergence as a world power with immense territorial possessions reflected God's providence and purpose. More specifically, Britain's imperial status and the unique advantages that came with it were "a trust given for missionary purposes," and failure to fulfill this imperial trusteeship "would be met by divine judgment on Britain as a nation."[13]

Such pro-imperialist convictions were well in keeping with the unbounded optimism and lofty visions of Victorian Britain. But, as an ideology, "divine providence" betrayed explicit acceptance of the link between empire and Christian mission. While it certainly provided grounds for advocacy of moral governance and imperial benevolence, it also fettered missionary action to political aggression and economic exploitation. European missionaries became strong advocates of empire and often requested colonial rule. In the 1890s the superintendent of the Wesleyan Methodist missions on the Gold Coast (now Ghana) intoned, "I should consider myself worse than despicable if I failed to declare my firm conviction that the British Army and Navy are today used by God for the accomplishment of his purposes."[14] He also welcomed what he termed "the most righteous invasion" of Ashanti (in 1895) and added, for good measure, that he would "like to see Britain in possession of the whole of Africa."

The doctrine of divine providence not only strengthened the mission–empire nexus; it also embodied, in thinly veiled form, the arrogance and racism that troubled both projects. This admixture of exalted idealism and ethnocentric conceit was immortalized in Rudyard Kipling's "The White Man's Burden," a poem that attracted considerable interest and controversy during the high imperialism period. The first verse read:

> Take up the White Man's burden—
> Send forth the best ye breed—
> Go, bind your sons to exile
> To serve your captives' need;
> To wait, in heavy harness,
> On fluttered folk and wild—
> Your new-caught sullen peoples,
> Half devil and half child.

---

13. For a thorough treatment of the doctrines of "divine providence" and "imperial trusteeship," see Stanley, *Bible and the Flag*, 67-70, 179-81.

14. Quoted in Andrew N. Porter, "Evangelical Enthusiasm, Missionary Motivation and West Africa in the Late 19th Century: The Career of G. W. Brooke," *Journal of Imperial and Commonwealth History* 6, no. 1 (1977).

But the Western idea that the fate of the world rests on the specific actions of a single self-identified nation (or peoples) took on an even more blatant racial representation in the concept of manifest destiny.

Where the doctrine of divine providence saw imperial expansion as serving a missionary purpose, the ideology of "manifest destiny" conflated imperial expansion *with* missionary purpose. In this regard it enshrined the ideals of Christendom more closely. "Manifest destiny" refers to the belief that God had chosen specific (Anglo-Saxon) nations, because of their unique or superior qualities, to fulfill his purpose in the world.[15] This ideology is manifestly rooted in the biblical concept of "chosenness" (of a nation or race). Embraced by the Puritans who migrated to the New World, it provided a rationale for colonial aggression against indigenous peoples and remains a peculiar element of American Christianity. This potent mix of racial superiority, territorial aggression or colonial expansion, and missionary enterprise was extolled in the writing of Rev. Josiah Strong (1847-1916), general secretary of the Evangelical Alliance (a coalition of Protestant missionary groups) in the United States. In his hugely popular book *Our Country: Its Possible Future and Its Present Crisis* (1885: 221, 222), written to stimulate missionary action, Strong intoned:

> Another marked characteristic of the Anglo-Saxon is what may be called an instinct of genius for colonizing. . . . He excels all others in pushing his way into new countries. It was those in whom this tendency was strongest that came to America, and this inherited tendency has been further developed by the westward sweep of successive generations across the continent. . . .
>
> This race of unequaled energy, with all the majesty of numbers and the might of wealth behind it—the representative, let us hope, of the largest liberty, the purest Christianity, the highest civilization—having developed peculiarly aggressive traits calculated to impress its institutions upon mankind, will spread itself over the earth.

Strong's views reflect the degree to which racism and racial perspectives had become entrenched in Western minds (nurtured by evolutionary theory) and fully woven into the structures of empire by the end of the nineteenth century.[16] Ultimately, however, European notions of chosenness, innate superiority, and the God-given right to rule others were rooted in an imagination nurtured by Christendom. Racialist ideologies such as manifest destiny were the fruit of a Christian ideal that sanctioned territorial aggression and countenanced both political dominance and cultural expansion as a strategy of mission. In addition to casting racial difference as a basis for divine preference, the doctrine of manifest destiny fundamentally confused the universality of the gospel with the universal spread of a particular expression of it.

---

15. See Bosch, *Transforming Mission*, 298.

16. See Andrew N. Porter, *Religion Versus Empire? British Protestant Missionaries and Overseas Expansion, 1700-1914* (New York: Manchester University Press, 2004), 283-87.

Andrew Walls argues that the evangelical emphasis on the depravity of the entire human race "shielded the first missionary generation from some of the worse excesses of racism."[17] That may be so, but the Western voices raised in defense of non-Western values and cultures were few and far between. As mentioned earlier, Henry Venn (Church Mission Society [CMS] secretary, 1840-1872) admonished CMS missionaries to "study the national character of the people among whom you labor, and show the utmost respect for national peculiarities." But such perspectives were exceptional and went largely unheeded. Cultural and racial superiority remained far more prevalent in Western missionary attitudes precisely because the missionaries (even the most high-minded) were products of their social environment. Josiah Strong's views were not the musings of an eccentric; they exemplified the ideological certainties of the period and reflected the dominant outlook of the white mainstream, from which the majority of American evangelicals were drawn. Importantly, such notions enjoyed wide currency in the decades leading to a massive increase in the American Protestant missionary involvement in China—this at a time when Chinese immigrants in America met with xenophobic hostility and racial rejection.

But the point I wish to make is much broader than Western missionary attitudes. The fact that Britain was the world's economic superpower from the early nineteenth to the early twentieth century had a lot to do with its status as the world's premier missionary-sending nation. Similarly, American dominance replaced British preeminence in global mission enterprise—in 1900 there were ten thousand British missionaries overseas; by 1940, America had the lead with over twelve thousand missionaries (thirty-five thousand by 1980)—in large measure because the United States, itself a colonial power, also succeeded Britain as the world's new superpower. In essence, Western missionary enterprise, both Roman Catholic and Protestant, reflected the intimate association between mission (the spread of the Christian faith) and imperial expansion.

All this is not to suggest that Protestant missionary initiatives were wholly motivated by imperial designs. As noted elsewhere, the missionary impulse is intrinsic to the Christian faith, and missionary activity has often outdistanced the reach of empire or formal territorial control. From the start, Protestant missionaries penetrated and conducted successful operations in places as far-flung as the Arctic, Africa, and the Far East well in advance and beyond the ken of imperial government. In fact, nineteenth-century faith missions were partly motivated by "a determination to operate in isolated and unfamiliar territory, as far as possible beyond any European influence or colonial rule"[18]—though this aspiration overlooked the fact the distinction would be lost on non-Western peoples. In fact, Hudson Taylor's China Inland Mission, perhaps the best known example of faith missions, was made possible by the "unequal treaties" imposed on China by European military aggression and commercial ambitions. Further, faith mission-

17. Andrew F. Walls, "The Evangelical Revival, the Missionary Movement, and Africa," in *Evangelicalism: Comparative Studies of Popular Protestantism in North America, the British Isles, and Beyond, 1700-1990*, ed. Mark A. Noll, D. W. Bebbington, and George A. Rawlyk (New York: Oxford University Press, 1994), 310.

18. Porter, *Religion Versus Empire?* 194.

aries in West Africa and China were hardly free from the arrogance and paternalism that characterized the Western missionary project in general.

The Role of Migration

European missionaries not only benefited from the projection of Western political power; they also formed a segment of the massive tide of European movement that characterized the second phase of international migrations. It is no coincidence that the most extensive missionary movement in history corresponded with the largest migration movement in history: *one in five Europeans migrated between 1800 and 1925.* The tide and flow of missionary activity were an undercurrent in the much broader sweep of migration movements. Both were shaped by technological and demographic developments; both were made possible by enormous economic inequalities and military superiority. To the extent that the European missionary movement reflected larger migration trends, its shape and size were also affected by migrant flows. The two ebbed and flowed together.

Eventually European migration movements began to decline after the outbreak of the First World War. Many European migrants returned home for military service, and though the warring powers used forced labor, the numbers involved were relatively small. By the 1920s increased hostility toward immigrants led traditional immigrant nations like the United States and Canada to pass restrictive immigration laws which stemmed immigrant flows considerably. The new laws privileged European migrants, but the onset of the Great Depression, followed by the Second World War, stifled voluntary European movement even further. One major exception was France, which, owing to huge war casualties and population decline, recruited just under two million foreign workers from East European countries in the interwar years. After a period of unprecedented mobility, international migrations slowed down drastically; and so, interestingly, did European missionary enterprise—though new American evangelical missionary initiatives gradually came to the fore.

The Limits of Empire

In part because of its strong association with the projection of Western political power, the Western missionary encounter with the non-European peoples has long been depicted as a one-directional movement, entirely shaped by the exploits and accomplishments of Western agents. This approach implicitly portrays non-Western peoples as passive, dependent, and exploited and treats the unique histories of non-Western societies as a subplot in a drama dominated by Western initiatives. This is a gross distortion of history. Interestingly, Andrew Porter (2004) notes that imperial historians are now paying increasing attention to the impact of empire on the imperial powers themselves. The foreign missionary, as Andrew Walls explains, has perforce to live on terms set by other people in order to have long-term effectiveness; and this "implied a readiness to enter someone else's world instead of imposing the standards of one's own. It meant learning another's language, seeking a niche within another's society, perhaps accepting a situation of dependence."[19]

In truth, the strong association with colonial domination meant that Western missionaries occupied positions of control and authority far removed from the notions of submission to local entities. Yet, as we have seen, the control mechanisms of Western missions proved inadequate in the face of indigenous appropriation of the gospel. In the West African context, for instance, the variety of responses subordinated under Ethiopianism (see pp. 304-5 below) severely undermines the notion that the black element was a passive or expendable element in the solvent of Western imperial domination.

Undoubtedly, the vision, sacrificial devotion, and tremendous courage of European missionaries who took the gospel to distant lands where they had to contend with all manner of dangers and adversity is one of the most remarkable chapters in Christian history. But much missionary historiography obscures the fact that the spread of Christianity in the non-Western world has largely been the work of non-Western agency.

We would be hard pressed to identify a mass movement in the history of Christian expansion that was led or sustained by foreign missionary agency. Modern African Christianity, notes Andrew Walls, "is not only the result of movement among Africans, but it has been principally sustained by Africans and is to a surprising extent the result of African initiatives."[20] In the African experience, African agents, serving as catechists, schoolmasters, and interpreters, formed the main vanguard of the Christian advance. In the second half of the nineteenth century and the early years of the twentieth, the Sierra Leone colony (in West Africa), "probably produced more missionaries, ministerial and lay, per head of population than any other country in the world."[21] Brian Stanley adds that "in most of the notable areas of church growth" on the African continent, "the overwhelming majority of missionary faces were black."[22] In 1906, for instance, notes Stanley (1990), the CMS (the largest British Protestant mission agency) had 8,850 accredited "native agents" compared to 975 European missionaries—nine Africans for every European.

Africa is also a notable example of the fact that throughout the non-Western world the most extensive and dynamic growth of the Christian faith took place *after* the collapse of empire or after the end of formal colonial rule. Interestingly, this was also true of the mass conversion of Germanic tribes, much of which took place after the collapse of the Roman Empire. In China, too, Christianity not only survived the expulsion of Western missionaries and bloody persecution of the church under Communism but continued to flourish and expand through

---

19. Walls, *Cross-Cultural Process*, 199, 220.

20. Walls, *Missionary Movement*, 86.

21. Walls, "Mission and Migration," 9.

22. Stanley, *Bible and the Flag*, 71-72. See also Roland Anthony Oliver, *The African Experience* (London: Pimlico, 1994), 210; Adrian Hastings, *The Church in Africa, 1450-1950* (Oxford: Clarendon, 1994), 437f.; Ogbu Kalu, "Colour and Conversion: The White Missionary Factor in the Christianisation of Igboland, 1867-1967," *Missiology* 18, no. 1 (January 1990), 61-74.

indigenous initiatives and a massive underground movement. Today, as many as three hundred million Chinese may be Christian.[23]

All this is to say that the contribution of the Western missionary has every-where been more catalytic than comprehensive. Like colonialism, with which its fortunes were intricately tied, Western missions represent only a brief episode in the history of non-Western societies and in the life of the non-Western church. And while it is true that the present global spread of Christianity would be well-nigh inconceivable without imperial expansion, the appropriation of the gospel by great masses of people in non-Western societies had little to do with the struc-tures of empire. As Andrew Porter comments, the history of Protestant missions leaves us with a paradox; for "indigenous choices and capacity for resistance or adaptation shaped a process of cultural exchange which often bore little relation to broader imbalances of material power between colonizers and the colonized."[24] In fact, nowhere do the reality and function of empire play a decisive role in the spread of the Christian faith. The reverse was often the case.

Unintended Consequences of Empire

European movements and resettlement fostered a new world order, transformed global interactions, and reconfigured cultural and demographic landscapes. That story is a major chapter in the history of globalization, and for many it was the only chapter that mattered. But, as I argue in the first part of this book, under-standing globalization as a one-directional, managed, process reflective of Euro-pean/Western domination is shortsighted. Events and processes that are truly global in scope and impact cannot be adequately explained by the needs and initiatives of select actors or, for that matter, by singular starting points.

Europe's imperial project instigated vast and complex movements of non-European peoples in the nineteenth and twentieth centuries. But the sheer scale of demographic redeployment and the complex diversity of cultural interactions involved placed potential outcomes beyond conventional human controls or colonial designs. Even in the Americas, where European expansion appeared to sweep all before it, it was not quite an all-conquering force. Empire building faced limitations imposed by a variety of local factors and forms of resistance. Unintended consequences are crucial to the story. European initiatives unleashed powerful forces of change that have acted back on Europe and shaped the emerg-ing world order in significant ways.

The story of how the explosive rise in the volume of intercontinental migra-tion under the aegis of European colonial expansion had many unforeseen and unforeseeable consequences is perhaps best illustrated by British efforts. By the early twentieth century the British empire encompassed almost a third of the earth's inhabited surface and roughly a quarter of its population (well over five

---

23. See "Survey Finds 300m China Believers," *BBC News Online,* February 7, 2007; Robert Pigott, "China Tour Showed Christian Growth," *BBC News Online,* October 31, 2006.

24. Porter, *Religion Versus Empire,* 322.

hundred million people). As the world's first global empire, British colonial and power structure was pervasive, extending to the control of schools, taxes, laws, and local government in far-flung domains. In addition to huge investments in transport and communications technologies, managing this extensive dominion also required the export of British models, ideologies, and institutions. The British system of education, the centerpiece of which was the English public and grammar school, proved exceptionally durable and invariably survived the decolonization process.

But the overseas territories that formed the British empire in the late nineteenth century were acquired mainly through the principle of effective occupation,[25] treaties, and consolidation. Direct military conquest had little to do with the process. The main effort at conquest took the form of three bloody and unsuccessful military campaigns in Afghanistan (in 1842, 1880, and 1919). The racist notion of "white man's burden," used to provide ideological rationalization for the scramble for colonial possessions, reflected the conviction that particular peoples of European extraction were destined to exercise dominance over others for the latter's own good. Yet effective colonial governance required accommodations with local authorities and extensive reliance on preexisting indigenous institutions.

For Britain, whose homegrown population in 1900 was only about forty million, indirect rule was an indispensable strategy. Such was the nature and extent of the British empire that by the end of the nineteenth century the Queen of England had more Muslim subjects than any other ruler.[26] Yet, as noted earlier, the hold that Islam exerted over economic life and instruments of local government in parts of Africa necessitated heavy concessions, including prohibitions against Christian proselytism. The highly celebrated British educational system did not replace Islamic schools; it was erected alongside them. In fact, the umbrella of protection provided by colonial governance allowed African Islam to flourish more than at any time previously. In India, too, colonial policy-making helped to ferment Hindu consciousness. As Vinoth Ramachandra explains, it was under British rule that "'Hindu' became a category for people in India who were not Muslims, Christians, Sikhs, Jains, Parsis or Buddhists." Thus, modern state institutions of the British empire, not religious tradition, are to thank for the powerful currents of nationalism and national identity which bedevil political government in India today.[27]

The new immigrant communities created by the inexhaustible labor demands of the colonial economic machinery also reconfigured the global cultural landscape and remade the world in their own way. Drawn by reward-for-labor schemes, millions ended up in foreign lands without the means to return and slowly formed new communities. In many parts of the world these newly inserted non-European immigrant communities would have an indelible impact on their new cultural and

---

25. First established by the British in 1580, this principle, whereby Western European powers agreed that the first nation to occupy a territory had sovereignty over it, was reinforced by the Berlin Conference of 1885.

26. Walls, "Africa as the Theatre of Christian Engagement with Islam," 167.

27. See Ramachandra, *Faiths in Conflict?*; also Walls, "Mission and Migration," 9.

economic environment in the long term, notwithstanding the fact that colonial policies often contributed to tense relations with the wider indigenous society. Despite racist oppression and the indignity of servitude, the descendants of African slaves developed religious and cultural forms that immeasurably enriched the variegated streams of American society. In East Africa, Asian immigrants became influential economic brokers.

Then, as now, the migrant experience deepened rather than lessened ethnic consciousness or homeland ties. Utilizing the same communication infrastructure that made large-scale transoceanic migration possible, non-European migrants in distant lands became powerful agents for cultural, economic, and political change in their homelands. Through transnational ties, many contributed to the rise of nationalist consciousness and influenced movements toward political independence. Ideologies and transatlantic movements that emerged out of the black experience in America exerted considerable influence on the development of African nationalism within church and society.[28] Similarly, political movements in nineteenth-century China (along with commercial growth) were greatly bolstered by the remittances and support provided by Chinese migrants.[29] Thus, when the Kuomingtang rose to power in China in 1927, they renewed ties with Chinese immigrants in the United States and incorporated them into a new nationalist movement.[30]

Even more crucial, the dismantling of European colonial structures from the late 1950s set powerful forces in motion within the non-Western world that had global ramifications. Mass immigration from the colonies to Britain had already begun by the late 1940s and was galvanized by the attraction of labor opportunities in Britain in the wake of the Second World War. The colonies and former possessions of the British empire in Africa, the Caribbean, and Asia were constituted into a British Commonwealth (later "Commonwealth of Nations"), and possession of a British passport granted their citizens unhindered rights to enter Britain. Pushed out by troubled postcolonial economies, many Commonwealth subjects emigrated en masse to Britain to seek work and a new future. By 1970 they numbered approximately 1.4 million. In 1972, when Ugandan dictator General Idi Amin expelled eighty thousand African Asians—people whose settlement in East Africa was a direct result of British imperial policies—the British government faced a major crisis. Many of the deportees held British passports. Amid feverish public debate, Britain admitted twenty-eight thousand in two months—the largest intake of the decade. The backlash to the influx of these new immigrants was fierce. Shunned by the wider population and labeled "ethnic minorities," they crowded into Britain's declining towns and created a distinctive

---

28. See Hanciles, *Euthanasia of a Mission*, 147-95; also J. Mutero Chirenje, *Ethiopianism and Afro-Americans in Southern Africa, 1883-1916* (Baton Rouge, LA: Louisiana State University Press, 1987); Kalu, "Ethiopianism in African Christianity."

29. See Spellman, *Global Community*, 135.

30. Nina G. Schiller, "Transmigrants and Nation-States: Something Old and Something New in the U.S. Immigrant Experience," in *The Handbook of International Migration: The American Experience*, ed. Charles Hirschman, Philip Kasinitz, and Josh DeWind (New York: Russell Sage Foundation, 1999), 100, 103.

underclass. In particular, the growth of black communities triggered the rise of racial violence and riots in cities like Birmingham and Nottingham.

But we are getting ahead of the story. The point at issue is that in the long run empire building had important and profound consequences for the empire builders. The very same structural linkages and international connections instituted to serve the imperial project became critical components in new unanticipated trends and developments that had important global ramifications and from which the initial actors could not insulate themselves. In this case the rise in nonwhite immigration, mainly from its ex-colonies, dramatically transformed Britain's religious, cultural, and racial landscape with important consequences for its future.[31]

Global Migrations (from the 1960s)

For over four centuries, European colonial expansion stimulated an unprecedented rise in international migrations. Yet decolonization and the formal end of empire have witnessed an even greater intensification of migratory flows. From the 1960s, international migrations have escalated in volume, velocity, and complexity and transformed into a truly global phenomenon no longer dominated by European needs and initiatives. The direction and composition of migration movement have also radically altered. Until the late 1950s international migration chiefly involved movement from the highly developed, politically powerful nations to areas in the non-Western world characterized by agrarian (or precapitalist) systems and relatively weak political institutions. Since the 1960s, migrant movement has been predominantly from areas with weak economic and political systems to the centers of global dominance and advanced industrial growth. The vast majority of migrants now come from the non-Western world, and the main destination countries include the European nations that have previously been the main emitters of international migrants.

But demographic patterns and economic considerations remain unchanged. Now, as previously, international migration flows are from densely populated parts of the world to areas of relatively low population density. Just as millions of Europeans once braved perilous conditions and horrible dangers to seek a better future and fortunes outside Europe, millions of non-Europeans are now desperate enough to endure all manner of hardship and even imperil their lives in a bid to reach Europe and North America. *If wealthy Western nations are now troubled by a massive and unstoppable influx of nonwhite immigrants, it is partly because non-Western societies were once troubled and overrun by Western migration and colonial expansion.*

This historic reversal in the direction of international migrations is rooted

---

31. For a brief overview, see Michael S. Teitelbaum and J. M. Winter, *A Question of Numbers: High Migration, Low Fertility, and the Politics of National Identity*, 1st ed. (New York: Hill & Wang, 1998), 50-51.

in a complex array of factors and processes.[32] But colonialism and the global economic expansion of Western powers are pivotal. Throughout history, massive displacements and population movement have accompanied the collapse of empire. Thus, the timing and extraordinary scale of contemporary migrations are not quite so surprising. What astonishes is the long-term directional reversal in global migratory flows. That takes a bit more explaining.

We must remind ourselves that until the 1960s, international migration was shaped by the needs and purposive designs of European imperialism; designs that were coercive, extremely violent, and utterly exploitative. This imperial project also fomented a new world order characterized by advanced communication technologies, new modes of travel, an interstate system, and unprecedented global interconnectedness. These developments set the stage for a new age of migrations. But it is the political and economic structures associated with them that have largely determined the present direction of global migratory flows. We have space only for a brief overview of the political and economic factors associated with Western empire building which help to explain the dimensions and direction of the current "age of migration." (The demographic factors are covered in chapter 8.)

Political Factors

The late-nineteenth-century scramble for colonies by European powers (and Japan) artificially created some fifty so-called nation-states—statehood being a modern European ideal. The vexing and often very violent process of state formation continued throughout the twentieth century. Worldwide, the number of states tripled from fifty in 1900 to 190 by the 1990s.[33] Then came decolonization, a process almost everywhere compromised by Cold War politics as the various powers manipulated their withdrawal to protect their interests and postcolonial influence. Furthermore, in Africa and Asia, rapid decolonization left in its wake a host of fragile "nation-states," many of which lacked "assimilative power" or the means to effectively contain deep ethnic tensions or harmonize competing religious blocs.[34] In many ex-colonial territories, the process of nation-state formation involved discrimination against, or vigorous suppression of, minority groups. Abruptly rendered defenseless by decolonization, some territories were promptly annexed or invaded with impunity by adjacent powers. To cite a few, China annexed Tibet in 1950, while Indonesia invaded Irian Jaya and East Timor in 1963 and 1973, respectively. Political chaos and widespread ethnic conflicts triggered massive population displacements and migrant movements.

---

32. On this, see Castles and Miller, *Age of Migration*, 67-103; Nikos Papastergiadis, *The Turbulence of Migration: Globalization, Deterritorialization, and Hybridity* (Malden, MA: Blackwell, 2000); Spellman, *Global Community*, 151-65.

33. See Schaeffer, *Understanding Globalization*, 11f., 298; Kennedy, *Preparing for the Twenty-First Century*.

34. See McNeely, "Determination of Statehood."

The rising tide of global migrations intensified with the end of the Cold War and the rapid collapse of the Soviet Union in 1991. Communist control and ideology had viciously suppressed ethnic identities and brought diverse peoples under a single system of government. With the disintegration of this political structure, nationalist divisions and historic boundaries were immediately reasserted, leading to widespread conflicts and people displacements. Almost overnight, millions of "Soviet citizens"—including twenty-five million Russians, seven million Ukrainians, and two million Belarusians—became foreigners in newly formed republics. This trend continued throughout the 1990s as the spread of democratic reforms and the creation of independent states triggered a sharp rise in separatist nationalist movements and bitter ethnic wars. The bloody disintegration of the Federal Peoples Republic of Yugoslavia, which saw three to five million people uprooted, represents one of the most spectacular examples. This federation was officially "non-aligned" at the time of its fateful breakup, but its political life was strongly influenced by communism and developments within the communist world.

Between 1945 and 1991, the spread of Western-style democracy stimulated the rise of numerous separatist or independent movements as "ethnic protests for autonomy and secession, wars of national irredentism and explosive racial conflicts . . . proliferated in every continent."[35] As Schaeffer (1997) observes, most failed because they represented minority groups or lacked superpower support. Political instability, military coups, civil wars, ethnic clashes, and tribal insurgence became all too common as the world's newest "states" struggled to deal with the legacies of colonialism and to grapple with the elusive ideals of statehood and democracy. The tide of displaced and uprooted peoples rose to a cascading flood, and the words "refugee" and "asylum seeker" became prevalent terms of reference in the lexicon of the international media. Later commentators would go so far as to describe the twentieth century as "the century of the refugee."[36]

By the 1970s wealthy Western countries had become target destinations for a growing tide of nonwhite migrants. This movement from the "margins" is as critical to the new world order as Western economic dominance. "Never before" note Castles and Miller, "has international migration seemed so pertinent to national security and so connected to conflict and disorder on a global scale."[37] American journalist Robert Kaplan similarly reflected that "the political and strategic impact of surging populations will be the core foreign-policy challenge from which most others will ultimately emanate."[38]

---

35. Smith, *Nationalism and Modernism*, 2.

36. Andreas Demuth, "Some Conceptual Thoughts on Migration Research," in *Theoretical and Methodological Issues in Migration Research: Interdisciplinary, Intergenerational and International Perspectives*, ed. Biko Agozino (Brookfield, VT: Ashgate, 2000), 22; also Khalid Koser and Helma Lutz, "The New Migration in Europe: Contexts, Constructions and Realities," in *The New Migration in Europe: Social Constructions and Social Realities*, ed. Khalid Koser and Helma Lutz (New York: St. Martin's Press, 1998), 1.

37. Castles and Miller, *Age of Migration*, 283.

38. Robert Kaplan, "The Coming Anarchy," in *Globalization and the Challenges of a New Century: A Reader*, ed. Patrick O'Meara, Howard D. Mehlinger, and Matthew Krain (Bloomington: Indiana University Press, 2000), 42.

Economic Realities

Global economic realities have played an even more central role in stimulating the mammoth tide of migration and mobility that has characterized the international order in the last five decades. That story is also rooted in historical antecedents and European initiatives. European colonialism brought major benefits to non-Western territories—among these, superior educational systems, technological development, advanced medical services, scientific knowledge, and infrastructural development. But European powers did not acquire far-flung territories and erect an elaborate worldwide capitalist system for the benefit of the subjected peoples (whom they often despised). What European powers created was an integrated political and economic system in which European nations, to borrow a page from Marxist analysis, constituted the *core*.[39] This core embodied superior military strength, concentration of capital, sophisticated technologies, and complex economic activities. It dominated and fully exploited the system. The colonies and dependencies constituted the *periphery*, a sphere characterized by much weaker political machineries and relatively simple technologies. The periphery provided cheap labor (including slaves), cheap staples, and raw materials or primary products on which the core economies thrive.

In the majority of cases the colonial era lasted less than a century, a fraction of the history of colonized territories. Yet few would dispute the fact that colonialism had a deleterious effect on the former colonies while it bolstered Europe's economic growth and industrial revolution. The African slave trade is only one prominent example of how the human costs on one side of the equation were directly related to huge profits on the other side. In Eric Williams's telling observation, "the increase in wealth for the few whites was as phenomenal as the increase in misery for the many blacks."[40] The industrial output of non-Western territories declined sharply under colonial rule since their productivity, in scale and diversity, was tailored to the needs of the controlling powers or otherwise undermined (even destroyed) by European priorities. It is striking to note that "in 1750, just before the beginning of the British industrial revolution, third world industrial output per person was almost as high as Britain's and substantially higher than in the American colonies. During the nineteenth century, though, third world industrialization declined, so that by 1900 it was just 2 percent of the British level."[41]

The colonial infrastructure was also characterized by lopsided modernization patterns that witnessed the rise of urbanized centers of economic and political power, typically close to the coast, while the interior languished in premodern conditions—often with European mission stations as the main symbols of

---

39. See Immanuel Wallerstein's "world system theory" ("The Rise and Future Demise of the World Capitalist System," in *The Globalization Reader*, ed. Frank J. Lechner and John Boli [Malden, MA: Blackwell, 2000], 57-63); also Thomas R. Shannon, *An Introduction to the World-System Perspective* (Boulder, CO: Westview, 1996). For a helpful critique of Wallerstein's theory, see Peter Beyer, *Religion and Globalization* (London: Sage, 1994).

40. Eric E. Williams, *Capitalism and Slavery* (New York: G. P. Putnam, 1980), 25.

41. Isbister, *Promises Not Kept*, 94f.

modernity. The impoverishment of the countryside contributed to massive rural-to-urban migrations that often formed the first link in the chain that led to international movement. Additionally, the uneven development between the capital and the countryside factored into intractable socioeconomic divisions and fueled tribal jealousies that continue to haunt ex-colonies long after the end of colonialism. The colonial bureaucracy also fostered the rise of an elite indigenous middle class who inevitably craved and subsequently inherited the unfair advantages exemplified by colonial rule.

Such was the nature of colonial dominance that even symbols of progress came with a heavy price. The implementation of public health measures, for instance, lowered mortality and triggered unprecedented population explosion throughout the non-Western world. Improved medical services are hardly a bad thing—though, truth be told, it did at the time put the collective noses of the local deities and witchdoctors out of joint! But, as John Isbister observes, this development was not accompanied by any change in the standards of living of the inhabitants.[42] Thus, whereas "in Europe and North America, increased longevity had been an integral part of a long process of social change; in the third world, increased longevity was bestowed from outside the social system" (Isbister 2001: 97). In fact, in many places it coincided with European land grabs and forcible displacement of people from the most fertile lands. More people on less land is a recipe for poverty anywhere in the world. Ironically, therefore, improved medical services actually contributed to the economic impoverishment and the huge social problems that came with rapid population growth, reduced productivity, and massive internal migrations.

Care must be taken to avoid the egregiously lopsided analysis, still popular in some circles, that lays the entire blame for the calamities and misfortunes that have overtaken many former colonies at the collective feet of former colonial masters. The postcolonial saga of chronic misrule, systemic corruption, extreme socioeconomic divisions (the richer the natural resources of the country, the wider the internal economic division), inadequate investment in human resources, and the perpetuation of a culture of exploitation cannot simply be attributed to imperialism.[43] Yet the colossal economic poverty that is the common experience of so many former colonies has some of its roots in European colonialism and the pervasive structures of domination and exploitation within the contemporary global order that are its legacy.

The newly independent states fashioned by decolonization found themselves within a new global order dominated by Western nations and institutions—a structure that, like the colonial system it purportedly replaced, is built on inequality. Their integration into this global economic system largely on terms shaped by the priority and agenda of the former colonial rulers typically left their *periphery* status unchanged. They were essentially excluded from "playing a central role in the growth mechanisms of the world economy and achieving meaningful partici-

---

42. Ibid., 97f.

43. For a thoroughgoing analysis of the African situation, see George B. N. Ayittey, *Africa in Chaos* (New York: St. Martin's, 1999).

pation in decision making (to the extent that political control is being exercised at all)."[44] As Raymond Baker demonstrates vividly, the complicity of Western governments, banks, and corporations in the enormous outflow of illicit financial flows (at the staggering rate of $500 billion a year) from poorer non-Western countries to Western countries is a major contributing factor to the crippling economic malaise and political instability that plague non-Western societies.[45] He adds pointedly that this global system of illicit financial flows was "developed in the West and advanced by the West."

The lot of the "periphery" is now all too familiar. Explosive population growth, precipitous economic decline, chronic internal crises (including the spread of disease and environmental degradation), rising debt burdens, grievous misrule, and shrinking export earnings have mired all but a few of the former colonies in horrendous poverty. Dependence on primary commodities (chiefly agriculture and minerals) remains a major handicap. By 2001 some thirty-five countries in Latin America, Africa, and Asia still received two-fifths or more of their export earnings from one or two agricultural or mineral products.[46] Economic and political factors are often deeply interrelated. Political misrule and harsh international regimes led to heavy debt burdens and heavy cuts in public spending, which deepened economic poverty and triggered massive social unrest. In response, governments devoted even more hard-earned foreign currency (or secured more loans) to equip the police and military, increasing the debt burden even further. An estimated 10 percent of "third world debt" is spent on arms, and research indicates that the majority of states involved in wars also carry heavy debt burdens.[47] This vicious cycle of instability, economic suffering, and social upheaval formed a taproot for the steady tidal flow of international migrations.

The Case for the Missiological Study of Migration

By the 1980s Africa, Latin America, the Caribbean, and Asia had become net exporters of millions of people to Western countries, initially as labor migrants and subsequently as asylum seekers but increasingly and predominantly as economic migrants—though, as I show in the next chapter, these categories of migrants tend to be misleading. Argentina's economic collapse at the turn of the twenty-first century, for instance, saw thousands of Argentines queuing up at foreign embassies in Buenos Aires, seeking a passport or a visa. So strong was the incentive to leave that members of the country's 250,000-strong Jewish community were "prepared to brave Palestinian suicide bombers and join the 80,000

---

44. Mittelman, *Globalization Syndrome*, 241.

45. See Baker, *Capitalism's Achilles Heel*, 186-206, 240-61.

46. Brubaker, *Globalization at What Price?*; cf. Kennedy, *Preparing for the Twenty-First Century*, 193-227.

47. See Elizabeth G. Ferris, *Beyond Borders: Refugees, Migrants and Human Rights in the Post-Cold War Era* (Geneva: WCC Publications, 1993), 84-85.

Argentines living in Israel."[48] More recently, precipitous economic decline combined with despotic political rule has seen a swelling of Zimbabwean emigrants, one-third of whom have ended up in Britain.[49]

Once again, the paradoxes of globalization are salient. The economic motivations driving international migrations are shaped by the juxtaposition of division and integration at the heart of global processes which express themselves most visibly in new social hierarchies and a widening North–South divide. As media coverage of emigration attempts shows, considerable numbers of people in the South are determined and desperate enough to risk death in their efforts to gain access to countries that afford better livelihoods, security, and access to resources that would infinitely improve the fortunes of their children. *According to one estimate, an average person from the poorest one hundred countries could increase his or her income five or six times by moving into one of the twenty-two richest countries.*[50]

For millions of inhabitants in the poorer countries, especially young people and professionals, increasing global interconnectivity and constant access to (Hollywood-mediated) images of hyper-prosperity and opportunities of life in the West contrasts sharply and grotesquely with the bleak economic environment and dim future prospects that frame their daily existence. As the cumulative theory (discussed in chapter 8) suggests, every act of migration enhances the propensity for more migration. Once households and communities are connected to wealthy foreign lands by the successful migration of their members, the migration compulsion among those left behind can become overwhelmingly intense. And the urge to move is often commensurate with the level of consciousness of the gap between what is and what could be. This is why the mechanics of global integration and division perpetuates migrant flows. What it does not explain is why some move and others do not. But even the best theories of migration fail to shed complete light on this fascinating question.

The next chapter explores the issue of contemporary international migrations, specifically South–North migration, in some detail. The fact that the direction of interregional migratory flow is now primarily south to north and east to west, where it was once primarily north to south, has profound implications for global religious expansion. For, in addition to its economic and demographic significance, the North–South divide is also of great religious importance, most notably so in the case of Christianity and Islam. It is a most extraordinary historical coincidence that the momentous "shift" in global Christianity's demographic and cultural center of gravity to the southern continents occurred at almost precisely the same time as the equally momentous reversal in the direction of international migrations. *This means that, as in the previous five centuries, global migration movement is matched with the heartlands of the Christian faith and the chief sources of missionary movement.* Thus, in the same way that unprecedented

---

48. "Emigration from Latin America: Making the Most of an Exodus," *The Economist*, February 23, 2002, 41.

49. See "So Where Are Zimbabweans Going?," *BBC News*, November 8, 2005.

50. Philip L. Martin, "The Impact of Immigration on Receiving Countries," in *Immigration into Western Societies: Problems and Policies*, ed. Emek M. Uçarer and Donald J. Puchala (Washington: Pinter, 1997), 18.

European migrations from Christianity's old heartland provided the impetus for European missionary movement, phenomenal migrations from Christianity's new heartlands (in Africa, Latin America, and Asia) have galvanized a massive non-Western missionary movement.

While this assessment makes sense from a missiological point of view (in an abstract sort of way), it presents a major problem. Missiologists take great pride in the multidisciplinary nature of mission studies. As well they might. The discipline of missiology (the science of missions) is notoriously multifaceted and readily encompasses theology, history, cultural anthropology, development economics, world religions, linguistics, urban studies, even sociology. But Western missiology has paid scant attention to international migrations. Much blame for this singular lack lies with my own discipline: history. Quite remarkably, given the critical role that migrations have played in the expansion of the Christian faith from its very inception, one is hard-pressed to find a book on the history of Christianity or Christian missions that addresses the fascinating links between migration and mission or incorporates the concept of Christianity as a migratory religion within historical analysis. Yet this correlation is intrinsic to the spread and impact of Christianity from its earliest beginnings. The very name "Christian" is linked to migrant refugee movement (Acts 11:19–26); and to repeat that memorable depiction of second century Christians, "though they are residents at home in their own countries, their behavior there is more like that of transients."[51]

Partly because the Western missionary project (which dominates the discipline of missiology) overlapped so extensively with visible structures of economic and political dominance, the inattentiveness to the impact of mobility, transience, and uprootedness on missionary enterprise has not been critical. But such an omission would be most damaging to the study of the newly emergent non-Western missionary movement. No dimension of contemporary experience captures more fully the magnitude, momentum, and motivations of this movement than migration.

In the chapters that follow I provide in-depth analysis of some of the most critical aspects of South–North migrations: including the theoretical models that best capture its complex dimensions and causative factors, its structure and composition (who migrates and why, where they go, what happens when they leave, etc.?), particular trends and trajectories (including the high rate of female migration and factors that affect flows), the complicated impact on source countries, and the significance of transnationalism. This general overview is then followed by a detailed examination of the African experience. Africa epitomizes the inextricable link between mission and migration: not only is it a major heartland of Christianity, but it is also a theater and source of international migrations. How and why this is so are of critical importance for understanding Africa's role in the non-Western missionary movement. Some readers may well find this extensive coverage of migration and related phenomena distracting, but I am convinced that without a thorough grasp of key factors and issues central to contemporary migration, the study of the new missionary movement would be most defective.

---

51. "Letter to Diognetus," 144-45.

8

South–North Migration

Old Story, New Endings

I cannot rest from travel: I will drink life to the lees. . . .
For always roaming with a hungry heart much I have seen and
    known;
Cities of men and manners, climates, councils, governments,
Myself not least, but honour'd of them all. . . .
                    —Alfred Lord Tennyson, "Ulysses"

According to UN estimates, international migrants totaled 191 million in 2005. This number, which represents 2.95 percent of the world population or roughly the size of Brazil's population, may seem inconsequential. Yet it means that one in thirty-four persons on the planet lives outside his/her land of birth or citizenship; which underscores the notion that few people in the world today are immune to the effects of migration. It is no small matter that the number of international migrants in the world increased by 150 percent in the last four decades or more than doubled in the thirty-year period from 1975 to 2005. In truth, the majority of international migrants are concentrated in certain regions—over 45 percent are in Europe and North America—but international migration has never been as pervasive or momentous, and there are ample indications that current trends will persist for the foreseeable future. If anything, as Stephen Castles and Mark J. Miller (1998) affirm, the various stimuli and pressures associated with worldwide mobility—including the potent combination of global integration, global demographic imbalances, and global economic disparities—appear to be intensifying.

For all this, a fulsome assessment of the dimensions of these incredibly complex and variegated movements is impossible. Credible statistics are lacking in many parts of the world, and the rising tide of undocumented workers and "irregular" (or illegal) migrants compounds the difficulty of accurate assessment. Quite simply, it is difficult to count people who are motivated to hide from authorities. Partly for these reasons, statistical data on international migrants in the world today are nearly always deficient, necessitating conjectures and educated guesses.

The multiplicity and variegated nature of contemporary movements also pose definitional and conceptual challenges that are further complicated by the variety of disciplinary approaches. The most common terms used are "migrants," "refugees," "asylum seekers," and (from the early 1990s) "internally displaced peoples." Within this framework, it is estimated that by the early 1990s there were seventeen million refugees and asylum seekers in the world, twenty million internally displaced peoples (IDPs), thirty million "regular" migrants, and another thirty million migrants with an "irregular" status.[1] Others estimate that in the early 1990s, before they were identified by the UNHCR (United Nations High Commissioner for Refugees) as a separate category "internally displaced peoples" who represent the vast majority and fastest-growing category of migrants numbered roughly one billion—eight times the number of international migrants or, incredibly, one in six of the entire human population.[2] The latest UN data on migrant stock in the world indicate that between 1960 and 2005 the numbers of international migrants and refugees in the world (asylum seekers are not identified as a separate category) rose from 75.5 million and 2.2 million to 191 million and 13.5 million, respectively.

By any reckoning the figures associated with migration and displacement in the world today are staggering. Yet analysis and application of the relevant data depend greatly on one's understanding of the various categories and forms of migration. The traditional distinction between *migrants* (those who "choose" go to another country for primarily economic or personal reasons) and *refugees* (those "forced" to leave their countries for primarily political reasons) has come under vigorous critique. Many scholars argue that motives for migration are much too complex and diverse for such a simple dichotomy. International migration often involves a complex web of obligations, pressures, and opportunities that make it impossible to disentangle elements of "compulsion" and "expulsion." The patterns of South–North migration, argues Elizabeth Ferris, "make it clear that most people leave their countries not because they want a *better* job, but because they simply cannot survive at home."[3] Thus, even economic migration is "forced" in some sense, and not all the people affected by political persecution or natural disaster necessarily migrate. Indeed, why some people *do not* migrate is a far more perplexing issue.

It is also worth noting in passing that, despite excited xenophobic foreboding within Western societies about the threats posed by uncontrolled nonwhite immigration, the full brunt of the global refugee crisis is being borne by the poorest nations of the world. Most migrants—including the bulk of the world's seventeen million officially registered refugees and asylum seekers—stay in their region of origin. Sub-Saharan Africa, with an estimated thirty-five million migrants, has the largest numbers of any continent, followed by Asia and the Middle East.[4] By 1995, Africa was home to about a third of the world's refugees and asylum seekers—more than twice the numbers accepted in the developed countries

---

1. Ferris, *Beyond Borders*, 10.

2. Demuth, "Some Conceptual Thoughts on Migration Research," 22. This extraordinary figure points to the pervasiveness and significance of interethnic conflicts. In 1999 the Kosovo–Albanian conflict alone produced over 750,000 IDPs.

3. Ferris, *Beyond Borders*, 10.

4. See Mittelman, *Globalization Syndrome*, 59; also Ferris, *Beyond Borders*, 130f. This figure represents about 8 percent of the population of sub-Saharan Africa.

of Europe, North America, and Oceania combined[5]—though the numbers had declined by 2000.

Studies of international migration are also beset by ideological factors. The legal criteria used to identify "migrant," "refugee," or "asylum seeker" vary considerably from country to country.[6] Many wealthy industrial nations have employed increasingly narrow descriptions and criteria for these categories as part of efforts to control nonwhite immigration. As we shall see, classification incompatibilities in immigration data kept by various Western destination countries also pose serious impediments to assessing international migration. Needless to say, whether one is defined as a refugee, an asylum seeker, or an economic migrant can make the difference between entry or deportation. And since international migration by definition implies crossing national border(s), legal definitions of these terms also determine legality or illegality. All these factors make international migration an intensely political issue. For purely political reasons, migrant figures may also be understated to forestall adverse public reaction or may be inflated because the number of "refugees" a country can claim affects the amount of international assistance that is given.

In truth, the complexities of the global order are such that the term *migrant* necessarily encompasses a wide range of types and experiences. Transient people, as Nicholas Van Hear recognizes, come in a variety of categories: permanent emigrants and settlers, temporary contract workers, professionals, business or trader migrants, students, refugees, asylum seekers, and cross-border commuters. They also shift between categories over a period of time, so someone who enters a country as a student may subsequently overstay or seek permanent residence and eventually become a naturalized citizen.[7] And, partly because of the racial and cultural distinctiveness of new immigrants, they tend to be identified with migration long after the physical act of migration is over, so that migrant children born in the country of destination (and considered "citizens" in some countries) are still described as "second- or third-generation migrants."[8]

All things considered, the fairly generic definition of international migrants as *people who have lived outside their homeland for one year or more* remains perhaps the most functional. In my view it renders it unnecessary to distinguish diverse forms of transience beyond the time element, and it implicitly focuses on the experience of uprootedness, regardless of the degree of choice or compulsion. In this study I have also avoided using the labels "sending" and "receiving" or "host" (to describe countries on either side of international migration movement). I consider such descriptors misleading and unhelpful, especially when applied to South-to-North migration. The poorer developing countries of the South have strong reasons to bemoan the steady emigration of their citizens and could hardly be described as "sending" them, while the term "host" society suggests a wel-

---

5. See Ferris, *Beyond Borders*, 94; Castles and Miller, *Age of Migration*, 91.

6. See Hania Zlotnik, "Trends in South to North Migration: The Perspective from the North," *International Migration* 29, no. 2 (1991): 317-31.

7. Nicholas Van Hear, *New Diasporas: The Mass Exodus, Dispersal and Regrouping of Migrant Communities* (Seattle: University of Washington Press, 1998), 41.

8. Papastergiadis, *Turbulence of Migration*, 55.

come that is seldom present in destination countries. It is common knowledge that the wealthy developed countries of the North have implemented increasingly restrictive policies aimed at curtailing nonwhite immigration, often in response to vigorous public anti-immigration sentiments. I have therefore employed the descriptors "origin" or "source" and "destination" or "country of settlement" to describe the constituent societies and countries of international migration.

Mapping New Trends: Reality in the Way of Theory

The unprecedented nature of current trends and patterns of international migration has stimulated fresh analyses that furnish new conceptual tools and challenge old paradigms. In particular, theories about the nature, origins, and processes of international migration have come under vigorous assessment and reappraisal within migration studies.[9] This discussion has been enriched by new efforts to incorporate interdisciplinary perspectives.[10] Of interest here are efforts to develop a theory of international migration that provides the best explanatory model of its complex, multilayered dimensions. Douglas Massey argues that, to be adequate, such a theory must contain four critical elements:[11]

1. A treatment of the structural forces that promote emigration from developing countries
2. A characterization of the structural forces that attract immigrants into developed countries
3. A consideration of the motivations, goals, and aspirations of the people who respond to these structural forces by becoming migrants
4. A treatment of the social and economic structures that arise to connect areas of out- and in-migration.

There is room here only to provide a brief summary of some the most prominent theories and perspectives.

The *neoclassical economic* perspective (the oldest and best known) explains international migration in terms of the supply and demand for labor. It includes theories that emphasize the tendency for people to move from densely to sparsely populated, or from low- to high-income, areas. The best known is the "push-pull" theory, which argues that migrant movement is a combination of "push" factors

---

9. Independent articles are too numerous to name. For published books, see, among others, Charles Hirschman, Philip Kasinitz, and Josh DeWind, eds., *The Handbook of International Migration: The American Experience* (New York: Russell Sage Foundation, 1999); Van Hear, *New Diasporas*; Castles and Miller, *Age of Migration*, 19-29; Papastergiadis, *Turbulence of Migration*, 30-37; Cornelius et al., eds., *Controlling Immigration*.

10. See Caroline Brettell and James Frank Hollifield, eds., *Migration Theory: Talking across Disciplines* (New York: Routledge, 2000); also Biko Agozino, *Theoretical and Methodological Issues in Migration Research: Interdisciplinary, Intergenerational and International Perspectives* (Brookfield, VT: Ashgate, 2000).

11. Massey, "Why Does Immigration Occur?" 50.

(including overpopulation, poverty, low income, lack of economic opportunity, religious persecution, and political oppression) and "pull" factors (including political freedom, high labor demand, opportunities for professional fulfillment and economic advancement, etc.). This "push-pull" model basically conceptualizes international migration in terms of individual choice, that is, movement based on rational, calculated, assessments of the costs involved and the potential benefits. This understanding is now widely rejected as inadequate and simplistic. Contrary to its main assumption, it is rarely the poorest or neediest people from the least-developed countries who migrate. The individualistic focus also overlooks historical causes of migration and ignores the central role of social networks. "Push" and "pull" factors do exist, but migrant choices and movements are subject to many constraints. This helps to explain why migrants go to certain countries (including densely populated ones like the Netherlands) and not others.

The *historical-structural* approach focuses on the unequal distribution of economic and political power. Rooted in Marxist analysis, it argues that migration is a form of cheap labor, driven not by individual choices but by uneven development; the unequal distribution of political power reinforces a stratified economic order in which poor countries remain trapped in their poverty while the rich countries get richer. Immanuel Wallerstein's "world systems theory," which explains how wealthy (capitalist) areas and poor (agrarian or precapitalist) regions are incorporated into a global market economy based on dependency, exemplifies this perspective. Proponents maintain that under colonialism the expansion of the capitalist economy into precapitalist societies inevitably caused disruptions and dislocations that created a mobile population prone to migrate. Subsequently, the past colonial relationship between the "core" and "periphery" creates cultural and ideological affinities (including language, education, and even currency) that influence economic penetration and facilitate migration. Additionally, the penetration of poor regions by wealthy foreign companies from the "core" areas (to take advantage of low wages, for instance) undermines the local economy, destabilizes social organization, and mobilizes or instigates migrant movement. The migrants move in the opposite direction (toward the capitalist core) utilizing the transportation and communications infrastructure created by capitalist economic expansion in the first place.

Essentially the historical-structural approach explains international migration mainly in terms of capitalist expansion and initiatives from the "core" states. Its assessment of international migration focuses almost exclusively on dominant structures and external forces. This approach diminishes the significance of more subjective elements, those subtle influences and complex motivations that contribute to migrant action and movement. Its treatment of the role of the state also leaves unanswered questions: Why does migration persist even when the economy in the core state stagnates? Given the deterministic role of core (Western) states, how do we explain their inability to effectively regulate immigrant flow? And why do states often favor or even encourage certain types of migrants while rejecting others?

The *social-capital* and *cumulative-causation* theories share common arguments and are best treated together. Social-capital theory draws attention to the

significance of intangible resources within family, communities, and networks
for international migration. Social capital—which can be described as relationships among persons that translate into tangible benefits or advantages—reduces
the costs of migration and increases the likelihood of further migration from
the same social network. In effect, social capital significantly augments migrant
movement. The first migrants from a community bear the fullest costs of migration because there are usually no social connections on which to draw to facilitate
their movement. But "migrants are inevitably linked to non-migrants, and the latter draw on the obligations implicit in relationships such as kinship and friendship to gain access to employment and assistance at the point of destination."[12]
Migrant networks lower the potential costs of international migration and also
potentially increase its benefits. In time, the growing numbers of people seeking
entry to a destination country may lead to the rise of private industries and organizations that service the migration demand and/or profit from it.

The cumulative-causation theory argues that over time international migration becomes self-sustaining or self-perpetuating. This happens in a number of
ways. The first migrants may be temporary workers or even visitors who plan
on a single trip. But the experience of social mobility and the exposure to higher
standards of living make repeated movement more likely, and each successive act
of migration increases the probability of further migration, which may end in permanent settlement. Similarly, the migration of the relatively well educated, professionals, and highly motivated people from the sending community stimulates
further migration, as costs and risks fall. On a long-term basis this process reinforces the productivity of the destination countries but simultaneously lowers the
productivity of the source region. Corresponding depletion in human resources
and productivity in the source countries contributes to economic stagnation and
stimulates further migration. Within destination societies also, immigrants tend
to be recruited into particular jobs that acquire the stigma of being "immigrant
jobs." Native workers become increasingly reluctant to fill those jobs, creating a
labor scarcity that reinforces the demand for more immigrants. However, the processes of cumulative causation can reach a point of saturation within a particular
community; and when that happens "migration loses its dynamic momentum for
growth" (Massey 1999: 46).

Both the social-capital and cumulative-causation theories depict migration as
a selective process and emphasize the role of individual or family decisions in
international migration. This perspective is one-sided. Neither gives much attention to the function of states or governments in implementing restrictive policies
aimed at stemming or regulating migrant flows. The role of historical processes
is also ignored. Furthermore, the sustained flow anticipated by the cumulative-
causation theory seems most pertinent when the countries of origin and destination are adjacent or at least located in the same region.

A more recent approach described as the *migration-systems theory* seeks to
examine both ends of the migration flow and study all the linkages between the
places concerned, whether within specific regions or between different regions.

---

12. Ibid., 34f., 44.

It makes two important arguments about international migrations. First, they "generally arise from the existence of prior links between sending and receiving countries based on colonization, political influence, trade investment and cultural ties." Second, such movements stem from the interaction of large-scale institutional factors (such as global economic structures or interstate relationships) and informal social networks developed by the migrants themselves (including personal relationships, family, and community ties). These informal networks not only link migrants with nonmigrants but also "provide the basis for processes of settlement and community formation in the immigration area" allowing migrant groups to develop their own social and economic infrastructure such as places of worship or ethnic food stores.[13]

Importantly, the migration-systems theory not only recognizes the role of the state in shaping migration patterns—an element largely overlooked in the other theoretical models—but it also attests that migrant decisions are usually made not by individuals but by families. Moreover, it incorporates the four elements that Massey insists must be included in a satisfactory theoretical account of international migration. The migration-systems theory provides perhaps the most comprehensive account simply because its seeks to address the deficiencies in the other models while incorporating their main arguments.

Ultimately, however, the multiplicity of theoretical accounts points to the immense complexities of contemporary international migration and, by implication, the inadequacy of monocausal explanations. But all the available theories contribute in some measure to our understanding of international migration, in part because each illuminates particular types of experiences or applies to a specific region.

South–North Migration: An Overview

Since the 1960s, nonwhite migration from less developed to highly developed countries—involving swelling tides of guest workers, labor migrants, asylum seekers, political and economic refugees, as well as family reunification—has become a dominant element in international migration trends. South-to-North migration is clearly rooted in global realities: primarily demographic imbalances, increasing global connectivity, and the daunting economic divide (or "the differential wealth and opportunities in the two worlds"[14]). Quite simply, the combination of global integration and the ever-widening divide between the wealthy industrial North and the nations of the "developing" South has transformed the former into a veritable magnet for migrant movement. But while the radical reversal in the direction of international migration in the postcolonial era is momentous, it should not obscure the fact that two critical and interrelated

---

13. See Castles and Miller, *Age of Migration*, 23-26.
14. R. T. Appleyard, "Summary Report of the Rapporteur," *International Migration* 29 (1991): 334.

dimensions of global migrations remain as salient as they were in previous centuries: namely, economic motivation and demographic imbalance. Having considered economic factors in the previous chapter, we turn briefly to the issue of demographic imbalance.

Demographic Imbalance

In a world where the richest 1 percent receive as much income as the poorest 57 percent,[15] the inverse relationship between demographic growth and economic development is a potent catalyst in the buildup of pressures that stimulate mass migration. In the poorer developing nations of the South, demographic expansion, anemic economic conditions, and sociopolitical turmoil generate intense pressures for migrating to the much wealthier, stable democracies in the North, where low fertility has also created huge labor demands.

The reverse flow of international migrations coincides uncannily with the onset of population stagnation and decline in Western societies. According to the Population Reference Bureau, the rate of population growth in more developed countries "peaked during the 1960s, at about 2 percent annually, and has declined since."[16] By the early 1990s it was already clear that the vast proportion of all future global population growth would take place in developing countries (of the South): over half in Asia and one-third in Africa.[17] By 1999, eighty-two million people were being added every year in less-developed countries compared to about 1.5 million in more developed countries.[18] With Africa, Asia, Latin America, and the Caribbean accounting for more than 80 percent of the world's population (see figs. 3 and 4), the pattern and volume of international migrations—and the attendant impact on world affairs—are unlikely to change any time soon.

The impact of such massive demographic growth on the development of the world's poorest countries is complex, but it will certainly compound existing socioeconomic problems and generate greater pressures to migrate. Nowhere is this more obvious than Africa, the world's fastest-growing continent. By 2005, an estimated 42 percent of Africa's population was under fifteen years of age, and Africa was home to ten of the eleven countries with the highest fertility rates in the world, with Niger (at eight lifetime births per woman) recording the highest of all.[19] Its roughly eight hundred million people (in 2000) are expected to increase by 65 percent to 1.3 billion in 2025 and by a further 45 percent to 1.9 billion by 2050.[20] While relatively wealthy countries like South Africa will

---

15. *Human Development Report 2001* (New York: Oxford University Press, 2001), 19.

16. *World Population: More Than Just Numbers* (Washington, DC: Population Reference Bureau, 1999).

17. See Kennedy, *Preparing for the Twenty-First Century*, 24.

18. *World Population: More Than Numbers.*

19. *2005 World Population Data Sheet* (Washington, DC: Population Reference Bureau, 2005).

20. World Population Prospects: The 2000 Revision in the United Nations—these estimates are

Figure 3
World Population Growth (1750-2150)

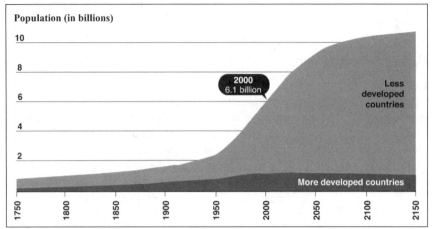

Source: United Nations, *World Population Prospects, the 1998 Revision; and estimates by the Population Reference Bureau.*

Figure 4
Demographic Estimates and Trends for Africa, Asia, Latin America, and the Caribbean

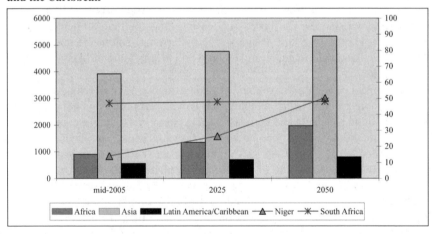

experience very modest population increase, the vast majority of African nations (like Niger) will experience significant growth (see fig. 4). Given existing social pathologies, this trend will likely translate into even greater poverty, escalating instability, and further out-migration movements.

---

based on a median variant; *World Population Data Sheet* (Washington, DC: Population Reference Bureau, 2005).

In sharp contrast, wealthy industrial countries, which constitute 17 percent of the world population are currently experiencing stagnant or negative population growth. It is projected that between 2005 and 2050 Europe will experience a 10 percent decline in population growth while North America's population will increase by 39 percent.[21] The overall picture for developed countries, however, is one of arrested growth. In most, the birthrate has dropped well below the replacement rate of 2.2 live births per woman of reproductive age. This trend potentially translates into severe labor shortages and economic constriction due to decreasing numbers of young people able to replace or support an aging population.

The economic and long-term geopolitical implications of this demographic disparity are complex. But, at the very least, they point to the profound significance of South–North migration for wealthy countries. In the period 1960 to 2005, the United States experienced a 60 percent increase in its population (from roughly 186 to 298 million); the corresponding demographic increase in Europe was 22 percent.[22] Over the next forty or so years the rate of growth in the United States is expected to be much slower (at 30 percent). But the contrast with Europe, where a 10-percent demographic *decline* is projected from 2005 to 2050, is striking. A crucial difference between the two regions is *immigration*. Quite simply, "America's immigration outstrips Europe's and its immigrant population is reproducing faster than native-born Americans."[23] In short, immigration will play a dominant role in America's projected growth.[24] By contrast, increased barriers to immigrant entry in Europe (since 1950) have contributed greatly to that continent's decline in population.

It is noteworthy that Germany, the world's third-largest economy, faces the prospect of having almost half its adult population aged sixty-five or over by 2030, which means that, over the next fifteen years, it will need to receive a million working-age immigrants each year just to keep a workforce at roughly the current level. Trends in the rest of Europe are hardly more promising. It is estimated that to maintain the age structure in the European Union, given fertility and mortality levels in 1996, would "require 7 million immigrants per year by 2024."[25] At present, immigration in the European Union remains well below one million. Some demographers confirm that large sustained immigration could have an impact on a population (in terms of size and age structure) similar to increased fertility. Yet growing anti-immigration sentiments in Europe, which has seen a fierce backlash against immigration and foreigners, act as a major impediment. The recent electoral defeats and reversal of fortune experienced by

21. *World Population Data Sheet.*

22. *Trends in Total Migrant Stock: The 2005 Revision.*

23. "Special Report: 'Demography and the West,'" *The Economist*, August 24, 2002, 20.

24. James P. Smith and Barry Edmonston, eds., *The New Americans: Economic, Demographic, and Fiscal Effects of Immigration* (Washington, DC: National Academy Press, 1997), 3.

25. Charles B. Keely, "Demography and International Migration," in *Migration Theory: Talking across Disciplines*, ed. Caroline Brettell and James Frank Hollifield (New York: Routledge, 2000), 56.

far-right political parties with an anti-immigration stance in Austria, France, and
Holland complicates analysis.

Frustratingly for Western governments, the general trend toward increasing global interchange and communication is at odds with the amount of effort
needed to control and provide surveillance of borders.[26] Many wealthy Western
countries have erected ever-higher barriers to stem this flow—transforming the
world into less a global village than a "gated community"[27]—but the impulses
stimulating mass migration are often too strong for restrictions to be fully effective, and none more so than demographic and economic factors.

Statistically Speaking

In the event, the closing decades of the twentieth century witnessed a tremendous increase in the immigrant populations of Europe and North America. Once
lower than Africa's, Europe's stock of international migrants rose to 7.7 percent
by 2000—nearly four times that in Africa (2 percent). Between them, Europe
and North America had 96.9 million migrants by 2000—more than half of the
estimated 175 million migrants worldwide.[28] The dismantling of the Soviet
Union and the redefinition of borders are contributing factors to the massive
increase in Europe's migrant stock—but so is the dramatic rise in South–North
immigration.

The year 1990 provides a significant reference point for the trend. By 1990,
Africa, Asia, Latin America and the Caribbean all show a *downward turn* in
their stock of international migrants, just when the migrant stock in Europe and
North America increases sharply. In 2005, Europe and North America accounted
for over eighty-seven million (45.8 percent) of the international migrants in the
world—up from 35.5 percent in 1960. Taken as a whole, these estimates point to
a gradual upsurge in non-Western migrant flows to the wealthy industrial nations
since 1960, a pattern that intensifies from about 1990 despite efforts within destination countries in the North to impose tighter and more restrictive immigration
policies.

For all this, non-Western immigrants constitute a small, if rapidly growing,
percentage of the populations in wealthy industrial countries—typically less
than 10 percent. Yet statistics do not tell the whole story. By their very existence,
the new immigrants have altered the face of many Western societies. In addition, higher birthrates and a disproportionately youthful population, as well as
continued influx, all point to a lasting and growing presence. By 2000, the new
immigrants and their children constituted about 20 percent of the American pop-

---

26. It is sobering to note that more than 1.3 million people, 340,000 vehicles, and 58,000 ship-
ments are estimated to enter the United States every day. See David Sanger and Eric Schmitt, "A
Nation Challenged: The Borders—Bush Leans toward New Agency to Control Who and What
Enters," *New York Times*, March 20, 2002.

27. Scott, "Great Divide in the Global Village," 160.

28. Philip Martin's estimation that "migrants in industrialized democracies" number about fifty
million is clearly off the mark. See Martin, "Impact of Immigration on Receiving Countries," 21.

Figure 5

Immigrants as Percentage of Total Population of United States, Netherlands, Germany, and Italy

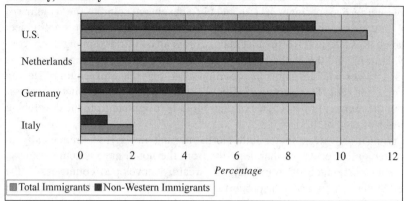

ulation.[29] Indeed, it is precisely because their unprecedented numbers portend major transformations of the ethnic, racial, and religious composition of Western populations that they are widely viewed in Western societies as a threat to livelihoods, cherished ways of life, and national identity.[30]

Andreas Demuth calculates that international migration accounted for 45 percent of the overall population growth in the more developed regions of the world between 1990 and 1995.[31] He notes, however, that only 10 percent of migrants from the poor countries of the world end up in the wealthy nations of the north. This figure is impossible to reconcile with Emek M. Uçarer's claim that South–North movement represents 40 percent of transboundary flows.[32] Such analytic disparities point to the fluidity and complexity of international migrations. The levels of non-Western migrants within Western nations have never been higher, yet determining the patterns, types, and composition that characterize such movements could not be more complex.

One major source of difficulty is the irreconcilable classification systems among destination countries. The United States, Canada, and Australia define an immigrant as someone born abroad to noncitizens—which links migrant identity to country of birth. But most European countries define immigrant status based on ethnicity or the immigration status of the parent,[33] while the traditional immigration countries only identify the migrant origins of persons admitted as

29. Rubén G. Rumbaut and Alejandro Portes, "Ethnogenesis: Coming of Age in Immigrant America," in *Ethnicities: Children of Immigrants in America*, ed. Rubén G. Rumbaut and Alejandro Portes (Berkeley: University of California Press, 2001), 7.

30. See Keely, "Demography and International Migration," 57.

31. Demuth, "Some Conceptual Thoughts on Migration Research," 21.

32. Emek M. Uçarer, "The Coming Era of Human Uprootedness: A Global Challenge," in *Immigration into Western Societies: Problems and Policies*, ed. Emek M. Uçarer and Donald James Puchala (London: Pinter, 1997), 1.

33. William J. Carrington and Enrica Detragiache, "How Extensive Is the Brain Drain," *Finance & Development* 36, no. 2 (1999): 48.

permanent residents.[34] Some countries, for example, Britain, determine migrant origin either by citizenship or by country of previous (or intended) residence. Given that many international migrants pass through multiple "transit" countries before long-term or permanent settlement in a developed country, the "country of birth" categorization is the most reliable since, unlike citizenship, it is not subject to change. It is also noteworthy that many European countries (among them, Germany, Britain, and the Netherlands) include incoming and outgoing migrants as well as citizens who are returning or emigrating, regardless of length of stay, in their migrant data. The incompatibility of these approaches complicates assessment of the number or percentage of migrants who originate from the developing countries of the South.

It is clear, however, that South–North migrant flows rose dramatically in the postcolonial period, so that migrants from the South have accounted for an increasing percentage of immigrants in wealthy, developed countries. In the United States, for instance, the proportion of migrants from the developing world rose from 40 percent in 1960 to 90 percent in 1990.[35] In Canada and Australia, where the *proportion* of migrants originating in developing countries was relatively lower in the early 1960s to begin with (8 and 12 percent, respectively), the rises have been much more striking: to 70 percent and roughly 52 percent, respectively.[36] Although the problems of data incompatibility must be borne in mind, European countries also registered a significant rise in the number of migrants originating in the South, even if the numbers and proportion were not nearly as substantial or consistent.[37] In Britain, where the proportion of migrants from developing countries remained quite high (compared with most European countries), there was a general decline from around 64 percent in the late 1970s to 48 percent in the late 1980s. As Hania Zlotnik points out, the fact that U.K. data classify immigrants by country of previous residence introduces significant bias into the assessment, since it would include British citizens returning from the developing world. My analysis, however, suggests that the migrant inflows for the U.K are much higher.

In order to provide a more up-to-date estimation of South–North migration (from 1990 to 2005), I have utilized data provided by the Migration Policy Institute for five major destination countries in the North: Australia, Canada, Germany, the United Kingdom, and the United States. Since the data source lists the number of migrants from specific source countries (as well as regional totals), I have calculated the approximate number of non-Western migrants simply by eliminating migrants from the United States, Canada, Europe, Australia, and New Zealand. Specifically, my assessment tracks movement from the following regions: Africa, the Caribbean, Central America, South America, Asia, Oceania, Melanesia, Micronesia, Polynesia. Included also are migrants classified as either

---

34. Zlotnik, "Trends in South to North Migration."
35. Ibid., 318.
36. Ibid., 319.
37. Ibid., 319-20. Zlotnik limits her analysis to five European countries: Belgium, Germany, Netherlands, Sweden, and the United Kingdom.

"stateless" or from "an unknown foreign country" (categories that are unlikely to include Westerners).

This approach has some obvious drawbacks: migrants from wealthy industrial nations like Japan and Korea are included, while migrants from developing countries in Eastern Europe are excluded. Moreover, the incompatibilities and vagaries in immigrant classification among the five countries imposes limitations on the accuracy of the final estimation.[38] That said, migrant data are notoriously imprecise, and the aim here is less to provide an empirical evaluation than to illustrate the general trend. The analysis serves a useful purpose insofar as it affords an overview of the volume and significance of South–North migration.

Among the five countries in our data sample, only the United States shows a decrease in non-Western migrant flows (from almost 1.7 million in 1991 to just over 800,000 in 2004). But, to put this in perspective, this decline in absolute numbers reflects an overall trend in U.S. immigrant flows—the percentage of non-Western migrants changes little over the same period (see fig. 6). Furthermore, the volume of non-Western migrants admitted to the United States far exceeds the comparable intake for any of the other four nations in the data sample in any given year within the period (and is often more than all the rest put together). Significantly, the United Kingdom registers the greatest increase of non-Western migrant inflows: numbers more than tripled from 43,790 in 1991 to over 114,000 in 2004. The increases indicated for Australia, Canada, and Germany are much more modest.

Figure 6

Inflow of Non-Western Migrants as a Percentage of Total Migrants to Australia, Canada, Germany, the United Kingdom, and the United States (1994 to 2004)

	1994	1995	1996	1997	1998	1999	2000	2001	2002	2003	2004
Australia	71.0	70.9	74.5	75.5	75.9	79.2	82.0	84.6	82.0	79.0	77.4
Canada	81.7	79.8	81.2	81.4	77.6	78.3	80.3	82.2	82.7	82.6	81.6
Germany	27.8	31.1	35.7	35.0	32.0	31.6	34.8	36.9	37.0	36.3	
United Kingdom	84.9	84.2	84.6	84.6	80.2	83.1	86.5	83.8	85.3	83.9	77.4
United States	79.7	82.1	83.8	85.0	85.4	85.3	83.5	82.5	82.8	85.2	85.9

---

38. The Australian data, for instance, include foreign-born children of Australian citizens, while the U.K. figures mainly comprise people granted permanent settlement but who were initially admitted into the United Kingdom on a temporary basis. The data on Canada and the United States is limited to immigrants granted permanent residence and therefore exclude significant numbers of migrants like students and professionals on work visas and their family members—all of whom may be legally resident for prolonged periods of time. Furthermore, not only are numbers typically rounded up but, even more crucially, the exact number of immigrants from certain countries is suppressed for reasons of confidentiality or security.

As figure 6 indicates, non-Western migrants represent a strikingly high percentage of migrant flows for the five countries in our sample. Germany records the lowest percentages—ranging from 27 to 37, although Germany's non-Western migrant stock is exceeded only by the United States. For Australia, Canada, the United Kingdom, and the United States, non-Western migrants constitute at least 70 percent of all immigrants from 1994 to 2004. The figures indicated for the United States and the United Kingdom average above 80 percent; those for Australia and Canada are only fractionally lower.[39] This assessment points to the massive upsurge in South–North migrations, albeit with some ebb and flow, over the last four decades.

Impact of Migration on Source Countries

The links between migration and development—or, more precisely, the impact of out-migration on developing countries—remains a matter of vigorous debate and the focus of voluminous literature. A fulsome assessment of the complex and often highly technical arguments animating this discourse is beyond the scope of this study. What follows is a critical assessment of those aspects of South–North migration that are held to have the most significant impact on source countries. An underlying concern, however, is to highlight the capacity of global migration movements to link the fate of distant communities. In this regard, the following aspects of South–North migration deserve brief consideration: (1) the "brain drain/gain" question; (2) remittances; (3) social network; (4) female migration; and (5) transnationalism.

"Brain Drain" or "Brain Gain"

The term "brain drain" was reportedly coined by the British Royal Society in the 1950s to describe the flow of scientists from Europe to North America.[40] Britain, for instance, lost 16 percent of its PhDs between 1952 and 1961, half of them to the United States. Since the late 1960s, however, the term has been employed almost exclusively as a reference to the increasing international flows of highly skilled and educated migrants from the developing countries of South to the industrial wealthy countries of the North. The direction and extensity of such skilled migration reflect wider trends within global migrations, of which the following stand out:

---

39. For reasons not apparent, the percentages represented in our data set are difficult to reconcile with Zlotnik's analysis, which stipulates a sharp decline to 48 percent for the United Kingdom in the late 1980s—unless, of course, the figures rebounded just as sharply by the early 1990s.

40. See B. Lindsay Lowell, Allan Findlay, and Emma Stewart, "Brain Strain: Optimising Highly Skilled Migration from Developing Countries," Institute for Public Policy Research, 2004, 3. Jean-Baptiste Meyer, however, dates official use of the term to 1963 (Jean-Baptiste Meyer, "Network Approach Versus Brain Drain: Lessons from the Diaspora," *International Migration* 39, no. 1 [2001]: 95). See also Rubén G. Rumbaut, "Origins and Destinies: Immigration, Race, and Ethnicity in Contemporary America," in *Origins and Destinies: Immigration, Race, and Ethnicity in America*, ed. Silvia Pedraza and Rubén G. Rumbaut (New York: Wadsworth, 1996), 28.

- Skilled migration among developed countries continues but remains a small part of the overall trend. For the most part, the phenomenon involves unidirectional flows from poorer, developing countries to wealthy industrial nations. It is largely a function of the massive inequalities in wealth and income, and the vast technological and digital divide, between North and South.
- Owing to the costs and complexities of international migration, migrants are drawn disproportionately from middle-income groups, which include professionals and those with advanced education.
- (The very rich also have the resources to migrate but typically lack the motivation or the need to seek the rewards of a better life abroad. Research also indicates that low levels of education often acts as a barrier to international migration.)
- For a complex number of reasons (including information access, resources, and ambition) the propensity to migrate increases with educational attainments. Thus, for developing countries migration rates tend to be highest among educated and professional groups. In other words, as a group, highly skilled immigrants typically represent a higher percentage of immigrants from a given country than they do of the source country's population.
- Owing mainly to changes in immigration regulations (from the late 1980s), skilled migrants comprise an increasingly greater proportion of South–North migration. Many destination countries—notably the United States, Canada, and Australia but also a growing number of European countries—have introduced highly restrictive and "quality selective" immigration policies, which target the highly educated or skilled and discourage unskilled flows.

These factors point to the progressive escalation of skilled (South–North) migration over the last three decades as part of processes of contemporary globalization. It is often recalled that, whereas the total number of highly skilled South–North migrants was estimated at 300,000 for 1961-1972, in 1990 the United States alone had more than 2.5 million highly educated immigrants.[41] Yet precise calculations of the scale and magnitude of skilled migration are bedeviled by a number of problems: there is no uniform system among destination countries for defining and classifying immigrants; immigration data from some countries omit the educational level of immigrants; and few source countries monitor out-migration or record return migration (with the exception of rare occasions when it is associated with special programs).[42]

In recent years there have been significant attempts to provide a meaningful quantitative assessment of skilled migration. A 1998 study of emigration from sixty-one developing countries to OECD (Organization for Economic

41. Frédéric Docquier and Hillel Rapoport, "Skilled Migration: The Perspective of Developing Countries," 2005, 5— PDF version available online (see bibliography).

42. See Piyasiri Wickramasekara, "Policy Responses to Skilled Migration: Retention, Return, and Circulation," ILO, 2002.

Co-operation and Development) countries concluded that the largest flows of highly educated migrants, in absolute terms, are from Asia.[43] Significantly, however, the highest migration rates (i.e., as a percentage of the source country's population) are to be found in the Caribbean, Central America, and Africa. The number of African migrants to the United States, for instance, is small compared to that from other regions, yet the rate of skilled African immigration is among the highest—95,000 individuals out of a total of 128,000 African migrants (or 74 percent) had tertiary education. Indeed, the study concluded that "migration of low-educated Africans is almost nil." It also confirmed that the United States, Australia, Canada, France, and Germany account for about 93 percent of total migratory flows to OECD countries.

A more thoroughgoing study conducted in 2004 estimated emigration rates of skilled workers for 170 countries in 1990 and 190 countries in 2000.[44] Here, too, the destination nations were limited to OECD countries. The study estimated that the total stock of adult immigrants (over twenty-five years of age) in OECD countries was 39.8 million in 1990 and 58.5 million in 2000. Highly skilled immigrants represented 37 percent of the OECD immigration stock in 2000 (up from 33 percent in 1990)—though only 9.1 percent of the world labor force had tertiary education.[45] On a country-by-country basis, the intensity of skilled emigration correlates to country size in two different ways: in absolute numbers, larger countries are most affected; whereas in relative terms (as a proportion of the labor force) smaller countries are the most affected. In relative terms, Africa and Asia showed the highest rates of skilled emigration:

- In 2000, highly skilled workers in Asian countries constituted only 6 percent of the entire Asian population but made up 43.5 percent of Asian emigrants.
- African nations accounted for seven of the ten countries in the world (with total populations exceeding 4 million) most affected by skilled migration.[46]

Admittedly, such assessments of migration suffer from data limitations. Importantly, the underrepresentation of low-skilled migrants in data samples reflects the fact that this group is the most likely to be undocumented. Yet the statistical evidence pointing to a tremendous flow of skilled migration from developing to developed countries is undeniable. Even the more conjectural estimation

---

43. William J. Carrington and Enrica Detragiache, "How Big Is the Brain Drain?" International Monetary Fund, 1998—available online (see bibliography). The study was purposefully restricted to individuals over twenty-five years of age.

44. Frédéric Docquier and Abdeslam Marfouk, "Measuring the International Mobility of Skilled Workers (1990-2000): Release 1.0," The World Bank, 2004—PDF version available online (see bibliography).

45. Ibid., 22.

46. The study also concluded that there is "a decreasing relationship between emigration rates and country population sizes" (p. 31); specifically that "small countries with a population below 4 million are the most affected" (p. 29).

that in 2001 nearly one in ten tertiary-educated adults born in the developing world resided in North America, Australia, or Western Europe denotes a movement of extraordinary scale.[47] And it is noteworthy that skilled migrations from the Caribbean and Western Africa are among the highest of all regions in the South.

Assessment of the impact on developing countries of this massive depletion of human capital has exercised economic analysts and other experts for over four decades. Whether the "brain drain" is wholly detrimental to developing countries or has some beneficial effects remains a vexed question, though recent evaluations tend to emphasize positive aspects.[48] Arguments focused on the adverse impact of skilled migration typically incorporate the following assertions:

- First and foremost, skilled migration represents a heavy loss of costly investments in subsidized education and training.
- Skilled migration diminishes the pool of taxpayers and potential leaders.
- By depriving the government of taxable income, skilled migration increases the fiscal burden on those left behind.
- By reducing the human capital stock—in this case of invaluable skills and professional experience—skilled migration severely curtails the country's productivity and growth prospects.
- The scarcity of skilled labor negatively impacts the productivity of unskilled labor and contributes to domestic inequality or income disparities.
- The depletion of professional skills contributes directly to the decline of essential services in health and education.
- High levels of out-migration can have tremendous inimical impact on social structures in the area of origin, by depriving families and communities of critical leadership or imposing enormous strains on marriages.
- Migrant remittances (which arguably offset the negative effect of brain drain) decline over time.

On the other side of the debate are proponents who argue that skilled migration affords a number of substantial benefits for developing countries. As such, they favor descriptions like "brain gain," "brain strain," or "brain circulation," to highlight the limited negative impact of skilled migration and the fact that it involves two-way or multiple flows.[49] Arguments focused on the positive benefits of skilled migration include the following assertions:

- In situations where the highly educated are unable to find stable employment, migration provides rewarding opportunities unavailable at home and alleviates unemployment or underemployment.

---

47. Lowell, Findlay, and Stewart, "Brain Strain," 9.

48. For an overview of the "traditional" and "modern" (or revisionist) views, see Wickramasekara, "Policy Responses to Skilled Migration," 1-13; Docquier and Rapoport, "Skilled Migration," 3-4, 15f., 24-35; and Riccardo Faini, "Is the Brain Drain an Unmitigated Blessing?" UNU/WIDER (United Nations University/World Institute for Development Economics Research), 2003.

49. On this, see Lowell, Findlay, and Stewart, "Brain Strain," 6-25.

- Better brain drain than brain decay.
- Skilled migration can stimulate an increase in the skilled stock of developing countries because potential workers are motivated to pursue higher education in the hope of working abroad. And since only a percentage of this skilled workforce can emigrate, there is a cumulative increase in the country's human capital. Also known as the theory of "optimal brain drain."[50]
- Skilled migration can lead to the formation of diaspora networks (of intellectuals and skilled professionals) involving emigrants and nonemigrants, which facilitate the feedback or circulation of knowledge and technology and promote integration into the global economy.[51] Such transnational connections, it is argued, benefit developing countries at little or no cost and turn brain drain into brain gain or brain circulation.
- While research indicates that return migration of the highly skilled is negligible unless prompted by sustained economic growth in the source country, migrants who return after acquiring additional knowledge and skills abroad can contribute to knowledge/technology diffusion and the creation of businesses or trade networks.
- The portion of migrant earnings (remittances) sent from the developed country to the area of origin is a vital source of revenue for developing countries—far more than foreign aid.

Remittances are widely recognized as possibly the most significant single source through which skilled migration benefits developing countries. Yet the "benefits" of migrant remittances are widely debated. The key issue is whether such remittances offset the negative effects of the "brain drain." That question has no straightforward answers.

Remittances

Migrant remittances through formal channels were estimated at $93 billion in 2003,[52] and at $167 billion (by the World Bank) in 2005. Since many migrants do not use official channels to remit funds and some remittances are sent in the form of goods, the real volume is definitely much greater. But even this partial picture indicates higher revenue than the total flow of official development assistance. Indeed, while aid to developing countries decreased during the decade of the 1990s, remittances almost doubled.[53] Remittances to India, for instance,

---

50. According to one study, 30 percent of Indian doctors surveyed acknowledged that the prospect of emigration affected the effort they put into their studies. See Docquier and Rapoport, "Skilled Migration," 16.

51. For a treatment of the emergence and significance of "highly skilled diaspora networks," see Meyer, "Network Approach," 97-108. Studies show that some immigrants constantly move back and forth between home and host country. A survey of Chinese immigrants in Silicon Valley revealed that 50 percent of those surveyed return to their home country at least once a year on business, and 5 percent do so at least five times a year. See "Special Report. The Longest Journey: A Survey of Migration," *The Economist*, November 2002, 12.

52. Lowell, Findlay, and Stewart, "Brain Strain," 23.

53. Peter Gammeltoft, "Remittances and Other Financial Flows to Developing Countries,"

exceed $9 billion per annum—six times the amount it receives in foreign aid. In 2004, Ghanaians abroad remitted over $1 billion, much of it used to generate small businesses in the country.[54] In several smaller countries remitted funds are a bigger source of foreign exchange than foreign investment or even exports. Pakistan, for instance, is said to have in some years "received more capital in migrants remittances than the state has allocated for national development at the federal and local levels."[55]

But, while the amount of remitted funds is impressive by any measurement, the impact and actual benefit of the remittances themselves remains a matter of vigorous argument.[56] Many contend that remittances are an unpredictable or volatile source of income; that they are spent on consumer goods, result in little or no capital investment, increase dependency, and exacerbate inequalities within the recipient societies. Others counter that each dollar sent home translates into three or four dollars of growth as it works its way through the local economy, that remittances ease foreign exchange constraints, are potential sources of capital investment, help to raise the standard of living of recipients, and improve income distribution. In sub-Saharan Africa there is strong evidence of remittance use for investment with education as a priority.[57] As with any worldwide phenomenon, each of these arguments has merit and applicability in different contexts.

A more fundamental question, however, is whether remittances increase with the educational level of migrants. Here, too, the complex array of factors that impinge on the subject defy straightforward analysis. Greater earning ability means that skilled migrants are able to send more, sometimes to reimburse the family for funding of (or sacrifices made for) their education.[58] They can also utilize more sophisticated financial flows, such as remittance-backed bonds and foreign currency accounts, and can invest in business or philanthropic ventures.[59] At the same time, highly educated migrants tend to emigrate with their immediate family, which lessens familial obligations and translates into lower remittances. They are also more likely to migrate on a more permanent basis and arguably remit less and less with the progressive weakening of ties to the home country.[60] Yet a higher earning capacity allows skilled (South–North) migrants to visit the home country more frequently.

A range of other complex factors and context-specific elements also trouble

---

International Migration 40, no. 5 (2002): 182f.

54. Micah Bump, "International Migration in Africa: An Analysis Based on Estimates of the Migrant Stock," Migration Policy Institute, 2006.

55. Mittelman, *Globalization Syndrome*, 23.

56. For a useful summary of the arguments, see Sharon Stanton Russell, "Migration Remittances and Development," *International Migration* 30 (1992): 267-87; also Sharon Stanton Russell, Karen Jacobsen, and William Deane Stanley, *International Migration and Development in Sub-Saharan Africa*, 2 vols., Africa Technical Department series, World Bank Discussion Papers (Washington, DC: World Bank, 1990), 1:23-36.

57. Russell, Jacobsen, and Stanley, *International Migration and Development in Sub-Saharan Africa*, 1:32f., 35.

58. See Docquier and Rapoport, "Skilled Migration," 25.

59. Lowell, Findlay, and Stewart, "Brain Strain," 24.

60. Faini, "Is the Brain Drain an Unmitigated Blessing?" 8.

clear-cut generalizations about skilled migration and remittances. Skilled or not, whether migrants have work permits or permanent residence, whether they have spouses back home, whether they are young and single, whether they are male or female (women tend to remit more funds and more faithfully than men), whether they have children of their own in the society of settlement are all critical factors for remittance sending.[61] Also germane is whether higher education or advanced skills were acquired in the country of origin or country of destination. Evidence indicating that some two-thirds of PhD holders of foreign origin in the United States earned their degree after they arrived in the United States is telling.[62] This offers further confirmation of the widely held view that migrants are "driven to uncommon performance," if only to overcome adverse conditions and thrive in a highly competitive environment.

In summary, assessments of the impact of skilled migration on development are bedeviled by fragmentary and conflicting evidence. In addition to the data limitations, however, analysis is often undermined by a restrictive theoretical framework that treats skilled migrants as so many *individual* goods (or capital), without reference to vital social networks which continually shape their decisions and interactions. International migration has complex social dimensions that help not only to determine the composition and direction of migratory flows but also frame the complex web of relationships and networks that link migrants to potential migrants and shape enduring links between societies of destination and societies of origin.

Social Networks

In the late nineteenth century, Rev. Josiah Strong, a prominent American evangelical, commented that "every foreigner who comes to us and wins success . . . becomes an advertiser of our land; he strongly attracts his relatives and friends, and very likely sends them money for their passage."[63] This insight affirms the critical role of social networks in migration to America over a century ago. Yet, until recently, international migration was often depicted in individualistic and mechanistic terms: migrant movement was seen as either the product of external pressures or deliberate individual calculation. More recent assessments have illuminated the critical role of informal social networks and interpersonal ties as well as the salience of intangible realities such as "the transmission of ideas, stories told by other migrants, rumors of opportunity, the strutting of returnees . . . and the complex levels of influence exerted by the media."[64] Needless to say, contemporary migrants are far better informed about opportunities abroad than earlier generations of European migrants were, and the propensity to migrate is significantly

---

61. For useful comments, see, among others, Richard Black, "Soaring Remittances Raise New Issues," *Migration Information Source*, 2003—available online (see bibliography); Kimberly Hamilton, "Migration and Development: Blind Faith and Hard-to-Find Facts," Migration Policy Institute, 2003—available online (see bibliography).

62. See Meyer, "Network Approach Versus Brain Drain," 98, 100.

63. Strong, *Our Country*, 47.

64. Papastergiadis, *Turbulence of Migration*, 47.

influenced by the fact that the transportation revolution has collapsed distance and lowered the costs of travel dramatically.

From a social perspective, the decision to migrate is usually made by families or household units, not autonomous individuals—in part because of the costs and risks involved. Indeed, studies show that migration sometimes functions as a household strategy to overcome local economic constraints.[65] Informal social networks, kinship or obligatory ties, and preexisting relationships dictate migration patterns to a significant extent and link migrants to potential migrants.

Long before the act of migration and long after settlement in the destination society, strong social networks shape the experience of migration and implicate societies of origin. The need to provide children with good education and better opportunities often factors heavily into decisions to migrate; and the new transnational cultural identities and social relationships formed by immigrant children often determine permanent settlement. To be sure, an unprecedented proportion of contemporary international migration is geared to permanent settlement in the destination society. Once in the destination country, migrants are under obligation to send remittances, and many continue to play an active role in home or homeland matters. Family reunification extends the process further, as immigrants bring or sponsor spouses, children, or other family members. Some marry other immigrants (often from a similar cultural background) who bring their own social ties into the new relationship.

Female Migration

Attentiveness to the significance of social networks has also contributed to fresh appraisals of female participation. In the traditional conception, international migration mainly involves enterprising males who leave their family behind for an unknown future in a foreign land. In this scenario feminine involvement is passive; females accompany or subsequently join pioneering male migrants. Despite the data deficiencies that plague migrant statistics, this understanding has turned out to be erroneous.[66] By 1990 female migrants accounted for virtually half (49 percent) of the world's migrants, up from 47 percent in 1960. Females not only make up half of the world's migrants but also constitute the majority of the world's refugees and displaced peoples.[67] Nikos Papastergiadis (2000) reports that Filipino women account for 80 percent of all migrants from the Philippines, and André Jacques indicates that 90 percent of Ethiopian refugees in Somalia in

65. See Partricia R. Pessar, "The Role of Gender, Households, and Social Networks in the Migration Process: A Review and Appraisal," in *The Handbook of International Migration: The American Experience*, ed. Charles Hirschman, Philip Kasinitz, and Josh DeWind (New York: Russell Sage Foundation, 1999), 57; John A. Arthur, *Invisible Sojourners: African Immigrant Diaspora in the United States* (Westport, CT: Praeger, 2000), 28, 82.

66. Pessar, "Role of Gender"; Annie Phizacklea, "Migration and Globalization: A Female Perspective," in *The New Migration in Europe: Social Constructions and Social Realities*, ed. Khalid Koser and Helma Lutz (New York: St. Martin's Press, 1998).

67. Papastergiadis, *Turbulence of Migration*, 48; Ferris, *Beyond Borders*, 108; Phizacklea, "Migration and Globalization," 22.

1986 were women and children.[68] The figures vary across regions, but only in Africa and Asia do male migrants constitute a clear majority. Everywhere else, female migrants equal or outnumber male migrants (most noticeably in Europe).

The fact that female migrants constitute a majority (52.4 percent) of all migrants in developed countries (compared to 44.7 percent in the developing world) suggests that female migrants form a significant proportion of South–North migration.[69] Misleadingly dubbed the "feminization of migration"—misleading because the number of female migrants has closely matched that of males for almost half a century—this trend is shaped by a number of factors. Family unification policies in Western countries since the early 1970s play a significant role. In France, for instance, the percentage of women in the total foreign population increased to 42.6 percent by 1982.[70] Zlotnik (1991) argues that greater access to a variety of educational and employment opportunities also attracts many women to developed countries as social actors in their own right.[71] Certainly, as changing economic patterns within developing countries negatively impact household incomes, an increasing proportion of women are emigrating alone in response to job opportunities abroad—notably in medical, care-giving, and domestic services.[72] Certainly, changes in the family structure in affluent Western countries have resulted in a vastly increased demand for migrant domestic workers, large percentages of whom are undocumented. At the same time, global economic realities have also contributed to a massive rise in the number of women exploited (as illegal or undocumented migrants) in the prostitution and entertainment industries. The numbers involved are staggering—in many Western countries foreign prostitutes far outnumber local prostitutes.[73]

Transnationalism

International migration patterns are also shaped by enduring cultural (and ideological) linkages rooted in prior colonial relationships among various regions and countries. The administrative models, educational systems, and language of public life in many former colonies are legacies of colonialism. Inevitably, Indians, Pakistanis, and many Africans grow up speaking English, pursue British-style educational degrees, and have a vague consciousness of being part of the British Commonwealth (a gross misnomer). More of their numbers migrate to Britain than anywhere else. For similar reasons, citizens of Senegal, Algiers,

---

68. André Jacques, *The Stranger within Your Gates: Uprooted People in the World Today* (Geneva: World Council of Churches, 1986), 55.

69. For data on the percentage of female migrants in various parts of the world, see *Trends in Total Migrant Stock: The 2005 Revision.*

70. M. Lemoine, "Effects of Migration on Family Structure in the Receiving Country," *International Migration* 27 (1989): 272.

71. See also Silvia Pedraza, "Origins and Destinies: Immigration, Race, and Ethnicity in American History," in *Origins and Destinies: Immigration, Race, and Ethnicity in America,* ed. Silvia Pedraza and Rubén G. Rumbaut (New York: Wadsworth, 1996), 14.

72. See Aderanti Adepoju, "South–North Migration: The African Experience," *International Migration* 29, no. 2 (1991): 213; also Phizacklea, "Migration and Globalization," 32f.

73. See Papastergiadis, *Turbulence of Migration,* 40-41.

and Morocco tend to predominate in France. For a while, Cold War geopolitical relationships also exerted some influence on international migrant movement. Until the late 1980s, scholarships for study and advanced training in the Soviet Union or the United States reflected efforts by the two superpowers to expand ideological influence. More recently, the prevalence of American cultural influence through its dominance of mass media, as well as other specific economic and military partnerships, has contributed to the recent increase of Asian and Latin American immigration.

Transformations in global communications and transport infrastructure have also had a profound impact on the nature and dynamic of contemporary migration, enabling fixed social and religious networks and interactions that transcend national boundaries and geographical distance. The social ties and networks that contemporary migrants forge between societies of origin and settlement, regardless of distance and national boundaries, are more pervasive and entrenched than at any time previously. For new migrant communities, identity formation and cultural distinctiveness are no longer bounded by geographical location or social space. Becoming migrants or permanent residents outside the homeland does not necessarily translate into complete cultural isolation, severed household ties, and erosion of identity. As Papastergiadis explains, "separation is . . . not so much an indication of loss and deprivation as the strategic luxury of economic optimization and risk minimization."[74] This aspect of global migrations, which began to attract scholarly attention in the 1990s, has been described as "transnational migration" or "transnationalism." Transnationalism, according to Nina G. Schiller, implies that "even though migrants invest socially, economically, and politically in their new society, they may continue to participate in the daily life of the society from which they migrated but which they did not abandon."[75]

Quite literally, an ever-increasing number of households in the South have at least one family member or close relative with whom they have close ties living in the North. Such linkages form the foundation of a vast and dynamic transnational reality. Transnationalism, as Schiller explains, is not to be equated with the deep nostalgia that many immigrants feel for home. Not every international migrant is a transmigrant. Transmigrants "are people who claim and are claimed by two or more nation-states, into which they are incorporated as social actors, one of which is widely acknowledged to be their state of origin."[76] Transmigrants are often bilingual, able to lead dual lives move easily between cultures, and frequently maintain a home in two countries. They help to link the fate of distant communities.

Empirical assessment of transmigration is impossible, but even by this strict

---

74. Ibid., 45.

75. Schiller, "Transmigrants and Nation-States," 94. See also Meyer, "Network Approach Versus Brain Drain"; Kathleen Newland, "Migration as a Factor in Development and Poverty Reduction," Migration Policy Institute, 2003—available online (see bibliography); Alejandro Portes, "Immigration Theory for a New Century: Some Problems and Opportunities," in *The Handbook of International Migration: The American Experience*, ed. Charles Hirschman, Philip Kasinitz, and Josh DeWind (New York: Russell Sage Foundation, 1999), 29.

76. Schiller, "Transmigrants and Nation-States," 96.

definition, the phenomenon is regarded as a widespread and pervasive component of global migrations. Innumerable studies confirm that the new immigrants establish and maintain transnational social networks that, at the very least, involve occasional visits home and remittance obligations. For increasing numbers of people, affirms sociologist John Tomlinson, "the comforting, familiar character of the cultural settings [they] routinely move amongst conceals the influences of distant social forces and processes."[77] Indeed, for some groups of immigrants, settlement in a wealthy industrialized country elevates their social status back home and enhances their capacity for political and economic participation. John Arthur notes of African immigrants in the United States that, partly because many harbor strong intentions of returning, they

> maintain close connections with social and political issues at home. . . . Fund-raising to support political and social causes at home is common. They lobby political leaders at home through letter writing and sponsorship of political activities in the host society. These forums are intended to call attention to particular issues at home and to formulate and coordinate action. The immigrant groups are a force to be reckoned with in African internal politics—a special constituency of well-off people in America whose voices are having an impact on African social and political policies.[78]

But transnationalism as a dimension of migration is hardly a new phenomenon. Even before the age of steam, the processes of globalization had influenced the emergence of migrant communities, which, though separated by considerable distance from their original homeland, maintained an active network of communication and interpersonal interaction.

In the early eighteenth century, for instance, a highly effective transatlantic communications network, characterized by prodigious personal (religious) correspondence, newspaper coverage, and social relationships was maintained by English Dissenters, New England Puritans, and Scots Presbyterians.[79] The seeds of this "triangular exchange" lay in the large-scale migration and refugee movement that began with the exodus of disgruntled Puritan separatists from England in the 1620s and 1640s. A sense of collective solidarity with "dissenting" groups back in England—groups that shared deeply felt spiritual disaffection with, and

---

77. John Tomlinson, *Globalization and Culture* (Chicago: University of Chicago Press, 1999), 106f.

78. Arthur, *Invisible Sojourners*, 91; also 138f. Jean-Baptiste Meyer also argues, based on research among South African expatriates, that links with the home country tend to be more personal and family oriented than professional; yet, "when called to participate in a national support scheme, like diaspora knowledge networks, they react positively and become unexpectedly involved" (Meyer, "Network Approach Versus Brain Drain," 100).

79. See John Walsh, "'Methodism' and the Origins of English-Speaking Evangelicalism," in *Evangelicalism: Comparative Studies of Popular Protestantism in North America, the British Isles, and Beyond, 1700-1990*, ed. Mark A. Noll, D. W. Bebbington, and George A. Rawlyk (New York: Oxford University Press, 1994), 19-37.

opposition to, the "established" Anglican Church—fostered a remarkably strong network of exchange and common expectation which flowered in the transatlantic eighteenth-century evangelical revival. It is said of George Whitefield (1714-1770), the foremost evangelist of the revival and one of the greatest itinerant preachers in Christian history, that he could step easily from one side of the Atlantic to the other, "from London to Boston, Lowland Scotland, South Wales, Philadelphia, or South Carolina, with little or no spiritual culture shock, feeling himself a fully passported citizen of a transatlantic revival community."[80]

In time, technological innovations in oceanic travel, notably the use of steam from 1850, saw the emergence of even more robust transnational communities linked to migration. Long-distance travel became more predictable, levels of communication and migrant remittances increased considerably, and many European migrants to the United States came as sojourners or seasonal migrant laborers who returned home as frequently as once a year.[81] As noted in chapter 7, the new globally dispersed immigrant communities created by the needs of European empire building often became active agents of political change in their homeland. Finding themselves economically exploited and politically marginalized in American society, many European migrants in the United States cultivated strong homeland identities and actively participated in homeland nationalism.[82]

Transnationalism was also an important dimension of Western missionary expansion. The traditional Western missionary was essentially a transmigrant, one who claimed and was claimed by two societies, with strong ties and commitment to both. On a wider canvas, the Western missionary movement not only played a crucial role in the spread of Western values throughout non-Western societies but also helped to shape public opinion and deepen knowledge of non-Western cultures at home. In many ways it linked the destinies of two worlds.

Needless to say, contemporary globalization has revolutionized the nature and significance of transmigration and transnationalism.[83] The tremendous rise in the magnitude, multiplicity, and extensity of transnational networks in the last half century stems from a number of factors: the phenomenal levels of international migration; radical transformations in the volume and velocity of global financial

---

80. Ibid., 19; see also Henry S. Stout, "George Whitefield in Three Countries," in *Evangelicalism* (see n. 79).

81. Richard D. Alba and Victor Nee, *Remaking the American Mainstream: Assimilation and Contemporary Immigration* (Cambridge, MA: Harvard University Press, 2003), 146; also Schiller, "Transmigrants and Nation-States." Schiller notes that between 25 and 60 percent of European immigrants who settled in the United States in the early twentieth century made at least one return trip.

82. Schiller, "Transmigrants and Nation-States," 100-105.

83. For a thorough discussion, see Caroline B. Brettell, "Theorizing Migration in Anthropology: The Social Construction of Networks, Identities, Communities, and Globalscapes," in *Migration Theory: Talking across Disciplines*, ed. Caroline Brettell and James Frank Hollifield (New York: Routledge, 2000) 105-6; Pyong Gap Min, "Contemporary Immigrants' Advantages for Intergenerational Cultural Transmission," in *Mass Migration to the United States: Classical and Contemporary Periods*, ed. Pyong Gap Min (New York: AltaMira Press, 2002).

flows (in which MNCs and TNCs play a crucial role); the diminished capacity of nation-states to regulate global flows in goods and services; the implementation by an increasing number of countries of dual-citizenship policies; the espousal of multiculturalism as an official policy by some Western governments; and major technological advancements in communication, transportation, and mass media, which translate into the dissolving of distance, unprecedented global connectivity, and deterritorialization.[84]

In short, today's migrants (or transmigrants) have tremendous capacity to form enduring cultural, social, and political ties with their homeland. Most are able to maintain exceptional levels of connectivity (through long-distance telephone calls, e-mails, and faxes), and many fashion multilayered identities informed by selective adaptation to their country of settlement while preserving a distinctive ethnic identity (reinforced through travel, ethnic media, the Internet, and the accessibility of homeland products like food, music, and dress). Immigrant congregations play a vital role in this regard. Whether or not the descendants of the new immigrants will sustain current levels of transnationalism, much less emulate the transmigration of their parents, remains an open question—though there is some indication that immigrant children may also maintain or renew transnational ties and networks.[85] The point at issue is that global migration movements irreversibly and meaningfully link the fate of distant communities. And it is not only the societies of origin that are greatly impacted. As we shall see (chapters 11 and 12), in important respects, the impact of South–North migration on the societies of settlement is arguably even more profound and transformative.

---

84. Deterritorialization (or delocalization) is a feature of globalization in which a group's or individual's strongest social bonds, including cultural identity and political loyalty, are dissociated from the inhabited geographical space or immediately surrounding community. Products can also be deterritorialized. For more on this phenomenon, see Tomlinson, *Globalization and Culture*, 106; Arjun Appadurai, "Disjuncture and Difference in the Global Cultural Economy," in *The Globalization Reader*, ed. Frank J. Lechner and John Boli (Malden, MA: Blackwell, 2000).

85. See Schiller, "Transmigrants and Nation-States," 96. Alba and Nee, who query the distinctiveness of contemporary transnationalism, compared to previous eras, see this as a crucial query (*Remaking the American Mainstream*, 149-53).

9

African Migrations

A Single Bracelet Does Not Jingle

For always roaming with a hungry heart much have I seen and
  known—
Cities of men and manners, climates, councils, governments. . . .
Come, my friends, 'Tis not too late to seek a newer world.
                              —Alfred Lord Tennyson, "Ulysses"

No region in the world exemplifies the view that migration is "an irrepressible human urge" more clearly than the African continent. Mobility, it is said, is "deeply ingrained in African societies."[1] African peoples are perpetually on the move, and migration (inter- and intra-continental) represents one of the most conspicuous and recurring themes of Africa's history. Yet, even for this most mobile of continents, the last three to four decades have witnessed a phenomenal rise in the volume and scope of migrant movement, as escalating conflicts, brutal regimes, and economic collapse have induced massive displacements of peoples and population transfers. This chapter provides a brief overview and analysis of the African experience, with a focus on the complex interaction of internal dynamics and global processes of change that account for the prominence of Africa and Africans in South–North migrations.

A Mobile Continent

In the precolonial context, African migrations were stimulated by a range of circumstances: including population increase, the search for food and adequate resources (or more productive habitats), environmental disasters like famine or flooding, commerce, and warfare. People movements were free ranging and often covered wide areas. Only terrain or hostile reaction by other groups restricted choice of movement. Given the limits of technology, migrant movement in this

---

1. Han van Dijk, Dick Forken, and Kiky van Til, "Population Mobility in Africa: An Overview," in *Mobile Africa: Changing Patterns of Movement in Africa and Beyond*, ed. Mirjam de Bruijn, Rijk van Dijk, and Dick Foeken (Boston, MA: Brill, 2001), 14; see also Aderanti Adepoju, "Migration in Africa: An Overview," in *The Migration Experience in Africa*, ed. Jonathan Baker and Tade Akin Aina (Uppsala: Nordiska Afrikainstitutet, 1995), 87.

period, unless provoked by warfare or trauma, tended to be sporadic and grad-ual. Recurrent patterns of migration were common among traders, fishermen, nomadic farmers, pastoralists, and (notably in the trans-Saharan region) reli-gious clerics. Migrations were predominantly communal—involving an entire clan, tribal group, or village—rather than individual. Indeed, except in cases of abduction or capture by hostile groups, individual migration was practically non-existent. H. W. O. Okoth-Ogendo observes that such "collective migration made social interaction among various [tribes] more readily acceptable" and contrib-uted to "the rich linguistic and cultural heritage observable throughout Africa, especially south of the Sahara."[2]

One of the best-known and most-extensive episodes of people movement in Africa is the Bantu migration. The term "Bantu" is a linguistic reference denot-ing the strong affinity of the four hundred or so languages spoken throughout the subregion by over one hundred million people. From around 3000 to 2000 B.C.E. successive waves of migrants, probably driven by the need for more land to support a fast-growing population, emerged from around the present Nigerian-Cameroonian border and slowly spread southwards in an unsystematic three-pronged pattern that penetrated as far as Angola and Namibia, through central Africa, southeastward to the Lake Victoria region, and as far as Zimbabwe and South Africa. Over a period of at least two thousand years these groups of migrants, believed to possess superior agricultural skills and (in the later stages of their migration) iron weaponry, gradually intermingled with, displaced, or absorbed the indigenous peoples they encountered.[3] Bantu migrations radically transformed the sub-Saharan region. The Bantu migrants disseminated or intro-duced advanced skills in agriculture and metallurgy and dispersed new ideas of sociopolitical organization which arguably contributed to the subsequent devel-opment of great kingdoms in eastern and southern Africa.

Out-migration of Africans during this period was largely a function of the Afri-can slave trade, which took three main forms: trans-Saharan, East African, and Atlantic. The Atlantic slave trade exceeded the other two in volume and impact. It involved the forcible transcontinental movement of some ten to twelve million Africans and was characterized by exceptional levels of cruelty and waste. Com-pared to the total African population, the estimated number exported in connec-tion with the slave trade appears insignificant. However, the slave trade was most intense between 1700 and 1850, and the greatest number of slaves were taken from relatively few and often relatively small areas; this means that "wherever slaving struck at a people who were comparatively few or economically weak it left an empty land."[4] The majority of slaves came from western Africa and the principal markets were on a three-thousand-mile coastline between Senegal and Angola.[5] Between 1700 and 1709, writes John Thornton (1998: 100), "somewhere

---

2. H. W. O. Okoth-Ogendo, "The Effect of Migration on Family Structures in Sub-Saharan Africa," *International Migration* 27 (1989): 310.

3. Basil Davidson, *Africa in History: Themes and Outlines* (New York: Simon & Schuster, 1995), 20-22.

4. Davidson, *African Slave Trade*, 120; also idem, *Africa in History*, 217.

5. Davidson, *African Slave Trade*, 121; Thornton, *Kongolese Saint Anthony*, 100.

around 70,000 people were exported from Kongo—on average, nearly 7,000 per year from a population of something around 600,000." Moreover, the impact of the African slave trade on Africa went well beyond depopulation, endemic warfare, or economic underdevelopment. It also laid the foundation for economic dependency and contributed to the attitudes of racial superiority that flowered with extensive subjugation of African peoples in the colonial period.

Migration in the Colonial Period (c. 1800-1960s)

From the start, the European colonial encounter with Africa stimulated growing internal migrations. One of the earliest and most significant examples of these was the recapture of African slaves by British naval vessels (off the coast of West Africa), after Britain declared slavery illegal in 1807. This liberation saw the transfer of thousands of liberated African slaves (an estimated sixty-seven thousand by 1840) to Freetown, in the British colony of Sierra Leone. The trauma of displacement and involuntary migration—the loosening of the bonds to the old gods in their various homelands[6]—contributed to mass conversions to Christianity among this "receptive" population. By 1820, Freetown boasted more African Christians than the rest of tropical Africa.[7] Subsequent migration by large numbers of Africans from this group, through repatriation initiatives, would play a hugely significant role in the spread of Christianity throughout West Africa and beyond.[8]

But the overall impact of colonialism on African migrations was hardly benign. The colonization of Africa by European powers culminated in the 1890s with aggressive partitioning—dubbed "the scramble for Africa." With colonial subjugation came the establishment of new administrative apparatuses involving new legislative regimes, enforced arbitrary territorial boundaries, imposed taxation, and organized military expeditions to "pacify" recalcitrant groups. The colonial economy also saw the rise of foreign export, massive appropriations of land, forced labor, exploitation of rural areas, and growth of the urban sector. All this portended far-reaching socioeconomic transformations that radically affected migration patterns and brought about new forms of interaction between Africa and the outside world.

The arbitrary imposition of fixed territorial boundaries, with scant regard for either preexisting ethnic or tribal heterogeneity or the distribution of natural resources, ruptured the internal cohesion of many communities and deprived others of ready access to vital resources. Colonial boundary control also interfered with previous patterns of free movement and effected new forms of migration within most regions. Generally speaking, population movements were now linked to the economic strategies and priorities of the colonial rulers.[9]

---

6. Walls, "Mission and Migration," 9.

7. Paul E. H. Hair, "Freetown Christianity and Africa," *Sierra Leone Bulletin of Religion* 6 (December 1964): 16.

8. See Jean Herskovits Kopytoff, *A Preface to Modern Nigeria: The "Sierra Leonians" in Yoruba, 1830-1890* (Madison: University of Wisconsin Press, 1965).

9. Adepoju, "Migration in Africa," 90.

In eastern and southern Africa, forced labor and extensive appropriation of land caused massive displacements and contributed to institutionalized labor migration. The rise of an urban sector and the economic development of coastal areas where the colonial administrative infrastructure was heavily concentrated, stimulated new flows of migration from the relatively deprived hinterland and gave rise to "international" migration—notably from landlocked countries to "areas of prosperous agricultural activity" in coastal regions.[10] In Ghana (then the Gold Coast), for instance, the development of gold mines and cocoa farms in the southern region attracted predominantly male migrants from surrounding colonies like the Gambia, Sierra Leone, Upper Volta (now Burkina Faso), Togo, Nigeria, Ivory Coast, Mali, and Benin.[11] By 1913, over four thousand foreign migrants were estimated to be working in the Gold Coast colony. The numbers continued to rise sharply. The 1931 census indicated that there were 289,217 foreign migrants in the Gold Coast—the majority of them from French colonies in the region.[12]

Spontaneous and unregulated migration by tribal groups persisted in many areas; but under the colonial regime migration was now more individual, male-dominated, and geared toward wage employment. It was also largely short-term, cyclical, and predictable. A pattern of temporary migration emerged in which labor migrants left home for plantations, mines, or coastal economic zones and returned after a period of service, only to set out again. The duration of the cycle was determined by a variety of factors, including residency restrictions (in apartheid South Africa) and the seasonal nature of particular industries.[13] The construction of railways and extensive road networks linking the hinterland to coastal areas and capital cities also contributed greatly to the volume and velocity of migration movement and fostered new modes of social interaction.

In West Africa, the rapid development of secondary and tertiary education (under the aegis of energetic missionary societies) combined with extensive involvement in transregional trade to foster the rise of an indigenous middle class. The spread of Christianity in the region using African agency and the presence of African-Americans (former slaves), many of whom rose to prominent positions in society,[14] contributed to a sense of community that transcended colonial boundaries. Promising Africans were sent abroad for advanced theological training, and successful African merchants sent their children to Britain to train as doctors and lawyers.[15] The exalted benefits of Western education (intimately linked to missionary Christianity) ushered an expanding class of Africans into the world of Western civilization, literature, and technology. This emergent African middle class read English newspapers keenly and assiduously emulated English manners and customs—even while they eagerly championed African ide-

---

10. Ibid.

11. Bump, "International Migration in Africa."

12. Ibid.

13. See Okoth-Ogendo, "Effect of Migration on Family Structures," 310f.

14. See Chirenje, *Ethiopianism*; also Hanciles, *Euthanasia of a Mission*, 94-103, 132-35.

15. See Hanciles, *Euthanasia of a Mission*, 153-70; Akintola J. G. Wyse, *The Krio of Sierra Leone: An Interpretive History* (Washington, DC: Howard University Press, 1991), 33-59.

als and identity.[16] In short, the colonial and missionary encounter *expanded the world of the African and the African sense of the world*, and in doing so sowed the seeds for future international migration.

Postcolonial Migration (from the 1960s)

Analysis of postcolonial African migrations is beset by innumerable complexities.[17] While fragile and porous national borders greatly facilitate migration flows, the majority of African states lack reliable census or demographic data. In many areas, societies in adjacent territories (separated by a "national" border) share common customs, language, and ethnic identity. In such circumstances, distinguishing immigrants from the native population, much less distinguishing between different types of migrants, becomes problematic, and the distinction between internal and international migration is greatly blurred.[18] Moreover, since few African governments have or enforce strict immigration laws, much international migration on the continent occurs "outside a regulatory framework."[19] A major 1990 World Bank study of international migration in sub-Saharan Africa concluded that "data on migration flows among countries are virtually nonexistent."[20]

On account of these severe data limitations, studious analysis of the African experience involves general estimates incorporating educated guesses and conjecture.[21] By 1990, sub-Saharan Africa contained some thirty-five million international migrants or almost 50 percent of the world total (though it accounted for less than 10 percent of the world population). Between 1986 and 1987 alone, "the estimated number of persons displaced by civil strife, persecution, drought, or other national disasters rose from 8.9 million to 12.6 million" (Russell et al. 1990: 1:1). In the same period, the number of officially recognized refugees increased by 15 percent. By 1995, the number of refugees in Africa was estimated at 6.4 million; and almost 40 percent of these were displaced within their own countries. But, mainly due to the resolution of some long-standing conflicts in the late 1990s, this number had declined to 3.6 million by 2000. East Africa emerged in the 1980s as the most volatile region, generating 80 percent of sub-Saharan Africa's refugees; by 2000, it still hosted 46 percent of the refugees in Africa.

The highest concentration of migrants, however, is in West Africa, a region with a long history of migration linked to trade, religious proselytization, and economic interdependence. Outbreaks of violent intra-state conflicts in the 1990s

---

16. See Hanciles, *Euthanasia of a Mission*, 155-64.

17. For a comprehensive and detailed analysis of international migrations in Africa (including country-by-country assessments), see the two-volume study published in 1990 by the World Bank—Russell, Jacobsen, and Stanley, *International Migration and Development in Sub-Saharan Africa*.

18. Adepoju, "Migration in Africa," 93; also Russell, Jacobsen, and Stanley, *International Migration and Development in Sub-Saharan Africa*, 1:3, 14.

19. See Zlotnik, "Trends in South to North Migration."

20. Russell, Jacobsen, and Stanley, *International Migration and Development in Sub-Saharan Africa*, 1:3.

21. Among useful sources, see ibid., vol. 101; Zlotnik, "Trends in South to North Migration"; Ferris, *Beyond Borders*, 129-68; Adepoju, "Migration in Africa."

(notably in Liberia, Ivory Coast, and Sierra Leone) triggered massive refugee movements.[22] By 2000, West Africa was home to 20 percent of the continent's refugee population. With an estimated migrant stock of 2.3 million, Ivory Coast had more migrants than any other African country (almost twice as many as South Africa, the next highest); and the five West African countries of Ivory coast, Burkina Faso, Nigeria, Guinea, and Ghana accounted for almost 45 percent of the migrant stock of the top fifteen African countries.[23] By 2000, West Africa had more international migrants (6.7 million) than any other region on the continent.[24]

Intra-State Conflict

Among the causative factors of mass migrations in Africa in the postcolonial period, the failure of the African state is the most elemental.[25] Throughout the world, the postcolonial period witnessed a massive global upsurge in the tide of migrants as post-independent states succumbed to overwhelming political and economic crises (see pp. 173-74 above). But nowhere was the scale and scope of the problems assailing newly independent states as extensive and catastrophic as in sub-Saharan Africa—not least because Africa boasted the largest number and concentration of colonized states.[26]

All over the continent, the process of decolonization marked a new chapter of political chaos and enduring economic hardship. The "national borders" artificially created under colonialism left many new "states" with little internal coherence. At the same time, the legacy of colonial policies and the political structures imposed by foreign powers—ranging from parliamentary democracies to Marxist-socialist experiments—often became blunted instruments wielded by self-serving factional groups. On the other side of the equation, traditional power structures, implacable intertribal antagonisms, and long-standing inequalities exerted a latent but pervasive influence on enduring political volatility. To be sure, political incompetence aside, the gravitation to one-party or authoritarian systems of government in much of Africa appears to owe as much to the fact that colonial and other foreign models exemplified this approach as to the intertribal animosities and monopoly of power associated with the traditional environment.

---

22. For a brief but helpful analysis of political instability in West Africa from the 1980s, see Jeff Drumtra, "West Africa's Refugee Crisis Spills across Many Borders," Migration Information Source, 2003.

23. "Estimated Number of International Migrants at Mid-Year, by Countries in Africa: 2000," Migration Information Source (2006).

24. "Estimated Number of International Migrants at Mid-Year, by Regions in Africa: 1990 and 2000," Migration Information Source (2006).

25. For an incisive treatment, see Ahmednasir M. Abdullahi, "The Refugee Crisis in Africa as a Crisis of the Institution of the State," International Journal of Refugee Law 6, no. 4 (1994): 567; also Aderanti Adepoju, "Preliminary Analysis of Emigration Dynamics in Sub-Saharan Africa," International Migration 32, no. 2 (1994); and John K. Akopari, "The State, Refugees and Migration in Sub-Saharan Africa," International Migration 36, no. 2 (1998): 211-36.

26. As late as the mid-1940s only five of Africa's now fifty-three countries were independent nation-states.

With almost predictable regularity, one state after another experienced profound political malfunction: signaled by power-mongering, partisan rule, politics of exclusion, monopolization of a country's resources by a particular ethnic group, and repressive authoritarian government. The postcolonial African state, notes John Akopari, "has shown a fundamental incapacity to either fairly distribute its meager political and economic resources among diverse social constituents, or promote fair competition for these resources."[27]

The litany of intra-state conflict and political upheavals in Africa is well documented. Post-independent African states have very seldom gone to war with each other; rather, suggests Elizabeth Ferris (tongue-in-cheek), they force other governments to do what they want by the less costly means of displacing massive sections of their population. In the postcolonial era, most states have been engulfed by political strife and anarchic disorder involving military coups, civil war, or some other form of armed insurgence. In 1966 alone five African governments were toppled by military juntas in just three months with remarkable ease, and by 1976 there had been forty-five military coups in over nineteen African countries. In the last four decades, this cycle of wretched paroxysms has generated extraordinary levels of migration and dislocation on the African continent.

Wars of liberation, notably against white minority rule in Zimbabwe and South Africa, destabilized great sections of their respective populations. The same white governments also intimidated radical elements (typically black urban intellectuals) and passed discriminatory laws that forced many political activists into exile. When the tables turned under majority black rule, thousands of whites migrated. Yet, in many cases, the attainment of independence intensified rather than resolved internal conflict and rendered the political destiny of the nation even more troubled. In the former Portuguese colonies of Angola and Mozambique, armed struggle against colonial rule gave way to full-blown civil wars that lasted more than two decades (fueled by interethnic hostility as well as Cold War politics) with devastating consequences. Millions of people were rendered homeless and hundreds of thousands became refugees in neighboring countries. By 1988, Mozambique, already the second largest supplier of labor to South Africa, was the foremost source country for international migrants within sub-Saharan Africa, accounting for 30 percent of all refugees.[28] More than 1.1 million people fled the fighting between the Mozambican government and rebel guerilla movements. In 1991, its refugee population was estimated at close to 1.5 million.[29]

Africa's longest-lasting conflict, the Ethiopia–Eritrea war, is a singular

---

27. Akopari, "State, Refugees and Migration," 214.

28. Russell, Jacobsen, and Stanley, *International Migration and Development in Sub-Saharan Africa,* vol. 1. In the late 1980s, Mozambican migrants in Zimbabwe were actively persecuted by the Zimbabwean government as sympathizers of RENAMO (an insurgent guerilla group backed by South Africa and opposed to the newly independent, Marxist-oriented Mozambican government), and thousands were forcibly repatriated. Others, including legal migrants working in the agricultural sector, were placed in refugee camps. A decade later (in the 1990s), relations between various countries in the East and Central African region deteriorated over accusations that one or the other was harboring or aiding rebel groups. See Russell, Jacobsen, and Stanley, *International Migration and Development in Sub-Saharan Africa,* 2:120-21.

29. See Adepoju, "Migration in Africa," 103.

example of intra-state political strife that escalated into a full-blown inter-state warfare. Colonized by Italy in 1885 and absorbed as a British protectorate after Italy's defeat by the Allied forces in 1941, Eritrea was conjoined to Ethiopia as part of a federation by the United Nations in 1962. When Ethiopia's harsh totalitarian regime under Haile Selassie revoked the federation scheme and annexed its smaller neighbor, Eritrean exiles (with Syrian and Iraqi support) resorted to armed struggle. The ensuing Eritrean war of independence lasted thirty years (1962-1991) and generated vast numbers of refugees in Africa—between 1.1 and 1.4 million.[30] Amidst brutal fighting, Ethiopia expelled seventy-seven thousand Eritreans and Ethiopians of Eritrean origin, and the protracted war triggered colossal internal displacement in both countries as civilians fled the war zone.

Similarly, in Somalia, independence from colonial regimes in 1960—Somalia was formed out of a union of territories colonized by Britain, France, and Italy—gave way to brutal internecine strife, political disintegration, and the demise of what passed for a "state." Interclan and interfactional fighting caused at least half a million deaths, about two million displaced, and massive refugee flows. By 1988, Somalia was the fifth largest refugee-sending nation in Africa.[31] It remains an anarchic political aberration: relatively homogenous (by African standards) yet bitterly divided along tribal lines in ways that defy pacification and international intervention. At the time of writing it is still without a national government.

In Uganda (1979), Liberia (1990), and Rwanda (1994), the state also collapsed amidst bloody violence and armed insurgence. Civil wars marked by horrific brutality followed in Sudan and Sierra Leone.[32] The Sierra Leone civil war, which was triggered by the Liberian conflict, lasted almost ten years (1991-2000) and created about half a million refugees.

But few of Africa's many conflicts have received the attention and coverage of the Rwandan crisis triggered by the death of President Juvenal Habyanrimana in April 1994. Depicted as "the purest genocide since 1945,"[33] the brutal conflict between the Hutus (who account for 85 percent of the population) and minority Tutsis remains perhaps the epitome of ethnic hatred on the continent. The outbreak of civil war between the two groups saw hundreds of thousands murdered and millions of people driven from their homes. The conflict generated a immense refugee crisis that engulfed neighboring states and embroiled them in the conflict, effectively widening the scale of upheaval and dislocation.

According to one estimate, in 1991 some 5.3 million refugees were distributed among twenty-three countries in Africa, with Malawi alone hosting almost a million.[34] In some instances the migrant influx provides the destination country with much-needed labor—skilled and unskilled. But, with most African

---

30. Russell, Jacobsen, and Stanley, *International Migration and Development in Sub-Saharan Africa*, 2:23.

31. Ibid., 15.

32. For a helpful synopsis of these conflicts and their impact on African migration, see Akopari, "State, Refugees and Migration."

33. "Rwanda Remembered," *The Economist*, March 27, 2004, 11.

34. Cited in Adepoju, "Migration in Africa," 103.

countries experiencing widespread poverty combined with surging population growth, the sudden influx of large numbers of migrants critically overburdens scant resources and facilities. For international migrants, therefore, the tragedy of displacement and dislocation is often compounded by the extreme poverty and inadequate infrastructure of the destination country. Moreover, in both western and eastern Africa—the regions most affected—the conflicts have spilled across many borders. As a result, many countries (such as Ethiopia, Sudan, Burundi, and Sierra Leone) have been in turn, or at the same time, both "source" and "destination" for international migration flows.

Increasingly, traditional attitudes of hospitality have given way to public discontent and strong xenophobia. Hostility and tension invariably flare up when impoverished local populations see refugees receiving generous food aid and external assistance. In conflict zones, national governments often view a large influx of refugees as a security threat, since they can provide cover for armed militias. Everywhere, sizable immigrant populations in Africa are favorite scapegoats for politicians, who blame them for economic recession, the spread of HIV/AIDS, or rising criminal activity.

Economic Crises

In Africa, political independence fueled high expectations based on the belief that, with Africans in control of their destinies, economic prosperity and development would follow. Up to the 1960s a worldwide boom in trade and corresponding demand for commodities allowed African nations (major producers of primary goods) to thrive. Buoyed by economic conditions, many African governments acquired huge loans from Northern banks to finance expensive national building projects and conspicuous consumption. The worldwide drop of commodity prices in the 1980s (due, in part, to oversupply) sent African economies into recession. At the same time, developed countries raised interest rates to fight inflation. The combination of falling prices and increased rates exacerbated the debt burden of African nations and undermined the ability of governments to repay their loans. Worse still, the high interest rates of Western banks acted like a magnet attracting capital from around the world, including huge public funds and reserves diverted by corrupt third world government officials to personal accounts.

Over the next three decades the economic situation grew more calamitous and tragic, threatening the very survival of African populations. With their sources of livelihood destroyed or threatened, Africa's predominantly rural populations migrated to the cities in unprecedented numbers. This trend contributed to joblessness, urban poverty, high crime rates, and social decay—ripe conditions for discontent and political protest. Deeply indebted and heavily dependent on foreign capital, African governments (including illegitimate regimes) quickly depleted their foreign exchange reserves and acquired new loans to get their finances in order, feed their burgeoning populations, and buy foreign goods.

In order to service their debts or acquire further loans, however, many African governments were forced to submit to the "structural adjustment program" imposed by the International Monetary Fund. As already noted in chapter 1, IMF conditionalities—which required currency devaluations, deep cuts in public spending, the removal of subsidies on health, education, and major food items, elimination of protectionist barriers to Northern goods, and vigorous privatization—failed to solve the debt problem. These measures not only exacerbated already adverse economic conditions but also served to integrate deeply impoverished economies into a system dominated by wealthy industrial nations, in a manner that amounted to recolonization.

In Africa and elsewhere, the economic impact was immediate and catastrophic. Rapidly growing populations were deprived of the very resources they needed for survival and human development. The standard of living dropped precipitously, accompanied by rising unemployment, reduced wages, massive inflation, and severe income inequalities. Teachers, healthcare providers, and other civil servants often went unpaid and unable to perform their jobs. The political upheaval and social unrest triggered by these untoward developments were typically met with brutal repression. Interestingly, the IMF program either emasculated already weakened governments or strengthened authoritarian regimes (as was the case in Ghana). The combination of widespread economic malaise, festering unrest, and dysfunctional political leadership became a time bomb within many African societies. It exploded in different countries at different times, but with quite similar results: a breakdown of the political order, civil strife, interethnic hostility, and (frequently) armed insurgence. The tremendous devastation that inevitably accompanied such turmoil not only intensified the economic crisis but also sabotaged prospects for development.

By the mid-1990s, Africa had the worst statistics on the planet with regard to population increase, living standards, and violence. Infrastructural collapse, retarded economic growth, environmental degradation, and a high incident of deadly diseases were all active agents in a calculus of unmitigated hardship. The Human Development Index, published annually by the United Nations, rates countries worldwide on the basis of life expectancy, adult literacy, daily supply of calories, access to safe water and under-five mortality. In 1998, according to the Index, Africa was home to twenty-five of the thirty least developed countries in the world, with six of the bottom ten located in West Africa.[35] By 2005, Africa accounted for thirty of the thirty-two countries ranked lowest in human development. The twenty-four least-developed nations in the world were African, and of these twelve (or half) were in West Africa.

The West African region's manifest economic underdevelopment helps to explain why it has the highest concentration of international migrants in Africa. The region forms a microcosm of the African dilemma—that complex linkage between colonial cartographical constructs, failed states, anarchic disorder, economic decline, and international migration. Moreover, West Africa has the greatest cluster of Lilliputian states. Few of them are viable as autonomous entities, and in the postcolonial period many have failed to achieve or sustain genuine

---

35. See also Sadig Rasheed and Eshetu Chole, "Human Development: An African Perspective," Occasional Paper 17, Human Development Report Office.

national unity or statehood. In the late 1990s American journalist Robert Kaplan concluded that the region was "becoming the symbol of world-wide demographic, environmental, and societal stress, in which criminal anarchy emerges as the real 'strategic' danger"; that "disease, overpopulation, unprovoked crime, scarcity of resources, refugee migrations, the increasing erosion of nation-states and international borders, and the empowerment of private armies, security firms, and the international drug cartels are now most tellingly demonstrated through a West African prism."[36]

Environmental Degradation

Widespread environmental pressures and the repeated occurrence of ecological disasters also contribute to major population displacements in Africa. Millions of Africans are threatened by famine every year, and displacement of whole communities as a result of drought or climatic variations is a regular occurrence in parts of the continent. In the Sahelian region, continuous desertification generates migration pressure both southward into West Africa and northward toward North Africa and ultimately Europe.[37] From 1982 to 1986, severe drought in eastern and southern Africa caused widespread famine and resulted in massive migrations.[38]

There are strong interrelated links between environmental degradation, political conflict, and economic deterioration. In their desperate need for foreign currency and short-term economic growth, impoverished African governments overexploit natural resources and routinely ignore environmental regulations. Land shortages and diminished resources linked to environmental degradation not only contribute to economic underdevelopment but can also precipitate competition, violent conflict, and displacement.[39] Ecological considerations are arguably an important factor in Sudan's protracted civil war; and in Somalia, where "moderate" droughts occur every three to four years and major ones every eight to ten years, ecological stresses are linked to abject poverty and political conflict, perpetuating regular cycles of displacement and migration.[40]

By 2000, the total number of international migrants within Africa (including refugees) had risen to sixteen million (up from nine million in 1960).[41] Of the major regions in the developing world, only the much larger Asian continent has more international migrants. Even so, there were already indications (in 2000) that the long-standing trend of steady increase in the stock of African migrants

---

36. Kaplan, "Coming Anarchy," 44-76; for the book version, see Robert Kaplan, *The Ends of the Earth: A Journey to the Frontiers of Anarchy* (New York: Vintage Books, 1996).

37. Adepoju, "Preliminary Analysis of Emigration Dynamics in Sub-Saharan Africa," 210, 213.

38. Russell, Jacobsen, and Stanley, *International Migration and Development in Sub-Saharan Africa*, 2:37.

39. See Akopari, "State, Refugees and Migration," 219f.

40. Adepoju, "Preliminary Analysis of Emigration Dynamics in Sub-Saharan Africa," 210.

41. "International Migration: Facts and Figures," International Organization for Migration, 2005; also, Zlotnik, "Trends in South to North Migration."

was slowing down. The continent's share of international migrants worldwide decreased steadily from 14 percent in 1980 to 9 percent in 2000, and, partly because of Africa's explosive population growth in the same period, the percentage of international migrants on the continent dropped from over 3 percent of the overall population in 1980 to 2 percent in 2000. Still, international migration in Africa itself remains fluid, voluminous, and unpredictable.

African Migrations and the Missionary Impulse

Throughout Africa, the word "missionary" still evokes images of a European person—such is the combined impact of the Western colonial and missionary projects on popular consciousness. Yet, in the history of African Christianity, the majority of Africans have heard the gospel from other Africans (often catechists, schoolmasters, and traders). With the emergence of prophet-healing movements in the early twentieth century, African missionary initiatives grew in significance and visibility. The massive migrations throughout the continent in recent decades have also stimulated an extraordinary and unprecedented expansion of the African missionary movement. It takes little stretch of the imagination to reason that the extraordinary tidal waves of human migration that have characterized the continent in the postcolonial era are one reason why Christianity is growing faster in Africa than anywhere else. Migrants travel with their religion, and the opportunities for intercultural diffusion of ideas (including religious ideas) are vastly expanded in the sustained encounters with new groups of people that migration often involves.

Demonstrating this migration–religious expansion nexus in the contemporary African context would require extensive field research and documentation well beyond the scope of this work. As part of my research, however, I interviewed seventeen African Christian leaders and pastors (in Kenya and Ghana) in the spring of 2004. Each of these leaders presided over, or was associated with, African ministries or churches that exemplify sustained international mission (see Appendix 1).

There was emphatic consensus that extraordinary African migrations in the last three decades have, more than any other single factor, helped to foment a new epoch of African missionary expansion. Migrant movement has also seen a spectacular rise in the internationalization and global extension of Africa-based ministries and churches. In the words of Dr. Tokumbo Adeyemo, general secretary of the Association of Evangelicals in Africa (AEA) for twenty-five years, Africa had made the transition *from mission field to missionary force.* Two brief illustrations must suffice.

Christian Migrants in Kenya

Until the 1980s, Kenya's relative political stability and well-developed infrastructure made it one of Africa's lowest migration countries. Kenyans who left for higher education abroad, because of Kenya's overburdened tertiary institutions, generally returned. The 1990 World Bank study on international migration in Africa reported that immigration levels in Kenya were considered "insignificant and satisfactory" by the Kenyan government.[42] By the end of that decade, however, Kenya's political and economic situation took a dramatic downturn, even as terrible catastrophes convulsed the region. By 1995, Kenya's international migrants had risen (by 150 percent) to 365,509, from an estimated 145,626 in 1990; its refugee population rapidly escalated within the same period, from 13,452 to a staggering 243,544.[43] The refugees who flooded Kenya were escaping violent conflicts in Uganda, Burundi, Ethiopia, Somalia, and Sudan. The country also acted as a transit point for the resettlement of refugees in other countries.[44]

In Nairobi, Kenya's capital, the Ethiopian and Eritrean communities included large numbers of Christians who had fled persecution by the Marxist Communist government (which came to power in 1975). They established large Christian fellowships, which splintered and grew into a number of churches. The largest of these is the Ethiopian Evangelical Fellowship Church with a regular attendance of about seven hundred (in 2004). Significantly, Ethiopian and Eritrean Christian migrants have discovered that missionary efforts among co-nationals are possible on a scale and effectiveness that were inconceivable back in their homelands. To be sure, some are being "converted" from the Orthodox faith (which evangelical Christians view as sterile ritualism); but many new converts, notably among the younger generation, were either nominal believers or non-Christians when they left their homeland. The crises of migration and uprootedness, and the attendant search for meaning, are the main reasons for this openness to new or renewed religious commitment among the immigrant community.

Exploits of a Ghanaian Missionary

Few accounts of individual African missionary endeavor amidst political upheaval are as compelling as that of Apostle Michael Ntumy, the current chairman of the Church of Pentecost, Ghana's largest Protestant body. In 1988, Ntumy was sent as a missionary to Liberia (Buchanan city), where he planted four vibrant churches in his first year. In December 1989, when the bloody Liberian civil war broke out, he made the fateful decision to stay (along with his wife, Martha, and their four young children) "for the sake of my church members." Over the next year and a half, Ntumy experienced the horrific carnage of the war, including the summary execution of other Ghanaian nationals at the hands of rebel groups incensed by the military intervention of the Ghanaian-led ECOWAS (Economic Community of West African States) Monitoring Group (ECOMOG). Held hostage with thou-

---

42. Russell, Jacobsen, and Stanley, *International Migration and Development in Sub-Saharan Africa*, 2:25.

43. *Trends in Total Migrant Stock: The 2005 Revision.*

44. Kenneth Okoth, "Kenya: What Role for Diaspora in Development?" *Migration Information Source*, 2003.

sands of refugees in a camp where starvation and disease took hundreds of lives (an average of six a day), Ntumy secured the permission of the camp commander to hold regular church services and prayer meetings.[45]

Having a captive audience surrounded by death and destruction could be construed as a winning evangelistic formula. Ntumy himself confesses that "the more people died the more receptive to the Gospel the survivors became."[46] But in a context suffused with religiosity and supernatural symbolism—many combatants claimed ritual protection from bullets—the many instances of miraculous provision and deliverance, after seasons of prayer and fasting, proved equally efficacious. Ntumy's ministry made so many converts (even among the rebel soldiers) that he organized a Bible class for their instruction. In the end, even the rebel captors attributed their hostages' survival and eventual evacuation to "the hand of God." Ntumy continued pastoral ministry among the refugee converts until he escaped the country in March 1991. Six months later, he was reassigned to the Ivory Coast where he learned to speak French fluently and planted 278 churches in five years.

Ultimately, the flood of African migrations in recent decades has multiplied the number of de facto African missionary agents and missionary encounters in myriad ways that are impossible to document. Even formal missionary operations overlap with clandestine initiatives. The Nigeria-based Redeemed Christian Church of God (RCCG) established a branch in Kenya through planned missionary action in 1995; but its regional coordinator, Pastor Prince Obasi-ike, has utilized refugee presence and movement to establish RCCG branches in Uganda and Burundi. In Ghana, Rev. Dr. Aiyelabowo, founder of the Triumph Global Ministries, conducted an evangelistic campaign at the Buduburam Refugee Camp (in Ghana's central region) in October 2002. The outcome was a church that grew to five hundred members within two years.

A complex picture emerges in which intra- and inter-continental movement, refugee influx, repatriation, and even the experience of political anarchy have all been turned to missionary purpose. The point at issue is that if African missionary initiatives have grown in scope and significance over the last couple of decades, migration movement has been a prime catalyst. This is also true of global expansion, for Africa also generates significant outflows of intercontinental migrants to western Europe and North America.

South–North Migration: The African Experience

With perhaps the most mobile population in the world, the highest population growth of any region, and the largest number of countries ranked lowest in

---

45. Ntumy confirmed the details of his experiences in a personal interview. He also published a detailed account. See Michael K. Ntumy, *"Flamingo," The Camp of No Return: A Missionary's Account of God's Liberation during the Liberia War* (Accra, Ghana: Pentecostal Press, 1994).

46. Ibid., 78.

the Human Development Index (2005),[47] Africa has disgorged unprecedented numbers of its inhabitants in the last four decades. Calamitous economic conditions in the subregion, epitomized by widespread unemployment, severe income inequalities, impoverishment of the middle class, declining standards of living, and low human development have generated an uncontrollable tide of economic migrants pushed to ever more extreme acts of desperation in their efforts to leave the troubled continent.

Here the social dimensions of migration are especially pronounced. The decision to move is intimately framed by family considerations and the family's survival needs. Young women make horrendous sacrifices and undertake brutal toil simply to earn enough for a hazardous boat trip to mainland Europe (run by unscrupulous migrant smugglers) in pursuit of a better life for their children. They embark on that first step on the journey of international migration knowing that they will likely be raped at night or, as likely as not, end up being thrown into the sea if the weather gets too inclement. And unbeknownst to many, what awaits them at the end of a perilous journey, is not the lucrative employment and transit to Europe promised by unscrupulous traffickers but hostility, degraded existence, and sexual slavery.[48]

Many young African men leave behind stable jobs and settled families, drawn by the allure of a better life (framed by images seen on TV screens), their own unrelenting inner ambitions, or a youthful determination to prove themselves and claim manhood. Many more repeatedly brave death and maiming at the hands of border police because they can no longer live with themselves or look suffering elders in the eye when memories of a prosperous past fade and the vibrant hopes of a better future slowly evaporate as the land is ravaged by factional politics and local industry is devastated by decisions made in a plush Western office. Unrelenting streams of desperate African migrants try to enter Europe illegally, and hundreds perish in the process.[49] As one immigrant put it, ever so poignantly, "*they say that to die once is better than dying ten times in the face of your parents' pity.*"

I have argued in this book that the traditional distinction between "forced" migration (or refugee movement) and "voluntary" migration (movement based on choice) can mislead. My perspective is informed by the complexities of the African experience. Undeniably, untold millions involuntarily abandon homes and livelihood in response to brutal violence, persecution, and ecological disaster. Yet, for masses of people, the irrepressible urge to "move" can also stem from reduced life expectancy, a sense of hopelessness about the future, the widespread disempowerment that accompanies failed political leadership, desperation borne of misfortune and abject poverty, or even the inability to provide basic necessities for family. In such cases, some planning may be involved, but the degree of choice is greatly constrained by imminent "threats" and the potential consequences of failure to move. Obviously, secondary factors such as financial

---

47. See *Human Development Report, 2005* (New York: UNDP, 2005). The other two are Yemen and Haiti.
48. See Jenny Cuffe, "African Dream of a Better Life," *BBC News Online,* June 16, 2007.
49. "Africa Invests to Stop Migrants," *BBC News Online,* August 22, 2007.

resources or access to a preexisting migrant network do enter the equation—which is one reason why even in times of calamity some people within the same social context fail to move. But it is often the case that included among those who are "forced" to move (by the outbreak of civil war, for instance) are many who failed, or resisted pressures, to move earlier.

It greatly complicates assessment of migrant motivations if many who fail to move are ultimately forced to move, or if failure to move reflects a lack of means rather than a lack of motivation. In many instances also, "voluntary" international migrants become "refugees" in their destination country simply because an outbreak of civil strife in their homeland renders the decision to return virtually suicidal. And, having experienced the initial trauma of uprootedness, many international migrants are conditioned to move again and again. In my view, a conceptual framework oriented around "choice" is invalidated when countless numbers leave the relative safety of their homeland to brave the most treacherous conditions, even risk life and limb, in sheer desperation to gain access to more developed countries in mainland Europe or elsewhere.

African migrants are widely dispersed among the wealthy industrialized countries of the North, but the patterns of emigration track with general trends in contemporary global migrations. This means at least four things.

1. Colonial and historical links have largely shaped the direction of South–North migration—Britain has mainly attracted migrants from Anglophone countries, France from Francophone countries, Portugal from Lusophone countries, Belgium from its former colonies of Rwanda and Zaire, Italy from Ethiopia, and so on.
2. The magnitude of migrant flows escalated during the period from the mid-1970s to the early 1990s when Africa's political and economic crises intensified.
3. As industrial nations have implemented tougher immigration regimes, family members, students, and professionals (rather than refugees or asylum seekers) constitute an increasing proportion of migrant inflows.
4. Females constitute a growing proportion of migrants—from 42 percent in 1960 to 46.7 percent by 2000[50]—as African women play more strategic economic and decision-making roles in a context were massive male unemployment has undermined traditional gender functions within the family.[51]

The numbers presented in figure 7 detail the African migrant stock in eight major destination countries—United States, Canada, Australia, Britain, Netherlands, Germany, Sweden, and Italy—and are intended to provide a general picture. A fairly straightforward profile of African South–North migration emerges from this data sample. With an estimated 1.1 million foreign-born Africans (in

50. Zlotnik, "Trends in South to North Migration."

51. See Aderanti Adepoju, "Changing Configurations of Migration in Africa," Migration Policy Institute, 2004; also Adepoju, "South–North Migration," 213, 217f.

Figure 7
African Migrant Stock in Eight Industrialized Countries

Country	Year	Number of African Foreign-Born	African Country with the Majority	Percentage of entire African Migrant Population	Total Foreign-Born Population	Africans as a Percentage of Total Foreign-Born Population	African Foreign-Born as a Percentage of Total Population
United States	2005	1,160,000	Nigeria	(13.8%)	35,157,000	3.3	0.40
Canada	2001	304,680	S. Africa	(12.2%)	5,647,125	5.4	1.02
Australia	2001	184,182	Egypt	(18.2%)	4,105,688	4.5	1.06
United Kingdom*	2001	834,107	S. Africa	(17%)	4,896,581	17.0	1.41
Netherlands	2003	301,964	Morocco	(54.1%)	1,714,155	17.6	1.87
Germany	2002	308, 238	Morocco	(25.9%)	7,335,592	4.2	0.37
Sweden	2001	57,316	Somalia	(23.5%)	1,027,974	5.6	0.64
Italy	2003	401,442	Morocco	(42.5%)	1,503,286	26.7	0.72

Source: The global database of the "Migration Information Source," published by the Migration Policy Institute. See Web site http://www.migrationinformation.org/GlobalData/
* The published data only list select (presumably the chief source) countries.

2005), the United States is the chief destination among industrialized countries for African migrants. But it is only recently so. More than half of this number arrived in the United States between 1990 and 2000, when the African foreign-born population doubled.[52] Britain, the leading colonial power in Africa, comes close to the U.S. numbers with over 800,000 African migrants, of whom (as in the case of Canada) South Africans form a majority. Of the eight countries in the data sample, it is only in the United States that West Africans constitute the majority (some 23 percent) of the total African migrant population. One in every seven foreign-born Africans in the United States is Nigerian.

Yet, while the United States boasts the largest African migrant population, it is possible to argue that African migrants constitute a more visible presence in the United Kingdom than any other Western nation, if the following factors are taken into account: the destination country's population size, estimated number of for-eign-born Africans, their percentage of the total migrant stock, and their percent-age of the entire population. The estimated stock of African migrants in the United Kingdom is slightly lower (at 834,107) than that of the United States but African nationals in the United Kingdom constitute a much higher percentage (17 percent) of the foreign-born population. The African percentage of the foreign-born popula-tion is highest in Italy (26.7 percent), but the actual numbers are less than half that of the United Kingdom, with which Italy shares a similar general population size.

---

52. See David Dixon, "Characteristics of the African Born in the United States," *Migration Information Source* (January 2006); also Elizabeth Grieco, "The African Foreign Born in the United States," *Migration Information Source* (September 2004).

Growing Numbers

African migrant inflow or entry data are a potentially unreliable means for assessing migrant stock (the number of migrants resident within a country) for a number of reasons: the data preclude information about returnees (migrants who subsequently returned home) or émigrés (those subsequently moved to another country);[53] and they do not necessarily indicate which destination countries attracted the most African migrants since they reflect only the numbers of those granted entry. But, while significant fluctuations in the data set point to the futility of predicting migration patterns, the overall trend is one of increased African migrant influx in industrialized countries over the last fifteen years. The growth trend appears strongest in the United States, which remains for now and the foreseeable future home to the largest population of African migrants among the wealthy industrialized countries in the North. (See chapter 13 for a detailed treatment.)

That said, the overall size of the African component in South–North migration is impossible to calculate with any certainty, in part because of the near absence of emigration policies or figures within African countries. The total volume of African migrant stock reflected in the eight destination countries in figure 7 is roughly 3.5 million. This figure is obviously inadequate. Major destination countries of African immigration such as France and Spain are not included because of limited data. Western government agencies (by their own admission) sometimes downplay immigrant statistics or mask total figures in order to protect certain groups or avoid adverse public reaction to burgeoning nonwhite immigration. Additionally, millions of African migrants are unaccounted for by "official" figures owing to their illegal or undocumented status. In sum, official immigration data, including those presented here, are pale shadows of a much larger reality.

Even with these important caveats, it is difficult to imagine that the African migrant stock in the wealthy industrial countries of the North exceeds fifteen to twenty million. At fifteen million (a conjectural figure), Africans would constitute roughly 25 percent of the overall number of adult immigrants (aged twenty-five and above) living in OECD countries in 2000.[54] There are no secure grounds to assume that Africans constitute such a huge percentage of South–North migration; yet, even if they did, the migrants involved would represent less than 2 percent of the entire African population. Undoubtedly, this fictitious African migrant stock would continue to expand rapidly through birthrates and family migration. But population growth on the African continent itself will almost certainly be higher. In sum, *the actual number of people lost to the continent through South–North migration is arguably negligible in terms of absolute numbers.*

---

53. This limitation is offset in the case of the United Kingdom and the United States by the inclusion in the data of migrants who gained permanent residence or long-term settlement. The five countries included in the sample are those for which the relevant data are available.

54. The total estimated figure is 58.5 million (Docquier and Rapoport, "Skilled Migration: The Perspective of Developing Countries," 6).

But because of Africa's massive and expanding population size, the question of how many Africans are South–North migrants is conceivably of less importance than which particular types of Africans migrate. Economic stagnation and low human development on the continent mean that international migrants are drawn disproportionately from middle-income groups that include professionals and the highly skilled. Thus, statistical estimations of Africa's skilled migration tend to be the gloomiest.

Migration by Natural Selection?

After decolonization, many African countries gave high priority to educational development, and by the mid-1980s literacy levels had improved substantially in many parts of the continent. Indeed, in most African countries education "expanded faster than the absorptive capacity of their economies."[55] The problem of job scarcity and unemployment for the highly trained and educated worsened rapidly with economic collapse and the bitter pill of "structural adjustment programs." Retrenchment and wage freezes deepened daily hardship; currency devaluations rendered salaries worthless; and "living wage" became an unfunny oxymoron. In such calamitous developments lay the roots of the massive African "brain drain." To put it simply, improved access to higher education following independence created an expanded class of skilled professionals and highly trained Africans technicians who, faced with distressing economic conditions and blighted prospects, emigrated in vast numbers—initially to other African countries but increasingly to wealthy developed countries (a pattern partly fostered by "quality selective" immigration policies).

The health and educational sectors were among the hardest hit precisely because they were most dependent on government subsidies and investment. In many countries the university system fell into ruins and the health system declined precipitously.[56] Migration became a survival mechanism. Faced with the prospects of woefully under-resourced tertiary education, tens of thousands of African students vied for scholarships and places in universities and institutions of higher learning in wealthy industrial countries. Even now, as we shall see, African students studying abroad remain pivotal to the growth of South–North migration.

Compared to other major regions in the world, a larger proportion of Africa's total migrant pool is made up of professionals.[57] Of the thirty countries (population size at least four million) with the highest rates of skilled migration in the world, fourteen (almost 50 percent) are in Africa.[58] In 2000, highly skilled work-

---

55. Adepoju, "South–North Migration," 208.

56. As George Ayittey notes (*Africa in Chaos*), buildings are dilapidated, books are unavailable, professors are unable to do research, dormitories are overcrowded, laboratories lack basic chemicals, and electricity and running water are in short supply.

57. See Ikubolajeh Bernard Logan, "The Brain Drain of Professional, Technical and Kindred Workers from Developing Countries: Some Lessons from the Africa-US Flow of Professionals (1980-1989)," *International Migration* 32, no. 4 (1992): 293.

58. Docquier and Marfouk, "Measuring the International Mobility of Skilled Workers," 32.

ers in Africa constituted 3.6 percent of the population, but the tertiary-educated group accounted for 31.4 percent of African immigrants in OECD countries.[59] A 1998 study noted that while the number of African migrants to the United States is quite small compared to flows from other regions, 95,000 out of a total of 128,000 African migrants (or 74 percent) had tertiary education.[60] By 1987 some 30 percent of Africa's professional/skilled people (nearly 70,000) had left for Europe,[61] and more recent estimates suggest that the continent loses over 20,000 skilled personnel to developed countries every year (up from 1,800 a year on average from 1960 to 1975).[62] It is also worthy of note that of all African regions, West Africa boasts the highest rates of skilled migration. In 2000, over 25 percent of West African immigrants in OECD countries had tertiary education (only the Caribbean registered a higher rate).

The Story of Ghana

By 2000, Ghana had the highest skilled migration rate for countries in West Africa with a population of over four million;[63] and, worldwide, only Haiti and Somalia had higher rates.[64] Up to the mid-1960s, Ghana was a major country of immigration, thanks to cocoa agriculture and gold mines. In 1969, confronted with major economic collapse, the Ghanaian government (under Dr. K. A. Busia) initiated the expulsion of foreign migrants, the majority of whom were Nigerians. At the same time, Ghanaians began to leave in increasing numbers to seek employment elsewhere in the region. An estimated two million Ghanaians left between 1974 and 1981.[65] Among their primary destinations was Nigeria, which had a booming oil economy in the 1970s. When the oil crises of the 1980s sent the Nigerian economy into recession and caused widespread unemployment, successive Nigerian governments ordered a mass expulsion of all foreign workers (in 1983 and 1985).

Among the expellees were over one million Ghanaians. With its economy in ruins and unemployment at unprecedented levels, the enforced repatriation of its citizens abroad could not have come at a worse time for Ghana. The event precipitated an escalation of Ghanaian emigration to other parts of Africa and to industrial nations. Political turmoil in the country also generated tens of thousands of asylum seekers (estimated at over 90,000). By the mid-1990s,

---

59. Ibid., 22.

60. Carrington and Detragiache, "How Big Is the Brain Drain?" 14. Indeed, the study concluded that "migration of low-educated Africans is almost nil" (ibid.).

61. Adepoju, "South–North Migration," 211; see also Ferris, *Beyond Borders*, 131.

62. Dhananjayan Sriskandarjah, "Reassessing the Impacts of Brain Drain on Developing Countries," Migration Policy Institute, 2005; See Docquier and Marfouk, "Measuring the International Mobility of Skilled Workers," 3.

63. See Docquier and Marfouk, "Measuring the International Mobility of Skilled Workers," 18-19. Gambia and Cape Verde have the highest rates of skilled migration, but both have populations of under four million (or 1.6 million and 420,000, respectively).

64. Docquier and Rapoport, "Skilled Migration," 9.

65. Van Hear, *New Diasporas*, 73-74; Bump, "International Migration in Africa."

between 10 and 20 percent of Ghanaians were living abroad. In the late 1990s, migration to industrial nations intensified: between 1996 and 2001 the number of Ghanaian immigrants in the United States quadrupled from 24,000 to 97,000; migration to Italy almost doubled, and Ghanaians, according to some observers, are the largest and longest-serving African immigrant community in the United Kingdom.

Ghana's skilled migration was severe. Micah Bump (2006) records that of the total number of medical personnel trained between 1995 and 2002, over 20 percent (including 69.4 percent of medical doctors) emigrated, as did some fourteen thousand teachers trained in its institutions between 1975 and 1981. Almost 20 percent of its nurses/midwives also left for greener pastures. For all this, the Ghanaian experience challenges "zero-sum" arguments, which infer that skilled migrants are lost to one society and gained by another. It furnishes a striking example of how global financial networks allow a goodly proportion of South–North migrants to function as an "important developmental resource" for their home societies (through remittances and investments).

Ghanaian immigrants maintain robust and sustained homeland connections through social networks, remittances, and financial investment. They remit money for much longer than any other immigrant community, and their remittances exceed revenue from tourism and more than double foreign direct investment. In 2004, a staggering 1.2 billion U.S. dollars flowed into the country through official channels alone. Not only that, Ghanaian returnees (who numbered about fifty thousand in 1999) bring back vital skills and investments, which contribute to job creation. In 2002, President John Kufuor's government passed the Ghana Dual Citizenship Regulation Act in direct recognition of the Ghanaian diaspora's huge contribution to economic development. This measure signified an enlarged conception of nationhood in which national identity and citizenship were no longer understood in terms of exclusive sovereignty.

The merits of dual citizenship remain a matter of debate,[66] but such measures only serve to bolster an established trend. The fact is that African immigrants in Western societies display a strong propensity for transnational ties and identities. Two elements help to account for this. The first has to do with the fact that African societies are marked by strong communal ties and deeply rooted kinship bonds. With the possible exception of refugee movement, it is a rare African migrant whose journey is unattended by the bonds of kinship and social capital. The decision to migrate and the journey that ends in settlement in a foreign country are typically framed by family support, facilitated by preexisting social networks (including religious and/or tribal organizations), and invested with unshakable kinship obligations.

Second, regardless of economic status or educational attainment, Africans

---

66. While other countries such as Sierra Leone have followed Ghana's example, dual citizenship remains a subject of vigorous debate in some African countries like Tanzania. Detractors argue that it sanctions a dilution of the spirit of patriotism, increases exposure to international criminal activity, and makes it easier for foreign elements to exploit the limited resources of developing countries.

experience social marginalization, race exclusion, and institutionalized discrimination in Western societies, which impede full integration into the mainstream society and effectively diminish the premigration status of individuals. Maintaining strong homeland connections and involvement becomes central to the immigrant's sense of status, owing to what Boris Nieswand terms the *"paradox of migration."*[67] The immigrant inhabits two social-status systems, both rooted in the experience of migration, with contradictory attributes: in the African context the very act of migration confers enhanced status because the migrant is perceived as successful and wealthy; in Western society, however, the immigrant is marginalized and socially excluded. Transnationalism, as such, makes it possible for "denial of status in the affairs of the host country [to be] compensated for by the status that is derived from meeting culturally defined expectations" in the society of origin.[68] In one context the migrants are virtually invisible, in the other they are likely to receive too much attention and too many demands.

John Arthur observes that the average African immigrant in America "often does not aspire to naturalize or assimilate," that most have a singular goal: to achieve economic independence and self-sufficiency and funnel their assets to Africa to start a business or retire.[69] This may be overstated. But it is noteworthy that social and political activism by African immigrants living in the United States is mainly confined to Africa, that "most consider participation in the economic development of their countries of origin paramount," that the majority plan to repatriate to Africa after their children have left home, and that "becoming citizens of the United States even strengthens their ties to the motherland because their new status in America provides them with political and economic advantages at home."[70]

Transnationalism has far-reaching implications for the African encounter with Western societies. It potentially transforms the experience of assimilation by strengthening cultural identity or ancestral ties and may well prove critical in identity formation among second-generation immigrants. The fact that increasing numbers of African migrants are simultaneously incorporated into two different societies will certainly shape the long-term impact of the African missionary movement and significantly extend its transformational capacity within global Christianity—not least because it will act as a conduit of ideas, experiences, and influences between different worlds.

---

67. Boris Nieswand, "Charismatic Christianity in the Context of Migration: Social Status, the Experience of Migration and the Constructions of Selves among Ghanaian Migrants in Berlin," in *Religion in the Context of African Migration*, ed. Afeosemime U. Adogame and Cordula Weisskèoppel (Bayreuth: Eckhard Breitinger, 2005), 255.

68. Arthur, *Invisible Sojourners*, 88.

69. Ibid., 128.

70. Ibid., 91, 129, 135, 139.

10

The Emperor Has New Clothes

Assimilation and the Remaking of the West

> We may well ask . . . whether this sweeping immigration is to for-
> eignize us, or we are to Americanize it. . . .
> Foreigners are not coming to the United States in answer to any
> appetite of ours, controlled by an unfailing moral or political instinct.
> They naturally consult their own interests in coming, not ours. The
> lion, without being consulted as to time, quantity, is having the food
> thrust down his throat, and his only alternative is, digest or die.
> —Rev. Josiah Strong, *Our Country* (1885)

In the 1880s, Josiah Strong (1847-1916), a prominent American evangelical
spokesman, identified immigration as one of the great perils that confronted the
American nation and threatened its very survival.[1] By then America was the
chief country of immigration, absorbing over one million European migrants a
year on average. Strong highlighted three main reasons for this massive influx:
(1) the attraction of America's spaciousness, civil liberties, and prosperity;
(2) "expellant forces from Europe" including dense populations, social discontent, and political upheavals; and (3) increasing facilities for travel combined
with drastic reductions in travel costs. Interestingly, he also noted that the United
States contributed directly to the massive immigration influx through the production and exportation of "labor-saving machinery": production increases its
demand for labor while exportation decreases the demand for labor in the Old
World. With the foreign stock already accounting for 34 percent of the entire
population, Strong warned that the rising tide of immigration, unless checked
by Congress, would have a profoundly adverse impact on the moral and political
life of the nation.

Strong characterized the typical immigrant as "a European peasant," whose
horizon is narrow and whose moral and religious training has been meager or
false. He was adamant that immigration furnished "the greater portion of our
criminals" and steadily augmented the masses of people who were illiterate, "little acquainted with our institutions," and "controlled largely by their appetites

---

1. On Strong's views, see his controversial but best selling book *Our Country: Its Possible
Future and Its Present Crisis* (1885). The other "perils" Strong identified were Romanism, religion,
the public schools, Mormonism, intemperance, socialism, wealth, and the city.

and prejudices."[2] His admonitions came at a time when doctrines of manifest destiny and Anglo-Saxon supremacy were far more entrenched and pervasive than at present. As general secretary (1886-1898) of the Evangelical Alliance for the United States, a coalition of Protestant missionary groups, Strong enjoyed widespread circulation of his views and contributed to a climate of opinion that favored the imperial designs of President Theodore Roosevelt (with whom Strong shared a close friendship).[3] His calls for legislative action against the rising tide of immigration went largely unheeded at the time; but, as we shall see below, they gave expression to a strong undercurrent of xenophobic apprehension that eventually instigated drastic measures against the newcomers in the 1920s.

If Strong were still alive a century later, he would find reassuring echoes of his theme of America's chosenness and call to global dominance, but the immigration landscape would surely give him apoplexy—not because of the numbers of immigrants (which are comparable to estimates in his own day) but because the racial composition and cultural diversity of present immigration represents a radical development that would have been unimaginable and deeply objectionable to the good citizens of late-nineteenth- and early-twentieth-century America.

America as an Immigrant Nation

America has been and remains the definitive immigrant nation. With the exception of Native Americans, who constitute less than 1 percent of the entire population,[4] every American is an immigrant or descended from immigrants. Immigration is integral to American society and lies at the heart of its multicultural and multiracial identity. Immigrants, it is observed, have "transformed America into a very diverse nation whose resilience and problems *both* often stem from that diversity."[5] Indeed, it is not too far-fetched to suggest that all major transformations of American society are ultimately linked to immigrant infusion and migration movement. The history of America is a history of migration and immigrants. Not only is immigration central to the emergence, character, and development of the American nation, it is also crucial to its future.

There have been, generally speaking, four major immigration episodes over the course of America's history, each episode composed of distinct ethnic and cultural groups, and each wave also fomenting new transformations in American society. The first wave (roughly 1620-1850) dates to the initial migration of northwest Europeans who populated the colonies of the New World. An estimated one million immigrants came to America during the colonial period—about half of whom came as indentured servants. By 1819, when formal efforts were made

---

2. Strong, *Our Country*, 59.

3. Strong was a fervent advocate of American imperialism. "If I read not amiss," he declared, "this powerful race will move down upon Mexico, down upon Central and South America, out upon the islands of the sea, over upon Africa and beyond. And can any one doubt that the result of this competition of races will be the 'survival of the fittest'?" (Ibid., 223).

4. *The American Indian and Alaska Native Population: 2000* (Census Bureau, 2002).

5. Pedraza, "Origins and Destinies," 3.

to count immigrants, another 250,000 foreign-born had arrived by ship.[6] These immigrants fundamentally shaped the nation's core institutions, religious life, and cultural outlook. Their descendants, dubbed the "Protestant Establishment," "represented the owners and executives of most industrial and commercial properties . . . , were sovereign indirectly if not directly over most important political structures (except in the cities)" and "certainly dominated the majority of elite circles from coast to coast."[7] This dominance lasted until the 1960s.

The second wave (1619-1850) was the forced migration of thousands of African slaves. Strangely, other classifications (like that provided by Silvia Pedraza) do not identify forced transatlantic migration of Africans as a major immigration episode in American history.[8] This wave overlapped with the first wave but was absolutely distinct from it. By 1800, America had one of the largest communities of Africans anywhere in the world outside Africa. In 1790, when the first census was taken, African Americans numbered about 760,000 or 19 percent of the population. By 1900, the black population had reached 8.8 million. Despite enslavement, racial oppression, and political exclusion, American blacks have impacted American society and culture in profound ways; most prominently in the areas of music (spirituals, jazz, rhythm and blues), art (dance, language, and literature), science (by 1913 over one thousand inventions were patented by black Americans), and religion (black spirituals, the emergence of American Pentecostalism).[9] The experience, actions, and aspirations of blacks have contributed to some of the most profound and historic developments in the political, social, and economic life of the country. The civil rights movement (c. 1955-1968), for instance, fundamentally transformed the political landscape, instigated significant constitutional reform, and contributed lasting changes to the social order.

The third major immigration wave (1881-1930) saw over twenty-seven million immigrants arrive mainly from southern and eastern European nations.[10] Among the main source countries were Italy, Austria-Hungary, present-day Poland, and Russia. Drawn by the huge labor demands of America's rapidly expanding economy, these European immigrants came as migrant laborers. The majority, as Josiah Strong recognized, were poor, low-skilled peasants.[11] But included in

---

6. Ibid., 4.

7. Langdon Gilkey, "The Christian Congregation as a Religious Community," in *American Congregations*, ed. James P. Wind and James Welborn Lewis (Chicago: University of Chicago Press, 1998), 102.

8. See Pedraza, "Origins and Destinies."

9. See John A. Davis, "The Influence of Africans on American Culture," *The Annals* 354 (July 1964): 75-83. Though often ignored, the black spirituality nurtured among African slaves and reflective of the African religious heritage formed a critical component in the emergence and spread of Pentecostalism in America. See Allan Anderson, *An Introduction to Pentecostalism: Global Charismatic Christianity* (New York: Cambridge University Press, 2004), 43f.

10. From the mid-nineteenth century, the Lutheran and Reformed communities in America were augmented by a massive influx of Germans, Scandinavians, and Dutch. I have not identified this movement as a unique immigrant wave because the immigrants were joining preexisting communities of their own nationals. See Wade Clark Roof and William McKinney, *American Mainline Religion: Its Changing Shape and Future* (Piscataway, NJ: Rutgers University Press, 1987), 89.

11. Ewa Morawska, "East Europeans on the Move," in *The Cambridge Survey of World Migration*, ed. Robin Cohen (New York: Cambridge University Press, 1995), 97-102.

their number were some 1.5 million Jews fleeing anti-Semitic violence at the turn of the century in Europe (especially in Russia). Unlike other immigrants, these Jews came to America as political refugees. They were also urbanized and highly literate. Additionally, goodly numbers of Chinese and Japanese immigrants arrived on the West coast, chiefly as laborers. Utterly marginalized and grievously exploited—a 1790 federal law limited citizenship to whites—they existed as a veritable underclass. Native hostility to their presence led to the passing of a series of acts, including the Chinese Exclusion Act of 1882 and the Gentlemen's Agreement of 1907, which stifled further influx. (Interestingly, as noted earlier, this transpired at a time when American Christian missions to China were gathering momentum.)[12]

In addition to making a vital contribution to the growth of America's urban-industrial economy, this wave of immigration significantly reshaped American society. America's lofty Protestant ethos was forever transformed by the massive infusion of Catholics and Jews. Its culture and urban landscape took on a new vibrant diversity as multiethnic immigrant communities spread and settled throughout its vast mass. Its way of life and livelihoods were profoundly enriched by the infusion of an immeasurable cornucopia of new customs, conventions, and style (in music, literature, the arts, movies, philosophy, cuisine, even language). Even its educational and political structures were impacted. A 1965 article in *Time Magazine* reflected on the contribution of this third immigrant wave thus:

The newcomers inestimably enriched the U.S., making it the most incredibly diverse nation on earth. . . . [They] . . . helped to build the great cities and shift the balance of American life away from the farm. . . . The list of immigrants and their sons who helped to mold American art and industry, politics and science is endless. There were Steel Magnate Andrew Carnegie (Scotland), Fur Trader John Jacob Astor (Germany), Inventor Alexander Graham Bell (Scotland), the Du Ponts from France and Yeast Tycoon Charles L. Fleischmann from Hungary. German-born Albert Einstein, Hungarian-born Edward Teller and Italian-born Enrico Fermi helped the U.S. to unlock the atom's secrets. There have been more immigrant musicians than one can shake a baton at, from Irving Berlin (Russia) and Victor Herbert (Ireland) to Artur Rubinstein (Poland) and Dimitri Mitropoulos (Greece).[13]

Acclaimed "the largest migration of people in all recorded history" — though, in truth, there were also high rates of return[14]—this third wave was characterized by record levels of migrant influx. From 1900 to 1920, over fourteen million men, women, and children (85 percent of whom came from Europe) poured into the

---

12. The percentage of American missionaries in China increased from 35 percent (of the total) in 1905 to 51 percent by 1922.

13. "Historic Homage," *Time Magazine*, October 1, 1965.

14. Between 1880 and 1930, for instance, an estimated one-quarter to one-third of European immigrants reportedly returned home permanently (Schiller, "Transmigrants and Nation-States," 98).

United States. The immigration flood was abruptly curtailed in the 1920s, when restrictive immigration acts (in the form of a "national origins" quota system) imposed strict limits on immigration from southern and eastern Europe as well as Asia. These measures were blatantly ethnocentric and racist. By then close to 80 percent of the population was made up of Anglo-Saxon Protestants who traced their ancestry to northern and western Europe. The measures were intended to protect their racial and cultural dominance. In the short run, the onset of the Great Depression followed by the outbreak of the Second World War rendered the immigration restrictions moot. But for the next half century, migratory flows to the United States (and the nation's migrant stock) declined drastically (see fig. 8).

Figure 8
International Migrants as Percentage of Total Population of the United States (1900-2005)

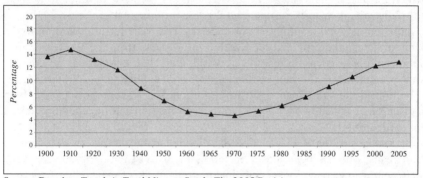

Source: Based on *Trends in Total Migrant Stock: The 2005 Revision*.

The fourth wave of immigration (1965-present), with which this study is primarily concerned, is unparalleled in American history by virtue of its enormous cultural diversity, variegated social composition, and the geographical spread of source countries. In the four decades spanning 1965 to 2005, America resumed its status as the chief destination of the world's international migrants. By 2005, the United States was home to 38.4 million migrants (up from 23 million in 1990) or one in five of the world's migrant population.[15] The United States accounts for between 35 and 49 percent of international migrants (on average) within the top ten destination countries in the West from 1960 to 2005. International migrants account for about 13 percent of the American population,[16] and the total "immigrant stock" (including U.S.-born children of immigrants) is estimated at over one-fifth of the entire U.S. population.[17]

Unlike in previous waves of immigration, however, the overwhelming majority of the current waves of immigrants—90 percent of whom arrived after 1960—are of non-European stock and come from over 150 countries. Slightly

---

15. *Trends in Total Migrant Stock: The 2005 Revision*.

16. Others estimate that one in ten Americans is foreign born. See Diana L. Eck, *A New Religious America: How a "Christian Country" Has Now Become the World's Most Religiously Diverse Nation* (San Francisco: Harper, 2001), 2.

17. Rumbaut and Portes, "Ethnogenesis," 7.

more than half (52 percent) come from Latin America and the Caribbean, and nearly a third (29 percent) come from Asia and the Middle East. This extraordinary development is linked to the Immigration and Nationality Act of 1965 (also known as the Hart-Celler Act) initiated by President John F. Kennedy and implemented by his successor.

The Significance of the 1965 Immigration Act for the United States

The 1965 act marks a momentous turning point in U.S. immigration history. It overturned previous restrictive immigration acts (of 1924 and 1952) and specifically abolished the forty-year-old national origins quota system under which 82 percent of visas went to northern and western Europe, 16 percent to southern and eastern Europe, and 2 percent to the rest of the world. It also eliminated national origin, race, or ancestry as a basis for immigration to the United States, and provided for 120,000 immigrants from the Western Hemisphere, 170,000 from the rest of the world. Outside the Americas no country was to exceed 20,000—though this limit was not applied to the Western Hemisphere until the subsequent 1976 Immigration Act. Most important, the 1965 legislation gave heavy priority to family reunification and included provisions for skilled immigration.

It is suggested that the legislation was directed mainly at eastern and southern Europeans, who had been most affected by the nativist immigration acts of the 1920s but who were no longer principal migrants.[18] This can be only partly true. The new legislation was passed at a time when American society was convulsed by issues of racism and social inequality as a result of the civil rights movement (c. 1955-1968), and its passing reflected a wider public debate. The aim was less to attract new immigrants than to bring immigration policy into line with broader currents of cultural reform by abolishing odious immigration regulations that effectively barred certain races and nationalities. Whatever the case, *the most important consequences of the 1965 amendment were entirely unforeseen*. These included the dramatic rise in nonwhite immigration from Asia, Latin America and the Caribbean, the ripple effects around the world, and the attendant transformations of American society.

But the passing of the 1965 act does not by itself adequately explain the volume, origins, and composition of the new immigrant flows. The historic forces unleashed by the legislation are far too potent and complex to be explained by the act alone. It is noteworthy that many of the poorest countries in the world are underrepresented among the new immigrants and that a good proportion are drawn (or self-selected) from the educated, professional, relatively wealthy sectors of the societies of origin. This formation contradicts the core claims of the

---

18. See Roger Waldinger and Jennifer Lee, "New Immigrants in Urban America," in *Strangers at the Gates: New Immigrants in Urban America*, ed. Roger D. Waldinger (Berkeley, CA: University of California Press, 2001), 33.

classical "push-pull" theory of immigration (discussed in chapter 7). Newer theories which highlight the importance of social networks and the self-perpetuating capacity of international migrations are more instructive. But most crucial are explanations that highlight macro processes; for global economic inequalities, demographic trends, decolonization, and new state formation are pivotal to the pattern and composition of the new immigration flows to the United States.

As we have seen, the *migration-systems theory* explains that global migrations are rooted in "prior links between sending and receiving countries based on colonization, political influence, trade investment and cultural ties" (Castles and Miller, 1998: 24). The main sources of post-1965 immigration (legal and illegal) have been those countries which share strong links with the United States based on a history of American military, economic, and colonial involvement.[19] These include countries with whom the United States shares deep structural linkages, reflected in external intervention or colonization—such as Mexico, the Philippines, and South Korea—as well as other Asian countries like Cambodia, Vietnam, or China, whose citizens are favored by the strong anti-communist orientation in American foreign policy. Still others like Taiwan and India reflect connections forged through foreign aid, trade, and direct investment. In Rumbaut's apt observation, "as the United States has become more deeply involved in the world, the world has become more deeply involved in America."[20]

Assimilation in Question

Like previous waves, post-1965 immigration also portends significant transformations of American society. Indeed, the impact on the religious landscape is likely to be more extensive than that of the third wave, and the demographic implications are even more profound. But, precisely because of its predominantly nonwhite nature and immense religio-cultural diversity, the assimilation or integration of the new immigrants into the mainstream (traditionally Anglo-Saxon) cultures of Europe and North America has emerged as one of the most widely debated issues of contemporary migration. (It should be noted that the popular apprehension about the capacity of the new immigrants to adapt to the customs and institutions of Western societies severely undermines the notion of an emerging single global culture.) Due to the limits of space, the following assessment is confined to the American experience, though key points of argument and the general conclusions apply to other Western democracies (see chapter 11).

Until the 1980s, the dominant theory of assimilation (in the United States) held that new immigrants will be completely assimilated, in terms of culture, education, and other social indicators, within three to six generations—the more racially distinct the group the slower the process. This "straight line" model of assimilation reflected the ideology of "Anglo-conformity," which combined views on the superiority of Anglo-American culture with the conviction that

---

19. See Rumbaut, "Origins and Destinies," 24, 28-31.
20. Ibid., 24.

middle-class Protestant whites of British ancestry are the "normative standard by which other groups are assessed and toward which they aspire."[21] In this perception, assimilation was a wholly one-directional and one-sided process. It required immigrant groups to gradually abandon (or "unlearn") old cultural traditions and homeland values in favor of new (superior) ones. And this development, once set in motion, moves inevitably and irreversibly. Within this framework, the dominant or core culture, envisioned as a culturally homogenous mass, remains unaffected and unchanged. (The reader may note a strong correlation between this ideology and the convictions that frame the universal civilization thesis discussed in chapter 2).

This theory of assimilation made no allowance for the possibility that the new ethnic or racial communities would make a positive contribution to the dominant society. Indeed, since full assimilation was understood in terms of *individual* mobility (at the expense of ethnic loyalty), the dissipation of the immigrants' collective identity was expected.

In the course of the twentieth century, alternative models of assimilation emerged.[22] By mid-century the "melting pot" ideal, which envisaged American society as the distinct creation of the cultural and organic amalgamation of diverse peoples, was hugely popular. But the exact nature of this "syncretic" American product remained ambiguous, and the model suffered from faddishness. It had waned by the 1990s. The "cultural pluralism" (or "multiculturalism") model rejects the very notion of a homogenous core and depicts American society as a mosaic of diverse races and ethnicities, all of which preserve their distinctive cultures alongside that of the dominant culture. In other words, immigrant cultures are not absorbed by a stable core; rather these distinct, equal, and autonomous cultures contribute to a fluid and dynamic whole in which their constitutive elements are constantly reshaped and remolded by interaction with each other and the host society. This multicultural model has received strong critique. Not only is the assumption that the constitutive elements of American society are equal highly debatable, but some immigrants also fear that it sanctions unequal status and inequitable treatment by local authorities.[23] Moreover, the concept rather ignores the experiences of immigrant children. Still, multiculturalism emerged as the most popular alternative to Anglo-conformity.

For all that, Anglo-conformity has remained the dominant model of assimilation in America. Its canonical status was bolstered by Milton M. Gordon's influential 1964 treatise, *Assimilation in American Life*. Drawing on earlier studies, Gordon outlined an assimilation framework that distinguished between the cultural and social dimensions.[24] In his analysis, *acculturation* or "cultural assimi-

---

21. Alba and Nee, *Remaking the American Mainstream*, 2, 3.

22. For a helpful overview, see ibid., 23-27; Min Zhou, "Segmented Assimilation: Issues, Controversies, and Recent Research on the New Second Generation," in *The Handbook of International Migration: The American Experience*, ed. Charles Hirschman, Philip Kasinitz, and Josh DeWind (New York: Russell Sage Foundation, 1999), 199-201; Pedraza, "Origins and Destinies."

23. See Jytte Klaisen, "The Two-Way Street to Integration for Europe's Muslims," *Faith & International Affairs* 4, no. 3 (Winter 2006): 18.

24. See also Herbert J. Gans, "Towards a Reconciliation of 'Assimilation' and 'Pluralism': The

lation," the adoption of the language, values, and cultural patterns of the core culture (i.e., the predominantly Anglo-Saxon middle class) by minority groups, was the first stage in the assimilation process. Acculturation need not be accompanied by other forms of assimilation and could last indefinitely. The next and more definitive stage was *structural assimilation*, when the immigrants became fully "incorporated" into the normative structures and major social institutions (civic, educational, and occupational) of the host society. This dimension was accompanied by the erosion of the immigrant culture and ethnic identity, considerable decline in prejudice and discrimination, and increasing intermarriage. Gordon's framework preserved the notion of Anglo-conformity. Not only was the process of assimilation largely inevitable (at least in the cultural stage) and one-directional, but the core culture also remained largely unaffected—its religious life being the sole exception.[25]

In recent years, however, this classical assimilation theory has come under fierce and sustained criticism.[26] Critics denounce its deeply ethnocentric and ideological bias, its blatant disregard of the variegated cultural streams and diverse ethnic elements that define American society, its inattentiveness to the capacity of new groups to maintain durable ethnic communities in the face of racial rejection, its blinkered framework (evident in assumptions about an ideal or inevitable outcome), and its failure to recognize alternative modes of incorporation into the dominant culture. For some, the very notion of assimilation (indissociable from the concept of Anglo-conformity) seems passé, an obsolete construct that served ideological purposes and now has limited application to the complex, multilayered cultural interactions associated with post-1965 immigration.

The issues are awfully complicated and data restrictions (too few of the second generation have reached adulthood as yet) invite caution. For now, the distinctiveness of contemporary mass immigration forms the fulcrum of the assimilation debate, which is to say that analytical comparisons between the new wave of (post-1965) immigrants and the previous wave of (early-twentieth-century, predominantly European) immigrants inform every major assessment. On one side of the debate are proponents who see strong historical parallels between past and present immigration. And since historical correspondence invites conceptual concurrence they postulate or anticipate patterns of assimilation for the new

Interplay of Acculturation and Ethnic Retention," in *The Handbook of International Migration: The American Experience*, ed. Charles Hirschman, Philip Kasinitz, and Josh DeWind (New York: Russell Sage Foundation, 1999), 161-71.

25. Milton M. Gordon, *Assimilation in American Life: The Role of Race, Religion, and National Origins* (New York: Oxford University Press, 1964), 109.

26. See, among others, Barbara Schmitter Heisler, "The Sociology of Immigration: From Assimilation to Segmented Integration, from the American Experience to the Global Arena," in *Migration Theory: Talking across Disciplines*, ed. Caroline Brettell and James Frank Hollifield (New York: Routledge, 2000), 77-96; Alejandro Portes and Rubén G. Rumbaut, *Legacies: The Story of the Immigrant Second Generation* (Berkeley: University of California Press, 2001); and Alba and Nee, *Remaking the American Mainstream*; Charles Jaret, "Troubled by Newcomers: Anti-Immigrant Attitudes and Actions during Two Eras of Mass Emigration," in *Mass Migration to the United States: Classical and Contemporary Periods*, ed. Pyong Gap Min (New York: AltaMira, 2002), 21-63.

immigrants that conform to past experience. On the other side of the debate are those who emphasize discontinuity between past and present immigration and argue that the distinctiveness of the new immigrants—in origin, composition, and urban concentration—requires fresh approaches to the assimilation question and new conceptual models.

Between these two positions are a range of voices that call attention to the applicability of aspects of both continuity and discontinuity arguments. Some, for example, like renowned American sociologist Herbert J. Gans, suggest that the two positions are readily reconciled if greater attention is paid to the critical distinction between *cultural assimilation* (or acculturation) and *social assimilation*. What follows is an attempt to summarize the main arguments and points of debate as they apply generally—that is, without focusing on the experiences of any particular immigrant group.

Continuity Arguments

The most prominent proponents of the continuity position are Richard Alba and Victor Nee, who co-authored a major study titled *Remaking the American Mainstream: Assimilation and Contemporary Immigration* (2002).[27] Alba and Nee share some of the criticisms of the classical assimilation model—notably the notion that assimilation is an inevitable process that produces an ideal or universal outcome—but they contend that what is needed is a revision or a more up-to-date formulation of the theory, not wholesale disavowal. They are convinced that assimilation, defined as "the decline of an ethnic distinction and its corollary cultural and social differences," "is likely to remain a central process in the adaptation of [contemporary] immigrants and their descendants," albeit with "divergent outcomes in American society." The theory of assimilation they propose includes the following assertions:

- The process is incremental and intergenerational.
- It occurs at different rates between and within different ethnic and racial groups.
- The nature of the mainstream into which groups are assimilating is changed in the process.[28] (Importantly, this "mainstream" is envisioned not as the restricted, static ideal assumed in the concept of Anglo-conformity, but as a "highly variegated" entity, a composite culture.)

The Assimilationist Model

The reformulation of the classical assimilation model proposed by Alba and Nee is predicated on the conviction that there is strong continuity between past and

---

27. See also Richard Alba and Victor Nee, "Rethinking Assimilation Theory for a New Era of Immigration," in *The Handbook of International Migration: The American Experience*, ed. Charles Hirschman, Philip Kasinitz, and Josh DeWind (New York: Russell Sage Foundation, 1999), 137-60.

28. Alba and Nee, *Remaking the American Mainstream*, 11-13, 38f.

present immigration. The authors insist that assertions about the uniqueness of contemporary migration have gone too far. In their view, while patterns of assimilation between past and present immigrants will not necessarily produce identical outcomes, claims about the distinctiveness of contemporary immigration "generally overlook the complexity of the historical record and oversimplify the European American experience in particular."[29]

Now, as then, assimilation is contingent on purposive actions and decisions taken by individuals and groups, either in an effort to maximize the benefits of immigration or as a result of institutional mechanisms present in American society. Basically, whether they want to assimilate or not, individual decisions and actions taken in pursuit of normal goals—such as acquiring a good education, getting a better job, moving to a nicer neighborhood—produce assimilation as an unintended result. Group assimilation also ensues when an ethnic group adopts strategies aimed at creating better opportunities of success or survival, such as emphasizing educational achievement or distancing themselves from other, less-favored immigrant groups.

The process of assimilation is promoted not only by individual action or group strategies but also by institutional mechanisms within advanced industrial societies. For instance, despite widespread anti-immigration sentiments, a continued influx of new immigrants and the possibility of long-term settlement are ensured if not encouraged by legal safeguards and constitutional rights. As a case in point, regulatory changes in 1952 granting citizenship rights to Asian immigrants for the first time radically altered paths to assimilation for those groups. Civil rights laws that enforce racial equality, encourage equal employment opportunity, and punish discrimination against marginalized groups also create an environment highly conducive to assimilation. Alba and Nee (2002) acknowledge that racism persists in American society, that many immigrants encounter glass ceilings in the workplace, and that vested interests and customs impose powerful constraints that limit the implementation and impact of institutional change. Nonetheless, they argue, profound changes have occurred in the institutional environment that encourage the assimilation of the new immigrants.

As a result of this assortment of individual, group, and institutional mechanisms, claim the authors, assimilation "will remain a central social process in the adaptation of immigrants and their descendants . . . in American society."[30] At the same time, because assimilation is the end-product of a variety of causes, it is neither inevitable nor irreversible. Rates of assimilation within and across ethnic groups will vary considerably—some Hispanics will live in segregated communities while many others will be integrated into white neighborhoods. In the final analysis, however, Alba and Nee are convinced that the available data on the descendants of present and previous immigrants indicate continuity in assimilation between past and present. They conclude that many descendants of post-1965 immigrants will be fully assimilated into American society.

What, then, of the capacity of assimilation to transform the "mainstream"?

---

29. Ibid., 156.
30. Ibid., 59.

For the authors, the American mainstream is a "composite culture . . . made up of multiple interpenetrating layers [which] allows individuals and sub-populations to forge identities out of its materials to distinguish themselves from others in the mainstream . . . [yet] in ways that are recognizably American."[31] Here, too, the authors see strong continuity between past and present. In the early twentieth century, the massive influx of predominantly Catholic and Jewish immigrants met with rigorous hostility because of America's self-identity as a white, Protestant nation (and possibly deeply rooted memories of bitter religious wars in post-Reformation Europe). Over time, however, the immigrants' religions became part of the American mainstream, even if those religions were also transformed in the process[32]—as in the emergence of Reform Judaism. Further, over time interfaith marriages also became increasingly accepted. As a result, the mainstream became more diverse "in the ethnic origins of those who participate in it," and the identity of the majority group was reconstituted.

This transformation of the mainstream, contend the authors, will continue with the new immigrants. Now, as then, assimilation will be marked by the crossing, shifting, and blurring of racial/ethnic boundaries which define the dominant group. As individuals or groups become part of the dominant group, their ethnic origins (or their more exotic aspects) will be reduced to symbolic reference or will become "socially 'invisible.'" In particular, interracial marriage and residential mixing will help to reduce the social and cultural distances between different groups.[33] The authors acknowledge the implausibility of this scenario for visibly nonwhite immigrants; but they insist that even the boundaries between blacks and other groups will become blurred, and they speculate that race/ethnicity will lose some of its salience. Indeed, they posit the notion that acceptance by the dominant culture of "a majority culture that is racially diverse" may be one way in which assimilation transforms the mainstream.

The continuity arguments proffered by Alba and Nee represent a constructive refurbishment of the classical assimilation theory. The argument that assimilation is frequently an unintended consequence of normal aspirations and motivations is insightful, while the reference to institutional mechanisms implicates the state as a significant actor in the assimilation process without validating state-led efforts at assimilation. And few would argue that rates of assimilation among contemporary immigrant groups will be uneven or will yield divergent outcomes—indeed this is a claim shared by critics of assimilation (see below).

It seems to me, however, that the authors give insufficient weight to what they acknowledge as "potentially important" distinctions between past and present immigration. Many crucial conclusions are based on the contention—chiefly extrapolated from past European immigration—that assimilation will redefine the racial categories, and that "boundary crossing" or "boundary blurring" between the new groups and the mainstream will attenuate the rigid racial dichotomy that plagues American society. In addition, while a strong case is made for

---

31. Ibid., 13.
32. See also Gordon, *Assimilation in American Life*, 110.
33. Alba and Nee, *Remaking the American Mainstream*, 260-67.

some reconstitution of the mainstream as it expands to absorb the new minority cultures, important differences between past and present are overlooked. For instance, even though the absolute numbers of past and present immigrants are comparable, the new immigrants and their children account for a much lower percentage of the total population—20 percent in 2000, compared to about 35 percent by 1900—simply because the U.S. population is now roughly four times what it was in 1900.[34] To put the matter differently, by 1910 the foreign-born population (excluding their children) represented almost 15 percent of the population compared to 10.4 percent in 2000. Whether this translates into a lower overall impact and influence on the mainstream culture or national life is a matter of debate.[35] Paradoxically, because of the current decline in the fertility rates of the native population, contemporary immigration plays a greater role in population growth than it did during the previous wave.[36]

The case for assimilation is also weakened, in my view, by questionable claims: notably the assertion that interracial marriages will contribute to the assimilation of the new immigrants.[37] The authors readily admit that interracial marriages still represent a very small percentage of all marriages in the United States—2.2 percent in 1992—and, to their credit, they also acknowledge that more research is necessary before confident projections can be made about marriage patterns and assimilation. Even so, they suggest that changes in marriage patterns in American society—marriage between individuals with similar educational attainment is increasing—will impact ethnic identification among the new immigrants. To gauge the significance of this point it is important to bear in mind that intermarriage is considered "the best and most easily available indicator of social assimilation."[38] This is one reason why studies about the marriage patterns of immigrant groups and subgroups have proliferated. But bold conclusions are sometimes drawn from quite limited trends such as shifts in rates of in-marriage within minority populations.

Ultimately the data on exogamy (marital and nonmarital union between people of different racial/ethnic backgrounds) is subject to methodological and interpretative complexities. Current prognostications are beset by at least two major

---

34. See Rumbaut and Portes, "Ethnogenesis," 7; Strong, *Our Country*, 55; also Kevin Jernegan, "A New Century: Immigration in the U.S.," *Migration Information Source* (2005); *Profile of the Foreign Born in the United States: 2000* (Washington, DC: U.S. Census Bureau, 2001), 9.

35. See Min Zhou, "The Changing Face of America: Immigration, Race/Ethnicity, and Social Mobility," in *Mass Migration to the United States: Classical and Contemporary Periods*, ed. Pyong Gap Min (New York: AltaMira, 2002), 66.

36. See Smith and Edmonston, eds., *New Americans*, 2.

37. Alba and Nee, *Remaking the American Mainstream*, 260-67. Compare the findings of the panel on the demographic and economic impacts of immigration instituted by the National Research Council. Utilizing the highly problematic approach of calculating persons in the population with multiple ancestry, this panel projected an increase in interracial marriages from 7 percent in 1995 to 21 percent in 2050 (with the highest percentages occurring among Asians and Hispanics) (Smith and Edmonston, eds., *New Americans*, 113-23).

38. David E. López, "Social and Linguistic Aspects of Assimilation Today," in *The Handbook of International Migration: The American Experience*, ed. Charles Hirschman, Philip Kasinitz, and Josh DeWind (New York: Russell Sage Foundation, 1999), 219.

problems. First, the vast majority of second-generation immigrants have yet to reach adulthood, which makes judgment about their marriage patterns premature and highly speculative. (Incidentally, the view that exogamic practices among descendants of contemporary immigrants will contribute to their assimilation is somewhat at variance with the argument that ethnic identification will likely erode among those same descendants as a result of assimilation, since exogamy assumes stable ethnic/racial categories.) Second, sustained demographic growth (due in part to higher fertility rates) and constant cultural replenishment through continued influx of new immigrants suggests an alternative possibility: that interracial marriage will often be a product, rather than a causative factor, of social assimilation. Surely, this much is signified by wider trends pointing to an increase in marriages between individuals with high educational attainment.

High levels of intermarriage between racial and ethnic groups will undoubtedly blur racial distinctions and ethnic identification, but racial identification remains as cogent as ever. Significantly, "interracial marriages are highest between whites and Asian Americans followed by whites and Hispanics and lowest between whites and blacks."[39] In 1990, 97 percent of whites and 94 percent of blacks still married within their own groups; the comparable rates for Asians and Hispanics was 70 percent and 73 percent, respectively.[40] Furthermore, much research on exogamy overlooks the central role that religion plays in immigrant identity and social formation. As Helen R. Ebaugh and Janet S. Chafetz indicate (based on a Houston study), marriage within the faith is quite strong among immigrant communities. In other words, objections to marrying *outside* the faith are often stronger than objections to marrying someone from another race or ethnicity. In some instances, therefore, an interracial marriage may mask the strengthening of the immigrant community's religious identity.[41]

In the final analysis, Alba and Nee's strongly optimistic assessment of the prospects of assimilation is less than convincing because it downplays rather that addresses cogent impediments: among these, that post-1965 immigration is predominantly nonwhite; that the new ethnic communities are being constantly replenished by new immigrant influx; and that racial distinctiveness is a more salient factor now than it was previously.

It is noteworthy that the assimilation of previous waves of European immigration did little to transform the social marginality or cultural distance of African Americans and other nonwhite groups. The racial environment has changed in significant ways, but it seems unwise to discount the possibility that current nonwhite immigration will reinforce the racial divide between the mainstream and a culturally diverse majority. There is no credible reason to discount a scenario in which new assimilation patterns simply shift this binary divide so that the predominantly white mainstream is reconstituted to include Hispanic and other self-defined whites. Already, in high immigration cities the growing presence of

---

39. Alba and Nee, *Remaking the American Mainstream*, 265.
40. Smith and Edmonston, eds., *New Americans*, 370.
41. See Helen R. Ebaugh and Janet S. Chafetz, *Religion and the New Immigrants: Continuities and Adaptations in Immigrant Congregations* (New York: AltaMira, 2000), 401f.

immigrants has stimulated large out-migration by non-Hispanic whites so that those cities have become "less white" and "more colored."[42] As we shall see, this social segmentation of American society represents the most formidable challenge for missionary-minded immigrant churches intent on reaching the wider American society.

Discontinuity Arguments

Critics of the old assimilation paradigm maintain that the distinctiveness of, and radically different environment encountered by, the new immigrants requires fresh tools of analysis.[43] They recognize that earlier immigrant groups from southern and eastern Europe encountered widespread prejudice and discrimination from mainstream Protestant Americans because of differences in culture, language, religion, and ethnicity. By the third or fourth generation, however, historical circumstances and basic racial affinity with the dominant society had combined to erode their particular cultural traditions and ethnic distinctiveness. They became indistinguishable from, and fully accepted by, other white Americans. A similar trajectory of near universal, "straight-line" assimilation for post-1965 immigrants is ruled out by a number of factors. Several stand out.

First, and foremost, the new immigrants reflect a more extensive diversity of cultures and social classes. Partly as a result of immigration policies, a sizable proportion arrive as highly educated and highly skilled middle-class professionals whose encounter with American society is radically different from that of low-wage, unskilled immigrants. Such major disparities rule out a universal outcome.

Second, the fact that they are overwhelmingly non-European means that the immigrants and their communities will remain ethnically distinguishable and racially distinctive—black immigrants more so—no matter how long they live in America or assiduously assimilate. Indeed, there is a strong likelihood that social exclusion and persistent racial discrimination will prompt their descendants to emphasize ethnic particularity and cultivate homeland or "primordial" ties.

Third, the numbers and diversity of contemporary immigrants is constantly replenished by new waves of new immigrants.[44] Government legislation in the 1920s drastically stemmed European migrant inflow; and the lack of cultural replenishment contributed to a high rate of assimilation. A similar hiatus in contemporary immigration, it is argued, appears quite remote for a number of crucial reasons: Western governments lack the will or effective instruments to curtail immigrant flows completely; the pressures and inequalities that fuel global migration flows remain unchanged. If anything, the outlook for critical factors

---

42. See Zhou, "Changing Face of America," 75-79.

43. See Portes, "Immigration Theory for a New Century"; Ebaugh and Chafetz, *Religion and the New Immigrants*, 456; Min, "Contemporary Immigrants' Advantages for Intergenerational Cultural Transmission,"135-60; Zhou, "Segmented Assimilation."

44. The panel sponsored by the National Research Council also concluded that the number of potential U.S. immigrants will increase in the foreseeable future (Smith and Edmonston, eds., *New Americans,* 79).

like the North–South economic divide are decidedly pessimistic, and, barring a global catastrophe of biblical proportions, demographic imbalances will definitely persist into the next century. Alba and Nee (2003) rightly contend that a decline in the attractiveness of the United States as a migrant destination or improved levels of development in countries of origin (as happened in the case of Japan and South Korea) may cause significant shifts. Yet such changes have to be global in scope to effect a reversal in current trends.

Fourth, the new immigrants enter a society that has changed in significant ways from that encountered by the previous wave of immigrants in the early nineteenth century. Increasing cultural diversity and the impact of social reform initiatives like the civil rights movement have engendered greater tolerance of ethnic diversity within American society and have prompted a deliberate strategy of multiculturalism at governmental levels. These developments signify a shift in the ideological climate from the dominant social policy of "Anglo-conformity."[45] The impact is seen in institutional developments such as affirmative action, bilingual education programs, diversified college campuses, and the addition of minority and ethnic studies to the liberal arts curriculum. As a result of such systemic transformations within the host society, contemporary immigrants face considerably less pressure to assimilate to a white middle-class culture, compared to earlier immigrant groups. (It is interesting to note that both continuity and discontinuity arguments arrive at conflicting conclusions from the same starting point).

Fifth, the structures of globalization provide the new immigrants with significant advantages over past groups to transmit their language and culture to subsequent generations.[46] Major transformations within the global system of communication and transportation have revolutionized the experience of transnationalism (see pp. 202-6 above). Today's immigrants are afforded greater resources to maintain transnational identities or to forge multiple social networks, so that aspects of their daily lives and decision making are subject to distant influences and obligations. Moreover, a goodly proportion of post-1965 immigrants have settled in parts of the country that have close physical proximity to their homeland: many Latino and Caribbean immigrants have settled in border states and cities like New York, while Asian immigrants predominate on the West (Pacific) Coast. This pattern of settlement reflects and reinforces transnational ties and identities.

Sixth, post-1965 immigration is characterized by higher levels of population concentration and residential segregation.[47] In 1910, approximately 57 percent of the immigrant population resided in six major immigrant states, whereas in 1990 nearly 75 percent of the immigrant population was concentrated in six (of the fifty) states: California, New York, Florida, Texas, New Jersey, and Illinois.[48]

---

45. Min, "Contemporary Immigrants' Advantages for Intergenerational Cultural Transmission," 146f.

46. For a detailed discussion, see ibid., 135-60.

47. Ibid., 137; see also Alejandro Portes and Rubén G. Rumbaut, *Immigrant America: A Portrait* (Berkeley: University of California Press, 1996), 28-56.

48. Min, "Contemporary Immigrants' Advantages for Intergenerational Cultural Transmission," 137.

The new immigrants are far more likely to live in the largest metropolitan areas than the native population. And the convergence of specific immigrant groups in certain suburbs, cities, or regions of the country underscores the centrality of social capital and social networks in the flow and formation of immigrant communities. The largest Arab immigrant community in North America, for instance, is concentrated in the Detroit metropolitan area,[49] while the largest black immigrant population (3.5 million) is to be found in New York. In addition, 29 percent of Mexican immigrants have settled in Texas and 39 percent of Asian and Pacific Islander groups reside in California (18 percent in Los Angeles).

In 1980 California replaced New York as the chief immigration state, and by 2004 it was home to 29 percent of the foreign-born population.[50] In 2000, Los Angeles and New York, which together had 13.3 percent of the entire U.S. population, had 33.1 percent of its foreign-born population.[51] The high concentration of America's newcomers in large metropolitan areas, which native Americans arguably find increasingly unattractive, has a twofold significance. Some argue that high concentrations of particular immigrant groups facilitate the use of a common language,[52] enhance the preservation of culture, and regulate the pace of acculturation.[53] It often also coincides with residential segregation and the formation of ethnic enclaves stamped by homeland ethos and mores. At the same time, such high concentration means that the impact of contemporary mass immigration on much of the United States is minimal or gradual, but tremendously magnified in a few regions.[54]

Some of the discontinuity arguments summarized above are stronger than others. The claim that there has been an ideological shift from Anglo-conformity to multiculturalism depends on narrowly interpreted events and developments. It is highly questionable whether state legitimation of cultural pluralism has had any significant long-term impact on popular attitudes, much less on the rigid, dichotomous, racial classification that characterizes the wider American society. Indeed, "multicultural" policies have evoked vigorous mainstream reactions against bilingual education and affirmative action. While there is no gainsaying the remarkable growth of cultural diversity in America, to suggest that this has transformed traditional views on "straight-line" assimilation seems unsafe. Alba and Nee (2003) are closer to the truth when they observe that, for many Americans, endorsement of cultural diversity is largely symbolic—signifying a limited openness to foreign food, ethnic music, and holiday customs.

Further, the distinctiveness of some aspects of contemporary experience can

---

49. Rumbaut, "Origins and Destinies," 32.

50. Jernegan, "A New Century"; *Profile of the Foreign Born*, 14-15.

51. *Profile of the Foreign Born*, 16.

52. In the United States, between 1980 and 1990, Spanish speakers grew by 50 percent (30 percent of New York is Hispanic), Chinese speakers by 98 percent, Korean speakers by 127 percent, and Vietnamese speakers by 150 percent (Wallraff, "What Global Language?").

53. Portes and Rumbaut, *Immigrant America*, 54.

54. Roger D. Waldinger, "Strangers at the Gates," in *Strangers at the Gates: New Immigrants in Urban America*, ed. Roger D. Waldinger (Berkeley: University of California Press, 2001), 2.

be exaggerated. Residential segregation, for instance, was also conspicuous in the previous wave. In the mid-1880s, Josiah Strong denounced the "unhappy tendency towards aggregation" among European immigrants and complained that "certain quarters of many cities are, in language, customs and costumes, essentially foreign" and set apart "from Americanizing influences."[55]

From a different perspective, Herbert Gans argues that the comparisons between the two periods suffer from differences in the origins of the two sets of researchers, which in turn influence their findings.[56] Very few of the researchers who studied the early-twentieth-century immigrants shared the same background as the immigrants, and the earliest studies began in the 1920s (forty years after the first eastern and southern European immigrants arrived in large numbers). This meant that most of the researchers were *outsiders* who did not speak the immigrant languages, and much of their data came from the second generation. As a result of these limitations, the immigrant culture appeared fairly homogenous, and public acculturation was more visible than ethnic retention. Accordingly, such studies strongly emphasized assimilation. Researchers of contemporary immigration, however, are largely *insiders*, who often share the same ethnic or racial background and values of the groups they study, and they obtain their data directly from the first generation. As a result, suggests Gans, they are far more conscious of ethnic solidarity and see less evidence of social and economic assimilation. In short, the rejection of "straight-line assimilation," while understandable may yet be contradicted when the second generation reaches the same stage of maturity as the European immigrants studied by previous researchers.

This argument raises deeper questions about empirical research and analytical subjectivity—how the researchers' own conscious or subconscious proclivities shaped their study, for instance—which falls outside our purview. But it raises the question of why the current immigration debate is polarized even among researchers and, like all continuity arguments, it plays down historical or contextual distinctions.

It would be unwise to ignore the fact that there are strong parallels in the predicaments and prospects faced by past and present migrants.[57] In the early twentieth century, nativist hostility toward new immigrant groups and xenophobic fears about the perceived threats they pose to the political order, national safety, economic security, and cherished sociocultural ideals of the dominant culture were as common as they are today. Even present forebodings about the spread of terrorist networks and deep anxieties about the capacity of global interconnectedness to facilitate the spread of deadly diseases echo the reactions of previous generations. But the peculiarities of the contemporary situation are critical: the immense cultural and social diversity of post-1965 immigrants; lower rates of return migration (or emigration); the fixation on illegal immigration; a decline in

---

55. Strong, *Our Country*, 60f. He added, in typically alarmist vein, "in some cases 100,000 or 200,000 acres in one block, have been purchased by foreigners of one nationality and religion; thus building up states within a state, having different languages, different antecedents, different religions, different ideas and habits, preparing mutual jealousies, and perpetuating race antipathies."

56. Gans, "Towards a Reconciliation of 'Assimilation' and 'Pluralism.'"

57. See Jaret, "Troubled by Newcomers," 21-63.

discriminatory laws against immigration and immigrants; diminished (governmental) will to restrict legal immigration; unprecedented levels of "nonimmigrant" arrivals (visitors, tourists, and students); concerns about overpopulation;
and crucial changes in America's position in the world.[58] Even if powerful pressures for one-way assimilation still exist in American society, the dynamics and
particular attributes of post-1965 immigration strongly militate against uniform,
rapid, or wholesale integration of the new immigrants.

Segmented Assimilation

Strong skepticism about the contemporary relevance of Anglo-conformity or
"straight-line assimilation" has yielded alternative perspectives or models. The
most compelling of these is the "segmented" or selective assimilation model for-
mulated by sociologists Alejandro Portes and Min Zhou.[59] In this model, straightforward acculturation and acceptance by the American mainstream are only one
of the possible outcomes for the new immigrants. Contemporary immigrants are
"being absorbed by different segments of American society, ranging from affluent middle-class suburbs to impoverished inner-city ghettos,"[60] and these distinct
patterns of adaptation produce divergent outcomes. Segmented-assimilation
theory maintains that the form and degree of assimilation are contingent on a
number of complex factors, four of which are considered crucial: (1) how the
first generation of immigrants are received;[61] (2) the relative pace of acculturation among parents and children; (3) the particular challenges confronted by the
second generation in their bid for adaptation; and (4) the economic resources and
social capital available within the immigrant family and community.

In the final analysis, the "segmented-assimilation" model demonstrates that
assimilation into the mainstream is only one among possible forms of assimilation. (As we shall see in chapter 13, this model best captures the African
immigrant experience.) Its framework identifies at least three "multidirectional
patterns" of adaptation: (1) upward mobility and economic integration into the
normative structures of middle-class America; (2) downward mobility involving parallel integration into the underclass; and (3) economic integration into
middle-class America combined with deliberate preservation of the immigrant
community's values and solidarity. The model is not without limitations. The
impact that immigrant parents have on the assimilation pattern of the second
generation is perhaps overstated. Alba and Nee contend that it stipulates "rigid
ethnic/racial boundaries and economic segmentation" and paints "an excessively
pessimistic future for central-city minority youths."[62] It is, however, noteworthy

---

58. On these, and for an in-depth comparison of the past and present immigration realities, see
ibid., 30-36, 52-54; also Zhou, "The Changing Face of America," 66-68.

59. See Zhou, "Segmented Assimilation"; Portes and Rumbaut, *Legacies*, 44-69; also Heisler,
"The Sociology of Immigration," 79ff.

60. Zhou, "Segmented Assimilation," 210.

61. On this, see also Portes and Rumbaut, *Immigrant America*, 82-92.

62. Alba and Nee, *Remaking the American Mainstream*, 8, 161f.

that the segmented-assimilation framework eschews the negative view of immigrant ethnicity and culture enshrined in the traditional assimilation paradigm.

Despite their incompatibility, each model ("assimilationist" and "segmented assimilation") contributes a critical insight to the study of contemporary immigration. The latter highlights the fact that the process of incorporation into a diversified and fragmented American society is shaped by a range of "complex and involuntary forces," while the former upholds the possibility that the mainstream culture is transformed as it absorbs new ethnicities and cultures. Importantly, both share one fundamental conclusion: namely, that assimilation among contemporary immigrants in the American context will produce divergent outcomes and proceed at different rates among and across ethnic groups. The assimilation debate will no doubt continue for the foreseeable future, and the polarized perspectives that currently dominate the field may yet be challenged (or possibly augmented) by other approaches. What seems certain is that America's future is tied in many ways to the fate and fortune of its new immigrants. This is perhaps most obviously true of American religious life, which is examined in some detail in chapter 12.

A New (Missionary) Encounter?

The notion that assimilation leaves neither the immigrant cultures nor the dominant mainstream culture unchanged has significant implications for understanding the "missionary" potential of post-1965 immigration. Already, the new immigrants have transformed America into the most religiously diverse nation on earth.[63] The African immigrant churches, which are given detailed attention in the final section of this book, are characterized by a strong missionary vision that echoes the exalted aims of the earlier and still forceful Western missionary movement. Whether this African religious phenomenon will have a wider, cross-cultural religious impact is something we will explore fully later on. Such religious initiatives form part of a remarkable and growing trend within the American Christian experience, a trend that has seen the burgeoning of Hispanic and Asian communities of faith (primarily of the Pentecostal variety) throughout the American religious landscape.

As many of these churches become more established and adapt to the demands of their new environment, their ability to reach the wider population will arguably increase. Not only do they provide alternative centers of Christian community and spirituality, but their impact is also likely to produce what some scholars describe as the "de-Europeanizing of American Christianity."[64] For analysts convinced that the end of the Cold War signifies the triumph of Western ideals and the inevitable surrender of non-Western cultures to the juggernaut of Western

---

63. Eck, *New Religious America*, 4.

64. Fenggang Yang and Helen Ebaugh, "Transformations in New Immigrant Religions and Their Global Implications," *American Sociological Review* 66 (April 2001): 269-88; also, R. Stephen Warner, "Coming to America," *Christian Century*, February 10, 2004, 23.

secularism or worldviews, the trends denoted by the new immigration must occasion discomfort. America's economic dominance clearly facilitates the global spread of American cultural goods—which, to reiterate an earlier point, does not in itself equate to cultural homogenization. But equally important, if not more so, America's supremacy and democratic ideals also provide the ideal environment for the incubation, renewal, and global spread of minority faiths.

How this is so is perhaps most effectively demonstrated in the case of Islam, to which we now turn. A whole chapter on Islam in a study that explores the links between migration and Christian mission needs explanation. I have argued repeatedly that, because the North–South divide within the contemporary world order is as religious as it is economic or demographic, South–North migration must be considered a religious movement. The growth of Muslim populations in Europe and North America provides the most conspicuous example of this trend. Not only does it demonstrate the unanticipated consequences of European empire; it also represents an important illustration of "globalization from below." Furthermore, the complexities and tensions that bedevil the encounter between Islam and Western society (where the ghost of Christendom still lingers) expose the inherent inadequacies of the single-global-culture ideal linked to secularization theories and allows for a more penetrating analysis of the assimilation question than is possible with the new Christian immigrants. At the same time, an assessment of the impact of Islam on Western societies helps to highlight the considerable importance of the massive influx of non-Western Christians for the future of Western Christianity.

Part III

MOBILE FAITHS

11

Immigration and Religion

Reflections on Islam

There is one Islam, and the fundamental principles that define it are those to which all Muslims adhere. . . . Western Muslims, because they are undergoing the experience of being established in new societies, have no choice but to go back to the beginning and study their points of reference in order to delineate and distinguish what in their religion is unchangeable (*thabit*) from what is subject to change (*mutaghayyir*), and to measure, from the inside, what they have achieved and what they have lost by being in the West.

—Tariq Ramadan,
Western Muslims and the Future of Islam (2005)

In the first part of this book I argued that, far from fulfilling expectations of a single global civilization, the global spread of socioeconomic modernization may be contributing to a widening of cultural disparities between the West and non-West. In Western societies, the process of modernization has witnessed distinctive cultural changes associated with the secular ideal of liberal democracy: notably stronger individualism, a greater push for gender equality, sexual permissiveness, a weakening of the institution of marriage, as well as greater tolerance of divorce, abortion, and homosexuality. Non-Western societies are not static, but they remain resistant to secularization (at least Western forms of the phenomenon) and retain strong allegiance to religious systems and traditional values. Present trends indicate that this cultural cleavage will steadily widen as younger generations in the West become more liberal and secular while their counterparts in the non-West (especially within the Islamic societies) remain deeply traditional.[1] Rapid population growth within the strongly religious non-Western societies combined with stagnant or negative demographic patterns within increasingly secular Western nations will further accentuate the divide.

This widening gap in religiosity between the West and non-West is supremely relevant to any assessment of the potential impact of nonwhite migration on Western societies. Owing to the pervasive religiosity of the non-Western world, the South-to-North migration movement is essentially a religious movement. This is to say that, in addition to the economic and cultural benefits that the new immi-

---

1. See Norris and Inglehart, *Sacred and Secular*, 217.

grants bring, they are also impacting Western societies in fundamental ways related to religious life. Generally speaking, their communities and ways of life represent a visible alternative to the hedonism and libertinism of secular society, and their cultural values have contributed to fresh debates within Western society about cherished liberal democratic principles like freedom of (religious) expression and individual rights. Most notably, the dilemmas posed by radical Islam have already "forced plenty of Western countries to sacrifice some liberties in the name of security."[2]

My main contention, however, is that contemporary global migrations implicate the West as a site of new religious interactions that portend long-term transformations of Western societies. In truth, the penetration of Western societies by religious impulses and initiatives from the non-Western world has a long history and represents a poorly researched aspect of Western colonial expansion and contemporary globalization. While not all such movements are religious—the spread of Japanese management practices is a nonreligious example of globalization from below—a good many relate to spiritual life. These processes have been termed "globalization from below" or "alternative globalizations."[3] Some, like American sociologist Peter Berger, admit that such cultural movements signify "alternative paths to modernity" or the possibility of "alternative modernities," which seems to imply that they may appropriate values associated with modernity without surrendering religious vitality. Asia, for instance, is a leading emitter of highly influential religious or pseudo-religious and cultural movements, including well-known examples from India such as New Age or the Hare Krishna movement. Key elements and practices of these movements have been incorporated almost seamlessly into modern Western societies. New Age, for instance,

> has affected millions of people in Europe and America, both on the level of beliefs (reincarnation, karma, the mystical connections between the individual and all of nature) and of behavior (meditation, yoga, shiatsu, and other forms of therapeutic massage; tai-chi and the martial arts; generally the use of alternative medical traditions of Indian and Chinese provenance).[4]

Global migrations have greatly intensified the push and potential of "globalization from below." But, unlike the New Age movement, which lends itself to the privatization of religion engendered by secularism, more robust religious systems such as Islam threaten the ideals of Western secularism more directly. As

---

2. See "Turkey and Europe: Coming Apart?" *The Economist*, May 6th, 2006, 16.

3. Berger, "Cultural Dynamics of Globalization," 12.

4. Ibid., 13f. The lesser-known Sai Baba movement, which Berger describes as a supernaturalistic alternative to the modern scientific worldview (p. 12), has two thousand centers in 137 countries—many in Europe and North America—and as many as seventy million devotees (though twenty million is thought to be closer). For a treatment, see Tulasi Srinivas, "'A Tryst with Destiny': The Indian Case of Cultural Globalization," in *Many Globalizations: Cultural Diversity in the Contemporary World*, ed. Peter L. Berger and Samuel P. Huntington (New York: Oxford University Press, 2002), 89-116.

David Masci comments, Europe's troubled relationship with Islam stretches back over thirteen hundred years and is "marked by countless wars and occupations as well as a vibrant, steady cultural exchange."[5] In the contemporary period, massive Muslim migrations to the West represent a long-term process of exchange and influence that is perhaps even more profound than military conquest. The story is complex and still unfolding in ways that reveal important distinctions between the Western European and American experiences. In both contexts, however, the growing presence and transformative impact of Islam continues to animate serious public debate about "national" or cultural identity.

Islam in Europe

Britain had presided over the largest empire in history, and its dismantling precipitated a flood of workers and aspiring citizens from far-flung lands. By 1981, there were 1.5 million non-European immigrants in Britain (60 percent from Africa and South Asia). The migrant influx from struggling democracies and impoverished economies in former territories in Africa, the Caribbean, and Southeast Asia was unprecedented. The Muslim incursion even more so. At the height of British colonial rule, the Queen of England had more Muslim subjects than any Muslim ruler, and colonization of Muslim lands also opened Britain to Muslim incursions. Thus, Muslim immigration and settlement in Britain date to the late nineteenth century.[6] But the most significant growth of the Muslim population came from successive waves of post–Second World War immigration.

The partitioning of India (and the creation of Pakistan) caused massive displacements that coincided with the guest worker program and stimulated huge migrations to Britain, especially from the Punjab. Decolonization in Africa also contributed to a steady rise of Asian migrants from East African countries culminating in the exodus from Uganda under General Idi Amin in 1972 (see p. 171 above). From the 1960s, also, British universities attracted a growing foreign student population from wealthy Muslim countries. At the same time, the decrease in the flow of mainly Christian Caribbean immigrants—caused by the passing of the 1965 Immigration Act in the United States—translated into a sharp increase in the percentage of Hindu and Muslim immigrants, mainly from India and Pakistan. Overall, the Muslim population surged from roughly 21,000 in 1951 to an estimated 369,000 in the early 1970s.[7]

Like Britain, other Western European countries also witnessed a massive influx of migrants from their former colonies, many of whom enjoyed or acquired citizenship rights. By the mid-1970s, Britain, France, and Germany each had minority populations in excess of four million.[8] France's factories attracted about

---

5. David Masci, "An Uncertain Road: Muslims and the Future of Europe," The Pew Research Center, 2005, 2.

6. See Ataullah Siddiqui, "Muslims in Britain: Past and Present" (1995), http://www.islamfortoday.com/britain.htm.

7. Masci, "Uncertain Road," 5.

8. Castles and Miller, *Age of Migration*, 72.

one million guest workers, mainly from former colonies in North Africa.[9] The new minority communities were predominantly Muslim.

Exactly how many Muslims there are in Europe, or the European Union, is impossible to ascertain because European nations do not require new immigrants to indicate religious identity. Nor do they include the estimation of religious affiliation in population censuses. French law, in fact, prohibits identifying citizens on the basis of national origin, race, or religion.[10] Thus, statistical assessments of the Muslim population typically involve estimates extrapolated from national origin figures. For example, since 98.7 percent of the Moroccan population is Muslim it is assumed that the same percentage of Moroccan immigrants within a given European country are Muslim. Such estimates usually take no account of immigrant reverts (those who abandon their faith) or native converts (members of the native population who embrace Islam as a result of Islamic missionary activity, intermarriage, spiritual quests, etc.); and they obviously exclude substantial illegal immigration from Muslim countries. Moreover, Muslim leaders and far-right politicians inevitably inflate the figures to press their causes.[11]

The most recent estimates put the Muslim population in the European Union at roughly thirteen to fourteen million or about 3 percent of the EU's total population (of 457 million)[12]—some assessments put the figure as high as 5 percent (or twenty million).[13] It is widely recognized that such figures are imprecise; but even the highest estimates suggest a relatively insignificant minority.[14] Once again, statistical representation belies a number of crucial considerations that explain the combustive nature of the current debate and controversies surrounding Muslim minorities. For instance, 2005 estimates of the total Muslim population *in all of Europe* (not just with the EU) range from 20.5 million (or 5.4 percent) to 51 million (roughly 7 percent). When Turkey is included, even the more conservative estimates stipulate close to 90 million Muslims (20 percent of the total population in Europe).

The singular focus on recent Muslim immigration (from the 1950s) also obscures the fact that the Islamic presence in Europe has a long history. Russia is home to an estimated 12 to 20 million Muslims with a history dating back to the tenth century. They constitute approximately 14 percent of its population and represent Russia's largest religious minority. Bosnia and Kosovo also have sizable Muslim populations dating to the Ottoman period in the sixteenth and

9. Stéphanie Giry, "France and Its Muslims," *Foreign Affairs* 85, no. 5 (September/October 2006): 90.

10. Ibid., 87.

11. Jytte Klausen, "The Two-Way Street to Integration for Europe's Muslims," *Faith & International Affairs* 4, no. 3 (Winter 2006): 15.

12. See "A Civil War on Terrorism," *The Economist*, November 27, 2004, 56; also Frank J. Buijs and Jan Rath, "Muslims in Europe: The State of Research," Institute of Migration and Ethnic Studies, University of Amsterdam, 2002, 7.

13. Masci, "Uncertain Road," 1.

14. See "Muslims in Europe: Country Guide"; "European Muslim Population," Muslim Population Worldwide, 2005 (see bibliography for Web site).

seventeenth centuries. The tacit assumption that the Islamic world and the West are discrete geographical entities neglects these historical realities.

Historical misconceptions also persist in current attitudes to the Muslim population in countries like Britain, France, and Germany, where Muslims are persistently branded as "immigrants" or "foreigners." After half a century of immigration, these communities now span at least two-to-three generations, and it is estimated that about 50 percent are European-born nationals[15]—including half of France's estimated five million Muslims and most of Britain's estimated 1.6 million Muslims. Europe's Muslims, in other words, include millions of full-fledged citizens who can use their voting rights with significant electoral impact.[16] Omer Taspinar explains that this voting power and gradual mastery of the mechanics of lobbying are some reasons why "the Muslim street in Europe is on its way to having more political weight than the Arab street of Egypt or Saudi Arabia."[17] Among other things, the political integration of Europe's Muslims will have a major impact on Europe's political outlook and foreign policy—on the Middle East question, for instance—in ways that may well trouble the transatlantic relationship between Europe and the United States.

If the presence of sizable Muslim communities in many European countries is largely a function of colonialism and past immigration policies, the future of European Islam is strongly tied to demographic factors. Owing to religious values and a youthful population, birthrate among Europe's Muslims is significantly higher than among the native population. In Amsterdam, for instance, the most common name for newborn boys is Mohammed.[18] The number of Muslims on the continent has tripled in the last thirty years; and an even higher rate of growth is forecast for the near future.[19] Various estimates maintain that, if present trends continue, Europe's Muslim population will double by 2015 and conceivably constitute a majority in a matter of decades.[20] Soon, some major European cities will have majority Muslim populations.

This historic turn of events was largely unforeseen and unforeseeable. Little over a century ago, Western Europe was dealing with the effects of overpopulation and the burdens of imperial expansion (see chapter 7). It had exported tens of millions of its peoples, along with its religion and culture, to much of the non-European world. Now, with its native population steadily shrinking at a rate that will see a further 3.5 percent reduction over the next decade, its need for substantial immigration is enormous. Yet, far from being a welcome presence, its mainly Muslim immigrants and their descendants have encountered hostility and rejection. (This was the case even before the monstrous terrorist attacks on the United

15. Masci, "Uncertain Road," 11.

16. For more on this, see Omer Taspinar, "Europe's Muslim Street," The Brookings Institute, 2003 (see bibliography).

17. Ibid.

18. Buijs and Rath, "Muslims in Europe," 8.

19. Masci, "Uncertain Road," 1.

20. Taspinar, "Europe's Muslim Street"; Daniel Pipes, "Muslim Europe," New York Sun, May 11, 2004; "Special Report: Islam, America and Europe," The Economist, June 24, 2006, 30.

States in September 2001, following which attitudes hardened even further.) The reasons for Western Europe's complicated relationship with its Muslim population are partly historic and partly cultural. They are also thoroughly religious and reflect acute religious divisions.

The Assimilation Question: From Benign Neglect to Hostile Embrace?

From the outset, Muslim minorities across Europe have existed as segregated and marginalized communities, viewed by the native population with attitudes ranging from amused curiosity to xenophobic hostility. Well into the 1980s, Europe's Muslim minorities were regarded as "a temporary phenomenon that will eventually go away."[21] Few entertained the notion that they constituted a permanent feature of European society, much less a source of demographic makeover or a critical element in the continent's future. The new Muslim immigrants settled in industrial areas in or close to cities with other foreign workers. Over time, their numbers grew; but the manufacturing jobs that had attracted the first generation slowly disappeared, and native Europeans moved out. This process transformed areas of original settlement into Muslim enclaves distinguished from surrounding communities by exotic sights and smells as well as low education and joblessness.

By the 1970s and 1980s, a new generation of European-born Muslims was reaching adulthood. They were European citizens "who speak only European languages and, except for their religion, are indistinguishable from others."[22] Unlike their immigrant parents, whose original intentions of returning to their homelands was now a forlorn hope, the new and subsequent generations of Muslims conceived of their future and prospects only in terms of life within Western society. Yet, faced with a European reluctance to embrace difference, many turned to a rediscovery of their origins and an affirmation of their Islamic identity.[23] Social exclusion also reinforced a propensity for self-segregation, which helps to account for a pattern of high Muslim concentrations in specific urban areas. In the English city of Bradford, for instance, Asians, mostly Pakistani Muslims, account for 24 percent of the population,[24] while in Saint-Denis, an industrial suburb north of Paris, a third of the residents are of Arab origin.[25] Within these communities, Muslims attend to their affairs, build mosques, and establish organizations to cater to their religious life and social needs.

On the whole, even though Western European countries claim to be liberal democracies, Muslim minorities have faced racial prejudice, widespread discrimination, and human rights abuses. But, until recently, official government policy toward Muslim minorities varied among Western European countries. Four main approaches were evident: tacit rejection (Germany, where *jus sanguinis* laws restricted citizenship to ethnic Germans or people of German

---

21. Masci, "Uncertain Road," 7.

22. "Islam in Europe," *The Economist*, April 15, 2006, 55.

23. Tariq Ramadan, *To Be a European Muslim: A Study of Islamic Sources in the European Context* (Leicester, England: Islamic Foundation, 1999), 114.

24. Buijs and Rath, "Muslims in Europe," 8.

25. Osnos, "Islam Shaping a New Europe."

descent); benign neglect (Italy and Spain); active tolerance or a policy of multiculturalism (Britain, Holland); aggressive assimilation (France). Multiculturalism, a model in which immigrants retain their distinctive culture and traditions while adopting the language and core values of the country in which they live, appeared to be the most successful approach, even though it still left minorities at the bottom of the economic pile.

But, as Muslim communities became more visible and their particular needs as a segment of society less easy to ignore, popular attitudes of xenophobic rejection hardened and public opinion coalesced around the notion that Muslim communities constituted a "problem." (It is only fair to add that the Iranian Revolution of the late 1970s was also fomenting a more radical Islamic consciousness worldwide that was militantly anti-Western.) By the early 1990s, far-right politicians and nativist political parties had begun to exploit growing fears about the perceived threats posed to European ways of life by the new minorities, and some (like Jean-Marie Le Pen's National Front in France) gained mainstream prominence by stereotyping immigrants and proclaiming anti-immigration policies.

In public rhetoric, the popular misconception of Islam as a uniform, foreign entity was combined with the equally mythical notion that European society constitutes a monolithic cultural mass. This made for heightened social tensions and a climate of mutual suspicion. A vicious circle emerged in which European calls for the subjugation of Islam fostered a greater determination among Muslims to preserve their distinctive traditions and identity, which in turn fueled European concerns about the capacity of Muslim minorities to adapt to the ideals and institutions of modern, secular Western societies. As Jytte Klausen indicates,

> Western European reaction to the growth of Islam has been fairly uniform: Controversies have broken out over religious holiday schedules, accommodations for prayers, the wearing of Muslim dress in the workplace, the provision of building permits for mosques, the public ownership of all available cemeteries, concerns about animal rights that disallow ritual slaughter, issues of pastoral care for Muslims who are in prison or receiving social services, the teaching of religion in public schools, and divorce law and other family law issues.[26]

The Radical (Islamic) Element

In short, Europe was already fretting about its Muslim population when the gruesome September 11 (2001) attacks by Islamic terrorists on the World Trade Center and the Pentagon in America radically altered the stakes. Throughout the Western world, this event turned the spotlight on Muslim populations more brightly than ever before and fueled new levels of public anxiety about Muslim minorities. At a time when anti-immigration sentiments were already widespread and

---

26. Klausen, "Two-Way Street to Integration," 16.

fully exploited by right-wing political parties, xenophobic rejection grew alarmingly amidst calls for the preservation of Western ways of life.

Subsequent events only served to reinforce the notion that Western institutions and ways of life (including liberal democracy and Christianity) were under perilous threat from the growing Islamic presence. The Madrid train bombings on March 11, 2004, were followed eight months later by the murder of Dutch film-maker Theo van Gogh on the streets of Amsterdam by Mohammed Bouyeri, a twenty-six-year-old Dutch-Moroccan Muslim.[27] Then came the deadly bombings of a London bus and three underground trains, on July 7, 2005, by three British-born Muslims (of Pakistani descent) and a Jamaican-born convert to Islam. The following September, a Danish newspaper, the *Jyllands-Posten*, published satirical cartoons of the Prophet Mohammed ostensibly to teach Muslims that free speech was a key element of Danish (and Western) democracy. The global tensions and violent reactions triggered by this provocative act were still raging when France was convulsed by two weeks of rioting and violence after two teens of North African decent met their deaths in Clichy-sous-Bois, a suburb of Paris, while fleeing from the police. The French incident inspired similar riots in impoverished immigrant communities across Europe.

Unlike the 2001 terrorist attacks in the United States, the events in London, Spain, and the Netherlands involved nationals born and raised in the country they attacked. This aspect both mystified and enraged public opinion. Surprisingly, the most volatile reactions took place in Holland, a country renowned for its attitude of tolerance and vigorous policy of multiculturalism.[28] The murder of van Gogh unleashed widespread outrage across the country. The fact that his killer, in addition to being a Dutch citizen, was allegedly part of a larger terrorist cell (linked to Hezbollah) that included two Dutch-American converts to Islam,[29] triggered violent reactions against Muslims. In the weeks that followed the murder, over twenty attacks and counterattacks (involving the use of bombs and arson) took place against mosques, Islamic schools, and churches around the country.[30] The large Moroccan community was often singled out, but public and government rhetoric focused on the forcible integration of immigrant minorities. What this meant remained ill-defined. After all, Mohammed Bouyeri (subsequently sentenced to life in prison for van Gogh's murder) had not been a marginalized individual but a student who did well in school, spoke excellent Dutch, and was active in community affairs.

In England, where the July 7 attacks killed fifty-six and injured some seven hundred people, leaders within the Muslim community were quick to condemn the terrorist act. While tensions between Muslims and non-Muslims rose palpably, there was no significant anti-Muslim backlash. But throughout the continent a rash of new government policies were hastily implemented to deal with

---

27. Van Gogh's movie had outraged Muslims with his inflammatory depictions of Islam. See "The New Dutch Model?" *The Economist*, April 2, 2005, 24.

28. Joanne van Selm, "The Netherlands: Death of a Filmmaker Shakes a Nation," *Migration Information Source* (October, 2005).

29. "New Dutch Model?" 26.

30. Van Selm, "The Netherlands: Death of a Filmmaker"; also Masci, "Uncertain Road," 7.

the Islamist threat. These included antiterrorist measures aimed at rooting out radical Muslim elements, more rigorous immigration and asylum restrictions, strenuous guidelines for acquiring (and retaining) citizenship, and new rules of deportation. The fact that some of these measures violate human rights laws have added to widespread resentment and have blunted studious efforts to court or affirm Muslim organizations. Muslims in Britain hardly speak with one voice and reactions to government action cover a wide spectrum; but opinion polls indicate that British Muslims, especially the younger generation, feel more alienated than ever before.

Throughout Western Europe, government policy making has tried, with varying degrees of coherence, to address the integration of Muslim minorities— amidst feverish public debate about the capacity and willingness of Muslims to adopt core European values such as tolerance, gender equality, and freedom of speech.[31] In countries with significant Muslim populations (France, Germany, Britain, and the Netherlands among them), the clamor for "a more aggressive insistence on western liberal values" was accompanied by widespread disavowal of multiculturalism as a viable alternative.[32] Reflecting the entrenched view of Muslims as foreigners and Islam as *a problem*, Europeans renewed their demand for minorities (including Muslims) to "learn our language, our history, our culture, and live by our laws and values."[33]

But the reality on the ground is exceedingly complex. In the first instance, the persistent image of Islam as a monolithic entity further bedevils calls for strict assimilation. (Indeed, the difference between Muslims, Sikhs, and Hindus is often lost on native Europeans.) The Muslim communities in Europe are the product of immigration from more than thirty different countries: from highly secular Turkey to Islamist publics like Iran and Algeria. This makes for a religion of great cultural, ethnic, and ideological diversity. The assumption that such a heterogeneous mass can be squeezed into a European mold—even if such a mold existed—reflects a certain kind of naïve idealism. Generally speaking, Europe's Muslims can be divided into five major categories:[34] (1) the sizable Muslim inhabitants of European countries like Bosnia, Albania, and Russia; (2) first-generation immigrants; (3) Muslims born in Europe, one or two generations removed from the immigrant generation, who have never lived anywhere else; (4) European converts, some two-thirds of whom are male;[35] (5) largely secular Muslims. Ultimately, the clamor for the integration of Muslims into European society misconceives reality: Islam is in many ways already European.

Vociferous, if often vague, assumptions about one-sided assimilation ("they"

---

31. James Hampshire and Shamit Saggar, "Migration, Integration, and Security in the U.K. Since July 7," Migration Policy Institute, March 1, 2005.

32. "Civil War on Terrorism."

33. "Top 10 Migration Issues of 2006: Good-Bye Multiculturalism—Hello Assimilation?" *Migration Information Source* (September 1, 2006).

34. "Islam in Europe," 55.

35. Based on Larry Poston's rather limited and possibly outdated study; see Larry Poston, *Islamic Da'wah in the West: Muslim Missionary Activity and the Dynamics of Conversion to Islam* (New York: Oxford University Press, 1992), 164f.

should be like "us") bespeak cultural intolerance fed by widespread perceptions of Muslims as backward and fanatical. Such assumptions are unmindful of the fact that even uncompromising integration of non-Western minorities will have implications for European society. In the Netherlands, for instance, the new emphasis on integration in government policy making has necessitated unprecedented and unfamiliar steps: including the offer of subsidies to universities to open theological departments to train Muslim prayer leaders, calls for the return of the death penalty, debate over strengthening the country's blasphemy laws (to protect Islamic sensibilities), and parliamentary consideration of stringent anti-terrorism laws intended to curb deeply cherished civil liberties.[36]

The new calls for assimilationist integration also overlook the fact that it is the very conditions of security and freedom provided by Western European societies that allow its Muslim communities to thrive. Islamic scholar Tariq Ramadan argues that, despite long-standing socioeconomic grievances like high unemployment, racism, and exclusion, the great majority of Muslims in Europe do not in fact face "specific religious discrimination" on a regular basis. He adds that while religious duties and commitment are difficult to maintain in highly secularized modern European societies, Muslims are generally allowed to practice their religion in relative freedom and to "live in an atmosphere of *security* and *peace*."[37] Thus, while conditions in Europe pose significant challenges to faithful adherence to Islam, Europe also provides an environment that is in crucial ways more hospitable for the practice of Islam than some parts of the Muslim world.

Western Europe's (Religious) Identity Crisis

It is perfectly understandable that European government policies and much public rhetoric on the Muslim question have stressed cultural integration and security concerns. But the most critical issues in the overwrought relations between Europe and its Muslim population relate to religiosity—the fear that the practice of Islam threatens secular values—and religious identity. Thus, even the shift of emphasis from integration to strict assimilation has expressed itself most obviously in open hostility toward visible religious symbols of Islam—notably the headscarf, the veil, and the *burqa* (a full dress worn by Muslim women from central and south Asia which covers the entire person except for a small slit for the eyes). In March 2004, the French government passed a law banning Islamic headscarves in public schools, claiming that visible religious symbols violated the French principle of secularism.[38] About the same time, some German states banned the Muslim headscarf while mandating the crucifix in public schools on the grounds that Germany is a "Judeo-Christian country."[39] In Britain, lead-

---

36. "New Dutch Model?" 26.

37. Ramadan, *To Be a European Muslim*, 121-22.

38. The headscarf issue has a long history in France, where three Muslim girls were expelled from a high school for wearing scarves in 1989 (Patrick Simon, "French Muslims: Government Grapple with Integration Pains," *Migration Information Source* [2003]).

39. "German State Backs Headscarf Ban," *BBC News,* April 1, 2004; also Klausen, "Two-Way Street to Integration for Europe's Muslims," 13.

ing Labor Party politician Jack Straw excited a public row when he declared in the fall of 2006 that Muslim veils reinforce separateness and hinder community relations.[40]

The eruption of headscarf controversies in Western European countries over the last two to three years may reflect a newfound consciousness that Islam is now a permanent feature of European society. It also signifies that the rapid growth of its Muslim population has left Western Europe with an identity crisis. Western Europe is a secular society haunted by a religious past and now confronted with the possibility of a religious future (at least a future in which religion plays a significant role). Negative attitudes to Islam are rooted as much in a consciousness of ancient rivalries as in resentment of the threat that a self-confident religion poses to secular certainties. Stephanie Giry hints at this religious crisis when she points out that, because of long-standing distrust of Islam and the entrenched view that Islam is a barrier to Frenchness, "religion may be as enduring a fault line in France as race is in the United States."[41]

This identity crisis is evident in the vexed question of Turkey's accession to the European Union. Despite its secular identity, Turkey is a Muslim country with a population of seventy million. Not only would its accession cause a massive increase in the EU's Muslim population; it would also see Turkey replace Germany (within a decade or two) as the Union's largest country, effectively transforming the nature of European identity. As David Masci reminds us, the European Union was originally a Roman Catholic venture aimed at creating a "visible unity of Christendom."[42] More than sixty years after its creation, the EU is decidedly secular—its constitution excludes any reference to God or Christianity—but its sense of identity is still shaped by a shared Christian past. Christendom is long dead, but the *ghost of Christendom* lives on. Indeed, its subliminal presence provides some comfort—eerie and perhaps unloved, but familiar.

In this regard, the growing presence of Islam, a faith that mirrors the vision of Christendom, is deeply unsettling in an almost atavistic way. In Europe, Islam evokes old questions (related to religion and national identity and the place of religion in public life or civil society) and threatens to breathe new life into an old ghost. From this perspective, the "clash of civilizations" model, which postulates a confrontation between a Christian West and a non-Western Islam, is misleading. For what Muslim immigrants and their descendants have encountered in Western Europe is a secular society in which Christianity is in fact an increasingly marginalized faith. If the very public religiosity of Muslim minorities has evoked cultural angst and profound questions about European identity, it is because that identity, while now decidedly secular, is haunted by a religious past.

Take traditionally Catholic Spain. As in much of Europe, secularization has penetrated deeply into Spanish society, but Christian institutions, symbols, and

---

40. "British Muslims: Deconstructing the Veil," *The Economist*, October 14, 2006.

41. Giry, "France and Its Muslims," 90.

42. Masci, "Uncertain Road," 15. It is interesting to note that the EU's strong Catholic identity was one reason why Britain's application for EU membership in the 1960s was vetoed by France.

traditions remain defining elements of Spanish self-identity. In fact, the expulsion of the last Muslim (Moorish) ruler from mainland Europe (Granada to be precise) in 1492 is a deeply cherished memory. Little wonder, then, that the growing presence of Muslims immigrants makes for acutely complex relationships, even though Spain's Muslim population remains quite modest—some one million or 2.3 percent of the population.[43] In 2003, a mosque was erected in modern Granada, and the call of the muezzin was heard in that city for the first time in over five centuries.[44] Spanish minds were still struggling to digest this reality when Islamist extremists bombed trains in Madrid in March 2004 and al-Qaeda (the militant Islamist organization behind the September 11 attacks) called for a holy war to re-conquer Muslim lands. As elsewhere in Western Europe, the actions of the radical sector became a defining element in public opinion of the wider Islamic whole. It also provided ample fodder for a "clash of civilizations" rhetoric and fed nativist fears about a revival of historic antagonisms.[45] Yet Spain's historic Christian identity is threatened less by radical Islam than by radical secularism.

In this respect, the maelstrom of debate and controversy surrounding the growth of Islam signifies to some extent the struggle within Europe to come to terms with the limits of modern secularism. To the bewilderment of highly secular Europeans, religious devotion and affiliation among Muslim groups remain strong decades after settlement within modern industrial society. To be sure, assessments of the level of religiosity among Europe's Muslims tend to be conflicting. Tariq Ramadan asserts that fewer than 40 percent of Europe's Muslims attend mosque regularly, though 70 percent fast during the holy month of Ramadan.[46] Yet one survey found that 80 percent of Muslims in London attend mosque regularly.[47]

The point at issue is that Europe's Muslims, by their presence and growth, signify the resilience of religion and the endurance of religious commitment. That avid religiosity should flourish practically unchecked within modern industrial society—not only among less modernized, or "backward," groups but also among urbanized European-born Muslim youths and the highly educated[48]—repudiates fundamental assumptions about secularization. Strikingly, while the majority of non-Muslims in Western countries think that Islamic devotion is incompatible with life in modern society, the majority of European Muslims (57 percent in Germany, 71 percent in Spain, 72 percent in France) are convinced that it is compatible.[49] In fact, the fortunes of Islam in Europe also signify that modern secular society itself contains the conditions necessary for religious growth or revival.

---

43. "Muslims in Europe: Country Guide."

44. See "Spain and Islam: Al-Andalus Revisited," *The Economist*, July 30, 2005, 216.

45. A 2006 Pew survey found that "positive opinions of Muslims have declined sharply in Spain over the previous year (from 46 percent to 29 percent)" ("The Great Divide: How Westerners and Muslims View Each Other," Pew Research Center, 2006, 2).

46. Ramadan, *To Be a European Muslim*, 121.

47. "Decline in Churchgoing Hits Church of England Hardest," *The Guardian*, April 14, 2001, 4; Masci, "Uncertain Road," 6.

48. See Berger, "Desecularization of the World," 7f.

49. "Great Divide," 23.

Not only is Islam thriving in Europe, but it is also the fastest growing religion on the continent. This growth is fueled by high birthrates, a revitalization of the faith among Muslim youths, as well as increasing conversions among the native population. In France, Islam is the second largest religion after Catholicism, the traditional faith.[50] By 1986, attendance at Sunday Mass in France was as low as 13 percent;[51] more recently an estimated 60 percent of French people report that they never attend church.[52] Thus, practicing Muslims may well outnumber committed Catholics. At the very least, religion plays a more vital role in the daily lives and attitudes of Muslims than it does among Catholics.[53] In Britain similarly, Muslims attend mosque more regularly than Christians attend church. Up to a point, Islam may also be benefiting from the decline in European Christianity. A 1991 study of converts to Islam in Britain found that 94 percent came from Christian backgrounds (73 percent from the Church of England).[54] Disillusionment with faiths such as Christianity or Judaism and disillusionment with Western society were among the major reasons for conversion.[55] Considering that membership of Roman Catholicism (the continent's largest denomination) has declined by more than 30 percent in the last twenty-five years,[56] the potential impact of Europe's burgeoning Muslim population on the continent's religious landscape will be nothing short of momentous.

Interestingly, the revival of Europe's historic Christian identity, at least the vital elements necessary to arrest de-Christianization, may come less from European sources than from non-European initiatives: namely, the *increasing immigration of Christians from Latin America and Africa*. Stimulated by migration, African immigrant churches in particular have mushroomed in unprecedented fashion throughout continental Europe, and the number of African Christians is thought to be in excess of three million.[57] In Britain, the European country with the longest ties to modern African Christianity, the establishment of African immigrant churches dates to the early 1960s, and they are thought to number up to three thousand congregations.[58] This astounding figure is difficult to reconcile with another estimate which indicates that some 705 "Black Majority Churches" (churches whose composition is made up of more than 50 percent of people of African or African Caribbean heritage) have been founded in Britain since 1948

---

50. Simon, "French Muslims."

51. Wilson and Siewert, eds., *Mission Handbook*, 26.

52. Davie, *Europe,* 6.

53. Giry, "France and Its Muslims," 93.

54. See Colin Chapman, *Islam and the West: Conflict, Coexistence or Conversion?* (Carlisle, England: Paternoster, 1998), 60-61.

55. Ibid., 61-73. On the whole, "net defections from Christianity—converts to other religions or to irreligion"—in Europe and North America are estimated at 1.8 million a year. See Barrett, Kurian, and Johnson, *World Christian Encyclopedia*, 3.

56. See Osnos, "Islam Shaping a New Europe."

57. Report of the Council of African Christian Communities in Europe (CACCE) at the 1999 meeting in Belgium, quoted in Gerloff, "Religion, Culture and Resistance," 277.

58. Gerrie ter Haar, *Halfway to Paradise: African Christians in Europe* (Cardiff: Cardiff Academic Press, 1998), 92.

with a combined membership of just over seventy thousand.[59] It is beyond dispute, however, that nonwhite, mainly immigrant, churches (the majority of which are black and Pentecostal) have grown explosively in recent decades in major Western European cities.[60] Significantly, members of these churches, who are mainly middle-class professionals and graduates,[61] reject secularism while they embrace economic modernization.

A European Islam?

Traditional Muslims conceive of Islam as a single community of believers, the *ummah*. From this perspective, a "European Islam" is problematic; it is far more appropriate to speak of Islam in Europe. However, because of the increasing numbers of Muslims who are taking up permanent residence in non-Muslim societies, minority Muslim groups now account for a third of the world's Muslim population—only about 18 percent of Muslims reside in the Arab world.[62] Living as Muslims in a non-Muslim (or Western) context necessarily stimulates a reformulation of what it means to be Muslim and a member of the *ummah*. This identity formation inevitably draws on the values and norms of the non-Muslim context (in this case, Europe). At the same time, it is liable to produce "a religious identity that is not linked to a given culture and can therefore fit with every culture."[63] In effect, the encounter with European society may be contributing to the emergence of a form of Islam that is more adaptive and, consequently, more global.

Tariq Ramadan, a strong advocate for a European Islam, emphasizes the distinction between the religion of Islam and its cultural expressions. Islam, he insists, "is not a culture . . . , the essence of Islam is religious."[64] He even condemns the notion that any particular context or culture (including Arab culture) is authentically Islam and argues that Islam's "potential for adaptation" was what "allowed Muslims to establish themselves in the Middle East and in Africa and Asia and, in the name of one and the same Islam, to give their identity concrete reality in specific and diverse shapes and forms."[65] For, while "Islam, with its Islamic sources, is *one and unique* . . . ; its concretization in a given time and place is by nature *plural* [italics in the original]." On this basis, "there should be

---

59. Sturge, *Look What the Lord Has Done!* 31, 91-93.

60. See "London Is Different!"; also ter Haar, *Halfway to Paradise*.

61. Sturge, *Look What the Lord Has Done!* 110. In Britain recently, John Sentamu, the Ugandan-born Archbishop of York broke with a tradition of gentile suggestions when he publicly condemned secularism and the erosion of Christianity in Britain ("Onward Christian Soldiers," *The Economist*, November 18, 2006).

62. Olivier Roy, *Globalized Islam: The Search for a New Ummah* (New York: Columbia University Press, 2004), 18.

63. Ibid., 24.

64. Tariq Ramadan, *Western Muslims and the Future of Islam* (New York: Oxford University Press, 2005), 214.

65. Ibid., 78, 85.

an Islam rooted in the Western cultural universe, just as there is an Islam that is rooted in the African or Asian tradition."[66]

Ramadan explains that Muslim believers everywhere in the world belong to the *ummah* which is one body, one community of believers bearing witness before all the whole world. But this Islamic identity in no way contradicts the obligations of citizenship, since the teaching of Islam requires Muslims to abide by the contracts or agreements they enter into (including travel visas) and to respect the legal and constitutional framework of the country in which they are citizens. The constitutions of the Western democracies do sanction particular actions or behaviors that contradict the Islamic faith, but Muslims are not under any compulsion to undertake those actions. Where they feel compelled to act against their religion or conscience—which rarely happens—every effort must be made to determine possible forms of adaptation (with the help of Muslim jurists) aimed at a satisfactory solution.[67] For Ramadan, then, Muslim citizens in the West must not only take their duties as citizens seriously; they also bear the challenging responsibility of shaping a "Western-Islamic identity," one that fully integrates their faith into the fabric of Western culture.[68]

It is impossible to determine the extent to which Ramadan's inviting proposals (represented here in simplified form) have spread among ordinary Muslims in Europe. As we shall see below, his thinking about the nature of Western Islam is at odds with that of French scholar Olivier Roy. Importantly, Ramadan's arguments explicitly refute claims by radical Islamic elements that as Muslims they are subject only to Islamic law and jurisprudence and cannot be bound by constitutions of a secular state. In other words Islamic extremism cannot be explained or justified on the basis of a conscientious rejection of the permissiveness and hedonistic materialism of Western society. But, as Ramadan recognizes, the challenges of fashioning a Western Islamic identity in a largely hostile secular environment are enormous and complex.

Taken together, Muslims represent Europe's largest minority population.[69] This minority status and experience, rooted in migrant movement, plays a critical role in Muslims' search for an Islamic identity, or an identity as European Muslims. Not all of Europe's burgeoning youthful Muslim population inhabit a "parallel universe" of social exclusion, high unemployment, and relative poverty, but anecdotal evidence suggests that most do. Most are also caught between the traditionalism of their parents and a hostile secular culture disdainful of religiosity. In this cauldron of disenfranchisement and acute cultural tension, younger generations of European Muslims are compelled to fashion an Islamic identity that reflects both their experience as alienated minorities and the pressures of modern industrial society. They feel the powerful, unrelenting, and ubiquitous pull of European culture and values, mediated through educa-

---

66. Ibid.
67. Ibid., 89–96.
68. Ibid., 97.
69. "Islam in Europe," 55. Even though populations in Bosnia and Albania are excepted.

tion, television, entertainment, even sport, but they also remain conscious of their distinctiveness.

The available evidence suggests that patterns of adaptation among Muslims defy the two main stereotypical images of religious zealot and backwardness.[70] *Financial Times* journalist Gautam Malkani draws attention to a "pliable popular culture" created by second- and third-generation South Asian youths in Britain which allows them "to coexist and integrate with mainstream Britain instead of living in a state of victimhood or voluntary segregation."[71] Still, many Muslims also retreat into seclusion or isolation in an effort to protect themselves from a culture considered dangerous—a reaction that, for a tiny minority, does lead to extremism and radicalization. Many others are simply swept along, unable or unwilling to maintain the demands of spiritual life in Europe's forbidding environment. Still others may even go so far as to denounce or reject their religious or cultural heritage altogether. Ramadan advocates what he calls "selective development," a process in which the community of faith fashions a new Muslim personality which draws on both Islamic sources and the materials of Western culture.[72]

Meanwhile, the experience of social rejection, the pervasive secularity, and the acute need for a sense of belonging have helped to produce a revival of Islamic devotion and practice among younger, European-born Muslims.[73] The children and grandchildren of Muslim immigrants have fully embraced religion and show a pattern of increasing participation in religious activities such as daily prayers, mosque attendance, and fasting during Ramadan.[74] But the precise nature of a "European Islam" remains vague and indeterminate. Analysis is bedeviled by conflicting signs and trends. On the whole, European Muslims appear to favor a moderate version of Islam—for instance, most express favorable opinions of Christians and are more positive (than their counterparts in Muslim republics) in their views of Jews.[75] Yet, in countries like Britain, younger Muslims are gravitating to more radical expressions of the faith.

According to a 2007 survey of one thousand Muslims from different age groups in Britain, "support for Sharia law, Islamic schools and wearing the veil is much stronger among younger Muslims," who are also "much more likely than their parents to be attracted to political forms of Islam."[76] British-born children of Muslim immigrants increasingly wear the veil when, in fact, their mothers did not.[77] Not only is the veil for them a badge of religious identity, but it also represents, within a modern framework, a kind of conservative feminism[78]—a reaction

---

70. See Timothy G. Ash, "What Young British Muslims Say Can Be Shocking—Some of It Is Also True," *The Guardian*, August 10, 2006.

71. Gautam Malkani, "Sounds of Assimilation," *New York Times*, August 19, 2006.

72. Ramadan, *Western Muslims and the Future of Islam*, 221.

73. Ramadan, *To Be a European Muslim*, 120.

74. Osnos, "Islam Shaping a New Europe."

75. "Great Divide," 5, 11.

76. "Younger Muslims 'More Political,'" *BBC News*, January 29, 2007.

77. "British Muslims: Deconstructing the Veil," 63.

78. Ash, "What Young British Muslims Say Can Be Shocking."

to pervasive lasciviousness which reduces women to sexual objects. Research also shows that with the exception of Muslims in France (who are almost evenly split), Muslims in Europe tend to identify themselves as Muslim first—81 percent in Britain, 69 percent in Spain, and 66 percent in Germany—and citizens of their particular European country second.[79] European studies scholar Timothy Ash offers three possible explanations for the conspicuous response in Britain: first, British Muslims are predominantly from South Asia (Pakistan, India, and Bangladesh), whereas their counterparts in France hail from the Maghreb; second, British Prime Minister Tony Blair's foreign policy and alliance with America in the global war on terror has hardened resentments; third, Britain has one of the most libertine societies in Europe, and Muslims, who live mostly in urban areas, are reacting "against this kind of secular, hedonistic, anomic lifestyle."[80]

The debate on the nature of European Islam is bound to continue for some time. For now, what remains certain is that the growth of Islam is critical to Europe's future and European identity. For Islam, too, expansion in Europe raises significant challenges related to a reformulation of core ideals and the emergence of new identities. In a sense, the tensions generated *within* each "civilization" by the new encounter may turn out to be far more consequential than a clash *between* them (typically understood in terms of a zero-sum dualistic competition for global dominance). Whatever its nature turns out to be, a "European Islam" will impact both Europe and the Islamic world.

Islam in the United States

A number of critical factors distinguish the American and European contexts with regards to the encounter with Islam. Unlike Europe, where Muslims constitute the vast majority of all immigrants and represent the largest minority group, Muslims in America constitute a tiny fraction of post-1965 immigration and represent only one of numerous minority groups. The relatively higher percentages of Muslim groups in individual European countries like Britain (3 percent), France (8 percent), and the Netherlands (3.6 percent) translates into a far more visible presence than in the United States, where the Muslim community arguably constitutes less than 2 percent of the entire population—though social composition may be more consequential.

By and large, Europe's Muslims are crowded into highly visible, often run-down neighborhoods characterized by high unemployment and low income.[81] In the United States, where quality selective policies (which focus on the highly educated and highly skilled) shape nonwhite immigration, Muslim immigrants and their descendants tend to be educated professionals living in middle-class suburbs. They also hail from twice as many different countries as Muslims in

79. "Muslims in Europe: Economic Worries Top Concerns about Religious and Cultural Identity," Pew Research Center, 2006, 3.

80. Ash, "What Young British Muslims Say Can Be Shocking."

81. Roy, *Globalized Islam*, 100.

Europe and possibly represent the most diverse Muslim population in the world: a stunning assortment of cultures, ethnicities, languages, and ideologies. But perhaps most significant of all, American Muslims find themselves in an environment where religious liberty and expression are valued and religious difference is accepted.[82]

It is not all disparity, however. As in Europe, estimates of the Muslim population in America are generally conflicting and imprecise. American Islam has also experienced accelerated growth in recent years, more than other religious traditions associated with post-1965 immigration.[83] (Muslim immigration declined significantly in the wake the 9/11 attacks as a result of heightened security procedures, but the numbers of immigrants from Muslim countries have rebounded since 2004.)[84] While Americans are far more comfortable with public religiosity, the public square is increasingly secular and Muslims are viewed with hostility and suspicion. In the United States, too, the nature and expression of an Islamic identity remain a fraught question.

Attending the Faith

Estimations of the number of Muslims in America range from three to ten million. Of these, immigrant Muslims represent 70 to 75 percent (two-thirds of whom are from South Asia and one-third from the Middle East and Africa), while American converts or indigenous Muslims account for the remaining 25 to 30 percent.[85] American converts to Islam include hundreds of thousands of white Americans, but the vast majority are African Americans. A 1992 study found that over 60 percent are male and the average age at the time of conversion was twenty-nine.[86] Driven by immigration and conversion, Islam is arguably the fastest growing religion in the United States.[87] Astonishingly, Muslims in America (even by the most conservative estimates) outnumber Episcopalians and outnumber members of the Presbyterian Church USA.[88] Islam is also poised to replace Judaism as the second-largest religion in the country. As in the case of Europe, America is now part of the Muslim world.

---

82. See Peter Skerry, "The American Exception," *Time*, August 21, 2006; "Special Report: Islam, America and Europe," 30.

83. Guillermina Jasso et al., "Exploring the Religious Preferences of Recent Immigrants to the United States: Evidence from the New Immigrant Survey Pilot," in *Religion and Immigration: Christian, Jewish, and Muslim Experiences in the United States*, ed. Yvonne Yazbeck Haddad, Jane I. Smith, and John L. Esposito (Walnut Creek, CA: AltaMira, 2003), 221; also "Introduction," in ibid., 1-18, here 12.

84. Andrea Elliott, "More Muslims Arrive in the U.S., after 9/11 Dip," *New York Times*, September 10, 2006.

85. M. A. Muqtedar Khan, "Constructing the American Muslim Community," in *Religion and Immigration: Christian, Jewish, and Muslim Experiences in the United States*, ed. Yvonne Yazbeck Haddad, Jane I. Smith, and John L. Esposito (Walnut Creek, CA: AltaMira, 2003), 176.

86. Poston, *Islamic Da'wah in the West*, 164, 166.

87. Harold A. Netland, *Encountering Religious Pluralism: The Challenge to Christian Faith & Mission* (Downers Grove, IL: InterVarsity, 2001), 9f.

88. Eck, *New Religious America*, 2. Such comparisons tend to have more propaganda, than factual, value. The fallacy in this case lies in implicitly treating Islam as a denomination.

Partly because of this rapid growth, the formation of a cohesive Muslim community in America faces significant challenges in at least three areas.[89] First, though mainly Sunni, immigrant Islam is characterized by a complex ethnic, linguistic, racial, and sectarian diversity. With representatives from more that sixty nations,[90] it includes virtually every movement in the Muslim world, including those deemed "heretical." In many respects, Islam in America is a microcosm of global Islam. Second, integrating this diverse immigrant body with indigenous Muslim communities has proven extremely difficult. Third, the climate of suspicion and antipathy engendered within the general public by the stereotypical and negative depictions of Islam and Muslims in the mainstream media deters many Muslims from fully identifying with their communities.

The enduring tensions between the immigrant and indigenous Islamic communities has a lot to do with socioeconomic and ideological differences. On the one hand, immigrant Muslims in America tend to be among the best educated (because restrictive immigration policies favor highly skilled professionals) and reportedly have "at least ten times the wealth of the African, Hispanic, European, and Native American community."[91] They also tend to be more focused on foreign policy issues and overseas events. American (predominantly black) Muslims, on the other hand, are largely drawn from the poorer sections of American society, burdened by inferior educational attainments as a whole, and far more sensitive to experiences of racism and oppression within American society. These divisions remain difficult to bridge, and some suggest that the unilateral decision by immigrant Muslims to support George W. Bush in the 2000 elections may have caused irreparable/lasting damage.[92]

America's predominantly Christian ethos, and the fact that immigrant Muslims hail from countries Americans consider unfriendly, make integration and acceptance within American society a daunting prospect for serious Muslims. In turn, significant proportions of the Muslim community view America as an imperialistic, anti-Islam colossus intent on spreading its particular (immoral or objectionable) values around the world. Yet, for the majority of Muslims, American's multicultural diversity, liberal democracy, and tolerance of religious plurality provide an environment that is far more conducive to building Islamic institutions and reconstituting Islamic movements than is conceivable in much of the Muslim world where fixed ideologies and repressive political instruments militate against such initiatives. Put differently, the hostility and prejudice that many

89. For a helpful overview, see Aminah Beverly McCloud, "Islam in America: The Mosaic," in *Religion and Immigration: Christian, Jewish, and Muslim Experiences in the United States*, ed. Yvonne Yazbeck Haddad, Jane I. Smith, and John L. Esposito (Walnut Creek, CA: AltaMira, 2003), 163, 164, 167.

90. Yvonne Yazbeck Haddad, "Make Room for the Muslims?" in *Religious Diversity and American Religious History: Studies in Traditions and Cultures*, ed. Walter H. Conser and Sumner B. Twiss (Athens: University of Georgia Press, 1997), 218.

91. McCloud, "Islam in America: The Mosaic," 172.

92. Ibid.

Muslims experience in America are nothing compared to the stifling character of despotic regimes in many parts of the Islamic world.[93]

In a word, the United States provides an enabling environment in which Islam is able to thrive and in which, thanks to the filtering process of immigration mechanisms, gifted Muslim professionals and intellectuals (some of whom came to the country as students) can pursue a revival of Islam and the reformulation of an Islamic identity.

Becoming American

Perhaps because of the plethora of minority groups and variety of religions that characterize American society, Muslims do not feel the same intense pressures to assimilate as their European counterparts. Yet, in a bid to fit in and avoid discrimination, thousands of Muslims in America make rigorous efforts to adapt: they Americanize their names (from Alhaji to "Al," Osama to "Sam," Mohammed to "Moe"), give up Islamic habits in food and dress, and distance themselves from the Muslim community. But the enlargement of this community in the last three decades, the continued experience of hostility in the public domain, and forceful American involvement in the Islamic world have helped to stimulate a widespread determination among the new Muslim immigrant communities to preserve religious values and reconstruct an Islamic identity, and even to impact American society.

To this end, there has been a huge drive toward institutional development. Islamic centers and schools have proliferated throughout the country. Over two thousand centers and twelve hundred schools have been established, and the first Islamic seminary in the United States (Zaytuna Institute, California) was founded in 1996.[94] Additional organizations provide intellectual vision, emphasize spiritual renewal, provide means of combating prejudice against Islam, generate copious publications, utilize a wide array of media communication technologies, and encourage political mobilization.[95] Muslim student organizations are also proliferating on U.S. campuses and are quite successful in promoting Islam.[96] Prison ministries, in particular, have proven to be a most effective avenue for Islamic "*da'wah*" (missionary activity).[97]

For this new generation of immigrant Muslims, the task of forging an identity as American Muslims has entailed not only experimentation with new institutional models but also major ideological shifts. The leading intellectuals among them, many of whom are alumni of American universities, promote a different kind of activism, one far removed from the media stereotypes of intolerant jihadists and terrorists. For them, the pressures and implacable constraints of the

---

93. Khan, "Constructing the American Muslim Community," 180.

94. Laurie Goodstein, "U.S. Muslim Clerics Seek a Modern Middle Ground," *New York Times*, June 18, 2006.

95. See Khan, "Constructing the American Muslim Community," 183-88; also Poston, *Islamic Da'wah in the West*, 122-30.

96. Roy, *Globalized Islam*, 212f.

97. Poston, *Islamic Da'wah in the West*, 127.

immigrant experience in America have enforced not mindless assimilation but a sophisticated ideological reorientation: a rethinking of ingrained hostility toward the West and a reinterpretation of Islamic ideals to meet the exigencies of life in a modern, predominantly non-Muslim context.

Naming American Islam

French scholar Olivier Roy (2004) is adamant that Islam in the West has become secularized (or Westernized). He argues that it is Western "not to the extent it changes its theological framework, but because it expresses that framework more in terms of values than of legal norms."[98] Thus, in order "to recast a Muslim identity in terms of compatibility with a Western conception of religion," being Muslim is defined in terms of values (or ideal norms) such as chastity for women, defense of the family, and opposition to legalizing homosexuality, "instead of interdicts and obligations."[99] More precisely, the experience of "deculturation"—by which Islam's religious tenets are disconnected from a given culture—forces Muslims to focus on the religious element in Islam and, however unwillingly, to utilize patterns established within Western societies for other religions. This process, in Roy's view, effectively secularizes Islam, since religion becomes separated from other spheres of social life.[100] Muslims, for instance, find themselves increasingly aligned with conservative Christians and Jews, often on issues that until recently had no equivalent in Islam (defining abortion as a mortal sin, for instance).

At first glance, Roy's arguments appear to be in tension with those of Tariq Ramadan (reviewed above), at least insofar as they imply that Islam has an ideal culture, which Ramadan refutes. From the same standpoint—namely, that Islam has an inherent capacity to adapt to different cultures—both scholars emphasize different sides of the same experience. Roy is convinced that adaptation to Western society Westernizes the faith, while Ramadan insists that Islam's ability to adapt to Western culture enhances its capacity to impact or influence Western society. In Ramadan's thinking, Muslims must find ways to adapt, live harmoniously within their environment; but this is not to suggest that they should "submit" to it. "On the contrary, once their position is secure, they should be a positive influence within it."[101] But Roy's argument proves unstable, since it also concedes that "deculturation" produces stronger emphasis on the religious elements of Islam. In other words, it fosters religiosity and religious renewal by producing a stress on personal experience and personal faith. It may even produce an inward-looking community given to isolationism and anti-intellectualism. We are therefore left with an irreconcilable scenario in which the disentangling of religion and cultural identity among Western Muslims not only secularizes their faith but also radicalizes it and pits it against secular society.

---

98. Roy, *Globalized Islam*, 32.

99. Ibid., 132, 335.

100. Ibid., 334. As he puts it, Islam is reduced to a "mere religion separated from other socio-cultural fields" (p. 128).

101. Ramadan, *Western Muslims and the Future of Islam*, 73, 80.

Yet there is much validity to Roy's argument. There can be no doubt that outside the cultural matrix that defines social organization and religious life in the Muslim world, major adaptations and remodeling of the practice of faith become mandatory. This process of selective adaptation and experimentation has been most conspicuous and extensive in the creation of Islamic centers or mosques and congregational life.[102] American Islam is being significantly shaped and influenced by the American context. Adaptive changes include the creation of a professionalized clergy;[103] the transformation of the mosque into a community center where marriage ceremonies and funerals take place (as well as non-mosque activities such as soup kitchens);[104] the emergence of congregational membership; the adoption of Sunday for religious activities (including the implementation of Sunday schools for religious instruction); the adoption of evangelical phrases such as "'born-again' Muslims, 'salvation,' and realizing the 'Kingdom of God' on earth";[105] and a much expanded role for imams to include missionary activities, not unlike that of Western evangelists.

Some point out that such structural adaptation or institutional flexibility is not a novel phenomenon within Islam.[106] Yet this process of adaptation within immigrant communities in the United States has resulted in what is referred to as "the mosque movement": a movement that "promotes a vision of the mosque as the center for organized community activities" (understood as its original role) and aims to spread the new experiment in the Muslim world. Through the immigrant experience therefore the mosque has emerged "not so much as a transplant but a new creation with a revitalized function and role in society."[107] Far from being assimilated within a Western prism, Islam has experienced "new birth" and renewal through the immigrant encounter.

Others are even more insistent on the nature and emergence of a specific American Muslim identity. Muqtedar Khan argues that the new generation of American Muslims "are not satisfied with the mere preservation of Islamic identity. They want it accepted and recognized as a constituent element of the American identity itself," presumably as an American religion. To this end,

> they have rejuvenated the tradition of *ijtihad* (independent thinking) among Muslims and now openly talk about . . . interpretation of the Shariah for places where Muslims are in the minority. They have emphasized Islamic

---

102. See Rogaia M. Abusharaf, "Structural Adaptations in an Immigrant Muslim Congregation in New York," in *Gatherings in Diaspora: Religious Communities and the New Immigration*, ed. R. Stephen Warner and Judith G. Wittner (Philadelphia: Temple University Press, 1998), 235-61, esp. 232-33.

103. Islam makes no provision for an official priesthood, and mosques in the Islamic world do not have professional ministers: imams are not professional religious leaders but "local leaders recognized for their extensive knowledge of the . . . Qur'an" (ibid., 253).

104. See Poston, *Islamic Da'wah in the West*, 95-96. Poston contends that, while the transformation of the mosque into an "Islamic Center" has allowed it to meet certain needs, it has also "weakened its specifically religious character." One survey reported that 55 percent of U.S. mosques run a soup kitchen for the poor.

105. Haddad, "Make Room for the Muslims?" 232.

106. Abusharaf, "Structural Adaptations," 251.

107. Haddad, "Make Room for the Muslims?" 235.

principles of justice, religious tolerance, and cultural pluralism. They have Islamized Western values of freedom, human rights, and respect for tolerance by finding Islamic sources and precedents that justify them. . . .

[They] are not Americans who are Muslims or Muslims who are born in America. They are American Muslims. They believe in Islam, they are democratic, they respect human rights and animal rights, and they share a concern for the environment. . . .

[They] are as Islamic as any Muslim and as American as any American. . . .[108]

If previous generations sought to modernize Islam, argues Yvonne Haddad, a professor of Islamic history at Georgetown University, the current generation "seeks to Islamize modernity."[109] She explains that America's determination to influence third world leadership and attract foreign students to its universities has made it a major center of Muslim intellectual activity, to the extent that it has "replaced France as the primary center for Islamic intellectual reflection."[110] The Zaytuna Insitute, America's first Islamic seminary, was founded by two American converts to Islam: Sheik Hamza Yusuf and Imam Zaid Shakir. Sheik Yusuf was raised Greek Orthodox and named Mark Hanson at birth; Shakir is an African American who was baptized Ricky Mitchell and grew up in Georgia's housing projects. Their vision, according to a *New York Times* report, is to teach American Muslims "how to live their faith without succumbing to American materialism or Islamic extremism."[111] As in Europe, the most dynamic centers and sources of an American Islam are those that take the process of fruitful adaptation seriously. Sheik Yusuf and Mr. Shakir, both of whom "spent years in the Middle East and North Africa being mentored by formidable Muslim scholars" represent the face of an American Islam that is equally at home in the Muslim and the modern world.[112]

In the final analysis, the long-term settlement of Muslim populations in Europe and North America and the complex interactions between Islam and modern Western secular culture make the West a vital part of the Islamic world and have, arguably, transformed Islam into a "Western religion." At the very least, self-satisfied claims about the global spread and imposition of Western culture and values look increasingly whimsical and myopic when massive migration movements steadily introduce non-Western cultures and religious expressions into European societies, transforming the collective image and religio-social landscape. Importantly, the presence of these vibrant religious minorities in Europe and North America highlights the permanence of religious trends within global processes and the enduring significance of religious communities. It is a safe prediction, therefore, that whatever else Western societies might look like in the future, the religious element will remain robust.

---

108. Khan, "Constructing the American Muslim Community," 186.
109. Haddad, "Make Room for the Muslims?" 231.
110. Ibid., 223.
111. Goodstein, "U.S. Muslim Clerics Seek a Modern Middle Ground," *New York Times* (June 18, 2006).
112. Ibid.

12

Sacred Canopies

Immigrant Congregations and American Religious Life

On the American scene two kinds of churches, sometimes overlooked by historians, have exercised enormous influence in shaping Christianity in the United States: the immigrant church and the American-born church.

—Wengert and Brockwell, *Telling the Churches' Stories* (1995)

An intense interest in the religious meaning of their break with the past lay behind the preoccupation of both clergy and lay emigrants with religious organizations. . . . The concrete symbols of order or hope that the village church and priest and the annual round of religious observances had once provided seemed far away; yet the mysteries of individual existence as well as the confusing agonies of anomie cried out for religious explanation. For this reason . . . migration was often a theologizing experience.

—Timothy L. Smith, "Religion and Ethnicity in America" (1978)

We have already taken account of the fact that, as a manifestation of Christendom, the Western missionary movement took the form of unidirectional territorial expansion from a fixed geographical ("Christian") center. In addition, the Bible-inspired vision for the worldwide spread of the gospel was inextricably linked with the universal spread of Western (or European) culture (see chapter 4). The story line remained the same irrespective of whether the dominant missionary nation was Britain or America. The American evangelical leader Rev. Josiah Strong (1847-1916) proclaimed Anglo-Saxons "the great missionary race," among whom was to be found "most of the spiritual Christianity in the world," and on whom depended the evangelization of the world.[1] He was also convinced that God was "preparing in our Anglo-Saxon civilization the die with which to stamp the peoples of the earth."[2] This perspective has remained a mainstay of

---

1. Strong, *Our Country*, 209. "I believe," he added, "it is fully in the hands of the Christians of the United States, during the next ten or fifteen years, to hasten or retard the coming of Christ's kingdom in the world by hundreds, and perhaps thousands of years" (p. 227).

2. Ibid., 214.

American missionary thinking and the study of American (or Western) missions. It leaves no room for the possibility that missionary action could flow in the reverse direction or, strangely for a nation founded by religious migrants, that America itself might be a *missionary-receiving* nation.

In concert with the prevalent understanding of "Christian missions," the dominant hermeneutic of mission studies holds that Christianity's global spread was largely a Western project, a function of European (or American) initiatives and cultural expansion.[3] In effect, Christ's work and influence in the world are exclusively linked with the culture, initiatives, and achievements of particular Western nations. While this self-serving perspective no longer goes unchallenged,[4] it remains entrenched. In Strong's day, the influx of non–Anglo-Saxon immigrants (predominantly Catholics) was widely viewed as a threat to America's "Christian" culture and its universal mandate. The immigrants were thus either to be assimilated, rejected, or at the very least marginalized. A century later, this approach remains strongly evident. Yet it is possible to argue that, then as now, massive immigrant incursions revitalized American religious life, reinforced its Christian ethos, and arguably renewed missionary consciousness within its churches.

This chapter provides an overview of the impact of successive waves of immigration on American religious life and the missionary function of immigrant congregations within American society. This historical assessment is used to explicate the missionary role and significance of post-1965 Christian immigrants and their descendants. The view taken here is that contemporary nonwhite immigration will arguably have an impact on the American religious landscape that surpasses all but that of the original European migrants who laid the foundation of America's religious culture. This argument reflects broader themes of this book, namely, that non-Western initiatives and movements are among the most powerful forces shaping the contemporary world order. More specifically, that migrant movement from the new heartlands of Christianity (in southern continents) to the old centers where the faith is experiencing dramatic erosion and marginalization constitutes a missionary movement; and that this development, in turn, implicates the West as a new frontier of global Christian expansion.

Immigrant Congregations and American Religious Life

Religious assembly and affiliation constitute the most powerful means available to immigrants in their search for self-identity, communal acceptance, and social

---

3. See Kenneth S. Latourette, "Christ the Hope of the World: What Has History to Say?" *Religion in Life* 23, no. 3 (Summer 1954): 323-33. For a critique, see Jehu J. Hanciles, "New Wine in Old Wineskins: Critical Reflections on Writing and Teaching a Global Christian History," *Missiology* 35, no. 3 (July 2006): 361-82.

4. Among others, see Walls, *Missionary Movement in Christian History*, 143-59; Andrew F. Walls, "Eusebius Tries Again: The Task of Reconceiving and Re-Visioning the Study of Christian History," in *Enlarging the Story: Perspectives on Writing World Christian History*, ed. Wilbert R. Shenk (Maryknoll, NY: Orbis Books, 2002): 1-21; Wilbert R. Shenk, "Recasting Theology of Mission: Impulses from the Non-Western World," *International Bulletin of Missionary Research* 25, no. 3 (July 2001): 98-107; Robert, "Shifting Southward."

integration. Religious congregations serve to facilitate the immigrants' assimilation into American life while simultaneously allowing them "to nurture their
ethnic ties even as they ease their adjustment into their new country."[5] Unsurprisingly, given America's status as a "nation of immigrants," congregations or
voluntary religious associations have been foundational to American religious
life. Historian E. Brooks Holifield reports that "for most of the past three hundred years, from 35 to 40 percent of the [American] population has probably
participated in congregations with some degree of regularity."[6] In that expanse
of time, the role and function of the congregation within American society have
changed remarkably: from the "comprehensive congregation" of the colonial era,
which was socially obligatory and embraced every colonist, to the more recent
"participatory congregation" typified by its multipurpose function (including a
wide array of social services and recreational activities).[7] What has remained
unchanged is the role of the religious congregation as a vital source and expression of community throughout the nation's history.

But there is also a case to be made that *immigrant congregations potentially
have a missionary function*, not only because they represent the most effective
instruments through which immigrants can impact the wider society but also
because immigrant churches model religious commitment, apply the message of
the gospel directly to daily exigencies, and comprise communities that interact
on a daily basis with other marginalized segments of society. This is perhaps
most apparent in the American situation because, in addition to an ingrained pro-
clivity for voluntary association, its strong immigrant ethos has allowed American society to develop a greater capacity for religious pluralism than any other
country in the Western world. So much so that in the contemporary period many
immigrant groups (including Muslims) find that the United States affords them
greater freedom of religious expression and better opportunities for religious
engagement than they had experienced in their homelands.

The point has already been made that where large-scale immigration is
involved assimilation is seldom a "straight line" or one-sided process of change
(see arguments in chapter 9). Patterns of assimilation or modes of incorporation
into any society are subject to broader historical forces and complex contextual
factors that produce divergent (even unexpected) outcomes—including the possibility that the dominant society is also transformed through the incorporation
or assimilation of new immigrants. This is most applicable to religious life. In
his influential 1964 volume on assimilation in America, sociologist Milton M.
Gordon argued that the impact of minority group cultures on American society
has been "significantly extensive" *only* in "the area of institutional religion."[8]

---

5. Gregory Rodriguez, *Tamed Spaces: How Religious Congregations Nurture Immigrant
Assimilation in Southern California* (The Davenport Institute, Pepperdine University School of
Public Policy, 2004), 9.

6. E. Brooks Holifield, "Toward a History of American Congregations," in *American Congregations*, ed. James P. Wind and James Welborn Lewis (Chicago: University of Chicago Press, 1998),
24.

7. Ibid., 28-47.

8. Gordon, *Assimilation in American Life*, 109.

We have already seen (chapter 9) that each of the previous waves of immigrants transformed American society in lasting ways. And it is worth reiterating that massive Christian immigration throughout the nineteenth century almost certainly curbed the subsequent decline of Christianity in America. How each wave directly impacted its religious life, primarily through voluntary religious association, is also worth a brief overview.

Northwestern Europeans

The earliest immigrants (not counting the "native" Americans who were also migrants) were predominantly Protestants from northwestern Europe whose vision of religious community conformed to the Christendom ideal of one congregation for each community or village. Some variant of this ideal persisted long after diverse congregations began to coexist.[9] The earliest Protestant groups were Episcopalians, Presbyterians, and Congregationalists. Subsequent waves of European migration brought Methodists, Baptists, Reformed Churches, and Lutherans. Together, these "mainline" Protestant groups dominated America's national and religious life until the early twentieth century.[10] Successive waves of migration constantly swelled this white Anglo-Saxon Protestant (WASP) population, and later immigrants sometimes impacted the religious culture in unexpected ways.

In the early twentieth century, for instance, the plight and experience of European immigrants contributed to the emergence of the "social gospel movement," which had a transformative impact on American Protestantism and American missionary enterprise. Significantly, Walter Rauschenbusch (1861-1918), who is considered the movement's most outstanding prophet, was born to immigrant parents and, as pastor of the Second German Baptist Church in New York City for over ten years, witnessed firsthand the predicament of immigrants and other disadvantaged groups who were ignored by the Protestant establishment.

On the whole, however, this Anglo-Protestant population constituted the religious mainstream with which other immigrant groups had to contend for power and influence. Not until the 1960s would the mainline denominations and churches associated with this Protestant establishment begin to experience a significant loss of religious vitality, regular attendance, and membership. That development is linked to possibly the most extensive makeover in America's religious life since its nation's founding. But we are getting ahead of the story.

Enslaved Africans

The second wave of immigrants (1619-1850) comprised enslaved Africans, who embraced Christianity in their hundreds of thousands from the late eighteenth century. Their conversion to Christianity signaled the end of American evan-

---

9. Holifield, "Toward a History of American Congregations," 29.

10. See Roof and McKinney, *American Mainline Religion*, 72-90; also Gilkey, "Christian Congregation as a Religious Community," 102f.

gelicalism as a white religion,[11] though their understanding and application of the gospel message were in some ways radically different. The emergence and growth of black Christianity contributed to a tremendous increase in the number of congregations, as religious protest and the structures of racial segregation stimulated the emergence of a black church movement. Some 931 separate black congregations were already in existence by the American Civil War (1860-1865).[12] By 1900, 17 percent of the nation's roughly 212,200 local churches were black congregations (at a time when blacks accounted for less than 11 percent of the American population).[13]

Black Christianity melded elements of the Anglo-American tradition out of which it emerged and a deep-seated African religious ethos.[14] Partly for this reason, its efforts to establish a unique identity over against the dominant European-American religious establishment generated "similarity and dissonance."[15] Yet, as the one institution (in a segregationist society) over which blacks had complete control, black churches became the foremost expression of black solidarity, "the single most important vehicle for the exercise of an independent social and cultural life."[16] From the start, the existence of black churches bore glaring testimony to the limitations of Anglo-conformity and the Christendom ideal. Black Christianity signified *anti-Christendom* in at least two ways: first, in its rejection of a Christian identity stamped by cultural domination and wedded to political control; second, in its purposeful refusal to sacrifice spiritual selfhood and vernacular Christian expression to the debilitating confines of a monolithic, territorially-bound, ideal.

Estimates in the 1920s and 1980s confirm that throughout the twentieth century over 85 percent of black church members belonged to black denominations.[17] According to the Baylor study *American Pietism in the 21st Century* (2006), 62.5 percent of blacks belonged to black Protestant churches in 2005. This state of affairs accounts for the assertions by Roof and McKinney that black churches are "effectively cut off socially and religiously from white America."[18] This is only partly true. Even while it remained distinctive and largely separated from the dominant mainstream, black Christianity has had a significant impact on American society and its religious heritage. Robert Franklin argues that white

---

11. Mark A. Noll, *The Rise of Evangelicalism: The Age of Edwards, Whitefield and the Wesleys,* A History of Evangelicalism 1 (Downers Grove, IL: InterVarsity Press, 2004), 177; cf. Holifield, "Toward a History of American Congregations," 39.

12. Holifield, "Toward a History of American Congregations," 37.

13. Mark A. Noll, *The Old Religion in a New World* (Grand Rapids: Eerdmans, 2002), 121.

14. See Milton G. Sernett, "Black Religion and the Question of Evangelical Identity," in *The Variety of American Evangelicalism*, ed. Donald W. Dayton and Robert K. Johnston (Downers Grove, IL: InterVarsity, 1991), 136; Robert Michael Franklin, "The Safest Place on Earth: The Culture of Black Congregations," in *American Congregations*, ed. James P. Wind and James Welborn Lewis (Chicago: University of Chicago Press, 1998), 259.

15. Sernett, "Black Religion," 135.

16. Ibid., 141.

17. Roof and McKinney, *American Mainline Religion*, 140.

18. See ibid., 140.

congregations with a substantial black membership are directly affected by the latter's dynamic religious tradition.[19] On a wider canvas, black initiatives and spirituality contributed to the development of the holiness movement and acted as a major stimulus in the emergence of American Pentecostalism, which marked a watershed in the history of American Christianity and galvanized American foreign missions. The impact of Pentecostalism on the growth of congregations (both "black" and "white") was nothing short of momentous. The main black Pentecostal denomination, Church of God in Christ, grew from ten congregations in 1907 to some forty-five hundred churches by the 1980s.[20]

Black churches are now a prominent and critical feature of the American religious life. Their significance is often overlooked not only because of their distinctiveness from the dominant culture but also because their contribution to America's religious heritage has often been indirect. Among other things, their very presence and proliferation bear testimony to the disfiguring impact of race and racism on American Christianity. Black congregations, asserts Franklin, "made claims upon the nation's identity, conscience, and moral obligation to practice fairness and mercy toward its most disfranchised citizens. Their *public mission* was to compel America to become America for everyone."[21] Perhaps the crowning achievement of this "public mission" was the civil rights movement, which emerged out of the black churches and, even if questions persist about its legacy, marked a historic turning point in American society and cultural history.

Eastern Europeans

Between 1881 and 1930, over twenty-seven million migrants from southern and eastern European nations arrived in America. The impact of this third wave of immigration on America's religious life was directly linked to the fact that the majority of these European immigrants were Roman Catholic. (Only a small fraction, fewer than 6 percent, were Jews). In 1790, when the first official census was taken, there were an estimated thirty-five thousand Roman Catholics among the American population, less than 1 percent of the total. They remained a distrusted and often persecuted minority. By 1850 their number had risen to just over a million, gathered in 1,221 parish congregations. The massive influx of Catholic immigrants in the late nineteenth century, however, caused an inevitable explosion in the numbers—to an estimated thirteen million (one in eight of the population) by 1890. Because of their multinational origins, the flood of immigrants also increased the variety of Catholic parishes and congregations. Each national group—among them Italians, Poles, Czechs, Slovaks, Croatians, Hungarians, Lithuanians, Ukrainians, and more—insisted on worshiping in its own gathered community so as to preserve language and distinctive traditions. National (or ethnic) parishes proliferated rapidly.

---

19. See Franklin, "Safest Place on Earth," 259.

20. Roof and McKinney, *American Mainline Religion*, 141; see also the COGIC Web site, http://www.cogic.org/history.htm.

21. Franklin, "Safest Place on Earth," 258 (emphasis added).

As noted earlier, the burgeoning Roman Catholic population attracted the condemnation of Rev. Josiah Strong, who identified "Romanism" as one of the eight major perils that seriously threatened America's well-being and supremacy.[22] By the outbreak of World War I, 35 percent of Roman Catholic congregations still conducted their services in a language other than English.[23] Foreign language usage declined over time but the ethnic and cultural diversity of the Catholic population remained a prominent feature of American society. From the 1920s, restrictive immigration policies stemmed flows from eastern Europe, but immigration from French Canada, Mexico, and Puerto Rico continued to swell the Catholic element. In addition to extensive "parish missions," or nationwide evangelistic revivals, aimed at establishing the faith among the burgeoning Catholic immigrant population,[24] large numbers of converts were also made from among the black population. As a religious institution, the Roman Catholic Church became strongly associated with the lower classes and impoverished immigrant groups in urban areas. Meanwhile, the proportion of Roman Catholics within the population continued to grow vigorously. By 1950, one in four Americans identified as Catholic, making the Roman Catholic Church the largest single religious group in the country.[25] And as its numbers increased, so did the church's influence. In fact, the massive Catholic growth contributed to the erosion of Protestant cultural domination.

The election (in 1960) of John F. Kennedy, a Roman Catholic, as president of the United States exemplified wider transformations. Some argue that it marked the end of an era, that it witnessed the demise of the centuries-old religious power base preserved by the Protestant establishment.[26] At the very least it signified a profound shift in America's religious culture. By the 1970s, Catholics (like Jews a little earlier) had "moved into the mainstream socially, culturally and religiously" and matched Protestants in education, occupational status, and income.[27] The Protestant center shifted, then gradually collapsed, giving way to a religious "mainstream" characterized by unprecedented plurality. Once again, large-scale immigration had irrevocably transformed the American religious (and, to a lesser extent, its cultural and political) landscape. Langdon Gilkey contends that there is a clear connection between the decline in mainline Protestant denominations and the erosion of Protestant dominance in economic, social, and political structures of American life.[28]

---

22. Strong, *Our Country*, 62-91. He denounced Roman Catholicism as incompatible with good citizenship and liberty of conscience and insisted that "the avowed purpose of Romanists [is] to 'make America Catholic'" (p. 84).

23. Roof and McKinney, *American Mainline Religion*, 118.

24. See Roger Finke and Rodney Stark, *The Churching of America, 1776-1990: Winners and Losers in Our Religious Economy* (New Brunswick, N.J.: Rutgers University Press, 2002), 117-23.

25. Gordon, *Assimilation in American Life*, 195.

26. See Roof and McKinney, *American Mainline Religion*, 15f.; also Gilkey, "Christian Congregation as a Religious Community," 103f.

27. Roof and McKinney, *American Mainline Religion*, 16.

28. Gilkey, "Christian Congregation as a Religious Community," 103-4.

The Missionary Element

These historical examples demonstrate that immigration and immigrant churches have played a significant role in shaping American religious life. Their missionary function is less explicit. But, then as now, immigrant churches were bastions of fervent religiosity and "communities of commitment."[29] Immigrant congregations bore faithful witness to the claims of the gospel, experienced significant growth through innovative ministries, catered to the most urgent needs of the most vulnerable communities, provided religious instruction and training for the next generation of Americans, and supplied vital social services that contributed to public well-being. It is significant that Catholic congregations, made up predominantly of immigrants, were the first to keep their churches open throughout the whole week.[30] This simple act signified the centrality of religion within the immigrant community. As other traditions adopted this practice, the "social congregations" became a dominant feature in American religious life. In this sense, the realities of the immigrant religious community transformed the role of the church within American society.

It would be a gross misnomer to label black churches as immigrant churches, yet so much about the formation and function of black congregations, including their emphasis on self-identity and sense of belonging, echoes the immigrant experience. The black church tradition, writes Franklin, demonstrates to the wider culture "that congregations are places where alternative cultures may be nurtured, prophetic language and action shaped, and liberating visions celebrated."[31] Significantly, weekly church attendance among black Protestants (43.1 percent) remains higher than the national average (36 percent), and the percentage of blacks who pray at least once a day (74.1 percent) is higher than evangelical Protestants (67.1), mainline Protestants (44.1), Catholics (46.1), or Jews (32.8).[32] There are few better models within the American experience of the intrinsic bond between the church and the wider community than that epitomized by the black church. This quality, affirm Roof and McKinney, has "served to buffer somewhat the trends towards greater religious individualism dominant in the society."[33]

Perhaps of even greater significance than the missionary function of immigrant congregations within American society is the tremendous boost that the immigrant Christian influx gave to the overseas or foreign missionary movement in America. From the very start, the black church movement stimulated African American missionary consciousness and initiatives. As early as the 1770s, John Marrant, a free black from New York City, started preaching to American Indians. In 1783, some ten years before William Carey sailed for India, Rev. George Liele (1750-1825), a former slave who converted to Christ in 1772 and became ordained as a Baptist minister in 1775, left America and settled in Kings-

---

29. Smith, "Religion and Ethnicity in America," 1178.
30. Holifield, "Toward a History of American Congregations," 38.
31. Franklin, "Safest Place on Earth," 257.
32. *American Pietism in the 21st Century*, 14.
33. Roof and McKinney, *American Mainline Religion*, 91.

ton (Jamaica) as missionary. Liele became America's first overseas missionary. By the time the first European missionary arrived in Jamaica, he had a church of more than five hundred members.

But black Christians focused their missionary energy mainly on Africa. To be sure, the number that went out officially as missionaries remained small—just over 115 African Americans went to Africa as missionaries by 1900.[34] Lack of resources was a major impediment. Until the black churches became sufficiently well established to form their own mission agencies, missionary-minded blacks depended on white organizations that readily funded them, owing to the lack of white volunteers and the relatively lower costs of supporting blacks.[35] The majority labored in either Sierra Leone or Liberia. Among the most successful were Joseph and Mary Gomer, who, under the auspices of the United Brethren, served among the Mende people on the Island of Sherbro (south of the Sierra Leone peninsula) from 1871 to 1892.[36] Both Alexander Crummell and Edward W. Blyden, two of the most influential black leaders of the period, were also sponsored by white denominations. William Sheppard, the most celebrated of African American missionaries in Africa, labored in the Congo among the Kuba people as a missionary of the Southern Presbyterian Society for two decades. His pioneering spirit, evangelistic efforts, and campaign on behalf of the Africans against colonial atrocities have prompted fascinating comparisons with the famed Scottish missionary-explorer David Livingstone.[37]

Eventually black mission agencies overtook white institutions in their support of missionary work in Africa. Between 1880 and 1900 the African Methodist Episcopal (AME) Church had at least sixty missionaries in Africa.[38] During this same period, Bishop Henry M. Turner of the AME Church initiated many efforts at missionary emigration (some linked to South Africa) and organized the emigration of over three hundred American blacks to Liberia in 1896.

But the missionary vision of the black church was grounded in the conviction that black Christians (the descendants of ex-African slaves) were God's chosen instruments for the redemption of Africans. The dominant missionary approach until well into the twentieth century was emigration—a prominent example of the strong links between migration and mission (see chapter 13). Not all were driven by missionary motives, but as many as twelve thousand blacks emigrated to Africa under the auspices of the American Colonization Society, which

---

34. See David Killingray, "The Black Atlantic Missionary Movement and Africa, 1780s-1920s," *Journal of Religion in Africa* 33, no. 1 (February 2003): 22.

35. Before 1880, reports Walter L. Williams, "almost all black evangelists working among indigenous Africans were supported by white churches" (*Black Americans and the Evangelization of Africa, 1877-1900* [Madison: University of Wisconsin Press, 1982], 9).

36. On the success and significance of the Gomers' missionary endeavors, see Williams, *Black Americans and the Evangelization of Africa*, 16; also Ogbu Kalu, "Black Missionaries and White Abolitionists: The Careers of Joseph and Mary Gomer in the Good Hope Mission, Sherbro, Sierra Leone, 1871-1894," *Neue Zeitschrift für Missionswissenschaft* (June 2003): 161-74.

37. See William E. Phipps, *William Sheppard: Congo's African American Livingstone*, 1st ed. (Louisville, KY: Geneva, 2002).

38. Williams, *Black Americans and the Evangelization of Africa*, 44; Phipps, *William Sheppard*, 58.

founded Liberia in 1821. Much earlier, the arrival in the Sierra Leone colony of eleven hundred black Christians from Nova Scotia (in March 1792)—as part of a British experiment to Christianize Africa—marked the establishment of the first black church in modern Africa; and their efforts to evangelize recaptured African slaves arguably signified the beginning of the "modern" missionary movement.[39]

The third wave of immigrants to America saw a record influx of over fourteen million people (mainly from Eastern Europe) between 1900 and 1920. The fact that this development coincided with the most extraordinary explosion in the number of American mission agencies and overseas missionaries forces may not be insignificant. Prior to 1900, there were only fifty-six American mission agencies; from 1900 to 1960 204 new mission agencies were founded (seventy in the 1950s alone).[40] This massive surge, which continued into the 1980s, is obviously linked to complex historical factors: the most obvious include the post–World War II boom and the rise of the Pentecostal-charismatic movement.[41] But the main source of growth came from non-denominational agencies that surged from fewer than thirty in 1900 to almost two hundred by 1960 and over 550 by 1998.[42] Given the injection of vitality and innovation that immigration gives to religious life, the immigrant element cannot be ruled out. Since the majority of immigrants in this case were Roman Catholic, it is hugely significant that the number of Roman Catholic overseas missionaries exploded from a handful in 1918 to over ninety-six hundred by 1968.[43]

"Communities of Commitment"

The New Christian Immigrants and American Christianity

It is one of the most striking coincidences of contemporary globalization that the decline of the Christian faith in North America has corresponded with a phenomenal influx of Christian migrants. (The concurrence is more remarkable in the United States than in Europe, where the greater proportion of new immigrants are Muslim.) To restate the basic facts (see chapter 10): by 2005, the United States was home to one in five of the world's migrant population (or 38.4 million)—up from twenty-three million in 1990[44]—and immigrants accounted for about 13 percent of the American population. America's total "immigrant stock" (including U.S.-born children of immigrants) is estimated at over one-fifth of the entire population.

---

39. See Lamin O. Sanneh, *Abolitionists Abroad: American Blacks and the Making of Modern West Africa* (Cambridge, MA: Harvard University Press, 2001), 62. It certainly predates the founding of the missionary societies associated with the eighteenth-century evangelical revival. See also Jehu J. Hanciles, "Back to Africa: White Abolitionists and Black Missionaries," in *African Christianity: An African Story*, ed. U. Kalu Ogbu (Trenton, NJ: Africa World Press, 2007), 167-88; A. F. Walls, "A Christian Experiment: The Early Sierra Leone Colony," in *The Mission of the Church and the Propagation of the Faith*, ed. G. J. Cuming (London: Cambridge University Press, 1970), 107f.

40. Siewert and Welliver, eds., *Mission Handbook 2001-2003*, 36.

41. Ibid.

42. Ibid., 39.

43. Wilson and Siewert, eds., *Mission Handbook*, 575.

44. *Trends in Total Migrant Stock: The 2005 Revision*, 3.

Unlike previous waves of immigration, however, the overwhelming majority of post-1965 immigrants are of non-European stock and come from over 150 countries. The non-Western origins and incomparable diversity of post-1965 immigrants are crucial considerations in estimating their long-term impact on America's religious landscape. So is the indication that the majority are *Christian*.

According to 1996 data reported in the New Immigrant Survey (2001), some 65 percent of the new immigrants self-identify as Christian.[45] These data are old enough to invite caution and the sampling was limited to immigrants granted permanent residence in a two-month period. But the results strongly correlate with the fact that many of the main source countries of migration to the United States are predominantly Christian. Not surprisingly, Mexico, the leading source country of immigration, is the top country of origin for both Catholic (28 percent) and Protestant (12.4 percent) immigrants. Other top countries of origin for Catholics were the Philippines, Poland, the Dominican Republic, and Vietnam; for Protestants they were Jamaica, the former Soviet Union, the Philippines, and Ghana.[46] Much has been made of the fact that the percentage of Christians among the new immigrants is lower than that within the United States (typically cited at 82 percent). But this comparison seriously underestimates the nature of American Christianity's decline in vitality, attendance, and membership (see pp. 115-19 above). Moreover, not only are the levels of religious commitment among immigrants much higher, but untold numbers also become Christian or renew their Christian commitment after they arrive in the country.

Recent studies (including the 2006 Baylor report discussed in chapter 5) indicate that 25 to 36 percent of Americans attend church regularly and less than half (47.2 percent) identify themselves as Bible believing. Comparative research among many immigrant communities is lacking, but anecdotal evidence suggests that the rates of church attendance are much higher among immigrant communities. Some 75 percent of Korean Americans, for instance, belong to Christian congregations,[47] and my own research among African immigrant churches (discussed in chapter 15) indicates that 45 percent of church members attend the midweek service. Certainly, the vigorous growth of immigrant churches and congregations in metropolitan centers throughout the country over the last three to four decades suggests that they represent the most dynamic and thriving centers of Christian faith in America.

Selling Birthrights for Lentil Stew?[48]

Inevitably, some assessments of the religious encounter between the new immigrants and American society are shaped by the kinds of premises expressed in the

---

45. Jasso et al., "Exploring the Religious Preferences of Recent Immigrants," 221; also Warner, "Coming to America," 20-23.

46. Jasso et al., "Exploring the Religious Preferences of Recent Immigrants," 226. The top source countries for Orthodox Christians are the former Soviet Union (56.9), Ethiopia (9.7), and Romania (7.4).

47. Alan Wolfe, *The Transformation of American Religion: How We Actually Live Our Faith* (New York: Free Press, 2003), 216.

48. See Genesis 25:29-34.

classical assimilation or Anglo-conformity theories. These assessments anticipate the inevitable one-sided integration of the new immigrants into American society at the expense of their collective identity and culture. In other words, the pressures immigrants face to adapt their Christian experiences and institutions to American culture and its dominant Protestant ethos will prove decisive. By the same token, the possibility that the new Christian immigrants will have an enduring impact on American religious life is discountenanced or downplayed. This viewpoint is evident in political scientist Alan Wolfe's *The Transformation of American Religion* (2003), in which a whole chapter is devoted to post-1965 immigration.

Wolfe acknowledges that the plurality of religions represented among the new immigrants "poses enormous challenges for American pluralism" because it significantly reduces the nation's dominant Judeo-Christian self-understanding.[49] He also contends, rightly, that the encounter with a society radically different from the one they left behind is bound to impact the ability of the new immigrants to practice their religion as previously. But he insists that the "necessity of choice"—a reference to the *individual* need for belonging, the cultural constraints imposed by long-term settlement within American society, and eagerness to enjoy the material benefits life in America offers—forces many immigrants to either switch their faith before they arrive in the United States or shortly after. This argument bears a strong similarity to Alba and Nee's new assimilation theory (see pp. 238-43 above), which maintains that whether America's new immigrants want to assimilate or not, *individual* decisions and actions taken in pursuit of normal goals produce assimilation as an unintended result. In Wolfe's assessment, the very act of movement itself forces assimilative change: "some people will want to change their faith as they change their country." Thus, "it need not take two or three generations before religion's collective identity gives way to an individual need to belong in an often strange new land."[50] As he puts it, they become American by becoming Christian.

Wolfe presents no concrete evidence to support the problematic claim that some immigrants switch their faith (presumably to one of the many varieties of American Protestantism) before they arrive. But he cites the higher percentage of Christian allegiance and church attendance among Korean, Taiwanese, Chinese, and Hispanic immigrants (compared to percentages in their respective home countries) as proof that some people switch their faith "when they switch their residence."[51] Moreover, it is to evangelical Protestantism that the new immigrants and their descendants are predominantly attracted. He alludes to the fact that second-generation Korean Americans have abandoned the churches of their parents (in a "silent exodus") to form English-language congregations in which Koreanness is downplayed and contemporary forms of worship are preferred. He surmises that the large number of conversions reported among Latinos (from Catholicism to evangelical Protestantism) represents "a mechanism through which immigrants from relatively poor backgrounds assimilate into American society."

---

49. Wolfe, *Transformation of American Religion*, 243.
50. Ibid., 225.
51. Ibid., 216-25.

The paucity of the ethnographic data (mainly individual interviews) on which Wolfe appears to base these weighty assessments must be noted in passing.[52] But threadbare substantiation is only part of the problem. Wolfe's secularist/materialist explanation makes no room for the possibility that the innate religiosity and deep spiritual orientation of immigrants and their descendants are cogent factors in the spectacular growth of immigrant congregations, or that religious conversion among immigrants is much more likely to be prompted by religious reasons, even if materialistic motivations cannot be ruled out entirely.

Crucially, recent studies indicate that the overwhelming majority of Hispanics (82 percent) who convert from Catholicism to evangelicalism "cite the desire for a more direct, personal experience with God as the main reason for adopting [their] new faith."[53] It has also been noted that Mexican immigrants in the United States practice a more church-centered form of Catholicism than they do in Mexico, where Catholicism is the national faith and expressions of the faith permeate all of life.[54] This means that rates of church attendance are higher for Mexican immigrants in the United States than they are for their counterparts in Mexico. In other words, being in the United States, where Roman Catholicism is a minority faith, did not prompt mass switching to the predominant Protestantism; rather it fostered institutional adaptation and enforced more intentional forms of religious allegiance to Catholicism. This development coheres with the argument that religious commitment intensifies with the migration experience.

Immigrant congregations continue to flourish not only because they function as sites of religious conversion and religious renewal but precisely because they help to preserve ethnic identity. When huge numbers of Korean, Taiwanese, or Chinese immigrants become Christian, rejecting their culture in order to better assimilate into American society may be the last thing on their mind. They join the immigrant congregation because the church is often the only social institution on American soil that incorporates aspects of the culture they left behind (including the vernacular and traditional customs) and provides vital communal support related to jobs, family life, and the challenges of adaptation.[55] Since most immigrants experience downward social mobility and marginalization in America, the sociocultural solidarity provided by the immigrant church is as vital as its religious resources. Wolfe's reference to a "silent exodus" from Korean immigrant churches—which appears anecdotal—also misleads. Other studies indicate that "rejection of all things Korean usually continues until members of the second generation reach adulthood," when direct experience of social marginality and nonacceptance "leads second-generation Koreans to re-evaluate their ethnic identity.[56]

It is also possible to argue that the adaptations made by children of Korean

---

52. Especially when it is considered that his conclusions include not only Christian but Buddhist and Muslim immigrants as well.

53. *Changing Faiths: Latinos and the Transformation of American Religion*, The Pew Research Center, 2007, 42.

54. Rodriguez, *Tamed Spaces*, 12.

55. See ibid., 15.

56. Ebaugh and Chafetz, *Religion and the New Immigrants*, 120-21.

and Chinese immigrants are motivated as much by a desire to fit into their new context as by missionary commitment, which is to say that it allows them to evangelize other second-generation Koreans more effectively and even to attract non-Korean and non-Chinese Americans. (Incidentally, the same argument applies to cultural adaptations made by Muslims and Islamic institutions in America.) Equating English usage with abandonment of Korean or Chinese culture, as Wolfe does, is troublesome (see arguments on pp. 71-74 above). There is a case to be made that institutional adaptation by descendants produces an impact that is not entirely dissimilar to that of the ethnic congregations established by their parents—it increases their capacity to reach others like them.

Wolfe admits that American evangelical Protestantism has historically proven flexible in matters of doctrine and practice, but he balks at the notion that it is flexible enough to accommodate the diverse expressions of non-Western Christianities. This seems to underline his conviction that the onus of change and conformity lies mainly on the new immigrants and their descendants. This understanding is far from original, but it reflects inattentiveness to processes of globalization, which allow immigrant communities robust access to homeland resources through social networks and modern telecommunications. It certainly ignores the profound implications that momentous demographic and cultural shifts within global Christianity have for the religious encounter between new Christian immigrants and American Christianity.

The fact that many mainline denominations in non-Western countries have a solidly evangelical ethos complicates the view that American evangelicalism presents a unique attraction—incidentally, mega-churches are a more uniquely Korean than American phenomenon.[57] While some immigrant groups (such as Koreans and Chinese) hail from countries where Christianity is a minority faith the non-Western expressions of faith now flourishing in American cities represent the new face of global Christianity. From a global perspective, Anglo-American evangelical Protestantism is the *minority faith*. Not only is it arguably experiencing decline, it is also confronted by new Christian expressions that are growing much faster, with far-reaching implications for the American experience. Stephen Warner affirms that "although it may not be apparent, in many congregations American Christians are increasingly people of color."[58]

Longing for Belonging

If the changing face of American Christianity is not as apparent as it could be, this is partly because the new immigrants tend to form separate congregations. This also makes it easy to overlook the fact that many immigrants experience rejection and discrimination when they seek membership or participation in American churches—even when they are committed Christians or seasoned

---

57. By 2002, of the eleven largest mega-congregations in the world, ten were in the city of Seoul, which also boasted "the largest Pentecostal, Presbyterian, and Methodist congregations in the world and the second largest Baptist" (Timothy K. Park, "A Survey of the Korean Missionary Movement," *Journal of Asian Mission* 4, no. 1 (2002): 113.

58. Warner, "Coming to America," 23.

ministers who speak excellent English. Thus, the suggestion that the new immigrants will be compelled by impervious cultural forces to individually conform assumes that they are welcome in the first place. The harrowing experiences of rejection, marginalization, and prejudice that non-Western Christian immigrants often encounter in their efforts to become involved in or join churches in the West (especially Protestant evangelical communities) is poignantly captured in the real-life story of an Asian migrant whom I shall call Samantha (not her real name).

I met Samantha on my travels, and our many conversations inevitably turned to issues of spiritual journeys and the Christian migrant experience. I was profoundly struck by both her natural gift for eloquent prose and her capacity to combine nuanced self-analysis with critical commentary on the wider currents that have shaped her interactions and encounters as a migrant. Here is her story:

> I'd never thought of myself as an "immigrant." Immigrants are driven from their homes by war, natural catastrophe, persecution. Immigrants seek better opportunities for themselves, for their families, in someone else's country. Being an immigrant presupposes a singular place of origin—a homeland where you feel most truly yourself, somewhere that connects you with biological ancestors and a cultural heritage. This homeland is a place you hark back to and yearn for. It's a pivotal reference point. It's that sense of belonging which is jolted and displaced when you move away from it.
>
> I was just someone who "moved around a lot." Up until I was 18, my parents' decisions determined where I lived. Our family straddled two countries (in Australasia) for most of my youth. Adjusting to new faces, a new school, new ways of life—to cultural dissonance—was part and parcel of my upbringing; it became second nature to me. My childhood was also spent in a chaotic and volatile family environment. I discovered early on that I did not 'belong' in one place or one culture, nor did I "belong" to one set of people or ethnic group. Others used "home" and "family" to understand and convey a sense of themselves, but I was troubled by how little these words really defined who I was. In my own "homeland," I was already feeling disoriented, displaced. . . .
>
> By the time I was 18, I had experienced a range of Christian traditions in Western countries. At each place, I discovered I didn't really fit in. I was a Protestant at the convent schools; at the Anglican school and church in Australia, I was a foreigner; being more comfortable with English, I was a linguistic anomaly at the Chinese-speaking Presbyterian church; and at the Methodist church in Asia, I was privileged and "Westernized." Of course, feeling different or out of place is every adolescent's prerogative. I didn't think too much of it; at least not until I made a conscious choice to leave for college/university in the United States by myself.

In the interest of space, I have omitted Samantha's account of the U.S. phase of her journey, which lasted seven years (four of them spent as a university student). In California, she found "family" within the campus Christian group, grew in Christian ministry, discovered the appeal of "liberation theology," and had life-transforming experiences working in the inner city during summer projects. Once outside the university setting, however, she struggled to find a church that offered "community." Eventually, she move to England to pursue a master's degree. Her story continues:

I was 26 when I packed up my suitcases, bid adieu to the life I'd built in the U.S., and headed off to an old university town in England. I remember being full of fresh hopes and naiveté, thinking perhaps I would finally find a sense of belonging in a place where the intellectual and Christian traditions were equally strong. I thought for sure I'd find a church that would not only understand and appreciate the experiences and gifts I could offer, but also value and nurture who I was for myself.

Soon after arriving, I joined a large charismatic Anglican church. The congregation was lively, the worship contemporary, and the preaching substantive. It seemed the right place for me. They even had a ministry for single professionals in my age range! The stereotypical English reserve was hard to crack, but I felt it had to be only a matter of time before I'd find "kindred spirits" and meaningful connections at the church.

But that first year was tough. As an "international student," I was immediately slotted into an "international Alpha course." Never mind that I'd been a committed Christian all my life. I attended the first session and found it geared towards non-Christian foreigners and newcomers living in an English-speaking country for the first time. It was not for me. I soon discovered that the student ministry catered only to undergraduates and the "young professionals" ministry—primarily consisting of English working people—had little room for a postgraduate foreigner.

I made efforts to get to know the church's leadership team, to speak with them about the various ministries and what my place might be. (Although I had volunteered in various capacities, I was left feeling no less isolated than before.) The ministers were gracious and well intentioned but the conversations yielded nothing concrete, with no real understanding of where I was coming from.

In one instance, several non-Brits had shared with me their struggles with the pressure to conform to the prevailing white, evangelical, English church culture. After what I thought was an engaging discussion with one minister on this issue of "diversity" (or lack thereof), he asked me to do a reading that Sunday. That was it.

A year or so later, I was finally approached to help at an Alpha course, in the kitchen. While I appreciated being asked, it seemed yet another "hoop" to jump through before I could be "trusted" to do any direct ministry. While I understand the rationale for caution, I also felt what I had to give, as well as to receive, was being dismissed and eroded over time. It was as if because I was someone who defied their established ministry structures—i.e., as a native-English-speaking Asian with an already robust Christian background—they did not know what to do with me. If they couldn't convert me or teach me English, what else could they do with me? Because I wasn't going to return to my "home country," they couldn't even train me to proselytize "my people." I'd never felt so adrift, so cut off from my primary source of Christian teaching and fellowship.

I wouldn't have made it through that first year if it weren't for the handful of Christians at my college and, perhaps ironically, my non-Christian house-mates.

After my master's degree, I decided to continue with the doctorate. This required conducting extensive fieldwork. My research focus was on contemporary religious experience, so I joined a Christian staff group living and working at a pilgrimage site in the U.K. The staff are hired by an ecumenical Christian community which believes that commitment to justice and peace is an imperative of the faith. Departing from the strict evangelicalism of past churches where "evangelism" and "mission" were limited only to "saving souls," I found this holistic understanding of Christianity refreshing and radical. Their ecumenism and hospitality meant I was welcomed and accepted as I am. I felt trusted and affirmed in a way I'd never felt at the previous church (although I'd been there almost two and a half years). I no longer felt like a "project" or a tolerated inconvenience. For all the flaws [of] this group . . . , at least I was given the chance to be an equal participant in the life of Christian fellowship.

My fieldwork completed, I returned to the university town once again. I found it impossible, however, to return to that particular Anglican church, to a community that had made it so hard for a newcomer—and not a very shy one at that!—to feel included. I'm not as angry or as bitter, but I still feel a sadness; it was a loss of sorts, for both sides. My experiences in the U.S. and the U.K. have led me to believe that the established church and I—and people like me—are sorely impoverished by such (mis)encounters. And sometimes, I feel very tired. I know no church is faultless and that there are other churches, but the string of hurtful experiences has left me wondering: What does the life of the church mean for someone like me? After all, when I finish my doctorate, I'll probably have to move again. Will I encounter yet another (Western) church that sees me as "the other," only to convert or to "civilize"? Will I be a perpetual stranger, even amongst my fellow sisters and brothers in Christ?

[One] Sunday, I stepped into the Franciscan church in my neighborhood. Being a first-timer, I sat at the back trying to be inconspicuous. Halfway through the service, a collection was taken. I didn't realize there was a second collection, so when the offering bag came round again, I could only smile sheepishly at the verger. Afterwards, I noticed him walking back towards me. Then he leaned over and quietly asked if I would like to carry the Eucharist to the priest. I was astonished. At the previous church, it had taken almost two years before I was "allowed" to help with the Communion. Not being Catholic, I had to say no, but I was deeply touched and honored by his simple gesture. It didn't matter who I was or where I'd come from. I didn't have to prove anything to him. What mattered was that I was there, a part of the worshiping body, and I had something to offer.

Yes, I suppose I am an immigrant. But an accidental one. My faith journey, corresponding with the physical movements from one country to another, has been rich and surprising. I remember how acutely I used to wish for that one special place I could genuinely call "home"; then I realized how privileged I am to be able to call many places "home." As a Christian, the church has been a major reason for that sense of security and hopefulness I feel no matter where I am in the world. As an immigrant, however—with the evangelical world only feeling increasingly more exclusive and alienating to me—I'm not so sure.

The De-Europeanization of American Christianity

Few would question the fact that the massive immigrant influx is rapidly changing the face of American Christianity. Only 19 percent of new immigrants identified themselves as Protestant, according to the 1996 data, considerably less than the estimated percentage within the native population (roughly 61 percent).[59] Yet the impact of the new immigrants on American Protestantism is considerable. In thousands of churches and Christian communities across the country, the language of worship, theological orientation, and modes of interaction draw on decidedly foreign elements and seek to replicate non-Western preferences.

In 2000, 51 percent of the foreign-born population in the United States were from Latin America (up from 9.4 percent in 1960).[60] The tremendous growth of the Hispanic population continues to fuel the establishment of increasing numbers of Latino-oriented churches in many major Christian traditions. By 1998 there were seven thousand Hispanic/Latino Protestant congregations nationwide, most of them Pentecostal and/or evangelical.[61] But the fastest-growing churches in America over the last two decades have been Korean. By 1990, there were over two thousand Korean congregations belonging to various Protestant denominations nationwide; more than eight hundred can be found in Southern California alone.[62] The recently formed Korean Presbyterian Church in America has more than two hundred congregations throughout the country; and the three hundred ethnic Korean congregations in the Presbyterian Church (USA) "represent the fastest-growing sector of that denomination."[63]

---

59. See *American Pietism in the 21st Century*, 8. According to this study, American Protestantism comprises mainline Protestants (22.1 percent), evangelical Protestants (33.6 percent), and black Protestants (5 percent).

60. See "Region and Country or Area of Birth of the Foreign-Born Population: 1960 to 1990," U.S. Census Bureau, 1999; "United States: Stock of Foreign-Born Population by Country of Birth as a Percentage of Total Foreign Born, 1995 to 2005," Migration Policy Institute, 2006.

61. R. Stephen Warner, "Immigration and Religious Communities in the United States," in *Gatherings in Diaspora: Religious Communities and the New Immigration*, ed. R. Stephen Warner and Judith G. Wittner (Philadelphia: Temple University Press, 1998), 5.

62. Rodriguez, *Tamed Spaces*, 15.

63. R. Stephen Warner, "The Place of the Congregation in the Contemporary American Reli-

The Korean and Hispanic examples illustrate a much wider trend. Across all Protestant groups (mainline or evangelical), the new congregations or "ethnic" churches formed by the new immigrants have produced new fervor and growth along with unprecedented cultural diversity. Within the Lutheran Church Missouri Synod "ethnic" congregations increased from 48 in 1998 to 204 in 2004, and new U.S. Christian and Missionary Alliance congregations worship in twenty-eight languages every Sunday.[64] Since 1993, adds Edith Blumhofer, the Assemblies of God "has closed, on average, more than 40 majority-white congregations each year while opening an annual average of 87 ethnic churches."[65]

The impact of the new immigrants on American Christianity is even more conspicuous in the case of Roman Catholicism, the church with the most enduring ties to immigrant communities. By the 1980s, most of the nation's larger Catholic dioceses were losing numbers and closing schools.[66] Post-1965 immigration has helped to reverse this trend. According to the 1996 data, the five top countries of origin for Catholic immigrants are Mexico (27.6 percent), the Philippines (12.6), Poland (7.4), the Dominican Republic (6.1), and Vietnam (5.5).[67] Even more important, the proportion of new Christian immigrants who identified themselves as Catholic (42 percent) was much higher than that among the native population (22 percent).

Latinos now account for a third of all Catholics in the United States, and studies indicate that this Latino segment will continue to rise for the foreseeable future.[68] Even if one must allow for large post-immigration defections to vibrant charismatic churches—a high proportion of Hispanic evangelicals (43 percent) are converts from Catholicism[69]—the huge boost provided by massive Hispanic immigration is a major reason why the Roman Catholic Church in the United States has avoided the fate of Catholicism in Europe (which has reportedly declined by more than 30 percent in the last twenty-five years).[70] In Los Angeles, where Catholicism is the most common faith among newcomers, there are now more Catholics than there are Episcopalians nationally; also, white Catholics are considerably outnumbered by both Latino Catholics (who make up 70 percent) and Asian Catholics.[71]

Perhaps even more significant than the numerical impact of massive Hispanic immigration is the fact that it is also transforming Catholicism in America through distinctive cultural expressions of Catholicism. By 1998, Mass was being celebrated in Spanish in some thirty-five hundred Catholic parishes throughout

---

gious Configuration," in *American Congregations*, ed. James P. Wind and James Welborn Lewis (Chicago: University of Chicago Press, 1998), 57, 77.

64. Edith Blumhofer, "The New Evangelicals: They Don't Think Like Billy Graham," *Wall Street Journal*, February 18, 2005.

65. Ibid.

66. Rodriguez, *Tamed Spaces*, 12.

67. Jasso et al., "Exploring the Religious Preferences of Recent Immigrants," 226.

68. *Changing Faiths*, 12-13; cf. Putnam, *Bowling Alone*, 76.

69. *Changing Faiths*, 39.

70. Osnos, "Islam Shaping a New Europe."

71. See Rodriguez, *Tamed Spaces*, 12.

the United States.[72] The rise in the number of Hispanic churches/parishes shows no signs of slowing down soon. Not only do they serve a sizable and surging foreign-born population, but they are also quite popular among native-born Catholics: 77 percent of immigrants attend churches with a strong Hispanic orientation, and so do 48 percent of native-born Catholics. In Los Angeles county, reports Gregory Rodriguez, roughly three-quarters of the archdiocese's parishes have at least one Mass in Spanish.[73] But Hispanic churches represent only one of a broad array of ethnic constituencies within the Los Angeles archdiocese. Mass is celebrated each week in forty-two different languages using thirty-eight distinct liturgies.

The new immigrants also bring with them new devotional expressions and spirituality. Stephen Warner writes that Latino piety "is more devotional, more home-centered and less parish-centered, more visual and less verbal than the rites inspired by Vatican II."[74] In Southern California, thanks to a huge Hispanic population, "nearly every grocery store stocks devotional candles for the home," and "images of the Virgin of Guadalupe, the patroness of Mexico, are painted on walls in Mexican neighborhoods."[75] Moreover, rites and feast days are more likely to reflect the inculturation of "pre-Christian symbols and traditions" from the Latin American world—a potent reminder for white Christians of the degree to which primal spirituality is also reflected in Western religious observances. Furthermore, 54 percent of Hispanic Catholics identify themselves as charismatics who, in addition to the traditional Catholic teachings, emphasize recurrent spiritual renewal, the in-filling of the Holy Spirit, divine healing, prophecies, speaking in tongues, and divine revelation. Charismatic believers are more than twice as prevalent among Latino immigrants as among non-Latino Catholics.[76]

In sum, the impact of new Christian immigrants and their descendants on American Christianity is profound and far-reaching. The majority are, broadly speaking, evangelical in faith and practice. This means among other things that they are Bible believing, emphasize evangelism (or conversion through faith in Jesus Christ), uphold strict moral lifestyles, and affirm divine intervention in daily life. But the fact that a goodly proportion of the immigrant Christians can be described as evangelical does not mean that their religious practices and institutions can be seamlessly absorbed (or assimilated) into Anglo-American evangelical Protestantism. Indeed, their presence exposes the erroneousness of indiscriminately applying Western categories or labels to non-Western phenomena. The overtly evangelical ethos of non-Western Christianities reflects the dominance of evangelical initiatives within the Western missionary movement, which took the message of the gospel to distant lands. But the forms of Christianity that prevail in Africa, Asia, and Latin America have been decisively shaped by the experiences, priorities, worldviews, and primal spirituality of those contexts.

Frequently labeled "conservative," the religiosity and social attitudes of these

72. Warner, "Immigration and Religious Communities in the United States," 5.
73. See Rodriguez, *Tamed Spaces*, 12.
74. Warner, "Coming to America," 23.
75. Rodriguez, *Tamed Spaces*, 12.
76. *Changing Faiths*.

new Christian immigrants are much more complex. While their religious life reflects familiar attitudes on biblical authority and sexual morality, it also often incorporates indigenous traditions, a distinctive spirituality, and a much stronger communal (less individualistic) ethos. Warner notes that "family practices, gender attitudes and sexual mores are typically more supportive of parents' prerogatives, less in tune with feminist assumptions, and decidedly less accepting of homo-sexuality than is the case for many white American religious communities."[77] On the whole, the new immigrant Christians "are expressing their Christianity in languages, customs, and independent churches that are barely recognizable, and often controversial, for European-ancestry Catholics and Protestants."[78] More-over, coming from countries with a history of colonialism and societies plagued by social injustice and political oppression, the new Christian immigrants (and their descendants) tend to be decidedly "liberal" on political and economic issues. Indeed, Blumhofer (2005) observes that they "have very little time for the much-publicized conservative interests that mobilize white middle-class church members" and "often pour money and energy into programs focused on their countries of origin."

The distinct forms of Christianity modeled in immigrant communities will undoubtedly undergo processes of adaptation and change (beyond the superfi-cial adoption of English language); and the end products are certain to differ in important ways from the original versions. In this sense at least, they reflect a form of mission in which the church is "born anew," not merely transplanted through "expansion." At the same time, forces of transnationalism and transmi-gration will help to sustain synergy between new and old. Thus, a seminal essay on the subject concluded that while many immigrants adapt their religions to the social conditions of the host country, the overall impact is what might be termed the *de-Europeanizing* of American Christianity.[79]

Assessing the Missionary Function of
the New Christian Immigrant Congregations

I have argued in this study that, owing to the pervasive religiosity of non-Western societies, South–North migration movement is essentially a religious movement. Insofar as it involves Christians, however, this movement is also a missionary movement, based on the fundamental premise that *every Christian migrant is a potential missionary.* For those who are attentive to the new reality, it is clear that "missionary initiatives from the churches in Asia, Africa, and Latin America are at the cutting edge of the Christian world mission."[80] Yet, for reasons outlined at the beginning of this chapter, the notion of non-Western missionary initia-tives impacting Western society goes against the grain, even though missionary

---

77. Warner, "Coming to America," 23.
78. Ebaugh and Chafetz, *Religion and the New Immigrants,* 14.
79. Yang and Ebaugh, "Transformations in New Immigrant Religions," 271 (emphasis added).
80. Shenk, "Recasting Theology of Mission," 98.

initiatives from the old heartlands of Europe and North America may already be of diminishing significance. Nonetheless, precisely because the heartlands of global Christianity are now in the South, contemporary South–North migrations form the taproot of a major non-Western missionary movement. The new Christian immigrants and their descendants will clearly have a lasting impact on the American religious landscape. How that impact also translates into a missionary encounter is indicated by a number of considerations.

First and foremost, the new immigrant congregations are performing a vital missionary function by their very presence. Migration, it must be said, can cause or contribute to erosion of faith: long-term isolation can weaken religious allegiance; alternative religious systems may become more attractive; marrying someone of a different faith can lead to abandonment of old belief systems; the sheer busyness and pressures of life in Western society can interfere with regular Sunday worship. But it is a well-attested fact that the experience of migration (even planned movement) tends to intensify religious consciousness, foster religious commitment, and increase the possibilities of religious conversion.[81] As Timothy Smith put it, "migration [is] often a theologizing experience" (1978: 1175). And the large numbers of converts won by immigrant churches, primarily from within the immigrant population, testify to their missionary function.

Interestingly, Wolfe provides the most widely used data in this regard.[82] He reports that while Christians make up only 25 percent of South Korea's population, some 75 percent of Korean Americans are Christian. This disparity is only partly explained by the fact that a high proportion of immigrants from South Korea are urban, educated, and Christian. A goodly percentage become Christians after they arrive in the United States. High rates of conversion to Christianity are recorded also among Taiwanese and Chinese immigrants. Only 2 percent of the Taiwanese population is Christian; yet 25 to 30 percent of Taiwanese immigrants in the United States are Christian, and as many as two-thirds of the members of Taiwanese Christian congregations are converts. According to the New Immigrant Survey, the highest proportion of immigrants who reported "no religion" originated from the former Soviet Union (23 percent) and China (22 percent). However, Chinese immigrants in America find Christianity more attractive than Buddhism or Daoism, the most popular traditional faiths in mainland China.[83] By 1988, the United States had seven hundred Chinese Protestant churches.

Of course, the ethnic factor and language barrier not only confine the ministry and outreach of most immigrant congregations to specific national groups, but they also help to explain the high conversion rate these congregations enjoy. Yet, even by evangelizing other immigrants—many of whom are far more open to religious conversion than they were before they migrated and would not otherwise be won to the Christian faith—these congregations represent a cutting edge of Christian growth in America. *They are Christianizing groups whom Ameri-*

81. See Ebaugh and Chafetz, *Religion and the New Immigrants*, 401.
82. Wolfe, *Transformation of American Religion*, 111.
83. Rodriguez, *Tamed Spaces*, 15.

can missionary agencies expend enormous amounts of resources and effort to reach in distant lands, often with modest results.

Second, the new immigrant congregations represent the face of Christianity to a goodly proportion of the nation's disadvantaged and marginalized population. As American Pentecostal-charismatic churches have struggled to maintain membership numbers or decamped to the suburbs (reflecting white-flight from the nation's cities), charismatic immigrant congregations are increasingly filling in the void. Predominantly located in urban neighborhoods and often forced to occupy the most unlikely places—cramped living rooms, hotel ballrooms, thousands of storefronts, rented halls or office buildings, even ornate churches whose membership has declined—they serve constituencies (both immigrant and native) long abandoned by more established and affluent American congregations. Often they represent the main forms of evangelical ministry and outreach within the areas and sections of the American population least impacted by the dominant culture.

This type of missionary engagement is typically described as "incarnational." It may also be termed *witness as withness* (see also p. 365 below).[84] This approach to mission reflects the experience of Christians who grow up in contexts of religious plurality (where all too often Christianity exists as a minority faith) and are accustomed to relational, non-confrontational, forms of proclaiming their faith. Where Western missions are deeply marked by a focus on distinction and difference (territorial, cultural, and racial), the non-Western approach is prompted by quite dissimilar contexts and understanding of the church and focuses on acceptance of diversity and interpersonal exchange. This form of witness emphasizes effective presence and participation as the basis for proclamation (1 Pet 3:15, 16).

Third, the new Christian immigrants encounter a society in which Christianity has suffered considerable decline in numbers and influence, where also there is no longer a dominant or cohesive religious "mainstream." Not only that, many of the new immigrants also hail from centers of vibrant Christian growth—including some who come from countries with a minority Christian population, like Korea and China—and they embody a brand of Christianity that is strongly evangelistic or conversionist. This makes it more likely (compared to late-nineteenth and early-twentieth-century European immigrants) that their congregations will develop specific strategies for effective cross-cultural outreach or mission beyond fixed ethnic constituencies. Quite frankly, America's diminished (or diminishing) "Christian" condition makes its easier to conceive of it less and less in terms of its missionary-sending heritage and more and more in terms of its missionary needs. As we shall see, the notion of America as a major "mission field" is well entrenched among African immigrant pastors and their congregations. This new perspective is another major reason why the new

---

84. I owe this phrase to Martha Fredericks, who uses it to describe Anglican Christian witness, involving the establishment of a Christian village (Kristikunda) among the Muslim Fula and Madinka peoples in the Gambia. "The witness," she writes, "took the form of with-ness, a qualified presence" (Martha T. Frederiks, *We Have Toiled All Night: Christianity in the Gambia 1465-2000* [Zoetermeer: Boekencentrum, 2003], 326).

immigrant congregations are likely to serve a missionary purpose beyond cultural self-maintenance and renegotiation of self-identity.

Fourth, the new immigrant congregations are more attuned to religious plurality than American Christians are. Post-1965 immigration has transformed the United States into the most religiously diverse nation on earth. This means that the greatest challenges to the church's witness will come from growing secularism as well as from a new and vibrant religious plurality. The number of secularists is growing, to be sure. Indeed some interpret the fact that 15 percent of the new immigrants report no religion (compared to 12 percent of the native-born population) as an indication that immigration may also, paradoxically, contribute to the growth of secularism.[85] But the rise in religious conversion among the new immigrants after their arrival in the United States and the large numbers of native-born Americans who convert to the religions that the immigrants bring with them to the United States (Islam and Buddhism, in particular) represent strong countertrends.

In the event, religious plurality is a new experience for the vast majority of Americans (including American Christians); and it presents unprecedented challenges to the American church in terms of its mission and self-understanding. A goodly proportion of the new Christian immigrants, on the other hand, hail from countries where the life of faith is forged in settings marked by daily interaction with other major faiths. Living next door to an avid Muslim or Hindu family is not a new experience for them, nor is waking to the sounds of the minaret—indeed, some might welcome its familiar tones. The capacity of these growing and dynamic Christian immigrant groups to maintain effective Christian witness in the face of religious plurality enhances their missionary capacity.

Secularist skeptics who expect proxy "clash of civilizations" between Nigerian Christians and Nigerian Muslims in downtown Dallas or Chicago, for instance, will be sorely disappointed. For one thing, this saturnine expectation ignores the fact that religious plurality in many parts of the world is not attended by the specter of "crusade." For another, the economic and political considerations that lie at the root of religio-ethnic conflicts in places like northern Nigeria are simply not present in America. If anything, what should keep secularists awake at night is the likelihood that sincere Christians and devout Muslims will make common cause against the secularist agenda.

Fifth, like thousands of immigrant communities before them, the new immigrant congregations represent centers of change and transition. In this case, however, the much stronger forces of transnationalism greatly enhance their capacity for sustained missionary engagement not only with American society but also within the wider global context. Given America's heavily segmented social landscape and the prospects of continued immigrant influx through social networks and family reunification, the new immigrant churches will remain urban-based for the foreseeable future. This means that they will continue to inhabit the most strategic intersections of mobility, dynamism, and change within American society. As veritable centers of transmigration or transnationalism, immigrant

---

85. See Jasso et al., "Exploring the Religious Preferences of Recent Immigrants," 218, 222.

congregations have great potential to play a critical role in global Christian missions. Many African immigrant pastors, for instance, find that living in America produces avenues and resources for global outreach unavailable to them before they moved. Writes Afe Adogame:

> The significance of local and global networks among African churches in both home and host contexts cannot be overemphasized. Such networks are assuming increasing importance for African migrants. The range and nature of ties include new ecumenical affiliations, pastoral exchanges between Africa, Europe, and the US, special events and conferences, prayer networks, internet sites, international ministries, publications, audio/video, and tele-evangelism. The "flow" between the links is two-directional, sending and receiving—globally and locally.[86]

The possibility that the missionary function of the new Christian immigrant congregations will fade after the first generation is worthy of brief comment. Dorothy Bass reminds us that deliberate efforts to transmit particular traditions from one generation to the next take place not only in immigrant congregations but in all American congregations.[87] But perhaps more than most, immigrant churches are typically sites of intergenerational conflict and cultural tension. While the new immigrants and their descendants are nurtured by the spirituality and cultural values brought from their homelands, they also experience the pull of cultural adaptation—more intensely so among the younger members or generation. But the likelihood that the new immigrants and their descendants will experience selective assimilation, in which varied patterns of acculturation produce divergent outcomes between different immigrant groups and even within the same group (see discussion on pp. 247-48 above), makes the question of how well immigrant descendants will maintain the religious commitment of their parents quite complex.

Undoubtedly, some immigrants are only too eager to discard restrictive or exploitative traditional customs in favor of secular liberal values, though many soon discover that such assimilative moves do not immunize them against xenophobic intolerance or racial rejection. But immigrants who abandon their culture in favor of efforts at wholesale assimilation are unlikely to be found within immigrant churches in any significant numbers. Immigrant congregations almost by definition function as cultural centers where immigrants nurture ethnic connections, intentionally preserve aspects of their cultural values, and socialize the next generation. Yet they also attract because they provide immigrants with a safe place from which to negotiate adaptation and incorporation into American

---

86. Afe Adogame, "Contesting the Ambivalences of Modernity in a Global Context: The Redeemed Christian Church of God, North America," *Studies in World Christianity,* vol. 10, no. 1 (2005): 29.

87. Dorothy C. Bass, "Congregations and the Bearing of Traditions," in *American Congregations,* ed. James P. Wind and James Welborn Lewis (Chicago: University of Chicago Press, 1998), 178. These, she explains, often involve some form of schooling—Sunday schools, Bible classes, Catholic parochial schools, Hebrew schools, and so on. Even the home school movement, popular among some evangelical groups, reflects efforts to shape the next generation.

society.[88] In other words, the new immigrant churches play multiple roles within the immigrant community. But perhaps the most important factor in the ability of the new immigrant congregations to preserve and pass on their religious commitment to the next generation is transnationalism.

The congregations and communities established by the new immigrants are more strongly enmeshed in transnational networks than those of earlier immigrants. The strength and durability of transnational networks vary among the foreign-born population, but, as argued in chapter 8, transnational networks will likely shape the assimilation pattern of immigrant children and help to foster enduring ethnic identities. We have also seen that transnationalism is particularly vital among African migrants not only because African life and societies are marked by strong social ties but also because Africans invariably experience social marginalization and other forms of discrimination in Western societies, which impede full integration (see pp. 227-28 above). For many, this state of affairs engenders or reinforces continued interest in, and the maintenance of strong connections with, the homeland. This trend will be further reinforced by continued increase in the number of countries that sanction dual citizenship.

By reinforcing the capacity for African migrants to remain key actors in the socioeconomic and political life of their respective home countries even when they become full-fledged citizens of foreign countries, dual citizenship could have far-reaching implications for the African encounter with Western societies. It bolsters transnationalism, potentially transforms the experience of assimilation by strengthening cultural identity or ancestral ties, and may well prove critical in identity formation among second-generation immigrants. Sustained access to African homelands will also shape the long-term impact of the African missionary movement. Perhaps most important of all, insofar as it buttresses transnational identities and transmigration, such measures will significantly extend the transformational capacity of the African missionary movement within global Christianity, not least because it will act as a conduit of ideas, experiences, and influences between different worlds.

The rest of this book is devoted to detailed examination of African (Christian) immigrants in the United States: their profile, assimilation patterns, religious congregations, troubled relations with African Americans, and their missionary engagement with American society. African immigrants in the United States remain one of the least studied groups, and the significance of their rapidly proliferating religious communities within the American religious landscape has received little scholarly attention.[89] Yet a number of factors point to their significance:

- the prominence of Africa and Africans within contemporary migration
- the emergence of Africa as a major heartland of contemporary Christianity

---

88. See Rodriguez, *Tamed Spaces*, 15.

89. The volume edited by Jacob K. Olupona and Regina Gemignani, *African Immigrant Religions in America* (2007), is the first major publication on the growth and significance of African immigrant religious communities (Christian and Muslim).

- the fact that the United States is now the primary destination for Africans who migrate to Western industrial nations
- the fact that African foreign-born (mainly from West Africa) constitute one of the fastest growing immigrant groups in the United States
- the interesting possibility that the presence of a sizable African American population will shape the assimilation patterns, social mobility, community formation, and religious impact of the new African immigrants.

It is no secret that African immigrant churches are among the fastest growing because they reproduce or exhibit the same vitality and dynamism that are present in the homelands of immigrant members and also because they draw on a widening base of immigrants hungry for religious association and participation. Less well known is the fact that African immigrant congregations also represent a prominent example of how South–North migration provides the structure and impetus for a full-fledged, if largely unstructured, non-Western missionary movement.

13

On the Road with the Ancestors

America's New African Immigrants

> Coming from where he did, he was turned away from every door like
> Joseph. . . .
>   He didn't know what it was to be black 'til they gave him his
> change but didn't want to touch his hand.
>   To even the toughest among us that would be too much.
> —Helen Folasade Adu ("Sade"), *Immigrant* (2000)

The presence of Africans in the United States dates to the period of slavery (1619-1865) and constituted the second major immigration wave in America's history (see chapter 9). The forcible transplantation of African slaves to American plantations formed part of an Atlantic trading system known as the "Triangular Slave Trade." It was so named because it took the form of a triangular system that straddled the Atlantic. Each side of this trading system generated tremendous profits for European merchants: The three sides involved were (1) the export of cheap manufactured goods from Europe to Africa; (2) the purchase of captured slaves on the African Coast and their transportation across the Atlantic, where they were exchanged for minerals and foodstuffs in the West Indies and Americas; (3) finally, the sale of slave-grown American and West Indian products (notably sugar and tobacco) to European markets.

The first African slaves arrived in Virginia in 1619. For the next 250 years, enslavement and brutal oppression were the norm for Africans living in the United States. Slavery and slave ownership became solidly entrenched in American society, and the church was fully complicit in its enforcement. Exactly how many of the estimated ten to twelve million African slaves who landed in the New World were dispatched to plantations in the American colonies (later the United States) is impossible to say. By 1800, America had one of the largest communities of Africans anywhere in the world outside Africa. In 1790, when the first census was taken, Africans numbered about 760,000 or 19 percent of the population. By 1865, when slavery was officially abolished with the passage of the Thirteenth Amendment to the U.S. Constitution, there were roughly 4.5 million Africans in the United States (about 14 percent of the population).

Within the burgeoning African population in the United States there emerged impulses and movements that acted back on the African continent. Arguably the most significant were the ideologies and missionary initiatives that flowed out of the black religious experience and contributed important elements to the development of modern African Christianity. From the start, black Christianity in the United States evinced a strong missionary consciousness that was supremely expressed in a desire "to win Africa not only for Africans, but for Christ, by mass emigrations from the West and by forging bonds of friendship and collaboration between Africans and African-Americans."[1] This missionary impulse stimulated emigration by individual blacks, the vast majority of whom went under the auspices of the American Colonization Society (ACS) established in 1816 with the express aim of "civilizing and Christianizing Africa through the instrumentality of emigrants from the United States."[2] In 1821, the ACS founded a colony for freed American blacks on the west coast of Africa. It was given the name Liberia.

In the final analysis, the number of African Americans who went to Africa as missionaries was fairly small (see pp. 283-85 above), and the black missionary impulse went into terminal decline after the Great Depression of the 1930s. It must also be acknowledged that, with few exceptions, black emigrants and missionaries invariably saw themselves as representatives of Western civilization and shared the extremely negative views of African cultures prevalent among their white counterparts, even if they must be credited, as Wilmore insists, with trying to accomplish abroad "what they could scarcely do for themselves at home."[3] Indeed, in Liberia, the attitudes of cultural superiority and social distance assumed by the black settlers hardened into enduring sociopolitical divisions that contributed to the recent brutal civil war (1989-1996). American blacks in Liberia viewed Christianity "as a badge of their higher status, many settlers were opposed to the idea of incorporating the indigenous population into their communities."[4] Yet, quite paradoxically, this black transatlantic movement brought with it ideological influences, notably Ethiopianism, which presented African Christians in the colonial context with a potent instrument of religious protest and resistance to white colonial domination.

The concept of "Ethiopianism" (derived from the biblical use of "Ethiopia" to describe black Africa) emerged out of the black experience in the New World as a symbolic expression of racial identification, spiritual aspirations, and religious protest. As an ideology, Ethiopianism embodied affirmation of the African heritage (including a celebration of the ancient African churches), rejection of white domination or racial oppression, and a conviction that Africans must take the lead in the Christianization of the African continent. As a movement, Ethiopianism championed racial equality, defended African capa-

---

1. Gayraud S. Wilmore, *Black Religion and Black Radicalism: An Interpretation of the Religious History of African Americans* (Maryknoll, NY: Orbis Books, 1998), 126.

2. See Joseph R. Coan, "Redemption of Africa: The Vital Impulse of Black American Overseas Missionaries," *The Journal of the Interdenominational Theological Center* 1, no. 2 (Spring 1974): 28; Sanneh, *Abolitionists Abroad*, 192-203.

3. Gayraud S. Wilmore, "Black Americans in Mission: Setting the Record Straight," *International Bulletin of Missionary Research* 10 (July 1986): 98-102.

4. See Peter B. Clarke, *West Africa and Christianity* (London: Edward Arnold, 1986), 40.

bility, and called for the formation of a genuine African Christianity (at least one freed from imposed European forms and control). It also anticipated the conversion of the entire African continent to Christianity as part of an "Africa for Africans" campaign. In West Africa, the two men who emerged as leaders of the earliest prophet-healing movements had been solidly exposed to Ethiopian ideals: William Wadé Harris (1860-1929) was closely associated with Edward Blyden (the most masterful advocate of Ethiopianism in West Africa) prior to the events that triggered his remarkable ministry; and the movement spearheaded by Garrick Sokari Braide (c. 1882-1918) was condemned as resurgent Ethiopianism. In South Africa, Isaiah Shembe (d. 1935), founder of the Zulu-based Ama-Nazaretha movement, was originally a member of the African Native Baptist Church linked to Ethiopianism.[5]

This movement provided inspiration for many of Africa's religious innovators in the colonial era. Its ideals arguably found realization in the emergence and phenomenal growth of African initiated churches (commonly AICs) which were most prominent in the areas where the Ethiopian movement was strongest. Moreover, its critique of the European missionary project and calls for African forms of Christianity anticipated, by almost a century, the emergence of third world theologies and calls (in the 1970s) for a moratorium on Western missions. Ethiopianism has a lot to do with the transformation of Christianity in Africa from a religion identified with Western culture and hegemony into a popular African religious movement. Above all, it enshrined a prophetic vision that is now being fulfilled in the momentous rise of African Christianity and its new global missionary initiatives. Strikingly, these new African missionary initiatives (from Africa to America) also involve emigration and mission. Ethiopianism has come full circle.

Introducing America's New Africans

Apart from the establishment of the Liberian settlement in 1821, America had no formal ties with the African continent during the colonial period. Founded by private philanthropic interests, Liberia was not a colonial project, and it became the first African settlement to secure its political independence when its American settlers declared it a republic in June 1847. The lack of formal colonial ties is one reason very few Africans visited the United States during the nineteenth century—at a time when a goodly number of Africans (from West Africa) went to Britain to be trained as doctors, lawyers, even printers, when also wealthy African merchants visited England at their own expense. Even after emancipation in 1865, the inflow of Africans to the United States remained insignificant. In the final decades of the nineteenth century, from 1870 to 1900, only 1,565

---

5. For more on Ethiopianism, see George Shepperson, "Ethiopianism: Past and Present," in *Christianity in Tropical Africa*, ed. Christian G. Baëta (London: Oxford University Press, 1968), 249-64; Hanciles, *Euthanasia of a Mission*, 147-95; Chirenje, *Ethiopianism and Afro-Americans in Southern Africa*; Kalu, "Ethiopianism in African Christianity."

Africans entered the United States (see fig. 9)—an average of roughly fifty a year. Between 1900 and 1950, the numbers improve considerably to an average of 625 a year. But, at 0.2 percent of total immigration, the African element remained inconsequential—Chinese immigrants were three times the number of Africans. Moreover, few immigrants from Africa were black Africans; the majority were from Egypt and South Africa.[6]

Figure 9

African Immigration to the United States (1820-2000)

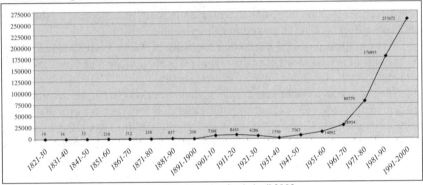

Source: Based on USCIS "Yearbook of Immigration Statistics," 2003.

Not until the 1960s, in the wake of African independence, do the numbers of African immigrants to the United States increase appreciably. U.S. immigration data do not indicate the proportion of immigrants who are white, but based on the countries of origin of the *African foreign-born* in the United States during the 1960s and 1970s,[7] it is reasonable to conjecture that African immigration to the United States remained predominantly white—many presumably fleeing black rule or black liberation struggles on the continent.[8] Some 65 to 80 percent of the African foreign-born in the United States for that period came from northern Africa (mainly Egypt), South Africa, and Cape Verde.[9]

Black Africans began to feature prominently in the African migration to the United States after the 1970s, when the flow of African immigrants increased

---

6. April Gordon, "The New Diaspora: African Immigration to the United States," *Journal of Third World Studies* 15, no. 1 (1998): 84.

7. In the U.S. census data, "foreign-born" describes those within the population who were not citizens at birth. It covers those classified as immigrants (legal or illegal) as well as naturalized citizens.

8. Gordon, "New Diaspora," 84.

9. Campbell J. Gibson and Emily Lennon, "Historical Census Statistics on the Foreign-Born Population of the United States: 1850-1990," U.S. Bureau of the Census, 1999. Cape Verde has a huge foreign population, and it is safe to assume that Cape Verdean migrants to the United States would be predominantly white. April Gordon explains that captains of American whaling ships began recruiting Cape Verdeans as sailors as early as the seventeenth century, and many later settled in the United States ("New Diaspora," 93).

most dramatically. The number of African immigrants admitted to the United States during the decade of the 1970s increased by 64 percent over the previous decade, and the influx continued to rise sharply (see figure 9). In the closing decade of the twentieth century, thirty-eight thousand Africans were admitted annually on average—a higher level of African intake than at any other time in America's history (including the period of slavery).[10] By 2003, African immigrants accounted for 7 percent of all immigrants admitted to the United States (up from 2.3 percent in 1990).[11] In 2002 alone, when the volume of African immigration reached a record high, 60,269 Africans were admitted into the United States—more than double the number admitted during the entire decade of the 1960s (or 75 percent of the total admittance from 1971 to 1980).

Time and Tide

A number of complex factors, reviewed in previous chapters, help to account for the dramatic increase in the level of African migration to the United States after 1970. During the slave-trade era, the African population in the United States grew faster than anywhere else outside Africa. But, because of America's lack of external intervention in Africa during the colonial era, postcolonial African migrations to America were a mere trickle compared to Europe. In addition, until the oil crisis of the early 1970s, European powers actively recruited African labor from their former (or existing) colonies to help rebuild economies devastated by the Second World War. But, as we have seen, deep racial tensions and mounting anti-immigration reactions—against "unassimilable" nonwhite populations—caused former colonial powers to take vigorous steps, from the 1970s, to limit or stem African immigration. Significantly, Europe's declining need for African labor migrants and its anti-immigration backlash coincided with the deepening of African political troubles and economic woes, which generated an unprecedented flood of international migrants.

The flow of African migrants to Europe remained high—with family reunification, refugee movement, and illegal overstays forming the greater proportion. Migrants from drought-prone northern Africa became especially prominent. But, with emigration to Europe increasingly difficult, the 1965 amendment to U.S. Immigration policy had an impact on African migration flows as powerful as that generated by European colonial linkage.[12] (For more on the 1965 amendment, see pp. 234-35 above.) The impact was not immediate. Until the 1970s, Europe

---

10. For a similar conclusion, see Joel Millman, *The Other Americans: How Immigrants Renew Our Country, Our Economy, and Our Values* (New York: Penguin Books, 1998), 179.

11. "Yearbook of Immigration Statistics," United States Citizenship and Immigration Services, 2003.

12. This amendment abolished the forty-year-old national origins quota system under which 82 percent of visas went to northern and western Europe, 16 percent to southern and eastern Europe, and 2 percent to the rest of the world. It also eliminated national origin, race, or ancestry as a basis for immigration to the United States. It stressed family reunification, provided for 120,000 immigrants from the Western Hemisphere, 170,000 from the rest of the world (outside the Americas no country was to exceed 20,000), though this limit was not applied to the Western Hemisphere.

(and wealthier African nations like Nigeria and South Africa) remained the logical destinations for international African migrants. Moreover, the 1965 amendment privileged family reunification, which had limited benefits for potential African immigrants—in 1960 the African foreign-born community in America was tiny (fewer than forty thousand) and predominantly white. In fact, while the 1965 amendment laid the dominant framework that still governs U.S. immigration policy today, subsequent immigration legislation was in some ways far more critical for the post-1970s rise in African migrants.

The Refugee Act of 1980 is a case in point. Prior to this act, the U.S. definition of "refugee" was narrowly applied to persons fleeing countries with a communist government or the Middle East. Thus, Cubans and Nicaraguans were recognized as refugees or asylum seekers but not Haitians or Salvadorians fleeing oppressive and despotic regimes. The 1980 act was intended to change this skewed definition to conform to the United Nations Protocol on the Status of Refugees. It also provided for fifty thousand refugee visas annually (with provisions for exceeding that limit). The new policies contributed to an increase in African immigration, even if refugee approval was largely determined by U.S. foreign interests and Cold War politics. This helps explain why, despite the fact that the largest proportion of the world's refugees were African, the vast majority approved by the United States from 1987 to 2001 came from Communist Southeast Asia (27 percent) and Eastern Europe (49 percent). Throughout the entire period (1985-2005), at a time when African societies were convulsed by political upheavals and accounted for 27.5 percent of the world's total refugee population,[13] African refugees accounted for only 6 percent of the U.S. total.

Over time, the number of African refugees approved for settlement in the United States increased appreciably from 1,974 (or 3 percent of the total) in 1987 to 20,014 (30 percent of the total) in 2000. But, of those admitted, the majority—35 percent of the 1991-2000 total—were from Marxist Ethiopia.[14] And the high number of Somali refugees reflects America's fateful involvement in Somalia's protracted and messy civil war in the early 1990s.

Meanwhile, the extensive and diverse influx of nonwhite immigrants made possible by the 1965 amendment triggered nativist and anti-immigration reactions in the United States. Rising public resentment over illegal or undocumented immigrants led to the passing of the Immigration Reform and Control Act (IRCA) in 1986. This act implemented a major amnesty program that allowed immigrants who had "resided continuously in the United States in an unlawful status" since January 1982 to legalize their status as permanent residents. It also imposed stiff fines for employment of illegal immigrants. Between 1989 and 1991, when the vast majority of applications were processed, almost 2.5 million immigrants benefited from the IRCA provisions—primarily Hispanics, who accounted for 89 percent of the total.[15] But the impact on African immigrants was quite significant. The 36,736 African immigrants who took advantage of the IRCA (between 1989 and 1991)

13. *Trends in Total Migrant Stock: The 2005 Revision.*
14. "Yearbook of Immigration Statistics."
15. "I.R.C.A. Legalization During Fiscal Years 1989 to 1991," U.S. Census Bureau, 2000.

represented roughly 9.7 percent of African immigrants in the United States. It is a sobering fact that one in ten African immigrants was in the country illegally at the time, even if a goodly number were probably visa overstayers.

The IRCA, however, fell short of intended objectives.[16] Four years later, renewed efforts to curb illegal immigration led to the 1990 Immigration Act. This act included two stipulations that had a much greater impact on African immigration than the IRCA amnesty. First, it increased the total number of immigrants admitted on the basis of skills, qualifications, and wealth to 675,000 per annum (outside family reunification) starting in 1995. Second, it launched a new "diversity" program to encourage immigration from countries with low emigration to the United States (countries that benefited little from the family reunification and labor requirements). The new program provided for fifty-five thousand diversity slots per year, to be awarded by lottery. It was gradually introduced beginning in 1992.

Africans have benefited from the new "diversity" initiative more than any other immigrant group. In the ten-year period 1996 to 2005, African immigrants represented under 6 percent of all immigrants admitted to the United States but accounted for roughly 31.5 percent of all "diversity" visas. In all, 168,219 Africans were admitted to the United States as part of this program during this period. Among the classes of admission identified within U.S. immigration data, only family reunification (admittance of "immediate relatives of U.S. citizens") has been a greater source of African immigration.

Importantly, family ties account for the bulk (62 percent) of African immigration. "Spouses" account for 17 percent of African immigrants between 1996 and 2005; and virtually all African foreign-born (98.3 percent) live in households of which 70 percent are family households and over 80 percent include a married couple.[17] Owing to the high premium that Africans in general set on education as a means of social status and economic advancement, a high proportion of family-related/sponsored immigrants are students or relatives with good prospects of pursuing advanced education. In fact, over 90 percent of African foreign-born in the United States have at least a high school education. John Arthur found that "the majority of African immigrants currently living in the United States entered the country with student visas (a nonimmigrant status), completed their education, and then overstayed their visas."[18] This also suggests that African immigration is greatly driven by young adults.

The relatively low percentage of African immigrants admitted as highly skilled professionals is striking, especially when it is considered that educational attainments among African immigrants are higher than any other immigrant group, and that 40 percent of African immigrants (aged sixteen and over) in the United States work in management and professional occupations.[19] This disparity confirms that very few African professionals are recruited outside the United

---

16. In California, for instance, discontent with illegal immigration led in 1994 to the passage of Proposition 187 aimed at curtailing illegal immigration by depriving undocumented immigrants medical and other public services and denying state resources or social services to their children.

17. "Foreign-Born Profiles," U.S. Census Bureau, 2000.

18. Arthur, *Invisible Sojourners*, 20.

19. "Foreign-Born Profiles" (2000).

States—perhaps a reflection of the weak trade and investment ties between America and African nations. In effect, most highly skilled African immigrants in the United States were originally admitted in one of the other categories (as students, refugees, family members, or through the diversity program). In the final analysis, there is no escaping the fact that while economic considerations and education aspirations are pivotal factors in African migration to the United States, the movement itself is *socially defined, network-driven, and framed by family ties or obligations.*

Clearly, post-1965 U.S. immigration policies have had a dramatic impact on the rise in African immigration, an impact that is comparable in its significance to the role that colonization has played in African migration to Europe. Cold War politics and U.S. involvement in a number of African countries—among these, Ethiopia, Egypt (recipient of massive U.S. foreign aid after the Camp David Accords), and Somalia—have contributed in great measure to the rising tide of African immigration. Yet it remains an intriguing fact of history that momentous changes in U.S. immigration policies coincided with a phenomenal tide of migrants generated by widespread political and economic cataclysms on the African continent. It is no less intriguing that the civil rights movement instigated by African Americans helped to set in motion processes that opened the way for another epochal influx of Africans in America.

Profile of America's New Africans[20]

In the U.S. census data, the term "foreign-born" is used to describe those in the population who were not citizens at birth, including "legal nonimmigrants" such as refugees, students, or those on work visas. By comparison, the term "natives" describes persons born in the United States or abroad to a parent who is a U.S. citizen. (The children of immigrants born in the United States are U.S. citizens). In what follows, the terms "foreign-born" and "immigrant" population are used interchangeably.

Africa has not been, comparatively speaking, a major source of post-1965 immigrants to the United States. From 1960 to 2000, the level of African admittance remained lower than any of the other four main regions of immigration to the United States (Europe, Asia, Latin America, and the Caribbean). In 2000, 51 percent of the foreign-born population in the United States were from Latin America (up from 9.4 percent in 1960), 25.5 percent were from Asia (up from 5.1 percent in 1960), 15.3 percent were from Europe (down from 75 percent in 1960), and 2.3 percent were from Africa (up from 0.4 percent in 1960).[21] But African immigration has risen steadily and significantly. In 1960, the African foreign-born in the United States was a puny 35,355 (0.4 percent of the entire

---

20. Unless otherwise indicated, the discussion in this section draws on data from "Profile of the Foreign-Born Population in the United States: 2000," U.S. Census Bureau, 2001.

21. See "Region and Country or Area of Birth of the Foreign-Born Population: 1960 to 1990"; "United States: Stock of Foreign-Born Population by Country of Birth as a Percentage of Total Foreign Born, 1995 to 2005."

foreign-born population). By 1980, the Africa immigrant population had more than quadrupled, and over the next two decades (by 2000) it increased by a further 250 percent. From 1996 to 2005, over half a million Africans took up legal permanent residence in the United States.[22] By 2005, the African foreign-born in the United States had grown to 1.2 million and accounted for 3.5 percent of the foreign-born population.[23] Admittance of African immigrants in 2005 alone accounted for 8 percent of the total.

The newness of African immigration affects assessment. At present, more than 80 percent of the African foreign-born population arrived in the country after 1980; and a good proportion (37 percent) had been resident in the country for less than five years. Even so, the huge rise in African immigration in recent decades means that the United States is now the chief destination of contemporary African migration. By 1990, the number of African immigrants being admitted to the United States far exceeded that of any other industrial nation. America is once again (and for the foreseeable future) home to a burgeoning population of African migrants. According to data from the *U.S. Census 2000,* the proportion of the population claiming "African" (distinct from "African American") ancestry grew by 381 percent between 1990 and 2000—a rate of growth surpassed only by those of Latin American ancestry.[24] This trend has led at least one scholar to suggest that black Africa "will likely be the last source of new Americans,"[25] a reference to the fact that the other major continents are already well represented.

The top ten source countries of African immigration to the United States for the fifteen-year period (1989-2003) are listed in fig. 10. Immigrants from Nigeria outnumber all other nationalities within the African foreign-born population, followed (in decreasing order) by Ethiopians, Egyptians, and Ghanaians. By 2005, Nigerians represented 13 percent of all Africans foreign-born legally resident in the United States.

In terms of regional representation, the majority of the African immigrant population in the United States comes from Anglophone (or ex-British colonies in) West Africa. Here, too, the growth is fairly recent—almost 60 percent of West African immigrants arrived after 1990. This surge is explainable by two key developments: first, the 1990s witnessed the eruption of calamitous civil wars, political turmoil, and economic crisis in the region; second, the quality selective emphasis of the 1990 Immigration Act (see p. 309 above) opened the way for skilled migration from a region that boasts perhaps the most extensive educational system in sub-Saharan Africa dating back to the colonial period (see pp. 225-26 above). Interestingly also, the current dominance of immigrants from West Africa evokes historical parallels to an earlier era when the majority of ✓ slaves on American plantations came from West Africa.

---

22. "2005 Yearbook of Immigration Statistics," U.S. Census Bureau, 2005.

23. "Place of Birth for the Foreign-Born Population," U.S. Census Bureau, 2006.

24. Angela Brittingham and G. Patricia de la Cruz, "Ancestry: 2000," U.S. Census Bureau, 2000, 4. To put this in perspective the average growth rate for the total population is 13 percent.

25. Millman, *Other Americans,* 192.

Figure 10

Top Ten African Countries Represented in U.S. Admittance Figures (1989-2003)

Country of Birth	1989-2003	Percentage of Total
Nigeria	105,674	17.4
Ethiopia	76,343	12.6
Egypt	67,958	11.2
Ghana	54,852	9.0
South Africa	36,736	6.1
Morocco	33,731	5.6
Somalia	30,765	5.1
Liberia	26,115	4.3
Sierra Leone	19,133	3.2
Cape Verde	13,705	2.3
Africa Total (all countries)	607,001	100.0

Source: Based on USCIS "Yearbook of Immigration Statistics," 2003.

The Fortunes of African Communities

With a median age of 36.1, the African foreign-born are among the most youthful of America's new immigrants.[26] In 2000, 12 percent were under eighteen, 8.7 percent were between the ages of eighteen and twenty-four, and 69 percent fell within the ages of twenty-five to fifty-four.[27] The low proportion of African foreign-born in the eighteen to twenty-four age range underscores the fact that African migration to the United States is dominated by persons in their prime of life—young adults and young families. Adult males outnumber adult females, but only marginally. The fact that females account for only 45 percent of the African immigrant population has a lot to do with the fact that a great proportion of female immigrants are admitted under family reunification provisions. And family reunification among the African foreign-born is in turn impacted by the low rate of naturalization among African immigrants. Naturalization significantly improves family reunification efforts; but among African immigrants who entered the country before 1980, only 14 percent had naturalized by 2000.[28]

According to the 2000 census data, the educational attainments of African foreign-born (age twenty-five and older) are the highest among all foreign-born

---

26. Only Latin Americans have a lower median age (34.2) ("Foreign-Born Profiles" [2000]).

27. There are fewer persons aged "65 and over" among African foreign-born than in any other immigrant group.

28. See "Foreign-Born Profiles" (2000). John Arthur attributes this to the "sojourner" status adopted by many African immigrants, a defiant assumption that their stay in the United States is temporary, or the "belief that one day economic and political conditions in Africa will improve and they will be able to go home" (*Invisible Sojourners*, 145).

and exceed even that of the native American population. Among African immigrants, 94.9 percent have a high school qualification or higher (compared to 67 percent among all foreign-born and 86.6 percent among the native population). About half (49.3 percent) boast a bachelor's degree or higher (compared to 25.8 percent among all foreign-born and 25.5 percent among the native population). A fairly high proportion of African immigrants (36.5 percent) are employed in the managerial or professional occupations—compared to Asians (38.7 percent) and Latin Americans (12.1 percent). Almost the same numbers of African foreign-born are employed in support (technical, sales, or administrative) and service (or maintenance) occupations—22.1 percent and 20 percent, respectively.[29] In general, the African foreign-born are more likely to be gainfully employed (70 percent) than any other immigrant group, including Europeans.[30] They are also more proficient in English than the overall foreign-born population, a quality attributable to the high proportion of African immigrants from ex-British colonies.

Despite these attainments, the average income of an African immigrant household in the United States ($36,371) is not appreciably different from that of the overall foreign-born population ($36,048). Poverty rates among African immigrants are among the lowest—13.2 percent, compared to Asian immigrants (12.8), Latin American immigrants (21.9), and Caribbean immigrants (20.6). But African immigrants are the least likely to own their own homes—38.2 percent, compared to Asian immigrants (52 percent), Latin American immigrants (41.2 percent), or Caribbean immigrants (42.6 percent).

The discrepancy between the high skill level of African immigrants (on average) and their relatively low economic achievement within American society can be explained by a number of factors. First, African immigration is the most recent. Even after twenty years of residence, immigrants are more likely than the native-born to be poor and to work in low-status jobs.[31] Second, naturalization among African foreign-born is relatively low—37 percent compared to Asian immigrants (47.1 percent), European immigrants (52 percent), Caribbean immigrants (46.5 percent), and Latin Americans (28.3 percent). Research indicates that foreign-born who become naturalized citizens have a slightly higher income on average than natives. Third, unlike all the other major immigrant groups, the new African immigrants lack an extensive and entrenched social network. This is, at least partly, a function of the multiplicity of African ethnic groups, though African immigrants also participate in social networks that transcend tribe and nationality. Still, despite sizable Nigerian and Ethiopian communities in different parts of the United States, there is no Nigeria- or Ethiopia-town.

---

29. Millman, possibly with New York in mind, notes that "Ghanaians are big in taxi driving, Nigerians in healthcare," while the Senegalese dominate commerce and petty trade (*Other Americans*, 175, 179).

30. "Foreign-Born Profiles" (2000); also Dixon, "Characteristics of the African Born in the United States."

31. Rumbaut, "Origins and Destinies," 38.

Developing Social Networks

In their groundbreaking study, Alejandro Portes and Rubén G. Rumbaut argue that the absence of dense social networks among African immigrants may help to explain why, "despite very high levels of educational attainment and high proportions in declared professional occupations, Nigerian household incomes are significantly lower than Jamaican and amounted to only 80 percent of the national median in 1989." [32] Fifty percent of Jamaican immigrants are concentrated in New York City, where they have established, along with other West Indian groups, well integrated ethnic communities involving a relatively high proportion of professionals and entrepreneurs. [33] This well-developed social network helps to shield immigrants from discrimination and rejection in the wider marketplace and cushions the crisis of social adaptation. The wide array of Jamaican-owned businesses ensures a fairly high rate of self-employment and economic participation, which, in turn, engender successful incorporation into American society.

The wide geographical dispersion of African immigrants and the recency of arrival help to explain why, despite their swelling numbers, their communities lack highly developed social and economic networks. African foreign-born in the United States are heavily concentrated in metropolitan areas, but their communities are scattered around the country. [34] The 2000 census indicates that no state had fewer than 150 Africans. This geographical dispersion is attributable in part to the high percentage of refugees and tertiary-level students within the African immigrant influx: refugees are dependent (at least initially) on government settlement schemes, while acceptance by diverse educational institutions determines student location. There is also some indication that Africans spread out the longer they live in the United States. For example, according to the U.S. Census (2000), 30 percent of African immigrants had resided somewhere else in 1995 than they did in 2000.

The majority of African foreign-born live in two regions: the South (35 percent) and the Northeast (31 percent). [35] According to the 2000 census, one-third of the estimated 881,300 African foreign-born (a low figure) lived in just three states: New York (116,936), California (113,255), Texas (64,470), followed by Maryland (62,688). Since early immigrants tend to settle in locations close to

---

32. Portes and Rumbaut, *Immigrant America*, 90.

33. See also Martin Frazier, "Continuity and Change in Caribbean Immigration," *People's Weekly World Newspaper* (September 1, 2005).

34. Jill Wilson, "African-Born Residents of the United States," Migration Policy Institute, 2003.

35. Nolan Malone et al., "The Foreign-Born Population: 2000," U.S. Census Bureau, 2003, 4, 6. The South region of the United States includes the states of Alabama, Arkansas, Delaware, Florida, Georgia, Kentucky, Louisiana, Maryland, South Carolina, Tennessee, Texas, Virginia, West Virginia, and the District of Columbia (equivalent to a state); the Northeast region includes the states of Connecticut, Maine, Massachusetts, New Hampshire, New Jersey, New York, Pennsylvania, Rhode Island, and Vermont.

national embassies,[36] the highest proportion of African immigrants (i.e., as a percentage of the surrounding population) are to be found in Washington, DC, and Maryland.[37] But there are numerous African immigrant enclaves in major metropolitan areas across the country. Joel Millman identifies the Ghanaians of East Orange, New Jersey, who number about three thousand; the Liberian refugee community in New York's Staten Island; the sizable Nigerian community in Silver Spring, Maryland; and "Houston's Nigeria 'hood [with] perhaps 100,000 immigrants spread over several west-side wards."[38]

These African communities are scarcely a decade old, and even the larger ones are dwarfed by the surrounding metropolitan population. There are more African immigrants in New York (roughly 11 percent of the total African immigrant population) than in any other U.S. city, but within New York itself this African element is diminutive: it represents 1 percent of the total population and 3 percent of all the foreign-born population.[39] Still, the last decade or so has witnessed a tremendous increase in the number of African-owned businesses, typically in large metropolitan areas across the country. These range from taxi services to clothing stores and restaurants, and they provide a modicum of self-employment. The business acumen and sophisticated entrepreneurship of the Senegalese community in New York is depicted in rich detail by Millman (1998). But, unlike the Senegalese, few African immigrants had business experience prior to coming to the United States.[40] And, owing to the challenges they face getting financial credit and bank loans, most African businesses are family based or small cooperative ventures. But what they lack in ready capital and experience, African immigrants more than make up for in a determined work ethic, a strong sense of community, and a motivation to succeed.

It seems only a matter of time before the burgeoning African foreign-born population develops entrenched and extensive socioeconomic networks. As stated above, 62 percent of African immigration is driven by family ties. This means that new African immigrants are largely dependent on existing social networks and family connections for initial settlement and incorporation into American society; and the vast majority take up residence in areas where there are other African immigrants. While African immigrant communities may lack the economic advantages that the older, geographically concentrated, and more established Caribbean communities enjoy, most African immigrants look to immigrant networks or associations (including churches, as we shall see) for identity formation, economic survival, spiritual nurture, cultural sustenance, and successful adaptation. Such immigrant associations provide vital support in the face of cultural isolation and social marginalization; and to the extent that they frame the crisis-ridden process of settlement and engagement with the wider society, they also have an important bearing on the process of acculturation.

---

36. Arthur, *Invisible Sojourners*, 44.
37. Wilson, "African-Born Residents of the United States."
38. Millman, *Other Americans*, 179.
39. Wilson, "African-Born Residents of the United States."
40. Arthur, *Invisible Sojourners*, 106.

The Assimilation Question

Despite the fact that it is home to one of the most diverse mainstream societies in the industrial world, American society is beleaguered by rigid racial dichotomies. As discussed in chapter 10, the expectation that new immigrants will gradually and inevitably abandon their cultures and ethic identities in the process of becoming fully incorporated into the dominant white Anglo-Saxon society (a pattern known as "Anglo-conformity") remains prevalent. This notion has come under severe criticism in recent years for its ethnocentric and ideological bias, and newer constructs like the "segmented assimilation" model not only emphasize alternative modes of incorporation but also recognize the capacity of the new, predominantly nonwhite, immigrant groups to maintain durable cultural and ethnic identities.

The data on the African foreign-born population in the United States illustrates the argument that contemporary immigrants are "being absorbed by different segments of American society, ranging from affluent middle-class suburbs to impoverished inner-city ghettos."[41] African immigrants are unlikely to be unemployed, but they are found in a wide range of occupations, from the highest to the lowest paid. To analyze family income figures is to see a picture of diverse economic fortunes. While quality selective immigration measures mean that African immigrant figures include disproportionate numbers of the highly skilled and educated, a range of complex factors impact reception and modes of incorporation into American society. The process is also attended by latent tensions.

Heavy emphasis on educational pursuits and accomplishments means that most African immigrants are thoroughly exposed to the values and norms of American society. In fact, since education is the main vehicle for social mobility as well as economic and cultural integration, African immigrants who lack educational credentials tend to experience downward assimilation into the underclass. Yet even the most Americanized discover that studious assimilation does not immunize them from xenophobic intolerance or social rejection. And the deeply alienating experience of racism and racial discrimination tends to stimulate renewed consciousness of African identity and strengthen ethnic solidarity.

Similarly, though a good proportion of African immigrants are drawn from the most Westernized segment of their home country's population, the cross-cultural experience tends to induce a profound appreciation for, and attachment to, aspects of their indigenous culture. African immigrants work assiduously to gain economic incorporation and social mobility, yet most define their socioeconomic status not in terms of American ideals (like individualized material comfort) but according to "the status identity they were culturally accustomed to while living in Africa."[42] High levels of English proficiency among African immigrants removes a major barrier to acculturation among first-generation immigrants, but "parents stress the necessity of preserving their African heritage and culture

---

41. Zhou, "Segmented Assimilation," 210.
42. Arthur, *Invisible Sojourners*, 88.

among the second generation" in the belief that an African identity "is vital for the cultural survival of their children" in America's diverse society.[43]

The encounter with American society also challenges the unequal gender relations, hierarchical kinship structures, and ethnic divisions common among African groups. This allows many, especially the women, to exchange restrictive traditional structures or roles for the far more affirming and egalitarian American value system. At the same time, African immigrant families and communities self-consciously emphasize and uphold African cultural values in reflexive response to what is widely perceived as the low moral values and permissive ethos of American culture. John Arthur found that, while African immigrant women redefined their roles and ideals, "they are fiercely traditional and deeply committed to African values when it comes to household organization, child raising, styles of dress, and expectations about children."[44]

In short, like other post-1965 immigrant groups, African families and communities place great premium on cultural preservation. This inevitably engenders segmented assimilation. Families and individuals negotiate a new identity or status, which draws on homeland materials while adopting or incorporating values and norms within the host society conducive to their advancement and aspirations. In his seminal study of the new African immigrants within American society, John Arthur concludes that "the majority of African immigrants have been able to preserve their traditional cultures."[45] He adds:

> Participation occurs only to the extent that it facilitates the achievement of cultural and economic goals, mainly in the pursuit of education and access to the labor market. This kind of selective adaptation is deliberate and designed chiefly to minimize social contacts with the host society. African immigrants engage the host society selectively, confining themselves to those carefully chosen domains of the host society that render them more likely to accomplish their goals.[46]

From a different perspective, Bosah Ebo (a professor of communications) found that African immigrants develop "co-cultural communication" patterns that involve regularly switching between two cultural modes—"Western" and "indigenous"—in order to fulfill expectations associated with both cultures.[47] Thus, they dress in Western attire, adopt Western etiquette, perform Western-style weddings, and refrain from holding hands with members of the same sex in public (a display of hospitality in many African societies but a mark of homosexuality in America) in order to "'fit' into the social milieu of the host culture." But they also observe African customs (like child-naming), eat indigenous food at

---

43. Ibid., 113f.
44. Ibid., 118, 122.
45. Ibid., 107.
46. Ibid., 143.
47. See Bosah Ebo, "Adaptation and Preservation: Communication Patterns of African Immigrants in America," in *The Huddled Masses: Communication and Immigration*, ed. Gary Gumpert and Susan J. Drucker (Cresskill, NJ: Hampton, 1998).

home almost daily (which explains the proliferation of African food stores), favor traditional dress and music in their celebrations, and order their lives around an extended family structure in order to preserve allegiance to indigenous cultures. The longer immigrants stay in the new environment, argues Ebo (1998: 71, 73), the better they get at "co-cultural comfort" (or selective assimilation): "knowing how to satisfy the cultural expectations of the host society and at the same time fulfill their desire for indigenous affiliation."

It is impossible to say with any certainty how these segmented patterns of assimilation prevalent among new African immigrants will impact the cultural integration and identity formation of the second and subsequent generations. There is little doubt that the children of African immigrants will become more assimilated than their parents, at least insofar as their cultural identity will be more American than African. But this is not to say that their incorporation into a diverse and pluralistic American society will be straightforward or predictable. There is much to be said for the argument that, since race identification will continue to pose a challenge to social acceptance and social mobility, assimilation to African American society (more on this below), while retaining a strong ethnic identity, is most likely.[48] But, since young adults dominate the African immigrant population—in 2000, 67 percent were between the ages of twenty-four and fifty-four[49]—the impact of the economic resources and social capital of the parents on the assimilation patterns of the next generation may be quite substantial. In this regard, two aspects of the contemporary African immigrant experience may prove significant: transnationalism and religious association.

We noted in chapter 8 that African immigrants have a strong propensity for transnationalism: the simultaneous incorporation and active involvement in both the society of settlement and the society of origin. Transnationalism facilitates selective adaptation within the first generation of immigrants and will arguably have some impact on the acculturation patterns of the second generation. Indeed, in some cases, maintaining strong homeland ties partly reflects the widespread desire among African immigrants that their children retain some African values and preserve an African identity. While only the better-off African immigrants can afford the expense of periodic family trips to Africa, many more are forced by economic circumstances or other considerations to send their children back to Africa to be raised by the extended family.[50] The point is that sustained cultural, social, and political ties with the homeland by the first generation is likely to contribute to the self-understanding and sense of identity of the next generation.

For the majority of African immigrant children, however, sustained exposure to African values and culture is mediated through immigrant religious associations, of which the immigrant congregation is the most prominent. Among the new immigrants, religion plays a critical role in expressions of ethnic and transnational identity as well as in social adaptation and community formation. More-

---

48. Min, "Contemporary Immigrants' Advantages for Intergenerational Cultural Transmission," 150.

49. "Foreign-Born Profiles" (2000).

50. Arthur, *Invisible Sojourners*, 96f.

over, in major cities throughout the Western world immigrant religion is stimulating "a remarkable and exuberant expansion of churches, mosques, Buddhist
temples, and synagogues, many of them designed to serve growing orthodox
populations and new immigrants."[51] These new immigrant congregations function as primary centers for preserving ethnic identity and negotiating modes of
incorporation into the host culture. Immigrant churches, which form the focus of
the next two chapters, provide the main sites of acculturation and spiritual orientation for the next generation of Africans (and future American citizens).

African and American, Not African American

The vast majority of African immigrants in the United States (certainly from
the 1980s) are black or dark-skinned. In a context where racial identification and
residential segregation significantly shape economic and social integration, the
single most important impediment they face in their efforts to adapt to American
society is racial exclusion and prejudice. (As we shall see later, this impediment
also poses challenges to missionary action.) Wealthy African immigrants can
be found in suburbs across the nation, but African immigrant communities are
mainly located in urban areas that have "racially diverse and minority populations, especially cities with a large Africa-American, Caribbean and Hispanic
presence."[52] For African immigrants, racial identification not only potentially
encumbers "upward mobility and economic integration into the normative structures of middle-class America"; it also generates pressures for downward mobility into the African American urban (sub-)culture. Caribbean immigrants face a
similar problem. As Arthur (2000) explains, their common experience as immigrants in America and a shared history of colonial domination help to account for
the close relationship between African and Caribbean immigrants.

Because of the obvious racial affinity between African immigrants and African Americans, the wider society tends to regard the two as a single group. This
notional blending not only contributes to the invisibility of African immigrants
but also imposes a stereotypical minority status on them. To be sure, the uniformly negative images of Africa and Africans (as diseased, primitive, destitute,
barbarous) prevalent in American society means that African immigrants are
liable to be relegated to a marginalized status anyway—doubly condemned on
racial and cultural grounds. But the point at issue is that the deep-seated racial
dynamic of American society adds to the difficulties of assimilation or inculturation for African immigrants, even if it is true that "becoming an American
includes learning about American race classification systems and about American racial attitudes and prejudices."[53]

To make matters worse, the growing presence of the new African immi-

---

51. Joel Kotkin and Karen Speicher, "God and the City," *God and the City* 10 (October/Novem-
ber 2003): 34-39.

52. Arthur, *Invisible Sojourners*, 45.

53. Smith and Edmonston, eds., *New Americans*, 394.

grants in American society has not so far been met with either cordial acceptance or fraternal embrace by African Americans. After almost three decades
of encounter and enforced interaction (by virtue of race identification and urban
concentration), the relationship between the two groups is, generally speaking,
fraught with tension and misunderstanding, even hostility in some situations.
This mutual alienation is not always evident or present everywhere, but it is a
real and growing problem;[54] and for both groups the fact that it is there at all is as
unexpected as it is bewildering. But the tensions are, generally speaking, rooted
in conflictual attitudes or expectations between the two groups in at least three
main areas: racial identity, economic opportunity, and cultural heritage.

The first is related to the issue of racism. The self-identity and outlook of
African Americans is profoundly shaped by the history of slavery, the retarding
effects of institutionalized racism, and the ignominies of life as a suppressed
racial minority. The new African immigrants, however, come from countries
where blacks form the majority population, control power, and occupy the dominant positions in society—South Africa and Zimbabwe (before 1980) being
notable exceptions. Thus, few have prior experience of racism or racial discrimination, and most learn "what it means to be black" for the first time in their
encounter with American society. But, while they also suffer from the adversities
inflicted by racism, African immigrants generally do not feel disempowered by it
and therefore tend to minimize its potential impact on their destiny and prospects
in American society. Partly for this reason, few feel compelled to fight racial
discrimination, and many consider the African American focus on it obsessive.
The latter, for their part, charge Africans with obliviousness to the insidiousness
of the race problem and poor appreciation for the hard-won battles against racial
discrimination.

The second area of tension between the two groups is economic in nature.
Informed by media images of African American superstars in sports and entertainment, African immigrants are stunned by the level of poverty and joblessness within African American communities, especially in the inner cities. Since
their own migration is partly driven by the collapse of African economies, African immigrants view the United States as a land of economic opportunity and
advancement, a country where industry and enterprise are rewarded. Due to high
skill levels, a heavy emphasis on educational pursuits, and a determination to succeed, a good many achieve decent living standards and social mobility within a
matter of years after their arrival as immigrants. These achievements predispose
them to share the view (common among whites) that American blacks, especially
those in the inner cities, are indolent, indifferent to economic and educational
opportunities, and given to complaining. Such attitudes make for poor relations
with African Americans, who denounce this view as arrogant and accuse African
immigrants (who tend to be preoccupied with economic needs and obligations in

---

54. For a summary account of differences separating the two groups, see Arthur, *Invisible
Sojourners,* 77-86; see also David D. Daniels, "African Immigrant Churches in the United States
and the Study of Black Church History," in *African Immigrant Religions in America,* ed. Jacob K.
Olupona and Regina Gemignani (New York: New York University Press, 2007), 47-60.

their homelands) of failing to invest in the surrounding community. Moreover, those at the lower end of the labor market harbor a fear that the influx of African immigrants costs them jobs and overwhelms limited social services.

Perhaps surprisingly, given the common ancestry and heritage of the two groups, the third area of dissonance revolves around cultural differences. African immigrants are surprised to discover that most African Americans share the stereotypically negative images of Africa held by the American public, and that, while many make much of their African heritage, they remain ignorant about African history (including the long-term impact of colonial domination) and African cultures. A typical African American rejoinder is to point to the immigrants' poor knowledge of the historical forces (including slavery, violence, and racial oppression) that have shaped the "black" experience in America. But, dismayed by the prevalence of single parenthood, teenage pregnancy, high rates of school dropout, and erosion of parental authority within African American communities, African immigrants respond by stressing their distinctive cultural identity and making strenuous efforts to inculcate African cultural values in their children. Indeed, as Arthur notes, "concerns about the influence of the urban minority culture on the lives of their children are fundamental to the flight of middle-class African immigrant families to the suburbs."[55] Chief among these concerns are what they consider the worse aspects of African American urban subculture—epitomized by misogynistic gangsta rap music, juvenile delinquency, low regard for education, and distinctive clothing.

Whether the prevailing atmosphere of conflict and tension between African immigrants and African Americans will give way to convergence is left to be seen. There is also no gainsaying the fact that the children of African immigrants will draw on aspects of the African American cultural heritage as part of their efforts to negotiate a new identity within America's multicultural landscape. Already, the gravitation of second-generation African immigrants toward the urban hip-hop culture is a major source of inter-generational conflict.[56] My own speculation is that convergence may be the fruit of rediscovery and shared expectations. As both groups learn more about and from each other, it is not unlikely that they will form alliances to address critical political and economic issues in their respective homelands. As African immigrants become stakeholders in American society, they may increasingly discover that racism and cultural segregation represent greater barriers to integration and other aspirations than first imagined, while African Americans may find that making common cause with the new Africans rather than viewing them as competitors or usurpers has political, economic, and cultural benefits.

An even stronger argument can be made that association and collaboration between the fast-growing African immigrant churches and black churches (especially the Pentecostal-charismatic type) holds the most promising avenue to breaking the current trend of disengagement and guardedness (if not mistrust) between the two groups. From a purely academic point of view, the areas of con-

---

55. Arthur, *Invisible Sojourners*, 114.
56. Ibid., 99, 113-17.

vergence between the two Christian communities seem quite obvious and quite strong, and they may yet provide durable building blocks for long-term engagement and collaboration. Three deserve mention.

First, there is the issue of *a shared ancestry*. The majority of African Americans hail from West Africa, and there is increasing interest among them in tracing their ancestry. The fact that the majority of the new African immigrants and the vast majority of African immigrant churches are also West African in origin provides a meaningful historical connection and a useful starting point for exploring community. Ghana, as we have already noted, is a major source of African Christian immigrants in the United States; and Ghana, because of its pivotal role in the African slave trade, looms large in the African American imagination as a major symbol of cultural and racial ancestry.

Second, it is noteworthy that the two groups share *deep spiritual and cultural affinities* reflective of their strong family resemblance. This needs qualification, for, as noted above, there are considerable cultural tensions between the two. Ironically, it is precisely because African immigrant churches and black churches serve so effectively as sites of cultural preservation and social cohesion within their respective communities that robust association is rendered difficult. At a basic level, both groups of Christians are attracted by a common spirituality and strong sense of community; yet they often find, on closer inspection, that their cultural universes are poorly aligned. It is therefore not uncommon to find African immigrant churches in predominantly black neighborhoods which attract very few African American families. Further, while large numbers of the new African immigrants have found a spiritual home in black Pentecostal-charismatic churches, anecdotal evidence suggests that involvement is not always sustained beyond a few years.

There is no getting away from the fact that black Christianity has incorporated significant elements of the Anglo-American tradition out of which it was formed. But it is also indelibly stamped by its African religious ethos.[57] And, like the most dominant forms of African Christianity, black Christianity also reflects *anti-Christendom* (see p. 280 above), which is to say that it is divested of political power, nurtured by suffering and subjugation, resistant to secularization, and forced to do mission from positions of vulnerability and need. Clearly also, black spirituality draws heavily on African worldviews, and to the extent that it has preserved its anchorage in the African primal world, it furnishes natural avenues of fellowship and solidarity with African congregations. This much is indicated by the prevalence of Pentecostal forms and expressions within both groups. There are daunting cultural gaps in the areas of language, attitude to sexuality and wealth, work ethic, and self-identity. Yet the semblance of cultural kinship is strong, and the degree of overlap in vital areas is considerable: including sense of community, attitude to eldership, music and worship, spirituality, healing and deliverance, cognizance of suffering, reading of the Bible, the rarity of genuine atheists among these groups, and pervasive religiosity.

---

57. See Sernett, "Black Religion and the Question of Evangelical Identity," 136; Franklin, "Safest Place on Earth," 259.

Third, renewed awareness of *the legacies of history* may instigate mutual interest above and beyond the challenges of the present. For the most part, both groups are unaware of the strong historical linkages between their two Christian-ities and the significant contribution that early African American Christian ideas (of religious protest and resistance to white domination) made to the emergence of African Christianity as an African religion. In Liberia, admittedly, the experi-ment in political and religious association sowed bitter seeds of antagonism that unraveled badly a century and a half later. But African immigrants are also gen-erally unaware of the momentous gains of the civil rights movement—including the historic amendments to immigration legislation that opened the way to new African immigration.

A greater appreciation for these legacies of history might encourage a stronger interest among African immigrant Christians in partnering with black churches in the latter's efforts to address the daunting socioeconomic crises confronting black communities. At the same time, African immigrant Christians, who are no strangers to nurturing faith and commitment in contexts of suffering and despair, bring new perspectives and insights that may help to widen the vision of the black church beyond the suffocating preoccupation with racial resistance to a greater appreciation of the vast resources provided by religious heritage. This also extends to theological engagement. As the renowned African American his-torian Gayraud Wilmore has noted, "the theological program of African scholars to Africanize Christianity has much to say to African American scholars who want to indigenize the Christian faith in the culture of the black America."[58]

I am conscious that the above perspectives and arguments project consider-able optimism in the face of growing alienation and mutual mistrust between the new African immigrants and African Americans. But it is important to recall that black Americans have historically been open to the influence and contribu-tion of other black immigrants:[59] Edward W. Blyden, the African statesman and architect of pan-Africanism, was Liberian; W. E. B. DuBois's father was Haitian; and Marcus Garvey, whose brand of African nationalism helped to inspire the Nation of Islam, was Jamaican. Moreover, a goodly number of black leaders and icons of the civil rights movement were first- or second-generation immigrants, including Malcolm X, Louis Farakhan, Harry Belafonte, Sidney Poitier, and Stokely Carmichael.

The situation on the ground shows little signs of improving; and, as noted earlier, the same tensions are evident within American Islam (see p. 271 above). It would be tragic indeed if the enormous potential that can be unleashed by col-laboration and partnership is sabotaged by the dilemmas and disaffection that ultimately stem from the fact that these two groups were *separated at birth*! My sanguine academic musings aside, it seems to me that the Christian communities on both sides are faced with a tremendous opportunity to model reconciliation and peace as part of their witness. That is not a matter of choice or preference; it is a scriptural mandate!

---

58. Wilmore, *Black Religion and Black Radicalism*, 281.
59. See Orlando Patterson, "The New Black Nativism," *Time*, February 19, 2007, 44.

14

Have Faith, Will Travel

African Migrants and the Making of a New Missionary Movement

> To start a congregation is a strong statement of commitment, and
> no small job. A remarkable degree of passion . . . is indispensable.
> . . . Congregation founders are not after the formation of a social
> club, which can usually be accomplished more easily by other readily
> available means. They are trying to make possible the vital living of
> their religious lives in a new place.
>
> —Dorothy C. Bass, "Congregations and the Bearing
> of Traditions," 174

The data presented and examined in this (and the following) chapter represent
the fruit of the Mobile Faith Project, which was launched in the fall of 2003. This
project broadly explores the South–North migration movement of Africans and
seeks to evaluate the missionary dimensions of rapidly expanding African immigrant churches in the United States. It is predicated on two interrelated assumptions: first, that Christian expansion and migratory movement have historically
been intimately intertwined; second, that massive migration from the southern
heartlands of Christianity to the old centers where the faith is experiencing dramatic erosion (though more obviously so in Europe than the United States) constitutes a de facto missionary movement of immense significance for the study of
contemporary global Christianity.

There is no hard data on the percentage of African foreign-born in the United
States who are Christian. But a number of salient factors indicate that the vast
majority of African immigrants are drawn from Christian rather than Muslim
Africa. In striking contrast to Europe, Christians form the great majority of
America's new immigrants. Ghanaians accounted for 4.4 percent of all Protestant Christian immigrants admitted to permanent residence in July and August
1996, according to data published in the New Immigrant Survey (2001).[1] Quality-

---

1. Jasso et al., "Exploring the Religious Preferences of Recent Immigrants," 226. Only Mexico
(12.4 percent), Jamaica (12.0), the former Soviet Union (6.2), and the Philippines (5.5) were higher.
But given that the number of African immigrants increased in unprecedented fashion after the mid-
1990s, this sampling is inadequate.

selective immigration requirements favor a higher inflow of Christian Africans for the simple reason that "Christianity is the dominant faith among the educated class in much of sub-Saharan Africa."[2] Among African immigrants in America, Muslims are more likely to convert to Christianity than the other way around. Furthermore, the rapid expansion of African immigrant churches since the 1970s points to a growing African Christian presence.

What is presented here is a preliminary assessment of the movement in the American context utilizing extensive ethnographic research in the form of thoroughgoing interviews of African pastors, participant observation of church functions, and official congregational surveys. The research covered seventy-one African immigrant churches (in Los Angeles, New York, Philadelphia, New Jersey, Washington, DC, and Chicago) with a total of roughly fourteen thousand members (see Appendix 2).

The study singles out African immigrant churches that are strongly missionary in outlook and function—churches, in other words, that consider intercultural engagement or outreach beyond the African immigrant constituency a primary objective. This requirement implicitly creates a typological restriction: the vast majority of churches that exhibit this "missionary" propensity are Pentecostal-charismatic–type churches. This should come as little surprise. The expansion and impact of Pentecostal and Charismatic movements are most commonly shaped by individual or spontaneous initiatives that discountenance rigid institutional or denominational control mechanisms. In addition, the emphasis on lay participation and the efficacy of individual empowerment (through the anointing and gifts of the Holy Spirit) within such movements translates into a religious form that is infinitely portable or, to coin a phrase, *migration-ready*. If Pentecostalism is a "religion made to travel," it is not only because its expressions and core practices draw on the deep reservoir of primal spirituality present in all cultures but also because ordinary believers make ordinary decisions based on the direct experience of the Holy Spirit in their lives. The fact that the empowerment of the Holy Spirit has a primarily missionary function (Acts 1:8) is the root source of the movement's missionary vitality.

Christian believers who uproot themselves and migrate to a distant land to preach the gospel in response to the Holy Spirit's directive are not unusual. In fact, stories of such movement are fairly common within the Western missionary project in which missionary movement has traditionally been shaped by economic realities to a significant extent. Among non-Western Christians, however, the missionary narrative is undergoing significant revisions—some might even argue that the new initiatives and experiences amount to a new narrative. It is emerging as largely a story of masses of Christians forced to migrate to distant lands by factors already examined in this book; Christian believers who travel

---

2. Jacob K. Olupona and Regina Gemignani, "Introduction," in *African Immigrant Religions in America*, ed. K. Olupona and Regina Gemignani (New York: New York University Press, 2007), 13. It is noteworthy that "a large percentage of West African Muslims [in the United States]—if not the majority—have never been to school." See Linda Beck, "West African Muslims in America: When Are Muslims Not Muslims?" in *African Immigrant Religions in America*, ed. Olupona and Gemignani, 185.

with a faith that is strongly missionary in orientation. The practicalities of how they fulfill the missionary mandate, or (more accurately) the missionary capacity of the communities of worship they form, are the main focus of the project.

Appropriate nomenclature for these churches and movements must remain open to scholarly discussion until more extensive research generates critical consensus. I personally find the acronym "AIC" hard to resist because of instant recognition. Most readers will be fully aware that AIC is an established (if now possibly outmoded) abbreviation for African initiated churches, which became a major phenomenon in African Christianity in the first half of the twentieth century. In my usage the term "African immigrant congregations" refers to churches or assemblies established by African foreign-born Christians whose membership was drawn primarily from, or included, a large proportion of African immigrants—at least initially. That said, the descriptor "African" is utilitarian rather than definitive—at least one African pastor rejected its inclusion in the congregational survey heading because it conveys a semblance of exclusivity that his ministry eschews.

Four Types of African Immigrant Churches

In my preliminary assessment, there are four main types of African immigrant church formation within Western societies. First, there is what I would term the *Abrahamic* type: independent churches that have their origin in the initiative of an individual African migrant. These churches or congregations embody predicament and promise, reflect spontaneous movement, and typically trace their origin to an individual's response to a divine call. The majority of African immigrant churches established in Europe and North America fall under this category. They originate as individual efforts, typically by long-stay migrants (including students, refugees, professionals, or others on long-term job-related assignments such as diplomatic service). Such informal individual initiatives are the most preponderant and yet the most difficult to track.

The second type of African immigrant churches or ministries can be grouped under the *Macedonian* type. By this I mean to suggest that they reflect to some degree the biblical account (Acts 16:9-10) of Paul's vision in which the apostle received a memorable plea from a man of Macedonia, "Come over . . . and help us." These churches or congregations exemplify planned or structured official initiatives or responses, which is to say that they come into existence through the missionary-sending initiatives of ministries or movements that are African founded (or African led) and African based. Invariably the leaders of such African ministries are consciously acting on the conviction that God has called them to proclaim the gospel in the West. But, quite often, the "call" comes not from Westerners but from members of the movement who have migrated to the West and who request pastoral oversight for an expanding Christian fellowship they have already established.

The *Abrahamic* and *Macedonian* type churches are strongly interrelated. Almost invariably, it is the migration of individual members that provides the primary stimulus for international missionary efforts by African churches and ministries. In effect, many *Macedonian*-type churches or congregations owe their existence to the same spontaneous migrant movement that accounts for *Abrahamic*-type churches. Both typically involve new African immigrants who, having failed to find meaningful Christian fellowship or avenues for ministry within American churches, start a regular Bible study or prayer meeting in their homes and invite new converts or other believers to join. The vast majority of African immigrant churches start this way: as a group of committed Christian immigrants meeting in someone's living room on a regular basis.

The third category of African immigrant church formation might be termed the *Jerusalem* type: African-established or African-led churches with significant African membership that are associated with Western mainline denominations and operate under their ecclesiastical structure and polity. Commonly designated "ethnic churches" in the United States, many perform a strong missionary function and often represent a singular form of vital growth within their respective denominations. However, denominational identity, organizational restrictions, and limited autonomy may complicate efforts to evaluate their true missionary capacity. For one thing, the distinction between "ethnic churches" and other churches within the same denomination with significant numbers of African members seems notional. Also included in this category are those Christian communities established with the worthy but narrow objective of serving specific African immigrant groups. The best examples of these are Ethiopian Orthodox churches (of which there are a good many in the United States) that focus almost exclusively on Ethiopian communities and use Amharic as the language of worship.

The fourth type I have in mind reflects church association rather than church formation, but it is worthy of mention because of its inherent missionary potential. I would describe this as the *Samuel-Eli* type: a reference to churches, typically mainline denominations, that attract significant numbers of African members whose active involvement can generate evangelical vitality, contribute new expressions of spitituality, and influence worship styles. An infusion of Christian immigrants has regenerated many a moribund (often long-established) congregation in Western societies. In their aged ecclesiastical traditions, dimming spiritual discernment, and tragic captivity to secularism, many Christian communities in the West evoke the biblical story of the old priest Eli and his sons (1 Samuel 2:12-26). Like Eli's sons, the decline of Christianity is often exemplified by lifestyles and life choices that show "no regard for the Lord" or treat the divine or transcendent with contempt. The enfeebled entreaties of Eli (symbolic of the many Western churches) do little to change the situation—not least because Eli also partakes of the illicit offerings. But, as I have argued elsewhere in this volume, evaluations of contemporary Western Christianity must reckon with the presence of "Samuels": growing immigrant presence that signals the promise of uncorrupted youth and the untapped potential of new spiritual vitality.

All these diverse expressions and models of the African missionary movement deserve scholarly assessment in their own right. But it is the *Abrahamic* and *Macedonian* type churches or congregations that form the focus of this study, for the simple reason that they form the vanguard of the African missionary movement. For more on *Macedonian*-type churches or congregations, see chapter 15.

This chapter evaluates the *Abrahamic* model and provides a synoptic sketch of the missionary-pastors whose vision, sense of missionary vocation, and resourcefulness define the movement and hold the key to its potential impact. Limitations of space prohibit an individual portrayal of the seventy-plus pastors in the study. The assessment that follows provides a detailed portrait of select pastors with a focus on the factors or events that instigated migration, the considerations that governed the founding of a church, and the pastors' understanding of the missionary task. This is followed by a general overview of the traits, approaches, and outlook that define the movement's leadership and hold the key to its prospects.

Out of Liberia

Liberia's seven-year civil war (1989-1996) claimed 250,000 lives and produced over one million refugees. This bloody and brutal conflict was rooted in almost a century and a half of bitter ethnic hostility fueled by the mistreatment of the native population by the early American settlers and the political dominance exercised by the latter's descendants (Americo-Liberians), who constitute 5 percent of the population. The immediate causes of the war, however, were the widespread intertribal violence, pogroms, and sizable refugee movement that followed in the wake of the bloody 1980 coup by master sergeant Samuel Doe of the marginalized Krahn tribe. The civil war is officially dated to December 1989, when an insurgent group (the National Patriotic Front of Liberia) formed by Charles Ghankay Taylor, an Americo-Liberian and one of Doe's former Lieutenants, entered Liberia from neighboring Ivory Coast in an effort to topple Doe's regime. Taylor failed to capture the capital, Monrovia, but soon controlled much of the countryside and strengthened his power base by exploiting the country's considerable natural resources, with the help of American and French firms.[3]

The following year one of Taylor's aids, Prince Johnson, broke away to form a splinter "guerilla" group. Johnson subsequently captured and publicly executed Samuel Doe—a gruesome act captured on video—plunging the nation into political cataclysm. Ironically, the demise of the state and the rise of warlordism saw Liberia more closely incorporated into global economic networks that were used by various warlords to gain enormous wealth, even as the country disintegrated into anarchy. More than half of the country's three million people fled their homes.

Bishop Darlingston Johnson
(Bethel World Outreach Church, Maryland)

As in much of sub-Saharan Africa, the most dynamic and conspicuous centers of religious vitality in Liberia by the 1980s were the largely apolitical charismatic-Pentecostal churches which proliferated in the country's capital, Monrovia. One

---

3. Paul Nugent, *Africa since Independence: A Comparative History* (New York: Palgrave Macmillan, 2004), 469.

of these was Bethel World Outreach, a vibrant and flourishing ministry headed by Dr. Darlingston Johnson (later bishop). Under Johnson's leadership, Bethel World Outreach had become one of the fastest-growing churches in the country, increasing attendance by over two thousand in less than three years. It held multiple services every Sunday at the Monrovia City Hall and had its own televised ministry. In October 1989, a Ghanaian assistant pastor prophesied during a worship service that Liberia would be plunged into a period of bloodshed and judgment before the year was out. The leaders of the church found this message difficult to digest, precisely because Bethel World Outreach was doing so well. Two months later Charles Taylor's army invaded Liberia and triggered a bloody civil war.

At the start, Liberians had no inkling of the ferocious violence and apocalyptic holocaust that were about to be visited on their nation. Pastor Johnson was part of a group of delegates formed under the auspices of the Liberia Council of Churches that (in early 1990) met with Samuel Doe in a futile effort to bring the warring factions to the negotiating table. Shortly after, an event took place that came to symbolize the diabolical barbarity of the seven-year conflict. In July 1990, hundreds of refugees from the Gio and Mano tribes who had fled Nimba county in northern Liberia arrived in Monrovia and took refuge in the Saint Peter's Lutheran Church.[4] On the night of July 29, 1990, just when the refugees were waiting in line for their meal, over two hundred of Doe's soldiers invaded the church and fell on the defenseless group with brutal savagery. By the time the commotion and screams were silenced, six hundred Liberians had been massacred and 150 others wounded. But the carnage had only just begun.

In 1990, just when the situation in his country was beginning to spiral out of control, Darlingston Johnson left Liberia to attend a conference in the United States organized by David T. Demola, the founder of Faith Fellowship Ministries World Outreach Center in Sayreville, New Jersey. That visit dramatically changed the course of Johnson's life and ministry.

Johnson grew up in a devout Presbyterian family of five children—both parents were elders in the church. He remembers his mother as a devout woman of prayer. When he was about five years old his aunt was instantly killed and his two older sisters were critically injured in a car accident; the girls remained in a state of unconsciousness for several weeks. Johnson's mother was inconsolable. Still in a state of hysteria, she went to the church, where she spent time weeping and praying. Suddenly, she stopped crying. She explained that she had heard an audible voice whisper into her ears, "Be still and know that I am God" (Psalm 46:10). Both sisters made a miraculous and full recovery. This incident left a deep impression on Johnson's young mind; as he put it, God "became very real to me." Nurtured in this Christian environment, Johnson grew up with a deep love for God and a strong belief in the efficacy of prayer. Answered prayer has shaped pivotal events in his life.

From an early age he wanted to become a preacher—an unusual ambition in a context where pastors were poorly paid. The ministry of Oral Roberts, regularly broadcast on Liberian television, became a strong influence on his sense of call-

---

4. These tribes were known to be sympathetic to Charles Taylor.

ing. By the time he finished high school, Johnson had his heart set on studying theology. The only school outside Liberia to which he applied was Oral Roberts University (ORU) in Tulsa, Oklahoma. In August 1977, his fervent prayers were answered when ORU offered him a full scholarship to study theology. He subsequently earned a B.A. degree with a double major in business administration and theology (summa cum laude), and he earned a master of divinity degree by 1984.

Characteristically, his search for a wife was also primarily a matter of prayer, and his subsequent decision an act of faith. About three months after he started praying for a wife, someone for whom he had much respect and to whom he had not spoken wrote him a letter from Liberia and mentioned the name of Chrysanthe Amet, a young Christian lady, who this person thought might make a suitable partner for him. Johnson was sufficiently impressed by this divine coincidence to contact Chrysanthe, and the two of them kept up a robust correspondence for about a year. The first time he saw her in person was when she came to the United States in 1982 for their wedding. Since then, Chrys, who also became a pastor, has been a faithful partner in ministry.

In the years that followed, Johnson completed a Doctor of Ministry degree at Phillips University (Enid, Oklahoma) before finally returning to Liberia in 1987. Thereafter, he took over the leadership of then Bethel Full Gospel Church and changed the church's name to Bethel World Outreach. This name change was prompted by a deeply founded conviction, nurtured during his ten-year stint in the United States, that he was called to global outreach.

"Don't Be Refugees, Be Missionaries"

Abandoning his hugely successful ministry in Liberia was the last thing on Pastor Johnson's mind when he left for the 1990 conference accompanied by Chrys. But while he was in the United States, Liberia suffered profound political and social disintegration. At first it seemed their prolonged stay would only last a matter of months, but Liberia's ruinous civil war worsened as the number of rebel groups multiplied. This dramatic turn of events transformed Johnson from nonimmigrant visitor in the United States to displaced refugee. He and his wife were now refugees, not because they had fled persecution or political conflict but because they had left a country to which it was now impossible to return. Distressed and stymied by these untoward developments, Johnson began to earnestly pray and ask God for direction. The divine response, he recounts, was clear and emphatic: *"Don't be refugees, be missionaries!"*

The substance of this divine directive was that rather than assume the role of passive or helpless victims, as the situation dictated, Johnson and his wife were to use this unique, tragedy-induced opportunity to fulfill God's call to mission. Johnson's hugely successful ministry in Liberia testified to his passion for evangelism, but the global vision he long harbored remained latent. It took the traumatic experience of becoming a refugee to bring the vision to full realization. As a migrant in the United States, he found himself in an environment that was radically different from the situation in Liberia, where he had made a name for himself and masterminded a successful ministry. He was not a typical migrant or refugee; this status was foisted upon him. Nonetheless, he could hardly have been immune to the psychological anguish common among immigrants from the developing world in advanced Western societies: the sudden sense of lowered status, marginalization, and diminished self. Yet, paradoxically, he was also now in a context that, in contrast to Liberia, held greater possibilities and resources for launching a global ministry. What was needed was boldness, enterprise, and a sense of calling; none of which Dr. Johnson lacked.

In 1990, according to immigration data, there were 11,455 Liberian foreign-born legally resident in the United States. Some had only just recently fled Liberia, including a few members of Johnson's church. They readily responded to Johnson's call for regular fellowship. In August 1990, seventeen Liberians attended the first fellowship service at Blackburn Center, Howard University (Washington, DC). After two months the group moved to Silver Spring, Maryland, and started meeting in a space that held forty people. At this point it was essentially a "Liberian" church, and perhaps for this reason growth was slow—at least compared to the explosive expansion of the former church in Monrovia. But Pastor Johnson remained committed to a global vision involving outreach to all nations. He was determined to supersede the "Liberian" image.

The first breakthrough came when a number of Francophone Congolese began attending the church. Through their presence and influence other nationalities were attracted. The successful implementation of home groups that met weekly for Bible study and fellowship provided a vital contact point with nonmembers and contributed to steady growth. To accommodate its growing membership, the church eventually moved (in February 1992) to an old movie theater on Georgia Avenue in the heart of Silver Spring's bustling business community. In the space of ten years, what began as a small Liberian fellowship flowered into a community of faith comprising people from forty-two nations. Bethel World Outreach Church is now one of the largest African immigrant churches in the United States. It boasts a membership of about three thousand, and average attendance at its three Sunday services (the earliest of which is conducted in French) is currently thirteen hundred. Its complex administrative structure requires a full-time staff of eight ordained ministers (each presiding over a major ministry) and two elders. At the head is the man affectionately known as Bishop Johnson.[5]

Bishop Johnson has a simple explanation for the success of his ministry and its missionary dimension: *"the principle of sowing and partnership"* derived from Philippians 4:15-19. He is a strong proponent of Oral Roberts's seed faith theology, which holds that investing or giving to God's work ("sowing in faith") yields a harvest of God's blessings and miraculous provision. The one who sows sacrificially (or as an act of faith) reaps a return multiplied many times over in the same

---

5. Dr. Johnson was consecrated "bishop" in Liberia in April 2000. The title "bishop" was unpopular with African Pentecostal groups (because of its association with the fossilized ecclesiastical structures of mainline denominations) until quite recently. The fact that alternative titles like "general overseer" were poorly recognized by ordinary people contributed to a change. On the African continent, the consecration of Pentecostal "bishops" was also popularized by the powerful Nigerian evangelist Benson Idahosa (d. 1998), who took on the title "archbishop" and consecrated a number of protégés as bishops.

way that seeds planted in the ground yield an abundance out of all proportion to their size. In Philippians 4:15-19, Paul specifically acknowledges the partnership and unsurpassed generosity of the Philippian Christians, who sent him "aid again and again." It is on this basis, posits Johnson, that Paul then goes on to declare, in that oft-quoted phrase, "*my God will meet all your needs according to his glorious riches in Christ Jesus*" (v. 19). The two aspects, he insists, are inseparably and vitally linked: God's abundant provision is an outcome predicated on the act of giving and partnership.

His embrace of the principle enshrined in this biblical passage makes Johnson an ardent advocate of self-support and a resolute opponent of chronic dependency in ministry. This principle is also central to his missionary vision. In a manner strongly reminiscent of the biblical considerations that animated "faith missions" from the nineteenth century, he understands the missionary vocation in terms of voluntary reliance on God's provision and the upkeep generated by the work of ministry itself (Matthew 10:9-10). This outlook precluded raising financial support among American churches, an option that Johnson believes would not only have subverted effective Christian ministry but also fostered a relationship of dependence and inequality—an application of the faith principle that Oral Roberts may not have had in mind.

The principle of "sowing and partnership" is also pivotal to Johnson's missionary outlook. From the start, Bethel World Outreach Church has devoted at least 10 percent of all income to outreach endeavors—in 2004 alone $300,000 went to "foreign missions." Partly because of this practice, missionary pastors commissioned from Bethel World Outreach Church, Maryland, have established churches in other parts of the United States as well as in Europe, the Caribbean, and Africa.[6] This global network of churches founded through Bethel World Outreach Church (Maryland) are conjoined in one organization: Bethel World Outreach Ministries International (BWOMI). True to Bishop Johnson's convictions, the relationship among the churches is devoid of structures of dependence or hierarchical subordination. New church initiatives only receive start-up support from Bethel World Outreach Church, and each individual church operates as an autonomous local entity. All abide by the *three-selfs* principle (self-supporting, self-propagating, and self-governing). Mutuality is a watchword. The BWOMI network exists for fellowship, accountability, partnership, and training. At this time of writing, BWOMI comprises 150 churches, three theological education institutions (including the Bethel University of Biblical Studies in Maryland), and a global membership in excess of twenty thousand.

Yet BWOMI is solidly African in membership, and while Bethel World Outreach Church (Maryland) is fully international, many of its sister churches in the United States are predominantly Liberian. The Maryland church has attracted quite a number of African American members and a few Caucasians, but West Africans constitute some 70 percent of the congregation. Regular outreach is a

---

6. All these churches carry the "Bethel" (family) name. There are eight churches in other parts of the United States, 140 churches on the African continent, and one each in the Caribbean and Europe. For details, see the Web site, http://www.bwochurch.org/index.php.

vital aspect of church life and it is at the center of an energetic global ministry. In that regard, the church evinces a missionary dynamism that many Anglo-American churches would envy. But insofar as its leadership and membership remain largely confined to an African base, the ministry falls short of the mandate enshrined in its name. Bishop Johnson expresses strong concerns about the church's entrenched "African" identity, which he attributes to the culturally segmented American landscape (more on this on pp. 371-72 below). Even the African Americans who attend, he concedes, are attracted by the church's African image. But he remains firmly committed to building a truly multiethnic church, one that is only 50 percent African.

To fulfill this vision requires, at the very least, an enlargement of the present physical facilities, which are already at capacity use; and there are plans under way to move to a more commodious campus, where greater provision will be made for ministry to the wider community. Meanwhile, Johnson has pushed forward with new steps toward missionary engagement. The third (12:45 P.M.) worship service on Sundays has been restructured to maximize its appeal to native-born Americans: it is led by young adults more acculturated to American ways, worship is American-styled, and the dress code is very informal. A special intercultural ministry advisory council has been set up to provide direction and guidelines on the best ways to minister to and attract non-African members, and the mission department in the church has started forming small groups based on national origin (including an American cohort) which meet monthly and fund mission-related projects aimed at co-nationals. In April 2007, Bethel launched a new 9:30 A.M. service in a predominantly white suburb as part of its strategic plan to reach non-blacks and non-Africans.

To his credit, Johnson recognizes that to reach non-Africans effectively ultimately requires visible non-African symbols and representation not only in the church's ministry but also in its leadership—presently only one member of the pastoral team is Anglo-American. Steps are under way to hire another Anglo-American pastor to assist with the new service and multiracial outreach. But it is possible to argue that by multiplying the number of African missionaries through its extensive ministries, Bethel World Outreach Church may already have contributed more to the transformation of the American religious landscape than present circumstances suggest.

Out of Nigeria

Nigeria is one of the world's largest oil producers and Africa's most populous state. It is a colossus in the West African region and has been the prime mover behind important initiatives for political stability and economic advancement in the region.[7] Yet, by the decade of the 1990s, Nigeria epitomized the economic failure, social disorder, and political repression that are the root causes of the

---

7. The twenty-first annual summit of the Economic Community of West African States (ECOWAS) in October 1998 devoted much of its time to panegyric affirmation of Nigeria's pivotal

extraordinary out-migration of Africa's middle class and skilled professionals in the postcolonial period. Between 1966 and 1998, the county was ruled by military dictators for all but a four-year interval of corrupt civilian rule. By the end of General Ibrahim Babangida's military dictatorship (1985-1993) the country was in profound economic and political crisis. Spectacular levels of corruption and massive self-enrichment within Babangida's regime were grotesquely combined with rigorous implementation of the IMF "structural adjustment program," which worsened the poverty and suffering of ordinary Nigerians.

The country's political predicament grew deeper still when the results of democratic elections in 1993 were abruptly abrogated by the military junta. Amidst the social upheaval that followed, General Sani Abacha, then Minister of Defense, seized power. Undoubtedly Nigeria's most brutal and corrupt ruler, Abacha instituted a reign of terror and political suppression. His intolerance of dissent saw the execution of nine Ogoni activists in Nigeria's oil-rich delta region, including internationally-recognized writer Ken Saro-Wiwa. In a five-year reign that ended with his untimely death under rather mysterious circumstances, Abacha also embezzled more funds (an estimated two to five billion dollars) than any other ruler in Nigeria's history.[8] Nigeria became a pariah state, and highly skilled professionals fled the country in staggering numbers.

Oladipo Kalejaiye (International Christian Center, Los Angeles)

Dr. Oladipo Kalejaiye grew up in a Christian home in Nigeria. His parents were "God-fearing" Methodists who took their faith seriously—his father still holds morning prayers every day at six o'clock. Yet, Kalejaiye grew up only nominally Christian and as an adult lived what he describes simply as a "wild life." He graduated from law school in 1982 and was awarded a scholarship to pursue advanced studies in Germany. After completing a doctorate in private international law at the University or Hamburg (in 1989), he returned to Nigeria and set up a law office. The following year, a childhood friend who visited him at his office shared the gospel with him. Kalejaiye did not make a commitment, but what he had heard unsettled him on a certain level and stimulated a process of self-examination. A month later, he woke up in the dead of night and, alone in his bedroom, committed his life to Christ. Conversion represented, in his words, "a 180 degrees turn." He went back to Germany to break off his engagement to a German woman and returned to Nigeria with all the zeal of a young convert.

Kalejaiye joined one of the several hundred parishes of the Redeemed Christian Church of God (RCCG), where he met and married his wife, Nonyelum (a dentist). He labored assiduously within the RCCG movement while practicing law. Such were his fervor and commitment that he was made an RCCG pastor in 1993 and was sent to Epe, a Muslim town on the outskirts of Lagos, to start a new church. By 1996 the church had one hundred members, and Kalejaiye

---

role in resolving regional conflict (conspicuously within the multinational ECOMOG intervention force) ("Nigeria and Ecowas Special Report," *West Africa*, October 19-November 1, 1998, 753-58).

8. For an account of the Abacha's venality, see Baker, *Capitalism's Achilles Heel*, 52, 60-64.

had planted two more churches—a remarkable accomplishment in a Muslim environment.

As a young lawyer and a devoted Christian, however, Kalejaiye faced formidable challenges in 1990s Nigeria to his career in private international law. Systemic corruption and institutionalized bribery made the practice of law a nightmare for scrupulous attorneys. Since over 90 percent of his clients were Europeans and Americans, Kalejaiye's cases attracted the attention of public officials determined to line their pockets. His outright refusal to pay bribes multiplied the roadblocks and severely hampered his law practice. He recalls that he spent enormous amounts of time in the court of appeal seeking to get unfair rulings against his clients overturned. One of his most famous victories involved the reversal of a fraudulent verdict in a big case that made the national headlines. But, in the prevailing climate, such successes hardened rather than softened the opposition he faced. One chief justice even threatened to teach him a lesson on the practice of law in "the real world." After six years of toil and frustration, Kalejaiye decided to come to California (with his wife and two young children) to continue his career.

His decision was influenced by two considerations. He regularly vacationed in California where he had a cousin, and California was one of only two states which allowed non-American lawyers to practice law after passing the state bar (the other was New York). Kalejaiye arrived in California in 1996 and set up a general law practice the following year after passing the state bar. The transition from Nigeria to California involved drastic change and significant loss of status. He had terminated a very promising career in Nigeria and, the fearsome challenges notwithstanding, had walked away from a lucrative practice with five other lawyers in his employ. His wife also ended a successful career as a dentist. As upwardly mobile professionals in their homeland, their daily lives included many privileges and comforts that were unattainable in America—back in Nigeria Kalejaiye had had a personal driver, and their household staff had included a nanny, a housekeeper, a housemaid, and a gardener. The transition from this standard of living to life as an African immigrant family in America was radical, to say the least; but it afforded important compensations, including peace of mind, a relatively stable environment, and unique opportunities for ministry.

Even before he passed the California state bar, Kalejaiye had begun to give serious attention to the matter of ministry. At the time there was no RCCG church in Southern California, so he actively considered starting his own church. Just then, he was approached by members of the Christ Apostolic Church (an African immigrant church) located in the Crenshaw district in south Los Angeles to be their pastor.[9] He explained his desire to found his own ministry but agreed to serve temporarily as their "spiritual adviser." In 1999, after three years, he finally left to start his own church.

---

9. Christ Apostolic Church (CAC) was established in 1941, as part of the *Aladura* ("praying people") movement, which emerged out of Nigeria in the 1920s. CAC is strongly Pentecostal with a strong emphasis on Bible study, divine healing, and education. It was one of the earliest ministries to establish African immigrant churches in the United States, where it now has some twenty-five churches.

"A People Belonging to God"

Like most African immigrant churches, Kalejaiye's International Christian Center began as a house fellowship meeting in his two-bedroom apartment. The first meeting involved fifteen people, but the group grew quickly. After four months, with the carpet in his apartment completely ruined, Kalejaiye incorporated the fellowship as a church and rented the banquet hall at the Hilton Hotel (Los Angeles Airport) for their weekly worship services. In 2000, he put his law practice on "inactive status" to take up full-time pastoral ministry for the first time in his life. The Hilton Hotel arrangement was intended to be temporary, since it limited the church's functions to one meeting a week. With a membership of around one hundred, the young church took the audacious step of purchasing a two-story structure in the city of Hawthorne, California, for $225,000. This move not only reflected the commitment of the church's core membership (which included many young professionals) but also signified confidence in Kalejaiye's missionary vision. He had included the descriptor "international" in the church's name to signal that it would not simply be a church for Nigerians, but rather one fully committed to "making disciples of *all* nations."

The purchase of the new property was all the more remarkable considering that International Christian Center was affiliated with the Redeemed Christian Church of God at the time, which meant it had to pay tithes to the parent body. In 2003, the remitted sum was $85,000. Between 2000 and 2003, International Christian Center also planted four other RCCG churches. However, Kalejaiye's relationship with RCCG soured over different approaches on matters pertaining to discipline within the church. International Christian Center has operated as an independent ministry since 2003.

The new building included a 350-seat sanctuary as well as offices and room for Sunday School. The purchase of its own property allowed the church to plan multiple weekly functions and diversify its ministries. This had a profound impact on its growth. By 2006 total membership was about four hundred. Two worship services are conducted each Sunday with attendances of 100 and 250 adults, respectively. The Sunday school attracts over eighty children. The bustling congregants, smartly-dressed ushers, energetic worship, and be-robed choir at Sunday services provide scant indication of the church's modest beginnings and remarkable growth. Yet, already in December 2004, when I first visited the church, there were obvious signs that the church had outgrown its current premises. The second service was packed to overflowing, and parking on the street outside is troublesome enough to deter casual visitors.

In his pastoral leadership, Pastor Kalejaiye places great premium on personal integrity, strict discipline, and high Christian standards. He applies the New Testament scriptures literally and he holds his church members to strict moral codes—dating without the prospect of marriage is strongly discouraged. His outlook evokes the scriptural view that Christians are "a people belonging to God" (1 Peter 2:9). The "strict discipline" rating by members of his church (53.5 percent) is much higher than the nationwide average (41.4 percent). While this puritanical approach to ministry undoubtedly costs him members, it means that his leadership inspires strong loyalty and respect. He informs me with a disarming smile that many members who leave because of his strict standards eventually return to the church after painful experiences.

Kalejaiye's high Christian principles (even by African Pentecostal standards) may be the product of a legal mind transformed by scriptural ideals. But when he criticizes the lax discipline, mediocre leadership, and corrupt practices which he insists characterize many African immigrant churches (he singles out the Nigerian-founded ones), Kalejaiye is not simply being judgmental; he is expressing a deeply felt aversion to laxity of any kind. He is even more critical of the widespread dilution of biblical standards within American churches.

Like other successful African pastors, Kalejaiye presides over a well-organized and efficiently run administrative structure. The leadership team consists of a board of six deacons including his wife. Though he has no formal ministerial training, Kalejaiye is a seasoned student of the Bible and a gifted teacher. His decision to found a church was informed by a strong missionary vision which remains compelling. At present less than 10 percent of the church's membership is American; the majority are Nigerian. Yet the man who appended the label "international" to the name of his church at a time when it was fifteen members strong and 100 percent African remains unshaken in his conviction that he is called to minister to people of "all nations," not solely to Africans. While fully alive to the challenges posed to his missionary vision within the American environment he is also determined to overcome them and expand his ministry cross-culturally.

The solution and strategies he articulates combine the spiritual and the pragmatic. Like other pastors in the study, he is convinced that this African missionary movement will have a major impact on American society. He informs me with quiet self-assurance that, since this African missionary movement is God-ordained, the various obstacles and impediments will be overcome. This observation is not speculative. It is stated with the matter-of-factness of a man who, despite advanced Western academic training, treats the spiritual dimension with utter seriousness. But he is one of the first to admit with refreshing candor that the intense African spirituality can be a turnoff. He cautions against what he calls "hyper-spirituality," an intense preoccupation with spiritual agency and experience which ignores the practical dimensions of effective ministry. He berates African pastors who emphasize prayer, fasting, and deliverance ministries but pay scant attention to organizational effectiveness, budgetary planning, and educational preparedness.

The centerpiece of his strategy for cross-cultural ministry and missionary expansion is the bilingual service. Initially, the first Sunday service incorporated Spanish translation in an effort to reach the surrounding Spanish-speaking community. Eventually, when it became clear that many in this target community have to work on Sunday mornings, this bilingual service was changed to Friday evenings. (Both Sunday services are now in English.) About fifteen Spanish-speaking members regularly attend on Fridays. The church recently bought wireless headphones, which are distributed during the service to facilitate bilingual fellowship. A Spanish-speaking minister is currently being trained to provide pastoral leadership for the Spanish-speaking community. His full-time appointment is likely to transform the church's missionary engagement.

Meanwhile, the church has already taken the momentous step of purchasing a $1.8 million property in close proximity to its current location; and almost the same amount has been spent on various construction projects necessary to prepare the site for occupation in December 2006. The move was necessitated as much by the need for bigger facilities—the new site houses two seven hundred-seat auditoriums—as it is by commitment to an intercultural missionary vision. Current ministries, such as the work among prostitutes, will be given a boost; but plans for the new structure include after-school programs, adult education for the Spanish-speaking community, and a homeless ministry. In seven years of ministry Kalejaiye has seen hundreds of lives transformed, but his most cherished vision—a church "populated by the people of the land"—remains unfulfilled. Yet, as he takes perhaps the most audacious step yet in his short missionary career, he remains as excited about the possibilities as ever.

Out of Congo

The Democratic Republic of Congo has a five-hundred-year Christian history that dates back to the sixteenth century Christian Kingdom of the Kongo. Today, its population of fifty-six million is 96 percent Christian, making it one of the most Christianized countries in Africa. It is also home to the largest Catholic church on the continent. European missionary efforts, in the wake of Belgian colonization, met with remarkable success among the Baluba people in the diamond-rich Kasai region (in the south-central part of the country). The Baluba converted to Christianity in huge numbers and became energetic missionaries of the faith.[10] Kasai became Congo's Christian center, producing the majority of the Congo's Christian leaders and a good proportion of its educated elite. In the chaotic period after political independence from Belgium (in 1960), when European missionaries and Western-educated Congolese were targeted in indiscriminate acts of violence (motivated by revenge and tribal hostility), some of the worse atrocities took place in Kasai province. Close to two hundred European missionaries and more than ten thousand Congolese Christians, both Protestant and Catholic, were massacred.

Belgian colonization of Congo (a country with vast mineral wealth) was brutally exploitative, sadistic (chopping off the limbs of men, women, and children was a common form of punishment for refusal to work), and genocidal (millions of Africans were wantonly killed). Independence in 1960 was followed by political upheaval. In 1965, Colonel Joseph Mobutu, commander-in-chief of the army, seized power (with American backing) and instituted one of the most venal and corrupt regimes in postcolonial Africa. His thirty-year rule

---

10. See John Baur, *2000 Years of Christianity in Africa: An African Church History* (Nairobi, Kenya: Paulines, 1998), 218, 220-21; also Peter Falk, *The Growth of the Church in Africa* (Kinshasa: Institut Supérieur Théologique de Kinshasa, 1985), 379.

was marked by one-party government and a personality cult. Seeking political legitimacy through national hero status, Mobutu embarked on a systematic campaign against all manifestations of Western influence and control within the country—including the church. In 1971, as part of an Africanization or "authenticity" drive, he changed the name of his country to "Zaire" and rechristened himself Mobutu Sese Seko (short version). All Congolese were required to renounce their Christian names. Observance of Christmas as a national holiday was abrogated, religious instruction in schools was replaced with "Mobutuism" (a vague anti-imperialist ideology), and public religious symbols were replaced with images of the president.

Through his extensive business empire and regular raids of the national bank—as much as $150 million was siphoned in one instance!—Mobutu became one of the richest men in the world.[11] His personal fortune (estimated at $5 billion!) was greater than the national debt. Institutionalized nepotism, systemic corruption, and unbridled self-enrichment among senior government officials and the higher echelons of the military created grievous economic disparities and set the conditions for precipitous economic decline. The oil crises of the early 1970s and the collapse of the price in copper sowed the seeds of rampant inflation and massive foreign debt. In 1989 development programs were canceled when the country defaulted on loans. The suffering and misery of the masses of people intensified greatly. Economic discontent and years of misrule also engendered armed insurgency among exiled opposition groups. An expensive but unsuccessful invasion of Angola to curb rebel incursions exposed the regime's fragility. By the 1990s, Mobutu's power had weakened considerably and was largely confined to the capital, Kinshasa.

The appalling conditions within the country stimulated increasing out-migration. In 1997, anti-Mobutu forces under Laurent Kabila captured the capital and set up a new government. But Congo's woes continued. The newly renamed Democratic Republic of Congo became engulfed in a brutal five-year war—termed "Africa's world war"—in which government forces supported by Angola, Namibia, and Zimbabwe were pitted against rebels backed by Uganda and Rwanda. As many as three million died, and many more were displaced in a conflict possibly prolonged by warring parties to exploit rich mineral resources.

Pastor Joe Kamanda (Schekina Christian Center, Chicago)

Pastor Joe Kamanda is a Baluba, and he exudes the self-confidence and enterprise associated with his ethnic group. Born into a devout Christian home—his father is an Assemblies of God bishop who also had a full-time job as director of a bank—Kamanda experienced personal conversion at the age of twelve and shortly thereafter felt called to full-time ministry. This "calling" was patently evident in an all-consuming passion for preaching the gospel. So intense was his desire to "win souls" that he had to be compelled by his parents to stay in school. The high school he attended at the time was an elite institution in the capital

---

11. Nugent, *Africa since Independence*, 236; Baker, *Capitalism's Achilles Heel*, 52, 138-43.

(Kinshasa) attended by the children of politicians and the high-ranking military officials. Kamanda promptly started a student prayer group that attracted up to three hundred members (half the student body) and met every day after school, sometimes for up to three hours. By the time he was fifteen, Kamanda had no doubt that evangelism and pastoral leadership were "my destiny."

The household he grew up in was far from wealthy, but his parents were hardworking and determined to give their children the best education they could afford. Their desire was that Kamanda attend the best business school, and the United States was the country of choice. Kamanda arrived in Chicago in early 1995, shortly after finishing high school, to pursue undergraduate studies in business management. He had no relatives or personal contacts in America and hardly any English (a subject he had hated in school). His intention was to acquire a bachelor's degree and return to Congo to help his father in ministry. He spent his first seven months enrolled in an English language school and thereafter studied business management at Triton College. Halfway through his program, however, his father quit his bank job and Kamanda was forced to abandon his studies and seek employment in order to support himself and raise the necessary funds for the completion of his degree. He has yet to return.

"For Such a Time as This"

Kamanda gained employment with Verizon Communications (the nation's largest local phone company), and over the next six years he worked his way up to regional manager (sales and marketing), overseeing operations in Illinois, Michigan, Indiana, Ohio, and Wisconsin. This was no mean achievement for an African immigrant who had been in the country for less than ten years; and he had the six-figure salary to prove it. In March 2002, two weeks after he got married to Ida, his Tanzanian fiancée, the Carolina branch where he was based at the time was shut down and Kamanda was offered relocation. He chose Chicago, the city he had come to regard as home away from home.

By now, Chicago, like many major cities in the United States, was a vibrant center of new immigrants, whose growing presence was inevitably marked by diverse centers of worship. Kamanda recalls that there were three to four French-speaking African immigrant congregations (including a Congolese church) at the time. All, however, operated as veritable ethnic enclaves, which provided for the religious and social needs of specific communities but made scant effort to reach out to the wider community. The vantage point afforded by a successful career in corporate America helped Kamanda to see that the younger French-speaking immigrants were poorly incorporated into American society and lacked both inspiration and direction. For many, inadequate English competency acted as a major barrier to social integration and adaptation.[12] Many lived lives characterized by quiet desperation—their desire to achieve personal goals, prosper, and

---

12. According to official immigration data, almost half (47.4 percent) of Congolese foreign-born in the United States "speak English less than 'very well'"—well above the African foreign-born average of 26.8 percent. See "Foreign-Born Profiles" (2000).

succeed constantly frustrated. The pastor in Kamanda rightly sensed that while regular Christian fellowship within their ethnic group met important needs, it also left major aspirations unattended to. Many, in fact, were already drifting away from church and had grown quite lukewarm in their Christian faith.

It was not the first time that Kamanda had noticed this undefined air of aimlessness among French-speaking African immigrants, who, as a group, faced particular challenges in building successful lives within American society. Employment with Verizon had involved periodic placement in different cities, and he had served as youth minister or assistant pastor in a number of churches (both white and African immigrant). These regular opportunities for ministry had helped to build an understanding about the expanded role that immigrant churches needed to play in the lives of immigrants. His own call to full-time ministry remained unfulfilled but undiminished. He did not realize it at the time, but his career in the corporate world had been an excellent training ground for ministry as a missionary-pastor. He now thoroughly understood both the world of the African immigrant and the wider American society. By the time he resettled in Chicago (in 2002), his experiences had forged in him a deep and passionate desire to minister to the needs of immigrants and bring the message of the gospel to Americans. But the vision had yet to crystallize.

In Chicago, Kamanda started ministry among French-speaking African immigrants. For almost a year he visited them in their homes, prayed with individuals, provided encouragement and spiritual counsel. This close interaction intensified his awareness of the urgent needs within the African immigrant community, and he now began to pray for a sense of direction. Given his successful career, starting a church was not an option he had seriously considered, but that was precisely the divine direction he received along with a revitalized call to full-time ministry. He envisioned what he termed a "holistic ministry"—a church where faithful proclamation of the gospel would be combined with solid teaching on how to apply biblical principles to the practical challenges of daily life, a worshiping community where individuals would be nurtured in the faith as well as on principles of success. In short, a ministry devoted to raising successful, confident African Christians, able to realize their full potential in American society. It suddenly occurred to him that what he envisaged, in fact, would be more accurately described as a "center" rather than a "church." The Schekina Christian Center (Chicago) was born.

In January 2003, Kamanda started a fellowship meeting comprising four adults and two children. After two months he withdrew all his savings, bought musical instruments, rented a hall, and held his first public worship service. Thirty people attended. Membership of the new church rose slowly. Nine months later, Kamanda quit his job at Verizon to serve as full-time pastor. Services were held in a small room at the Light of Christ Lutheran Church (rented for $100 a week). As a new pastor in charge of a fledgling church with a young family to care for (his first child was born in 2001), Kamanda had his work cut out for him. He worked long hours, prayed long hours, and drew on his considerable managerial skills to build the new ministry. After a little over a year, the ministry had outgrown the facility and it was necessary to find a bigger place. Finding affordable premises meant moving out of Chicago. In 2004, the growing church moved to Evanston, a predominantly white suburb about thirteen miles north of downtown Chicago. This move turned out to be ill-fated.

About this same time, Kamanda had grown increasingly restless with the fixed African identity of his ministry. The lack of outreach and inward-looking mind-set that characterized other African immigrant churches he had encountered had always been a source of disquiet; and now that he was heading his own ministry his sense of frustration had become unbearable. In words that echoed those of other immigrant African pastors, he emphatically declares that he is called to minister not only to his own people but to every race and nationality. The missionary vocation was important to him; the passion to win souls that had burned in the twelve-year-old now compelled the man. As he puts it, Jesus urged his disciples (in Acts 1) to start in Jerusalem, not *stop* there—in his case, ministry to French-speaking Africans constituted "Jerusalem."

Kamanda was also fully conscious that implementing this missionary mandate within a French-speaking African immigrant community had serious implications. His church, after all, had been born out of the urgent need for alienated French-speaking African immigrants to construct the cultural and linguistic space necessary to nurture their Christian faith, cater to their spiritual well-being, and develop the insights and skills necessary for successful incorporation into American society. The "center" was a place to be at home, a place of refuge from the alienation and daily indignities nonwhite immigrants in American society were exposed to. Missionary outreach meant giving up a "comfort zone," including that most prized ingredient: unencumbered fellowship and unfettered worship in a familiar tongue. After months of agonizing, Kamanda consulted with his leadership team and informed the church of his vision. To his surprise, the idea met with considerable enthusiasm. With the move to Evanston (in April 2004), the ministry seemed poised for major change. Mailings were sent out announcing the church to the wider public and a new awareness about inviting non-Africans spread through the membership.

The Evanston move did bring change—of the worse kind. The new facilities were bigger and self-contained; the church service was now bilingual—the sermon was preached in French with an English interpretation and half the worship songs were in English. But when it left Chicago the church essentially abandoned its core membership, many of whom lacked independent means of transportation. Utilizing public transportation to cover the long distance was a considerable burden, and plans to purchase a bus never materialized. Moreover, the Evanston location was in a depressed area of town that proved unappealing (even for members) and strategically ill-suited for outreach to nonimmigrant groups. Within a year, the membership had declined by about 60 percent. Kamanda describes this as the lowest point in the ministry. But the experience strengthened his resolve to build up the ministry's missionary function. After thirteen months, Schekina Christian Center moved back to Chicago. Sunday attendance tripled within three months, but the church's troubles were not over. The hall (or storefront) they rented was located opposite a synagogue, and the church's growing attendance created a parking congestion that displeased the synagogue authorities, who lodged a formal complaint with the City of Chicago. The church was forced to move again.

This time, Kamanda approached the leadership of the Light of Christ Lutheran Church, the church where his new ministry had rented a small room three years previously. His ministry had come full circle, but the situation within the Lutheran Church had altered drastically. With their Sunday attendance down to sixteen, the Lutheran Church leaders offered Kamanda the church's two hundred-capacity sanctuary and moved their own services to the small room that Schekina Christian Center had once rented. This remarkable turn of affairs provides a small cameo of the changing American religious landscape. In the space of four years, a young and struggling African immigrant church had grown to a membership of about 160, with average church attendance over one hundred, while a much wealthier and long-established mainline church had experienced significant decline.[13]

Kamanda immediately renewed efforts to pursue his missionary vision. By now, he had lived in the United States for over ten years and was thoroughly familiar with what he describes as the "materialized" or "counterfeit" gospel preached in American churches—a gospel stripped of offense and packaged in such a way as to make it amenable to a secularized society. Since he was often invited to preach and minister in American churches, he claims firsthand knowledge of the deep spiritual need and hunger that were evident among American churchgoers. In this regard Kamanda is adamant that African Christians have much to offer.

He offers that African ministries in the United States confront a society that has largely turned away from Christian ideals and where many churches have lost fidelity to the gospel. He is convinced that the "passion" and "fire" that characterize African Christianity make African Christians powerful missionaries. They have a lot to offer because they come with a "gospel of power." (See pp. 128-31 for a brief description of African Christianity.)

To enhance the missionary function of his ministry, Kamanda briefly experimented with two separate English and French services. Even though it attracted three American families, he found this approach limited and has resumed the bilingual format. He plans to wait until there is a sizable American membership in the church before attempting two separate services again. Of the one hundred or so people who regularly attend, only fourteen are Americans (and of these only two are white). The church is no longer limited to French-speaking Africans, and it is fully multinational, but it is a long way from fulfilling its founder's vision. Quite recently, Kamanda adopted the strategy of holding regular Bible study in the homes of his American members. When the first Bible study was held, he turned up expecting a handful of people. There were eighteen present,

---

13. According to its Web site, Light of Christ Lutheran Church is "a reconciling congregation of the Evangelical Lutheran Church in America," and its stated mission is to "proclaim God's Gospel of justice and mercy, celebrate the diversity of God's Creation and share God's abundant blessings as we grow in faith, hope and love" (http://www.loclc-chicago.org/).

and two subsequently attended the church. Like many missionaries before him he is learning to labor patiently and wait for the harvest.

(Meanwhile, in an unexpected development, the Lutheran Church offered Schekina Christian Center an opportunity to purchase the current building—one of the largest in North Chicago—for $2.5 million. At the time this manuscript was submitted for publication, Pastor Joe was in the process of raising the requisite down payment. He is absolutely convinced that this step would radically transform his ministry. How much so remains to be seen.)

An Appraisal of African Immigrant Missionary-Pastors

The three African missionary-pastors profiled here are representative of the leadership of the African immigrant church movement. Their stories (including the strong correlation between migration and divine re-commissioning), their vision, their missionary passion, and their commitment to devising strategies that will bridge the intercultural gap were unfailingly repeated in the seventy-plus interviews conducted. Their gifts and temperament have shaped the emergence of the movement, and the quality of their leadership will have a decisive impact on its future. But why start an immigrant church?

Scarcely any of the African pastors in the study came to the United States expressly to start a church. The immigration restrictions and strict visa requirements that have been implemented by Western democracies in response to non-white migration preclude the possibility of individual African Christians entering most countries as "missionaries," except under the auspices of an American church or denomination. Such arrangements are quite uncommon and are typically limited to mainline denominations. They also make for a very different kind of "missionary" encounter. In the event, the vast majority of African immigrant pastors experienced a "call" to start a church only after they got to the United States. In other words, these pastors are *migrants first*, missionaries second. They are missionaries because they are migrants. Their sense of missionary calling is framed by the experience of migration: as students, professionals, visitors, refugees or asylum seekers, lottery winners (through the diversification program), family members, and so on. And the fact that they can become full-fledged American citizens presents long-term missionary possibilities unavailable to most Western missionaries, who could never become citizens in many countries where they labor.

A general profile of all the pastors in the study reveals patterns and traits that reflect broad migration trends, and in a few cases put them in sharp relief. The majority (80 percent) arrived in the United States before 2000.[14] Almost half (47.9

---

14. The study did not attempt to verify either the current immigrant status of the pastors or their original visa status, though such details often emerged in the course of the interviews. By and large, virtually all the visa types were represented, and a good many pastors experienced significant difficulty changing their original visa status to permanent resident. The three pastors profiled at the beginning of this chapter entered the United States in different categories—student, visitor (turned refugee), and visitor (turned professional). As indicated in the previous chapter, African

percent) arrived in the United States in the 1990s, the decade in which political upheaval and economic collapse intensified in many parts of sub-Saharan Africa, notably in the West African region. For now the African immigrant church movement is dominated by West African pastors and congregations. Of the total pastors in the study, 88.7 percent are from English-speaking West Africa; 62 percent are Nigerian; and 24 percent are Ghanaian pastors. With only a few exceptions the pastors are male—though females form a slight majority (54.9 percent) of church attendance.

The data indicate that the educational level of the African foreign-born population in the United States is the highest in the country (among all foreign-born as well as the native population).[15] It should therefore come as no surprise that most of the pastors (57.8 percent) have a college degree, and *one in ten has a doctorate*. To impute a correlation between educational attainment and ministerial (or spiritual) effectiveness would be disingenuous and misleading, yet the fact that the leadership of this African missionary movement is dominated by men of recognizable intellectual ability must be considered one of its major strengths.

It is equally noteworthy that men with a business or managerial background, in banking, accounting, administration, and the like, constitute a clear majority (31 percent) among African immigrant pastors, followed by teachers (14.1 percent) and civil servants (7 percent). The overrepresentation of business skills is unsurprising for two reasons. First, and most obvious, U.S. immigration policies favor skilled immigrants. Second, and far more consequential, the successful establishment of an autonomous immigrant church in the American context requires innovativeness, self-motivation, sound leadership, an eye for good publicity, and business acumen—qualities that are nurtured by management and business training. As Dorothy Bass puts it, "to start a congregation is a strong statement of commitment, and no small job. A remarkable degree of passion . . . is indispensable" (1998: 174). Even so, it is startling to discover that fewer than 6 percent of the pastors in the study had a "religious" career or occupation prior to establishing an immigrant church; though the majority (70 percent) indicated that they had received "formal training" for ministry.[16] A significantly lower number (28.2 percent) had received what would be described as "formal missionary training."

It has to be said that, while ministry to the wider society invariably constitutes a key element in their original vision, few African immigrant pastors have the capacity to minister interracially or interculturally on an organized and sustained

---

foreign-born appear less inclined, on average, to became naturalized citizens than the foreign-born population as a whole.

15. See chapter 13. According to one 1998 study, 74 percent of African immigrants in the United States had tertiary education (Carrington and Detragiache, "How Big Is the Brain Drain?" 14).

16. While the study did not probe the nature of this formal training (whether it was academic, for instance), it was clearly understood as training provided by an established theological institution—as opposed to the informal in-house training provided by some churches or movements. This contradicts the widespread notion that African immigrant pastors are theologically ill-equipped. See Benjamin Simon, "Preaching as a Source of Religious Identity: African Initiated Churches in the Diaspora," in *Religion in the Context of African Migration*, ed. Afeosemime U. Adogame and Cordula Weisskèoppel (Bayreuth: Eckhard Breitinger, 2005), 289.

basis—at least not until they successfully negotiate the process of cultural adaptation and social incorporation themselves. In any case, as much as a missionary
vision is vital to their sense of calling, the immediate response is shaped (perhaps
constrained) by the struggles and needs of the immigrant community—including
a widespread longing for religious participation and culturally relevant forms of
ministry. Immigrant pastors are compelled to minister to people like themselves,
migrants who are displaced, who experience diminished status and alienation,
and who (like Samantha [see pp. 290-93 above]), often to find themselves spiritually homeless. They quickly discover that, in the crises-ridden encounter with
American society, many immigrants who once embraced the faith are in danger
of backsliding, and many who once rejected the gospel were now open to its
claims. In short, they become pastors because they are missionaries and fulfill
their missionary calling, at least initially, by becoming pastors. As one pastor
put it,

> We want to reach some Africans because they come over here and get lost
> in the crowd and stay away from church because no one knows them to
> challenge and encourage them to continue with the faith they had in Africa.
> We want to provide a cushioning for the social and economic pressures in
> this country by showing them what they need to do to survive the culture
> shock here. Our objective is to provide spiritual feeding such as teaching
> them the word of God and encouraging them to walk with the Lord so they
> do not lose the spirituality they had in Africa. We also want to reach our
> fellow Americans with the gospel of Jesus Christ. . . .

For these African pastors, therefore, the missionary call is invariably accompanied by an instinctive awareness that the African immigrant community
should form both the initial focus of ministry and the foundation on which to
build a more extensive missionary effort. This is not to minimize the missionary challenge involved in building a dynamic community of faith from what is
often an insignificant group of marginalized immigrants. This accomplishment
takes strong personal self-confidence, good networking skills, and a knack for
blending spiritual intensity with businesslike pragmatism. It is also informed by
racial pride.

As the segmented assimilation theory suggests, the immigrant's degree of
affinity with the dominant culture in terms of physical appearance, religion,
language shapes the mode of incorporation into American society. Even African immigrants who assiduously assimilate soon discover that "becoming an
American includes learning about American race classification systems and
about American racial attitudes and prejudices."[17] Thus, the very fact that they
are African profoundly impacts not only the process of integration and adaptation but also their approach to ministry and understanding of their missionary
calling.

As African immigrants, these missionary-pastors experience firsthand the

---

17. Smith and Edmonston, eds., *New Americans*, 394.

marginalization and exclusion that nonwhite immigrants commonly face in American society. Regardless of their natural ministry gifts, level of professional achievement, or educational attainment, being immigrants places significant limitations on their endeavors and forestalls the immediate realization of their missionary vision. The experience of racial discrimination and exclusion—which comes as a blow to West African immigrants in particular—reinforces racial identification and, ironically enough, animates missionary purpose. "Don't be refugees, be missionaries!": the divine message that galvanized Bishop Johnson's ministry (see p. 330 above) carries more than a hint of racial consciousness. It also celebrates African-ness.

For African immigrant pastors, therefore, being African (or black) is more than a badge of identity; it is a fundamental motivational force. Their success as Africans becomes part of the message, as it were, because it punctures the negative stereotypes of Africans (in American society) as dependent, backward, inferior, and underprivileged. All are impelled, in Bishop Johnson's words, not only to build a successful ministry but to do so in such a way that "it is clear that this is an African man, who has African roots, but whose ministry transcends the African constituency."

Here is how a few of the pastors articulated this commitment to reaching the wider American society:

America is now a mission field because it does not have the fire that she once had and continues to go down hill. Our kind of ministry is something people are looking for and yearning to have. . . . It is taking America time to accept what is happening in our ministries but eventually she would embrace the work God is doing through African churches.

America needs the gospel as much as any other society in the world. Americans are aware of what God is doing through the African churches. They call us for prayers, for counseling, for deliverance but they will not come to our churches. . . . They think Africans are inferior.

[America] is surely a mission field and God has us brought us here so that He can release his revival upon this nation. This nation needs the power of God and the gospel more than many people believe. Our ministries here are a great blessing and those who know are praying that God would raise up many more ministries like others in this country. . . . The American Christianity is too comfortable; the Christians do not realize the danger of being that way. . . . The church is supposed to be an example to the world but the church in America cannot be distinguished from the world.

The U.S. is a great mission field because God is not a priority here; instead materialism has taken over the lives of people. We are responding to these challenges by attempting to change the direction of the wind. We have opened our doors for early Morning Prayer meetings which are attended by

African Americans, Hispanics, Japanese, and Koreans. We believe through this multi-ethnic interaction we can impact this society for Christ.

American Christianity is saturated with . . . the American spirit of materialism. Many people are [so] busy chasing the dollar that God is given second place in their lives. God has called us from Africa and other places to help in reviving and redirecting the Christians to the true tenets of the Bible.

The United States is a mission field and a big one for that matter. I know many Americans will not agree with this. But if one considers the general and dominant culture in American and many European states now, it is clear that many have moved away from the Judeo-Christian religion. The formation of African churches here in the US is a stepping stone to evangelization of the American people.

Yet the fact remains that while the evangelistic efforts of African immigrant pastors are not limited to Africans it is Africans that they mainly attract—in the United States, at least. How quickly this scenario will change is difficult to predict. Much depends on the ability of these pastors to act as *cultural brokers* who can, on the one hand, nurture African spirituality and its distinctive ethos and, on the other, navigate the indeterminate gaps between that spirituality and the variegated religio-cultural landscape of the wider American society. For the majority of pastors, the conviction that they were called to be missionaries to the wider American society, and their confidence in fulfilling that mandate, has grown as they have become more culturally adapted and socially incorporated into American society. Evidence that African immigrant pastors who are more established within Western society are more adept at intercultural ministry is not hard to find.

Bishop Peter Morgan, head of Vision International Ministries, is a Ghanaian (from the Fante tribe) who experienced a "call" to ministry in 1979 while he was with the Assemblies of God. Shortly afterwards, he came to the United States to study theology at Seattle Pacific University but did not stay on after his studies were completed. He went to England, where he took over pastoral oversight of the struggling Holly Park Methodist Church in North London. It proved to be a daunting assignment, at least initially—Morgan recalls preaching to "empty pews" for months. By 1999, however, Holly Park Methodist Church was a thriving multiracial congregation with over 250 members. Morgan then felt another "call" to expand his ministry to the United States. Responding to this new vision, he moved to Los Angeles with his Ugandan wife, Sarah (also a pastor), and their seven children. In April 2000, after twenty-one days of prayer and fasting, Morgan started Vision International Ministries with a handful of individuals. Within the space of five years the church had grown to 250 adult members. But even more notable than the church's growth is its present composition. African immigrants (mainly from West Africa) form only a small minority (15 percent) of the church. About 80 percent of its membership is American and roughly 10 percent of attendance at its Sunday service is white (another 5 percent is Hispanic).

Bishop Morgan's Vision International Ministries has the highest number and percentage of Americans among the churches in our study. Accounting for his extraordinary cross-cultural appeal requires some conjecture, but two interrelated elements stand out. First, Morgan had already lived in a Western society for an appreciable length of time (at least ten years in England) before coming to the United States. He was already culturally adapted to Western ways of life and did not need the period of incubation that an African immigrant congregation provides. Second, Morgan directed his ministry to Americans from the beginning. Thus, his church included African immigrants from the start but was never confined to an African immigrant base. In his words: "I have been sent to America and to Americans. I am not sent to Africans in America. . . . I have not come here as a Ghanaian looking for Ghanaian immigrants to reach out to them."

The relative success of Morgan's initiative provides reasonable support for the view that with time and the benefits of cultural adaptation, African immigrant pastors will be better equipped to fulfill their missionary vision. In this sense, at least, the African immigrant church functions as crucial training ground and a springboard for wider missionary expansion. At the same time, the fact that Bishop Morgan was determined not to start an immigrant-only church points to the possibility that other African pastors may in the long run be inhibited from fulfilling their cross-cultural missionary vision by the peculiar demands and needs of the immigrant congregations over which they preside. In other words, what if the immigrant congregation itself becomes a pastoral detention center rather than a missionary springboard? This question can be answered fully only by examining the congregations themselves.

15

African Immigrant Churches in America

"Switch Off Mobile Phones—The Only Urgent Call Here Is the Voice of God"

Africa may yet prove to be the spiritual conservatory of the world . . . when the civilized nations, in consequence of their wonderful material development, shall have had their spiritual perceptions darkened and their spiritual susceptibilities blunted through the agency of a captivating and absorbing materialism, it may be, that they may have to resort to Africa to recover some of the simple elements of faith; for the promise of that land is that she shall stretch forth her hands unto God.

—Edward W. Blyden, "Africa's Service to the World" (1880)

As expected, the presence and growth of African immigrant congregations correspond to the general pattern of post-1965 African immigration. The earliest churches were established in the 1970s, and the vast majority are Nigerian founded. Females constitute a slight majority of the members (55 percent)—interestingly, only a small minority of church members (8.4 percent) think that appointing more women leaders would make the churches more effective (see fig. 12). Just over half of all members surveyed (52.9 percent) were in the thirty-one to fifty age bracket; and young adults (age fifteen to thirty) account for another 28.2 percent of members. In effect, the congregations are made up mostly of young families—over 80 percent are fifty years old or younger. The congregations also mirror the professional and educational profile of African immigrants. Many (42.7 percent) identify themselves as professionals; one in five (22 percent) are students; and one-tenth are self-employed. Only a small fraction (8.4 percent) are unemployed. Almost half of the churches in the study (48 percent) had one hundred to three hundred members; a tenth (11 percent) had three hundred to six hundred members.

Obviously, not all African Christian migrants establish separate centers of worship. As indicated by the "Samuel-Eli" model (see p. 327 above), countless thousands take up membership or participate in established American denominations and churches, where their presence or ministry often impacts the life and vitality of the congregation in innumerable ways. At the very least, suggests Andrew Davey, the mere fact of "a diversity of cultures within a congregation often leads to fresh understandings of the . . . practice of community as personal stories of migration and pilgrimage are retold against the backdrop of the biblical narrative."[1]

The Macedonian Model

As explained in the previous chapter, this study focuses on two types of African immigrant churches: *Abrahamic* and *Macedonian*. The former typified the establishment and growth of the three initiatives discussed in the previous chapter. Insofar as it reflects a planned (and commissioned) missionary response, two major movements are associated with initiatives in the United States that reflect the *Macedonian* model, namely, the Ghana-based Church of Pentecost (CoP) and the Nigerian-based Redeemed Christian Church of God (RCCG). Only the briefest account of the these ministries is possible here.

Church of Pentecost (Ghana)

The Ghana-based Church of Pentecost was established in 1937 through the ministry of the Irish-born Rev. James McKeown, originally of the Bradford Apostolic Church in Britain, who (unusually for a European missionary) resolved not to plant "an English oak on Ghanaian soil."[2] The new church was founded in the classical Pentecostal tradition, with major emphases on prophecy, healing, holiness, and evangelism. Nurtured on principles of inculturation and self-support, and spearheaded by indigenous initiatives, the church grew steadily. In 1962, the year it severed ties to the U.K. branch, it had a membership of twenty thousand. By 1987, it had grown to over 170,000 members, making it the fastest-growing church in Ghana. Under the leadership of the current chairman, Apostle Michael Ntumy, the church's adult membership surged from just over 450,000 in 1998 to 881,000 in 2002. The main cause of growth was personal evangelism.[3] Every member of the Church of Pentecost is trained to be actively involved in evangelism. The fact that many members retain this commitment after they leave Ghana underlines the argument that *every Christian migrant is a potential missionary*.

Church of Pentecost provides a classic example of how the extraordinary levels of African migration from the 1980s have radically transformed the outreach potential of African churches and Christian ministries.[4] The church leadership

---

1. Andrew P. Davey, "Globalization as Challenge and Opportunity in Urban Mission," *International Review of Mission* 88, no. 351 (October 1999): 386.
2. For a detailed history of this movement, see Emmanuel Kingsley Larbi, *Pentecostalism: The Eddies of Ghanaian Christianity,* Studies in African Pentecostal Christianity 1 (Accra, Ghana: C.P.C.S., 2001).
3. When he became chairman in 1998, Apostle Ntumy challenged every member to win one convert in the next five years (interview with Apostle Ntumy in Ghana, May 27, 2003).
4. Coincidentally, Ntumy's primary mission text, forged out of his own experience as a mis-

is strongly conscious of that fact. Interestingly, church annals record that a prophetic message received in 1948 had warned of this development. The prophecy
declared that God was going to instigate a worldwide spread of the church by
allowing life in Ghana to be very difficult; out of the subsequent "scattering" the
message of the Gospel will spread.[5]

By the end of the century, one in five Ghanaians was living abroad. (A brief
account of the event that triggered massive out-migration of Ghanaians from the
1970s is provided in pp. 226-27 above.) Ghanaians became the largest African
immigrant group in the U.K. In the United States, the number of Ghanaian immigrants increased fourfold between 1996 and 2001. Little wonder Ghana is identified in the New Immigrant Survey (2001) as one of the top five source countries
of Protestant immigrants in America.[6]

Dispersed throughout the world, Church of Pentecost immigrants evangelized
conscientiously, created small groups of new converts or started new churches,
and requested help from the mother church.[7] Church of Pentecost's highly centralized structure means that all churches established by its members form part
of the one polity. From the mid-1980s, under the stimulus of this extensive but
unstructured migrant movement, Church of Pentecost assemblies (as its individual churches are called) proliferated throughout Africa and beyond, in the
Middle East, Europe, and North America. Pastors sent out to assume charge
of churches founded by immigrants are always sent as "missionaries."[8] By the
end of 2002, 1,917 assemblies comprising 150,416 members had been established
outside Ghana. In 2003 alone, fifty-three new churches were opened and 6,405
new converts baptized.[9]

The first Church of Pentecost assembly in the United States dates to 1987 when
Ghanaian migrants in New York started a prayer group. When the group began
to expand, they requested a pastor from Ghana. Rev. A. K. Awuah was sent, and
the fellowship was registered as a church soon after he arrived in January 1989.
The new assembly grew vigorously with the upsurge of Ghanaian immigrants.
The congregation presently owns a huge structure in the Bronx (New York),
which boasts a six-hundred-seat auditorium and houses Church of Pentecost's
U.S. national headquarters. Other assemblies emerged in various parts of the
United States. By September 2005, Church of Pentecost (USA) comprised eighteen districts and seventy assemblies with a total of 10,882 members. In 2004
alone 504 new converts were baptized throughout the United States.

Church of Pentecost has an extensive missionary program, under which Gha-

---

sionary (see chapter 9), is Acts 16:9: "*Come over . . . and help us.*"

5. Interview (in Ghana) with Apostle Ntumy, May 27, 2003.

6. See Jasso et al., "Exploring the Religious Preferences of Recent Immigrants," 228f.

7. Opoku Onyinah, "Pentecostalism and the African Diaspora: An Examination of the Missions Activities of the Church of Pentecost," *Pneuma* 26, no. 2 (Fall 2004): 226.

8. Ibid., 228. It is worth adding that, in addition to providing pastoral assistance for the congregations established by its church members in the West, the church has officially commissioned
and sent missionaries to Australia, South America, Asia, and the Far East. See Jehu J. Hanciles,
"Beyond Christendom: African Migration and Transformations in Global Christianity," *Studies in
World Christianity* 10, no. 1 (2005): 93-113.

9. Onyinah, "Pentecostalism and the African Diaspora," 229.

naian missionaries have been officially commissioned and sent to Australia, South America, Asia, and the Far East. But it also consciously utilizes Ghanaian migration "as a springboard to contribute to the Christianization of the world through evangelism."[10] This approach is pragmatic and bears strong echoes of early Christianity, but it is troubled by a perennial missionary dilemma: how to increase the church's cross-cultural missionary function (so that it reaches more Americans) without alienating the core constituency on whose efforts missionary action depends.

Importantly, Church of Pentecost officially disavows a strategy of cultural expansion or imposition. This is hardly surprising. A formal strategy to replicate Ghanaian models in foreign lands would be a violation of the church's founding vision. Yet Opoku Onyinah, a senior Church of Pentecost pastor (and rector of the church's University College in Accra), insists that the church's heavily centralized administration imposes constraints on the overseas churches in their efforts to adapt to Western culture.[11] There is some truth in this. The church's strongly hierarchical leadership structure means that change and innovation tend to come from above, not from below. National bodies (like Church of Pentecost, USA) enjoy some autonomy, but their organizational structure duplicates that of the mother church in Ghana. Moreover, Church of Pentecost churches all over the world are integrated into the one body politic—no assembly is owned by, or registered in the name of, an individual. For now, however, the church's hierarchical structure serves its missionary outlook well, for the simple reason that the leadership has a strong and coherent missionary vision.

Apostle Albert Amoah, the national head of Church of Pentecost (USA), admits that less than 10 percent of the current membership is American, but he declares forcefully that "we have not come to establish a Ghanaian Church of Pentecost but an American Church of Pentecost."[12] He explains that the high incidence of first-generation Ghanaian immigrants who do not speak English has meant that some assemblies struggled to abandon transported Ghanaian forms, in language, worship, dress, and even duration of the Sunday service (which can last up to four hours).[13] But this is changing with the increase in numbers of a younger generation of Ghanaian immigrant and American-born Ghanaians. Nurtured on African spirituality and conscious of African values, but raised in the United States and educated in American schools, this group is only now beginning to train for positions of leadership and ministry in the church. They are also more interested, reports Apostle Amoah, in starting churches among Americans.

Apostle Amoah is adamant that developing a transcultural, transethnic identity is crucial to the church's mission and future. He is also convinced that it is possible for the church to culturally adapt while maintaining its core emphases

---

10. Ibid., 218.

11. Ibid., 238-39.

12. Interview at Church of Pentecost (USA) headquarters (New York), June 13, 2005.

13. See Daniel J. Watkin, "In New York, Gospel Resounds in African Tongues," *New York Times*, April 18, 2004.

on holiness, evangelism, prayer, and the baptism of the Holy Spirit. If these ingredients are maintained, he informed me, "the African element will not be lost."

The missionary commitment of the younger generation of Ghanaian Christians in the United States is a linchpin of Apostle Amoah's long-term vision. But this strategy reflects the American situation. In other parts of the world, Church of Pentecost has implemented cross-cultural missionary engagement from the start. In European countries like Italy, where Africans are viewed with disdain and largely confined to menial occupations, leadership by European nationals is considered a prerequisite for successful church planting, and close conformity to the local culture is strongly emphasized.[14] All five Church of Pentecost assemblies in the Ukraine are headed by Ukrainians. Even in the United States a number of assemblies are pastored by non-Ghanaian Africans, and some, like the assembly in South Bend (Indiana) have only a few Ghanaian members. One church in Atlanta is made up of Latinos. Now that the church is well established in the United States, the practice of sending missionaries from Ghana to head churches in the United States is resisted because it can retard cross-cultural ministry. Meanwhile, Church of Pentecost (USA) has already launched mission initiatives outside the United States in Guatemala, Dominican Republic, El Salvador, and Belize.

The Redeemed Christian Church of God (Nigeria)

The Nigerian-based Redeemed Christian Church of God (RCCG) was founded in 1952 by Pa Josiah Akindayomi (d. 1979), an illiterate charismatic healer. By then grassroots African Pentecostal (or prophet-healing) movements had proliferated in West Africa, and the new church experienced limited growth. That changed in 1980, when Rev. Enoch A. Adeboye, a former mathematics professor who had been Pa Akindayomi's interpreter, took over its leadership. Adeboye had a radical new vision for the church that involved its expansion from a small church dominated by uneducated and marginalized groups from the lower classes into a global movement. To this end he implemented a thorough modernization program designed to attract middle-class professionals, intellectuals, and other upwardly mobile groups into the church. He adopted a twofold structure of *classical* and *model* parishes: the former comprised churches that maintain the original lower-class membership and use of vernacular languages in their services; the latter comprises well-educated pastors and members who meet in urban areas, use English as the language of worship, and organize meetings (breakfasts, dinners, etc.) in the best of hotels to which other professionals and upwardly mobile groups were invited. Both sets of parishes retain the church's core emphasis on the power of the Holy Spirit, divine healing, and prophecy.[15]

The strategy worked superbly and marked a major tuning point in the life of

---

14. Interview with Apostle Stephen K. Baidoo (International Missions Director, Church of Pentecost) in Ghana, May 27, 2003.

15. Much later, a third entity called *Unity* parishes was added, aimed at counteracting the emergence of a two-tier system. This model comprises a combination of members from the first two and uses both English and the vernacular.

the RCCG. The influx of middle-class professionals not only changed the image of the church but also generated much-needed resources for expansion projects and mission. Evangelism, church planting, and discipleship are the primary focus of ministry. Adeboye also promoted a new principle of church growth—which I would term *the twelve-month pregnancy principle*—namely, that each church should give birth to another church after one year. The church's "mission statement" leaves no doubt about its strong commitment to evangelism:

> It is our goal to make heaven. It is our goal to take as many people as possible with us. In order to accomplish our goals, holiness will be our lifestyle. In order to take as many people with us as possible we will plant churches within five minutes walking distance in every city and town of developing countries; and within five minutes driving distance in every city and town of developed countries. We will pursue these objectives until every nation in the world is reached for Jesus Christ our Lord.[16]

Today, RCCG is recognized as one of the fastest growing and most popular Pentecostal churches in Nigeria.[17] The movement is a major phenomenon of African Christianity, and its development defies rigid classification. Its meetings and convocations are legendary. Its annual Holy Ghost Congress—an all-night prayer, healing, and miracle service lasting for three days every March—held at "Redemption Camp," the main RCCG center (located along the Lagos-Ibadan Expressway in Nigeria), attracts millions of participants.[18] As with other African Christian initiatives, RCCG's growth into a global movement was largely a function of massive African migrations.

As explained in the previous chapter, Nigeria's political and economic crises worsened with every passing decade after independence (in 1960). By the 1980s, Nigerians were leaving the country in staggering numbers. The sections of society most likely to migrate are the middle class and urban professionals; the same group, in other words, that constituted RCCG's new core membership. The steady migration of its members to other parts of Africa and other continents gave substantial impetus to RCCG's global expansion. Today, RCCG counts over six thousand parishes worldwide in more than eighty countries and claims a total membership in excess of two million. Almost everywhere, RCCG parishes are marked by its central features: dynamic worship, aggressive evangelism, an emphasis on church planting, all-night prayers, healing, and miracles. RCCG parishes throughout the world also send 20 percent of their tithes to headquarters; and much of this income is invested in further expansion schemes and missionary ventures.

Between 1989 and 2003, over 105,000 Nigerian immigrants were admitted into the United States. By 2005, Nigerians accounted for 13 percent of the African foreign-born population in the country—more than any other African

---

16. See Web site, http://home.rccg.org/MissionStatement/MissionStatement.htm.
17. Adogame, "Contesting the Ambivalences of Modernity in a Global Context," 30.
18. Ibid., 33.

nationality. This large Nigerian constituency has fueled the expansion of the movement in U.S. cities. Winners' Chapel, the first RCCG parish in the United States, was established in 1992 in Detroit (Michigan). It started as a fellowship group comprising twelve families led by James Fadele, an engineer employed by Ford Motors. Since then, RCCG parishes have multiplied and spread throughout the United States following the now familiar pattern in which Nigerian immigrants start a fellowship and later request the headquarters to send a pastor from Nigeria. To cite one further example, Jesus House (Chicago) started as a house fellowship of four Nigerian immigrants in July 1996. When the fellowship grew too large to meet in a house, a pastor was sent from Nigeria. When Pastor Bayo Adewole arrived in September 1996, he assumed leadership of a group comprising thirty members who met in a hotel in downtown Chicago. Today, Jesus House owns its own two-story building in Chicago and has an attendance of six hundred at its two Sunday morning services.

There are now 175 RCCG parishes in America with an estimated membership in excess of ten thousand.[19] These, together with another fifty parishes in Canada, comprise RCCG-North America (RCCG-NA). In the United States the vast majority of RCCG members are Nigerian; but the church evangelizes aggressively, attracts African Americans, Anglo-Americans, and Hispanics as members, and emphasizes a global vision. In the United States, RCCG has sensibly modified its church-planting objective from planting churches "within five minutes driving distance in every city and town" to planting one "within 30 minutes driving distance."[20] Whatever the prospects of this daunting vision, it signals the church's determination to impact American society. "The United States has become very slack," noted one of its pastors, "so God is making us bring worship and praise to them."[21]

In 2005, RCCG purchased about five hundred acres of land in Floyd, a largely rural area in North Texas about an hour's drive from downtown Dallas (which is home to ten thousand Nigerians).[22] This unprecedented move prompted considerable media interest, and elevated the ministry and expansion of African immigrant churches into public view flittingly. Believed to cost well over $1 million, this property is to be developed into "Redemption Camp" (patterned after the Nigerian original) incorporating RCCG-NA's headquarters, a conference center, a large dormitory, and a ten-thousand-seat sanctuary. Like other major African ministries in the West (including Apostle Sunday Adelaja's twenty-thousand-member church in the Ukraine and Rev. Matthew Ashimolowo's ten-thousand-strong congregation in the center of London), the construction of a large "sacred" place signals commitment to a sustained missionary encounter with American

19. Interview with RCCG Pastor Bayo Adewole, Jesus House (Chicago), June 24, 2005. No exact figures were available.

20. Adogame, "Contesting the Ambivalences of Modernity in a Global Context," 32.

21. Julia Lieblich and Tom McCann, "Africans Now Missionaries to the U.S.," *Chicago Tribune*, June 21, 2002, 1.

22. Simon Romero, "A Texas Town Nervously Awaits a New Neighbor," *New York Times*, August 21, 2005; Laolu Akande, "Redeemed Christian Church of God Buys Multimillion Dollar Property in Dallas, USA," Celestial Church of Christ, 2005.

society. Yet success will depend less on erecting multimillion dollar complexes than on its capacity to develop initiatives that can bridge the daunting cultural divide between Lagos and Dallas.

Minding Church Growth

African immigrant churches in the United States are overwhelmingly products of West African Pentecostalism and reveal some of its hallmarks: including personality-driven competitiveness and a propensity for endless replication—though, in fairness, these traits are also evident in worldwide Christianity. A few emulate American charismatic models, but most are decidedly African in their leadership, ministry, theology, and worship. As in other non-Western Christian communities, attentiveness to the supernatural and an intense focus on the spiritual dimension (as a cogent factor in everyday life) are hallmarks of identity.[23] This spiritual orientation is evident in the emphasis on deliverance (from demonic or evil spiritual forces and other identifiable forms of oppression), healing, and nightly prayer meetings. Church names such as New Anointing Deliverance Church, Full Deliverance Ministry, Abundant Life Ministries, Riches of Christ, and Living Waters Outreach also betray a decidedly African spiritual outlook. Given the inchoateness of the movement, the rate of growth of many of these African immigrant churches is astonishing.

The Mobile Faith Project included a congregational survey conducted between 2003 and 2005 that involved nineteen African immigrant churches (and 1,134 individual responses) in different parts of the United States. Based on the responses from the church members, three distinct elements appear critical for the growth of African immigrant congregations, not so much in terms of fixed principles as in the more basic existential sense of why people bother to attend or maintain regular attendance. These three elements were identified in our congregational surveys as the primary reasons for church attendance: "lively worship" (74.3 percent), "solid preaching" (64 percent), and meeting of spiritual needs (55.9 percent) (see fig. 11). It is important to note that each of these three elements represents an area of church life in which there is pronounced distinction between the post-Western Christianity of African immigrants and ways of doing church in a post-Christian (perhaps more accurately, post-Christendom) West. They also reflect areas in which the needs of the immigrant Christian community and the staple of American churches is most clearly misaligned.

Lively Worship

The functionality of music is universal. Like religion, music (in its endless variety of forms and expressions) pervades daily life in Africa. Religious ideas and

---

23. Peruvian theologian Miguel A. Palomino makes a similar point about Latino immigrant congregations in "Latino Immigration in Europe: Challenge and Opportunity for Mission," *International Bulletin of Missionary Research* 28, no. 2 (April 2004): 55-58, esp. 57.

memory are retained, celebrated, and transmitted through music, dance, and song. As John Mbiti explains, "African peoples are very fond of singing. Many of the religious gatherings and ceremonies are accompanied by singing which not only helps to pass on religious knowledge from one person or group to another, but helps create and strengthen corporate feeling and solidarity. . . . Music, singing and dancing reach deep into the innermost parts of African peoples, and many things come to the surface under musical inspiration which otherwise may not be readily revealed."[24] In African societies, moreover, the pervasiveness of music is a reflection not only of its intimate links with religion but also of the vital role it plays in expressing communal solidarity or affirming the social bond. Besides its entertainment value, offers Shlomit Kanari, "[African] music is bound up with social and family events. As part of the aural culture, music is important in inter-personal communication, in imparting meaning to social events, in creating a feeling of identification, and in conveying feelings and messages."[25]

Figure 11

African Immigrant Churches (U.S.): Members' Reasons for Attending Church

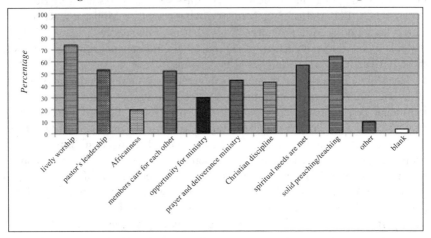

It is no secret that Africans have a strong propensity for exuberant and expressive worship. For African Christians, worshiping God through commu-nal singing and celebration is a vital part of congregational life and religious gathering. Worship styles vary from one Christian tradition to the other, but the African need for celebratory worship as part of religious participation is fairly unvarying. Extensive efforts by early European missionaries to suppress the full incorporation of African rhythms and sounds within the liturgy/worship

---

24. John S. Mbiti, *African Religions and Philosophy* (Portsmouth, NH: Heinemann, 1990), 67.

25. Shlomit Kanari, "Music and Migration: The Role of Religious Music in American Migrant Churches in Israel," in *Religion in the Context of African Migration*, ed. Afeosemime U. Adogame and Cordula Weisskèoppel (Bayreuth: Eckhard Breitinger, 2005), 270.

of the institutional church is one of the most grievous failings of the Western missionary movement. Those efforts were only partially successful, of course. In Africa today, familiar Western hymns and songs are liable to be sung or performed with musical expressions that reflect the rich sounds, rhythm, and harmony of the African musical culture. Of all the Christian traditions in Africa, however, none has appropriated music, song, and dance more thoroughly into regular worship than the African Pentecostal-charismatic movement. Music accompanies nearly all parts of the service.[26] Vibrant evocative worship is a mainstay of African Pentecostalism and a crucial reason for its widespread appeal and spectacular growth.

Like other peoples the world over, when Africans migrate they take their religion with them, which also means taking their music with them. Perhaps the most lasting legacy of the African slave trade was the transmission of African rhythms and musical sounds to the Americas and the West Indies, where their influence remains evident over three centuries later. Among African immigrants, a major reason for dissatisfaction with Western churches and a prime motive for regular attendance/participation in the African immigrant church is the form of worship. They are drawn as much by the familiar African sounds and expressions as by the atmosphere of celebration and the role music plays in strengthening the communal bond. Worship enriches their spiritual lives, "thereby enabling them to face practical life situations with fortitude and hope, in addition to conducting their Pentecostal life of witness with zeal."[27] Worship in African immigrant churches is better experienced than explained.

Pastor Kalejaiye's International Christian Center in Los Angeles, California, has the most dynamic worship of the many I have attended as part of this research. The singing and praising begin before the designated time of service (11:00 A.M.), and, once inside the church, the visitor is enveloped in sounds and rhythms that evoke unself-conscious involvement. The loudness and intensity discourage casual conversation. Nonparticipation is well-nigh impossible. Hardly anyone sits down during worship, which lasts roughly an hour broken up into two segments. Just one song could last for over ten minutes interspersed with instrumental interludes provided by a talented band ensemble. The all-female choir is robed in yellow gowns with red borders. Their song contribution is a fine blend of musical artistry and emotive worship. The congregation is not simply being entertained; it is being ministered to and invited into the intimacy of an encounter with the divine. The choir's rendition transitions seamlessly into more congregational worship. Words and music evoke stronger and stronger emotive self-expression and the total giving up of self. Worshipers break into "tongues"; many drop to their knees; hands are raised in supplication or praise. The moving of the Spirit is palpable—at least to this participant-observer. It was easy to see why, among the nineteen congregations that took part in the survey, the rating given to worship was highest in this church: 84 percent of respondents identified "lively worship" as the primary reason for their attendance.

---

26. Ibid., 271.
27. Onyinah, "Pentecostalism and the African Diaspora," 232.

Spiritual Needs

Philip Jenkins observes that "if there is a single key area of faith and practice that divides Northern and Southern Christians, it is this matter of spiritual forces and their effects on the everyday human world."[28] "Spirituality" is one of the most used and abused terms in the religious lexicon of modern Western society. The distinctiveness of African (essentially primal) spirituality perhaps lies in the fundamental belief that all reality is spiritual, which implicitly rejects the modern dichotomy between sacred and secular or between the supernatural/spiritual and worldly/material. This sense of "living in a sacramental universe where there is no sharp dichotomy between the physical and the spiritual" is nevertheless qualified by "a clear ethical dualism in respect of good and evil."[29] Indeed, the prevalent understanding in Africa of evil as a pervasive immanent force—reflective of the African belief in a densely populated spiritual universe—is one reason why Pentecostal movements, which maintain that the power imparted by the Holy Spirit in the life of the believer ensures victory over Satan or malignant spirits, have enjoyed such tremendous success.

African Christians place a premium on spiritual experience and vitality, specifically concrete experiences of divine power in everyday life; and African immigrant churches attract increasing membership because they take this feature of African Christianity very seriously indeed. Over half of church members in the study (55.9 percent) stipulate that their "spiritual needs" are being met. Like virtually all immigrant religious communities, African congregations act as a major social, spiritual, economic, and cultural resource. Members have access to multiple networks, solidarity groups, physical help, and vital support.[30] But there is also heavy emphasis on spiritual resources, on spiritual means and solutions: including discernment of harmful spiritual forces in everyday life, prayer, and fasting sessions, healing and deliverance, and other demonstrations of divine power.

These attributes are not considered exclusive of human resources (like medical care or legal consultation). The African worldview can be described as monistic, which is to say that spiritual power pervades and supersedes all things. For Christians, this translates into a focus on the power and authority of Christ who reigns over all creation and has conquered all things and who is at work in the life of the believer (Ephesians 1:18-23; Romans 8:31-39). In this unitary view, spiritual power and spiritual blessings trump all, but they are also manifested through material blessings and earthly success. This is why African Christianity can appear intensely spiritual and materialistic at the same time. The physical world is patterned on the spiritual realm. In its most rigorous application, repeated failure, constant setbacks, and lack of well-being signify spiritual malfunction.

---

28. Philip Jenkins, *The Next Christendom: The Coming of Global Christianity* (New York: Oxford University Press, 2002), 123.

29. See Harold W. Turner, "Primal Religions of the World and Their Study," in *Australian Essays in World Religions*, ed. Victor C. Hayes (Bedford Park, South Australia: Australian Association for the Study of Religions, 1977), 27-37.

30. See Onyinah, "Pentecostalism and the African Diaspora," 232-33.

Within this unitary framework, all forms of crises and hardship (from serious illness to immigration problems or wayward children) are addressed by spiritual as well as "earthly" means. Immigrants who fall out of official immigration status, for instance, will pursue legal help and seek strong prayer support at the same time. For the seriously ill, prayer and the laying on of hands are combined with antibiotics, chemotherapy, and CT scans. Western scholars who try to make sense of these multiprong approaches through an enlightenment worldview are likely to conclude that they "defy schematic interpretation."[31]

So the declaration that spiritual needs are being met implies that members experience spiritual growth and adequate spiritual support in times of crisis. Prayer and deliverance ministries feature strongly in the pastors' priorities. Most important, the need to cater to the spiritual nourishment and development of their members is the main reason why African immigrant churches hold more regular weekly gatherings for the whole church than the average American church. Research data reveal that 61 percent of the churches hold weekly prayer and fasting sessions;[32] 58 percent have a weekly Friday prayer meeting; 82 percent hold weekly Bible study meetings (either in the homes of members or in the church as part of a separate weekly meeting), and one-third hold regular mid-week services.

The rate of attendance at (or congregational participation in) the various weekly meetings is also relatively high: over 90 percent attend Sunday services; almost half of members (44.8 percent) attend the mid-week service; 16 percent participate in home groups; and one in four (26 percent) attend Friday prayer meetings. These figures provide an incomplete indication of the reality on the ground. Many of these meetings attract people who are not regular members of the church. Though 45 percent of church members attend the midweek service only a third of the churches hold one; roughly a quarter attend Friday prayer meetings but most churches (58 percent) have them.[33]

It is difficult to overemphasize the centrality of prayer (communal and individual) in the life of these churches. Vigorous, informal, collective praying forms part of every public gathering. Over half of the churches surveyed hold weekly Friday night prayer meetings that are attended in average by 25 percent of the members. The "intercessory prayer" ministry—a select group(s) that meets regularly to pray for the church and the needs of members—is more popular in the churches survey (90 percent have them) than any other form of ministry. More

---

31. Harvey Cox reflects on the same feature within Latin American Pentecostalism in *Fire from Heaven: The Rise of Pentecostal Spirituality and the Reshaping of Religion in the Twenty-First Century* (Reading, MA: Perseus Books, 1995), 172f.

32. At Bishop Darlingston's Bethel World Outreach Church, twenty-one days of fasting (during which participants eat one meal a day) are held twice a year, and one-week fasts are held three to four times every year.

33. In at least one church, more African nonmembers attended Friday prayer meetings than any other service. It is difficult to know what to make of the fact that more church members in churches located on the East Coast of the country (58 percent) affirm that "their spiritual needs are being met," compared to 44 percent of members in churches locate in Los Angeles.

than half the pastors in the study (55 percent) also identify prayer as one of their main ministry functions.

Slightly more than half (56 percent) also maintain a "deliverance" ministry, which emphasizes spiritual (as opposed to physical) healing, based on the conviction that the individual can be oppressed by or held captive to malignant spiritual forces that are often the cause of misfortune and chronic failure. Manifestations include addiction, barrenness, recurrent or incurable sickness, and mental instability.[34] That many African immigrant churches include the word "deliverance" in their names—as in New Anointing Deliverance Church—is ample testimony to the centrality of this feature in African Christian spirituality. As I explain below, even Sunday sermons tend to be strongly oriented to addressing the spiritual condition of the faithful, including an emphasis on the spiritual resources power available to the committed Christian.

Preaching of the Word

Preaching is the most important public function of the African immigrant pastor. (It is ranked relatively low in the ministry priority list mainly because, in practice, the distinction between preaching, teaching, and evangelism is an artificial one.) The Sunday sermon is the most strategic and fundamental form of ministry that the immigrant pastor performs on a regular basis. It is also the only ministry addressed to the entire community of faith. Thus, the quality of preaching not only contributes to regular attendance and membership commitment but also quite conceivably impacts the church's membership composition. Few other forms of ministry are as critical for nurturing spiritual growth and equipping members for daily Christian living. The Sunday sermon frames the church's self-understanding and spiritual outlook and offers a unique window on the pastor's vision. But the importance of preaching goes beyond the church's internal needs. As the most visible form of ministry, it showcases the quality of spiritual leadership and contributes to the church's missionary function. The sermon factors in the decision of first-time visitors to return or go elsewhere. It also arguably signals the pastor's readiness to minister beyond the African constituency.

On average, the sermons in African immigrant churches last thirty minutes to one hour and are dynamic, evocative affairs. The style is generally *ex tempore*, with the aid of notes, and dialogical responses (or shouts of encouragement and affirmation) from the congregation are common. What is striking is their content and focus. As Benjamin Simon attests (based on experience in Europe), sermons by African immigrant pastors "deal extensively with the religious, social and cultural problems of their audience."[35] Preaching is primarily directed at the host

---

34. For more on this, see Moses Biney, "'Singing the Lord's Song in a Foreign Land': Spirituality, Communality, and Identity in a Ghanaian Immigrant Congregation," in *African Immigrant Religions in America*, ed. Jacob K. Olupona and Regina Gemignani (New York: New York University Press, 2007), 268ff.

35. Simon, "Preaching as a Source of Religious Identity," 292; also, Biney, "'Singing the Lord's Song in a Foreign Land,'" 267.

of challenges that African immigrants face in building fulfilled lives in the new society.

African immigrants in Western societies are beset by innumerable hardships and struggles. These include painful cultural adjustments, the daily experience of rejection or alienation, demanding work schedules, mounting credit card debts, joblessness or employment insecurity, and raising a family in a permissive and individualistic society. Unaccustomed to taking regular vacation, African immigrants struggle mightily in the stressful pace demanded by a more individualistic, self-seeking, social environment. The attendant pressures impose unbearable tensions on marriages, create intense generational conflicts within family life, and even exert a terrible toll on spiritual well-being. In all these areas, immigrant pastors often face overwhelming demands as spiritual guides, community arbitrators, and therapists all rolled into one. All the pastors in the study indicated that marital problems (which often stem from role/status reversal in cases where the husband is unemployed), employment difficulties, and immigration-related troubles are among the most common problems they address on a regular basis. Fully 68 percent of the pastors identified "counseling" as a primary area of ministry; those identifying evangelism as a primary ministry approach 70 percent. Teaching, preaching, prayer, and deliverance ministries are seen as primary by 40 to 50 percent.

The pastor's aim, generally speaking, is to apply biblical insights to daily living, affirm the nature of victorious Christian living, and proclaim the efficacy of spiritual empowerment. This much is reflected in the sermon topics recorded in the course of this research: "Capture Your Season for Your Life" (Job 8:7); "Sword of the Spirit" (Hosea 4:6); "Time for Sober Reasoning" (Matthew 25:1-13); "The Power of the True Believer" (Luke 10:19); "Spiritual Warfare" (Ephesians 5); "The Anointing to Finish" (Genesis 37); "Strange Fire" (Leviticus 10); "Man in the Mirror" (2 Corinthians 3:15-18); "The Portrait of a Prevailing Church" (Acts 11).

The hermeneutic utilized by African immigrant pastors normally incorporates four elements: (1) a literal application of Scripture based on the conviction that the Bible speaks directly to current experience; (2) the view that all reality is spiritual; (3) an African understanding of evil as a pervasive immanent force; (4) the power imparted by the Holy Spirit in the life of the believer ensuring victory (over Satan or malignant spirits) and success.

Every Sunday, African immigrant pastors confront members whose lives are characterized by the struggle to succeed, various forms of hardship, the daily challenge of preserving self-esteem, the pain of social exclusion, racial discrimination, serious temptations to compromise ethical or traditional values (in a morally permissive and seductively consumerist environment), and the challenge of maintaining cultural dignity. As fellow immigrants (some of whom work part-time to support their family), the pastors have firsthand knowledge of the daily realities that confront church members, and this enhances the facility to inspire, encourage, warn, and stimulate. Sermons generally highlight the wiles of Satan or the power of evil, the empowerment of the Holy Spirit, and the need to live steadfast lives of holiness. The aim is generally to build self-esteem, encourage a positive and confident outlook, reinforce the strong sense of community, and promote a way of life that takes the ethical demands of the New Testament seriously. The survey revealed that among the theological themes emphasized by most pastors in their preaching were personal holiness, conversion, biblical soundnesss, and divine healing. More pastors (56 percent) identified personal holiness as a greater focus of their ministry than the other three—all of which were tied at 39 percent.

Assessing the Missionary Commitment

The data from individual interviews (of pastors) and congregational surveys leave no room for doubt that both the pastors and the regular members of African immigrant churches are strongly conscious of the need for intercultural ministry and missionary outreach. The views and vision of the pastors in this regard have already been reviewed in the previous chapter. It is worth noting in passing that being in the United States affords many African pastors unique opportunities to establish a full-fledged international ministry. Bishop Johnson provides only one example of the energetic church-planting ministries of African immigrant pastors. In our study more than half (53.5 percent) indicated that they are engaged in international ministry, which is to say that they have established churches in other Western countries (as well as in Africa) or that they regularly travel outside the United States for evangelistic ministry. Such efforts, it is important to clarify, are not limited to pastors with large churches and sizable budgets. In one year alone, Pastor Edward Odiakosa of the one-hundred member, predominantly Nigerian, Former and Latter Rain Church (Los Angeles), traveled to Cambodia, Italy, Austria, and London as part of an extensive international ministry.

But international ministry can be conducted during a few summer months in the year, and the better organized make extensive use of personnel and administrative resources available in the host context or environment. Active missionary engagement with the wider society in which the immigrant church is situated requires sustained effort and thoughtful long-term strategy amidst the enormous demands of presiding over an expanding congregation. Indeed, it is possible to argue that the immigrant congregation with its growing and extensive needs functions less as a launch pad for intercultural missionary enterprise than as a spiritual detention center of sorts, a flourishing but demanding locus of ministry that, for the pastor at least, ultimately inhibits missionary outreach beyond a predominantly African constituency.

Still, the missionary commitment of the pastors cannot be denied. Fully 70 percent of the pastors in the study identified "evangelism/mission" as a principal area of ministry—second only to "pastoral leadership. It needs to be said that the distinction between these forms of ministry (which include counseling, teaching, prayer, preaching, and deliverance) breaks down in practice. Depending on context and content, all serve a missionary purpose. While they are aware of personal ministry strengths or giftedness, these pastors do not compartmentalize the various aspects of their work. Every form of ministry is used as a basis for outreach and communicating the message of salvation. Certainly, all public events, including regular worship services, are clearly oriented toward exhorting the faithful and inviting the "unsaved" to respond to the claims of the Gospel and make the vital decision to follow Christ.

The unique challenges of serving a missionary purpose within the American (typically urban) context also compels some pastors to rethink the very nature of being church. Nigerian-born Pastor Tayo Badejoko of the two-hundred-member Courage Christian Center in downtown Philadelphia envisions his church as "embedded in the fabric of its community."[36] He gets this idea from the Old Testament portrayal of the tabernacle placed at the center of the journeying people of God. When the church decided to purchase its own building in 2005, the leadership was determined not to buy a church-looking building. What they purchased, for almost half a million dollars (the down payment was raised among members when the church was refused a bank loan), was an attractive, highly visible, glass edifice that could never be mistaken for a church structure. What Pastor Badejoko has in mind is not anonymous blending-in but a reconception of being "church" that allows the church space to serve the social needs of the surrounding community as well as house regular congregational activities. This understanding dissolves the popular demarcation between "church" and "mission"; it transforms the site of worship from a symbol of differentiation to one of integration.

This model or understanding of mission is shared by almost all the pastors in the study. It represents *witness as withness*, an approach to Christian mission that depends not on aggressive strategies, superior material resources, or sending structures but on sustained daily interaction with others who belong to the same neighborhood and deal with similar daily challenges. Missionary engagement in this sense focuses not on organizational "targets" or statistical goals but on a preparedness "to give an answer to everyone who asks . . . the reason for the hope that you have" (1 Peter 3:15 NIV). And where the Christendom model emphasizes cultural distinctiveness and aggressive expansion, this approach accepts cultural diversity and promotes mission as sustained interpersonal engagement.

The African Immigrant Congregation

The makeup, capacity (in material terms), and outlook of the congregation over which the pastor presides are also critical to the church's missionary function. Of special relevance are the level of missionary consciousness, openness to non-African members, property ownership (which significantly enhances the capacity for innovative ministry), and the resources to fund ventures or forms of ministry that take the church to the community. Even the residential patterns of the immigrant church members (whether they live in the vicinity of the church) as well as the type of neighborhood or community in which the church is located are crucial for cross-cultural missionary orientation insofar as they

---

36. Interview on June 10, 2005.

contribute to the degree of daily contact with non-African social segments of American society.

Unlike the vast majority of new immigrant (or "ethnic") churches in the United States, a high percentage of African congregations conduct their services in English—which removes a major barrier to cross-cultural ministry or missionary engagement.[37] All the churches in our study conducted their main services in English—though, as I explain below, English competence comes with its own built-in impediments. Of greatest significance is the attitude of church members to non-African membership and involvement. Three questions in the survey addressed this issue:

- Do you think the church should do more to reach non-Africans? (Answer: Yes, 85 percent; No, 3 percent; Not sure, 12 percent)
- Have you ever invited a non-African to this church? (Answer: Yes, 58 percent)
- How can this church be more effective in its outreach and ministry or increase its impact? (Answer: See fig. 12)

When these responses are combined with the finding that 40 percent of members would like so see their church more engaged in formal outreach and become more involved in the community (fig. 12), it adds up to a distinct interest in missionary expansion. Street evangelism by members is not uncommon. After ten consecutive evenings on the streets of downtown Silver Spring, Maryland, the evangelistic team at Bethel World Outreach ministries collected contact details from 1,132 respondents!

Confounding general expectation, only one in five members who attend African immigrant churches indicates "Africanness" as one of their main reasons for attending. This suggests a striking departure from the norm among immigrant churches. Equally significant, members who think that the church would increase its effectiveness ministry and outreach if it emphasized Africanness represent an insignificant minority (4.4 percent). At the same time, only a small minority were of the opinion that the church would become more effective if it became "less African" (see fig. 12). Two important conclusions can be drawn from these responses: first, that while the overwhelming majority of church members support cross-cultural outreach, they are somewhat ambivalent about how their church's African ethos would impact its missionary function; second, that there is a general willingness among members to make the cultural accommodations necessary for the church to reach non-Africans.

Evaluating the Missionary Challenge

On the whole, the members of African immigrant congregations tend to think that the capacity of their churches to impact the wider society depends on physi-

---

37. As noted in chapter 13, the new African immigrants are more proficient in English than the overall foreign-born population.

Figure 12

**African Immigrant Churches (U.S.): Members' Suggestions
for Increased Ministry Effectiveness**

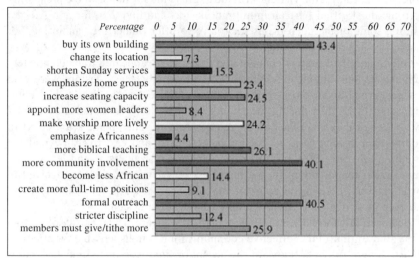

cal/material resources (building ownership, seating capacity, involvement in the community) and spiritual elements (biblical teaching, type of worship, greater evangelistic activity). Perhaps in part because of the limitations of research protocol, the data reveal very little awareness or recognition among church members (compared to the pastors) that systemic factors or broader trends within the American environment, including racial attitudes and social segregation, are liable to present major obstacles to cross-cultural missionary outreach. Three of these deserve brief examination.

Lost in Pronunciation

As noted above, immigrants from Anglophone Africa form the majority of the African foreign-born in the United States, and their level of English proficiency is higher than that of any other immigrant group.[38] Yet interviews with the pastors revealed that most had experienced a rather unexpected handicap in their efforts at cross-cultural ministry, namely, linguistic peculiarity. To ordinary Americans and people from other cultures, some types of African accent are difficult to understand—sometimes even for other Africans. This is less of a problem in ordinary day-to-day interaction, even though it promptly identifies the African immigrant as a foreigner—with sometimes undesirable consequences. But this linguistic distinction is much more difficult to overcome in public preaching, which, for most African pastors, tends to be an impassioned affair. To the amused

---

38. The percentage of African foreign-born who speak English very well (73.2 percent) is remarkably high compared to the total foreign-born populations (49 percent). See "Foreign-Born Profiles" (2000).

frustration of many African immigrant pastors, American visitors are likely to be impressed by their stage presence and endlessly fascinated by their particular "foreign" accent, yet the visitors struggle to grasp the substance of the preaching. Even the most gifted African immigrant pastors can find that, for non-African visitors, some of the deep truths they have to offer (under the "anointing," of course) are lost in pronunciation.

Only one or two pastors encountered in the study appeared to be completely oblivious to this linguistic handicap. Unsurprisingly, these pastors were also less concerned about cross-cultural ministry and outreach. While they communicated in English during the church service, they conducted their ministry as though they were back in an African setting. They made scant effort to modify their speech so as to communicate clearly and effectively beyond the co-ethnic universe. They used esoteric African colloquialisms and lapsed into their mother-tongue often. In one instance, the African researcher involved in participant-observation was a co-national (albeit from a different ethnic group), and even he struggled to entirely follow what was being said.

However, this form of cultural parochialism was rare. The majority of pastors in the study, mindful that effective communication is indispensable for effective ministry, were fully conscious of the accent or linguistic impediment. A number considered it their biggest challenge; and one pastor even commented wryly that he had considered voice training. Fortunately, this problem diminishes over time as the African pastors become attuned to subtle linguistic inflexions and acquire, usually by conscious effort, new speech patterns and verbal enunciation that bridge the communication gaps.

Race and Mission

In the predominantly white societies of Europe and America, most African immigrants discover what it means to be "black" for the first time in their lives. This experience can be either profoundly debilitating or psychologically liberating. In America, as in all Western societies, Africa is the face of poverty, disease, calamity, and degradation. Ingrained associations in the Western mind between black skin color and backwardness, extreme need, and inferiority are significant obstacles confronting the African missionary movement. Moreover, the degradation and violent oppression of blacks by whites in American history have done lasting harm to attitudes and social relations between the two groups. For this reason, the race factor has tremendous bearing on the missionary function and impact of the African immigrant churches.

The growth of these churches is hardly in doubt. Such are their dynamism and expansion that an accurate estimation of their numbers is daunting. (The 71 churches in this study had a combined membership of almost fourteen thousand.) But the new African immigrants join a native black population of over thirty-six million (roughly 13 percent of the total population) with its own particular history, cultural heritage, social institutions, and distinctive Christianity. If the new African immigrant population becomes culturally and socially integrated into this dominant black population, as some analysts speculate, it would render them invisible. For now, the degree to which the new African immigrants will inherit the marginalized and segregated status of the much larger African American group is difficult to determine. But it seems unlikely that they will transcend the rigid racial dichotomy that plagues American society.

As noted already, some scholars are convinced that race will become a diminishing problem as the assimilation of the new immigrants helps to bridge cultural distances. Maybe so. For the foreseeable future, however, African migrants, like the rest of the black population, will remain fully exposed to social marginalization, racial exclusion, and institutionalized discrimination. In this regard, it is worth reiterating that among most African immigrants, the experience of racial rejection strengthens rather than weakens racial identification and invites African consciousness. Most important, it often provides added motivation to succeed, which, for the African pastors, translates into a determination to prove that their ministry is effective enough to reach beyond the African constituency. As such, the experience of marginalization may prove to be double-edged: likely to stymie missionary outreach beyond other marginalized groups but also liable to imbue the more confident and highly skilled African pastors with added motivation to succeed as missionaries.

For all that, the new African Christians and the congregations they have formed represent a radical departure from the image, models, approaches, and strategies that have dominated the study of missions for the last five centuries. This non-Western missionary movement represents mission *beyond Christendom*: mission de-linked from structures of power and domination; mission undertaken from positions of vulnerability and need; mission freed from the bane of territoriality and one-directional expansion from a fixed center; mission involving agents who reflect the New Testament reference to the "weak things of the world" (1 Corinthians 1:27).

Almost four decades ago, John Fairbank, president of the America History Association at the time, observed that "the missionary in foreign parts seems to be the invisible man of . . . history."[39] By this he meant that the instrumental role of Western missionaries in shaping historical developments is typically overlooked by secular historians. This observation takes on added significance in relation to the new non-Western missionary movement. For these missionaries are invisible (so far) not only to the ivory towers of academic historical assessment but also to contemporary observers in the Western settings in which they function. Such is the entrenched view of missions as a Western prerogative and privilege that, at least in the United States, the notion of non-Western immigrant Christians fulfilling a missionary function within American society remains an implausibility for many. For the most part, when American churches give attention to nonwhite immigrants it is with a view to making converts out of them. In other words, the non-Western missionary in the West must get used to (at least

---

39. John K. Fairbank, "Assignment for the '70s," *American Historical Review* 74, no. 3 (1969): 877.

be prepared for) the experience of refusal of acceptance or denial of recognition from fellow Christians as well as non-Christians!

I argued in chapter 13 that African immigrant churches have much to gain from meaningful association and collaboration with the African American Christian community, and vice versa. At present the possibilities of this happening appear fairly bleak. Some of the churches in this study included significant numbers of African Americans,[40] but, taken across the board, the African American attendance is relatively low. It is not uncommon to find African immigrant churches in predominantly black neighborhoods which attract very few African American families. A mere handful of the pastors interviewed reported that they had collaborated with African American church leaders in the early stages of their ministry, but no long-standing association or partnership was reported. As a matter of fact, most African pastors appear leery of the African American "image" (see pp. 319-23 above) and tend to focus their energies on outreach to whites and Hispanics. Whether intentionally or not, African American pastors return the favor. Those with an interest in Africa tend to put more energy into building relationships (or setting up partnerships) with churches *in Africa*—a tendency informed by the general African American infatuation with the continent—and by and large ignore the burgeoning African immigrant churches in their midst.

It would be a mistake, of course, to treat either African immigrant churches or African American churches as homogenous units. The former are still in an early stage of formation and, with the exception of churches that are part of larger movements like RCCG or Church of Pentecost, they largely represent disconnected individual initiatives. The African American church is an infinitely more established phenomenon, but it is also variegated in its identity and expressions. In particular, it incorporates a burgeoning number of autonomous individual start-ups which exist alongside mainline denominations or movements. But both groups of churches tend to serve discrete communities with competing views of life in American society and disparate aspirations. Indeed, the determination of African immigrant churches and pastors to pursue cross-cultural ministries may contribute to existing tensions and disconnection.

Yet both groups have much to learn from each other about *mission from the margins*, not least because they share a marginalized status (in American society) along with the dilemmas and aspirations that come with racial rejection. This will remain true even in the likelihood that increasing numbers of the new African immigrants join the growing black middle class. On the ground, the presence, missionary fervor, and spiritual dynamism of African immigrant churches provide important correctives to African American views of African Christianity. At the same time, active collaboration with black churches would arguably bolster the efforts of African immigrant churches at cross-cultural ministry and missionary engagement. Black churches will find the presence and growth of African immigrant churches impossible to ignore, and African immi-

---

40. Bishop Morgan's Vision International Ministries in California boasts a membership that is *70 percent* African American. African immigrants, mainly from West Africa, form 15 percent, whites roughly 10 percent, another 5 percent is Hispanic. See pp. 348-49 above.

grant churches will likely discover that pursuing its missionary vision from the margins requires common ministry and witness with other marginalized groups as well as a greater willingness to invest in the underprivileged communities of American society. Alas, ordinary life is much more complex; for now, these two groups have yet to discover each other.

A Place to Feel at Home

Possibly the most formidable impediment that lies in the way of the cherished ideal of missionary outreach beyond the African constituency is not linguistic peculiarity, cultural adaptation, or even African spirituality; it is America's *segmented religious landscape*. As I have already noted, the massive influx of nonwhite immigrants appears to have reinforced rather than undermined the rigorous racial/cultural divisions that characterize American society. A major influx of nonwhite immigrants in an area invariably depresses the housing market and stimulates out-migration of non-Hispanic white residents. As a result, major immigrant cities have become "less white" and "more colored."[41] But the issue is broader than geography. One of the great paradoxes of American society is that while it can claim to be more diverse than any other nation on earth it is also arguably the most segregated—economically, socially, and racially.

This incongruity is pithily exposed by social commentator and *New York Times* columnist David Brooks, who writes:

> Maybe it's time to admit the obvious. We don't really care about diversity all that much in America, even though we talk about it a great deal. Maybe somewhere in this country there is a truly diverse neighborhood in which a black Pentecostal minister lives next to a white anti-globalization activist, who lives next to an Asian short-order cook, who lives next to a professional golfer, who lives next to a postmodern-literature professor and a cardiovascular surgeon. But I have never been to or heard of that neighborhood. Instead, what I have seen all around the country is people making strenuous efforts to group themselves with people who are basically like themselves. . . . The United States might be a diverse nation when considered as a whole, but block by block and institution by institution it is a relatively homogeneous nation.[42]

Brooks notes that while the number of middle-class and upper-middle-class African American families is rising, those families still tend to congregate in predominantly black neighborhoods. Moreover, as newly established suburbs grow and age they take on distinctive cultural personalities or become associated with particular ethnic groups.

This propensity among American inhabitants to cultural zoning or societal segmentation is powerfully demonstrated within congregational life and compo-

---

41. See Zhou, "Changing Face of America," 75-79.
42. David Brooks, "People Like Us," *Atlantic Monthly* 292, no. 2 (September 2003): 29.

sition. Dr. Martin Luther King's famous quip that "eleven o'clock Sunday morning is the most segregated hour" was a sharp critique of the hypocrisy and passivity of the Christian church in the face of institutionalized racism. But, despite the outstanding fruits of the civil rights movement, his condemnation remains a truism, one palpably underlined by phenomenal nonwhite immigration.

To reiterate, post-1965 immigration is characterized by high levels of population concentration and residential segregation;[43] moreover, while this trend fosters "segmented assimilation," it also means that the impact of contemporary mass immigration is greatest in specific regions (like Los Angeles, New York, or Washington, DC) but minimal or gradual in much of the country.[44] Undeniably, the convergence of specific immigrant groups in certain suburbs, cities, or regions of the country reflects the role of social networks in the flow and formation of immigrant communities. Such community formation is instinctual and critical to survival in an alien environment. In this sense at least, the new immigrants themselves contribute to the pervasive societal segregation, and the fact that America is a veritable nation of immigrants perhaps helps to account for this indelible feature. The distinctive groups of its rich mosaic of cultures are instinctively driven, through subliminal choice or the inflexible contours of the social environment, to be with and around others just like them. Brooks may be only partly right when he despairs that this is "human nature"; it is a quintessentially American trait. In the event, this situation is acutely reflected within the American religious landscape. Generally speaking, Koreans go to Korean churches, Hispanics attend Hispanic churches, very few Chinese Christians are to be found outside Chinese congregations, and so on. There are multicultural churches, to be sure, but even these tend to reflect egregious socioeconomic groupings, in the sense that their membership is often drawn from a particular social class.

The immigrant church, therefore, embodies profound paradoxes. While it plays a critical role in the lives of immigrants as they adjust to life in the new environment (by functioning as a site of cultural preservation and social adaptation), it also potentially limits full interaction with other major segments of the wider society. Put differently, if America's segmented religious landscape is a major reason why culturally distinctive congregations thrive, the same feature acts as a major embargo to intercultural engagement (missionary or otherwise). Further, while a widening base of immigrants hungry for religious association and a place to feel at home is responsible for their tremendous growth, successful intercultural missionary outreach requires sacrificing the immigrant ethos—a notion poignantly reminiscent of the challenge earlier Western missionaries faced in the choice between eliminating Eurocentric ideals or stifling the growth of the indigenous church.

This segregation of church or congregational life looms large in the minds of African immigrant pastors and is readily identified as the most difficult obstacle they have to overcome to fulfill their missionary vision. As Bishop John-

---

43. Min, "Contemporary Immigrants' Advantages for Intergenerational Cultural Transmission," 137; see also Portes and Rumbaut, *Immigrant America*, 28-56.

44. Waldinger, "Strangers at the Gates," 2.

son noted, the perception that his is an African church is taken *even by other Christians* to mean that "we are [exclusively] missionaries to our own people." The all-white Light of Christ Lutheran Church in Chicago will readily rent their facilities to Pastor Kamanda's predominantly African Schekina Christian Center or even offer them an opportunity to buy the building (see above). It is highly unlikely, however, that either side considered a merger of the two congregations as a present or future possibility. This scenario is replicated in cities throughout the country.

There are hopeful signs, however. The reach and influence of many African immigrant pastors extends beyond their congregations in extensive counseling ministries, regular community functions, or vicariously through the living witness of their members. As we have seen, there is some indication that African immigrant pastors who are more established within Western society are more adept at intercultural ministry. It also matters that pastoral ministry and missionary effort among African immigrants tends to inflame rather than quench the vision (among the pastors) to reach beyond the African constituency. For now, it is important to acknowledge that by presiding over the well-being of significant sections of the new immigrant communities, African pastors perform an important public service; and it ought not to be overlooked that their churches *provide the main sites of acculturation and spiritual orientation for new/future American citizens*. These are important beginnings.

The recency of the African immigrant church movement means that assessment of its potential must be tentative and provisional—even if it signifies bold initiatives. At this stage, much about the movement is inchoate, and its missionary prospects remain at the experimental level for the most part. Yet it is significant that both the pastors and the members of their congregations who participated in the study conceive of America as a vast mission field and demonstrated a strong missionary commitment. The long-term impact is left to be seen. What is certain is that this African missionary movement reveals, yet again, how migration movement is intimately linked with the long-term prospects of the Christian faith. Its ignoble beginnings may be deceptive, especially when compared to the relative splendor and prominence of the Western missionary movement. Yet all too often, the most momentous episodes in the history of Christian missions have been launched by small, insignificant initiatives, such as the ordinary actions of those unnamed migrant-refugees in first-century Antioch.

Conclusion

New Age, New Movement, Old Mission

We shall not cease from exploration, and the end of all our exploring
will be to arrive where we started.

—T. S. Eliot, "Little Gidding"

The popular and entrenched notion that the values, ideals, and institutions of
modern Western societies are destined to dominate the world, at the expense of
autochthonous or indigenous forms, is one of the most pervasive myths of the
contemporary era. Yet it has a certain allure. It is patently self-serving but also
powerfully seductive, for it promises a certain future based on a fixed, supposedly universal, ideal. This ideal, however flawed, offers a single path to prosperity and a single solution to the messy, cacophonous, unpredictable disorder and
unmanageable diversity that have always marked the human condition. It turns
out that this idea, which purports to bring history to an end (on terms dictated
by the hegemonic aspirations of a particular dominant group), is not that new.
It has dressed itself in many different garbs over the course of time—at times
even claiming divine clearance—but it is as old as the phenomenon of rampant
uncontrolled diversity it seeks to replace or dispel. That much is evident from the
biblical story of Babel.

Whose Future Is It?

In its most recent guise, this approach maintains that the processes of globalization mainly reflect Western dominance and expansion in such a way that a single
ideal outcome or condition is likely. This outcome is typically conceptualized
in terms of the emergence of a single global culture or a universal model based
on Western liberal secular values, and its inevitability is premised on Western
economic dominance. This line of thinking, as I have explained, is not only peculiarly Western but is also rooted in religious convictions spawned by Western
Christendom. It is redolent of well-known ideological concepts like "*padroado*,"
"manifest destiny," "divine providence," and "white man's burden." That these
religious convictions informed and, indeed, fueled European imperialism starting from the sixteenth century is a matter of record. Then, as now, the outcomes

tend to be palpably detrimental, even while they are pursued "for the good" of non-European peoples.

In the present era, belief in the universal applicability of the Western experience, ideals, and culture has been codified in secular rationalism, the dominant ideology of the Western academy and popular thinking. Among other things, its viewpoints

- account for religious dynamism mainly using materialistic or mechanistic explanations (poverty, human insecurity, rational choice, etc.);
- uphold the conviction that religious interest and involvement generally decline with human development or economic modernization;
- celebrate humanitarianism and human endeavor, individual choice, freedom of expression and democratic processes;
- utilize arguments that associate well-being with the technologies of modernity (and exclude religious faith);
- maintain the belief that human progress and development are a function of specific cultural attributes (chiefly those associated with modern culture or Western civilization);
- favor Westernization, cultural homogenization, or the emergence of a universal civilization based on the unidirectional spread of economic modernization and Western/American values;
- consider strong religious identity and commitment inimical to the liberal democratic project and a major cause of conflict and hostility in the world;
- tend to analyze religious expressions everywhere in terms of Western intellectual constructs and binary dichotomies: "fundamentalist," "Christendom," "crusade" "liberal/conservative," "sacred/secular," "modern/traditional," "church/sect," "church/mission," etc.

Not all secular assessments include all these views (some of which overlap), nor does acceptance of one or more imply acceptance of the rest. But since they form part of received (Western) academic wisdom, they are reflected in the writings of both self-confessed secular thinkers and convinced Christian scholars. Indeed, in its most insidious form secular rationalism functions less as a badge of ideological commitment than as a hermeneutic lens. This partly explains why the discrediting of once-dominant theories by non-Western experiences or realities tends to produce not their abandonment but revisions that purport to take account of fresh developments but leave the original premise or rationale intact. Instances of these include the update of the "secularization theory" by Pippa Norris and Ronald Inglehart, the revision of the "straight line assimilation" theory by Richard Alba and Victor Nee, the "next Christendom" construct by Philip Jenkins, and the even less credible "exporting the American Gospel" argument.

All these studies boast fastidious scholarship and powerful analyses. But they also demonstrate the inherent limitations of secular rationalism as a reliable frame of reference for explicating some major trends within contemporary globalization, especially those pertaining to religion and non-Western initiatives or impulses. The fundamental assumption that Western paradigms have universal validity contaminates understanding of non-Western realities. The dynamic and flourishing religiosity of non-Western societies cannot simply be explained in terms of low human development and poverty, and the realities shaping non-white immigration into Western societies render existing theories of assimilation unsustainable, even misleading.

Unfortunately, even assessments that take the religious dimensions of contemporary globalization seriously are weakened by the secular rationalist tendency to treat Western models or categories as definitive. This is evident in Olivier Roy's treatment of Islam in the West but even more so in Philip Jenkins's otherwise excellent appraisal of "Southern Christianity."

To repeat earlier arguments and conclusions here would be wearisome. A central thesis of this volume is that the prevalent theories within the globalization discourse which depict the phenomenon as a one-directional, Western- or American-dominated movement are seriously flawed not least because such views overlook the capacity of non-Western societies to adapt or resist Western flows and project alternative movements with potential global impact. As it happens, a thoroughgoing evaluation of earlier forms or epochs of globalization, in which Western initiatives and ideals were even more prominent or decisive, indicates that the impact and outcomes have been patently paradoxical.

For well over four centuries, the West, by virtue of superior technology, economic dominance, and military might, imposed its structures and spread its influence throughout much of the world. This imperial project was accompanied by an unprecedented missionary movement which spearheaded the global spread of both the Christian faith and Western cultural values. Then, as now, military superiority and economic dominance were liable to be confused with the efficacy and desirability of specific ideals and values. Still, the overall impact produced profound and lasting transformations of non-Western societies.

But the notion of the West as a colossus able to project its power and cultural values (deemed universal) while remaining serenely immune to the impact of outside forces and influences is a colossal self-deception. While Western colonialism and empire building created a new world order, it also produced unintended outcomes and stimulated processes of change that have acted reflexively on the West and portend major sources of transformation within Western societies. A world order simply created in the European image proved to be a mirage. In particular, Western expansion projects were attended by unprecedented levels of migrations and, in turn, galvanized massive people movements. The legacies of colonialism and the global economic structures erected by Western powers reinforced a new North–South divide. This divide is at once economic, demographic, and religious. It also provides the framework for a new era of global migrations in which Western societies that once exported their people and ideas in an effort at universal dominance now constitute the chief destination of a nonwhite migration of unprecedented magnitude. The "empire" not only struck back; it came to stay!

Similarly, the Christendom model was undermined by the very agents and process of exportation, and it was eventually bankrupted in the Western missionary encounter with non-Western societies. Attempts to impose Western Christian institutions and expressions not only failed but they also stimulated ethnic consciousness and unleashed powerful non-Western initiatives (ecclesiastical and political) that subverted structures of foreign domination. The long-term impact of the Western missionary movement was not the worldwide spread of one normative form of faith but the unprecedented growth of non-Western Christian forms that now represent the face of global Christianity. Given the demise of Western Christendom in its historical heartland, its global expansion would have seriously jeopardized Christianity's survival.

In fact, European migrations, missionary enterprise, and colonial expansion also had far-reaching implications for Europeans. The sustained encounter with other major religious systems such as Hinduism and Buddhism and the pervasive religious plurality in the non-Western world raised important questions about Western understandings of the Christian faith. The missionary effort profoundly transformed the status of women in Western societies, while the encounter with Africa and Asia revolutionized Western scholarship and led to the establishment of new disciplines such as anthropology, comparative religion, phenomenology of religion, linguistics, philology, and Asian studies. In addition, the emergence of new expressions of the Christian faith among non-Western peoples and the growth of new "theologies" underlined theology's contextual nature and discredited Western claims to universality.

My analysis has focused on international migrations partly because few aspects of contemporary globalization more fully expose the erroneousness of key tenets of secular rationalism and the sheer folly of the single global culture argument. The processes of globalization are collapsing distance and juxtaposing cultures in an unprecedented fashion and, especially for Western societies, posing profound questions related to cultural identity and managing religious plurality. Contemporary migration has helped to create new societies in which the cultural "other" is not a geographically distant curiosity or a random stranger one might perchance encounter on the street but a distinct, sizable presence within and impinging on the same social space (be it the neighborhood, the city, the province, or the country). The presence of vibrant, growing, non-white immigrant communities within Western societies puts the West and the non-West together in a manner that is without historical precedent and with profound long-term consequences. I have used a brief overview of Islam and a more extensive evaluation of transformations within global Christianity to make the case that the most critical aspects of this new encounter are religious and that it has significant missionary implications. This missionary component is most difficult to evaluate because of its newness. But its durability and long-term impact will both be shaped by demographic realities, the North–South religious divide, and transnational structures or identities (including dual citizenship).

Migration and Mission

The main arguments in this book revolve around the premise that migration movement has historically been a prime factor in global religious expansion—

preeminently so in the case of Christianity—and that current patterns of migration will have an incalculable impact on religious interactions in the course of the twenty-first century. The impact of global migratory flows on the structure and significance of the non-Western missionary movement is at the heart of our study. Over 65 percent of Christians now live outside the West, compared to about 14 percent in 1800. The fact that migrant movement from less developed countries (in the South) to highly developed countries (in the North) coincides with the emergence of the South as the new heartland of global Christianity is of profound significance. By 2000, more than 70 percent of immigrants arriving in the major destination countries in Western Europe and North America were from the non-Western world.

As I have shown, the conjunction between migrant movement (mobility) and God's salvific purpose or missionary expansion is deeply rooted in the biblical story and strongly manifested throughout Christian history. Throughout the Old Testament, God's plan of salvation and redemptive action repeatedly unfold within the trauma and travail of displacement, uprootedness, and migration. In the New Testament, the intersection of migration and mission is further extended and encapsulated in the establishment of the church, the new Israel, which, not unlike the old, comprises "aliens and strangers." From the outset, the spread of the gospel, including inception of the Gentile mission, was linked to migrant movement and networks. And, in the centuries that followed the fall of Jerusalem (in 70 C.E.), the faith spread mainly through kinship and commercial networks, migrant movements (some stimulated by persecution), and other forms of mobility.

In the thousand years from 500 to 1500, vast movements of peoples on the Eurasian landmass were critical to the Christian conversion of western European peoples, and the emergence of Christian communities across Asia and in South Arabia owed much to the vast network of trade routes by land and sea that acted as outlets for Christian migrant movement. The end of this thousand-year period also witnessed the beginning of that momentous expansion of Europeans from the heartlands of Christianity to other parts of the world. From about 1800 to 1914—the great ("long") century of Western missionary enterprise—up to 60 million Europeans left for the Americas, Oceania, and East and South Africa. In effect, the most remarkable of all migrations in known human history coincided with the greatest Christian missionary expansion to date. The net impact transformed the face of global Christianity.

In simple terms, from both a biblical and a historical perspective, *every Christian migrant is a potential missionary.* Precisely because the heartlands of global Christianity are now in the South, contemporary South–North migrations form the taproot of a major non-Western missionary movement. Among the swelling tide of guest workers, students, labor migrants, asylum seekers, political and economic refugees, and family members of previous migrants are innumerable Christians, each one a missionary in some sense. In Europe, where the largest church is African-founded and led, African Christians alone are thought to number in excess of three million. In the United States, where Hispanic, Korean, and Chinese congregations have proliferated vigorously, the religious landscape looks less and less European.

America may be the foremost missionary-*sending* nation in the world (see below), but patterns within contemporary global migrations have arguably transformed it into the foremost missionary-*receiving* country in the West. By the early 1980s it was estimated that some two-thirds of all legal immigrants worldwide came to the United States. Today, one in ten Americans is foreign born. Given the preoccupation with America's economic dominance, its central role in Western missionary expansion, and long-standing (rather racist) convictions about Anglo-conformity, it is hardly surprising that the immense impact of immigration on America's cultural and religious landscape gets so little attention. Yet America is the definitive immigrant nation. The history of America is a history of migration and immigrants, and American Christianity is a direct product of migration and refugee movement. In this book I have argued that not only is immigration central to the emergence, character, and development of the American nation, but it is also crucial to its future.

This is perhaps most clearly evident with regard to America's religious life. For the most part, accounts of American missionary expansion ignore ways in which initiatives or movements from outside may have impacted American religious culture itself and indirectly contributed to American foreign missionary enterprise. The Christendom understanding that conceives of "missions" in terms of expansion from a fixed geographical center helps to account for this. My own analysis examines how major immigrant waves in American history (including the enslavement of Africans) have constantly revitalized American religious life and also had a missionary impact on America society, through the formation of new congregations. My main contention, however, is that post-1965 immigration is likely to have a greater impact on the American religious landscape than that of any previous wave, with the exception of the earliest European migrants. Post-1965 immigration is predominantly nonwhite, more culturally diverse than any previous wave. It also includes significant representation from other world religions (already there are as many Muslims in America as there are Jews) and is characterized by more selective assimilation patterns. Perhaps most striking, it brings a massive influx of non-Western Christians at a time when American Christianity is experiencing decline.

Phenomenal levels of immigration have not only transformed America into the most culturally diverse nation on the planet; they are also rapidly changing the face of American Christianity. At the very least immigration is de-Europeanizing the American Christian experience. Immigrant congregations represent the fastest growing segment of American Christianity across all traditions, and they represent forms and expressions of the faith (in terms of spirituality, ritual, and worship) that may sometimes seem as foreign to native-born Christians as other religions—even though the majority are evangelical Christians. Above all, this unprecedented immigration of non-Western Christians represents a new missionary encounter with American society. Among other things:

- immigrant Christians and their descendants have a striking record when it comes to winning converts among immigrants.

- They encounter a society in which Christianity is experiencing decline in numbers and influence (and therefore more obviously a "mission field").
- They represent the face of Christianity to a goodly proportion of the nation's disadvantaged and marginalized population.
- They are far more attuned than American Christians to religious plurality, an area of increasing challenge for American Christianity.

The African Element

The prominence of Africa and Africans in global migrations and Africa's emergence as a major heartland of global Christianity make the African element quite apposite for illustrating how the emergence of the southern continents as the new heartlands of Christianity, combined with major South–North migratory flows, provides the structure and impetus for a full-fledged (but largely unstructured) non-Western missionary movement, one that points to the West as a major frontier of religious interactions and missionary engagement. A detailed mapping of the causative factors of mass migration within and from Africa—including the structures imposed by the colonial state, intra-state conflict, profound economic crises, and environmental degradation—highlights the conspicuousness of mobility and displacement within the African condition. Perennially convulsed by horrendous conflicts and civil strife, Africa has produced phenomenal tides of displaced peoples and massive migration movements. By 2000, Africa had more international migrants (including surging refugee populations) than any other continent, except the much larger Asia.

Indeed, it is possible to argue that the extraordinary tidal waves of human migration that have characterized the continent in the post colonial era are one reason why Christianity is growing faster in Africa than anywhere else. The African experience also illustrates why the traditional distinction between "forced" migration (or refugee movement) and "voluntary" migration (movement based on choice) is misleading, since the degree of choice is greatly constrained by imminent "threats" and the potential consequences of failure to move.

In addition to confirming the strong African element in South–North migration, the research data presented in this study confirm that since 1990 the United States has been the chief destination among industrialized countries for African migrants. The reasons for this are explored in great detail (see chapter 13). By 2005, the United States had the largest African foreign-born population of all industrialized nations. While African immigrants constitute a fairly low percentage of the overall foreign-born population, they constitute one of the fastest growing immigrant groups in the United States. With educational attainments that exceed all other foreign-born groups (even that of the native population), the new African immigrants are poised for economic integration into middle-class America. However, strong transnational ties or networks (fostered by dual-citizenship) and a propensity for selective adaptation, not to mention racial barriers to social mobility in American society, mean that assimilation patterns among

African immigrants remain segmented. At the same time, their absorption into American society is greatly complicated by the presence of the vastly larger and established African American population.

For now relations between the two groups, the new African immigrants and African Americans, are characterized by much tension, owing to divergent attitudes toward racism, disparate economic experience, and (surprisingly) cultural differences. I have argued that efforts at convergence by the Christian communities within the new African immigrants and African Americans ought to be viewed by both sides as a biblical mandate and that it holds the most promising avenue to breaking the current trend of disengagement. In my view, shared ancestry, spiritual and cultural affinity, and the legacies of history (including ties forged by migration and mission) are among possible elements that might, in time, transform the current climate of tension and suspicion to one of mutual identification and collaboration. Certainly, meaningful partnership and active collaboration and engagement between the fast-growing African immigrant churches and the more established black Churches would yield considerable benefits to both groups in the area of witness and ministry—not least because both groups must, perforce, undertake mission from the margins. But that is left to be seen.

Meanwhile, African immigrant churches are among the fastest growing in America's cities, where they increasingly exhibit a strong missionary consciousness. The last two chapters in this volume provided detailed portrayal of the lives and ministry of a number of new African pastors as well as in-depth analysis of the formation, structure, and missionary vision or purpose of these churches. My research amply demonstrates that the experience of migration is integral to the sense of calling and missionary commitment of African immigrant pastors and also that, while most preside of over congregations that are predominantly African, they definitely view the United States as a mission field and evince a strong determination to impact the wider society. But the formation and growth of African immigrant churches owe as much to charismatic leadership as to the cultural need and missionary consciousness of individual African Christian migrants. The greater proportion of these churches start as Bible study or prayer groups meeting in someone's living room, usually because members are quite dissatisfied with the levels of spirituality, worship, community, and ministry they experience in American churches.

If the ethnographic research findings examined here are anything to go by, the discontinuity between new immigrant and American congregations is most evident in the areas of worship, spirituality, and preaching of the Word. Rather surprisingly, only 20 percent of respondents indicate that they attend the immigrant church because of its "Africanness." The findings also show some ambivalence among members about whether the church's African ethos would be a hindrance or an asset to cross-cultural outreach. But more than half have invited non-Africans to attend their church, and the great majority (85 percent) want their church to do more to reach non-Africans. We are therefore left in no doubt about the missionary consciousness and commitment of the new African congregations.

But the challenges involved in a non-Western missionary encounter with

American society are as formidable as the idea itself is unconventional. Two stand out: (1) entrenched racism in American society; (2) its segmented religious/cultural landscape (see chapter 15). Both signify that in its encounter with Western society, the non-Western missionary movement is most clearly stamped by the experience of marginalization, powerlessness, and vulnerability, which are hallmarks of migration. Few other aspects of the movement more clearly expose its distinctness from Christendom.

Some Implications for Mission and Mission Studies

It is time to admit that the transformation of Christianity into a non-Western religion typified by diversity of expressions not only signifies the bankruptcy of the Christendom ideal but also marks the end of Western missionary dominance. As noted above, the misfortune that befell Western Christendom suggests that the successful transplantation of this model would surely have threatened the survival of the faith elsewhere. And, while the crowning of the southern continents as the new "center" of global Christianity needs to be qualified (as I argue below), there can be little doubt that the future of global Christianity is now inextricably bound up with non-Western initiatives and developments. This is supremely applicable to missionary enterprise.

The notion that mission is a Western (particularly) American prerogative and privilege—an assumption encouraged by global economic inequalities—remains entrenched. Career missionaries are thin on the ground, and the traditional missionary society has lost its edge.[1] But the proliferation of "short-term" missions—many of which amount to little more than Christian tourism with a touch of scheduled humanitarianism—suggests the enduring appeal of the missionary idea. In addition, the pervasive tendency to confuse American Christianity with American culture, as well as the persistence of catch phrases like "unreached peoples" or the "10/40 Window" (both of which reflect Western mapping of the world and ignore the living witness of Christians residing in non-Western contexts[2]), provide subtle indications of the lingering shadow of Christendom.

---

1. The number of long-term or "career" American missionaries has showed a steady decline since the 1980s (when the number of new mission agencies also peaked). Analyses of these trends are varying and occasionally conflicting. Among the most useful, see Robert T. Coote, "Taking Aim on 2000 AD," in *Mission Handbook: North American Protestant Ministries Overseas*, ed. Samuel Wilson and John Siewert (Monrovia, CA: MARC, 1986); idem, "The Uneven Growth of Conservative Evangelical Missions," *International Bulletin of Missionary Research* 6, no. 3 (July 1982): 118-23; idem, "Good News, Bad News, North American Protestant Overseas Personnel Statistics in Twenty-Five-Year Perspective," *International Bulletin of Missionary Research* 19, no. 1 (January 1995): 6-13; Scott Moreau, "Putting the Survey in Perspective," in *Mission Handbook 2001-2003: U.S. and Canadian Christian Ministries Overseas*, ed. John A. Siewert and Dotsey Welliver (Wheaton, IL: Billy Graham Center, 2000); Patrick Johnstone and Jason Mandryk, *Operation World: 21st Century Edition* (Waynesboro, GA: Paternoster, 2001), 4-6, 747-52.

2. For helpful comments, see Stan Guthrie, *Missions in the Third Millennium: 21 Key Trends for the 21st Century* (Waynesboro, GA: Paternoster, 2000), 57-63, 85-92.

Thus, even while they acknowledge the southward shift of global Christianity's center of gravity, many Western missiologists and missionary administrators are wrong-footed by it and somewhat nonplussed by the revolutionary sea-change in world missions that has seen the upsurge of non-Western initiatives that bear little resemblance, and owe little, to Western models and approaches.

Western missionary consciousness remains captive to the defunct Christendom concept with its territorial and triumphalist paradigms and an understanding of "missions" in terms of expansion from a fixed geographical center. If this approach persists in the face of the Western church's marginalization within global Christianity, it is largely because it depends less on religious capacity than on structures of global economic dominance for practical realization. In this regard, it is also possible to argue that Western missionary action and thinking have been secularized to some extent, at least insofar as it reflects overdependence on material resources, embodies structures of power, and confuses quantifiable measures of growth or human development (modeled on Western values) with missionary success.

There are those, of course, who have long recognized that the study of missions and the writing of Christian history need to give serious attention to the expressions and experiences of "the church outside Western Christendom," that, indeed, the dramatic shift that has transformed global Christianity into a non-Western religion calls for fresh missiological perspectives.[3] But, for now, mission and theological studies remain largely hostage to the kind of world vision shaped by secular rationalism—in which Western models and initiatives are considered definitive. Worse still, as I show in the case of Philip Jenkins's *The Next Christendom*, when non-Western Christian realities or initiatives do receive attention, analysis tends to be imprisoned within patently unhelpful Western categories and constructs such as "Christendom," "postmodern," "fundamentalist," and "conservative."

The reshaping of global Christianity has significant implications for the study of Christianity and the understanding of Christian missions. The old mental maps and conceptual wineskins quite simply will not do. If Western missiological thinking fails to detect, or struggles to understand, the nature and global significance of the new non-Western missionary movement, for instance, this is largely because the Western experience provides few obvious guidelines or models that can be usefully applied to the new realities. Quite frankly, the shift in perspectives and understanding that needs to accompany "the shift" within global Christianity may be nothing short of Copernican. But, as with many aspects of globalization, the dominant forces appear all too self-evident, strongly entrenched, and very much in control of the action.

In sheer numbers (based on "official" calculations), America has been the chief Western missionary-sending nation since the First World War,[4] though

---

3. Shenk, "Toward a Global Church History," 54.

4. After 1980, analysis of missionaries in the world, never fully empirical to begin with, became further complicated by the upsurge and varying definitions of "short-term" missionaries.

per capita assessments indicate that well over fourteen European countries and Canada were sending out more missionaries as a percentage of their population than the United States (with Ireland ranked highest) by 1980.[5] The claim that the United States "still remains the largest foreign missionary-sending nation (followed by South Korea)" is rather disingenuous, since that assessment is restricted to Protestant missionaries.[6] However, with close to thirty-three thousand "long-term U.S. personnel" serving overseas, the United States remains a major missionary-*sending* nation.[7] But the full picture is much more complex.

Statistics on foreign missionaries are notoriously inadequate because there are literally too many moving targets! They serve only to give a generalized, and often quite indistinct, picture. For what it is worth, the Korean international missionary force exploded in numbers from around five hundred in the mid-1980s to about fourteen thousand in 2006 (one in ten of whom are long term),[8] a faster rate of growth in missionary sending than any other country. The all-too-common observation that the Korean missionary force is second only to that of the United States and destined to pass it in the near future is both accurate and misleading. Misleading because the per head ratio of foreign missionaries to the Christian population tells a very different story: 1 to 900 for South Korea compared to 1 to 7,000 for the United States.[9] The fact is that the number of "foreign" missionaries officially sent by non-Western nations is increasing at an extraordinary rate. There were an estimated sixty-seven thousand Asian missionaries by 2000, and uncounted legions from Africa and Latin America.[10]

But all this is beside the point. Few doubt that "missionary initiatives from the churches in Asia, Africa, and Latin America are [now] at the cutting edge of the Christian world mission."[11] With millions of non-Western Christian migrants fulfilling a "missionary" function within their own continents and in Western societies, the inattentiveness within Christian historiography to the role and significance of migrants as key actors in the Christian missionary movement translates into a major analytical flaw—a deficiency evident in ongoing efforts to calculate the comparative numerical strength of the Western and non-Western mission-

5. See Barrett, Kurian, and Johnson, *World Christian Encyclopedia*, 804-5, 838-39; also Coote, "Taking Aim on 2000 AD," 79f. Comparable post-1980 data are lacking. Analysis of the number of "major mission institutions" sees the United States (with nine thousand) second only to Italy (with 13,500) but falling below sixtieth place in terms of number of the same institutions as a percentage of overall population. Islands excepted, Ireland ranked highest.

6. See Johnstone and Mandryk, *Operation World*, 6. It also disguises the fact that the North American Protestant missionary enterprise is losing momentum. See Robert T. Coote, "Shifts in North American Protestant Full-Time Missionary Community," *International Bulletin of Missionary Research* 29, no. 1 (January 2005): 12-13.

7. Moreau, "Putting the Survey in Perspective," 34.

8. See Julie Ma, "The Growth of Christianity in Asia and Its Impact on Mission," *Encounters Mission Ezine* 16 (2007). Some estimates put the figures much higher, at nineteen thousand.

9. For convenience I have use data from the *CIA World Factbook*, which states that Christians account for 26.3 percent of South Korea's forty-nine million population, and 78 percent (including Mormons) of America's 301 million population.

10. Ma, "Growth of Christianity," 3.

11. Shenk, "Recasting Theology of Mission," 98.

ary movements.[12] The largely unstructured, even clandestine, nature of the latter movement means that it is ultimately uncountable in an empirical sense.

The main problem is that Western missiologists are stuck with definitions, models, and instruments of measurement associated with Western operations and ill-suited for evaluation of new non-Western initiatives. For starters, the term "missionary" is generally linked with "command and go" structures and typically applied to individuals "sent" by an organization to a foreign country (usually outside the West). The initiatives, movements, and sheer numbers involved in the new Western missionary movement are of a scale and magnitude that defy statistical analysis; nor are they driven by the results-oriented calculations with which the American missionary movement is notoriously obsessed. The reasons are not hard to find: non-Western initiatives are disconnected from structures of domination and control, freed from the bane of triumphalism (and the militant aggression associated with it), less resource-dependent/-oriented, and bereft of a territorial understanding of mission. But these developments hint at something far more significant. The new "center" is radically different, and failure to appreciate this fact impoverishes our understanding of its profound historical implications

Understanding the "Shift": Marginalizing the Center

Without doubt, the global Christian landscape contemplated at the 1910 World Missionary Conference has altered radically and unrecognizably, but the global power structures (Christian and otherwise) that the Edinburgh meeting exemplified remain largely unchanged. The reshaping of global Christianity has rendered Western Christendom a defunct and meaningless conception; but, however marginalized the church and its institutions are within Western society, they remain associated with Western economic and political dominance and retain some of the old primacy. Within global Christianity, therefore, long-standing attitudes and assumptions related to Western supremacy, control, and monopoly of ideas are still entrenched. Thus, *while non-Western Christians now represent the face and future of global Christianity, the church in the non-Western world does not yet constitute its main driving force.*

The reasons for this are not hard to find: the entrenched forms of economic dependency (associated with developing economies and the legacies of Western colonial domination) apply no less to global Christian interactions than other international relations. The fact that the new southern heartlands of Christianity are characterized by acute poverty and powerlessness translates into meager resources for direct global influence, at least in a structured sense. Geographical distance, disparate experiences and expectations, and perennial factionalism greatly hinder the ability of the burgeoning Christian communities in the non-Western world to make common cause or else act concertedly to bring their

---

12. See Michael Jaffarian, "Are There More Non-Western Missionaries Than Western Missionaries?" *International Bulletin of Missionary Research* 28, no. 3 (July 2004): 131-32.

enormous spiritual and intellectual resources to bear on global Christianity.[13] "South–South" Christian partnerships are woefully lacking or difficult to sustain in part because poor telecommunications infrastructures within the new Christian heartlands remain a major impediment. The myriad and formidable challenges that the various Christian communities face in their own local contexts exhaust resources and foster self-preoccupation; similarly, the spiritual vitality and the extraordinary numerical growth of non-Western Christianity fully consume the energies of its leaders. And, truth be told, the ingrained supernaturalism of non-Western Christianity can dampen attentiveness to initiatives that require earthly machination.

In the event, contemporary global Christianity is decidedly polycentric.[14] The church in the southern continents can claim to have become only global Christianity's demographic, cultural, and spiritual center. Its intellectual and organizational center remains in the old heartlands—at least for now. To note this is not to minimize the profound historical significance of the recent shift. But it is of utmost importance that we recognize that the new heartlands of the faith in the non-West are radically different in character and function from the preceding heartlands in the West. The old heartlands exemplified domination and territorial control, national religion, cultural superiority, and a fixed universal vision. In acute contrast, the emerging heartlands of the faith embody vulnerability and risk, religious plurality, immense diversity of Christian experience and expression, and structures of dependency. These disparities necessarily translate into new forms and models of missionary function.

Perhaps this state of affairs reflects a state of historical transition. But the fact that the recent "shift" has taken place in a different era of globalization factors into its nature and distinctiveness. It is so far removed from "Christendom"—the unidirectional spread of one dominant form of faith—that some scholars even shy away from using the term "global Christianity" to highlight the distinction.[15] This is another way of saying that Western conceptual categories and experiences provide no secure basis for a full understanding of non-Western Christian realities. But as my arguments in this book show, globalization implies quite complex interaction and interdependence between the global and the local. It incorporates dominant processes, to be sure, but its dynamic renders the constructs of "margin" and "center" fluid and interchangeable. The new shape of global Christianity typifies this central paradox. Taken as a whole, it is marked by a complex interplay of domination and weakness, paternalism and marginalization. Its "center(s)" are also "margin(s)." To fully appreciate the nature and significance of the recent "shift" requires a recognition that, quite often, the tail is wagging the dog! The recent controversy within the worldwide Anglican Communion (the world's third largest affiliation of Christian churches) illustrates this situation.

As we have noted, the vast majority of the Anglican Communion's seventy-

---

13. Despite internal fissures, the old heartlands benefited from geographical proximity, uniform ideals, and a shared heritage, all of which aided efforts at global expansion.

14. See Shenk, *Changing Frontiers of Mission*, 174-76.

15. Sanneh, *Whose Religion Is Christianity?*, 23.

seven million members now reside in the non-West—one in five is Nigerian. African Anglicans number up to forty-four million (more than half), compared to 2.3 million in America. By virtue of numerical preponderance and spiritual dynamism, the younger churches in Africa and Asia represent the Communion's new center of gravity. But the traditional centers of power and control remain unchanged. Economic factors are germane. The Episcopal Church in the United States (hereafter Episcopal Church) provides at least 30 percent of the Anglican Communion's budget. Additionally, tens of millions of dollars flow annually from Episcopal dioceses and agencies in America "to support aid and development programs in the Communion's poorer provinces in Africa, Asia, and Latin America."[16] For the African Church, numerical strength is necessarily attended by economic dependence; for the Episcopal Church numerical marginality is greatly offset by economic power.

The theological storm that has engulfed the Anglican Communion since November 2003, when Rev. Gene Robinson, an openly gay priest, was consecrated in the Episcopal Church, reflects this complex dynamic. Anglican provinces and bishops in Africa have vociferously condemned the Episcopal Church's stance on homosexuality and same-sex union. They have also rejected the possibility of continued participation in the worldwide fellowship until the Episcopal Church rescinds its position.[17] In February 2007, after a five-day meeting in Dar es Salaam, Tanzania, top leaders of the Anglican Church issued the "Tanzanian Communiqué" which rebuked the Episcopal Church for its stance on homosexuality.[18] The communiqué demanded an end to the appointment of gay clergy and the blessing of same-sex couples and issued an ultimatum for compliance with the traditional Anglican position.

African Anglicans defend their position on the authority of Scripture and orthodox Anglican teaching. Yet the fact that the vast majority of African dioceses are dependent on diocesan partners in the United States for economic aid adds considerably to the tensions. Archbishop Peter J. Akinola of Nigeria, who heads the largest church within the Communion, has emerged as the fiercest critic of the Episcopal Church's position.[19] Coincidentally perhaps, his is the only self-supporting Anglican church in Africa. Not that others have sacrificed theological conviction to economic expedience. To date, the acute theological divisions have not affected the flow of vital funds, though allegations that African bishops have been bought by "favors" are not uncommon. At the very least, the one-sided economic relationships raise the stakes significantly. When Archbishop Henry

---

16. Laurie Goodstein and Neela Banerjee, "Money Looms in Episcopalian Rift with Anglicans," *New York Times*, March 20, 2007.

17. The "Road to Lambeth," a document published (in September 2006) for the Council of Anglican Provinces of Africa, declared: "We will definitely not attend any Lambeth Conference to which the violators of the Lambeth Resolution are also invited as participants or observers" ("The Road Towards or Away from Lambeth 2008?" http://www.anglican-mainstream.net/?page_id=1756 [accessed September 7, 2007]). See also "Communiqué from the House of Bishops of the Church of Nigeria," Anglican Communion Service, January 17, 2007.

18. "Primates Meeting Communiqué," Anglican Communion News Service, February 13, 2007.

19. Jenkins, "Defender of the Faith," 49.

Orombi of Uganda turned down money from the Episcopal Church because of its stance on homosexuality, a community development program involving families affected by HIV/AIDS had to be shut down.

Meanwhile, the Episcopal Church has remained largely unmoved by the censure of the "Provinces of the Global South." It has pressed ahead with the blessing of same-sex couples, and in August 2007 one lesbian priest was included among the five nominees for bishop in the Episcopal diocese of Chicago. Complicating the division further, up to one-tenth of the Episcopal Church's own dioceses have rejected the national church's stance on homosexuality,[20] and these dioceses have made common cause with the more orthodox African and Asian churches. In December 2006, two of the oldest and largest Episcopal congregations in the United States placed themselves under the authority of the Anglican Church of Nigeria. Subsequently, a number of American bishops have been ordained by African prelates, which means that while they preside over American congregations their allegiance is to the Anglican provinces in Africa.[21] By September 2007, some twelve American bishops were affiliated with African provinces (in Rwanda, Nigeria, Kenya, and Uganda) while serving American congregations.

It is possible to argue that the structures of globalization that allow the Episcopal Church to play an important (financial) role in the life of African dioceses have also facilitated direct intervention in the life of the Episcopal Church by African provinces (notably Archbishop Akinola's Nigerian Church). In the latter case, global migration patterns, rather than global economic inequalities, form the underlying cause. As I have explained elsewhere in this book, Nigerian immigrants constitute the greatest proportion of new African immigrants in the United States. By 2005, Nigerians accounted for 13 percent of all African immigrants legally resident in the United States. A good proportion (impossible to say how many) are practicing Anglicans. Their numbers led to the appointment of a Nigerian chaplain, Rev. Canon Gordon Okunsanya, to oversee their pastoral care. But, inevitably, this community of Anglican Nigerians—along with Anglican immigrants from other parts of the non-Western world—has been completely alienated by the theological stance of the Episcopal Church. Their plight became even more critical when Okunsanya's tenure was abruptly terminated amidst controversy, even as it became all too manifest that a change in the Episcopal Church's position was highly unlikely.

Ostensibly to cater to pastoral needs of this Nigerian community and to prevent the most disgruntled from leaving the Anglican Church altogether or becoming spiritually homeless, Archbishop Akinola established a missionary diocese in America. Named the Convocation of Anglicans in North America (CANA) and headquartered in Virginia, the new diocese came into existence in 2005. In May 2007, Akinola consecrated Rev. Martyn Minns, an Englishman who had worked

---

20. Sharon LaFraniere and Laurie Goodstein, "Anglicans Rebuke U.S. Branch on Blessing Same-Sex Unions," *New York Times*, February 20, 2007.

21. "U.S. Church Splits over Sexuality," *BBC News,* December 17, 2006; Neela Banerjee, "Episcopalians in Colorado Plan to Leave Denomination," *New York Times*, March 28, 2007; "U.S. Anglicans Join Kenyan Church," *BBC News,* August 30, 2007; "Kenya Consecrates Conservative U.S. Clerics as Bishops," *New York Times*, August 30, 2007.

among immigrants in Fairfax, Virginia, as the first missionary bishop of CANA. By the end of 2007, the convocation comprised over seven thousand members and fifty clergy in thirty-two congregations.[22] Other African provinces have also initiated similar missionary partnerships.

The interventions by African churches in the life of the Episcopal Church has met with resentment and has reinforced the lines of conflict. But it is important to note that the African bishops, who claim to be defending Christian orthodoxy, conceive of their initiatives in terms of missionary action and outreach. These African Anglican missionary initiatives embrace not only African immigrants but also American Anglicans. The United States, in short, is designated a *mission field*. Interestingly, the creation of CANA has been compared to the establishment of the first Anglican communities in the United States (in the seventeenth century) as "a missionary outpost under the Bishop of London, England."[23] Now, as then, the links between migration and mission are notable. Declared Archbishop Akinola: "we believe we are continuing the tradition of Missionary Bishops that has always been an essential part of Anglicanism."[24]

The Future in Retrospect

One of the chief lessons of the history of Christian missions is that more often than not theoretical formulation and formal strategy lag behind actual missionary enterprise. The full extent to which this non-Western missionary movement will break new ground in its vision, strategies, and even choice of scriptural texts (which will define its assumptions) is left to be seen. Questions about the assumptions, models, and even theology that will characterize the emerging non-Western missionary movement may not be fully answered for some time. But it is already evident that in its strategies, methods, and structures (or lack thereof), this non-Western missionary movement differs significantly from the Western missionary movement that preceded it. This is partly because it is shaped by factors, insights, and experiences that are in some ways radically different from those associated with the former.

There are areas of convergence of course, including the pervasive evangelical ethos, strong pietism, the efficacy of global migration, association with areas of significant population growth, and identification with the heartlands of the faith. But the areas of distinctiveness may prove far more consequential in the long run.

Fundamentally, the factors and considerations that framed the Western missionary movement—including the idea of Christendom, imperial expansion, political and economic dominance, and technological supremacy—are strikingly absent from the emerging Western missionary movement. Where enlightenment

---

22. "The Road Towards or Away from Lambeth 2008?"

23. See CANA Web site (FAQs)—www.canaconvocation.org.

24. "Church of Nigeria Elects Missionary Bishop for Convocation of Anglicans in North America," http://www.anglican-mainstream.net/?p=501 (accessed September 7, 2007).

certitudes (including the universal relevance of Western ideas and ideals), militarist triumphalism, and a rather secular emphasis on means and human calculations framed the Western movement, it is the experience of colonial domination, marginalization, and an intensely spiritual worldview that will provide the defining elements in the non-Western movement. Shaped by Christendom ideals, Western missions remain marked by an emphasis on distinctions and difference (territorial, cultural, and racial). Shaped by the experience of plurality and diversity, non-Western efforts are oriented toward relational presence and interpersonal exchange. Where the Old Testament-based notion of "divine providence" informed the Western movement, the New Testament emphasis on "weak things of the world" (1 Corinthians 1:27) will inform the thinking and outlook of non-Western missionaries.

Within the African migrant-missionary movement, relative economic poverty and political powerlessness rule out structures of dominance or control and make critical accommodation (not to be understood as total assimilation) to the host culture imperative. This necessarily stimulates faster patterns of indigenization. It is noteworthy that within European initiatives, the "*three-selfs*" strategy—of self-support, self-propagation, and self-governance—has proven intensely problematic to implement due in large measure to the attitudes of paternalism engendered by economic and political superiority. African immigrant churches (certainly those in the West) are self-supporting from the start, and some actually become sources of revenue for their home churches! Self-propagation is a major preoccupation, while irrepressible religiosity and deep spirituality invariably translate into evangelistic zeal. Most also emphasize the importance of indigenous leadership and oversight. In cases where the individual church is part of a larger African movement (such as Church of Pentecost or RCCG), autonomy can be restricted. But most African immigrant churches operate as autonomous entities and found autonomous congregations.

Informed by notions of Christendom, the Western missionary movement conceived of Christian faith in territorial terms and fostered an understanding of Christian mission in which the world is (territorially or geographically) divided into church and "mission field." This approach engendered a unidirectional flow of resources and ideas in which the West was the sender and the non-West the receiver. Within the emergent non-Western movement, however, each nation sends as well as receives missionaries. Never before has the course of missionary movement been this multidirectional, disparate, and global. In particular, African Christians conceive of the whole world (including Africa itself) as a mission field. Additionally, the African missionary movement is a church-based initiative that promotes church-centered engagement. This emphasis diverges sharply from the European missionary movement which emerged outside the existing church structures, operated almost exclusively through extra-ecclesial missionary orders or voluntary societies, and produced an entrenched church/mission dichotomy in both missiology and mission praxis.

The newer movement also exemplifies New Testament patterns and models of mission far more closely, with accompanying manifestations, such as an emphasis on demonstrations of (spiritual) power rather than material abundance, use of house churches, tent-making ministries, lay apostolate, informal and invisible structures combined with clandestine activities, prominent charismatic leadership, a consciousness of weakness and marginality. It is also reflective of the biblical paradigm of God's people as pilgrims, migrants, and refugees.

For all this it would be a mistake to glorify the still-inchoate non-Western missionary movement, to suggest that its distinctiveness from the still far more celebrated Western missionary effort confers on it special grace of divine favor. Undoubtedly, the emergence of the non-Western missionary movement in conjunction with global migratory flows represents a major turning point in the history of Christianity. Yet much about this movement remains uncertain, and the assessment provided in this study is intended to be preliminary, even provisional. What is not in doubt is that the future of global Christianity will be decided mainly by the outcome of such non-Western initiatives. This leads both post-Western Christianity and the post-Christendom West into uncharted waters. For the church in the West, it is, paradoxically, in this novel status of marginality—being divested of a long-standing position of domination and privilege—that it may yet experience the efficacy of that core scriptural motif of the people of God as strangers and pilgrims. Such is life beyond Christendom.

Appendix 1

List of African Christian Leaders and Pastors in Kenya and Ghana Interviewed in Spring 2004

Dr. Tewoldemedhin Habtu (Ethiopian), Lecturer, Nairobi Evangelical School of Theology, Kenya.

Pastor Oscar Muriu (Kenyan), Senior Pastor, Nairobi Chapel, Kenya.

Pastor Esther Obasi-ike (Nigerian), Redeemed Christian Church of God, Kenya.

Pastor Prince Obasi-ike (Nigerian), Regional Co-ordinator, Redeemed Christian Church of God, Eastern Africa Region, Kenya.

Rev. Muriithi Wanjau (Kenyan), Outreach Pastor, Nairobi Chapel, Kenya.

Dr. Tokumboh Adeyemo (Nigerian), former General Secretary of the Association of Evangelicals in Africa (AEA); currently Director, Centre for Strategic Thinking and Constructive Engagement, Kenya.

Bishop George Adjeman (Ghanaian), Regional Director, West African World Mission Agency, Winners Chapel, Ghana.

Rev. E. A. T Sackey (Ghanaian), Senior Associate Pastor, Lighthouse Chapel International, Ghana.

Rev. Dr. A. F. Aiyelabowo (Nigerian), Founder, Triumphant Global Ministries or Chapel of Triumph, Ghana.

Samuel Gyamfi (Ghanaian), General Secretary, Bethel Prayer Ministry International, Ghana.

Bishop Owusu Tabiri (Ghanaian), Founder, Bethel Prayer Ministry International, Ghana.

Bishop James Saah (Ghanaian), Christian Action Faith Ministries, Ghana.

Pastor Mensa Otabil (Ghanaian), International Central Gospel Church, Ghana.

Apostle Opoku Onyinah (Ghanaian), Principal, Pentecostal University College of the Church of Pentecost, Ghana.

Bishop Duncan-Williams (Ghanaian), Head of Christian Action Faith Ministries, Ghana.

Apostle Stephen K. Baidoo (Ghanaian), International Missions Director, Church of Pentecost, Ghana.

Apostle Michael Kwabena Ntumy (Ghanaian), Chairman, Church of Pentecost, Ghana.

Note: the official status/positions indicated here date to 2004.

List of Churches in the Study

Church	Pastor	Year Founded	Estimated Membership	Average Attendance	State	City
Abundant Life Miracle Center	Clement Nwanni	1998	30	40	CA	Los Angeles
African Christian Community Church	Kasereke Kasomo	2000	150	100	CA	Los Angeles
African Fellowship	Peter Kaimathiri	2001	120	60	PA	Marietta
All Grace Ministries	Emmanuel Oppong	1996	70	45	CA	Los Angeles
All Nations Assembly	Pastor Akano	2000	120	90	IL	LaGrange
Babalola Assembly		1998	50	40	IL	Chicago
Bethel World Outreach Church	Darlingston Johnson (Bishop)	1987	3000	1300	MD	Silver Spring
Celestial Church of Christ (Jericho Parish)	Evangelist Israel	1994	100	120	NJ	Newark
Chapel of Restoration	Daniel Ajayi-Adenira	1997	250	200	NY	Bronx
Christ Apostolic Church	Rotimi Akinwole	1989	250	180	CA	Hawthorne
Christ Apostolic Church (HQ)	Ezekiel O. Owoeye	1983	150	120	IL	Chicago
Christ Apostolic Church International	Daniel Omolaje	1991	70	50	CA	Long Beach
Christ Apostolic Church of America	Timothy Agbeja	1983	500	350	MD	Hyattsville
Christ Citadel International Church	Vincent Akosah	1997	130	120	CA	Los Angeles
Christ Harvesters' Church	Finnian Ebuehi	1996	50	50	CA	Bell Gardens
Christ Is Lord Ministries	Gibrilla Bangura	2004	130	180	VA	Springfield
Christ Temple	Samuel Olajide Ajibola	1989	250	200	IL	Chicago
Christ's Champions Ministries	Ezekiel Oyekale	2002	20	20	CA	Los Angeles
Church of Pentecost	Stephen Omane-Yeboah	1992	150	120	CA	Los Angeles

Church	Pastor	Year Founded	Estimated Membership	Average Attendance	State	City
Church of Pentecost	Maxwell Kushi	1991	250	350	IL	Chicago
Church of Pentecost	Peter Amposah	1991	450	350	NJ	Newark
Church of Pentecost (HQ)	Apostle Amoah	1987	800	550	NY	Bronx
Citygate Christian Center	Victor Airiohuodion	2001	65	55	CA	Bakersfield
Courage Christian Center	Tayo Badejoko	1999	200	120	PA	Philadelphia
Day Spring Church	Olu Obed	2003	80	65	NY	Roosevelt Island
Deeper Life Bible Church	Pius Elemchukwu Okoro	1994	150	50	IL	Chicago
DIOS International Missionary Church	Charles Fajinmi	1992	100	70	CA	Los Angeles
Dominion Chapel	Toyin Laoye	1995	800	550	NJ	Newark
Faith in Christ Evangelical Church	Akinjide Awojobi	1995	75	60	MD	Bladensburg
First Evangelical Church of West Africa	George Adekeye	1992	30	60	MD	District Height
Former and Later Rain	Edward Odiakosa	1986	100	80	CA	Los Angeles
Fresh Anointing International Church	Rev. Tsagli	2001	90	20	IL	Chicago
Full Deliverance World Ministries	Charles Azonwu (Bishop)	2001	150	100	CA	Los Angeles
Ghana Emmanuel Methodist Church	Nathan Addo Nartey	1998	100	50	NJ	Newark
Ghanaian Anglican Mission	Charles H. Holdbrooke	2001		80	NY	Brooklyn
Ghanaian Presbyterian Reformed Church	Samuel K. M. Atiemo	1991	135	89	NY	Brooklyn
Goodnews Evangelical Church	Sunday Bwanhot	1997	24	25	IL	Chicago
Gospel Faith Mission International	Joseph Dosumu	1989	65	30	CA	Los Angeles
Gospel to the Nations Ministries	Samuel Osamudia	1990	25	20	CA	Los Angeles
Heart of Worship Church	Kofi Peprah	2003	25	25	CA	North Ridge
House of Glory	George O. Akhigbe	2002	70	50	MD	Halethorpe
Household of Faith	Akin Gbenro	2003	150	120	IL	Calumet City

Church	Pastor	Year Founded	Estimated Membership	Average Attendance	State	City
International Central Gospel Church	Emmanuel Owusu	1995	150	65	NY	Bronx
International Chapel	Nimi Wariboko	1998		300	NY	Brooklyn
International Christian Center	Oladipo Kalijayi	1999	400	400	CA	Hawthorne
International House of Prayer for All People	Frederick O. Ogunfiditimi (Dr.)	1967	250	200	CA	Washington DC
Jesus Embassy	Niran Fafowora	1999	100	55	CA	Van Nuys
Jesus House Chicago	Bayo Adewole	1996	600	500	IL	Chicago
Joyful Nations Ministry	Adam Olayiwola	2001	50	30	CA	Ontario
Kenya International Community Church	Benson Andebe	1997	200	120	CA	Pomona
Kings Assembly	Bath Uzowuru	2001	120	100	CA	Moreno
Labour for Christ Ministry	Albert Asante	1993	120	85	CA	Los Angeles
Mighty Fortress Ministries International	Isaac Agyepong	2003	35	35	CA	San Dimas
Miracle Church of Christ	Eddie Okyere	1994	100	120	NY	Brooklyn
Morning Star Victory Church	Joseph Gichuhi	2003	30	30	CA	Buena Park
Mountain of Fire and Miracles	Lawrence Adetunji	1999	400	300	MD	Bowie
New Anointing Deliverance Church	John Okobi (Bishop)	1997	120	100	CA	Los Angeles
Oracles of God Mission Church (Glory Center)	Joshua Nathan	1991			MD	Lanham
Pentecost International World Church	James McKeown	2000	150	90	NJ	Newark
Rancho Church of the Living God	Steve Adarkwa	1993	100	80	CA	Rancho C.
Riches of Christ Fellowship International	John Egwuonwo	1988	100	50	CA	Los Angeles
Roger Park Congregation	Paul Olaniyan (Prophet)	1997	100	70	IL	Chicago
Royal Dominion Family Chapel	Femi Fatunmbi	1999	50	30	CA	Los Angeles
Schekina Christian Center	Joe Kamanda	2002	70	55	IL	Evanston

Church	Pastor	Year Founded	Estimated Membership	Average Attendance	State	City
Somerset Miracle International Church	Joseph Nzeketha	2000	45	50	NJ	Plainfield
Springs of Hope International Ministries	Lawrence Lasisi	2001	50	45	CA	Long Beach
St. Timothy's Episcopal Church	Stephen Mungoma	1925	135	30	CA	Compton
The Gospel Faith Mission International	Francis Aremo & P. Odagbodo	1984	300	250	MD	Brentwood
Trinity Circle Ministries	Prince Frimpong				MD	
Upper Room International Christian Fellowship	Blessing Ubani	1997	110	65	CA	Inglewood
Vision International Ministries	Peter Morgan (Bishop)	2000	250	180	CA	Los Angeles
Watchman Catholic Charismatic Renewal Movement	Timothy Okeke	2000	250	200	MD	New Carrollton

Select Bibliography

2005 World Population Data Sheet. Washington, DC: Population Reference Bureau, 2005.

"2005 Yearbook of Immigration Statistics," U.S. Census Bureau, http://www.census.gov/population/www/documentation/twps0029/tab03.html (accessed September 2006).

Abdullahi, Ahmednasir M. "The Refugee Crisis in Africa as a Crisis of the Institution of the State." *International Journal of Refugee Law* 6, no. 4 (1994): 562-80.

Abusharaf, Rogaia M. "Structural Adaptations in an Immigrant Muslim Congregation in New York." In *Gatherings in Diaspora: Religious Communities and the New Immigration*, ed. R. Stephen Warner and Judith G. Wittner, 235-61. Philadelphia: Temple University Press, 1998.

Adelaja, Sunday. "Go to a Land That I Will Show You." In *Out of Africa*, ed. C. Peter Wagner and Joseph Thompson, 37-55. Ventura, CA: Regal Books, 2004.

Adeney, Miriam. *God's Foreign Policy: Practical Ways to Help the World's Poor.* Vancouver: Regent College Publishing, 1998.

Adepoju, Aderanti. "South-North Migration: The African Experience." *International Migration* 29, no. 2 (1991): 205-21.

———. "Preliminary Analysis of Emigration Dynamics in Sub-Saharan Africa." *International Migration* 32, no. 2 (1994): 197-216.

———. "Migration in Africa: An Overview." In *The Migration Experience in Africa*, ed. Jonathan Baker and Tade Akin Aina, 87-108. Uppsala: Nordiska Afrikainstitutet, 1995.

———. "Changing Configurations of Migration in Africa." Migration Policy Institute, http://www.migrationinformation.org/Feature/print.cfm?ID=251.

Adogame, Afe. "Contesting the Ambivalences of Modernity in a Global Context: The Redeemed Christian Church of God, North America." *Studies in World Christianity* 10, no. 1 (2005): 25-48.

Adu, Helen Folasade. "Immigrant." *Lovers Rock.* New York: Sony Music, 2000.

"Africa Invests to Stop Migrants." *BBC News Online,* http://news.bbc.co.uk/2/hi/africa/6958164.stm (accessed August 2007).

Agozino, Biko. *Theoretical and Methodological Issues in Migration Research: Interdisciplinary, Intergenerational and International Perspectives.* Brookfield, VT: Ashgate, 2000.

Aids Epidemic Update: Special Report on Hiv/Aids. Geneva: UNAID/WHO, 2006. http://data.unaids.org/pub/EpiReport/2006/2006_EpiUpdate_en.pdf.

Ajami, Fouad. "The Summoning." *Foreign Affairs* 72, no. 4 (1993): 2-9.

Akande, Laolu. "Redeemed Christian Church of God Buys Multimillion Dollar Property in Dallas, USA." Celestial Church of Christ, http://www.celestialchurch.com/news/newsroom/rccg_buys_land.htm.

Akopari, John K. "The State, Refugees and Migration in Sub-Saharan Africa." *International Migration* 36, no. 2 (1998): 211-31.

Alba, Richard D., and Victor Nee. "Rethinking Assimilation Theory for a New Era of Immigration." In *The Handbook of International Migration: The American Experience*, ed. Charles Hirschman, Philip Kasinitz, and Josh DeWind, 137-60. New York: Russell Sage Foundation, 1999.

———. *Remaking the American Mainstream: Assimilation and Contemporary Immigration*. Cambridge, MA: Harvard University Press, 2003.

Albrow, Martin. *The Global Age: State and Society beyond Modernity*. Stanford: Stanford University Press, 1997.

The American Indian and Alaska Native Population: 2000. Census Bureau, 2002.

American Pietism in the 21st Century: New Insights to the Depth and Complexity of Religion in the U.S. Waco: Baylor Institute for Studies of Religion, 2006.

Anderson, Allan H. "A 'Failure in Love'? Western Missions and the Emergence of African Initiated Churches in the Twentieth Century." *Missiology* 29, no. 3 (July 2001): 275-86.

———. *An Introduction to Pentecostalism: Global Charismatic Christianity*. New York: Cambridge University Press, 2004.

Appadurai, Arjun. "Disjuncture and Difference in the Global Cultural Economy." In *The Globalization Reader*, ed. Frank J. Lechner and John Boli, 322-30. Malden MA: Blackwell, 2000.

Appleyard, R. T. "Summary Report of the Rapporteur." *International Migration* 29 1991): 333-39.

Arthur, John A. *Invisible Sojourners: African Immigrant Diaspora in the United States.* Westport, CT: Praeger, 2000.

Ash, Timothy G. "What Young British Muslims Say Can Be Shocking—Some of It Is Also True." *The Guardian*, August 10, 2006.

Ayittey, George B. N. *Africa in Chaos*. New York: St. Martin's, 1999.

Bainton, Roland Herbert. *The Reformation of the Sixteenth Century*. Enllarged ed., ed. Roland H. Bainton and Jaroslav Pelikan with a foreword and supplementary bibliography. Boston: Beacon, 1985.

Baker, Raymond W. *Capitalism's Achilles Heel: Dirty Money and How to Renew the Free-Market System*. Hoboken, NJ: John Wiley & Sons, 2005.

Barber, Benjamin R. *Jihad vs. McWorld: Terrorism's Challenge to Democracy*. New York: Ballantine, 1995.

———. "Beyone Jihad vs. McWorld." *The Nation* (2002). http://www.thenation.com/doc/20020121/barber.

Barnet, R., and J. Cavanagh. "Homogenization of Global Culture." In *The Case against the Global Economy and for a Turn toward the Local*, ed. Jerry Mander and Edward Goldsmith, x, 550. San Francisco: Sierra Club Books, 1996.

Barrett, David B. *Schism and Renewal in Africa: An Analysis of Six Thousand Contemporary Religious Movements*. Nairobi: Oxford University Press, 1968.

Barrett, David B., and Todd M. Johnson. "Status of Global Mission, A.D. 2006, in the Context of 20th and 21st Centuries." *International Bulletin of Missionary Research* 30, no. 1 (January 2006): 28.

Barrett, David B., George Thomas Kurian, and Todd M. Johnson. *World Christian Encyclopedia: A Comparative Survey of Churches and Religions in the Modern World*. 2nd ed. New York: Oxford University Press, 2001.

Bass, Dorothy C. "Congregations and the Bearing of Traditions." In *American Congregations*, ed. James P. Wind and James Welborn Lewis, 169-91. Chicago: University of Chicago Press, 1998.

Baur, John. *2000 Years of Christianity in Africa: An African Church History.* 2nd rev. ed. Nairobi, Kenya: Paulines, 1998.

Baylis, Phillipa. *An Introduction to Primal Religions.* Edinburgh: Traditional Cosmology Society, 1988.

Beatty, Jack. "Do as We Say, Not as We Do." *Atlantic Monthly* (February 2002): 24.

Beck, Linda. "West African Muslims in America: When Are Muslims Not Muslims?" In *African Immigrant Religions in America*, ed. Jacob K. Olupona and Regina Gemignani, 182-206. New York: New York University Press, 2007.

Bede. *The Ecclesiastical History of the English People.* The World's Classics. New York: Oxford University Press, 1994.

Bediako, Kwame. *Christianity in Africa: The Renewal of a Non-Western Religion.* Maryknoll, NY: Orbis Books, 1995.

———. "Understanding African Theology in the 20th Century." In *Issues in African Christian Theology*, ed. Samuel Ngewa, Mark Shaw, and Tite Tienou, 56-72. Nairobi: East African Educational Publishers, 1998.

———. *Theology and Identity: The Impact of Culture upon Christian Thought in the Second Century and in Modern Africa.* Regnum Studies in Mission. Irvine, CA: Regnum Books International, 1999.

Bello, Walden. "Structural Adjustment Programs: 'Success' for Whom?" In *The Case against the Global Economy and for a Turn toward the Local*, ed. J. Mander and E. Goldsmith, 285-93. San Francisco: Sierra Club Books, 1996.

Belloc, Hilaire. *Europe and the Faith.* New York: Paulist Press, 1920.

Berger, Peter L. "The Desecularization of the World: A Global Overview." In *The Desecularization of the World: Resurgent Religion and World Politics*, ed. Peter L. Berger, 1-18. Grand Rapids: Eerdmans, 1999.

———. "Four Faces of Global Culture." In *Globalization and the Challenges of a New Century: A Reader,* ed. Patrick O'Meara, Howard D. Mehlinger, and Matthew Krain. Indianapolis: Indiana University Press, 2000.

———. "The Cultural Dynamics of Globalization." In *Many Globalizations: Cultural Diversity in the Contemporary World*, ed. Peter L. Berger and Samuel P. Huntington. New York: Oxford University Press, 2002.

———, ed. *The Desecularization of the World: Resurgent Religion and world Politics.* Grand Rapids: Eerdmans, 1999.

Bergstrom, Lindsay, "Worldwide Baptists Survive, Reflect Century of Cultural Change." Associated Baptist Press, January 6, 2005. http://www.abpnews.com/184.article.

Beyer, Peter. *Religion and Globalization.* London: Sage, 1994.

Biney, Moses. "'Singing the Lord's Song in a Foreign Land': Spirituality, Communality, and Identity in a Ghanaian Immigrant Congregation." In *African Immigrant Religions in America*, ed. Jacob K. Olupona and Regina Gemignani, 259-78. New York: New York University Press, 2007.

Bjork, David E. "The Future of Christianity in Western Europe." *Missiology* 34, no. 3 (July 2006): 309-24.

Black, Richard. "Soaring Remittances Raise New Issues." *Migration Information Source* (2003). http://www.migrationinformation.org/Feature/print.cfm?ID=127.

Blumhofer, Edith. "The New Evangelicals: They Don't Think Like Billy Graham." *Wall Street Journal*, February 18, 2005.

Blyden, Edward Wilmot. *Christianity, Islam and the Negro Race* (London: W. B. Whittingham, 1888), 143.

Böhning, W. R. "International Migration and the Western World: Past, Present, Future." *International Migration* 16, no. 1 (1978): 11-22.

Bosch, David J. *Transforming Mission: Paradigm Shifts in Theology of Mission.* Maryknoll, NY: Orbis Books, 1991.

Bowen, John R. "The Myth of Global Ethnic Conflict." In *Globalization and the Challenges of a New Century: A Reader*, ed. Patrick O'Meara, Howard D. Mehlinger, and Matthew Krain, 79-89. Bloomington: Indiana University Press, 2000.

Brettell, Caroline B. "Theorizing Migration in Anthropology: The Social Construction of Networks, Identities, Communities, and Globalscapes." In *Migration Theory: Talking across Disciplines*, ed. Caroline Brettell and James Frank Hollifield, 97-135. New York: Routledge, 2000.

Brettell, Caroline, and James Frank Hollifield, eds. *Migration Theory: Talking across Disciplines.* New York: Routledge, 2000.

Brierley, Peter W. *U.K.C.H. Religious Trends No. 3.* London: Christian Research, 2001.

Bright, John. *A History of Israel.* 4th ed. Louisville: Westminster John Knox, 2000.

"British Muslims: Deconstructing the Veil." *The Economist*, October 14, 2006, 63.

Brittingham, Angela, and G. Patricia de la Cruz. "Ancestry: 2000." U.S. Census Bureau (accessed September 2006).

Brooks, David. "Kicking the Secularist Habit." *Atlantic Monthly* 291, no. 2 (March 2003): 26-28.

———. "People Like Us." *Atlantic Monthly* 292, no. 2 (September 2003): 29-32.

Brouwer, Steve, Paul Gifford, and Susan D. Rose. *Exporting the American Gospel: Global Christian Fundamentalism.* New York: Routledge, 1996.

Brown, L. David, Sanjeev Khagram, Mark H. Moore, and Peter Frumkin. "Globalization, NGOs, and Multisectoral Relations." In *Governance in a Globalizing World*, ed. Joseph S. Nye and John D. Donahue, 271-96. Washington, DC: Brookings Institution, 2000.

Brubaker, Pamela K. *Globalization at What Price? Economic Change and Daily Life.* Cleveland: Pilgrim, 2001.

Bruce, Steve. "The Demise of Christianity in Britain." In *Predicting Religion: Christian, Secular, and Alternative Futures*, ed. Grace Davie, Linda Woodhead, and Paul Heelas, 53-63. Burlington, VT: Ashgate, 2003.

Bühlmann, Walbert. *The Coming of the Third Church: An Analysis of the Present and Future of the Church.* Maryknoll, NY: Orbis Books, 1978.

Buijs, Frank J., and Jan Rath. "Muslims in Europe: The State of Research." Institute of Migration and Ethnic Studies, University of Amsterdam.

Bump, Micah, "International Migration in Africa: An Analysis Based on Estimates of the Migrant Stock." Migration Policy Institute, http://www.migrationinformation.org/Profiles/print.cfm?ID=381.

Burns, Timothy. *After History? Francis Fukuyama and His Critics.* Lanham, MD: Rowman & Littlefield, 1994.

Carpenter, Joel A. *Revive Us Again: The Reawakening of American Fundamentalism.* New York: Oxford University Press, 1997.

Carrington, William J., and Enrica Detragiache. "How Big Is the Brain Drain?" International Monetary Fund.

———. "How Extensive Is the Brain Drain." *Finance & Development* 36, no. 2 (1999), 46-49.

Carroll, Robert P. "Exile! What Exile? Deportation and the Discourses of Diaspora." In *Leading Captivity Captive: "The Exile" as History and Ideology*, ed. Lester L. Grabbe Lester, 62-79. Sheffield: Sheffield Academic Press, 1998.

Cary, Otis. *A History of Christianity in Japan: Roman Catholic, Greek Orthodox and*

Protestant Missions. New York: F. H. Revell, 1909; repr., Rutland, VT: C. E. Tuttle, 1976.

Castles, Stephen, and Mark J. Miller. *The Age of Migration: International Population Movements in the Modern World*. 2nd ed. New York: Guilford Press, 1998.

Changing Faiths: Latinos and the Transformation of American Religion. The Pew Research Center, 2007.

Chapman, Colin. *Islam and the West: Conflict, Coexistence or Conversion?* Carlisle, England: Paternoster, 1998.

Chirenje, J. Mutero. *Ethiopianism and Afro-Americans in Southern Africa, 1883-1916*. Baton Rouge: Louisiana State University Press, 1987.

"Christianity 'Almost Vanquished in U.K.,'" *BBC News Online*, http://news.bbc.co.uk/2/hi/uk_news/1527876.stm.

"A Civil War on Terrorism." *The Economist*, November 27, 2004, 56.

Clarke, Peter B. *West Africa and Christianity*. London: Edward Arnold, 1986.

Coan, Joseph R. "Redemption of Africa: The Vital Impulse of Black American Overseas Missionaries." *Journal of the Interdenominational Theological Center* 1, no. 2 (Spring 1974): 27-37.

"Communiqué from the House of Bishops of the Church of Nigeria," Anglican Communion Service, http://www.trinity-dublin.org/Documents/communique_house_of_bishops_of_the_church_of_nigeria.pdf.

Coote, Robert T. "The Uneven Growth of Conservative Evangelical Missions." *International Bulletin of Missionary Research* 6, no. 3 (July 1982): 118-23.

———. "Taking Aim on 2000 AD." In *Mission Handbook: North American Protestant Ministries Overseas*, ed. Samuel Wilson and John Siewert, 35-80. Monrovia, CA: MARC, 1986.

———. "Good News, Bad News, North American Protestant Overseas Personnel Statistics in Twenty-Five-Year Perspective." *International Bulletin of Missionary Research* 19, no. 1 (January 1995): 6-13.

———. "Shifts in North American Protestant Full-Time Missionary Community." *International Bulletin of Missionary Research* 29, no. 1 (January 2005): 12-13.

Cornelius, Wayne A., et al., eds. *Controlling Immigration: A Global Perspective*. 2nd ed. Stanford: Stanford University Press, 2004.

Cox, Harvey G. *Fire from Heaven: The Rise of Pentecostal Spirituality and the Reshaping of Religion in the Twenty-First Century*. Reading, MA: Perseus Books, 1995.

Cox, James L. "The Classification 'Primal Religions' as a Non-Empirical Christian Theological Construct." *Studies in World Christianity* 2, no. 1 (1996): 55-76.

Crowther, Dandeson C. *The Establishment of the Niger Delta Pastorate during the Episcopacy of the Rt. Rev. Bishop S. A. Crowther*. Liverpool: Thomson, 1907.

Cuffe, Jenny. "African Dream of a Better Life." *BBC News Online*, http://news.bbc.co.uk/2/hi/programmes/from_our_own_correspondent/6757657.stm (accessed June 2007).

Curtin, Philip D., S. Freierman, L. Thompson, and J. Vansina. *African History*. London: Longmans, 1991.

Daniels, David D. "African Immigrant Churches in the United States and the Study of Black Church History." In *African Immigrant Religions in America*, ed. Jacob K. Olupona and Regina Gemignani, 47-60. New York: New York University Press, 2007.

Daniels, Roger. *Coming to America: A History of Immigration and Ethnicity in American Life*. New York: HarperPerennial, 1991.

Davey, Andrew P. "Globalization as Challenge and Opportunity in Urban Mission." *International Review of Mission* 88, no. 351 (October 1999): 381-89.

Davidson, Basil. *The African Slave Trade.* Rev. and expanded ed. London: Little, Brown, 1980.

———. *Africa in History: Themes and Outlines.* London: Paladin Grafton Books, 1987; 1st Touchstone ed. New York: Simon & Schuster, 1995.

Davie, Grace. *Europe, the Exceptional Case: Parameters of Faith in the Modern World.* London: Darton Longman & Todd, 2002.

Davis, John A. "The Influence of Africans on American Culture." *The Annals* 354 (July 1964): 75-83.

Dawson, Christopher. *The Historic Reality of Christian Culture: A Way to the Renewal of Human Life.* New York: Harper, 1960.

De La Torre, Miguel A. *Reading the Bible from the Margins.* Maryknoll, NY: Orbis Books, 2002.

Demuth, Andreas. "Some Conceptual Thoughts on Migration Research." In *Theoretical and Methodological Issues in Migration Research: Interdisciplinary, Intergenerational and International Perspectives*, ed. Biko Agozino, 21-58. Brookfield, VT: Ashgate, 2000.

Dixon, David. "Characteristics of the African Born in the United States." *Migration Information Source* (January 2006), http://www.migrationinformation.org/Feature/print.cfm?ID=366.

Docquier, Frédéric, and Abdeslam Marfouk. "Measuring the International Mobility of Skilled Workers (1990-2000): Release 1.0." The World Bank, http://www-wds.worldbank.org/servlet/WDSContentServer/WDSP/IB/2004/09/22/000160016_20040922150619/Rendered/PDF/wps3381.pdf (accessed April 16 2006).

Docquier, Frédéric, and Hillel Rapoport. "Skilled Migration: The Perspective of Developing Countries," http://www-wds.worldbank.org/servlet/WDSContentServer/WDSP/IB/2004/09/22/000160016_20040922151739/Rendered/PDF/WPS3382.pdf (accessed April 16 2006)

Drane, John. *The McDonaldization of the Church: Consumer Culture and the Church's Future.* Macon, GA: Smyth & Helwys, 2001.

Drumtra, Jeff. "West Africa's Refugee Crisis Spills across Many Borders." Migration Information Source, http://www.migrationinformation.org/Feature/display.fm?ID=148.

Easton, M. G. *Baker's Illustrated Bible Dictionary.* Rev. ed. Grand Rapids: Baker Book House, 1981.

Ebaugh, Helen R., and Janet S. Chafetz. *Religion and the New Immigrants: Continuities and Adaptations in Immigrant Congregations.* New York: AltaMira, 2000.

Ebo, Bosah. "Adaptation and Preservation: Communication Patterns of African Immigrants in America." In *The Huddled Masses: Communication and Immigration*, ed. Gary Gumpert and Susan J. Drucker, 59-76. Cresskill, NJ: Hampton, 1998.

Eck, Diana L. *A New Religious America: How a "Christian Country" Has Now Become the World's Most Religiously Diverse Nation.* San Francisco: Harper, 2001.

Editorial. "Harvesting Poverty: Napoleon's Bittersweet Legacy." *New York Times*, August 11, 2003.

Ellis, Stephen. *The Mask of Anarchy: The Destruction of Liberia and the Religious Dimension of an African Civil War.* New York: New York University Press, 1999.

Epp, Frank H. "The Migration of the Mennonites." In *Mennonite World Handbook: A Survey of Mennonite and Brethren in Christ Churches*, ed. Paul N. Kraybill, 10-19. Lombard, IL: Mennonite World Conference, 1978.

"Estimated Number of International Migrants at Mid-Year, by Countries in Africa: 2000." *Migration Information Source* (2006), http://www.migrationinformation.org/Datatools/graphs/africa.4.shtml.

"Estimated Number of International Migrants at Mid-Year, by Regions in Africa: 1990 and 2000." *Migration Information Source* (2006), http://www.migrationinforma tion.org/Datatools/graphs/africa.4.shtml.

Etouga-Manguelle, Daniel. "Does Africa Need a Cultural Adjustment Program?" In *Culture Matters: How Values Shape Human Progress*, ed. Lawrence E. Harrison and Samuel P. Huntington, 65-77. New York: Basic Books, 2000.

"European Muslim Population," Muslim Population Worldwide, http://www.islamicpopulation.com/europe_general.html (accessed December 2006).

Eusebius. *The Life of the Blessed Emperor Constantine*. Internet Medieval Sourcebook. http://www.fordham.edu/halsall/basis/vita-constantine.html.

Faini, Riccardo, "Is the Brain Drain an Unmitigated Blessing?" UNU/WIDER, http://www2.gtz.de/migration-and-development/download/riccardo-faini.pdf (accessed April 25, 2006).

Fairbank, John K. "Assignment for the '70s." *American Historical Review* 74, no. 3 (1969): 861-79.

Falk, Peter. *The Growth of the Church in Africa*. Kinshasa: Institut Supérieur Théologique de Kinshasa, 1985.

Ferris, Elizabeth G. *Beyond Borders: Refugees, Migrants and Human Rights in the Post-Cold War Era*. Geneva: WCC, 1993.

Finke, Roger, and Rodney Stark. *The Churching of America, 1776-1990: Winners and Losers in Our Religious Economy*. 5th ed. New Brunswick, NJ: Rutgers University Press, 2002.

Fishman, Joshua A. "The New Linguistic Order." In *Globalization and the Challenges of a New Century: A Reader*, ed. Patrick O'Meara, Howard D. Mehlinger, and Matthew Krain, 435-42. Indianapolis: Indiana University Press, 2000.

Fletcher, Richard. *The Barbarian Conversion: From Paganism to Christianity*. New York: Henry Holt, 1997.

"Foreign-Born Profiles." U.S. Census Bureau, http://www.census.gov/population/www/socdemo/foreign/STP-159-2000tl.html (accessed September 2006).

Frank, Isnard Wilhelm. *A History of the Medieval Church*. Translated by John Bowden. London: SCM, 1995.

Franklin, Robert Michael. "The Safest Place on Earth: The Culture of Black Congregations." In *American Congregations*, ed. James P. Wind and James Welborn Lewis, 257-84. Chicago: University of Chicago Press, 1998.

Frazier, Martin. "Continuity and Change in Caribbean Immigration." *People's Weekly World Newspaper* (2005), http://www.pww.org/article/articleprint/7359/.

Frederiks, Martha T. *We Have Toiled All Night: Christianity in the Gambia 1465-2000*. Mission: Missiological Research in the Netherlands. Zoetermeer: Boekencentrum, 2003.

Friedman, Thomas L. *The Lexus and the Olive Tree: Understanding Globalization*. New York: Farrar, Straus & Giroux, 1999.

———. *The World Is Flat: A Brief History of the Twenty-First Century*. New York: Farrar, Straus & Giroux, 2007.

Friesen, J. Stanley. *Missionary Responses to Tribal Religions at Edinburgh, 1910*. New York: Peter Lang, 1996.

Frykenberg, Robert E. "India." In *A World History of Christianity*, ed. Adrian Hastings, 148-91. Grand Rapids: Eerdmans, 1999.

Fukuyama, Francis. "The End of History?" *The National Interest,* Special Edition (Summer 1989).

———. *The End of History and the Last Man.* New York: Free Press, 1992.

———. "Second Thoughts: The Last Man in a Bottle." *The National Interest* (Summer 1999).

Gammeltoft, Peter. "Remittances and Other Financial Flows to Developing Countries." *International Migration* 40, no. 5 (2002): 181-209.

Gans, Herbert J. "Towards a Reconciliation of 'Assimilation' and 'Pluralism': The Interplay of Acculturation and Ethnic Retention." In *The Handbook of International Migration: The American Experience,* ed. Charles Hirschman, Philip Kasinitz, and Josh DeWind, 161-71. New York: Russell Sage Foundation, 1999.

Garrett, Geoffrey. "Partisan Politics in the Global Economy." In *The Globalization Reader,* ed. Frank J. Lechner and John Boli, 227-35. Malden, MA: Blackwell, 2000.

Gerloff, Roswith. "Religion, Culture and Resistance: The Significance of African Christian Communities in Europe." *Exchange* 30, no. 3 (2001): 276-89.

"German State Backs Headscarf Ban." *BBC News,* http://news.bbc.co.uk/2/hi/europe/3591043.stm (accessed January 2007).

Gerstner, Jonathan N. "A Christian Monopoly: The Reformed Church and Colonial Society under Dutch Rule." In *Christianity in South Africa: A Political, Social, and Cultural History,* ed. Richard Elphick and Rodney Davenport, 16-30. Berkeley: University of California Press, 1997.

Gibbs, Eddie, and Ian Coffey. *Church Next: Quantum Changes in Christian Ministry.* Downers Grove, IL: InterVarsity, 2001.

Gibson, Campbell J., and Emily Lennon. "Historical Census Statistics on the Foreign-Born Population of the United States: 1850-1990." U.S. Bureau of the Census, http://www.census.gov/population/www/documentation/twps0029/tab03.html (accessed September 2006).

Giddens, Anthony. *The Consequence of Modernity.* Stanford: Stanford University Press, 1990.

Gilkey, Langdon. "The Christian Congregation as a Religious Community." In *American Congregations,* ed. James P. Wind and James Welborn Lewis, 100-132. Chicago: University of Chicago Press, 1998.

Giry, Stéphanie. "France and Its Muslims." *Foreign Affairs* 85, no. 5 (September/October 2006): 87-104.

Goodpasture, H. McKennie. *Cross and Sword: An Eyewitness History of Christianity in Latin America.* Maryknoll, NY: Orbis Books, 1989.

Goodstein, Laurie. "U.S. Muslim Clerics Seek a Modern Middle Ground." *New York Times,* June 18, 2006.

Gordon, April. "The New Diaspora: African Immigration to the United States." *Journal of Third World Studies* 15, no. 1 (1998): 79-103.

Gordon, Milton M. *Assimilation in American Life: The Role of Race, Religion, and National Origins.* New York: Oxford University Press, 1964.

Gort, J. D. "Theological Issues for Missiological Education: An Ecumenical-Protestant Perspective." In *Missiological Education for the Twenty-First Century: Essays in Honor of Paul E. Pierson,* ed. John Dudley Woodberry, Charles Edward van Engen, and Edgar J. Elliston, 67-75. Maryknoll, NY: Orbis Books, 1996.

"The Great Divide: How Westerners and Muslims View Each Other." Pew Research Center, http://pewglobal.org/reports/pdf/253.pdf.

Grieco, Elizabeth. "The African Foreign Born in the United States." *Migration Infor-*

mation Source (September 2004), http://www.migrationinformation.org/Feature/print.cfm?ID=250.

Guthrie, Stan. *Missions in the Third Millennium: 21 Key Trends for the 21st Century.* Waynesboro, GA: Paternoster, 2000.

Haddad, Yvonne Yazbeck. "Make Room for the Muslims?" In *Religious Diversity and American Religious History: Studies in Traditions and Cultures*, ed. Walter H. Conser and Sumner B. Twiss, 218-61. Athens: University of Georgia Press, 1997.

Hair, Paul E. H. "Freetown Christianity and Africa." *Sierra Leone Bulletin of Religion* 6 (December 1964): 13-21.

Halstead, T., and C. Cobb. "The Need for New Measurements of Progress." In *The Case against the Global Economy and for a Turn Towards the Local,* ed. J. Mander and E. Goldsmith, 197-206. San Francisco: Sierra Club Books, 1996.

Hamilton, Kimberly. "Migration and Development: Blind Faith and Hard-to-Find Facts." Migration Policy Institute, http://www.migrationinformation.org/Feature/print.cfm?ID=174 (accessed May 12, 2006).

Hampshire, James, and Shamit Saggar. "Migration, Integration, and Security in the U.K. Since July 7." Migration Policy Institute, http://www.migrationinformation.org/Feature/print.cfm?ID=383.

Hanciles, Jehu. *Euthanasia of a Mission: African Church Autonomy in a Colonial Context.* Westport, CT: Praeger, 2002.

———. "Beyond Christendom: African Migration and Transformations in Global Christianity." *Studies in World Christianity* 10, no. 1 (2005): 93-113.

———. "New Wine in Old Wineskins: Critical Reflections on Writing and Teaching a Global Christian History." *Missiology* 35, no. 3 (July 2006): 361-82.

———. "Back to Africa: White Abolitionists and Black Missionaries." In *African Christianity: An African Story*, ed. U. Kalu Ogbu, 167-88. Trenton, NJ: Africa World Press, 2007.

Harrison, Lawrence E. "Introduction." In *Culture Matters: How Values Shape Human Progress*, ed. Lawrence E. Harrison and Samuel P. Huntington, xvii-xxxiv. New York: Basic Books, 2000.

Hastings, Adrian. *The Church in Africa, 1450-1950.* Oxford: Clarendon, 1994.

———. *The Construction of Nationhood: Ethnicity, Religion, and Nationalism.* New York: Cambridge University Press, 1997.

———. "Latin America." In *A World History of Christianity*, ed. Adrian Hastings, 328-68. Grand Rapids: Eerdmans, 1999.

———. "The Clash of Nationalism and Universalism within Twentieth-Century Missionary Christianity." In *Missions, Nationalism, and the End of Empire*, ed. Brian Stanley, 15-33. Grand Rapids: Eerdmans, 2003.

Heisler, Barbara Schmitter. "The Sociology of Immigration: From Assimilation to Segmented Integration, from the American Experience to the Global Arena." In *Migration Theory: Talking across Disciplines*, ed. Caroline Brettell and James Frank Hollifield, 77-96. New York: Routledge, 2000.

Held, David, Anthony McGrew, David Goldblatt, and Jonathan Perraton. *Global Transformations: Politics, Economics and Culture.* Stanford: Stanford University Press, 1999.

Hertz, Noreena. *The Silent Takeover: Global Capitalism and the Death of Democracy.* New York: Free Press, 2001.

Hirschman, Charles, Philip Kasinitz, and Josh DeWind, eds. *The Handbook of International Migration: The American Experience.* New York: Russell Sage Foundation, 1999.

Hobsbawn, E. J. "The World Unified." In *The Globalization Reader*, ed. Frank Lechna and John Boli. Malden, MA: Blackwell, 1999.

Holifield, E. Brooks. "Toward a History of American Congregations." In *American Congregations*, ed. James P. Wind and James Welborn Lewis, 23-53. Chicago: University of Chicago Press, 1998.

Hoogvelt, Ankie. *Globalization and the Postcolonial World: The New Political Economy of Development*. Baltimore: Johns Hopkins University Press, 1997.

Howard, David M. *The Dream That Would Not Die: The Birth and Growth of the World Evangelical Fellowship 1846-1986*. Exeter: Paternoster, 1986.

Human Development Report 2000. New York: Oxford University Press, 2000. http://hdr. undp.org/en/media/hdr_2000_en.pdf.

Human Development Report 2001. New York: Oxford University Press, 2001. http://hdr. undp.org/en/media/completenew1.pdf.

Human Development Report 2003. New York: Oxford University Press, 2003. http://hdr. undp.org/en/media/hdr03_complete.pdf.

Human Development Report 2005. New York: UNDP, 2005. http://hdr.undp.org/en/ media/hdr05_complete.pdf.

Human Population: Fundamentals of Growth: Population Growth and Distribution. Population Reference Bureau, 2006.

Hunter, George G. *How to Reach Secular People*. Nashville: Abingdon, 1992.

Huntington, Samuel P. "No Exit: The Errors of Endism." *The National Interest* (Fall 1989).

———. *The Clash of Civilizations and the Remaking of World Order*. New York: Simon & Schuster, 1996.

"I.R.C.A. Legalization During Fiscal Years 1989 to 1991." U.S. Census Bureau, http:// www.census.gov/population/documentation/twps0009/ (accessed September 2006).

Iheanacho, Maureen, and Allison Howell. *By His Grace: Signs on a Ghanaian Journey*. Akropong, Ghana: Amara-Zaane, 2005.

"International Migration: Facts and Figures." International Organization for Migration http://www.iom.int/en/PDF_Files/wmr2005_presskit/wmr_facts_and_figures/ WMR_Facts_and_Figures.pdf.

Isbister, John. *Promises Not Kept: The Betrayal of Social Change in the Third World*. 5th ed. Bloomfield, CT: Kumarian Press, 2001.

"Islam in Europe." *The Economist*, April 15, 2006, 55.

Jacques, André. *The Stranger within Your Gates: Uprooted People in the World Today*. Risk Book Series 29. Geneva: World Council of Churches, 1986.

Jaffarian, Michael. "The Statistical State of the Missionary Enterprise." *Missiology* 30, no. 1 (January 2002): 15-32.

———. "Are There More Non-Western Missionaries Than Western Missionaries?" *International Bulletin of Missionary Research* 28, no. 3 (July 2004): 131-32.

JanMohammed, Abdul R. "The Economy of Manichean Allegory: The Function of Racial Difference in Colonialist Literature." In *"Race," Writing, and Difference*, ed. Henry Louis Gates, Jr., 58-106. Chicago: University of Chicago Press, 1986.

Jaret, Charles. "Troubled by Newcomers: Anti-Immigrant Attitudes and Actions during Two Eras of Mass Emigration." In *Mass Migration to the United States: Classical and Contemporary Periods*, ed. Pyong Gap Min, 21-63. New York: AltaMira, 2002.

Jasso, Guillermina, Douglas S. Massey, Mark R. Rosenzweig, and James P. Smith. "Exploring the Religious Preferences of Recent Immigrants to the United States:

Evidence from the New Immigrant Survey Pilot." In *Religion and Immigration: Christian, Jewish, and Muslim Experiences in the United States*, ed. Yvonne Yazbeck Haddad, Jane I. Smith, and John L. Esposito, 217-53. Walnut Creek, CA: AltaMira, 2003.

Jeal, Tim. *Livingstone.* New York: Putnam, 1973.

Jenkins, Philip. *The Next Christendom: The Coming of Global Christianity.* New York: Oxford University Press, 2002.

———. "Defender of the Faith." *Atlantic Monthly* 292, no. 4 (November 2003): 48-49.

Jernegan, Kevin. "A New Century: Immigration in the U.S." *Migration Information Source* (2005), http://www.migrationinformation.org/Feature/print.cfm?ID=283.

Johnstone, Patrick, and Jason Mandryk, Jason. *Operation World: 21st Century Edition.* Waynesboro, GA: Paternoster, 2001.

Kalu, Ogbu. "Colour and Conversion: The White Missionary Factor in the Christianisation of Igboland, 1867-1967." *Missiology* 18, no. 1 (January 1990): 61-74.

———. "Black Missionaries and White Abolitionists: The Careers of Joseph and Mary Gomer in the Good Hope Mission, Sherbro, Sierra Leone, 1871-1894." *Neue Zeitschrift für Missionswissenschaft* (June 2003): 161-74.

———. "Ethiopianism in African Christianity." In *African Christianity: An African Story*, ed. U. Kalu Ogbu, 227-43. Trenton, NJ: Africa World Press, 2007.

Kanari, Shlomit. "Music and Migration: The Role of Religious Music in American Migrant Churches in Israel." In *Religion in the Context of African Migration*, ed. Afeosemime U. Adogame and Cordula Weisskèoppel, 267-83. Bayreuth: Eckhard Breitinger, 2005.

Kaplan, Robert. *The Ends of the Earth: A Journey to the Frontiers of Anarchy.* New York: Vintage Books, 1996.

———. "The Coming Anarchy." In *Globalization and the Challenges of a New Century: A Reader*, ed. Patrick O'Meara, Howard D. Mehlinger, and Matthew Krain, 34-60. Bloomington: Indiana University Press, 2000.

Keely, Charles B. "Demography and International Migration." In *Migration Theory: Talking across Disciplines*, ed. Caroline Brettell and James Frank Hollifield, 43-60. New York: Routledge, 2000.

Kennedy, Paul. *Preparing for the Twenty-First Century.* New York: Vintage Books, 1993.

Khan, M. A. Muqtedar. "Constructing the American Muslim Community." In *Religion and Immigration: Christian, Jewish, and Muslim Experiences in the United States*, ed. Yvonne Yazbeck Haddad, Jane I. Smith, and John L. Esposito, 175-98. Walnut Creek, CA: AltaMira, 2003.

Killingray, David. "The Black Atlantic Missionary Movement and Africa, 1780s-1920s." *Journal of Religion in Africa* 33, no. 1 (February 2003): 3-31.

Klaisen, Jytte. "The Two-Way Street to Integration for Europe's Muslims." *Faith & International Affairs* 4, no. 3 (Winter 2006): 13-19.

Klaus, Byron D. "Pentecostalism as a Global Culture: An Introductory Overview." In *The Globalization of Pentecostalism: A Religion Made to Travel*, ed. Murray W. Dempster, Byron D. Klaus, and Douglas Petersen, 127-30. Irvine, CA: Regnum Books International, 1999.

Klausen, Jytte. "The Two-Way Street to Integration for Europe's Muslims." *Faith & International Affairs* 4, no. 3 (Winter 2006): 13-19.

Klein, Ralph W. *Israel in Exile: A Theological Interpretation.* Overtures to Biblical Theology 6. Philadelphia: Fortress, 1979.

Klinghoffer, David. "That Other Church." *Christian Century* 49, no. 1 (January, 2005): 62.

Kopytoff, Jean Herskovits. *A Preface to Modern Nigeria: The "Sierra Leonians" in Yoruba, 1830-1890.* Madison: University of Wisconsin Press, 1965.

Koser, Khalid, and Helma Lutz. "The New Migration in Europe: Contexts, Constructions and Realities." In *The New Migration in Europe: Social Constructions and Social Realities*, ed. Khalid Koser and Helma Lutz, 1-17. New York: St. Martin's, 1998.

Kotkin, Joel, and Karen Speicher. "God and the City." *God and the City* 10 (October/ November 2003): 34-39.

Kupchan, Charles A. "The End of the West." *Atlantic Monthly* (November 2002): 42-44.

Larbi, Emmanuel Kingsley. *Pentecostalism: The Eddies of Ghanaian Christianity.* Studies in African Pentecostal Christianity 1. Accra, Ghana: C.P.C.S., 2001.

Latourette, Kenneth S. "Christ the Hope of the World: What Has History to Say?" *Religion in Life* 23, no. 3 (Summer 1954): 323-33.

———. *The Thousand Years of Uncertainty.* Grand Rapids: Zondervan, 1970.

———. *Three Centuries of Advance, A.D. 1500-A.D. 1800.* Vol. 3, *A History of the Expansion of Christianity.* 3rd ed. Grand Rapids: Zondervan, 1970.

Lemoine, M. "Effects of Migration on Family Structure in the Receiving Country." *International Migration* 27 (1989): 271-79.

"Letter to Diognetus." In *Early Christian Writings: The Apostolic Fathers.* New York: Penguin Books, 1987.

Lieblich, Julia, and Tom McCann. "Africans Now Missionaries to the U.S." *Chicago Tribune*, June 21, 2002, 1.

Limburg, James. "Psalm 121: A Psalm for Sojourners." *Word & World* 5, no. 2 (1985): 180-87.

Logan, Ikubolajeh Bernard. "The Brain Drain of Professional, Technical and Kindred Workers from Developing Countries: Some Lessons from the Africa-US Flow of Professionals (1980-1989)." *International Migration* 30, no. 4 (1992): 289-312.

"London Is Different!" *Quadrant*, January 2007.

López, David E. "Social and Linguistic Aspects of Assimilation Today." In *The Handbook of International Migration: The American Experience*, ed. Charles Hirschman, Philip Kasinitz, and Josh DeWind, 212-22. New York: Russell Sage Foundation, 1999.

Lowell, B. Lindsay, Allan Findlay, and Emma Stewart. "Brain Strain: Optimising Highly Skilled Migration from Developing Countries." Institute for Public Policy Research, http://www.esa/population/publications/fourthcoord2005/P15_Lowell&Martin .pdf (accessed April 26, 2006).

Lyon, David. *The Steeple's Shadow: On the Myths and Realities of Secularization.* Grand Rapids: Eerdmans, 1987.

Ma, Julie. "The Growth of Christianity in Asia and Its Impact on Mission." *Encounters Mission Ezine*, no. 16 (2007).

MacMullen, Ramsay. *Christianity and Paganism in the Fourth to Eighth Centuries.* New Haven: Yale University Press, 1997.

Malone, Nolan, Kaari F. Baluja, Joseph M. Costanzo, and Cynthia J. Davis. "The Foreign-Born Population: 2000." U.S. Census Bureau, http://www.census.gov/prod/ 2003pubs/c2kbr-34.pdf (accessed September 2006).

Marshall-Fratani, Ruth. "Mediating the Global and Local in Nigerian Pentecostalism." *Journal of Religion in Africa* 28, no. 3 (1998): 278-315.

Martin, Philip L. "The Impact of Immigration on Receiving Countries." In *Immigration into Western Societies: Problems and Policies*, ed. Emek M. Uçarer and Donald J. Puchala, 17-27. Washington: Pinter, 1997.

Martinez, Andrés. "Who Said Anything about Rice? Free Trade Is about Cars and Play-stations." *New York Times*, August 10, 2003.

Masci, David. "An Uncertain Road: Muslims and the Future of Europe." The Pew Research Center, http://pewforum.org/publications/reports/muslims-europe-2005.pdf.

Massey, Douglas. "Why Does Immigration Occur? A Theoretical Synthesis." In *The Handbook of International Migration: The American Experience*, 34-52. New York: Russell Sage Foundation, 1999.

Mbiti, John S. *African Religions and Philosophy*. 2nd rev. and enl. ed. Portsmouth, NH: Heinemann, 1990.

McCloud, Aminah Beverly. "Islam in America: The Mosaic." In *Religion and Immigration: Christian, Jewish, and Muslim Experiences in the United States*, ed. Yvonne Yazbeck Haddad, Jane I. Smith, and John L. Esposito, 159-74. Walnut Creek, CA: AltaMira, 2003.

McNeely, Connie. "The Determination of Statehood." In *The Globalization Reader*, ed. J. Lechner Frank and John Boli, 199-206. Malden, MA: Blackwell, 2000.

Mengisteab, Kidane. *Globalization and Autocentricity in Africa's Development in the 21st Century*. Trenton, NJ: Africa World Press, 1996.

Meyer, Jean-Baptiste. "Network Approach Versus Brain Drain: Lessons from the Diaspora." *International Migration* 39, no. 1 (2001): 91-108.

Mignolo, Walter. "Globalization, Civilization Processes, and the Relocation of Languages and Cultures." In *The Cultures of Globalization*, ed. F. Jameson and M. Miyoshi, 32-53. Durham, NC: Duke University Press, 1998.

Míguez-Bonino, José. "Genesis 11:1-9: A Latin-American Perspective." In *Return to Babel: Global Perspectives on the Bible*, ed. John R. Levison and Priscilla Pope-Levison, 13-16. Louisville: Westminster John Knox, 1999.

Miller, Donald E. *Reinventing American Protestantism: Christianity in the New Millennium*. Berkeley: University of California Press, 1999.

Millman, Joel. *The Other Americans: How Immigrants Renew Our Country, Our Economy, and Our Values*. New York: Penguin Books, 1998.

Min, Pyong Gap. "Contemporary Immigrants' Advantages for Intergenerational Cultural Transmission." In *Mass Migration to the United States: Classical and Contemporary Periods*, ed. Pyong Gap Min, 135-60. New York: AltaMira, 2002.

Minogue, Kenneth. "Religion, Reason and Conflict in the 21st Century." *National Interest* (Summer 2003): 127-32.

Mittelman, James H. *The Globalization Syndrome: Transformation and Resistance*. Princeton: Princeton University Press, 2000.

Moravcsik, Andrew. "Striking a New Transatlantic Bargain." *Foreign Affairs* 82, no. 4 (July/August 2003): 74-89.

Morawska, Ewa. "East Europeans on the Move." In *The Cambridge Survey of World Migration*, ed. Robin Cohen, 97-102. New York: Cambridge University Press, 1995.

Moreau, Scott. "Putting the Survey in Perspective." In *Mission Handbook 2001-2003: U.S. and Canadian Christian Ministries Overseas*, ed. John A. Siewert and Dotsey Welliver, 33-80. Wheaton, IL: Billy Graham Center, 2000.

"Muslims in Europe: Country Guide," *BBC News*, http://news.bbc.co.uk/2/hi/europe/4385768.stm (accessed January 2007).

Neill, Stephen. *A History of Christianity in India: The Beginnings to A.D. 1707.* New York: Cambridge University Press, 1984.

———. *A History of Christian Missions.* 2nd ed. New York: Penguin, 1990.

Netland, Harold A. *Encountering Religious Pluralism: The Challenge to Christian Faith & Mission.* Downers Grove, IL: InterVarsity, 2001.

Netland, Harold A., and Craig Ott. *Globalizing Theology: Belief and Practice in an Era of World Christianity.* Nottingham: Apollos, 2007.

"The New Dutch Model?" *The Economist,* April 2, 2005, 24-26.

Newland, Kathleen. "Migration as a Factor in Development and Poverty Reduction." Migration Policy Institute, http://www.migrationinformation.org/Feature/print.cfm?ID=136.

Nieswand, Boris. "Charismatic Christianity in the Context of Migration: Social Status, the Experience of Migration and the Constructions of Selves among Ghanaian Migrants in Berlin." In *Religion in the Context of African Migration,* ed. Afeosemime U. Adogame and Cordula Weisskèoppel, 243-65. Bayreuth: Eckhard Breitinger, 2005.

"Nigeria and Ecowas Special Report." *West Africa,* October 19-November 1, 1998, 753-58.

Noll, Mark A. *American Evangelical Christianity: An Introduction.* Malden, MA: Blackwell, 2001.

———. *The Old Religion in a New World.* Grand Rapids: Eerdmans, 2002.

———. *The Rise of Evangelicalism: The Age of Edwards, Whitefield and the Wesleys.* A History of Evangelicalism 1. Downers Grove, IL: InterVarsity, 2004.

Norris, Pippa, and Ronald Inglehart. *Sacred and Secular: Religion and Politics Worldwide.* New York: Cambridge University Press, 2004.

Ntumy, Michael K. *"Flamingo," the Camp of No Return: A Missionary's Account of God's Liberation during the Liberia War.* Accra, Ghana: Pentecostal Press, 1994.

Nugent, Paul. *Africa since Independence: A Comparative History.* New York: Palgrave Macmillan, 2004.

Nye, Joseph S. "U.S. Power and Strategy after Iraq." *Foreign Affairs* 82, no. 4 (July/August 2003): 60-73.

Nye, Joseph S., and John D. Donahue, eds. *Governance in a Globalizing World.* Washington, DC: Brookings Institution, 2000.

Ohmae, Kenichi. *The End of the Nation State: The Rise of Regional Economies.* London: HarperCollins, 1995.

Okoth, Kenneth. "Kenya: What Role for Diaspora in Development?" *Migration Information Source* (2003), http://www.migrationinformation.org/Feature/print.cfm?ID=150.

Okoth-Ogendo, H. W. O. "The Effect of Migration on Family Structures in Sub-Saharan Africa." *International Migration* 27 (1989): 309-17.

Oliver, Roland Anthony. *The African Experience.* London: Pimlico, 1994.

Olupona, Jacob K., and Regina Gemignani, eds. *African Immigrant Religions in America.* New York: New York University Press, 2007.

———. "Introduction." In *African Immigrant Religions in America,* ed. Jacob K. Olupona and Regina Gemignani, 1-24. New York: New York University Press, 2007.

Onyinah, Opoku. "Pentecostalism and the African Diaspora: An Examination of the Missions Activities of the Church of Pentecost." *Pneuma* 26, no. 2 (Fall 2004): 216-41.

Osnos, Evan. "Islam Shaping a New Europe." *Chicago Tribune,* December 19, 2004.

Outram, Dorinda. *The Enlightenment.* New York: Cambridge University Press, 1995.

Papastergiadis, Nikos. *The Turbulence of Migration: Globalization, Deterritorialization, and Hybridity*. Malden, MA: Blackwell, 2000.

Park, Timothy K. "A Survey of the Korean Missionary Movement." *Journal of Asian Mission* 4, no. 1 (2002): 111-19.

Parratt, John, ed. *A Reader in African Christian Theology*. London: SPCK, 1987.

Pearse, Meic. *Why the Rest Hates the West: Understanding the Roots of Global Rage*. London: SPCK, 2004.

Pedraza, Silvia. "Origins and Destinies: Immigration, Race, and Ethnicity in American History." In *Origins and Destinies: Immigration, Race, and Ethnicity in America*, ed. Silvia Pedraza and Rubén G. Rumbaut, 1-20. New York: Wadsworth, 1996.

Pessar, Partricia R. "The Role of Gender, Households, and Social Networks in the Migration Process: A Review and Appraisal." In *The Handbook of International Migration: The American Experience*, ed. Charles Hirschman, Philip Kasinitz, and Josh DeWind, 53-70. New York: Russell Sage Foundation, 1999.

Phipps, William E. *William Sheppard: Congo's African American Livingstone*. Louisville, KY: Geneva, 2002.

Phizacklea, Annie. "Migration and Globalization: A Female Perspective." In *The New Migration in Europe: Social Constructions and Social Realities*, ed. Khalid Koser and Helma Lutz, 21-38. New York: St. Martin's Press, 1998.

Pigott, Robert. "China Tour Showed Christian Growth." *BBC News Online* (http://news.bbc.co.uk/2/hi/asia-pacific/6101786.stm) (accessed February 2007).

Pipes, Daniel. "God and Mammon: Does Poverty Cause Militant Islam?" *National Interest* 66 (Winter 2001/2002): 14-21.

Porter, Andrew N. "Evangelical Enthusiasm, Missionary Motivation and West Africa in the Late 19th Century: The Career of G. W. Brooke." *Journal of Imperial and Commonwealth History* 6, no. 1 (1977): 23-46.

———. *Religion Versus Empire? British Protestant Missionaries and Overseas Expansion, 1700-1914*. New York: Manchester University Press, 2004.

Portes, Alejandro. "Immigration Theory for a New Century: Some Problems and Opportunities." In *The Handbook of International Migration: The American Experience*, ed. Charles Hirschman, Philip Kasinitz, and Josh DeWind, 21-33. New York: Russell Sage Foundation, 1999.

Portes, Alejandro, and Rubén G. Rumbaut. *Immigrant America: A Portrait*. 2nd ed. Berkeley: University of California Press, 1996.

———. *Legacies: The Story of the Immigrant Second Generation*. Berkeley: University of California Press, 2001.

Poston, Larry. *Islamic Da'wah in the West: Muslim Missionary Activity and the Dynamics of Conversion to Islam*. New York: Oxford University Press, 1992.

"Primates Meeting Communiqué." Anglican Communion News Service, http://www.wfn.org/2007/02/msg00203.html (accessed September 7, 2007).

Profile of the Foreign Born in the United States: 2000. Washington D.C.: U.S. Census Bureau, 2001.

"Profile of the Foreign-Born Population in the United States: 2000." U.S. Census Bureau, http://www.census.gov/prod/2002pubs/p23-206.pdf (accessed September 2006).

Putnam, Robert D. *Bowling Alone: The Collapse and Revival of American Community*. New York: Simon & Schuster, 2000.

Ramachandra, Vinoth. *Faiths in Conflict? Christian Integrity in a Multicultural World*. Downers Grove, IL: InterVarsity, 1999.

Ramadan, Tariq. *To Be a European Muslim: A Study of Islamic Sources in the European Context*. Leicester: Islamic Foundation, 1999.

————. *Western Muslims and the Future of Islam.* New York; Oxford: Oxford University Press, 2005.

Rambo, Lewis R. *Understanding Religious Conversion.* New Haven: Yale University Press, 1993.

Ramsay, William M. *St. Paul: The Traveler and Roman Citizen.* 1898. Rev. and updated ed. Grand Rapids: Kregel, 2001.

Ransford, Oliver. *David Livingstone: The Dark Interior.* London: J. Murray, 1978.

"Region and Country or Area of Birth of the Foreign-Born Population: 1960 to 1990." U.S. Census Bureau, http://www.census.gov/population/www/documentation/twps0029/tab03.html (accessed September 2006).

Ritzer, George. *The McDonaldization of Society: An Investigation into the Changing Character of Contemporary Social Life.* Thousand Oaks, CA: Pine Forge, 1996.

Robert, Dana L. "Shifting Southward: Global Christianity since 1945." *International Bulletin of Missionary Research* 24, no. 2 (April 2000): 50-58.

Robertson, Roland. *Globalization: Social Theory and Global Culture.* London: Sage, 1992.

————. "Globalization and the Future of Traditional Religion." In *God and Globalization: Religion and the Powers of the Ethics of the Common Life*, ed. M. L. Stackhouse and P. J. Paris, 53-68. Harrisburg, PA: Trinity Press International, 2000.

Rodriguez, Gregory. *Tamed Spaces: How Religious Congregations Nurture Immigrant Assimilation in Southern California.* The Davenport Institute, Pepperdine University School of Public Policy, 2004.

Roof, Wade Clark, and William McKinney. *American Mainline Religion: Its Changing Shape and Future.* Piscataway, NJ: Rutgers University Press, 1987.

Ross, Andrew. *A Vision Betrayed: The Jesuits in Japan and China, 1542-1742.* Maryknoll, NY: Orbis Books, 1994.

Roy, Olivier. *Globalized Islam: The Search for a New Ummah.* New York: Columbia University Press, 2004.

Rumbaut, Rubén G. "Origins and Destinies: Immigration, Race, and Ethnicity in Contemporary America." In *Origins and Destinies: Immigration, Race, and Ethnicity in America*, ed. Silvia Pedraza and Rubén G. Rumbaut, 21-42. New York: Wadsworth, 1996.

Rumbaut, Rubén G., and Alejandro Portes. "Ethnogenesis: Coming of Age in Immigrant America." In *Ethnicities: Children of Immigrants in America*, ed. Rubén G. Rumbaut and Alejandro Portes, 1-19. Berkeley: University of California Press, 2001.

Russell, Sharon Stanton. "Migration Remittances and Development." *International Migration* 30, no. 314 (1992): 267-87.

Russell, Sharon Stanton, Karen Jacobsen, and William Deane Stanley. *International Migration and Development in Sub-Saharan Africa.* 2 vols. Africa Technical Department series, World Bank Discussion Papers 101-2. Washington, DC: World Bank, 1990.

Sanger, David, and Eric Schmitt. "A Nation Challenged: The Borders—Bush Leans toward New Agency to Control Who and What Enters." *New York Times*, March 20 2002.

Sanneh, Lamin. "Christian Missions and the Western Guilt Complex." *Christian Century* (April 8, 1987): 330-34.

————. *Translating the Message: The Missionary Impact on Culture.* Maryknoll, NY: Orbis Books, 1989.

————. *Abolitionists Abroad: American Blacks and the Making of Modern West Africa.* Cambridge, MA: Harvard University Press, 2001.

————. *Whose Religion Is Christianity? The Gospel beyond the West.* Grand Rapids: Eerdmans, 2003.

Saracco, Norberto. "The Liberating Options of Jesus." In *Sharing Jesus in the Two Thirds World*, ed. Vinay Samuel and Chris Sugden, 33-41. Grand Rapids: Eerdmans, 1984.

Sardar, Ziauddin, and Merryl W. Davies. *Why Do People Hate America?* New York: Disinformation Company, 2002.

Saul, John Ralston. "The Collapse of Globalism and the Rebirth of Nationalism." *Harper's Magazine* 308, no. 1846 (March 2004): 33-43.

Schaeffer, Robert K. *Understanding Globalization: The Social Consequences of Political, Economic and Environmental Change.* New York: Rowman & Littlefield, 1997.

Schiller, Nina G. "Transmigrants and Nation-States: Something Old and Something New in the U.S. Immigrant Experience." In *The Handbook of International Migration: The American Experience*, ed. Charles Hirschman, Philip Kasinitz, and Josh DeWind, 94-119. New York: Russell Sage Foundation, 1999.

Scott, Bruce. "The Great Divide in the Global Village." *Foreign Affairs* 80, no. 1 (January/February 2001): 160-77.

"Seeking Europe's 'Promised Land.'" *BBC News,* http://news.bbc.co.uk/1/hi/world/africa/4292840.stm.

Senior, Donald, and Carroll Stuhlmueller. *The Biblical Foundations for Mission.* Maryknoll, NY: Orbis Books, 1983.

Sernett, Milton G. "Black Religion and the Question of Evangelical Identity." In *The Variety of American Evangelicalism*, ed. Donald W. Dayton and Robert K. Johnston, 135-47. Downers Grove, IL: InterVarsity, 1991.

Shah, Timothy S. "Evangelical Politics in the Third World: What's Next for the 'Next Christendom'?" *Brandywine Review of Faith & International Affairs* 1, no. 2 (2003): 21-29.

Shannon, Thomas R. *An Introduction to the World-System Perspective.* 2nd ed. Boulder, CO: Westview, 1996.

Shenk, Wilbert R. "The 'Great Century' Reconsidered." *Missiology* 12, no. 2 (April 1984): 133-46.

————. "Toward a Global Church History." *International Bulletin of Missionary Research* 20, no. 2 (April 1996): 50-57.

————. "The Training of Missiologists for Western Culture." In *Missiological Education for the Twenty-First Century: Essays in Honor of Paul E. Pierson*, ed. John Dudley Woodberry, Charles Edward van Engen, and Edgar J. Elliston, 120-29. Maryknoll, NY: Orbis Books, 1996.

————. *Changing Frontiers of Mission.* American Society of Missiology Series 28. Maryknoll, NY: Orbis Books, 1999.

————. *By Faith They Went Out: Mennonite Missions, 1850-1999.* Occasional Papers, Institute of Mennonite Studies. Elkhart, IN: Institute of Mennonite Studies, 2000.

————. "Recasting Theology of Mission: Impulses from the Non-Western World." *International Bulletin of Missionary Research* 25, no. 3 (July 2001): 98-107.

————. *Enlarging the Story: Perspectives on Writing World Christian History.* Maryknoll, NY: Orbis Books, 2002.

————. "Contextual Theology: The Last Frontier." In *The Changing Face of Christianity: Africa, the West, and the World*, ed. Lamin O. Sanneh and Joel A. Carpenter, 191-212. New York: Oxford University Press, 2005.

Shepperson, George. "Ethiopianism: Past and Present." In *Christianity in Tropical Africa*, ed. Christian G. Baèta, 249-64. London: Oxford University Press, 1968.

Shweder, Richard A. "Moral Maps, 'First World' Conceits, and the New Evangelists." In *Culture Matters: How Values Shape Human Progress*, ed. Lawrence E. Harrison and Samuel P. Huntington, 158-76. New York: Basic Books, 2000.

Siddiqui, Ataullah. "Muslims in Britain: Past and Present" (1995), http://www.islamfor today.com/britain.htm.

Sider, Ronald J. *Rich Christians in an Age of Hunger: Moving from Affluence to Generosity*. Nashville: Word, 1997.

Siewert, J. A., and E. G. Valdez, eds. *Mission Handbook*. Monrovia, CA: MARC, 1997.

Siewert, John A., and Dotsey Welliver, eds. *Mission Handbook 2001-2003: U.S. And Canadian Christian Ministries Overseas*. Wheaton, IL: Billy Graham Center, 2000.

Simes, D. K. "America's Imperial Dilemma." *Foreign Affairs* 82, no. 6 (November/December 2003): 91-102.

Simon, Benjamin. "Preaching as a Source of Religious Identity: African Initiated Churches in the Disapora." In *Religion in the Context of African Migration*, ed. Afeosemime U. Adogame and Cordula Weisskèoppel, 285-300. Bayreuth: Eckhard Breitinger, 2005.

Simon, Patrick. "French Muslims: Government Grapple with Integration Pains." *Migration Information Source* (2003), http://www.migrationinformation.org/Feature/print.cfm?ID=153.

Sine, Tom. *Mustard Seed Versus McWorld: Reinventing Life and Faith for the Future*. Grand Rapids: Baker Books, 1999.

Smith, Anthony D. *Nationalism and Modernism: A Critical Survey of Recent Theories of Nations and Nationalism*. New York: Routledge, 1998.

Smith, Daniel L. *The Religion of the Landless: The Social Context of the Babylonian Exile*. Bloomington, IN: Meyer-Stone Books, 1989.

Smith, James P., and Barry Edmonston, eds. *The New Americans: Economic, Demographic, and Fiscal Effects of Immigration*. Washington, DC: National Academy Press, 1997.

Smith, Timothy L. "Religion and Ethnicity in America." *American Historical Review* 83, no. 5 (December 1978): 1155-85.

Song, Choan-Seng. "Genesis 11:1-9: An Asian Perspective." In *Return to Babel: Global Perspectives on the Bible*, ed. John R. Levison and Priscilla Pope-Levison, 27-33. Louisville: Westminster John Knox, 1999.

Southern, R. W. *Western Society and the Church in the Middle Ages*. Harmondsworth: Penguin, 1990.

"Special Report: Islam, America and Europe." *The Economist*, June 24, 2006, 29-31.

Spellman, W. M. *The Global Community: Migration and the Making of the Modern World*. Stroud, England: Sutton, 2002.

Srinivas, Tulasi. " 'A Tryst with Destiny': The Indian Case of Cultural Globalization." In *Many Globalizations: Cultural Diversity in the Contemporary World*, ed. Peter L. Berger and Samuel P. Huntington, 89-116. New York: Oxford University Press, 2002.

Sriskandarjah, Dhananjayan. "Reassessing the Impacts of Brain Drain on Developing Countries." Migration Policy Institute, http://www.migrationinformation.org/Feature/print.cfm?ID=324.

Stackhouse, Max L., and Peter J. Paris, eds. *God and Globalization,* vol. 1, *Religion and the Powers of the Common Life*. Harrisburg, PA: Trinity Press International, 2000.

Stanley, Brian. *The Bible and the Flag: Protestant Missions and British Imperialism in the Nineteenth and Twentieth Centuries*. Leicester: Apollos, 1990.

————. "Christianity and the End of Empire." In *Missions, Nationalism, and the End of Empire*, ed. Brian Stanley, 1-11. Grand Rapids: Eerdmans, 2003.

————. "Twentieth Century Christianity: A Perspective from the History of Missions." In *Christianity Reborn: The Global Expansion of Evangelicalism in the Twentieth Century*, ed. Donald M. Lewis, 52-83. Grand Rapids: Eerdmans, 2004.

————. "Defining the Boundaries of Christendom: The Two Worlds of the World Missionary Conference, 1910." *International Bulletin of Missionary Research* 30, no. 4 (October 2006): 171-76.

Stark, Rodney. "Secularization: The Myth of Religious Decline." *Fides et Historia* 30, no. 2 (1998): 1-19.

Stark, Rodney, and Roger Finke. *Acts of Faith: Explaining the Human Side of Religion.* Berkeley: University of California Press, 2000.

Stearns, Peter N. *Cultures in Motion: Mapping Key Contacts and Their Imprints in World History.* New Haven: Yale University Press, 2001.

Stout, Henry S. "George Whitefield in Three Countries." In *Evangelicalism: Comparative Studies of Popular Protestantism in North America, the British Isles, and Beyond, 1700-1990*, ed. Mark A. Noll, D. W. Bebbington, and George A. Rawlyk, 17-41. New York: Oxford University Press, 1994.

Strong, Josiah. *Our Country: Its Possible Future and Its Present Crisis.* New York: Baker & Taylor, 1885. Rev. ed., 1891.

Sturge, Mark. *Look What the Lord Has Done! An Exploration of Black Christian Faith in Britain.* Bletchley: Scripture Union, 2005.

Tamás, G. M. "A Clarity Interfered With." In *After History? Francis Fukuyama and His Critics*, ed. Timothy Burns, 81-109. Lanham, MD: Rowman & Littlefield, 1994.

Taspinar, Omer. "Europe's Muslim Street." The Brookings Institute, http://www.brookings.edu/views/op-ed/fellows/taspinar20030301.htm.

Taylor, John V. *The Primal Vision: Christian Presence amid African Religion.* London: SCM, 1994.

ter Haar, Gerrie. *Halfway to Paradise: African Christians in Europe.* Cardiff: Cardiff Academic Press, 1998.

Thornton, John K. *The Kongolese Saint Anthony: Dona Beatriz Kimpa Vita and the Antonian Movement, 1684-1706.* New York: Cambridge University Press, 1998.

Tiplady, Richard, ed. *One World or Many? The Impact of Globalisation on Mission.* Pasadena: William Carey Library, 2003.

Tomlinson, John. *Globalization and Culture.* Chicago: University of Chicago Press, 1999.

Trends in Total Migrant Stock: The 2005 Revision. United Nations, 2006.

Turner, Harold W. "The Contribution of Studies on Religion in Africa to Western Religious Studies." In *New Testament Christianity for Africa and the World*, ed. M. E. Glasswell and E. W. Fasholé-Luke, 169-78. London: SPCK, 1974.

————. "Primal Religions of the World and Their Study." In *Australian Essays in World Religions*, ed. Victor C. Hayes, 27-37. Bedford Park, South Australia: Australian Association for the Study of Religions, 1977.

Tutu, Desmond. "Black Theology and African Theology." In *A Reader in African Christian Theology*, ed. John Parratt, 46-55. London: SPCK, 1987.

Uçarer, Emek M. "The Coming Era of Human Uprootedness: A Global Challenge." In *Immigration into Western Societies: Problems and Policies*, ed. Emek M. Uçarer and Donald James Puchala, 1-16. Washington, DC: Pinter, 1997.

"United States: Stock of Foreign-Born Population by Country of Birth as a Percentage of

Total Foreign Born, 1995 to 2005." Migration Policy Institute, http://www.migra-tioninformation.org/GlobalData/countrydata/data.cfm.

"U.S. Anglicans Join Kenyan Church." *BBC News*, http://news.bbc.co,uk/go/pr/fr/-/2/hi/africa/6970093.stm (accessed August 31, 2007).

"U.S. Church Splits over Sexuality." *BBC News,* http://news.bbc.co,uk/go/pr/fr/-/2/hi/americas/6188465.stm (accessed 2007).

van Dijk, Han, Dick Forken, and Kiky van Til. "Population Mobility in Africa: An Over-view." In *Mobile Africa: Changing Patterns of Movement in Africa and Beyond,* ed. Mirjam de Bruijn, Rijk van Dijk and Dick Foeken, 9-26. Boston: Brill, 2001.

Van Hear, Nicholas. *New Diasporas: The Mass Exodus, Dispersal and Regrouping of Migrant Communities.* Seattle: University of Washington Press, 1998.

Vargas, Jose. "Bridging the Digital Divide in Latin America." *Global Future* (First Quarter, 2001): 16.

Verkuyl, Johannes. *Contemporary Missiology: An Introduction,* ed. Cooper Dale. Grand Rapids: Eerdmans, 1978.

Von Laue, Theodore H. *The World Revolution of Westernization: The Twentieth Century in Global Perspective.* New York: Oxford University Press, 1987.

Waldinger, Roger D. "Strangers at the Gates." In *Strangers at the Gates: New Immigrants in Urban America,* ed. Roger D. Waldinger, 1-29. Berkeley: University of California Press, 2001.

Waldinger, Roger D., and Jennifer Lee. "New Immigrants in Urban America." In *Strangers at the Gates: New Immigrants in Urban America,* ed. Roger D. Waldinger, 30-79. Berkeley: University of California Press, 2001.

Wallerstein, Immanuel. "The Rise and Future Demise of the World Capitalist System." In *The Globalization Reader,* ed. Frank J. Lechner and John Boli, 57-63. Malden, MA: Blackwell, 2000.

Wallraff, Barbara. "What Global Language?" *Atlantic Monthly* (November 2000): 52-66.

Walls, Andrew F. "A Christian Experiment: The Early Sierra Leone Colony." In *The Mission of the Church and the Propagation of the Faith,* ed. G. J. Cuming, 107-29. London: Cambridge University Press, 1970.

———. "The Evangelical Revival, the Missionary Movement, and Africa." In *Evangelicalism: Comparative Studies of Popular Protestantism in North America, the British Isles, and Beyond, 1700-1990,* ed. Mark A. Noll, D. W. Bebbington, and George A. Rawlyk, 310-30. New York: Oxford University Press, 1994.

———. "The Legacy of David Livingstone." In *Mission Legacies: Biographical Studies of Leaders of the Modern Missionary Movement,* ed. Gerald H. Anderson. Maryknoll, NY: Orbis Books, 1994.

———. "African Christianity in the History of Religions." *Studies in World Christianity* 2 (1996): 183-203.

———. *The Missionary Movement in Christian History: Studies in the Transmission of Faith.* Maryknoll, NY: Orbis Books, 1996.

———. "Africa as the Theatre of Christian Engagement with Islam in the Nineteenth Century." *Journal of Religion in Africa* 29, no. 2 (1999): 155-74.

———. *The Cross-Cultural Process in Christian History: Studies in the Transmission and Appropriation of Faith.* Maryknoll, NY: Orbis Books, 2002.

———. "Eusebius Tries Again: The Task of Reconceiving and Re-Visioning the Study of

Christian History." In *Enlarging the Story: Perspectives on Writing World Christian History*, ed. Wilbert R. Shenk, 1-21. Maryknoll, NY: Orbis Books, 2002.

———. "Mission and Migration: The Diaspora Factor in Christian History." *Journal of African Christian Thought* 5, no. 2 (December 2002): 3-11.

———. "Ecumenical Missiology in Anabaptist Perspective." *Mission Focus: Annual Review* 13 (2005): 191-98.

Walsh, John. "'Methodism' and the Origins of English-Speaking Evangelicalism." In *Evangelicalism: Comparative Studies of Popular Protestantism in North America, the British Isles, and Beyond, 1700-1990*, ed. Mark A. Noll, D. W. Bebbington, and George A. Rawlyk, 19-37. New York: Oxford University Press, 1994.

Warner, R. Stephen. "Immigration and Religious Communities in the United States." In *Gatherings in Diaspora: Religious Communities and the New Immigration*, ed. R. Stephen Warner and Judith G. Wittner, 3-34. Philadelphia, PA: Temple University Press, 1998.

———. "The Place of the Congregation in the Contemporary American Religious Configuration." In *American Congregations*, ed. James P. Wind and James Welborn Lewis, 54-99. Chicago: University of Chicago Press, 1998.

———. "Coming to America." *Christian Century,* February 10, 2004, 20-23.

Weeks, Priscilla. "Post-Colonial Challenges to Grand Theory." *Human Organization* 49, no. 3 (1990): 236-44.

Wengert, Timothy J., and Charles W. Brockwell, eds. *Telling the Churches' Stories: Ecumenical Perspective on Writing Christian History*. Grand Rapids: Eerdmans, 1995.

Wieseltier, Leon. "Spoilers at the Party." *National Interest* (Fall 1989).

Williams, Eric E. *Capitalism and Slavery*. New York: G. P. Putnam, 1980.

Williams, Walter L. *Black Americans and the Evangelization of Africa, 1877-1900*. Madison: University of Wisconsin Press, 1982.

Wilmore, Gayraud. "Black Americans in Mission: Setting the Record Straight." *International Bulletin of Missionary Research* 10 (July 1986): 98-102.

Wilmore, Gayraud S. *Black Religion and Black Radicalism: An Interpretation of the Religious History of African Americans*. 3rd rev. and enl. ed. Maryknoll, NY: Orbis Books, 1998.

Wilson, Jill. "African-Born Residents of the United States." Migration Policy Institute, http://www.migrationinformation.org/Feature/print.cfm?ID=147.

Wilson, Samuel, and John Siewert, eds. *Mission Handbook: North American Protestant Ministries Overseas*. Monrovia, CA: MARC, 1986.

Wolfe, Alan. *The Transformation of American Religion: How We Actually Live Our Faith*. New York: Free Press, 2003.

World Bank Development Report: Building Institutions for Markets. New York: Oxford University Press, 2002. http://www.worldbank.org/wdr/2001/fulltext/fm.pdf.

World Missionary Conference, 1910: Report of Commission 1—Carrying the Gospel to All the Non-Christian World. Edinburgh: Oliphant, Anderson & Ferrier, 1910. http://name.umdl.umich.edu/1936337.0001.001.

World Missionary Conference, 1910: Report of Commission 4—the Missionary Message in Relation to Non-Christian Religions. Edinburgh: Oliphant, Anderson & Ferrier, 1910. http://name.umdl.umich.edu/1936337.0001.001.

World Population: More Than Just Numbers. Washington, DC: Population Reference Bureau, 1999.

World Population Data Sheet. Washington, DC: Population Reference Bureau, 2005.

"World Population Growth, 1750-2150." Population Reference Bureau, http://www.prb
    .org/Content/NavigationMenu/PRB/Educators/Human_Population/Population_
    Growth/Population_Growth.htm.
World Population Prospects: The 2000 Revision in the United Nations.
Wyse, Akintola J. G. *The Krio of Sierra Leone: An Interpretive History.* Washington, DC:
    Howard University Press, 1991.
Yang, Fenggang, and Helen Ebaugh. "Transformations in New Immigrant Religions
    and Their Global Implications." *American Sociological Review* 66 (April 2001):
    269-88.
"Yearbook of Immigration Statistics." United States Citizenship and Immigration Services,
    http://www.uscis.gov/graphics/shared/aboutus/statistics/IMM03yrbk/2003IMM
    .pdf (accessed August 2006).
"Younger Muslims 'More Political,'" *BBC News,* January 29, 2007, http://news.bbc
    .co.uk/2/hi/uk_news/6308683.stm.
Zhou, Min. "Segmented Assimilation: Issues, Controversies, and Recent Research on
    the New Second Generation." In *The Handbook of International Migration: The
    American Experience*, ed. Charles Hirschman, Philip Kasinitz, and Josh DeWind,
    196-211. New York: Russell Sage Foundation, 1999.
———. "The Changing Face of America: Immigration, Race/Ethnicity, and Social Mobil-
    ity." In *Mass Migration to the United States: Classical and Contemporary Periods*,
    ed. Pyong Gap Min, 65-97. New York: AltaMira, 2002.
Zlotnik, Hania. "Trends in South to North Migration: The Perspective from the North."
    International Migration 29, no. 2 (1991): 317-31.

Index